REAL WORLD ILLUSTRATOR 9

Deke McClelland
Sandee Cohen

Peachpit Press

REAL WORLD ILLUSTRATOR 9

Deke McClelland, Sandee Cohen

Peachpit Press
1249 Eighth Street
Berkeley, CA 94710
510/524-2178
800/283-9444
510/524-2221 (fax)

Find us on the World Wide Web at:
http://www.peachpit.com

Peachpit Press is a division of Addison Wesley Longman

Real World Adobe Illustrator 9 is published in association with Adobe Press.

Project Editors: Corbin Collins, Cary Norsworthy
Copy Editor: Dave Awl
Production Coordinator: Kate Reber
Cover design: Earl Gee, Gee + Chung Design
Cover art and part opener art: Ron Chan
Interior design: Michele Cuneo and Mimi Heft
Compositor: Owen Wolfson
Indexer: Steve Rath

ISBN 0-201-70405-6

9 8 7 6 5 4 3 2 1

Printed and bound in the United States of America

ACKNOWLEDGMENTS

There are a few people who deserve some special mention for their help in the creation of this book. First, we'd like to thank all the staff at Peachpit Press, especially Corbin Collins and Cary Norsworthy, the project editors, and Marjorie Baer, Peachpit's executive editor. We thank Dave Awl, our copy editor, for his eagle eye and cheery notes. Also, thanks go to Kate Reber for her production guidance.

We'd like to thank Ron Chan for once again contributing the art for the cover and part openers. And we'd like to thank Luanne Seymour Cohen, author of *Design Essentials*, and Richard Koman of *Communication Arts* for their kind quotes that appear at the back of the book.

Thanks go to Barbara Obermeier and Michael Bierman for their technical expertise in reviewing the book. Also, thanks to the Illustrator team, especially Ted Alspach, Senior Product Manager, and Asako Yoshimuro, Product Manager, for answering our questions about the new features in Illustrator 9.

CONTENTS AT A GLANCE

TABLE OF CONTENTS

PART ONE STARTING 1

Chapter 1

Chapter 2

Chapter 3
Objects, Images, and the File Formats That Love Them 65

PART TWO CREATING 103

Chapter 4
Drawing the Simple Stuff 105

Chapter 5
Exact Points and Precision Curves 139

Chapter 6
How to Handle Typical Type 191

Chapter 7
Some of Your Wackier Text Effects 235

Chapter 8
This Is Your Brain on Graphs. 287

PART THREE
CHANGING 341

Chapter 9
Modifying and Combining Paths 343

Chapter 10
Developing a Flair for the Schematic 377

Chapter 11
The Magical World of Transformations 423

Chapter 12
Hog-Wild Special Effects 461

Chapter 15
Fills, Multi-Fills, and Fab Fills. 561

Chapter 16
Strokes and Brushes. 597

Chapter 17
Transparency 643

Chapter 18
Blends, Masks, and Ink Pen Fills 671

Chapter 19
Web Graphics and Animations. 717

Chapter 20
Working Smarter and Faster. 747

Chapter 21
Printing Your Illustrations 771

Index 807

INTRODUCTION

Deke's Story: Although I'm in my late thirties, a phase that's sadly unlikely to last too much longer, I sometimes feel like a crusty old codger who's witnessed more than anyone cares to hear recounted. For instance, I might venture that where computer graphics are concerned, you are spoiled rotten. Adobe Illustrator is a prime example of a professional-quality application that—despite any problems you may or may not have with it—performs without crashing and prints like a champ. You can get up in the morning, start working in the program, and expect to make substantial progress. The darn thing works.

It's quite a different story than when I was a boy. I don't think I could have endured desktop publishing back in 1986—before Illustrator hit the market—if I hadn't been a kid. When I began working as artistic director for a small service bureau, our world consisted of a laughably inept collection of software and hardware. We used PageMaker 1.2 to lay out pages. Sure, the files corrupted regularly and the program took an extra 15 minutes to print a page with a downloadable font on it, but it was better than facing the customer and admitting that desktop publishing was a cruel joke.

We used a program called FullPaint to create black-and-white bitmapped graphics because it could rotate a selection (an operation that MacPaint couldn't handle). We scanned images using a ThunderScanner, which boasted photocopier quality when it wasn't stretching and slanting photos as it curled them around its roller. Less than 100 fonts were available in all the world, most of which were clumsily executed by folks still learning their trade. For printing, we had a Linotronic 100 imagesetter—the number of which coincidentally corresponded to the thousands of dollars it cost—and a film processor that looked and acted like it had fallen off the back of a truck. And our best computer was a supercharged Macintosh 512K with a whopping 2 MB of RAM and two 400-K floppy drives. There wasn't such a thing as a hard drive.

The following year, we purchased better machines, upgraded PageMaker, and continued to pour expensive chemicals into our increasingly frightening processor. But the event that most changed how *I* worked was the arrival of Illustrator 1.0. It was the first drawing program that worked worth a hill of beans. MacDraw was nearly unusable; you couldn't get two lines to properly align. And though CricketDraw permitted gradations and type along a curve—both missing from Illustrator at the time—it crashed on the hour and absolutely refused to print to our imagesetter. Frankly, that program went a long way toward helping me loosen my fragile grasp on reality.

But Illustrator was an entirely different kind of program, unlike anything I had used before. Other programs supplied more features, but Illustrator had exactly what I needed, implemented in the most logical fashion. Most important, I could actually depend on the program. Call me a sentimental fool, but I have no memory of it ever once crashing or failing to print. It has always come through.

The new Illustrator is far more capable than its distant ancestor. And though nostalgia may cloud my judgment, it's frequently less logical and less streamlined. But it remains the most reliable application for printing computer-generated graphics that I've ever used. After nine years of writing, designing, and reworking this book, I have yet to conceive of a graphic that I couldn't manage one way or another. I can still open every illustration just as I originally created it, with no line, shape, or character of text missing or moving on the page. (I'd love to see *any* version of PageMaker do that.) And I know that everything I draw will eventually print, even if it requires some minor modifications. Mind you, I don't like every-thing about Illustrator—in fact, I would change quite a few features if I could—but this is an important program that has *never* been absent from any of my hard drives. Heck, I'd still be using Illustrator 1.0 if Adobe hadn't upgraded it.

Now, tell me honestly. I sound like I'm at least 86, don't I?

Sandee's Story: I was working at an advertising agency back in the mid-eighties. We used a program called LightSpeed to create color comps of our advertising layouts that we printed on a special color printer. We also used QuarkXPress to set black-and-white text for ads. (Foolishly, we would set the copy in XPress, then send a laser print of the copy to a type shop which would reset it using photolettering typesetting machines. We didn't trust service bureaus and imagesetters.)

After working for a while with those two programs, I went to the woman in charge of all the computers at the ad agency and asked her if there were any other pro-grams I could learn. (Learning new software was fun—like solving a puzzle.) She threw a box at me and said, "Here, you can try this. *Nobody* understands it." It was Illustrator 88. And like everyone else in the office, I too couldn't understand it. However, a short time later, Illustrator 3 came out as well as a book called *Mastering Adobe Illustrator 3.0* by Deke McClelland. That's when it happened: I finally understood the mysterious world of vectors and Bézier handles. In fact, I understood the concepts so well, that I now call myself a "vectorbabe."

Eventually, I left advertising and began teaching computer graphics and desktop publishing in New York City and around the country. Eventually I got to meet Deke (who's just as funny in person as he is in print). And today, I'm thrilled to be a part of the writing of this book!

Illustrator and You

Adobe Illustrator 9 is a drawing program for both the Macintosh and Windows compatible computers. The differences are few and are mostly related to things that are unique to a particular platform, such as the look and function of a palette's close box. The biggest of these differences is that Illustrator on a Mac employs the Command key (sometimes called the Apple key) and the Option key, whereas on a Windows machine Illustrator uses the Ctrl and Alt keys. Most of the time we write the keystroke combinations using the following shortcuts. "Cmd/Ctrl" means you should hold the Command key if you're on a Mac or the Ctrl key if you're working on Windows. When you see "Opt/Alt" it means you should hold the Option key if you're on a Mac, or the Alt key if you're on Windows. So the instruc-tion Cmd/Ctrl-click means Mac users would hold the Command key and click while Windows users would hold the Ctrl key and click. The instruction Cmd/Ctrl-Shift-N means Mac users hold Command-Shift-N and Windows users hold Ctrl-Shift-N. (If a keystroke is very long, we've divided it up into two different instructions, rather than tell you to hold Cmd/Ctrl-Opt/Alt-Shift-click.)

Also, the Windows users have a left and right mouse button. "Click" refers to the left mouse button. "Right-click" refers to the right button on the mouse. Since the standard Macintosh mouse only has one button, they use a different keystroke: "Control-click." This refers to holding the Control key on the Macintosh keyboard and clicking the mouse.

Regardless of your platform, you can use Illustrator to draw high-contrast graphics with perfectly smooth edges. You can also edit the outline of any shape long after you create it. You see Illustrator graphics every day in newspapers, magazines, print, and the World Wide Web. Artists use Illustrator to create diagrams, info-art, maps, logos, posters, photo-realistic renderings, and all sorts of other illustrations that defy categorization. You can even integrate photographs that were corrected and enhanced in Adobe Photoshop or a similar application.

Illustrator is a graphics workshop; it's as expansive, elaborate, and perplexing as any traditional workshop on earth. Like any powerful collection of tools, Illustrator demands your attention and rewards your understanding. That's why this book guides you through every feature of the program as if you've never seen a drawing application in your life. Regardless of your level of experience, you'll find yourself easily graduating into the advanced topics that consume most of the pages in this book. Every section explains not only how to perform a technique but also provides enough background so you know why you'd want to. Though we hope they're pleasing to look at, our figures aren't meant to amaze; they're included to educate. We want you to amaze yourself.

The Structure of This Book

Real World Illustrator 9 contains a total of 21 chapters organized into four distinct parts. Each part explores a simple concept in exhaustive and engaging detail. Our hope is that at the end of every part, you will feel confident enough with the material to see the gaps in our explanations. "Oh, sure, you can do *that*, but how about *this*, and *this*, and *this*?" Once you understand the topics, you can invent techniques on your own without the slightest hesitation.

- **Part One, Starting:** The first part's three chapters introduce the fundamental issues in Illustrator 9. We explain how Illustrator differs from other graphics programs. We introduce you to Illustrator's network of tools and palettes. And we tell you everything there is to know about the file formats included with Illustrator 9. If you're familiar with previous editions of Illustrator, this part will get you up and running in no time at all.

Part Two, Creating: These five chapters tell you how to create the basic type and graphic elements in Illustrator. We explain all the tricks you need to know to get the most out of tools like the polygon, star, and spiral. We make sense out of the pen tool and Bézier curves. Chapters 6 and 7 devote close to 100 pages to the topic of creating and editing text. And we close the part with a look at one of Illustrator's most overlooked features, charts and graphs.

Part Three, Changing: In sculpture, a substance like clay is considered "forgiving" by comparison to, say, marble, because clay permits you to modify your mistakes. By this standard, Illustrator provides the most forgiving environment possible. Nothing in Illustrator is permanent; everything you create is subject to adjustment. In Chapters 9 through 13, we tell you how to cut apart lines and shapes and how to put them back together again. we spend more pages discussing such essential features as compound paths and Pathfinder filters than any other book. We also make sense of Illustrator's transformation and special-effects capabilities. And this book spends an entire chapter showing you how to exploit the special relationship between Illustrator 9 and Photoshop as well as working with raster images within Illustrator.

Part Four, Coloring: We've devoted more than 200 pages to showing you how color works, how to use color, and how to print grayscale and color illustrations. Even if you weren't using Illustrator, you'll find a lot in Chapter 14 to help you understand working with color. (To keep the cover price as low as possible, we've put some of those illustrations into a special color insert in the middle of the book.) Chapter 17 looks at how the transparency options affects objects. However, coloring doesn't just mean color, so Chapter 18 covers blending colors and shapes as well as masks, opacity masks, and the ink pen effects. Chapter 19 covers creating Web graphics. We then cover printing in Chapter 20. Once you've made it through to Chapter 21, we'll show you all our techniques for working smarter and faster using styles and actions.

We've written the chapters so you can read them from beginning to end without finding the information either repetitive or overwhelming. If you prefer to read when you're stumped, you can look up a confusing topic in the index. Or you can simply browse through the pictures until you come to something that looks interesting. But no matter how you approach the text, we hope that it snags you and teaches you more than you bargained for. If you look up from the book at your watch and think, "Dang, I've got to get back to work!" then we've done our job.

Meet the Margin Icons

Throughout this book, we've designed two kinds of special text elements to attract your attention and convey fast information. The first are the figure captions. A caption is worthless unless it tells you something about the figure that you don't already know. Between the graphic and the caption text, an experienced user should be able to glean enough information to perform a similar effect in Illustrator. If you need to know more, the text contains the full story, including additional hints and details. But you shouldn't *have* to read if you don't want to.

The second special text element is the icon text. If a paragraph contains very important information or an offhanded aside that you can feel free to skip, we include an icon next to the paragraph to distinguish it from the surrounding text. If you already know Illustrator, you can get up to speed in Illustrator 9 by just reading these paragraphs.

Here are the four icons that you can expect to jockey for your attention:

This icon points out features that are new to Illustrator 9. Sometimes, the paragraph tells you everything you need to know about the new feature. Other times, the icon introduces several pages of text. Either way, you'll know it's something you didn't have in Illustrator 9 or earlier.

It seems like every book offers a tip icon. So we try to steer clear of the boring old tips that every Illustrator user hears a million times, and we concentrate on the juicy stuff that most folks don't know. But keep in mind, these are fast tips. For the more involved killer techniques, you have to read the text, too.

This icon explains an action to avoid. Few operations are hazardous in Illustrator, but many are time wasters. And you can bet that after we tell you what not to do, we include a preferable alternative as well.

Between the two of us, we've been using Illustrator and other programs for as long as they've been out. So occasionally we feel compelled to share our thoughts on a variety of subjects. Sometimes it's a bit of history, other times it's a thoughtful observation, and every once in a while it's just a complaint. Whatever it is, you can skip it if it gets on your nerves.

Contacting the Folks Who Are Responsible for All This

Deke has close to ten books on the market at any one time. These plus his magazine and speaking commitments keep him busier than he cares to admit—not to mention his newfound love for off-track Shetland pony racing simulations for UNIX-based machines. With one thing and another, he regrets that he can't talk to every reader. But he does invite you to submit your comments, questions, and general observations to his electronic mail account, which is accessible from his Web site, at http://www.dekemc.com.

He's not very regular about checking and responding to e-mail, so you can expect a delay of a week to a month, depending on what the current deadline situation is like. But you have his word. One day, when you least expect it, you'll hear back from him.

Sandee is far less busy with only five books out there. So it's much more likely you can contact her with comments and questions. You can find her through her Web site, at http://www.vectorbabe.com.

PART ONE
STARTING

CHAPTER 1

ILLUSTRATOR 9: WHAT IT IS

Illustrator—what is it, and what's new with version 9? That's the stuff of Chapter 1. This chapter provides a general overview of Illustrator 9, along with a brief history of the program.

If you've never used Illustrator before, we'll tell you what it is and why you've probably heard its name bandied about. We'll show you where it fits into the world of computer graphics. Along the way you'll find out about Illustrator's relationship to its more popular sibling, Photoshop—a graphics program with an entirely different purpose.

If you're a longtime Illustrator enthusiast, this chapter provides some amusing—if not terribly insightful—analyses along with a practical assessment of Illustrator 9's new capabilities. We even tell you which chapters to turn to for more information on Illustrator's new features.

Adobe: the "Microsoft of Graphics"

To truly understand Illustrator, you have to know a bit about the company behind it, Adobe Systems. One of the five largest software companies in this quadrant of the galaxy, Adobe is widely considered to be the one software developer that Microsoft cannot destroy. Adobe knows electronic graphics and design, and Microsoft never will. It's that simple.

Case in point: Photoshop, Adobe's phenomenally successful image-editing program, is widely considered the most powerful personal computer application for mucking around with computerized photographs. Photoshop is equally revered by expert and novice, young and old, educated and self-taught, primate and bottom-feeding slimefish. Photoshop isn't altogether perfect, but it has a universal appeal.

Microsoft, meanwhile, has squat. No high-end image editor now, and none planned for the future.

Adobe also makes Premiere, the number one program for editing computerized video sequences. Premiere needs a fast computer and an awfully big hard disk to run, and you need special hardware to capture the movies and then send them back out to videotape. But there's absolutely nothing like it for messing around with moving images and creating simple animated effects.

Microsoft is currently unaware of any need for a video editing package among the populace at large.

Are you beginning to see the trend? Adobe is absolutely steeped in the world of professional artistry and business graphics, and Microsoft hasn't even begun to compete. And perhaps it never will.

In the mind of your everyday, average industry analyst, Adobe is the "Microsoft of graphics." Like Microsoft, Adobe is a dominant force that not only lords over an entire discipline of computing with an iron fist, but also manages to consistently churn out quality software. Lesser companies regard Adobe with a combination of envy, respect, and fear. For better or worse, Adobe is currently where the artwork is.

Where Illustrator Fits In

Illustrator is important because its creation set current events in motion. Prior to Illustrator—back in the mid-1980s, when the world was learning to pronounce *Mikhail Gorbachev* and *Scritti Politti*—Adobe was a small company that had invented the PostScript printing language. PostScript revolutionized the world of typesetting and jump-started the career of at least one computer book author, but it didn't exactly make *Adobe* a household word (except in New Mexico, where adobe houses are quite common).

The problem with PostScript was its inaccessibility. In theory, PostScript let you design incredibly ornate, twisty-curvy lines and fill them with any of several million color options. But unless you wanted to resort to PostScript programming—the equivalent of instructing a friend to draw an object by reciting numerical coordinates over the phone—your options were limited to text surrounded by a few straight lines and rectangles.

Illustrator single-handedly changed all this. Before Illustrator, Macintosh graphics looked blocky and turgid; after Illustrator, most folks couldn't tell Mac graphics from those drawn with pen and ink. The transition couldn't have been more abrupt or more welcome.

Close, But Not Kin: Illustrator Versus Photoshop

Now in its thirteenth year, Illustrator is often seen as a kind of support program for Photoshop, thanks to the latter's dramatic and overshadowing success. Mind you, Illustrator's growth has been consistent and commendable over the years, and to this day it remains the world's most popular PostScript drawing program. But Photoshop manages to sell roughly twice as well as Illustrator, despite being nearly three years younger.

Truth be told, Adobe has tried to piggyback Illustrator on Photoshop's success. Since Photoshop was first released, Illustrator's popularity has mushroomed and the two programs have become more closely related. In fact, beginning with Illustrator 7, Adobe took this marriage one step further. Illustrator now has the look and feel of Photoshop. It still functions like Illustrator should, but the physical layout and the interface is similar to that of modern-day Photoshop. Adobe is simply trying to make Illustrator more accessible to the numerous Photoshop users.

Illustrator Does Smooth Lines, Photoshop Does Pixels

The easiest way to help you understand how Illustrator works is to start off by explaining how it *does not* work—which is precisely how Photoshop *does* work. As its name implies, Photoshop's primary purpose is to edit photographs. When you scan a photograph into a computer, the software converts it to a collection of tiny colored blocks called *pixels*. Each pixel is perfectly square, and one is perfectly adjacent to the next with no wiggle room between them. The purpose of Photoshop's hundred or so functions is to adjust the colors of these pixels. (The pixels in Photoshop should not be confused with Pixel—Sandee's cat—who hisses and spits if you try to adjust her colors.)

Although you can force Illustrator to edit pixels in a comparatively crude fashion, the main purpose of the program is to create line art. Each line, shape, and character of text is altogether independent of its neighbors. These independent elements are known collectively as *objects*, which is why Illustrator is sometimes called an *object-oriented* application. Illustrator keeps track of each object by assigning it a separate mathematical equation. (Don't worry, there is no math in this book. Well, none that's important, anyway.) Illustrator later prints the lines, shapes, and text by sending the equations to the printer and letting the printer figure it out. The result is uniformly smooth artwork with high-contrast edges and crisp detail.

The Right Tool for the Right Job

As you might imagine, this difference in approach leads to a difference in purpose. Pixels are great for representing continuous color transitions, in which one color gradually changes into another. Such color transitions are the norm in real life, which is why pixels are so well suited to photographs. (Experienced/pretentious computer artists have even been known to call photographs *continuous-tone images*, but for our purposes, just plain *image* will suffice.)

Likewise, Illustrator is perfect for high-contrast artwork, which can vary from schematic or cartoonish to just barely stylized. This kind of computer art is known as a *drawing* or *illustration*.

Take as examples the two graphics in Figure 1-1. Both depict a sea lion in an attitude of aquatic grace, to be sure. But whereas the first is a photograph snapped by Marty Snyderman and distributed on CD-ROM by Digital Stock Professional, the second is a line drawing created by Deke in Illustrator. To achieve the left-hand image, he converted the color image to grayscale, corrected the brightness and contrast, and sharpened the focus, all in Photoshop. To achieve the right-hand illustration, he had to meticulously trace the photograph in Illustrator and fill each shape with a different shade of gray.

Figure 1-1: A photographic image enhanced in Photoshop (left) compared with a line drawing created in Illustrator (right).

The first image looks like a photo. But although the second is a recognizable member of the wildlife community, it is obviously executed by human hands, not snapped with a camera. This is the most significant difference between Photoshop and Illustrator.

Flexible Resizing

Another difference is in the details. Photoshop's details can be grainy, but Illustrator's are forever smooth.

As you increase the size of a Photoshop image, the square pixels likewise grow and become more obvious. On the left side of Figure 1-2, for example, we've enlarged the sea lion image to 200, 400, and 800 percent. At each level of magnification, your eye is better able to separate the pixels into individual colored squares. As a result, a photograph looks great when printed at high resolutions, that is, when a lot of pixels are packed into a small space. But it begins to look coarse, jagged, and out of focus when printed at low resolutions, with fewer pixels per inch.

Illustrator art isn't like that at all. As shown on the right side of Figure 1-2, the drawing looks great no matter how much you enlarge it. Every line is mathematically accurate regardless of size. The downside, of course, is that it took Deke about five minutes to adjust the sea lion photo in Photoshop, but almost three hours to draw the sea lion in Illustrator. Apart from the photographic process itself, illustrations typically require a more sizable time investment than photographic images.

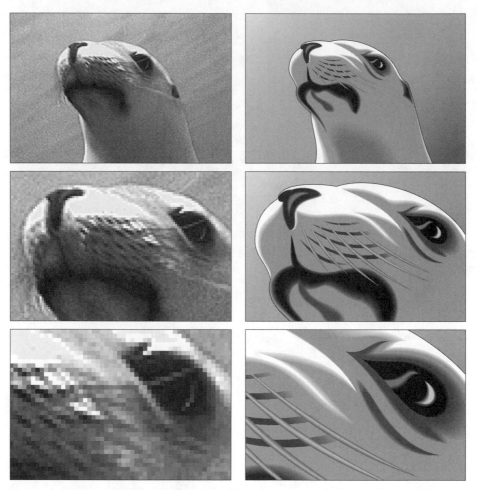

Figure 1-2: The results of magnifying the Photoshop image (left) and Illustrator drawing (right) to 200, 400, and 800 percent.

Objects and Pixels Together

The final difference between Photoshop and Illustrator is that Photoshop can handle only pixels, while Illustrator accommodates both pixels and vectors together. Don't get us wrong, Photoshop is several times more capable than Illustrator where pixels are concerned, but Photoshop doesn't do anything except pixels. With Illustrator, you can draw objects as well as import images from Photoshop or some other pixel editor. Figure 1-3 shows the object-oriented sea lion layered in front of the original Photoshop image, so that the image serves as a background.

Figure 1-3: This inspiring creature is the product of Photoshop and Illustrator working together.

But to interpret Illustrator's acceptance of pixels as an advantage over Photoshop's ignorance of objects misses the point. Illustrator and Photoshop are designed to work together, now more than ever before. There may even be times when you prefer to convert an entire illustration to pixels inside Photoshop, either to apply special effects that only Photoshop can handle or merely to simplify the printing process so the printer has to solve fewer equations. Illustrator and Photoshop are two halves of the artistic process, each taking up where the other one leaves off, each making up for the other one's weaknesses. It's the perfect marriage, and you're the happy beneficiary.

The Lowdown on Illustrator 9

 If you're coming to Illustrator as a total beginner, most of these descriptions of new features may seem like some bizarre foreign language. If you're familiar with previous versions of Illustrator, you should find most of these new features exciting developments. So exciting, we hope, that you'll rush to read the chapters that contain the explanations.

- **True transparency (Chapter 17):** Over the years Illustrator users would periodically approach their Adobe masters, like young Oliver Twist, hands outstretched, and in a plaintive whisper ask, "Please sir, I want some transparency." The Adobe masters scoffed and told them transparency was not possible due to the limitations of PostScript. Still-devoted Illustrator users watched in sorrow as their friends who used FreeHand and CorelDraw applied transparency to their illustrations. "Please sir, why can't we have what they have?" they politely asked. The Adobe lords thundered, "Those applications don't have *real* transparency. Their transparency features have limitations. We shall only provide transparency in Illustrator when we can do it right!" Well the time has come at last, and Illustrator 9 does have transparency—done right! Done without limitations! Done better than any other program around! It was a long time coming, but well worth the wait.

- **Live effects (Chapter 12):** With barely enough time for users to get used to live blends, Illustrator 9 goes even further with live effects. (Live blends were introduced in Illustrator 8 and allowed users to make changes to blends long after they were originally created.) What's a live effect? Well, if you've been working with Illustrator for a while, you may know that you can apply filters that make a simple circle look like the petals of a daisy. In older versions, applying those filters meant a permanent distortion of the circle; there was no way to go back the next day and change the effects of the filter. You had to redraw the circle and start from scratch. Live effects let you go back and change your mind the next day, and the next, and the next. They are the perfect solution for every artist and designer who ever had a client who said, "Can you make that just a little different?"

Figure 1-4: Notice how the beam of light from the bottom projector interacts with the art behind it, while the top beam does not. Before Illustrator 9's transparency, this effect would only have been possible in Photoshop.

- **Live shapes (Chapter 18):** If live blends mean the blend can be easily updated, and live effects mean the effect can be easily updated, do live shapes mean the shape can be easily updated? Well, sorta. Live shapes allow you to create a shape such as a rectangle or circle that gets tied to the size of another objects. Not impressed? OK, how about this: You can make a button to use in Web designs and if you change the text inside the button, the shape contracts or expands as necessary to fit the text. It's not just live, it breathes!

- **Illustrator gets Web-savvy (Chapter 19):** Although there were some primitive Web export features in previous versions, Illustrator 9 goes hog-wild when it comes to creating Web graphics: GIF or JPEG graphics, SWF animations, and SVG files. There's also new pixel preview, which helps you see how graphics will appear when converted into Web formats. Illustrator 9 is so Web-friendly that we've devoted an entire chapter to the subject.

- **Graphic styles (Chapter 20):** Another one of the top ten most-wanted features has been styles. Styles aren't a visible feature, like transparency. You can't look at an illustration and say, "Oh, look at those lovely styles." Styles are simply a way of automating the processes of applying colors and changing artwork. If that doesn't sound exciting, just wait till it's three in the morning and you've just discovered that the trees need to be browner, the grass greener, the sky bluer; the shadows need to be less obvious; and instead of red, the client wants a yellow brick road. When you can make all those changes in less than thirty seconds, that's when you'll see how exciting styles are.

- **Layer thumbnails (Chapter 10):** As we've mentioned, Illustrator keeps getting more and more like Photoshop. Layer thumbnails is a feature that comes straight from Photoshop into Illustrator 9. A *thumbnail* is a little drawing that represents the items on a layer. So if you're like Sandee, who never bothers to name her layers with descriptive names but winds up with *Layer 1, Layer 2,* and *Layer 2 copy,* you're going to love using the thumbnails to tell exactly what is on each layer.

- **Nested layers (Chapter 10):** If you're one of those people who routinely creates upwards of a hundred different layers in a document, you may find it time-consuming to scroll through an endless list of layers. Illustrator 9 lets you nest one layer as a subset of another. True, nested layers won't make your illustrations look any better; they just help you work faster.

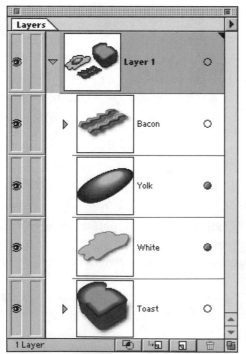

Figure 1-5:
The new layers palette in Illustrator 9 shows thumbnail previews of what's on each layer as well as nesting sublayers for easier organization.

Opacity and layer masks (Chapter 18): This is another feature that Photoshop users will recognize. Opacity masks allow you to use the light and dark values of one image to reveal portions of another image. Layer masks allow you to designate all the objects on one layer as the masks that hide areas of other layers.

Preview overprinting (Chapter 21): *Overprinting* is the term used to describe setting the colors of one object to merge with any objects below. Yet until Illustrator 9, there has never been a way to see the effects of overprinting onscreen. You had to wait till the artwork was actually printed to see how the overprinting would look. This isn't just a new feature to Illustrator 9; no other illustration or layout program currently has previews of overprinting onscreen. (Sandee put the word *currently* in the preceding sentence because she hopes to see other programs pick up this technology soon.)

RGB or CMYK workspace (Chapter 14): Once again a Photoshop feature gets imported into Illustrator. In this case it means that you can set a document so that all colors are either RGB or CMYK. What's the benefit? Well, if you're creating artwork for print separations, you don't have to worry about errant RGB colors messing up your color space. Web designers will also appreciate special gradients and patterns made with RGB, not CMYK colors.

Simplify path (Chapter 4): Seems like one of the simplest things to add to Illustrator would be a simplify command. Over and over Illustrator users would ask why it was that so many other applications had commands to remove excess points on a path, but not Illustrator. Well, it took a while, but the Adobe engineers have created the most sophisticated simplify path command ever seen.

Lassos (Chapter 5): Another one of the top ten features, Adobe didn't feel that one lasso was enough; so Illustrator 9 has two—one for lassoing objects, the other for lassoing points. These two lassos make it much easier to select objects in non-rectangular areas.

Customized keyboard shortcuts (Chapter 20): If you're just starting out working with computer graphics, the ability to designate your own keyboard shortcuts may not seem like a big deal. But as soon as you gain some experience, you'll understand why it is. For instance, let's say you're about to place a hundred or so images into an Illustrator document. Illustrator doesn't have a keyboard shortcut for the place command. But with Illustrator 9, instead of choosing Place from the menu a hundred times, you can simply assign your own keyboard shortcut to the command.

Growing up with Illustrator

The following is a brief history of how Illustrator has grown and changed through the years. Although it may not help you master the program, it might help you understand why a feature you've been waiting for still isn't in the program. After all, it's taken more than 13 years to get us to where we are today.

- **Illustrator 1.1:** Released in January, 1987, Illustrator 1.1 was called Adobe Illustrator, and a young man named Deke McClelland was there to witness it. (In a practice that continues today, Adobe did not advertise that this was the first version of the product. It simply left off the number and hoped you wouldn't notice. Internally, though, Adobe called it version 1.1.) Although there was a pen tool, Illustrator created only black-and-white artwork. Great for making your average, boring company logo, but little else.

- **Illustrator 88:** Adobe then skipped 87 versions of the program and came out with number 88. No, actually, when the second version of the program was released, Adobe had the bright idea that it should name the product with the year it was created. Illustrator 88 (Sandee started with this version) added color inside the program, and an outside program called Adobe Separator that could create color separations. However, you couldn't see the colors as you drew; you could only work in the artwork mode and then switch to color to preview your work. (This didn't bother Sandee at all because she only had a black-and-white Mac SE with a 6-inch screen.)

- **Illustrator 3:** It took two years for the next version to be released. By then the Illustrator team realized they had a problem with the year-naming convention. It was fine when Illustrator 88 was out and it was still 1988, but as the months went by in 1989, the number 88 on the package dated the product. People didn't like the idea of buying a program that they knew was over a year old. So Adobe changed the naming scheme and released Illustrator 3 in 1990. One of the new features Sandee remembers fondly was compound paths. Compound paths (covered in Chapter 9) allow you to punch holes in an object to see through to what is behind it. The hole in a donut is a compound path. Before compound paths, you had to do all sorts of strange things to make holes in objects. Sometimes Sandee goes back to old artwork and sees those primitive workarounds. It's like digging in an archeological site.

Illustrator 4: Ask Mac users what version came after Illustrator 3, and they'll say 5. But the answer is actually 4, released in 1992 for Windows only. Illustrator 4 was really like Illustrator 3 except for one important feature: You could actually manipulate artwork in the preview mode. Finally, you—or rather Windows users—didn't have to toggle back and forth to see how their blends looked. For all of 1992 Mac users grumbled that Adobe was favoring the Windows market.

Illustrator 5: Finally, in 1993, Adobe released version 5 for the Macintosh. Perhaps as a way to make up to their loyal Mac users, they went beyond working in the preview mode and added gradients, filters, multiple undos, a paintbrush, and many other tools and commands. Suddenly it was the Windows users who felt overlooked.

Illustrator 5.5: To make matters worse, the next version of Illustrator was again Mac-only. One of the most exciting and revolutionary features in 5.5 was the addition of the pathfinder filters (now pathfinder commands, covered in Chapter 9). Sandee vividly remembers an advertisement for the program that promised transparency. The problem was that the pathfinder "transparency" that you got using the mix hard or mix soft filters (now called just hard and soft) was actually a trick. Once you applied a pathfinder command to an object, you could never move it or change its color, or the transparency effect would be ruined. (Did we mention that Illustrator 9 finally has real transparency? Hallelujah!)

Illustrator 6: Released in 1996, Illustrator 6 was starting to work more closely with its first cousin Photoshop. Not only could you place TIFF images in Illustrator, but you could even apply Photoshop filters to them! New tools included the star and spiral tools, which replaced the star and spiral filters. (If you're wondering, Illustrator 6 was *still* Mac-only. Windows users were starting to get downright nasty.)

Illustrator 7: The version heard round the world. 1997 was the big shakeup in the life of Illustrator. First, Adobe swore that never again would Mac and Windows versions of the program differ. Illustrator 7 was the first totally cross-platform version of the program. Not a single feature was available on one platform that you couldn't find on the other. Every keystroke, every command, every shortcut had to be totally the same. The text tools were improved so that Japanese text could be set in English versions of the program. Illustrator 7 was also the big shakeup in the look of Illustrator. All the onscreen elements were redesigned to make them look more like their Photoshop counterparts.

Although it caused some confusion for longtime users, new users found it much easier to pick up the program. (This is the same philosophy behind Adobe InDesign, which looks and feels very similar to Illustrator.)

Illustrator 8: In 1998, Illustrator finally gave its users live blends. No more did we look at the blends in programs like FreeHand and CorelDraw and wonder when, oh when, would we have such features. Not only that, but Adobe leapt far beyond those programs with two new features never seen in any illustration program: brushes, which opened up all sorts of new looks for paths, and the gradient mesh, which added more airbrush-type blends to Illustrator.

And now, with the year 2000 upon us, once again we have a new version of Illustrator. What's the best new feature? Are there any problems that will need fixing for the next version? How will Illustrator 9 affect your style of art? How will it improve your life? The only way to answer these questions is to forge ahead. There's a lot to learn, so let's get going.

CHAPTER 2

WITNESS THE SPLENDOR THAT IS ILLUSTRATOR

Whenever folks speak about Illustrator, someone always seems to drop the word "elegant" into the conversation. And truly, it fits. Despite its occasional flaws, Illustrator has always delivered a rare combination of a logical interface and extremely reliable performance. And what, we ask you, could be more elegant than that?

But even an elegant application can bewilder and vex the user it has sworn to serve. The biggest strike against Illustrator is that it doesn't always work like other programs. Illustrator provides three different arrow tools where all other programs manage to make do with one. Many commands are missing from the menus, available only through floating palettes. You change the performance of many tools by clicking *with* them rather than double-clicking *on* them. The pen tool takes some getting used to with its Bézier control handles.

The end result is that the elegant Illustrator is hard to learn. But once you come to terms with it, which takes some concentrated and patient effort, you'll never go back to other illustration programs. This chapter introduces Illustrator to new users, reminds casual users how it works, and brings longtime users up to speed. Here's where we explain the interface, briefly describe the tools and palettes, and examine every single one of the preference settings in excruciating detail.

There is nothing that says you have to read this stuff sequentially. Feel free to skip around, read bits and pieces over the course of several weeks, or cut out the pages and paste them over your bathroom mirror. Follow whatever learning style makes you smart in the shortest amount of time.

Getting Illustrator Up and Running

Most folks are pretty clear on how to start up a program with the Mac OS or Windows system software, and Illustrator is no exception. For example, you can double-click the Adobe Illustrator icon, which looks as though someone dolled up her thumb to look like Venus. Or you can double-click an Illustrator file. Or you can drag some other file onto the Illustrator application icon. Some folks call this technique *launching* a program, others call it *running* a program—but whatever you call it, you have to do it before you can use Illustrator.

Setting Aside Memory

Prior to starting up Illustrator, Mac users may want to adjust the amount of memory (called RAM, like the sheep) that your Mac assigns to the application. To do this, first select the Adobe Illustrator application icon and choose File » Get Info » Memory. This brings up the dialog box shown in Figure 2-1. Change the Preferred Size value to assign more RAM to Illustrator. (Even though you can also change the Minimum Size value, don't do it! Lowering this value can wreak havoc on Illustrator's performance and may even prevent the program from running.)

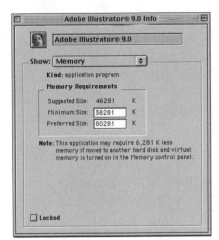

Figure 2-1: You can change the Preferred Size value, but leave Minimum Size alone.

The Splash Screen

After you launch Illustrator, the splash screen shows you that your computer is obeying your instructions. Little messages tell you that Illustrator is loading fonts or reading plug-ins. This is a perfect time to get a cup of coffee.

If you ever want to look at the splash screen again, choose About Illustrator from the Apple menu if you're on a Mac, or from the Help menu on a PC. There's no practical reason you'd ever want to do this, but there are a couple of silly features that you might find mildly amusing.

- Wait a while to see a list of credits. Whoopee.
- Press the Opt/Alt key to see the credits roll by quickly. Super whoopee.
- Click or press any key to make the splash screen go away.

There you have it, a bunch of silly information that won't do you a lick of good, except to clog your mind when you're in your dotage.

Onscreen Elements

 After the splash screen goes away, you will see the onscreen elements. Unlike the previous versions, Illustrator 9 does not automatically create a new illustration window. You have to choose the New command from the File menu and make a few decisions about the document. This may add a few seconds to your projects, so make sure you budget your time accordingly.

If you've been working on the Mac or Windows system for any amount of time, you're probably familiar with the basic desktop elements labeled in Figure 2-2. If you're new to the world of microcomputing or new to Illustrator, go ahead and read the descriptions. (Labeled items from the figure appear in italic type.)

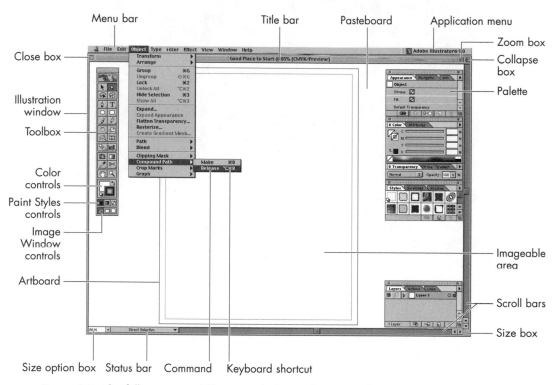

Figure 2-2: The fully annotated Illustrator desktop. This one is the Mac version.

The *menu bar* provides access to Illustrator's nine menus. Click a menu name to display a list of *commands* that perform various operations. To choose a command, drag your cursor on top of it so it becomes highlighted, then release. *Keyboard shortcuts* appear to the right of commands. If a command is dimmed (as Create Gradient Mesh is in Figure 2-2), it isn't applicable to the current situation and you can't choose it.

If a right-pointing arrowhead follows a command name, choosing the command displays a submenu of additional commands. To choose Object » Compound Paths » Release, for example, you would click the word Object in the Menu bar to open the Object menu. You would then move down to the Compound Paths command, then over to the submenu, and then click the Release command. This closes the menu and applies the command.

The *toolbox* includes 22 default tools and 31 alternate tools. To select a tool, click its icon. We introduce all 53 tools in the "Using Tools" section later in this chapter. The bottom portion of the toolbox offers three sets of controls. The *color controls* let you change the colors of an object's stroke and fill as well as interchange colors. The *paint styles controls* let you select a solid color, a gradient, or none (that is, see-through) for your fill or stroke. And in the final row, the *image window controls* give you control over the display of the foreground window.

The toolbox is known generically as a *palette*. In addition to the toolbox, Illustrator provides a number of other palettes, all of which are detailed in the "Using Palettes" section of this chapter.

The *illustration window* is the large window in the middle of the desktop. A window appears for every open illustration. The *title bar* lists the name of the document, the relative viewing size, the document color mode, and the type of preview currently chosen. If the illustration has not been given a name, the name appears as "Untitled art," followed by a number.

You can move the illustration window by dragging the title bar. Close the illustration by clicking in the *close box* in the upper left corner (or in the upper right corner in the Windows environment). Drag the *size box* in the bottom right corner of the window to enlarge or reduce the size of the window manually. Macintosh users can click the *zoom box* on the right side of the title bar to expand the window to fill the entire screen. Click the zoom box again to reduce the window to its previous size. For Windows users, this corresponds to the *maximize/restore box* that sits just to the left of the close box. To the left of that, Windows provides the *minimize box*, which reduces Illustrator to a button on the Windows taskbar without quitting the program. (The Macintosh equivalent is the *collapse box*, which hides the entire window with just the title bar visible.)

The page with the drop shadow in the middle of the window is the *artboard*. This represents the size of the drawing you want to create. Surrounding the artboard is the *pasteboard*. You can move objects out into the pasteboard if you like and these objects will be saved with your illustration, but they will not print. Experienced artists typically use the pasteboard as a storage area for objects they can't quite bear to delete. The dotted line around the *imageable area* shows the portion of the artboard your printer can actually print. Most printers can't print to the extreme edges of a page.

Together, the artboard and pasteboard are generically known as the *drawing area*.

- The *scroll bars* appear along the right and bottom edges of the illustration window, as they do in most Mac and Windows applications. They allow you to move your drawing with respect to the window to better see various portions of your illustration. Click one of the arrows at the end of a scroll bar to nudge the drawing a small distance; click in the gray area of a scroll bar to move the drawing a greater distance. Drag the tab in either scroll bar to move the drawing manually.

- The *size option box* in the lower left corner of the illustration window lets you change the view size of your artwork. Simply click the size option box, enter any permitted value, and hit Enter. You can reduce the view to as little as 3.13 percent of the actual size, allowing you to easily see the largest possible artboard size that Illustrator permits. Going to the other extreme, you can expand a square inch to a respectable 6⅓ square feet by choosing 6400 percent.

- The *status bar* just to the right of the size bar lists all kinds of moderately useful information about the program. Click the status bar to display a pop-up menu of status bar options, as shown in the top example of Figure 2-3. You can have the status bar list the active tool, the date and time, the amount of RAM going unused inside Illustrator, the number of available undos and redos, or the type of color profile assigned to the document.

Press the Option key (or the Alt key for Windows users) as you click the status bar to access the additional options shown in the bottom example of Figure 2-3. Most of these options are very silly—Random Number and Shopping Days 'til Christmas—but two are actually useful. If you use Illustrator on an older PowerBook, you might appreciate the Eyes option, which brings up a pair of eyes that follow your cursor around the screen. No more lost cursor! And if you can't get Illustrator to work correctly, then check out Ted's Home Number. You won't really get Ted, one of the Illustrator product managers—you'll get Adobe's technical support line.

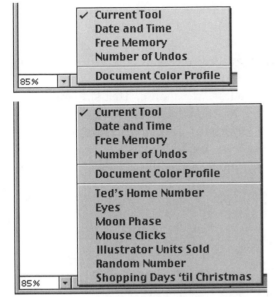

Figure 2-3:
The pop-up menus that
appear when you click (top)
and Opt/Alt-click (bottom)
on the status bar.

Using Tools

The toolbox, like any other palette, is entirely independent of all other desktop elements, so if you reduce the size of a drawing window the toolbox remains unchanged, with 22 tools visible and easily accessible. The toolbox serves, and is positioned in front of, any and all open illustrations. You can move the toolbox by dragging its title bar and hide it by choosing the Window » Hide Tools command. To redisplay the toolbox, choose Window » Show Tools.

> You can hide the toolbox and all other palettes by pressing the Tab key. Press Tab again to bring all the palettes back. To get rid of all palettes except the toolbox, press Shift-Tab (that is, hold the Shift key and then tap the Tab key).

As with other graphics and publishing programs, you select a tool in Illustrator by clicking on its icon in the toolbox. Illustrator highlights the active tool so it stands out prominently. Even folks in the next cubicle can't help but know which tool you're using.

The toolbox contains 22 tool *slots*. In addition to the default tools occupying these slots, Illustrator offers 31 alternate tools that are initially hidden. For example, Illustrator hides the polygon, star, and spiral tools under the ellipse tool slot. To use one of these hidden tools, you have to click and hold the ellipse icon to display a pop-up menu of alternates, as demonstrated in Figure 2-4. Select the desired tool as you would a command—that is, by highlighting the tool and releasing the mouse button. Slots that offer alternate tools have tiny right-facing arrowheads in their lower right corners.

Slots have an added benefit of letting you tear off the tools so they appear in their own little row. Just drag your cursor over to the *tearoff* icon (indicated by the small arrowhead) at the end of the slot. Release the mouse. That slot appears in its own little toolbar. (Despite the name, you don't actually *tear* the slot *off* the toolbar. You just choose it and it tears off by itself.) You can then position the slot anywhere on your window. You can even have multiple slots for the same tools. So on Independence Day, you can have star tools on all four corners of your screen.

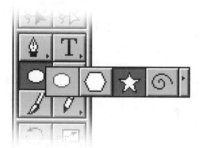

Figure 2-4:
To select an alternate tool, click and hold a toolbox icon that features a small arrowhead.

All 53 default and alternate tools appear in the composite screen shot in Figure 2-5. These tools, aside from the new ones, work just as they did in Illustrator 8.

Illustrator 9 adds two long-sought-after lasso tools. If you've ever spent too much time selecting and deselecting elements to get exactly the items you want, you're going to love riding the range with the lassos. The lasso tool (black arrowhead) selects complete objects, similarly to the regular selection tool directly above it. The direct selection lasso (white arrowhead) selects points and parts of grouped objects like the direction selection tool above it.

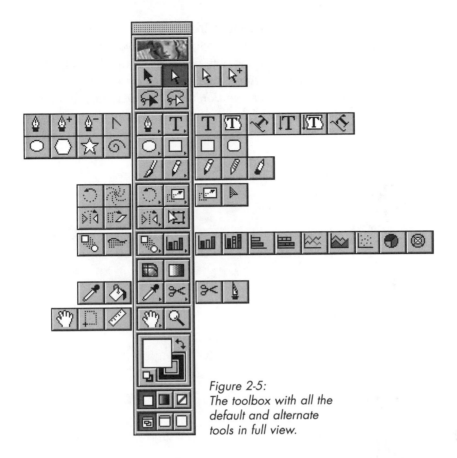

Figure 2-5:
The toolbox with all the
default and alternate
tools in full view.

Illustrator allows you to switch to any of the tools, or access the controls in the toolbox, by pressing the appropriate key, as shown in Figure 2-6. Many of the default settings are the same shortcuts Photoshop uses. They don't all make sense on first glance, but if you realize that the tool that makes rectangular areas is the *marquee (M)* tool in Photoshop, you'll understand why the rectangle tool uses the letter *M* in Illustrator. After all, the *R* key can't be assigned to the rectangle, rotate, and reflect tools simultaneously. Fortunately, Illustrator 9 lets you assign your own keys to any of the tools. So if you want to set *R* for *rectangle,* and *A* for rotate *around,* and *M* for reflect in a *mirror,* you can do so (Chapter 20).

Once again Adobe has changed the way the keyboard shortcuts access tools. In Illustrator 7 pressing a key several times cycled you to the next tool in the slot. In Illustrator 8 you had to add the Shift key with the letter to cycle through the slot. However, in Illustrator 9, the cycling is gone. You

have to assign specific keyboard shortcuts to most of the
alternate tools. (The only alternate tools that have default
shortcuts are the add point, delete point, and paint bucket
tools.) Perhaps Adobe assumes that because we can now
run with our own shortcuts, we don't need to cycle anymore.
The only exception is the F key, which does cycle through the
three window modes.

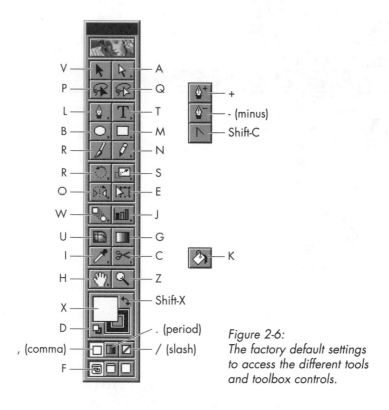

Figure 2-6:
The factory default settings
to access the different tools
and toolbox controls.

The following paragraphs explain how to use each of Illustrator's 53 tools in the
illustration window. For example, if an item instructs you to *drag*, click the tool's
icon to select it and then drag inside the drawing area; don't drag on the icon
itself.

These are intended as introductory descriptions only. If a tool name appears in
italics, that indicates that the tool's description appears elsewhere in the list.
Subsequent chapters contain more info, which is why we've included chapter
numbers in the descriptions.

Selection (Chapter 5): The selection tool—which is usually called the "arrow tool" in deference to its appearance—is active when you first start Illustrator. Use this tool to select objects that you've created so you can manipulate them. Click an object to select the entire object. Drag an object to move it. You can also use the selection tool to select text blocks.

Direct selection (Chapters 5 and 10): Click with this hollow arrow to select individual anchor points and segments in a line or shape. This is also the perfect tool for editing the Bézier control handles that govern the curvature of segments. Option/Alt-click while in this tool to access the *group selection* tool.

Group selection (Chapters 5 and 10): Click with this tool (or just Option/Alt-click with the direct selection tool) to select whole objects at a time. Though it frequently acts the same as the standard arrow tool, the group selection tool lets you select individual objects inside groups, whereas the arrow tool selects *all* objects in a group.

Lasso (Chapter 5): Drag with this tool to select entire objects within a non-rectangular area. When you release the mouse, any objects within the lasso area will be selected.

Direct selection lasso (Chapter 5): Drag with this tool to select the individual points within a non-rectangular area. When you release the mouse, any points or paths within the lasso area will be selected.

Pen (Chapter 5): This is Illustrator's most powerful drawing tool, the one that's most responsible for Illustrator's success. Use the pen tool to draw a line as a series of individual points. Click to add corners to a line, drag to add arcs. You can also Option/Alt-drag on an arc to change it to a cusp. Illustrator automatically connects your points with straight or curved segments. Option/Alt-click while in this tool to access the *convert direction* tool.

Add point (Chapter 5): Click a segment with the add point tool to insert a new point into a line. Option/Alt-click to access the *delete anchor point* tool.

Delete point (Chapter 5): Click a point with this tool to remove the point while leaving the line intact. That's why we'd rather call this the *remove point* tool—"deleting" a point would create a hole. Option/Alt-click to access the add anchor point tool.

Ⱶ   **Convert point (Chapter 5):** Use this tool to change a corner in a line to an arc or vice versa. Click an arc to make it a corner, drag on a corner to make it an arc.

T   **Type (Chapter 6):** Click with this tool and then enter text from the keyboard to create a line of type in the standard left-to-right format. To create a text block with type that automatically wraps from one line down to the next, drag with the type tool and then start banging away at the keyboard. You can also use this tool (or one of the other five type tools) to highlight characters in a text block—allowing you to edit or format them. Shift-click while in this tool to access the *vertical type* tool.

⟨T⟩   **Area type (Chapter 7):** Click a line or shape to create text that wraps inside an irregular boundary. Option/Alt-click to access the *path type* tool. Shift-click to access the *vertical area type* tool.

↝   **Path type (Chapter 7):** Click a line or shape to create text that follows the contours of the object, better known as text on a curve. Option/Alt-click to access the *area type* tool. Shift-click to access the *vertical path type* tool.

|T   **Vertical type (Chapter 7):** Very similar to the *type tool,* this tool arranges text vertically, the way Japanese script appears. Click with this tool and then enter text from the keyboard to create an ascending column of type. To create a text block with type that automatically wraps from one column to the next (from right to left), drag with the vertical type tool and then start them magic fingers fluttering. Option/Alt-click to access the *vertical path type* tool. Shift-click to access the *type tool.*

|⟨T⟩   **Vertical area type (Chapter 7):** Click a line or shape to create text that fills an irregular boundary column. Option/Alt-click to access the *vertical path type* tool. Shift-click to access the *area type* tool.

↜   **Vertical path type (Chapter 7):** Click a line or shape to create text that follows the contours of the object. As you probably guessed, one letter will stack upon the next to form a column that follows the curve. Option/Alt-click to access the *vertical area type* tool. Shift-click to access the *path type* tool.

○   **Ellipse (Chapter 4):** Drag with this tool, previously called the oval tool, to draw an ellipse. You can also Shift-drag to draw a circle or Option/Alt-drag to draw an ellipse from the center outward. Click with the tool to enter numerical dimensions for your ellipse.

Polygon (Chapter 4): When you drag with this tool, you draw a regular polygon, like a triangle or pentagon. Click with the tool to change the number of sides.

Star (Chapter 4): Drag with this tool to draw a star with symmetrical points. Option-drag to constrain the star so opposite arms are perfectly aligned, as for a five-pointed American star or a Star of David. Click with the tool to change the number of points.

Spiral (Chapter 4): Drag to draw a spiraling line, like a stylized pig's tail. To change the number of times the line twists inside itself, click with the tool in the drawing area.

Rectangle (Chapter 4): This tool works just like the ellipse tool, except that it makes rectangles and squares. Shift-drag to draw a square or Option/Alt-drag to create a rectangle from the center outward.

Rounded rectangle (Chapter 4): If you want your rectangles to have rounded corners, use this tool. To adjust the roundness of the corners of future shapes, click with the tool in the drawing area. Shift-drag to draw a rounded square. As you may have guessed, you can Option/Alt-drag to create a rounded rectangle from the center outward.

Paintbrush (Chapter 16): Referred to as the brush tool in previous versions of Illustrator, this tool creates an open path that is automatically styled with one of the calligraphy, artistic, scatter, or pattern brushes. Double-click the icon to set the sensitivity of the paintbrush. Like the *pencil* tool, the paintbrush can also be used to modify a previously-drawn brushstroke.

Pencil (Chapter 4): Formally known as the freehand tool, the pencil tool makes a freeform line when you drag with it, much as if you were drawing with a pencil. If you are not satisfied with the final result, simply drag over the part of your path you wish to correct and the offending snippet toes the line.

Smooth (Chapter 4): Use the smooth tool to reposition points and reshape paths quickly. After you drag with this tool, Illustrator will add or remove points (or even move points) in an attempt to streamline the path and smooth it out.

Erase (Chapter 4): With the erase tool, you drag over a segment of an entire path to remove it. This allows you to open closed paths and delete unnecessary paths easily.

Rotate (Chapter 11): This tool lets you rotate selected objects. Click with the tool to determine the center of the rotation, and then drag to rotate the objects around this center. Or just drag right off the bat to position the center of the rotation smack dab in the center of the selected objects. You can also Option/Alt-click with the tool or double-click the rotate tool icon in the toolbox to specify a rotation numerically.

Twirl (Chapter 12): This tool lets you twirl selected objects as if the objects were in a whirlpool. Click to set the center of the twirl and then drag to twirl, or just start dragging to twirl around the objects' exact center. To twirl numerically, Option/Alt-click with the twirl tool or choose Filter » Distort » Twirl. You can also use Effect » Distortion & Transform » Twirl to twirl an object without permanently distorting its shape.

Scale (Chapter 11): This tool and the two other transformation tools, *reflect* and *shear*, work just like the rotate tool. The only difference is that the scale tool enlarges and reduces selected objects.

Reshape (Chapter 5): Click and drag with this tool on an open path to deform the path in a freeform manner. The result of the deformation is entirely dependent on which points of the object were selected.

Reflect (Chapter 11): Use this tool to flip objects across an axis. Usually it's easiest to just drag with this tool, or Option/Alt-click to flip horizontally or vertically.

Shear (Chapter 11): Drag with the oddly named shear tool to slant or skew selected objects. The effects of Shift-dragging are generally easier to predict; when the Shift key is down, the shear tool slants objects horizontally or vertically.

Free Transform (Chapter 11): The free transform tool allows you to scale, rotate, reflect, and shear as well as properly four-point distort selected paths, all right on screen. A lame version of this tool that uses a dialog box is found under Filter » Distort » Free Distort. This is the Free Distort filter that was removed when the Free Transform tool was introduced in Illustrator 8. However, a live version of the Free Distort filter is found under Effect » Distortion & Transform » Free Distort. This allows you to transform an object without permanently changing its shape.

Blend (Chapter 17): The blend tool allows you to create custom gradations. After selecting two or more objects with one of the arrow tools, use the blend tool to click a point in one object, then click a point in the others. Illustrator creates a collection of intermediate shapes between the two objects and fills these with intermediate colors. Blends can also be created using the blend command.

Autotrace (Chapter 4): Click or drag within 6 screen pixels of a raster image to trace a line around the image. This tool is easily Illustrator's worst; you're almost always better off tracing images with the pen or pencil.

Column (Chapter 8): Drag with this tool to specify the rectangular boundaries of a standard column graph. Shift-dragging constrains the boundary to a square and Option/Alt-dragging forms rectangular boundaries from the center out. Illustrator then presents you with a spreadsheet in which you can enter your data. Double-click the graph tool icon in the toolbox to specify the options for the graph you want to create.

Stacked column (Chapter 8): This tool and the seven other graph tools that follow work just like the column graph tool, except that dragging with this tool specifies the boundaries of a stacked column graph.

Bar (Chapter 8): Drag with this tool to specify the boundaries of a standard horizontal bar graph.

Stacked bar (Chapter 8): Drag with this tool to specify the boundaries of a stacked horizontal bar graph in which each graph entity appears farther to the right.

Line (Chapter 8): Drag with this tool to specify the boundaries of a line graph—you know, your basic dot-to-dot with a few labels to make it look official.

Area (Chapter 8): Drag with this tool to specify the boundaries of an area graph. It's the color-within-the-lines evolution of the line graph.

Scatter (Chapter 8): Drag with this tool to specify the boundaries of a scatter graph, one in which only the points are plotted.

Pie (Chapter 8): Drag with this tool to specify the boundaries of a pie graph. Enough said.

Radar (Chapter 8): Drag with this tool to specify the boundaries of a radar graph. This is the ideal graph for confusing anyone attending your presentation.

Gradient Mesh (Chapter 15): Click inside an object to convert the object to a gradient mesh object and add a gradient mesh point. Drag to move a gradient mesh point. Click inside an existing gradient mesh object to add additional gradient mesh points. Option/Alt-click a gradient mesh point to delete it.

Gradient (Chapter 15): Drag inside a selected object that's filled with a gradation to change the angle of the gradations, as well as the location of the first and last colors. Shift-drag to constrain your drag to 45-degree increments.

Eyedropper (Chapters 6 and 14): Click or drag across text to copy the text attributes. These attributes can then be applied to other text using the *paint bucket*. Click an object to copy its fill and stroke attributes to the toolbox. You can also double-click an object to copy the colors from that object to all selected objects. Set the eyedropper options by double-clicking the icon in the toolbox.

Paint bucket (Chapters 6 and 14): Click or drag across text to apply the attributes copied by the eyedropper. Click an object with the paint bucket tool to apply the fill and stroke from the toolbox to the object. Set the paint bucket options by double-clicking the icon in the toolbox.

Scissors (Chapter 9): Click a line to cut it into two. Illustrator inserts two points at the spot where you click, one for each line.

Knife (Chapter 9): Drag with the knife tool to slice shapes into new shapes, just as if you had dragged through them with a real knife. The knife tool is a little *too* sharp though; it cuts through any objects in its path, whether they're selected or not.

Hand (Chapter 3): Drag with the hand tool to scroll the drawing inside the illustration window. It is much more convenient than the scroll bars. You can also double-click the hand tool icon in the toolbox to fit the entire artboard into the illustration window.

Page (Chapter 3): Drag with the page tool to move the imageable area within the artboard. Unless the artboard is larger than the printed page size, you don't have to worry about this tool. Double-click the icon in the toolbox to automatically reposition the imageable area to the lower left corner of the artboard.

Measure (Chapter 10): Drag with this tool to measure the distance between two points. Alternatively, you can click in one spot and then click in another. Illustrator displays the measurements in the Info palette.

Zoom (Chapter 3): Click with this tool to magnify the size of the illustration. (This doesn't affect the printed size of the drawing, just how it looks on screen.) Option/Alt-click to zoom out. You can also draw with the tool to surround the exact portion of the illustration you want to magnify. Double-click the zoom tool icon to view your drawing at the very same size it will print.

Using Dialog Boxes

When you choose any command whose name includes an ellipsis (…)—such as File » Save As… or Type » Find/Change…—Illustrator has to ask you some questions before it can complete the operation. It asks you these questions by displaying a dialog box.

A *dialog box* is a window that comes up on screen and demands your immediate attention. You can sometimes switch to a different application while a dialog box is on screen, but you can't do any more work in Illustrator until you address it, either by filling out a few *options* and clicking on the OK button, or by clicking on the Cancel button.

Options naturally vary from one dialog box to the next, but there are eight basic kinds of options in all. Figure 2-7 shows examples of these option types as they appear in two of Illustrator's dialog boxes. Also labeled is the title bar, which tops just about every dialog box these days. If the dialog box is blocking some important portion of your illustration, just drag the title bar to move it to a more satisfactory location.

Here's a quick run-down of the different kinds of dialog box options:

- **Radio buttons:** When you can select only one option from a group of options, a round radio button precedes each option name. To select a radio button, click either on the button itself or on the name of the option following the button. This deselects all other radio buttons in the group. A radio button filled with a black dot is selected; a hollow radio button is not.

- **Check boxes:** When you can select several options in a group, square check boxes come before the option names. To turn a check box on or off, click either on the box itself or on the option name. An *x* indicates a selected check box; a deselected check box is empty.

- **Pop-up menus:** A pop-up menu looks like a word in a box. Click the word or the triangle next to it to display a menu of options, as shown in Figure 2-7. Select the desired option from the menu just as you would a command from a menu.

- **Option boxes:** If a dialog box were a test, radio buttons, check boxes, and pop-up menus would be multiple-choice questions; whereas option boxes (also called *numerical fields* by the nerd faction) are fill-in-the-blank questions. Option boxes are typically reserved for numbers, such as dimensions or color percentages. To select the current value in an option box, double-click it. Enter a new value from the keyboard.

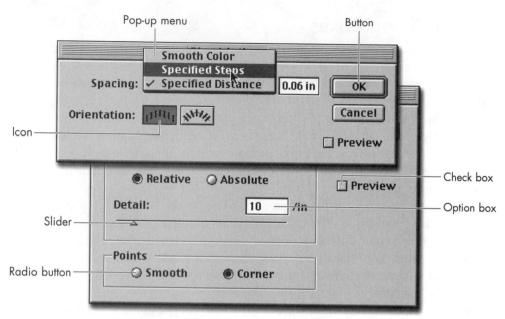

Figure 2-7: Two dialog boxes with the basic elements and options labeled.

 If a dialog box contains lots of option boxes, you can advance from one to the next by pressing the Tab key. To go in the other direction, press Shift-Tab.

● **Scrolling lists:** When Illustrator really wants to pack in a lot of options, it presents them inside a scrolling list. Use the scroll bar on the right side of the list to check out more options. Then click the option you want to use. When a scrolling list is in a dialog box, you can only select one option from the list. Palettes, however, display their own form of scrolling lists. These scrolling lists let you select multiple options by holding the Shift key to select contiguous listings or Cmd/Ctrl key to select non-contiguous listings.

 In most cases, you can select a specific option from a scrolling list by typing the first few letters of its name. For example, pressing the P key selects the first option whose name begins with a P. You may want to first make sure the list is active by clicking on it. If an option box is active, typing replaces the value instead.

- **Icons:** In a few rare cases, Illustrator just doesn't feel like being locked into all the other options it has at its disposal, so it resorts to small graphic icons. These icons are like radio buttons in that you can select just one icon from a group. Illustrator either highlights or underlines the selected icon.

- **Slider bars:** If you come across a horizontal line or colored bar with one or more triangles underneath it, you've encountered a slider bar. Drag the slider triangle back and forth to lower or raise the value, which is usually displayed in an option box. (You can also enter a different option box value if you prefer.)

- **Buttons:** Not to be confused with radio buttons, standard dialog box buttons look like words inside rectangles or rounded rectangles. Click a button to make something happen. Two of the most common buttons are OK, which closes the dialog box and applies your settings, and Cancel, which closes the dialog box and cancels the command. Some dialog boxes offer Copy buttons, which apply settings to a copy of a selected object.

Instead of clicking on the OK button, you can press the Return or Enter key. Press Escape or Cmd/Ctrl-Period to cancel the operation. Press Opt/Alt-Return or hold the Option/Alt key as you click the Return button to make a copy.

A dialog box that conveys information rather than requests it is called an *alert* box. As its name implies, the purpose of an alert box is to call your attention to an important bit of news. Some alert boxes warn you about the consequences of an action so you can abort it and avert a hideous outcome. Others are just Illustrator's way of whining at you. "I can't do that," "You're using me wrong," and "Don't you think I have feelings, too?" are common alert box messages. (Okay, that's an exaggeration, but it's not far from the truth.) The Disable Warnings setting in the General Preferences can help reduce Illustrator's complaints.

Using Palettes

A palette is nothing more than a dialog box that can remain open while you fiddle about inside the software. You can show or hide all of Illustrator's numerous palettes (including the toolbox) by choosing the appropriate command.

 To hide all palettes, including the toolbox, press Tab. To redisplay them, press Tab again. Illustrator displays only those palettes that were on screen before you pressed Tab the first time. If you press Shift-Tab, you hide all the palettes except the toolbox.

Figure 2-8 shows a couple of typical palettes from Illustrator. As you can see, palettes offer many of the same kinds of options that you find inside dialog boxes, including check boxes, scrolling lists, and the like. A bar tops off each palette. Drag the bar to move the palette on screen. Illustrator's palettes snap into alignment with other palettes; they also snap into alignment with the edges of the screen.

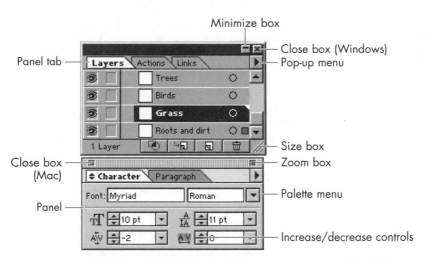

Figure 2-8: Two palettes with their cryptic options labeled.

Options vary more widely in palettes than they do in dialog boxes. Some are so specific to the function of the palette, there's no point in explaining them here. So for now, we'll just cover the ones that you see quite a bit in Illustrator and other applications (including Photoshop).

Close box: Mac users click in the close box in the left corner of the title bar to close the palette. Windows users will find their close boxes in the right corner.

Zoom box: Palettes offer zoom boxes, known as minimize buttons in Windows, on the right sides of their title bars. When you click in the zoom box, Illustrator changes the size of the palette, either making it larger to show the options or reducing its size to show just the panel tab. In the case of the Tabs palette, clicking in the zoom box aligns the palette with the active text block.

Palette menu: Click the right-pointing arrowhead located at the top right of any palette to display the palette menu, then drag to choose the desired command.

Size box: Drag the size box to change the size of particular palettes.

Increase/decrease controls: Some of the option boxes in palettes have controls that let you increase or decrease the values in the box. Click the up arrow to increase the value; click the down arrow to decrease it.

Pop-up menu: If you see a little down-pointing arrowhead in a box, this indicates a pop-up menu. Drag from the arrowhead to display the menu and select your favorite option.

After you enter a value into a palette's option box, you can press the Return or Enter key to make the value take effect and to return control to the drawing area. To make a value take effect and keep the palette in focus (that is, not return control to the drawing area), press Shift-Return.

When the drawing area is in focus, press Cmd/Ctrl-tilde (~) to return focus to the last-used palette. Illustrator will try to activate the last option you used in that palette. Because not all options remain active once you've selected them (such as the Gradient Type pop-up menu or the Caps and Joins buttons in the Stroke palette), it may highlight one of the palette's nearby option boxes instead.

Customizing a Palette's Appearance

Palettes allow you to change the attributes of your artwork on the fly, but they can also clutter up the screen and considerably limit your view. If you have tons of money to spend, you can always get a second monitor to display just your palettes while you work on your main monitor. Or you can change the look and construction of palettes so they take up less room on your screen.

The default arrangement of the palettes groups certain palettes together, as *panels* within a single palette. For instance, the color panel is grouped with the attributes panel. To change a panel's group, click and drag on the panel's tab and move the panel to its new location. One of three things happens. First, if you end your drag on an area free of palettes, you separate the panel from its original group. Second, if you move the tab onto another panel in a different palette, the panel you move will join the new group as the newest and rightmost member of that group. When you drag a panel onto a new palette, Illustrator will indicate that it is ready to let the panel join the destination palette's little family by ringing the palette with a strip of black, as shown in Figure 2-9. So if you really need to free up some screen real estate, you can group all your palettes into one humongous group.

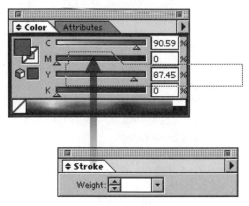

Figure 2-9:
The destination palette is ringed
with black when a new palette
is about to join the group.

The third result of dragging a panel is that you will *dock* the panel below a palette. Docking a palette results in a *meta-palette,* as shown in Figure 2-10. (OK, so maybe Deke did make up the term meta-palette, but you have to admit it did sound official. And maybe if he uses the term enough, someone from Adobe will offer him money to use the term in the next Illustrator manual.) Once you have formed a meta-palette, you have the option of adding palettes to either group, as described above, or even of making an *ultra-meta-palette* (yes, it's another Deke term) by dragging another palette onto the bottom of the meta-palette.

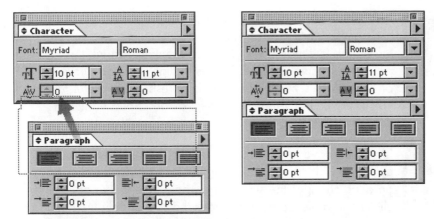

Figure 2-10: The destination palette displays a black bar at the bottom when a new palette is about to be docked. A docked meta-palette appears on the right.

Most of the palettes have more than one display size. For example, there are three different display sizes for the color palette: full options, basic options, and tab only. Full options shows all the color controls as well as the color ramp. Basic options contains just the color ramp. Tab only shows just the panel tab. If a palette has different display sizes, you will see two little arrows in the panel tab. Click the up or down arrows to cycle through the different sizes for the palette. Figure 2-11 shows the three different sizes for the color palette.

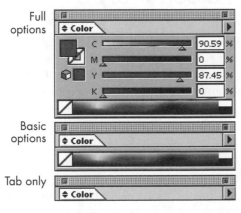

Full options

Basic options

Tab only

Figure 2-11: The three display options for the color palette.

Even if you don't see the arrows in the panel tab, double-click any panel's tab to reduce the palette and cycle through its different sizes. You will eventually shrink the palette to its smallest size, just as though you had clicked on the palette's zoom box. This is an especially useful function when you have meta-palettes, as described earlier in this section.

 Once you have formed a meta-palette, be sure to try double-clicking on all the tabs. In a regular palette, double-clicking on a tab changes the size of the whole palette; but double-clicking in a meta-palette changes the size of only the portion where that tab resides. The rest of the palette remains unchanged.

So what does all this mean? It means that you have considerably more freedom in designing your workspace. If you find that, for the most part, you use only the color, stroke, and layers palettes, then combine them into a single palette, a meta-palette, or even an ultra-meta-palette and close all the other palettes. With your single palette, controlled by a single zoom box, you'll have considerably more unobstructed space to create your artwork.

Accommodating Your Personal Style

No two folks draw alike. It's a cliché, but it happens to be true (except in the case of very close twins). For those who draw to a different drummer—in other words, all of us—Illustrator provides the File » Preferences submenu, which provides eight commands that allow you to edit a variety of attributes controlling Illustrator's performance. All of these commands affect Illustrator's *global* preferences—that is, preferences that affect every single illustration you create or edit in the future. (In the next chapter we discuss Document Setup and other commands that affect one illustration at a time.)

Choosing any of the commands in the Preferences submenu displays the corresponding dialog box; all of these boxes share a few identical elements. A pop-up menu appears at the top, and four buttons line the right side of each preference dialog box. The pop-up menu allows you to switch quickly to any of the other preference dialog boxes. The four buttons include both the standard OK and Cancel, which implement or ignore your changes while also closing the box, and the new Prev and Next. As you have probably surmised, clicking on Prev takes you to the previous preference dialog box, and clicking on Next advances you to the next box. Admittedly, this isn't the biggest improvement in software design, but it does make changing preferences a bit more efficient.

General Preferences

Choosing File » Preferences » General or pressing Cmd/Ctrl-K displays the General Preferences dialog box, shown in Figure 2-12. Here you can control the way some tools behave—the sensitivity of the pencil and autotrace tools, whether dialog boxes display warnings, plus much, much more.

The following list describes each option available in this dialog box. Of course, you may feel that you don't have the background to understand many of these options. But have no fear, each option is covered in context in one or more chapters, as the descriptions indicate. For now, content yourself with the certain knowledge that these pages contain an invaluable resource you can refer to over and over throughout your happy and productive illustrating years.

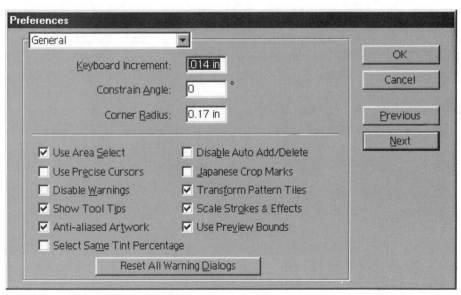

Figure 2-12: Here's where you make Illustrator conform to many of your idiosyncratic whims.

Here are the options, in their order of appearance in the General Preferences dialog box:

 Cursor Key (Chapter 10): Illustrator allows you to move selected objects from the keyboard by pressing one of the four arrow keys. Each keystroke moves the selection the distance you enter into this option box. The default value is 1 point, equivalent to one screen pixel at the 100 percent view size. That's a subtle nudge.

Constrain Angle (Chapters 4, 11, and others): If you press the Shift key while dragging an object, you constrain the direction of its movement to a multiple of 45 degrees; that is, straight up, straight down, left, right, or one of the four diagonal directions. These eight angles make up an invisible, er, thingamabob called the *constraint axes*. You can rotate the entire set of constraint axes by entering a value—measured in degrees—in the Constrain Angles option box. This value affects the creation of rectangles, ellipses, and text blocks, as well as the performance of transformation tools.

Corner Radius (Chapter 4): This option sets the default roundness for the rounded rectangle tool. A value of 0 creates perpendicular corners; larger values make for progressively more rounded rectangles. However, this is just the default setting. You can change the amount as you are working using the Rounded Rectangle dialog box. You never need to come back here to change the setting.

If you're wondering where the Use Bounding Box setting is, rejoice! Illustrator 9 has taken the setting out of the Preferences dungeon and moved it up to the View menu under the new name Show or Hide Bounding Box. Not only does this make it easier to turn the bounding boxes on or off, but you can even assign a keystroke to the command (Chapter 5).

Use Area Select (Chapter 5): This option controls how you go about selecting filled objects in the preview mode. When it's checked, you can click anywhere inside an object to select the object, so long as the object is filled. When the option is off, you can select an object only by clicking on its points and segments. Deke tells experienced users to leave this option off so they can select objects behind other objects easily without the fills getting in the way. Sandee keeps it on so she never has to worry about where she clicks.

Use Precise Cursors: When this option is checked, Illustrator displays crosshair cursors in place of the standard cursors for all drawing and editing tools. These special cursors let you better see what you're doing, but they're not so fun to look at.

In truth, there's no reason on earth to select this check box. Just press the Caps Lock key to access the precise cursors when the check box is off. If the check box has been mysteriously turned on, pressing Caps Lock displays the standard cursor.

Disable Warnings: Checking this box commands Illustrator to resist its temptation to tell you incessantly that you don't know what you are doing. For instance, clicking even slightly off an object's point with the convert point tool will by default result in Illustrator's scolding you. Disabling this warning won't correct the problem—you will still have to repeat the operation from the beginning—but you won't have to close the warning box first. Leave this on if you're just starting out so you have some idea of *why* Illustrator is yelling at you. Turn it off when you're fed up with the complaints.

Show Tool Tips: This option is responsible for those little yellow rectangles that pop up displaying the name of the tool or palette option when you hold your cursor over it. In the beginning, it's probably a good idea to leave this option selected. It helps beginners become accustomed to Illustrator's different features. Even experienced users can profit from it, because Illustrator now shows icons instead of names in palettes such as Pathfinder and Character. If the tips make you crazy, though, turn this off.

Anti-aliased Artwork (Chapter 13 and 18): With this option on, your document will have a smoother on-screen appearance. This gives you a better idea of what your vector artwork will look like when printed on a PostScript printer, because your final hardcopy will not have all the jagged imperfections that show up on-screen. This option doesn't affect placed graphics but it does impact the appearance of artwork you rasterize inside of Illustrator.

Paste Remembers Layers (Chapter 10): Select this check box if you want to paste objects back onto the layers from which they were originally copied. When this option is turned off, Illustrator pastes all objects onto the current layer, regardless of where they came from. This is just the default setting, though. There's a command in the layers palette that lets you override this setting.

Select Same Tint Percentage (Chapter 14): In old versions of Illustrator, there was a problem using the selection commands on tints of spot colors. If you had two objects filled with Pantone 185 and another filled with a 50% tint of Pantone 185, the select same fill color command would select all three objects as one. This option fixes that problem (finally!!!). Tints of colors have to have the same percentages before they are chosen by the selection commands.

Disable Auto Add/Delete (Chapter 5): By default, the pen tool will automatically change to the add point tool or delete point tool as the situation demands. For example, if you position the pen tool over a point of a selected path, the pen tool will temporally transform into the delete point tool, ready to out the damn spot. If you prefer the pen tool to limit its personalities to only one identity, check this box.

Japanese Crop Marks (Chapter 17): Instead of the typical crop marks you get when you choose Object » Cropmarks » Make, you'll get the Japanese-styled ones when this option is active. With this option selected, trim marks will also conform to Japanese styling. Japanese crop marks are a bit more involved and provide an additional center mark along each side, but they function just the same as the regular old crop marks.

Transform Pattern Tiles (Chapters 11 and 15): When an object is filled or stroked with a tile pattern, you can specify whether the pattern moves, grows, shrinks, or rotates as you move, scale, or rotate the object. Fortunately you can turn this option on or off in the transformation tools dialog boxes. This setting only affect transformations created manually.

 Scale Strokes & Effects (Chapters 11 and 16): This is the new name for the old Scale Stroke Weight. When you scale an object proportionally—so that both height and width grow or shrink the same amount—Illustrator can likewise change the thickness of the stroke or effects such as feathering that are assigned to the object. If you are working on a project where all strokes must be half a point, you want to turn this option off. Like the transform pattern tiles, you can turn this setting on and off in the transformation tools dialog boxes.

Use Preview Bounds (Chapter 10 and 11): This is the new name for the old Add Stroke Weight command. By default, both the Transform and Info palettes display a selected path's physical attributes without considering the path's stroke weight. For example, the Info palette would normally list a 40 point by 20 point rectangle with a 10 point stroke as having a width of 40 points and a height of 20 points. With the Use Preview Bounds option on, the Info palette would list this same rectangle with a height of 50 points and a width of 30 points. The 10 point stroke would add 5 points to each side. The reason for the name change is that the preview bounds can also apply to effects such as drop shadows, glows, and other effects that extend far beyond the boundaries of the original object. Good name change, Adobe!

 **Reset All Warnings Dialogs**: As you work in Illustrator, you will encounter various dialog boxes that Adobe thinks are giving you important information that will make you a happier and smarter Illustrator person. After a few dozen times reading the same dialog box, you may find yourself cursing at the screen. Sometimes, however, there is a little box that says "Don't show again." If you click that, you will never see that specific dialog box again. Unless you click this major button in the preferences—then you get to re-read all those informational messages you had forgotten.

Type & Auto Tracing

The next preference command, File » Preferences » Type & Auto Tracing, displays the lovely and functional dialog box shown in Figure 2-13. In this box you will find options related to text manipulation. If you're familiar with this dialog box from Illustrator 8, you can just skip to the next section. Nothing has changed here in Illustrator 9.

- **Size/Leading (Chapter 6)**: Just as you can nudge objects from the keyboard, you can likewise adjust the size and leading of selected text with keystrokes. To define the increment of each keystroke, enter a value in this option box.

- **Baseline Shift (Chapter 6)**: Baseline shift raises and lowers characters relative to the baseline, ideal for creating superscript and subscript type.

To define the increment for raising and lowering selected type, type a new value into this option box.

Tracking (Chapter 6): To keep large text looking good, you may want to adjust the amount of space between neighboring characters, called *kerning* or *tracking*. You can modify the kerning from the keyboard by the increment you enter in this option box. This value is always measured in 0.001 em space. (An em space is as wide as the current type size is tall.)

Greeking (Chapter 3): If text gets smaller than this value Illustrator shows the text blocks as gray bars, an operation called *greeking*. Both type size and view size figure into the equation, so that 6-point type greeks at 100-percent view size and 12-point type greeks at 50 percent. Greeking speeds up the screen display because gray bars are easier to draw than individual characters.

Type Area Select (Chapter 6): Just as the Area Select option of General Preferences gives you control over how you go about selecting filled paths, the Type Area Select option lets you choose just how careful you have to be when you're trying to select text and text blocks. When this option is deactivated, you have to click the path in which the type resides. With this option checked, you have a bit more freedom, since you need to click only within the bounding box that envelopes the type.

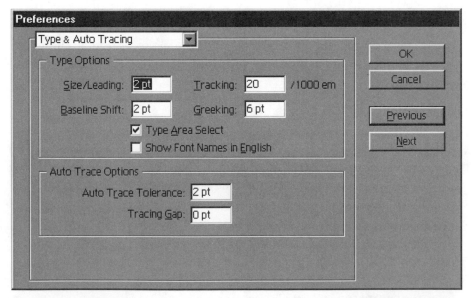

Figure 2-13: Fear not this dialog box, for it is your friend—for setting arrow key options and some text preferences.

- **Show Font Names in English (Chapter 6):** If you have fonts loaded on your system that use alphabets other than the Latin alphabet, check this option to force Illustrator to show the font in its English equivalent. This assumes that the font contains this information in its code; Illustrator cannot translate the fonts' names on its own.

- **Auto Trace Tolerance (Chapter 4):** This complex little option controls the sensitivity of *both* the pencil and the autotrace tools. Any value between 0 and 10 is permitted, and it is measured in screen pixels. Low values make the tools very sensitive, so that a pencil path closely matches your cursor movements or an autotrace path closely matches the form of the imported template. Higher values give Illustrator license to ignore small jags and other imperfections when creating the path.

- **Tracing Gap (Chapter 4):** Tracing templates frequently contain loose pixels and rough edges. Using the Auto Trace Gap option, you can instruct Illustrator to trace over these gaps. A value of 0 turns the option off, so that the autotrace tool traces rough edges as they appear in the template. A value of 1 allows paths to skip over single-pixel gaps; a value of 2 (the highest value allowed) allows paths to hurdle two-pixel gaps.

Units & Undo

The File » Preferences » Units & Undo command focuses on the units that Illustrator uses in different dialog boxes, as well as the number of undos that are at your disposal. Please take a moment to revel in the glory that is Figure 2-14.

- **General (Chapter 10):** Select Points/Picas, Inches, Centimeters, or Millimeters from this pop-up menu to specify the system of measurement to use throughout all dialog boxes (including this one) as well as in the horizontal and vertical rulers. Unlike the similar option in the Document Setup dialog box—which affects just the one drawing you're working on—this option applies to *all* future illustrations in addition to the one you're working on.

- **Stroke (Chapter 16):** Let's say you're one of those people who thinks in inches. Most likely you will want to set the general measurement to inches. But do you *really* want to specify stroke weights in inches? Not unless you enjoy thinking in hundredths of an inch. This setting gives you the luxury of defining strokes as points in an inches world.

- **Type (Chapter 6):** You *could* select an option from this pop-up menu to specify the measurement system used specifically for type. But no one in his right mind *would* do this, since points are the standard for measuring type in nearly every corner of the globe—the only exception to this rule is that a unit called Q (equal to .25 millimeters or roughly 1.4 points) has a strong foothold in Japan. Honestly, leave this option set to Points/Picas, the default. (Incidentally, this option controls the units used by three options in the General Preferences dialog box— Size/Leading, Baseline Shift, and Greeking.)

Numbers Without Units Are Points (Chapter 6): Though this may sound like a nonsensical mantra, it's meant to explain that, provided you've chosen picas as your general units, you have more freedom with the way you enter numbers into dialog boxes. With this box checked, Illustrator will assume that any number you enter into an option box without specifying a unit, such as 72 instead of 72 *pt*, should be in points and not picas. Otherwise, Illustrator will convert unitless numbers to picas—72 becomes 6p0 (6 picas and no points).

Minimum Undo Levels (Chapter 5): Here you enter the minimum number of undos and redos that Illustrator can perform in a row. Notice the word *minimum,* though. Most of the time Illustrator will give you far more than the minimum number of undos. However, if your graphics are very complex, Illustrator will lower the number of undos. This setting simply sets the absolute minimum number of undos you can have.

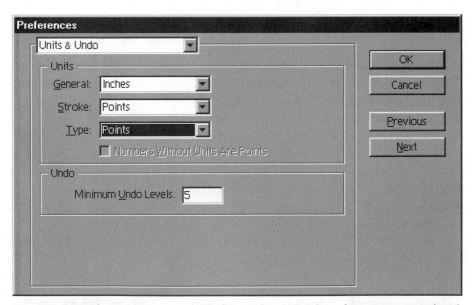

Figure 2-14: Release your inner child all over this dialog box, featuring unit and undo options.

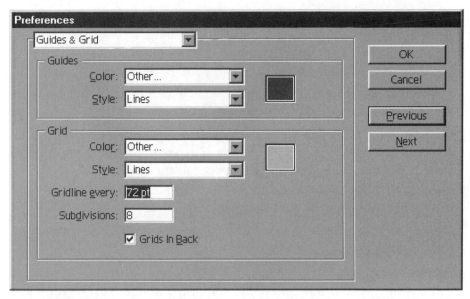

Figure 2-15: You can access even the most sublime details through Illustrator's Guides & Grid dialog box.

Guides & Grid

Descending the list, we find the File » Preferences » Guides & Grid command. This dialog box, shown in Figure 2-15, allows you to choose the color and style of both guides and grids. You can also set the size and spacing of a grid. To see the actual guides and grid, you must choose the corresponding Show command in the View menu.

- **Color (Chapter 14):** From this pop-up menu, choose from eight predefined colors for your guides and grids. If you prefer to define your own color, then either choose Other from the pop-up menu or double-click the color box just to the right of the menu. The Color dialog box will display, where you construct your own color by clicking on the spectrum in the upper right portion of the box. Also, if you become quite smitten with your creation, you can save it by clicking the Add to Custom Color button.

- **Style (Chapter 10):** From these pop-up menus, you decide whether your guides and grid will appear as dashed or solid lines. If you select the Dots option, you will see only the major gridlines and not all the additional subdivisions.

- **Gridline every (Chapter 10):** Enter the size that you want your square grids to be. You can specify the units of this number or simply enter a number and have Illustrator use whatever units you set in the Units & Undo Preferences dialog box.

- **Subdivisions (Chapter 10):** Here you state the number of times you want to divide your grid both horizontally and vertically.

- **Grids in Back (Chapter 10):** When you're using a grid, you have the choice of having the grid overlaid on the pasteboard, partially obscuring parts of your artwork, or having it appear in the background, giving your work the appearance of lying on top of graph paper. Simply select this option to place the grid in the background, where it's less intrusive.

Smart Guides

Provided you have selected the command (View » Smart Guides or Cmd/Ctrl-U), additional information and path outlines appear and disappear as you move your cursor over the different elements of your artwork. Smart guides are meant to help you align paths as you transform and move them by showing you when your transformation coincides with different intersection points within your artwork. Many people feel overloaded with information when they turn on the smart guides. The Smart Guides Preferences dialog box (shown in Figure 2-16) lets you control what type of information is displayed when you turn on the smart guides, as well as set the angles that the guides work along.

- **Text Label Hints (Chapter 5):** With this option selected, several different labels (including path, anchor, align, intersect, and page) may pop into view as you move your cursor or drag paths around the screen. They indicate that your cursor is over a special point of interest, aiding you in determining whether you have found the right spot. We suggest that you turn off this option. Artwork consisting of many paths is complex enough without the additional muddling these labels can add.

- **Construction Guides (Chapter 5):** One of the main functions of smart guides is the alignment guides that pop up as you move or transform paths. True to intuition, these guides spring forth to tell you when the present location is in alignment with your starting point. You use the Angles option (discussed below) to decide where to position these guides. If you want Illustrator to display even more alignment information, select the Construction Guides option. In addition to showing you when your present location is aligned with respect to your starting point, Illustrator also alerts you when you are in alignment with respect to various aspects of the other paths in your artwork. This allows you to position paths relative to two separate points.

Transform Tools (Chapter 5): Illustrator's alignment guides appear when you are manipulating a path with one of the arrow tools, or transforming a path with one of the four traditional transformation tools. If you want the alignment guides to appear only when you're using one of the arrow tools and not when you're using one of the transformation tools, simply deactivate this option.

Object Highlighting (Chapter 5): When this option is on, Illustrator highlights the outline of a path, making it appear to be selected as long as you position an arrow or transformation tool over the path. This is helpful when you're dealing with a number of overlapping paths, some of which are very small or just barely exposed. Otherwise, this option is better left off.

Angles (Chapter 5): With these six option boxes, you decide at what angles Illustrator will inform you whether your present on-screen position aligns with either your initial position or one of the points of some other path in your artwork—that is, provided Construction Guides is selected. You can choose from one of seven predefined sets of angles or enter the angular values that best suit your needs. Package designers and others creating 3D perspectives may want to set their own angles here.

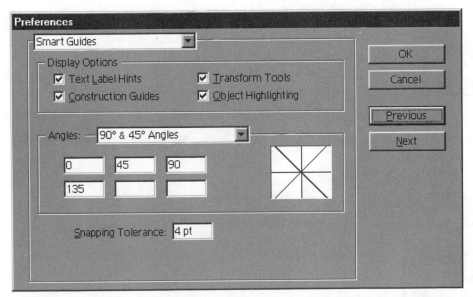

Figure 2-16: The smart guides preferences let you turn off or modify the feedback information given when smart guides is turned on.

Snapping Tolerance (Chapter 5): Here you decide within how many points (ranging from 0 to 10) you must position your cursor (that is, how close you must come to the various points of interest) before the alignment guides and text labels appear. The default value is 4 points. Higher numbers make the smart guides appear more readily; lower numbers mean you have to get closer to objects before the smart guides appear.

Hyphenation Options

Moving right along, you can choose File » Preferences » Hyphenation Options to exclude words from Illustrator's automatic hyphenating capabilities (covered in Chapter 7). Though most Illustrator users go their entire careers without ever giving a second thought to automatic hyphenation, you may feel compelled to rule out the occasional proper noun, so that Johnson never appears as John-son. Here's how:

1. Choose File » Preferences » Hyphenation Options to display the dialog box captured for time immemorial in Figure 2-17.

2. Select a language from the Default Language pop-up menu to determine which set of rules Illustrator uses to hyphenate your words. For example, you wouldn't want Hungarian hyphenation if you were writing in Finnish.

3. Enter the word you want to protect from hyphenation harm into the New Entry option box.

If you enter the word without any hyphens, it will never be hyphenated. If you place hyphens in the word, it will only be hyphenated at those places. So for example, if you enter the word *therapist* as *thera-pist*, it will only be hyphenated that way and never as *the-rapist*.

4. Click the Add button. The word appears in the scrolling list of Exceptions.

5. If you decide you've added a word in error, select it from the scrolling list and click the Delete button.

6. Click the OK button to exit the dialog box.

Your hyphenation information is saved with the application that created the file. If you transfer the file to a different computer, the text may hyphenate differently. If you share files with others, it's a good idea to make sure everyone sets the same hyphenation exceptions.

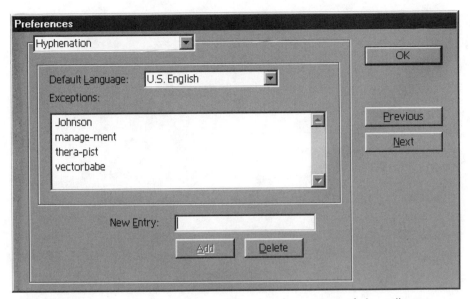

Figure 2-17: The Hyphenation Options dialog box lets you specify how Illustrator should hyphenate words and which words Illustrator should never hyphenate.

Plug-ins & Scratch Disk

These preferences are more maintenance issues that cover how Illustrator interacts with the rest of your computer. The Plug-ins command lets you direct Illustrator to the folder that contains the plug-ins you want to use. By default, all Illustrator plug-ins are installed in the Plug-ins folder inside the same folder that contains the Illustrator application. But because plug-ins consume a large amount of RAM, you may want to organize your plug-ins into a series of separate folders. This may make Illustrator perform faster or get it to work better on Macs with little memory. Then you can use the File » Preferences » Plug-ins command to tell Illustrator which set of filters you want to use the next time you start the program.

1.   Choose File » Preferences » Plug-ins. The dialog box shown in Figure 2-18 will appear.

2.   Click the Choose button and locate the folder that contains the set of plug-ins you want to use next.

3.   Click the OK button.

4.   Quit Illustrator by pressing Cmd/Ctrl-Q.

5.   Launch Illustrator again to load the program as well as the new set of plug-ins.

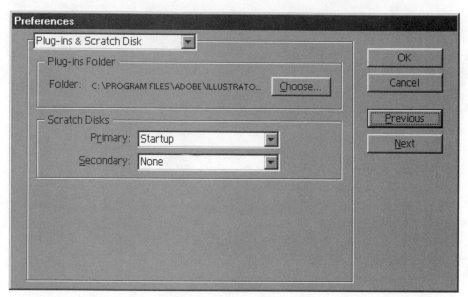

Figure 2-18: The Plug-ins & Scratch Disk dialog box enriches the Illustrator's body (hard disk space) and mind (memory allotments).

You also have the option of specifying the location of a primary and secondary *scratch disk*—the virtual memory that Illustrator uses when your RAM is full. Because virtual memory resides on your hard drive, reading and writing to virtual memory will slow Illustrator considerably. Choose the location of the first place that you want Illustrator to use for virtual memory from the Primary pop-up menu shown in Figure 2-18. From the Secondary pop-up menu you select the location of the scratch disk that supplements Illustrator's memory when the first scratch disk is full. If you have a second hard drive or another form of storage media, you can use this as your secondary scratch disk.

 When an application writes to the scratch disk, it likes to write in a contiguous area. (Hey, you wouldn't like it if you had to run all over your house just to write a letter to your folks.) Your scratch disks will be more contiguous if you regularly run utility programs to defragment your scratch disks. (Like organizing all your notepaper in one box.) If you feel Illustrator is acting sluggishly, make sure your scratch disks are defragmented.

Files & Clipboard

The final entry in the Files » Preferences submenu is the Files & Clipboard command. This command opens the Files & Clipboard dialog box (shown in Figure 2-19) that controls how files are named, how links are updated, and the format for items copied to the clipboard.

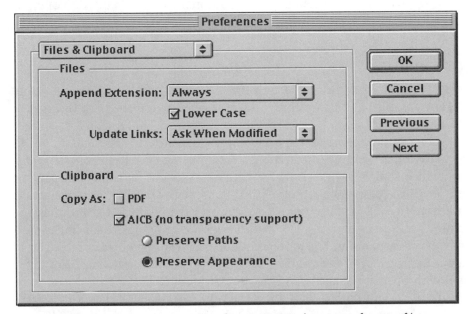

Figure 2-19: The Files & Clipboard preferences control aspects of saving files, linking files, and how images copied to the clipboard are handled.

- **Append Extension (Chapter 3):** This setting appears only in the Macintosh version of Illustrator. It allows you to automatically add the three-letter file extension to the names of saved and exported files. Windows users don't have this preference because all files automatically get the file extension added to the name of the file—that's one of the basic tenets of the Windows operating system. But the Macintosh doesn't use file extensions. If you routinely send files from the Macintosh to Windows, you probably should turn this option on.

- **Update Links (Chapter 13):** When you place images from other programs in Illustrator, they keep a link to the original file. If you modify the original file, the linked image needs to be updated in Illustrator.

This option controls how the updates happen: automatically, manually, or with a dialog box that asks if you want to update the modified links.

🌑 **Clipboard (Chapter 9):** This option controls how much information gets sent to the clipboard. This doesn't do anything if you copy from one Illustrator document to another. But if you copy from Illustrator, and then paste into other programs, you may need to set these options. For instance, older programs may not be able to handle PDF information or transparency. Changing your options here can help you copy and paste.

Color Settings

Not all preference settings reside with the Preferences command. In fact, some of the most complex and compelling lurk next door within the dark recesses of Edit » Color Settings.

The Color Settings command specifies how Illustrator manages colors inside any currently open or future illustrations. Very likely, you've heard of *color management*, which sometimes goes by the acronym *CMS* (short for color management system). And if you've heard it in the same context as most folks, your reaction may not have been altogether positive. When presented with CMS, most designers wrinkle their noses with disdain, shudder with fear, or cross their fingers and toss wreaths of garlic around their necks in hopes of warding off what must surely be the most pernicious of all possible technologies. Few folks welcome color management with open arms, and even fewer understand it.

Fortunately, where Illustrator is concerned, it's not really all that bad. So let's step back for a moment, forget everything we've heard or learned about CMS, and focus exclusively on what's going on inside Illustrator. For starters, what precisely does the Color Settings command do? The answer is: more than you may hope and less than you may expect.

First, the Color Settings command determines whether Illustrator modifies the colors in a graphic when opening or importing the artwork. Second, it determines how those colors are modified, with the ostensible goal of making sure that what you see on screen is more or less indicative of what you'll get on the Web or in print. And third, it tells Illustrator whether or not to append a few lines of code at the end of each file that explains the environment in which the illustration was last viewed and edited.

What Color Settings does *not* do is calibrate your monitor, your printer, or any other piece of hardware in your office. You can calibrate your monitor in a number of ways, including using a hardware puck or a piece of software such as Adobe Gamma. Calibrating a printer is typically the domain of the printer manufacturer or a commercial prepress technician. Illustrator can make use of this calibration data, but it cannot—nor should it—generate such data.

Of course, it's one thing to know what a command can and can't do; it's quite another to actually put it to use. Here's a blow-by-blow account of how to achieve accurate color in Illustrator 9:

1. Like Photoshop, InDesign, and other Adobe applications, Illustrator contains Adobe Gamma, which you can use to adjust the color on your monitor. We recommend you use it. On the Mac, go to the Apple menu, choose Control Panels, and then choose Adobe Gamma. On Windows, choose Settings from the Start menu, then choose Control Panel. Then double-click on the Adobe Gamma icon. From that point on, it's just a matter of reading the instructions and responding as directed. Our single suggestion—when you get to the screen with the View Single Gamma Only check box, turn it off. Then you can adjust the red, green, and blue settings independently, which is essential for getting the colors just right.

 In the end, Gamma asks you to save your characterization settings as either a ColorSync file on the Mac or an ICM file on the PC. Both formats are understood by most major graphics applications. This file defines your monitor's color space so that Illustrator can properly translate CMYK and even Web-based RGB colors so they look great on your particular screen.

2. Now that you've characterized your monitor, it's time to return to Illustrator and choose the Color Settings command from the Edit menu. Illustrator displays the Color Settings dialog box shown in Figure 2-20. The dialog box is filled with a million options, nearly all of which are dimmed. This is because, by default, the Settings option is set to Emulate Adobe Illustrator 6.0, which deactivates the color management functions and displays CMYK values on screen according to a generic color table. The upshot is that Illustrator leaves your colors absolutely unmodified when opening or placing artwork, just as in the good old days.

3. The problem with the good old days is they really weren't all that good. Selecting no color management is like forgoing the vegetables at dinner. It's all well and good to avoid the unpleasantness in the short term, but your poor diet and lack of color activism will come back to haunt you in the long run.

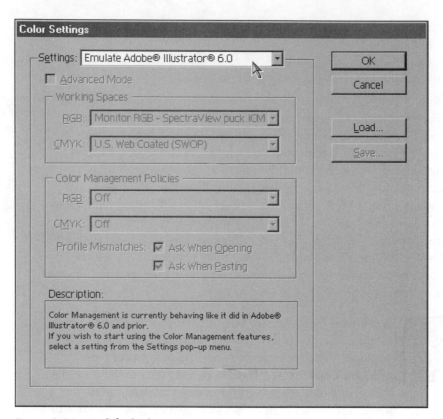

Figure 2-20: By default, the Settings option reads Emulate Adobe Illustrator 6.0, which turns most color management functions off.

 That's why we recommend you try a different option: If you mostly use Illustrator for creating screen graphics, select Web Graphics Defaults from the Settings pop-up menu. If you usually print your artwork, select the Prepress Defaults option that matches the little corner of the world you call home. Here in the States, for example, we select U.S. Prepress Defaults. In any case, Illustrator makes the other options in the dialog box available and fills them with predefined settings based on your selection, as in Figure 2-21.

4. At this point, you can press Enter to accept the default settings, or tweak the settings to make them better suit your needs. If you figure Illustrator knows best, skip to the end of the steps. If you choose to tweak, keep reading.

5. The 2 Working Spaces settings determine how Illustrator translates RGB and CMYK colors to the monitor space that you specified using Adobe Gamma. Adobe RGB (1998) is a fantastic RGB space for print professionals; the sRGB color space is well suited to on-line designers because it emulates a generic PC screen, typical of the monitors used by most Web surfers. State-side, the CMYK option is set to U.S. Web Coated (SWOP) both for print and Web professionals. If you print to a different commercial standard, select the appropriate option from the list.

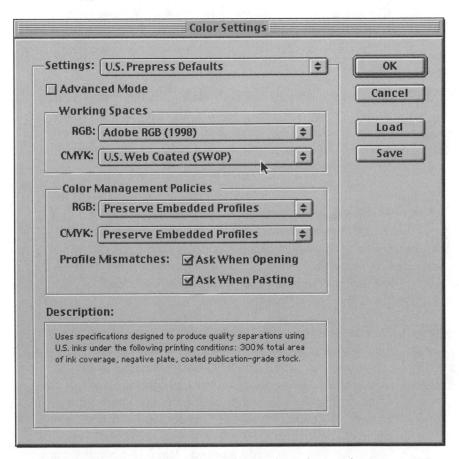

Figure 2-21: The best setting for print professionals working in the States is U.S. Prepress Defaults.

6. The next set of options, named Color Management Policies, controls how Illustrator interprets graphics that contain embedded profiles. A profile explains where a file came from so that Illustrator can make the required changes to display the artwork properly on your screen.

Print professionals will find both RGB and CMYK set to Preserve Embedded Profiles, which respects the original source of the artwork. Illustrator will not modify any actual color values, but it will massage the colors on-the-fly so they look right on your screen. Alternatively, you can also select Convert to Working Space to modify the colors as dictated by the Adobe RGB or Web Coated (SWOP) spaces selected in the previous step. For our part, we heartily recommend you leave both options set to Preserve Embedded Profiles.

Web folks will find the options set to Off. This means source profiles go ignored and no attempt is made to convert the colors onscreen. This makes sense on the Web, where exact color matching across the world's billion or so screens is very nearly impossible.

7. Last but not least are the Profile Mismatches options, which ask you what to do when opening or importing artwork that is profiled in a way that doesn't exactly match the settings you selected in Step 5. When turned on, Ask When Opening displays a message anytime you open an illustration with a non-matching profile; Ask When Pasting affects any artwork pasted, dragged and dropped, or imported using the File » Place command.

These options are good in spirit, but tiresome in practice. They both invoke the endless display of alert messages, even when opening illustrations that contain no profiles. Since Illustrator 9 is the first version of the program to support profiling, this means you see an alert each and every time you open a file created in Version 8 or earlier. Believe us, it gets old fast. Our recommendation is to turn both check boxes off and leave Illustrator to do what you told it to do in the previous step.

8. If you like pain, you can select the Advanced Mode check box at the top of the dialog box and make more work for yourself. This option lets you fine tune the exact manner in which Illustrator converts colors. If you're a color scientist, go nuts. Otherwise, leave well enough alone. Adobe's default color engine and Relative Colorimetric rendering intent are better suited to vector artwork than any of the alternatives.

9. That's it. When you're done, click the OK button. From this point on, the color settings are established and you shouldn't have to monkey with them ever again.

Clear as mud, eh? All right, that was a little dense, so here's a recap:

- Choose Edit » Color Settings
- Select the appropriate Web or Prepress option from the Settings pop-up menu
- Turn off both Profile Mismatch check boxes
- Click OK.

Now, you should be set until the next version of Illustrator comes along and makes us grapple with yet another set of entirely revamped color management options. Don't you just love upgrades?

The Prefs File

All global preference settings—including those specified in the General Preferences, Hyphenation Options, Plug-ins, and Color Settings dialog boxes— are saved on a Macintosh to a file called Adobe Illustrator 9.0 Prefs, located in the Preferences folder inside the System folder. On Windows, they are saved as the AIPrefs in the folder where you installed Illustrator. Illustrator also saves a list of open palettes, as well as the physical location of the palettes on screen, in the preferences file. These settings affect every file that you create or modify from this moment on (until you next change your preferences).

To reset all preferences and related dialog boxes to their original settings, quit Illustrator and drag the Adobe Illustrator 9.0 Prefs file into the Trash or rename the AIPrefs file. Then relaunch Illustrator; a spanking clean new preference file will be created. This can be a particularly good thing to do when Illustrator starts flaking out on you. If you've customized the program exactly the way you want, you probably don't want to lose those preferences. Make a backup copy of the preference file and save it on a backup disk. Then the next time the program starts acting flaky, most likely your preference file has gotten corrupted. Whip out your backup copy of the preference file and swap your nice clean preference file for the dirty old corrupted one.

Keep in mind, Illustrator updates the Adobe Illustrator 9.0 Prefs file *every* time you quit the program, and *only* when you quit the program. If you crash or force-quit Illustrator (by pressing Cmd-Option-Escape on a Mac or Ctrl-Alt-Delete on a PC), Illustrator leaves the preference file untouched. Therefore, if you want to force Illustrator to save your preferences, quit the program by pressing Cmd/Ctrl-Q.

If you're the adventurous type (Deke may be, Sandee isn't), you may want to try your hand at editing the Adobe Illustrator 9.0 Prefs file (or the AIPrefs file) in a word processor, such as Apple's SimpleText or Windows Notepad. After quitting Illustrator, open the Adobe Illustrator 9.0 Prefs or the AIPrefs file. You'll see a list of items in code. There's an item to turn off the splash screen (/showSplashScreen); you can even change the default typeface and size (/faceName and /faceSize). Limit your changes to numerical values and items within parentheses. In most cases, 0 means off and 1 means on. (If you totally muck things up, you can always throw away the Prefs file and let Illustrator create a fresh one.)

The Startup File

The other method for changing Illustrator's global preferences is to edit the startup files contained in the Plug-ins folder. You can change the custom colors, gradients, tile patterns, and path patterns available to every illustration. Perhaps more alluring, you can change the illustration window size, the view size, and the position of the artboard inside the window. Now, in Illustrator 9, you can edit the default style that controls the fill and stroke attributes that are applied to objects when you press the letter D. These are minor adjustments, of course, but even minor adjustments can go a long way toward creating a more comfortable environment.

1. Open the Adobe Illustrator Startup_CMYK or _RGB.

2. The file contains all kinds of styles, patterns, gradients, and colors. Read Chapters 14 through 16 for information about editing these or creating your own. Placement is not important; just fill a shape with whatever color, pattern, or gradation you want to add.

3. Size the illustration window as desired by dragging the size box.

4. Magnify the window to the desired view size using the zoom tool, as explained in Chapter 3.

5. Use the hand tool to scroll the artboard to the desired position (also described in the next chapter).

6. Use File » Document Setup and press the Page Setup button to make any desired changes to the size and shape of the artboard and imageable area. (For the third time, see Chapter 3.)

7. Choose View » Show Rulers or press Cmd/Ctrl-R if you want the rulers to come up every time you start Illustrator.

8. Close the file (Cmd/Ctrl-W) and press the Return key to save it to disk.

From now on, every new illustration you create will subscribe to these adjusted settings.

Online Updates

Once you have Illustrator installed, that doesn't have to end your relationship with Adobe. As long as you've got an Internet connection, Adobe has all sorts of information as well as updates to the program that you can download. Click the microscopic image of Venus at the top of the toolbox to open the Adobe Online dialog box. This screen provides access to Adobe's Internet-based resources, which include technical support, tips and tricks and information about upgrades and related products. If you have Internet access, launch your browser and switch back to Illustrator. Click the icon atop the toolbox and then click one of the options in the Adobe Online dialog box.

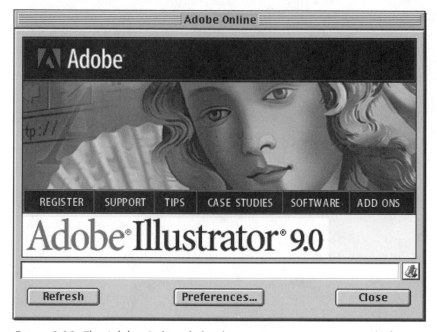

Figure 2-22: The Adobe Online dialog box connects you to a myriad of Web-based support services and information on updates.

CHAPTER 3

OBJECTS, IMAGES, AND THE FILE FORMATS THAT LOVE THEM

Decisions, decisions! When you first open Illustrator 9, you've got all your tools ready, but no document to start working on. Right away you need to make some decisions about your artwork, and you will keep making decisions as you work with the program. Some of these decisions are easy; others may confuse you. This chapter should make it easier to handle all your decisions.

The absence of an open document at startup is new in Illustrator 9. Previous versions gave you an artboard so you could immediately get to work. But today's Illustrator needs to know a little more about how you want to work before it will give you the artboard to start with.

At this juncture, you have the following options. You can:

- Ask (politely) to create a new document (Cmd/Ctrl-N).
- Open an illustration that you've previously saved to disk (Cmd/Ctrl-O).

However, every time you make a decision in Illustrator, more decisions will be available. It's like the show "Who Wants to Be a Millionaire?" where the first questions are easy but then you find yourself going for the big money—such as modifying the document, saving, or placing files. But unlike the game show, Illustrator has no audience poll and, unless you're lucky, no friends you can phone. Think of this chapter as all your lifelines.

Preparing a New Illustration

If all you ever do is open documents previously saved to disk, you can skip this information. But if you would like to start from scratch, you need to make some decisions about your document.

Creating a New Document

When you choose File » New (Cmd/Ctrl-N) you are confronted by the New Document dialog box as shown in Figure 3-1. Fortunately the decisions you make here can be changed easily later on. Press Cmd » Opt » N (Mac) or Ctrl » Alt » N (Windows) to bypass the New Document dialog box and use the settings from the previous document.

Figure 3-1: The first of many decisions you will need to make about your document. Fortunately, the ones in the New Document dialog box are easy to deal with.

Name: This one is easy; what name would you like the document to have? Because the default—"Untitled" followed by a number—is a rather bland name for a document, you should think of something snappy. Sandee has always liked the name "Guernica" but if you don't think you can live up to that, use something more descriptive like "Business Card" or "Lunch Menu."

 Don't let entering a name for the file fool you: Your file is not actually saved or written to disk when you give it a name here. The only thing that entering the name does is put the name up in the title bar of the document. You still have to perform the save command to actually make a permanent copy of the document on a disk.

 Color Mode: Don't panic, you don't have to take a course in color management to get this one right. Even if you guess, there are only two options, so you've got a fifty-fifty chance of being right. First, you need to decide whether Illustrator will limit your colors to either CMYK colors, which are usually used for print jobs, or RGB colors, which are used for Web graphics. So if your job is going to be separated by a commercial printing process, you should choose CMYK. If it's going to the Web, choose RGB. Wait, did we hear someone ask "What if the job is going to be printed *and* published on the Web?" In that case, you should choose CMYK—the needs of the commercial print job come first. It's not such a big deal if you have CMYK colors in a Web graphic, but RGB colors in a print job can cause problems when the illustration is separated.

 The ability to limit the document's colorspace is new in Illustrator 9. The reason was that after Illustrator 7 introduced RGB colors, many artists working on print documents complained that if they inadvertently chose RGB colors, their document wouldn't print correctly. So Adobe added this option to keep errant RGB colors from invading CMYK print jobs.

 Unlike what happens in Photoshop, in Illustrator choosing RBG doesn't make your file any smaller. There are no extra channels in Illustrator that make a CMYK file bigger than an RGB one.

⬤   **Artboard Size:** Sometimes you may care about the size of the artboard; sometimes you may not. It depends on what kind of document you want to create:

If you're creating a drawing, logo, or other graphic that you intend to place into a layout program such as InDesign or QuarkXPress, then you aren't interested in how big the artboard is in Illustrator. When you import an Illustrator drawing into page layout programs, all empty portions of the artboard are cropped away, leaving just the graphic itself. Heck, you can create the entire graphic in the pasteboard if you like. Therefore, the size of the graphic is all that matters.

But issues such as page size, orientation, and placement are important any time you are going to print directly from Illustrator or make a PDF file. These issues can also affect the size of Web graphics. For instance, if your page size is huge, you could end up with huge Web graphics as well.

Once you've made your selections in the New Document dialog box, click OK, and your document window appears. Now you're ready to hunker down and get to work. (For you page-conscious folks, Illustrator provides two dialog boxes—Document Setup and Page Setup—as well as one tool—the page tool. The following sections explain how these features work.)

The Artboard Versus the Printed Page

In Illustrator, you specify the size and orientation of the printed page in one step and the size and orientation of the artboard in another. This may seem flat-out bizarre—aren't the artboard and the printed page the same thing?—but it makes sense given Illustrator's flexible approach to pages. See, in Illustrator, you can create humongous pages, just shy of 19 by 19 feet—larger than many bedrooms. Because very few printers can handle this extreme page size, Illustrator lets you divide your artwork onto several printed pages if you so desire.

Now, you probably aren't looking to print 19-by-19-foot artwork, but you still might find a use for an artboard that's larger than the printed page.

Say that you want to create a 17-by-22-inch poster in Illustrator. Although this size is rather small for a poster—most are twice that large—it's awfully large for a printer. Office printers, for example, top out at 11 by 17 inches. This means you'll probably have to print your poster onto several pages and paste the pages together by hand (at least in the proofing stage).

In most cases, you'll want to specify the size of the printed pages first and then adjust the size of the artboard. You don't have to work in this order—you can keep adjusting the two back and forth until the dogs come home—but this is frequently the most logical order. It's also the order in which we discuss the commands in the following sections.

Setting Up the Printed Page

To specify the size of the pages Illustrator prints, you first need to make sure you have the proper printer selected. Mac people need to select the Chooser command from the Apple menu. On the left side of the Chooser dialog box you'll see a scrolling list of icons. These icons are *printer drivers*. Select the proper driver for your printer:

- If you're using a PostScript-compatible printer, select the PSPrinter icon. If PSPrinter is not available, select LaserWriter 8. (The two are virtually identical. PSPrinter comes from Adobe and is therefore probably more recent; LaserWriter 8 comes from Apple.)

- If you own a non-PostScript printer, select the icon named after your printer. It may even look like your printer.

After you select the proper driver, click the close box or press Cmd-W to close the Chooser dialog box.

Windows folks can change printers by clicking the Start button on the Windows Taskbar and then choosing the Settings » Printers shortcut. Double-click the Add Printer icon and follow the instructions in the Add Printer Wizard. You will have the opportunity to select a printer driver from a slew of drivers that come with Windows, or to add one that comes from your printer's manufacturer on a separate disk. After choosing a printer and finishing with the Add Printer Wizard, return to Illustrator.

Next, on the Mac choose File » Page Setup (Cmd-Shift-P); for Windows choose File » Print Setup (Ctrl-Shift-P). Different printer divers change the dialog box but for the time being, only two options in this dialog box matter: Size and Orientation. (For descriptions of the others, read Chapter 18.)

- **Paper Size pop-up menu:** From this menu—which goes by different names depending on which platform and operating system you're using—select the paper size you want to print on. As you might imagine, it's important to make sure your printer can handle the paper size you select. Don't select Tabloid (11 by 17 inches), for example, if your printer maxes out at Legal (8.5 by 14 inches). A4, B5, and others are European page sizes.

● **Orientation:** You can create an upright page (portrait) or turn it over on its side (landscape), depending on whether you want a page that's taller than it is wide (the default) or one that's wider than it is tall.

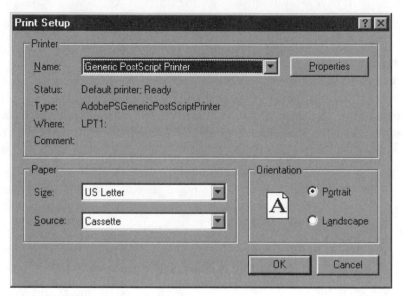

Figure 3-2: Whether it's called Print Setup on Windows or Page Setup on the Mac, here's where you change the page size and the orientation of the printed page.

After you respond to these two options, click the OK button or press the Return/Enter key. Illustrator automatically redraws the dotted outlines inside the artboard. One outline represents the border of the printed page, and the other represents the size of the imageable, or printable, area.

 If the size of the printed page is the same size as the artboard, you won't see the outside border of the printed page. You need to make the artboard bigger to see the border of the printed page.

Configuring the Artboard

To change the size of the solid-bordered artboard in the drawing area, either choose File » Document Setup, or press the two-handed key combination Cmd-Opt-P on the Mac or Ctrl-Alt-P on Windows. Most of the options in the Document Setup dialog box (shown in Figure 3-3) control the size and orientation of the artboard, as well as the relationship between the artboard and the printed page. Rather than handle the two other areas for the Document Setup dialog box here, we'll cover Printing & Export in Chapter 18 and Transparency in Chapter 17.

 If you're paying close attention you can see there's a Print Setup or Page Setup button in the Document Setup dialog box. It's a back door to the Print Setup area in case you realize you need to make some changes in that dialog box without leaving the Document Setup.

 In Illustrator 9 this dialog box is divided into three different sections. Since you're interested in the artboard, make sure artboard is chosen in the pop-up list.

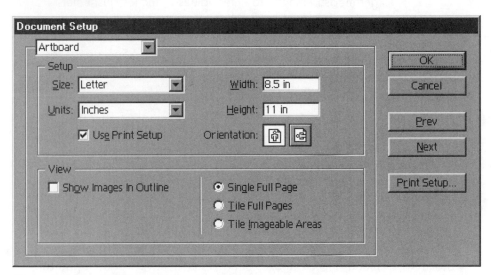

Figure 3-3: Use the Document Setup options to change the size and orientation of the artboard.

Here's how the Document Setup options work (in their order of appearance in the dialog box):

- **Size:** This pop-up menu lets you choose from a bunch of predefined artboard sizes.

- **Units:** Select an option from this pop-up menu to change the measurement system for the current drawing only (as opposed to the identically named option in the Units and Undo Preferences dialog box, which affects all drawings from now on).

- **Use Page Setup:** If you want to match the artboard to the printed page size, select this check box.

- **Width and Height:** If you don't want to use one of the predefined settings, specify the width and height of the artboard by entering values into these option boxes. It doesn't matter which value you enter first and which second—by default, the smallest value is treated as the width and the largest as the height. To change this, you have to select a different Orientation icon.

 Unless you've changed the measurement systems in the Units & Undo Preferences dialog box, the Dimensions values are probably listed in points. Although this is a good unit for precise measurements, few of us think in terms of points for larger measurements. To enter values in inches, just enter the value, followed by *in*. Illustrator automatically converts the measurement to points. You can also enter values in millimeters (*mm*) or picas (*p*). For example, *55p6* stands for 55 picas plus 6 points, which is 666 points or 9.25 inches. You can also enter *pt* for points.

- **Orientation:** Here you specify whether your artboard is taller than it is wide or vice versa. Be sure to select an option. Regardless of how you enter values in the Dimensions option boxes, Illustrator conforms to the selected orientation.

- **Show Images in Outline:** When this preference setting is turned off, a placed image does not display properly in the outline mode. Instead, it appears as a rectangle, bisected by two diagonal lines. When the check box is selected, Illustrator shows a monochrome version of the image in the artwork mode. Placed images of all varieties *always* show up in the preview mode—and of course they always print—regardless of the Show Images in Outline check box.

- **Single Full Page:** The three radio buttons next to the Show Images in Outline check box determine how Illustrator prints oversized artboards. Single full page is the default setting. It instructs Illustrator to display just one set of dotted lines and print just one page, regardless of the size of the artboard. Some artists like to use this option with a slightly oversized artboard so they can adjust the way the illustration fits on the page using the page tool.

Tile Full Pages: Select this option to display as many whole pages as will fit in the drawing area. No partial pages are allowed.

This is the option to select when creating a multipage document such as a newsletter. Illustrator numbers the page boundaries inside the artboard so you know the order in which the pages will print.

Tile Imageable Areas: By selecting the Tile Imageable Areas radio button, you tell Illustrator to chop up the artboard into as many imageable areas as will fit, thus ensuring no gap between an object printed half on one page and half on another.

Select the Tile Imageable Areas option when subdividing poster-sized artwork onto many printed pages.

Once you exit the Document Setup dialog box (by pressing Return/Enter, naturally), you'll see the altered page boundaries against the altered artboard. To adjust the position of the page boundaries, read on.

Positioning the Pages on the Artboard

You can't move the artboard. (That is, you can scroll around so that it looks like it moves inside the illustration window, but you can't actually change its location.) The artboard is always positioned smack dab in the center of the pasteboard. However, you can move the page boundaries with respect to the artboard using the page tool. (If you can't raise the bridge, lower the water.)

The page tool is the first alternate tool in the hand tool slot. Select this tool and then click or drag inside the artboard to set the location of the lower left corner of the imageable area of a printed page. If you selected the Tile Imageable Areas or Tile Full Pages option in the Document Setup dialog box, a network of page boundaries emanates from the point at which you release the mouse button.

To automatically line up the page boundaries with the lower-left corner of the artboard, double-click the page tool in the toolbox.

(If just one page boundary appears even though you selected the Tile Full Pages radio button, it's because this is the only whole page that fits at this location. Drag again with the page tool or increase the size of the artboard to see more pages.)

Always use the page tool to change the placement of an illustration on a page. It's generally easier and always faster than trying to move a huge squad of graphic objects and text blocks with the arrow tool. If you need more wiggle room, increase the size of the artboard one or more inches all around.

Hiding Pages and Artboards

If the dotted page boundaries get in your face, choose View » Hide Page Tiling to make them go away. This is, of course, merely a temporary measure. You can make the page boundaries reappear at any time by choosing View » Show Page Tiling.

As we mentioned before, if you're creating artwork that will be exported to a layout program, you don't need to be concerned with the artboard. Choose View » Hide Artboard. (If the idea of working without an artboard frightens you, choose View » Show Artboard to get it back.)

Opening and Placing

Illustrator lets you have multiple illustration windows open at a time. To create another empty illustration window, for example, you can choose File » New or press Cmd/Ctrl-N. You open an illustration saved to disk by choosing File » Open or pressing Cmd/Ctrl-O (the letter O), all without closing any open windows.

You can open four kinds of files in Illustrator:

- Drawings previously created in Illustrator.

- Drawings created in FreeHand or some other drawing program and saved in either the Illustrator file format or the format native to the other drawing program.

- Documents created in InDesign, QuarkXPress, or FreeHand and exported in EPS format, or documents converted to the PDF format.

- Images saved as TIFF, JPEG, or some other compatible format.

If you open an illustration (a line drawing saved in any of a number of different formats, including both the Illustrator and the FreeHand native formats), it pops up on screen in a new illustration window. You can edit any line, shape, or word of text as explained in the myriad chapters that follow. Similarly, you can open and edit the lines, shapes, or text from EPS documents. You can also edit the shapes and text inside opened PDF files, although it is possible that you may lose some objects in the PDF conversion.

When you open a TIFF file or another image, Illustrator displays the images in a new illustration window. You can move or transform (scale, rotate, flip, or skew) images, as well as apply Photoshop filters (as described in Chapter 13). But you can't edit them in the same way that you edit object-oriented illustrations.

If you want to add an illustration or image to the illustration you're working on, choose File » Place. Rather than creating a separate illustration window, Illustrator places the graphic in the foreground window. The graphic appears selected so you can begin working on it immediately. You can move or transform a placed graphic, but you can't edit it, even if the graphic was created using Illustrator. You can also apply Photoshop filters to placed images (unless the placed image is an Illustrator EPS, as this chapter explains later).

We discuss individual file formats and the special ways to deal with them later on in the section "Those Crazy, Kooky File Formats." But first, let's briefly go over the basics of opening or placing a file from disk. If you already know all about opening files, feel free to skip this section.

Using the Open Dialog Box

When you choose File » Open or File » Place, Illustrator displays the Open dialog box (shown in Figure 3-4) or the Place dialog box. These boxes are identical in form and function except for their names, of course, and the Place dialog box contains an additional option box, discussed below. Both Open and Place request that you locate and select the drawing that you want to work with. The dialog box lets you search through the folders on all available hard drives, CD-ROMs, and floppy disks. Sometimes you can even preview what the file looks like before you open or place it.

Using the Preview

The Open dialog box includes a thumbnail preview of the selected illustration or image. The beauty of the preview is that you don't have to open the graphic in order to remember what it looks like. Click the Show Preview button to open the preview area in the dialog box. In order to see the preview you have to have saved a thumbnail along with the file inside either Illustrator 6 or later (previous versions didn't support previews) or Photoshop 2.5.1 or later. Illustrator can also display the PICT previews included with some EPS files. If you turn the option off, the preview disappears and the Open dialog box collapses to save screen space.

Showing Files

The Open dialog box also has a pop-up menu where you can choose what types of files you want to see. The choices are:

- **All Readable Files:** This lets you see all files that Illustrator knows it can open. This option is the default and helps you focus on the files you want to work with.

- **All Files:** Choose this option to see all files in the current folder, whether Illustrator can open them or not. Every once in a while you may be lucky and you can force Illustrator to open a graphic that it doesn't think it can open.

- **File types:** You can also choose to display only a specific type of file that Illustrator knows it can open. For instance, you may only want to open CorelDraw files. You can choose that file type and only open those files. This list also helps you understand which file types Illustrator does recognize.

Figure 3-4: The Open dialog box is nothing more than a tool for locating graphics stored on disk.

The Place Options

The Place dialog box has additional options that aren't available in the Open dialog box: the Link, Template, and Replace check boxes.

Link

When this box is checked, Illustrator tags the physical location of the image or illustration without integrating it into the file, and the file's size therefore does not increase. Images so placed are considered linked. If you turn off this check box, Illustrator will save the placed item as part of your artwork—resulting in a larger file. These images are called "embedded images."

Template

If you choose this check box, the placed image acts as a template, ideal for tracing. Illustrator automatically creates a new template layer (directly below the current layer) expressly for this image. A template layer is automatically set as visible, locked, and non-printing. The image will be dimmed by 50 percent. (For more information on layers, see Chapter 4.)

Replace

Instead of simply placing an image, you can replace a previously placed image with a new one. First select the image that you want to replace in your artwork. Then choose File » Place, select the new image from the scrolling field, check the Replace check box, and press the Return/Enter key.

The Links Palette

Illustrator offers a palette devoted to the organization and keeping of all your placed images, linked and embedded. For each image you place in a document, Illustrator creates a *link* in the Links palette—this term is used for both linked and embedded images. The link includes the image's name and a thumbnail preview of the image, as shown in Figure 3-5.

The link may also include one of three small informational icons, labeled in Figure 3-5.

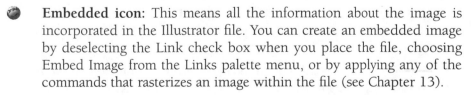 **Embedded icon:** This means all the information about the image is incorporated in the Illustrator file. You can create an embedded image by deselecting the Link check box when you place the file, choosing Embed Image from the Links palette menu, or by applying any of the commands that rasterizes an image within the file (see Chapter 13).

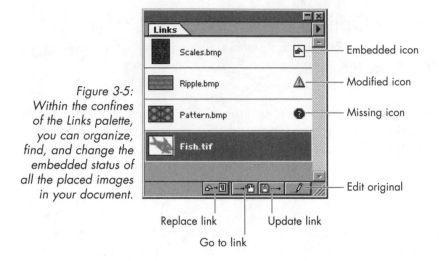

Figure 3-5:
Within the confines
of the Links palette,
you can organize,
find, and change the
embedded status of
all the placed images
in your document.

Modified icon: If you change a linked image outside of Illustrator, Illustrator displays the modified icon. This is a gentle reminder that you need to update the linked image.

Missing icon: This icon never shows up when you first place an image. It appears when you open a file that contains a linked image that Illustrator can no longer locate. Perhaps you've moved the file to a new location or—shudder!—you've thrown the file away. Whatever the case, this icon alerts you that the original is no longer available. You can either relink the image or replace it with another image.

No icon whatsoever: This lack of an icon tells you that you have a linked image in proper working order.

The Link palette's pop-up menu contains options that let you view and modify the images associated with the different links. The first six options require that either an image is selected in your document or that a link is selected in the Links palette. These options are:

Go to Link: With a link selected, choose this option (or click the second icon from the left along the bottom of the palette) and Illustrator will select the image associated with the link and center it in the document window.

Update Link: If you've modified the original file of a linked image currently open in Illustrator, this command lets you update the image. Select the image's link and choose this option (or click the second icon from the right along the bottom of the palette).

- **Edit Original:** Choose this option to open the original image in the application in which it was created. If the original image wasn't created on your computer, the image will open in the most appropriate application (as dictated by your operating system and the image's format). This option affects only linked images because embedded images, as integrated parts of your document, no longer have originals.

- **Replace:** If you decide that an image is wrong for your document, select its link from the Link palette and choose this option. The standard Place dialog box will display. Select the image that you'd prefer in the place of the original. As was the case when you placed the original image, you'll have the option of linking or embedding the new image via the Link check box.

- **Embed Image:** Choose this option to encode a linked image's information into your document. This embeds the image, just as though you had deactivated the Place dialog box's Link check box when first placing the image.

- **Information:** With a link selected, choose this option (or double-click the link) to display the Link Information dialog box. Here you'll find information about the image including its name, location on disk, size in bytes, kind (that is, its file format), creation and modification dates, and any changes you that made to its scaling or angular orientation.

- **Show:** You can opt to show all links in the Links palette or just those in which you are interested.

- **Sort:** Choose the appropriate option to sort the links by name, kind or status. Sorting links by status groups the links into those that are missing, modified or up-to-date.

Those Crazy, Kooky File Formats

For the record, *file formats* are different ways to save or export a file to disk. Just as Betamax and VHS are different videotape formats, TIFF and PCX are different image formats. By supporting a wider variety of formats, Illustrator can accept graphics from all kinds of Macintosh and Windows applications.

The following sections describe many of the formats Illustrator 9 supports, starting with the native Illustrator format and continuing through the others in alphabetical order. We'll tell you how each format works and what good it is, and we'll offer additional instructions as needed.

Native Illustrator

The native Illustrator format—the one Illustrator likes best—is a type of PostScript file. If you know how to program in PostScript, you can even open the file (as a text file) in a word processor and edit it line by line. There are seven variations on the basic Illustrator format, each corresponding to a different version of the software:

- **Illustrator 9.0:** This format saves every little thing you can do in Illustrator 9.

- **Illustrator 8.0:** This format does not support appearances, transparency, live object effects, and live raster effects.

- **Illustrator 7.0:** This format does not support the extended blend capabilities, gradient meshes, and specialized brushstrokes.

- **Illustrator 6.0:** This format does not support grids, the expanded template abilities, and some file formats. Otherwise, it is identical to the Illustrator 8 format.

- **Illustrator 5.0/5.5:** The Illustrator 5 format does not support imported image files or thumbnail previews.

- **Illustrator 4.0 (for Windows):** This Windows-only version of the Illustrator format is almost identical to the Illustrator 3 format. (Illustrator 4 also supported grids and TIFF templates—neither of which was possible on the Mac side until Illustrator 7—but this hardly matters format-wise.)

- **Illustrator 3.0/3.2:** This format doesn't support gradients, layers, large artboard sizes, tabs, and columns or rows. It converts gradient fills to blends and combines all objects onto a single layer. Objects in the pasteboard may be lost.

- **Illustrator 88:** This format does not support compound paths, area and path text, text blocks with more than 256 characters, custom guides, and charts. All paths remain intact, but they may not serve their original function. Text blocks are divided into pieces; area and path text may be broken up into individual letters.

- **Illustrator 1.0/1.1:** This format supports only paths and small text blocks. What it doesn't support could fill a book (such as this book): tile patterns, masks, placed EPS images, and colors (that's right, colors).

Although Illustrator can open both 88 and 1.0/1.1 files, it no longer allows you to save back to those formats. If there is some obscure reason you need files in those formats, use FreeHand 8 or 9, which do support saving files in those formats.

Acrobat PDF

In reality, a native Illustrator 9.0 file is actually an Acrobat 1.4 file hiding under an Illustrator icon. (Choose File » Open in Adobe Acrobat 4.0 and then choose Show All Files. You'll be able to view any Illustrator files directly in Acrobat.) This means that Illustrator files are already in the Acrobat PDF (*Portable Document Format*) and can be made part of a PDF pre-press workflow.

You can trade PDF files with other Mac and Windows users, and regardless of which program you used to create the original file or which fonts you used to format the text, all anyone needs to view the file is the Acrobat reader. Illustrator goes one better, letting you edit text and graphic objects within the Acrobat document itself.

Amiga IFF

The Amiga was an experiment in desktop computers pioneered by Commodore in the 80s. Adobe recognizes that there still may be many files originally saved in this format. To this end, Illustrator lets you open and save IFF (Interchange File Format) files. IFF is the Amiga's all-around graphic format, serving much the same function as PICT on the Mac.

AutoCAD Drawing (DWG) and AutoCAD Interchange (DXF)

AutoCAD is program used by engineers and architects. DWG is the standard file format created by AutoCAD. DXF is the tagged data format of those files.

BMP (BMP)

BMP is the native format for the cheesy little Paint utility that ships with Windows. BMP is the equal of PCX, supporting 16 million colors and high resolutions. If there is any way that you can avoid working with BMP files, do so. However, if you get a BMP image, rest assured that you can place it into your illustration.

Computer Graphics Metafile (CGM)

CGM is a vector-based file format that is used by a wide variety of programs. Think of CGM as the common language between different vector programs.

CorelDRAW 5, 6, 7, 8 (CDR)

Although it can't export in the CorelDRAW format, Illustrator does let you open files created in CorelDRAW versions 5, 6, 7, and 8. Of course, not all effects and attributes will translate correctly when opened in Illustrator.

Encapsulated PostScript (EPS)

The EPS format combines a pure PostScript description of an illustration with a preview so you can see what the image looks like on screen. Years ago EPS files were the only way to get Illustrator artwork into page layout programs. However, programs such as InDesign and PageMaker can now import native Illustrator files. If you are working with those programs, you should consider using the native Illustrator format. For other layout programs, such as QuarkXPress, use EPS files.

FilmStrip (FLM)

FilmStrip is the format used by Adobe Premiere and Adobe Photoshop. FilmStrip organizes frames into a long vertical strip. A gray bar separates each frame. Though Photoshop is a far more useful program for editing FilmStrip files, you can open and add to these files in Illustrator.

FreeHand 4, 5, 6, 7 (FH4, FH5, FH6, FH7, FH8)

Why would Adobe let you open FreeHand files in Illustrator? After all, isn't Macromedia FreeHand Illustrator's number one arch rival? Well, yes, but that doesn't mean you shouldn't be able to translate Freehand files into your own Illustrator artwork. Of course don't expect all the FreeHand attributes to make it across the border. But it does help greatly when you're working desperately Sunday night and need to add the client's FreeHand logo into your Illustrator page.

Graphics Interchange Format (GIF89a)

Originally designed for transferring compressed graphics with a modem, GIF is the most extensively used graphics format on the Web. It supports up to 256 colors and LZW compression, as does TIFF (mentioned below). Although you can use the Export command to create GIF images, you've got far more control if you use the Save for Web option explained in Chapter 19.

JPEG

Named after the folks who designed it—the Joint Photographic Experts Group—JPEG is the other widely used Web graphics format and is best used for compressing photographs and other *continuous-tone* images, in which the distinction between immediately neighboring pixels is slight. Any image that includes gradual color transitions qualifies for JPEG compression. JPEG is not well suited to screen shots, line drawings, and other high-contrast images. Like GIF images, you have much more control using the Save for Web option to create JPEG files.

Kodak Photo CD

Photo CD is the affordable photographic scanning technology that leaves some flatbed scanners in the dust. You can take a roll of undeveloped film, color negatives, or slides in to your local Photo CD dealer and have the photos scanned onto a CD-ROM at 2,048 by 3,072 pixels for $2 per photo. Each CD holds 100 images, allowing you to acquire a library of images without taking up a lot of room in your home or office. Better yet, Photo CDs are designed to resist the ravages of time and last well into the twenty-second century (longer than any of the people using them now).

Metafiles (WMF, EMF)

Metafiles are actually the broad description of any files that contain commands that are used to draw graphics. Strictly speaking, Illustrator files are a type of metafile. WMF stands for *Windows Metafile,* the 16-bit files used by the Windows operating system to display pictures. EMF stands for *Enhanced Metafile*, a more advanced form of the Windows metafile, which contains 32-bit information.

PC Paintbrush (PCX)

PCX doesn't stand for anything. Rather, it's the extension that PC Paintbrush assigns to images saved in its native file format. PCX is one of the most popular image file formats in use today, largely because PC Paintbrush is the oldest painting program for DOS. PCX images can include up to 16 million colors.

Photoshop 5 (PSD)

Illustrator can open and place images stored in Photoshop's native format. This means you do not have to save a copy of a Photoshop file as a TIFF or EPS in order to add it to Illustrator documents. Even better, you can open Photoshop files and any Photoshop layers can be converted into distinct images in Illustrator—complete with transparency, and with masks applied.

PICT (PIC, PCT)

The PICT (*Macintosh Picture*) format is a graphics exchange format Apple designed more than ten years ago and has updated irregularly over time. You can save both object-oriented illustrations and photographic images in the PICT format, but the format isn't ideally suited to either. Frankly, TIFF is better for images, and EPS is better for illustrations.

Pixar (PXR)

When it wasn't busy creating award-winning blockbusters such as *Toy Story, A Bug's Life* and *Toy Story 2,* Pixar created a few 3-D graphics applications for the Mac, including MacRenderMan, ShowPlace, and Typestry. The company works its own 3-D magic using mondo-expensive Pixar workstations. Illustrator can open a still image created on a Pixar machine.

Portable Network Graphics (PNG)

Designed to outperform and eventually replace GIF, PNG compression doesn't sacrifice quality and supports both 24-bit and 48-bit images. Thus, PNG files are larger than GIF, JPEG, or TIFF files (unless you are exporting a grayscale image), and are generally best suited for smaller images. Once again, although you can use the Export command to create PNG files, you have more control using the Save for Web dialog box. Although older browsers don't support PNG, the new versions do.

Scalable Vector Graphics (SVG) and Scalable Vector Graphics Compressed (SVGZ)

Welcome to the world of the future. Scalable Vector Graphics is a vector file format that can be coded directly into XML documents. SVG files offer many benefits over other formats: They are smaller than GIF or JPEG files, can be scaled up or down, can be made part of searches, and can handle animation. So why aren't there loads of SVG files posted on the Web? Because as of the publication of this book, most people don't have the browsers necessary to view SVG files. We aren't sure when support for SVG will be incorporated into the main browsers.

The release of Illustrator 9 may help make SVG more widespread. Not only can Illustrator create SVG files, it ships with a plug-in to let you view SVG files in a Web browser.

Shockwave Flash (SWF)

Oh, the drama! Oh, the competition! Until very recently it was hard to get anyone from Adobe to even *use* the term SWF—Macromedia's proprietary format for Web animations. Now there are *two* Adobe products—Illustrator and LiveMotion—that create SWF animations. (SWF animations are commonly called Flash files, but Flash (FLA) files are the native file format created by Macromedia Flash.) Why the switcheroo? Adobe decided that if you can't beat 'em, join 'em. Adobe knew that Flash (SWF) animations let you create very intricate animations with extremely small file size. So Illustrator lets you export as SWF animations (see Chapter 19).

Although Illustrator can create SWF animations, it doesn't let you create the buttons, actions, or scenes, nor add sounds that many finished SWF animations have. For that you'll need to use either Macromedia Flash or Adobe LiveMotion.

Targa

TrueVision's Targa and NuVista video boards let you overlay computer graphics and animation onto live video. The effect is called *chroma keying* because typically a key color is set aside to let the live video show through. TrueVision designed the Targa format to support 32-bit images that include so-called *alpha channels* capable of displaying the live video. Illustrator doesn't know a video from a rodeo, but it can place a still Targa image.

Tag Image File Format (TIFF)

Developed by Aldus (which is now part of Adobe) to standardize electronic images so you could easily import them into PageMaker, TIFF (*Tag Image File Format*) is one of the most widely supported formats across both the Macintosh and Windows platforms. Unlike PICT, it can't handle object-oriented artwork, but it is otherwise unrestricted, supporting 16 million colors and virtually infinite resolutions.

Photoshop lets you apply so-called LZW (Lempel-Ziv-Welch) compression to a TIFF image, which substitutes frequently used strings of code with shorter equivalents. This makes the files smaller on disk without altering so much as a single pixel. Imaging professionals call this kind of compression *lossless*, because it preserves the integrity of each and every scanned color. Illustrator likewise supports LZW compression. It also opens both the Mac and Windows varieties of TIFF, so you never have to worry about your Photoshop images' compatibility with Illustrator.

Getting Around in Illustrator

Illustrator works a lot like other graphics programs. You can zoom in to take a closer look at a detail and out to view your illustration in its entirety. You also can scroll the illustration to bring different bits and pieces into view. And if you own an older, slower machine, you can view objects in a special wireframe mode that speeds up screen display.

The next few sections explain how to get around quickly and expertly. If you don't know the keyboard shortcuts already, pay special attention to these. Using navigational shortcuts rather than selecting tools and commands expedites the artistic process more than any other single factor.

Fit-in-Window and Actual Sizes

Illustrator provides 23 preset *view sizes*, which are the magnification levels that Illustrator uses to display your drawing in the illustration window. Illustrator also allows any view size between 3.13 and 6400 percent by entering the value into the size option box or dragging with the zoom tool.

Assuming that you haven't altered the Adobe Illustrator Startup file, Illustrator displays every new illustration at a *fit-in-window size*, which reduces the artboard so it fits inside the illustration window. The specific magnification level required to produce the fit-in-window size depends on the size of your monitor and the size of the artboard. In Figure 3-6, for example, the artboard fits in the window at 50 percent magnification.

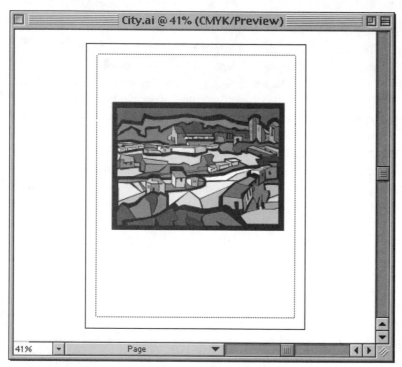

Figure 3-6:
A typical
illustration
viewed from
far away at fit-
in-window size.

You can return to fit-in-window size at any time by choosing View » Fit In Window or pressing Cmd/Ctrl-0 (zero). If this key equivalent doesn't necessarily remind you of anything, just double-click the hand tool icon in the toolbox. (To help you remember this shortcut, think of using that hand tool to *push back* the illustration.)

Another useful view size is *actual size*—or 100 percent view—which shows the visible details of your illustration on screen more or less as they will print. Figure 3-7 shows an example.

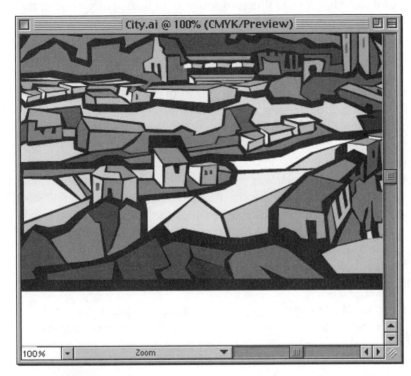

Figure 3-7: Switch to actual size to see your illustration at the size it will print.

Actual size is not an *exact* representation of your illustration, and even approximate accuracy assumes your monitor displays 72 pixels per inch. Many monitors can pack in more pixels, causing an illustration viewed at actual size to appear quite a bit smaller than it prints. If you want to get a truly accurate feel for how your illustration will print, print it (as described in Chapter 18).

You can switch to actual size by choosing the View » Actual Size command or pressing Cmd/Ctrl-1. (The number 1 stands for *one* hundred percent.) But if you can't remember any keystrokes, double-click the zoom tool icon in the toolbox (the one that looks like a magnifying glass).

Magnifying as the Mood Hits You

You can access each of Illustrator's 23 preset view sizes using the zoom tool. Select the zoom tool and click in the illustration window to magnify your drawing to the next-higher view size. For example, when you're viewing an illustration at actual size, clicking with the zoom tool takes you to 150 percent. Clicking again takes you to 200 percent. Each view affords greater detail but shows off less of your artwork.

Drag with the zoom tool to surround the portion of the illustration that you want to magnify with a dotted rectangle called a *marquee*. Illustrator zooms in until the surrounded area fills the entire screen, as demonstrated in Figure 3-8. Whereas clicking with the zoom tool lets you step through the 23 preset view sizes, the marquee takes you to the view size that most closely reflects the exact area you drag on. Notice that in the lower portion of Figure 3-8, which shows the result of dragging with the zoom tool, the size box indicates a view size of 478.38 percent. If you were to click with the zoom tool or click the Zoom In button inside the Navigator palette, the view size would step up to the next size, 600 percent.

Once you get a feel for marqueeing, try out the following techniques in mid-drag to make your zooms more precise:

- Mac users can press the Control key after starting the drag to create a marquee from the center outward. Windows users simply marquee as you normally would (depress the left button and drag with the mouse) and then, in addition, press and hold the right mouse button.

- Press the spacebar in the middle of a drag to move the marquee. To change the shape of the marquee again, just release the spacebar.

- If you decide in mid-drag that you don't want to magnify the illustration after all, drag back to the spot where you started so the dotted marquee disappears, and then release. Illustrator knows you chickened out and leaves the view size unchanged.

When you press the Opt/Alt key, the cursor displays an inset minus sign, showing you that it's all set to zoom out. Opt/Alt-clicking with the zoom tool reduces the view size to the next lower view size. You can see more of your artwork but less detail.

The zoom tool cursor is empty when your current view size is at either the maximum (6400 percent) or minimum (3.13 percent) level of magnification. At that point, you can zoom in or out no further.

Figure 3-8: Drag with the zoom tool to marquee the area that you want to zoom in on (top). When you release the mouse button, Illustrator magnifies the area to fill the window (bottom).

You can also zoom in and out using a whole mess of keyboard shortcuts:

- To access the zoom tool temporarily when some other tool is selected, press and hold the Cmd/Ctrl key and spacebar (the same shortcut as found in InDesign, PageMaker, Photoshop, and FreeHand). Releasing the keys returns the cursor to its previous appearance.

- You can also zoom in one level by pressing Cmd/Ctrl-+ (plus sign), the shortcut for View » Zoom In.

- Press Cmd-Opt-spacebar on the Mac or Ctrl-Alt-spacebar on Windows to get the zoom out cursor. Again, all the best applications use this shortcut.

- Or zoom out by pressing Cmd/Ctrl-– (minus sign), which selects the View » Zoom Out command.

Zooming by the Navigation Palette

Like other Adobe applications, Illustrator also gives you a Navigator palette to help you move around in your document. By default, the Navigator palette displays the active illustration's entire artboard and a red rectangular *window boundary*. This window boundary represents the current display of the illustration window. As shown in Figure 3-9, the window boundary is smaller than the artboard that it overlaps. This means that the corresponding illustration window shows only this portion of the artboard and a bit of the pasteboard that flanks it on one side.

Figure 3-9:
The Navigator palette lets you easily switch to any view size, including the preset values. The palette also allows you to scroll quickly to any location on the pasteboard.

The Navigator provides three ways to change the illustration window's view size:

- Click the zoom in button to magnify to the next larger preset view size. Click the zoom out button to reduce the view to the next smaller preset size.

- Click along the zoom slider to change the view size. Click all the way to the left to zoom in all the way to the smallest view size, 3.13 percent. Click all the way to the right to zoom out the maximum level of magnification, 6400 percent.

- Click the zoom option box and enter any value between 3.13 and 6400 to change the view size to that percent.

The Navigator palette offers a few other useful features:

- Click in the palette's window to reposition the boundary window such that it's centered on your click. Drag in the palette's window to move around the window boundary. As you drag, Illustrator will automatically update the illustration window to reflect your movements.

- Press the Cmd/Ctrl key while the cursor is over the Navigator palette's window, and it changes to a magnifying lens. Cmd/Ctrl-drag to change the size of the window boundary. This is similar to dragging with the zoom tool in the illustration window, except that the window boundary will always remain proportional to the dimensions of the illustration window.

- By default, the Navigator palette displays all the paths that will fit in its window at the current view size, including those that reside on the pasteboard outside the boundaries of the artboard. To see only those paths that appear on the artboard, choose View Artboard Only from the palette's pop-up menu. If any paths straddle the edge of the artboard, this option will truncate their appearance in the Navigator palette's window.

- Select Palette Options from the palette's pop-up window to change the color of the window boundary. You can choose from a list of predefined colors or create your own by double-clicking the color box.

 The Navigator can be enlarged so you can see more details in the artwork. This lets the palette act as a second window displaying your illustration. This way you can zoom in on one area of the illustration while keeping an eye out for the overall big picture.

Those of use who grew up on early versions of Illustrator used to create multiple views in a single illustration by choosing Window » New Window. Illustrator doesn't create a copy of the artwork, but rather makes a second illustration window that lets you track changes. There's no difference between this and creating a larger Navigator palette as mentioned in the previous tip.

Dragging the Drawing

Because most screens aren't as large as a full page, you probably won't be able to see your entire illustration at actual size or larger. Therefore, Illustrator lets you move the artboard inside the illustration window, a technique known as *scrolling*. It's like looking through a pair of binoculars, in a way. You can see the action more clearly, but you can see only part of the action at a time. To look at something else, you have to move the binoculars (and your head) to adjust your view. This is what happens when you scroll in Illustrator.

One method for scrolling the drawing area is to use the two scroll bars, located at the bottom and right side of the window. But only saps use the scroll bars, because Illustrator provides a better tool: the hand tool. The hand tool allows you to drag the drawing area inside the window. As you drag, the hand cursor changes to a fist to show you that you have the illustration in your viselike grip.

To access the hand tool when some other tool is selected, press and hold the spacebar. Then drag as desired. Release the spacebar to return the cursor to its previous appearance.

When a text block is active, pressing the spacebar results in a bunch of spaces. You can get around this by pressing the Cmd/Ctrl key, then pressing the spacebar, and then releasing the Cmd/Ctrl key. As long as you keep the spacebar down, the hand tool is yours and the text block remains active.

Changing the Display Mode

Another way to control what you see on screen is to change the *display mode*— that is, how you see individual objects on screen. You can select from two basic modes in Illustrator:

- In the *preview mode*, you see objects and text in full color, more or less as they will print. (Again, Illustrator does its best with this what-you-see-

is-what-you-get stuff. It's only software, after all.) Illustrator displays
your drawing in the preview mode by default, and you can return to it
at any time by choosing View » Preview or pressing Cmd/Ctrl-Y.

If you own a slowish computer, you may grow impatient with the
lethargic speed at which Illustrator draws objects on screen. To speed
things up, choose View » Outline or press Cmd/Ctrl-Y again.
Illustrator's *outline mode* is what other programs call a *wireframe* or *key-
line* mode: text appears in black, graphic objects have thin outlines and
transparent interiors, and there's not a color in sight. Figure 3-10 shows
how outline and preview modes compare.

*Figure 3-10: A relatively complicated illustration displayed in the sparse outline mode (top)
and the colorful preview mode (bottom).*

The outline mode used to be called the *artwork* mode in earlier versions of Illustrator. Someone at Adobe must have felt the term artwork was confusing. We agree; outline is a much better way to describe the display.

The outline mode is very fast, because Illustrator doesn't have to display complicated visual effects such as blends and gradients. However, it takes some time to get used to. You basically have to imagine how the colors, strokes, gradations, and other effects are going to look. That's why most experienced artists switch back and forth between the artwork and preview modes by pressing Cmd/Ctrl-Y.

Fortunately Illustrator lets you different preview options for different layers (see Chapter 10). So you can set the active layer to preview mode while other layers with gradients and blends are in the outline mode.

Creating a View You Can Come Back To

Do you find yourself switching back and forth between the same views over and over? First you zoom in on an individual leaf in a tree, then you scroll down and zoom out a little to examine the trunk, and next you zoom out two or three increments to take in the whole tree. Then you magnify the leaf again and start the process over. This kind of zooming and scrolling back and forth between key locations in your illustration can eat up all kinds of valuable drawing time.

Luckily, Illustrator has a solution. You can save specific views of your illustration and then return to them at the press of a key. When you choose View » New View, Illustrator asks you to name the current view of your illustration. Enter a name and press the Return/Enter key. Illustrator saves the view size, the relative location of the page in the illustration window, and even the display mode.

Illustrator appends the view name to the bottom of the View menu. From now on, you can return to this exact view size, page position, and display mode just by choosing the view name or by pressing Cmd-Opt-Shift or Ctrl-Alt-Shift along with a number. (Illustrator numbers views in the order of their creation.)

You can create more than ten views, but only the first ten are assigned keyboard shortcuts. All views are saved with the illustration, and change from one illustration to the next. That is, the views saved with one drawing will not necessarily be the views that are saved with any other drawing.

To change the name of a view, or to delete one or more views, choose View » Edit Views. Then select a view from the scrolling list in the Edit Views dialog box and enter a new name, or press the Delete key to get rid of it. If you want to delete many views at a time, you can Shift-click a view name to select consecutive views or Cmd/Ctrl-click to select one view here and another there.

Saving Your Work to Disk

Whenever the topic of saving files comes up, Deke is tempted to jump on a soapbox and recite broken-down slogans:

- Save your illustration early and often!

- The only safe illustration is a saved illustration!

- An untitled illustration is a recipe for disaster!

- If you're thinking of switching applications, hit Cmd/Ctrl-S! If you hear thunder, hit Cmd/Ctrl-S! If a child enters your room, hit Cmd/Ctrl-S!

If you see a man running down the streets screaming, "Cmd/Ctrl-S! Cmd/Ctrl-S! Cmd/Ctrl-S!" at the top of his lungs and shaking his hands in the air, you'll know that Deke has come to visit. (If you're wondering, Sandee has been known to strike her students with a wooden ruler when she sees unsaved work on their machines.) We're both absolutely despotic about saving, and with good reason. In our many years of writing, teaching, and creating artwork on computers, we've lost more work than anyone can measure. And all because we didn't save in time.

So save, for crying in a bucket. The file you lose might be your own!

Four Saves and an Export

If you think we're fanatics about saving, just look at Illustrator's File menu. There are four—count 'em—*four,* different commands with a Save in them: Save, Save As, Save a Copy, and Save for Web. And if that isn't enough, Adobe added an Export. When should you use what?

- **Save:** This is the command that writes the current information about the named file on the disk. If there is no file on the disk, then Illustrator treats the Save command as a Save As.

- **Save As...:** Notice the ellipsis? Anytime you see an ellipsis after a command name, you know there's a dialog box that follows. The command can't be completed until you do something with the dialog box. The Save As command is where you can name the file, make decisions about its format, and then write the file to disk. You can also use the Save As command to make different versions of your document. When you Save, Save As, or Save A Copy, you are creating a file that is in the Illustrator family: either an Illustrator file, an EPS file, or a PDF file. All three types of files can be opened and modified by Illustrator; not so with the Save for Web and Export commands.

 Remember, even if you named the file when you first opened the document, you must perform a Save As command to actually name the file on a disk.

- **Save A Copy…:** Most people with more than a year of computer experience wonder why anyone would want to save a copy? Doesn't Save As do that? Well, yes, but when you choose Save As, you change the name of the file you're working on. When you choose Save A Copy, you send a copy of the newly named file off to sit on the disk. But you're still working on the original file. The best way to think of Save a Copy is to imagine you're about to do something really strange to your document. Before you make that drastic move, use Save A Copy to make a copy of your work at that point under a name like "Before I messed up the art." Then you can do whatever you want to the file. Days later, when the client sees the bizarre version, you know you still have the safer version saved as a copy.

- **Save For Web…:** This command really isn't a save, but is an export. However, unlike the Export command, the Save For Web (see Chapter 19) opens up a large dialog box—actually a mini-program inside Illustrator—where you can play around with different Web formats, sizes, and optimization settings for Web files. People used to pay big money to get programs like Save For Web, and here it is, free with Illustrator.

- **Export:** The Export command gives you a list of different file formats that Illustrator can convert your file into. Most of these convert your elegant line drawings to pixelated facsimiles.

Using the Save Dialog Box

If the foreground image is untitled, as it is when you work on a new image, choosing File » Save or pressing Cmd/Ctrl-S displays the Save dialog box, shown in Figure 3-11. This is Illustrator's way of encouraging you to name the illustration, specify its location on disk, and select a file format. After you save the illustration once, choosing the Save command updates the file on the disk without bringing up the Save dialog box.

Choose File » Save As or press Cmd/Ctrl-Shift-S to change the name, location, or format of the illustration. Choosing the Save As command always brings up the Save dialog box. If you didn't give your document a name when you first created it, here's another chance. Use the navigation buttons to find the area where you want to save your file.

Mac users can choose to add a file extension to the name and have that extension in lowercase. This is extremely helpful if you routinely send your files to your Windows friends (like if Sandee sends Deke a file) or if you need to post your files on Unix servers that like lowercase extensions. (Windows users, you don't care about this because your files always get the file extension added automatically.)

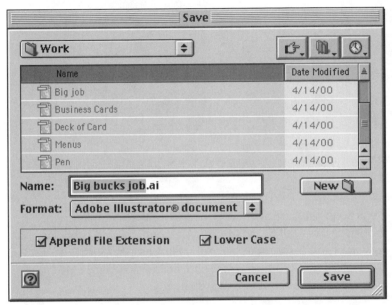

Figure 3-11: The Save dialog box lets you save a document from the current application.

Selecting a File Format

The most complex option in the Save dialog box is the Format menu that lets you specify the file format you want to use to preserve your illustration. Your choices are Illustrator, Illustrator EPS, or Acrobat PDF. (Because PDF files are so often used in pre-press, we cover them in detail in Chapter 21.) If you choose Illustrator, you are then faced with another dialog box where you need to set which version of Illustrator you would like to make your file compatible with, as shown in Figure 3-12. The only time you need to change the version compatibility is if you need to send your file to some poor soul who hasn't upgraded to Illustrator 9.

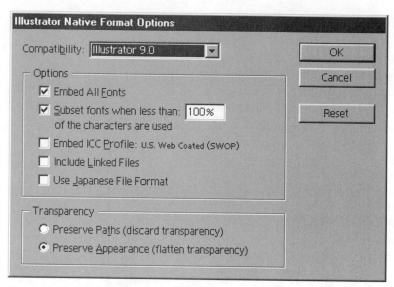

Figure 3-12: The Native Format Options dialog box lets you choose which version of Illustrator should be able to open and play with your file.

If you save an illustration in any format other than Illustrator 9 or Illustrator 9 EPS, make sure you have created a backup version of the illustration first in the Illustrator 9 format! Otherwise, you are needlessly and deliberately throwing away some amount of your hard work.

Compatibility: This list contains all the previous versions of Illustrator back to 3.0. If you don't care about previous versions of Illustrator, leave the most recent version selected so you don't lose anything.

Embed All Fonts: Don't get excited, this box doesn't do quite what you think it does. If you choose this option, Illustrator will include the fonts used with the file. However, that doesn't mean that you can send the file to someone to work on it who doesn't own the fonts. It only means that the fonts are included with the file if you place it into a layout program such as InDesign.

Subset fonts: Once you've decided to embed all fonts, you then have another question: How much of the fonts do you want to embed? For instance, if you have used a font for only one single character, do you really want to embed the entire alphabet and other characters in the font? This option lets you choose only those characters used. However, if you want to make sure the entire character set is included, set this to 100 percent.

- **Include ICC profile:** Check this if you want to keep the color management system attached to the file. Deselect this if you would like another application to handle the color management.

- **Include Linked Files:** Like the option to include fonts, this doesn't mean you can throw away the linked file if you are going to work on the file. (You need to embed the file to do that.) It means if you place it into a layout program, there's enough information to print the file.

- **Use Japanese File Format:** If you save in a version of Illustrator before version 6, you need to choose this if you want the Japanese file format. This is not the case for present day Illustrator, because now the Illustrator format is universal.

- **Transparency:** This option only shows up if you save in a version prior to Illustrator 9. You need to decide what to do with any objects that have a transparency, drop shadow, or other special effect assigned to them. Preserve Paths throws away the effect but keeps the path shapes. Preserve Appearance rasterizes the image. (Check out Chapter 17 for an in-depth look at the transparency features.)

Saving an EPS Illustration

To use an illustration in InDesign or QuarkXPress, select Illustrator EPS from the Format pop-up menu. After you click the Save button or press Return/Enter, Illustrator displays the EPS Format dialog box depicted in stunning detail in Figure 3-13. You can probably figure out the majority of these options on your own, but we may as well run through them, if only to eliminate all possible confusion.

- **Compatibility:** This menu is the same as the one for the native Illustrator format.

- **Preview:** These options control the screen preview that Illustrator attaches to an EPS file. If you're sending the file to a Windows machine, choose TIFF (8-bit Color). (Choose 1-bit only if the program you're sending the file to doesn't support color.) You can also set the preview to transparency or opaque if you choose the TIFF preview. If you're sending the file to a Macintosh machine, choose Macintosh 8-bit color.

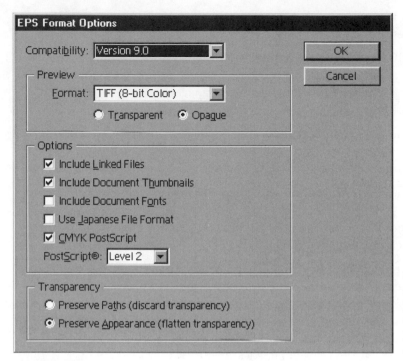

Figure 3-13:
Illustrator presents
you with a world
of options when
you're saving an
EPS file.

 If you are going to send your work to QuarkXPress on the Macintosh, you can choose the TIFF preview. QuarkXPress can handle the TIFF preview information.

 Remember, the preview doesn't change the actual information in the file. However, some non-PostScript printers do use the information in the preview to print the file.

 Include Linked Files: This is the same as the one for the native Illustrator format. Check this option if you would like to send just one EPS file.

Don't throw away the original file if you choose this option. You still have to have the original linked image if you want to edit your file.

- **Include Document Thumbnails:** Always select this check box. It creates a thumbnail of the illustration so you can preview it from the Open dialog box inside Illustrator, Photoshop, and an increasing number of other programs.

- **Use Japanese File Format:** Same story as in the native Illustrator dialog box.

- **Include Document Fonts:** If you use a font in your illustration that you're not sure is as popular with your audience as it is with you, check this option. The file will be a bit larger (depending on the size of the font file), but you ensure that your document will appear with the font you intended. Just remember, someone who doesn't own the fonts still won't be able to edit the file.

- **CMYK PostScript:** With this option selected, Illustrator will automatically convert RGB colors to their CMYK equivalents as needed.

- **PostScript Level:** When you send your artwork to a PostScript printer, there are different levels of PostScript that are used to print the file. Level 3 is the most sophisticated and can handle any effect or feature in Illustrator. Level 2 is less complex. Some features, such as the gradient mesh, are converted into raster images if the printer uses level 2. Level 1 is the most primitive. If you know your printer can handle level 3 information, choose it. If not, use level 2. Don't pick level 1 unless you've been specifically told to do so.

- **Transparency:** This is the same as the options in the native Illustrator dialog box.

Illustrator is pretty clever. In most cases you can just press the Return/Enter key to quickly get you out of the EPS Format dialog box. The default settings ensure there's no loss of information even if you weren't paying a lick of attention to what you were doing. That's the kind of service any decent program is all too happy to perform.

PART TWO
CREATING

CHAPTER 4

DRAWING THE SIMPLE STUFF

Heaven help the experienced artist who encounters Illustrator for the first time. If you've drawn with pencil and paper, or sketched inside a painting program such as Photoshop, but you've never used Illustrator before, now is a good time to open your skull, remove your brain, and replace it upside down. Drawing with an illustration program is a very different adventure, and though it pains us to say it, your previous experience is as likely to impede your progress as to expedite it.

Drawing in Illustrator is actually a three-part process: You draw lines and shapes, you manipulate these objects and apply special effects, and you stack the objects one in front of another like pieces of paper in a collage.

This means the lines and shapes are forever flexible. You can select any object and edit, duplicate, or delete it, regardless of its age or location in the illustration. (Sandee still plays around with the logo she created ten years ago, and every object responds exactly as it did the day she drew it.) Pencil and paper do not give you this degree of control.

But Illustrator's flexibility comes at a price. It takes a lot of time and a fair amount of object-oriented savvy to create even basic compositions. There are no two ways about it—Illustrator is harder to learn and more cumbersome to use than conventional artists' tools.

In this chapter, we explain how to use Illustrator's most straightforward drawing tools. If you're feeling a little timid—particularly after our pessimistic introduction—have no fear. With this chapter in front of you, you'll be up and running within the hour. If you're the type who prefers to dive right in and investigate basic functions on your own, you can discover how these tools work, largely without our help. For you, we explain options, suggest keyboard tricks, and point out small performance details that many novice and intermediate users overlook.

But before we start, we just want to take a few brief paragraphs to explain how lines and shapes work inside Illustrator. You'll better understand how drawing tools work if you first understand what you're drawing.

Everything You Need to Know about Paths

Any line or shape you create in Illustrator is called a *path*. (Now that we've introduced that word we'll stop saying "lines or shapes" all the time; the one word comprises both.) Conceptually, a path is the same as a line drawn with a pencil. A path may start at one location and end at another, as in the case of an open line. Or it may meet back up with itself to form a closed shape. (A piece of string is an open path; a rubber band is a closed one.) Paths can range in length and complexity from tiny scratch marks to elaborate curlicues that loop around and intersect like tracks on a roller coaster.

The cartoon face in Figure 4-1 contains 12 paths. Of the paths, 10 are open (lines) and 2 are closed (shapes). So that you can clearly distinguish open from closed, we've given the lines thick outlines and the shapes thin ones. The closed paths surround the face, with the white shape mostly covering the gray one. The open paths represent the face's features.

Figure 4-1: A simple cartoon composed of open paths (thick outlines) and closed ones (thin).

All paths—whether open or closed—are made up of basic building blocks called *anchor points* (or just plain *points*). The simplest line is a connection between two anchor points—one at each end. (Anyone familiar with a little geometry will recognize this principle: a minimum of two points are needed to define a line.) But Illustrator can just as easily accommodate paths with hundreds of points, one connected to another like dots in a connect-the-dots puzzle.

Points and Segments

Figure 4-2 shows the points required to create the cartoon face. We've applied thinner outlines to the lines and made the shapes transparent so you can better see the square points. The most complicated path contains 11 points; the least complicated contains two.

The bits of line between points are called *segments*. A segment can be straight, as if it were drawn against the edge of a ruler. A straight segment flows directly from one point to another in any direction. A segment may also curve, like the outline of an ellipse. Curved segments connect two points in an indirect manner, bending inward or outward along the way.

Figure 4-2: The small white squares represent the points needed
to create the cartoon in Illustrator.

Strokes and Fills

Although a line drawn with a dull pencil is heavier than a line drawn with a
sharpened one, the thickness of any line fluctuates depending on how hard you
press the pencil tip to the page. In Illustrator, the thickness (or *weight*) of an outline is absolutely consistent throughout the course of a path. In other words, different paths can have different weights, but the weight of each path is constant (as
Figure 4-1 shows).

 Just because the weight of each path is constant doesn't
mean that the appearance of the path has to remain constant. Illustrator's brushes allow you to have strokes that have
the appearance of different weights—even though the stroke
weight remains constant.

The thickness of an outline is called the *stroke*. In addition to changing the
weight of the stroke, you can change its color. Strokes can be black, white, gray,
or any of several million colorful variations.

You can also color the interior of a path by assigning it a *fill*. Like a stroke, a fill
may be black, white, or any color. In Figure 4-1, the shapes that encircle the face
are filled with white and gray. You can even assign a transparent fill, as in the case
of the shapes in Figure 4-2.

The Simplest of Simple Shapes

Illustrator offers three tools for creating rectangles and ellipses. The standard rectangle and ellipse tools appear by default in the third row from the top of the toolbox. The rounded rectangle is the alternative tool in the rectangle tool slot. You select it by clicking and holding on the rectangle tool slot, as shown in Figure 4-3. Now simply drag to the right until the rounded rectangle tool is highlighted.

 Here's a sneaky trick for choosing alternate tools in the toolbox. Hold the Opt/Alt key as you click the tool in the toolbox. This will toggle you through the tools in that slot.

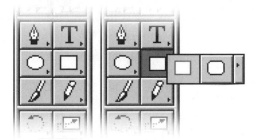

Figure 4-3: Illustrator offers three basic shape tools.

Drawing a Rectangle

To draw a rectangle, select the rectangle tool and then click and drag inside the drawing area. The point at which you start dragging sets one corner of the rectangle; the point at which you release sets the opposite corner, as shown in Figure 4-4. The two remaining corners line up vertically or horizontally with their neighbors. (Illustrator creates a fifth point called the *center point* in the center of the shape. If you move the rectangle or change its size, Illustrator repositions the center point so it remains in the center of the shape.)

You can also use the rectangle tool as follows:

- If you press the Opt/Alt key while drawing with the rectangle tool, the start point of your drag marks the center of the rectangle. As before, the release point becomes a corner point.

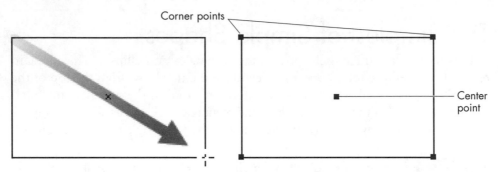

Figure 4-4: Drag from one corner to the opposite corner to draw a rectangle.

- Shift-drag with the rectangle tool to draw a perfect rectangle—also called a square. You can press and release the Shift key in mid-drag to switch between drawing a rectangle or a square. Isn't it great how Illustrator lets you change your mind?

- Opt/Alt-Shift-drag with the rectangle tool to create a square from center to corner.

- Press the tilde (~) key while dragging with the rectangle tool to create a series of rectangles, all of which border on a common point. Press Opt/Alt-~ while you drag to create a series of concentric rectangles.

- Press the spacebar while dragging to move the rectangle rather than change its size. When you get it positioned properly, release the spacebar and continue dragging or release.

Drawing by the Numbers

You can also enter the dimensions of a rectangle numerically. Click with the rectangle tool—that's right, just click inside the drawing area—to display the dialog box shown in Figure 4-5. Here you can enter values for the Width and Height options. After you press Return/Enter or click OK, Illustrator creates a rectangle to your exact specifications.

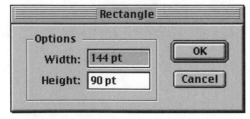

Figure 4-5:
Click with the rectangle tool to enter the exact width and height of your rectangle.

Want to create a square? You could enter the same value in both option boxes, but frankly that's too much effort. Just enter the desired size into the Width option box, and then click the word Height to duplicate the value. You can likewise duplicate the Height value by clicking the word Width.

 Because the Rectangle dialog box doesn't give any placement options, the point at which you clicked with the tool serves as the upper left corner point of the shape. If you want the click point to be the center of the shape, Opt/Alt-click.

Notice that both option boxes in Figure 4-5 includes the letters *pt*, an abbreviation for points (¹⁄₇₂ inch). This refers to the unit of measure you set using the General Units option in the Units & Undo dialog box. The unit of measure can alternatively be inches (*in*) or millimeters (*mm*).

You can enter spaces between the number and the measurement abbreviation, but you don't have to. If you enter a value without an abbreviation, Illustrator assumes the active unit of measurement—points, by default.

The exception to this is when you have selected picas for the General Units option and then elected to activate the Numbers Without Units Are Points checkbox—also found within the Units & Undo dialog box. Illustrator will then assume that any numbers you enter into the Rectangle dialog box (or any other dialog box for that matter) should be interpreted as points and not as picas.

You use the Rectangle dialog box only to create new shapes—not to modify existing ones. If you want to change the size of a rectangle you've already drawn, you can use any of the transformation options covered in Chapter 11. However, the easiest option is to use Illustrator's Transform palette (shown in Figure 4-6). Make sure the rectangle is selected so that its points are visible. (Use the arrow tool to click the shape if it is not selected.) Then, if the Transform palette is hidden, choose Window » Show Transform. Next, enter new values in the W and H option boxes. Illustrator resizes the rectangle automatically.

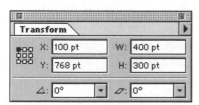

Figure 4-6:
The Transform palette offers the easiest way to change the dimensions of an existing rectangle—by modifying the W and H values in the Transform palette.

The reference points on the left side of the Transform palette let you choose the point around which the transformation should take place. The default position for the reference point is the center of the object. If you click the reference point icon, you can change that position to top or bottom, left or right, or side center.

Rounding off a Rectangle's Corners

To draw a rectangle with rounded corners, select the rounded rectangle tool from the rectangle tool slot and drag away. Illustrator creates a shape with eight points—two along each side with a curved segment around each corner—as in Figure 4-7.

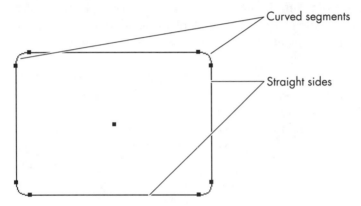

Figure 4-7: Illustrator uses curved segments to join straight sides in a rounded rectangle.

You control the roundness of the corners by changing the Corner Radius value in the General Preferences dialog box. You can also click with the rounded rectangle tool and enter a value into the Corner Radius option box.

Once you draw with the rounded rectangle tool, there is no way to change the roundness of the corners. Do not despair, though. Illustrator 9 now lets you add live rounded corners to rectangles (as well as other objects). Because this is a live effect (covered in Chapter 12), it means you can change the corner radius any time you want. (Deke is dancing and yelling in the background: "Thirteen years! I've waited thirteen years for this feature!")

Creating a Live Rounded Rectangle

Deke is so excited about the new live effect for rounded rectangles that he insists that we cover it here, rather than waiting for Chapter 12. So even though it's not quite in the right place, here goes.

Start by drawing a regular rectangle. With the rectangle still selected, choose Effect » Stylize » Round Corners. This opens the Round Corners dialog box, which has but one simple field in which to enter the radius amount. The plain rectangle is transformed into a rounded rectangle. Of course creating a rounded rectangle is easy; the hard part is making changes to the amount of rounding.

To change the size of the corner radius, you need to open the Appearance palette. (If you can't find the palette, choose Window » Show Appearance.) With the object selected, you will see a listing for Round Corners. Double-click the entry and the Round Corners dialog box appears again. Make whatever changes you want to the corner radius.

If you get totally tired of the rounded corners, drag the Round Corners listing into the Appearance palette's trash—instantly you've got your regular rectangle again.

Drawing an Ellipse

When it comes to drawing ellipses and circles, the ellipse tool is the one for the job. Simply click and drag along a diagonal line to form graceful and sublime rings of drawing excellence. Your ellipse fills the imaginary rectangle you create as you drag.

 If you're an old time Illustrator user, like Deke, you may remember that many years ago (before version 8) Illustrator drew ellipses from arc to arc with the imaginary rectangle inside the ellipse —not outside as it does now. Fortunately Deke was thrilled to find he can still draw the old way. Start your ellipse as you would normally—by dragging with the tool. Once you're into the drag, press the Cmd/Ctrl key. The ellipse will resize in accordance. Be sure to hold the Cmd/Ctrl key through the completion of the drag.

In most other respects, the ellipse tool works much like the rectangle tool:

- Opt/Alt-drag with the ellipse tool to create an ellipse outward from the center. As always, the release point becomes the middle of an arc, determining the size and shape of the ellipse.

- Shift-drag to draw a perfect ellipse (also called a circle). Opt/Alt-Shift-drag to draw a circle from the center point outward.

- Press the tilde (~) key while dragging with the ellipse tool to create a series of ellipses. Press Opt/Alt-~ while you drag to create a series of concentric ellipses.

- Press the spacebar while dragging to move the ellipse rather than change its size. When you get it positioned properly, release the spacebar and continue dragging or release.

- Click in the drawing area to bring up the Ellipse dialog box. It contains Width and Height options for specifying the width and height of the shape. The shape aligns to your click point by the middle of the upper left arc. If you Opt-click with the ellipse tool, the ellipse aligns by its center.

- Use the W and H values in the Transform palette to change the width and height of an ellipse that you've already drawn.

Simple Shapes at an Angle

Sandee remembers one class where a student was really having trouble drawing in Illustrator. In fact, she couldn't even get her rectangles to draw properly. They were all rotated like the one shown in Figure 4-8. Finally she discovered that the student wasn't completely incompetent. Someone had gone and changed the Constrain Angle value in the General Preferences dialog box.

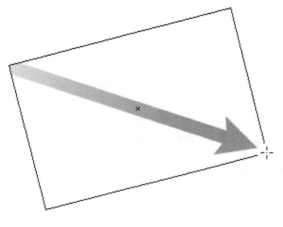

Figure 4-8:
The result of drawing a
rectangle after rotating the
constraint axes by 15 degrees.

Sandee always threatens to pull an April Fool's joke on the school where she teaches and change all the constrain angles to 1 degree—just enough to drive everyone crazy.

The *constraint axes* control the angles at which you move and transform objects when pressing the Shift key. But they also control the creation of rectangles, ellipses, and text blocks. If the Constrain Angle value is set to anything besides 0, Illustrator rotates a rectangle or an ellipse to that angle as you draw. The Constrain Angle value has no impact on the creation of stars, polygons, or spirals whatsoever—even if you hold down the Shift key while drawing one of these shapes, they will still align to the horizontal despite the option box's value.

If someone has indeed reset your Constrain Angle, press Cmd/Ctrl-K (or choose File » Preferences » General). Enter 0 into the Constrain Angle option box and press Return.

Polygons, Stars, and Spirals

Illustrator offers three tools that let you draw polygons, stars, and spirals by dragging in the drawing area. The new functions still leave a thing or two to be desired, particularly when it comes time to edit the paths (for example, you can't automatically change the number of points in a star after you create it). All three of these tools are alternates in the ellipse tool slot shown in Figure 4-9.

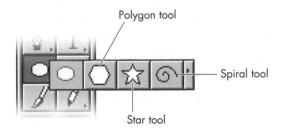

Figure 4-9: Illustrator offers three tools
for drawing polygons, stars, and spirals.

Drawing a Regular Polygon

A regular polygon is a shape with multiple straight sides—each side is identical in length and meets its neighbors at the same angle. An equilateral triangle is a regular polygon, as is a square. Other examples include pentagons, hexagons, octagons, and just about any other shape with a *gon* in its name. Figure 4-10 shows a few regular polygons for your visual edification.

To draw a polygon, select the polygon tool and drag in the drawing area. You always draw a polygon from the middle outward, whether you press the Opt/Alt key or not. The direction of your drag determines the orientation of the shape.

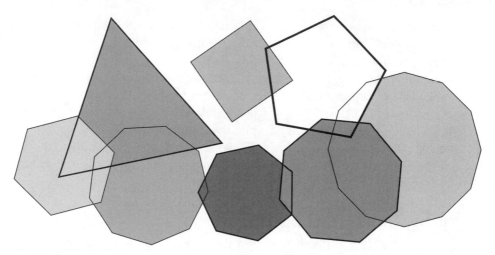

Figure 4-10: A whole mess of regular polygons, ranging from 3 to 12 sides.

By default, Illustrator draws hexagons (six-sided shapes) with the polygon tool. You can change the number of sides while dragging with the polygon tool by pressing the up and down arrow keys. The up arrow key adds a side; the down arrow key deletes one.

Another way to change the number of sides is to click with the polygon tool in the drawing area. Illustrator displays the Polygon dialog box, which lets you specify a *Radius* value and a number of sides.

- The Radius value is the distance from the center of the shape to any corner point in the shape. Therefore, a regular polygon with a radius of 100 points would fit entirely inside a circle with a radius of 100 points.

- You can enter any number of sides from 3 to 1000. Shapes with more than 20 sides look like circles with bumps.

As always, the values you enter into the Polygon dialog box affect all future polygons you create. You cannot make changes to an existing polygon using the Polygon dialog box. If you want to change the size of a polygon, use the scale tool, as discussed in Chapter 11. To change the orientation of a polygon, use the rotate tool, also covered in Chapter 11. But if you want to change the number of sides, you have to delete the polygon and redraw it.

Here are a few more (marginally useful) things you can do with the polygon tool:

- Shift-drag with the tool to constrain a polygon's orientation so the bottom side is horizontal. (This is the same way Illustrator draws a shape when you click with the polygon tool.)

- Press the spacebar while dragging to move the shape rather than change its size. When you get the polygon positioned properly, release the spacebar and continue dragging or release.

- Press the tilde (~) key while dragging to create a series of concentric polygons. This is a singularly bizarre technique. It's great for getting oohs and ahs from your friends, but it's rarely practical.

Drawing a Star

Illustrator lets you draw regular stars, in which each spike looks just like its neighbors. To draw a star, drag with the star tool, which is the second alternative tool in the ellipse tool slot. Illustrator draws the shape from the center outward.

You can modify the performance of the star tool by pressing the Cmd and Opt or Ctrl and Alt keys as you drag. But to explain adequately what you're doing, we need to conduct a small geometry lesson. A star is made up of two sets of points, one at the points where the spikes meet and one at the tips of the spikes. These points revolve around one of two imaginary circles, which form the inner and outer radiuses of the star, as pictured in Figure 4-11.

When you drag with the star tool, Illustrator scales the two radiuses proportionately, so that the inner radius is exactly half the outer radius (as in Figure 4-11). If you don't like this particular arrangement, you can gain more control in the following ways:

- Press Cmd/Ctrl while dragging to scale the outer radius independently of the inner radius. So long as the Cmd/Ctrl key is down, the inner radius remains fixed. You can even drag the outer radius inside the inner radius to make the outer radius the inner radius. Then you can adjust the inner radius while the outer one is fixed. To resize both radiuses proportionally again, release Cmd/Ctrl and keep dragging.

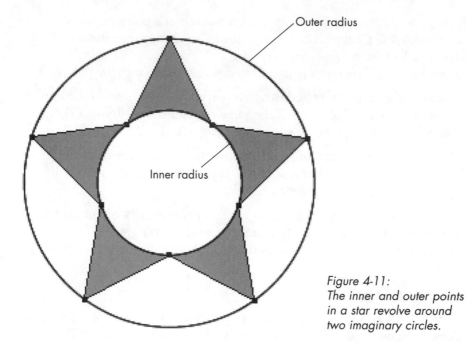

Outer radius

Inner radius

Figure 4-11:
The inner and outer points
in a star revolve around
two imaginary circles.

 Opt/Alt-drag to snap the inner radius into precise alignment so that opposite spikes align with each other. The top sides of the left and right sides of a five-sided star, for example, form a straight line.

 Because Cmd/Ctrl and Opt/Alt have mutually exclusive effects on a star, they cannot be in effect at the same time. If you do hold down both the Cmd/Ctrl and Opt/Alt keys, Opt/Alt takes precedent.

> **TIP**
>
> Say you used the Cmd/Ctrl key in conjunction with the polygon tool and went way too far with the outer radius, so that you could draw only stars consisting of a number of spindly arms emerging from the center. You would probably have a heck of a time correcting this problem with just the Cmd/Ctrl key. Here's the solution: Click and drag with the polygon tool. While dragging, tap both the Cmd/Ctrl key and the Opt/Alt key simultaneously. The star will return to a more regular shape.

As with the polygon tool, you can add or delete spikes from a star by pressing the up or down arrow key in mid-drag. You can also move a star in progress by pressing the space-bar or orient the star upright by pressing Shift. And—lest we forget the least important tip of all—you can press the tilde (~) key to create concentric stars.

Probably the funkiest of all the hidden tool tips is that in addition to creating the regular star, the star tool lets you draw a double star. That's the type of star where the lines are visible across each other—not that there's a huge demand for such a shape, but it is an interesting variation on the traditional star.

To draw a double star, here's what you need to do:

1. Drag with the star tool and hold down the mouse button throughout these steps.

2. Press the down arrow key until you have a three-sided star, the least number of sides permitted.

3. Tap both the Cmd/Ctrl and Opt/Alt keys.

4. Press the up arrow key until you've reached the desired number of sides. Once you're at four sides, you'll see the double star configuration.

5. Adjust the double star's size, placement, and orientation as you would a regular star's—with the Cmd/Ctrl key, Shift key, and space-bar, respectively.

To take full advantage of its duality, be sure to press the Cmd/Ctrl key while you're drawing a double star. This allows you to vary the size of one star independently of the other.

 If you tire of the double-star configuration and want to return to drawing more traditional ones, you simply need to tap both the Cmd/Ctrl and Opt/Alt keys once again. The star tool will then draw stars as usual.

Click in the drawing area with the star tool to bring up the Star dialog box. As shown in Figure 4-12, this dialog box permits two Radius values, one for the outer radius and one for the inner. You can also specify the number of spikes. (Illustrator calls these "points," so don't confuse them with the points between segments. There are twice as many points as spikes—for example, a path with five spikes has ten points.)

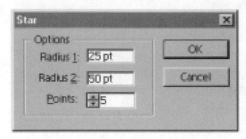

Figure 4-12:
You'll get a dialog box to
specify the precise inner and
outer radius values by clicking
with the star tool.

Creating a Spiral

Most folks look at spirals and think, "Why in tarnation would I want to draw that?" Spirals don't exactly lend themselves to a wide range of drawing situations, but both of us have become enthusiastic spiralists since their introduction. Deke adds spirals wherever he can; see if you can find the spiral in Figure 4-1.

But wouldn't you know it, spirals are one of the most difficult things to create in Illustrator. Oh sure, you can draw them easily enough; just drag with the spiral tool and the spiral grows outward from its center. But controlling the number of times the spiral wraps around itself requires a fair amount of dexterity and reasoning.

Let's start with the Spiral dialog box, shown in Figure 4-13. To access this dialog box, click with the spiral tool inside the drawing area. The Spiral dialog box contains these options:

- **Radius:** Enter a Radius value to specify the size of the spiral. This represents the distance from the center of the shape to the last point on the spiral.

- **Decay:** The Decay value determines how quickly the spiral loops in on itself. Small values result in short loops. Larger values—up to 99.99 percent—result in more tightly packed spirals.

Here's where things get weird. If you enter a value of 100 into the Decay option box, the spiral coils on top of itself, creating a circle. Values above 100 (up to 150 percent) turn the spiral inside out, looping it in the opposite direction and outside the radius.

- **Segments:** Enter the number of curved segments between points into the Segments option box. Each segment represents a quarter coil in the spiral.

- **Style:** Select a radio button to coil the spiral counterclockwise or clockwise. (This assumes a Decay value of less than 100 percent. If the Decay is higher than 100, the spiral coils in the opposite direction.)

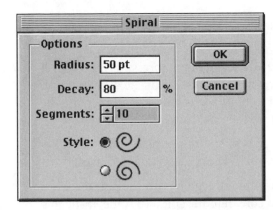

Figure 4-13:
The Spiral dialog box allows
you to specify the Radius and
Decay of the spiral.

By itself, an increased Segments value may not result in more coils. Strange, but true. You have to raise both the Decay and Segments values to wind the coils more tightly. This is because Illustrator drops segments when Decay is too low to accommodate them.

Once you've set the spiral dialog box, you can drag new spirals directly on the page. However, you might want to make your spiral experience more interactive. Fortunately Illustrator lets you control spirals as you drag.

Controlling Spirals on the Fly

By now you're probably thinking, "Whelp, that's it for spirals." But wait, there's more. As luck would have it, you can modify coils without resorting to the Spiral dialog box (Sandee's favorite way to doodle around in Illustrator). It takes a little getting used to, but it works. Here's how:

- When you drag with the spiral tool, you're changing the radius and rotating the spiral around. We just want to get that straight before we go any farther.

- Press the Cmd/Ctrl key while dragging to modify the decay. Drag outward to lower the decay; drag inward to raise it. If you drag inward past one of the coils, the spiral flips on itself, indicating a decay of more than 100 percent.

- Don't press the Cmd/Ctrl key the moment you start dragging or you'll pop the Decay value to some ridiculously low number such as 7 percent. Start dragging and then press Cmd/Ctrl in mid-drag. Release the key to modify the radius again.

- Press the up and down arrow keys while dragging with the spiral tool to raise and lower the number of segments in a spiral.

- You can also change the number of segments by pressing the Opt/Alt key. Opt/Alt-drag toward the center of the spiral to delete segments and reduce the radius. Drag outward to both add segments and increase the radius, thus better accommodating the new coils.

- If you press both Cmd/Ctrl and Opt/Alt simultaneously, Cmd/Ctrl takes precedence (unlike with the star tool, where Opt/Alt is dominant).

- You can also press the spacebar while dragging with the spiral tool to reposition the path. Shift-drag to constrain the spiral to some 45-degree angle.

- As if it's not goofy enough to be able to create concentric polygons and stars, you can create a series of spirals by pressing the tilde (~) key as you drag. Just the thing to embellish the next annual report.

Drawing Free-Form Paths

The tools we've discussed so far are all well and good. But Illustrator's true drawing power lies in its ability to define free-form lines and shapes. Such paths may be simple shapes such as zigzags or crescents, or they may be intricate polygons and naturalistic forms. It all depends on how well you can draw.

The pencil tool works much like a real pencil and lets you draw anything you want. Heck, the pencil cursor even looks like a pencil.

When you first choose the pencil tool, the pencil cursor displays with a small (almost microscopic) x in the lower right corner. This indicates you are drawing a new, independent path. As you drag with the tool, Illustrator tracks the cursor's motion with a dotted line. After you release the mouse button, Illustrator automatically assigns and positions the points and segments needed to create your path. The path created adopts the traditional fill and stroke characteristics as dictated by the values set in the various palettes (including the Color and Stroke palettes). For more information on fill and stroke, read the way-fab and truly meaty Chapters 14, 15, and 16.

Adjusting the Tolerances

Alas, automation is rarely perfect. (If it were, what need would these machines have for us?) Try as it might, Illustrator doesn't always do such a hot job of drawing pencil paths. When the program finishes its calculations, a path may appear riddled with far too many points, or equipped with too few.

Fortunately, you can adjust the performance of the pencil tool to accommodate your personal drawing style using the Fidelity and Smoothness Tolerances options found in the Pencil Tool Preferences dialog box. To change how the pencil tool works, double-click the pencil tool icon in the toolbox (Figure 4-14). This opens the Pencil Tool Preferences dialog box (shown in Figure 4-15).

Figure 4-14:
The pencil tool
lets you draw
free-form paths.

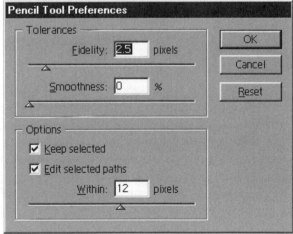

Figure 4-15:
In the Pencil Tool
Preferences dialog box,
you specify exactly how
Illustrator mimics your
mouse movements when
you're dragging with
the pencil tool.

In the Fidelity option box, either enter any value between 0.5 and 20, or if you prefer, use the slider bar to select a value within the same range. Illustrator measures the Fidelity value in screen pixels. Fidelity determines how far from the path the individual point may stray. A value of 2.5, for example, instructs the program to ignore any jags in your cursor movements that do not exceed 2.5 pixels in length or width. Setting the value to 0.5 makes the pencil tool extremely sensitive; setting the value to 20 smooths the roughest of gestures.

A Fidelity value of 2 or 3 is generally adequate for most folks, but you should experiment to determine the best setting. Keep in mind that Illustrator saves the

Fidelity value, and it remains in force until you enter a new value into the Pencil Tool Preferences dialog box.

Smoothness is the other tolerance value that affects the pencil tool's behavior. Smoothness dictates how many points are needed to complete the path. Smoothness ranges from 0 to 100 percent, a value you can enter into the Smoothness option box or set via the slider bar. The higher the value, the smoother the pencil path.

You can't alter either the Fidelity or the Smoothness value for a path after you've drawn it because Illustrator calculates the points for a path only once, after you release the mouse button.

The other features of this dialog box are worth mentioning. The first is the Keep Selected checkbox. When you select this option, a path remains selected just after creation, allowing you to extend or close it.

The second is the Edit Selected Paths. When this is selected, you have a choice as to how close the pencil tool has to come before it can modify selected paths. (Rather than clutter up the rest of this chapter with how to modify paths, we cover it all in great detail in Chapter 9.)

If you trust the Adobe engineers more than your own preferences, click the Reset button, which sets all the options back to their factory defaults.

Extending and Closing a Path

Normally, when you drag with the pencil tool, the result is an open path. This is true even if the starting point of your draw coincides perfectly with the final point. In this case, Illustrator will create two points so that the initial point overlaps the final point. This is not the limit of its capabilities, however: You can also use the pencil tool to create closed paths or extend any open path, lengthening it or even closing it.

To create a closed path from scratch, press the Opt/Alt key while dragging with the pencil tool and hold it through the completion of the drag. As you do this, the pencil cursor changes slightly. It still looks like a pencil, but now the eraser end is filled and a small *o* replaces the *x* that usually appears to the right, as shown in Figure 4-16. Upon your drag's completion, Illustrator automatically adds a segment that connects the first and last points. The right side of Figure 4-16 shows how Illustrator adds this segment. If the two endpoints coincide, holding the Opt key creates a single point that marks both the beginning and the end of the closed path.

On the other hand, if you want to extend an existing open path, select the path and position the pencil cursor over either end of the line. You'll know you're ready to go when you get the connect cursor (the standard pencil cursor without the *x*, as seen in Figure 4-17). Drag away—Illustrator treats your cursor movements as an extension of the existing path.

Finally, to close a selected open path with the pencil tool, you might think you need to hold the Opt/Alt key as in the case of creating a closed path from scratch. Amazingly, this is not so. In this case Illustrator understands that if you extend a path, you probably want to close it. So all you need to do is bring the pencil tool onto the open point and the path will close with a single point.

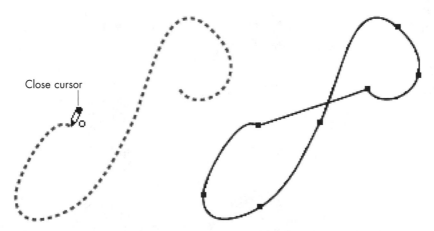

Figure 4-16: Hold down the Opt key while you drag with the pencil tool, and Illustrator automatically closes your path regardless of where you start and end your drag.

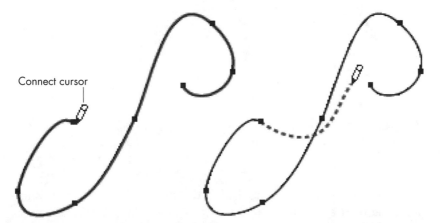

Figure 4-17: Drag from an endpoint to extend a path (left). Drag back to the other endpoint to close it (right).

Painting Paths

The paintbrush tool is the other free-form path creation tool. Like the pencil, the paintbrush follows your mouse movements. When you release the mouse, Illustrator automatically assigns and positions points and segments to the path. So what is the difference between the two tools?

The big difference between the tools is that the paintbrush automatically assigns a special type of strokes—called brushes—to the paths it draws. These brushes allow you to create the look of pen and ink, calligraphy, natural media, and even supernatural strokes. Figure 4-18 shows how applying brushes to a simple path can dramatically change the path's appearance.

Figure 4-18: The plain image on the left was changed by applying different brushes to the path. Nothing was moved, altered, or in any way changed except by applying the brushes.

Outside of automatically applying brushes to the stroke, there are many similarities between the paintbrush and the pencil. To open the paintbrush preferences, simply double-click the tool in the toolbox (Figure 4-19). This opens the preferences for the paintbrush (as shown in Figure 4-20).

Figure 4-19:
The paintbrush is a
slightly more expressive
version of the pencil.

Paintbrush Tool Preferences

Tolerances

Fidelity: 4 pixels

Smoothness: 0 percent

OK

Cancel

Reset

Options

☑ Fill new brush strokes
☑ Keep Selected
☑ Edit Selected Paths

Within: 12 pixels

Figure 4-20:
The preferences for the
paintbrush tool. Notice
the very slight differences
from those of the pencil
in Figure 4-15.

You can adjust the fidelity, tolerance, and edit distance, just as with the pencil. However, there is one setting for the paintbrush that is very different. When you draw with the pencil, it applies whatever fill and stroke settings are active to the path. The paintbrush will always apply a new stroke from the brush currently selected in the brushes palette. (We cover all of this in greater detail in Chapter 16.)

 Although Illustrator sets the Fill new brush strokes option to on as the default, you most likely will want to turn it off. Your paintbrush strokes will look more natural without the fill. Just remember that your fill color will become the color for the brush stroke.

The preference setting for the Fill new brush strokes option controls how the paintbrush swaps the new stroke. When this is selected, the paintbrush keeps whatever fill is currently selected. It then applies a stroke from the brushes list using the active stroke color. When this option is not selected, the paintbrush behaves more sophisticatedly so that you never have filled brushstrokes. First, it looks at if there is a stroke color. If there is, the paintbrush discards any fill, and keeps the stroke color applied to the color of the brush. Then, if there is no stroke color, it takes whatever color has been applied to the fill and applies it to the color of the brush. It then deletes the fill color. The benefit to all this is that you will always have pure brushstrokes without any cumbersome fills.

Tracing Templates—No Longer a Black-and-White Issue

Anytime you place a file into Illustrator or open a raster image, you have the option to make the image a template. Templates are images on special layers that make it (slightly) easier to trace images. The image used as a template can be black-and-white, grayscale, or color.

When the template image comes into Illustrator, it comes in on a new layer that is given special template status. A template layer is positioned under the current layer; is set not to print; any images on the layer are ghosted (dimmed) to 50% of their regular shades; and the layer is locked so you can't inadvertently move the image. You can set all these options yourself by creating a new layer, placing the image, and setting all the layer options, but it's much easier to just place the image as a template. If you are the do-it-yourself type, see Chapter 10, where all the options for layers are fully covered .

 Unfortunately, you still can't scan images directly into Illustrator. Ideally, you ought to be able to scan in some line art and make it into an illustration in minutes without opening other programs.

Using the Autotrace Tool

After placing or opening a template in your illustration (as described in the "Opening and Placing" section of Chapter 3), you can trace the edges manually using any of Illustrator's drawing tools. But if you want Illustrator to do the work for you, your only choice is the autotrace tool.

 If you're really serious about tracing and like to scan your own handiwork or do a lot of tracing, you'll want to check out Adobe Streamline. Not only can this dedicated tracing program trace multiple paths at once, it also gives you much more control over the tracing paths, and it can be set to trace an entire folder of images.

Uh, where were we? Oh, yes, *Illustrator's* autotrace tool. Well, despite its faults, we feel obliged to show you how to work with the autotrace tool. First, select the autotrace tool (the alternative tool in the blend tool slot) from the toolbox. Figure 4-21 shows just that, with a tracing template all ready to go in the background.

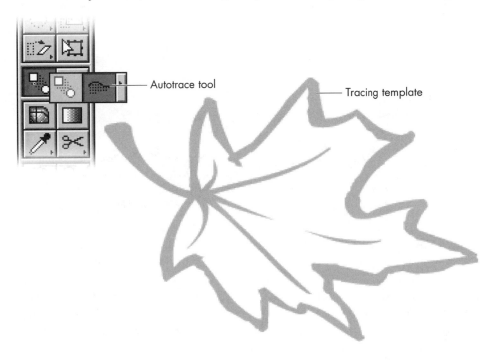

Figure 4-21: With a template image in place, select the autotrace tool.

You can use the autotrace tool in one of two ways:

- Click within six pixels inside edge of an area in the tracing template. Illustrator automatically encircles that area with a closed path.

- Drag from within six pixels of an edge to within six pixels of some other portion of that same edge. Illustrator traces an open path between the point at which you click and the point at which you release.

For example, to trace around the outside of the cactus, we clicked at the top just inside the edge. To trace the bottom crevice, we clicked inside that shape. The results of the two clicks are shown in Figure 4-22.

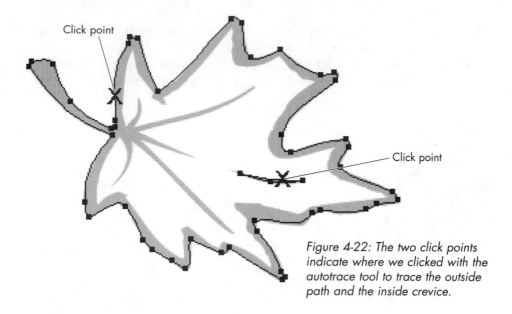

Click point

Click point

Figure 4-22: The two click points indicate where we clicked with the autotrace tool to trace the outside path and the inside crevice.

Dragging is a less common way to trace shapes, but it can be useful if you want to trace one portion of the template automatically and the rest manually. After you complete your drag, Illustrator traces a portion of the image, tracing clockwise around exterior edges, as demonstrated in Figure 4-23, and counterclockwise around interior edges. This is true even if it's tracing the longer of the two distances between where you started your drag and where you released.

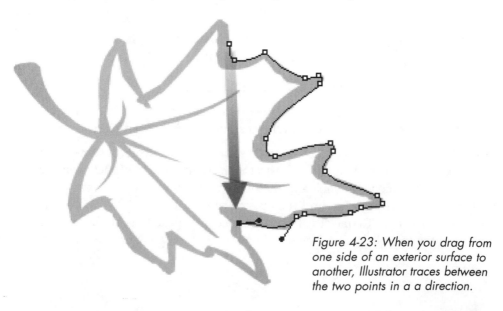

Figure 4-23: When you drag from one side of an exterior surface to another, Illustrator traces between the two points in a a direction.

You can temporarily hide a template layer to get a better view of your artwork. Click that layer's Visibility button—the eyeball on the left side—in the Layers palette. The template disappears. To bring the template back into view, click again where the eyeball was.

Adjusting Autotracing Sensitivity

If you are dissatisfied with Illustrator's tracing accuracy, you can adjust the autotrace tool's sensitivity by changing the Auto Trace Tolerance value in the Type & Auto Tracing Preferences dialog box. An Auto Trace Tolerance value of 0 instructs Illustrator to trace every single pixel of a bitmapped template. If you raise the value to 10, the software ignores large jags in the outline of a template and smooths out all kinds of details.

Generally speaking, it's better to have too many points than too few. After all, you can always delete points later. So for the most reliable autotracing, set the Auto Trace Tolerance value no higher than 2.

Tracing across Gaps

The autotrace tool is most effective in tracing the borders between the black and white areas in a template. But it can also trace gray areas and areas with broken or inconsistent outlines. To accommodate such rough spots, Illustrator provides a Tracing Gap option in the Type & Auto Tracing Preferences dialog box.

You can set this value to any value from 0 to 2. The default value of 0 instructs Illustrator to never pass over the gap. A value of 1 permits Illustrator to jump one-pixel gaps. If you raise the value to 2, Illustrator can jump a two-pixel gap. This is a useful setting when you're tracing photographs and other images with loose pixels.

Fixing Things

It happens—somewhere, sometime, somehow you're going to make a mistake. Perhaps you have created a pencil path that is too wobbly; perhaps you kept dragging with the pencil beyond where you should have; or maybe you just don't like one side of the line anymore. Whatever the reason, Illustrator gives you several tools and commands to make things right.

Smoothing, Erasing, and Reshaping

Once you have created a path, you may want to change it. Fortunately Illustrator provides you with several different tools and a special filter that can reshape, smooth, and erase existing paths. Two of the tools are the aptly-named smooth and eraser tools. These tools are found in the alternate slots for the pencil tool (Figure 4-24).

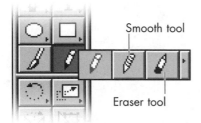

Smooth tool

Eraser tool

Figure 4-24: The smooth and eraser tools don't create new paths, but they help you modify existing ones.

The other two tools are the pencil and paintbrush. Not only can the pencil and paintbrush create paths, they can also reshape them.

All five tools work on any selected path—not just those drawn by the pencil or paintbrush.

Smoothing Things Out

The smooth tool works by modifying selected paths. As you drag across the path with the tool, the tool deletes points so that the modified path is closer to the path that you dragged. As Figure 4-25 shows, the smooth tool works by deleting excess points as well as moving others. Multiple passes with the smooth tool will make a path progressively smoother.

Double-click the smooth tool in the toolbox to open its preferences. There you can set the same Fidelity and Smoothness sliders found in the pencil tool preferences. The higher the Fidelity, the more the smooth tool will distort the selected path to the shape of the line that you draw with the smooth tool. The higher the Smoothness, the more the tool will move and delete points in the path.

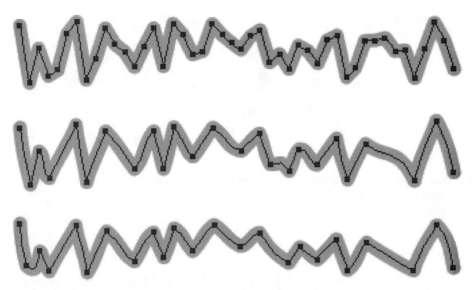

Figure 4-25: The smooth tool was dragged across the original path (top) at its highest setting. The middle example shows how the tool deleted many of the points. The bottom example shows how the smooth tool reshaped the path.

Erasing

Lady Macbeth would have loved the eraser tool (out, out, damn'd path!). The eraser tool lets you drag across the selected path and poof—in one simple sweep that portion of the path is gone.

Choose the eraser tool from the alternate slot of the pencil tool. (The cursor looks like a pencil turned upside down, with a black eraser.) Drag the eraser across or along a selected path. The eraser will delete that portion of the path. Unlike simply deleting a point (covered in Chapter 5), which will delete the segment till it reaches a new point, the eraser will add points at the position where you start and end the drag. As shown in Figure 4-26, the eraser tool can delete part of a path even if there are no anchor points.

 Click with the eraser tool on a selected path to delete the entire path. Poof! It's gone!

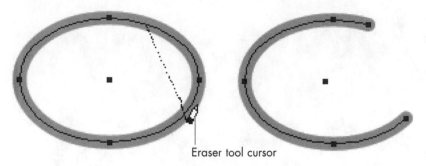

Eraser tool cursor

Figure 4-26: The eraser was dragged across the original path (left). That portion of the path was deleted and two new anchor points were added as endpoints to the path.

Reshaping

As you saw earlier, you can use the pencil to create or extend a path. You can also use it to reshape any selected path—even paths created by other tools besides the pencil. As shown in Figure 4-27, if you drag the pencil over a selected path, the path reshapes itself to follow the drag of the pencil.

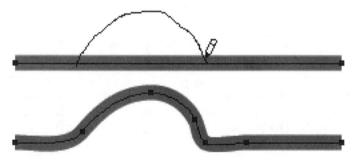

Figure 4-27: The pencil tool was dragged in an arc over the straight line (top). This resulted in a reshaped path (bottom).

The paintbrush can also reshape selected paths, but only those that have been styled with a brushstroke as explained in Chapter 16. The pencil can reshape any selected path, including those styled with brushes. (That makes the pencil more powerful than the paintbrush.)

Simplification

 Finally, it's here! Illustrator 9 introduces the simplify command. Although there have been several third-party filters (third-party means that other people besides Adobe created the filter) that have simplified paths, the new simplify command is free; it is automatically installed with Illustrator, and it is the most complicated simplify command ever. (Yes, we know that's an oxymoron.) What makes it so complicated, though, is its sophistication and power.)

If you draw your own shapes, you will most likely never need to simplify them. You will only create clean, simple, elegant paths. (That's why you are reading this book.) But many designers and artists receive files created from *CAD* programs (Computer Aided Design), such as AutoCAD, which add hundreds of unnecessary points. Others use clip art such as maps and cartoons that were created using programs such as Streamline that created many extraneous points. Still others inherit logos and other artwork designed by incompetent fools who added points willy-nilly.

So besides making selected paths look like the edge of a open zipper, why should you care if there are millions of points in your artwork? The primary reason is that it's easier to manipulate paths when they have fewer points. It's much easier to select one or two points (as explained in Chapter 5) if you don't have a huge pile of them in one microscopic section.

The other reason is that every single point takes up some part of the memory used to write the file. Excess points add to the file size; and the bigger the file, the more time it will take a print shop or a desktop printer to print the darn thing. And we promise you, you don't want to get a phone call at 11 o'clock at night from the manager of some service bureau who tells you, "Hey lady, yah file won't print."

If you have a path in need of simplification as shown in Figure 4-29, you can apply the simplify command by choosing Object » Path »Simplify. The simplify dialog box appears as shown in Figure 4-28. Adjust the settings as follows:

- Check **Preview.** This adds a display of the number of points in the original version of the object, as well as the number of points that will be in the object after you apply the command.

- Adjust the **Curve Precision** slider from 0% to 100%. This controls how close the simplified path should follow the original. Higher percentages leave more points on the path. Lower percentages remove more points and can cause greater distortion in the final path.

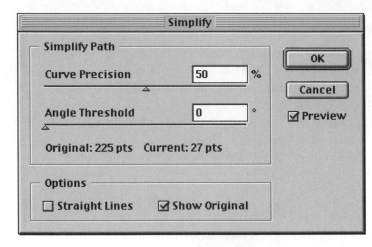

*Figure 4-28:
The simplify dialog
box is where you
can throw out
redundant points.*

*Figure 4-29: The outline of New York (top) has
far too many points. After the simplify filter was
applied (bottom) there are far fewer.*

- Adjust the **Angle Threshold** slider from 0 to 180 degrees. The controls the smoothness of the corner points. (We'll cover the different types of points in the next chapter.) The lower the Angle Threshold, the more likely sharp angles will be turned into smooth curves.

- Check **Straight Lines** to create straight lines between points.

- Check **Show Original** to add a red preview of the original path. This helps you see just how much your original artwork will be changed.

Yet One Tools Beats Them All

Before we close this chapter, we want to leave you with a parting bit of wisdom. We've tackled all but one of Illustrator's drawing tools, and that remaining tool—the pen tool—is far and away the best of all. It is infinitely more flexible than the rectangle, ellipse, and other shape tools, and more precise than the pencil, paintbrush, and autotrace tools. (The pen tool is also mightier than the sword tool, but that's another story.) It is, in fact, the only tool you really need. In fact, there was a time when the pen, rectangle, and ellipse tools were all Illustrator offered—yet there wasn't a thing you couldn't draw. And if you use either Adobe Photoshop or InDesign, they too use the same pen tool. So mastering the Illustrator pen can help you when working in other applications.

That's why the next chapter is so important. It shows you how to edit the paths you create with the tools in this chapter, and how to create more exacting shapes with the pen. These features require more work, but they'll reward your effort several times over.

CHAPTER 5

EXACT POINTS AND PRECISION CURVES

Much as Illustrator tries, at a price of $149–$399, it just can't live up to the 25¢ pencil when it comes to smooth, real-time drawing. Whether you use Illustrator's pencil, paintbrush, or autotrace tool, you still get the same thing—paths divided by anchor point. A drawing tablet helps, but only to communicate smoother lines to Illustrator; it doesn't help Illustrator better interpret your beautiful work.

There is hope for the future, of course. Today's Illustrator does a much better job of interpreting pencil paths than did Illustrator 88 (the first version to offer the tool). So one might expect Illustrator 2001 to perform even better and Illustrator 2525 to be right on the money. But in the meantime, we can either suffer with clunky paths, or we can fix them.

That said, it would be a sin if fixing paths weren't what this chapter is all about. We'll explore a whole mess of path-editing theories—you'll see how to move anchor points and bend segments to get lines as smooth as water droplets and as organic as flower petals. We'll also cover the pen tool, the only tool in all of Illustrator that lets you draw paths correctly the first time out. And just when you think Illustrator couldn't be any dreamier, we'll throw in some pointers for adding, deleting, and converting points.

If Illustrator is nothing else, it's the most excellent path creation and manipulation tool the world has ever enjoyed. This chapter tells why.

Selecting Like a House on Fire

 If you're an old-time user you might be tempted to skip this section. After all, what new features could Adobe have possibly added to Illustrator's robust selection tools? Well, cowboy, how 'bout two lasso tools for selecting non-rectangular areas—does *that* polish your saddle? So even though there's not much else that's new in this chapter, there's still reason to stick around.

The job of sprucing up paths rests on the shoulders of five very sturdy tools. These are the selection tools, available from the top four slots in the toolbox, as shown in Figure 5-1. Clicking or dragging on a point or segment with one of these suckers selects all or part of a path. The tools differ only in the extent of the selection they make.

Arrows or Lassos?

No, this isn't the prop department for an old Hollywood western; it's the two categories for selection tools in Illustrator. The arrows (also known as the selection, direct selection, and group selection tools) are the most powerful of selection tools. Not only can they select objects and points, but if you drag with them, they move things around.

Lassos (also known as the lasso and direct selection lasso) aren't as powerful as the arrow tools. They can only select things; if you want to move the selection around, you have to switch to an arrow.

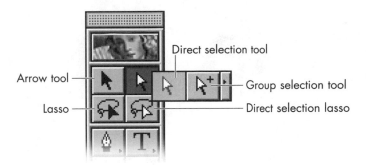

Figure 5-1: The three selection tools are all you need to move anchor points, bend segments, and otherwise whip paths into shape. The lasso tools select but don't move points and paths.

 Ordinarily you would see a bounding box around objects that are selected using the selection tool. This bounding box can be used to scale or rotate selected objects. However, we both feel that the bounding box gets in the way of working with selection basics. So we've hidden it from these illustrations. To hide (or show) the bounding box, choose View » Hide (or Show) Bounding Box. Or take the time to memorize the vital keystroke Cmd-Shift-B on the Mac or Ctrl-Shift-B on Windows.

The Plain Black Arrow Tool

The selection tool—which we call the arrow tool to distinguish it from its selection pals—is the most straightforward of the bunch. When the arrow tool is active, you can click anywhere along the outline of a path to select the path in its entirety. If the Use Area Select check box is turned on inside the General Preferences dialog box, you can also click inside the path to select it, provided the path has a fill (as discussed in Chapter 15). All points become visible as filled squares, as Figure 5-2 demonstrates.

After selecting a path with the arrow tool, you can move it, apply a transformation, or perform any other manipulation that affects the path as a whole. You cannot move points or bend segments. If the path has been grouped with other paths (as explained in Chapter 10), the arrow tool selects the entire group, prohibiting you from altering one grouped path independently of another.

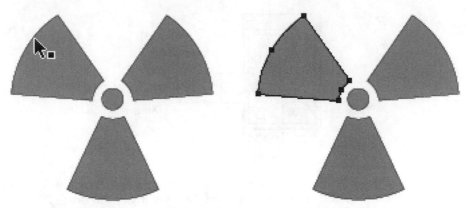

Figure 5-2: Click any part of a path with the arrow tool (left) to select the entire path (right).

Here are a few other ways to select paths with the arrow tool:

- When you click a path, you not only select the path you click, you also deselect any previously-selected path. To select multiple paths, click the first path and then hold the Shift key as you click each additional path you want to select (this is called a *Shift-click*). The Shift key prevents Illustrator from deselecting paths as you click new ones.

- Another way to select multiple paths is to *marquee* them. Drag from an empty portion of your drawing area to create a dotted rectangular outline, called a marquee. You select all paths that fall even slightly inside this outline when you release the mouse button. In Figure 5-3, for example, Sandee dragged midway across the left side and circle shapes.

- You can combine marqueeing with Shift-clicking to select multiple paths. You can also drag a marquee while pressing Shift, which adds the surrounded objects to the present selection.

- If you Shift-click an object that is already selected, Illustrator deselects it, as discussed in the upcoming section "Deselecting Stuff That You Want to Leave as Is."

 To access the arrow tool temporarily when some other tool is active, press and hold the Cmd/Ctrl key. Release the key to return to the last tool you used. If pressing Cmd/Ctrl gets you one of the hollow selection cursors instead, press Cmd/Ctrl-Tab and then press Cmd/Ctrl again. To switch to the arrow tool without having to hold modifiers, press the V key.

Mac users, take note: If the preceding tip doesn't work, it's because the Mac OS has taken over the use of Cmd-Tab for switching between open applications. Fortunately Adobe recognized the situation and has added Ctrl-Tab to also switch between the arrow tool and the hollow arrow tools.

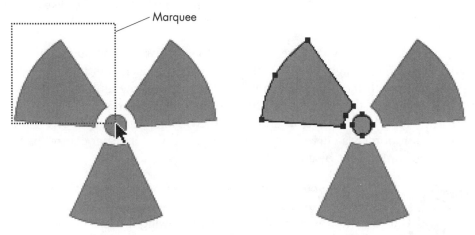

Marquee

Figure 5-3: By marqueeing partially inside two of the blades and the center circle shapes (left), Sandee selected them both (right).

The Hollow Direct Selection Tool

The direct selection tool is the hollow (white) arrow in the upper right corner of the toolbox. Click with the direct selection tool to select an individual point or segment in a path. If you click a point, you select the point; if you click a segment, you select the segment. This works even if the path that contains the point or segment is part of a group.

 As you work with the selection arrows you will notice little squares that appear next to the cursor. These boxes indicate what type of object the arrow is over. When the cursor is over any point, a small white square appears, as shown in the left two examples of Figure 5-4. Move it over a segment of a path and a black square joins the cursor, as you can see in the top right example of Figure 5-4. Move it over a filled area (when Use Area Select is turned on) and it also displays the black square. These cursors inform you that if you click with the mouse, you will select the intended element.

Turning Use Area Select on or off is a very personal choice—so personal it's not polite to ask someone their preferences. One of us likes Use Area Select turned on. She likes the fact that she can just click inside an object to select it. The other likes it turned off. He wants to be able to select through to objects behind others. However, because this is such a sensitive topic, we won't tell you which one of us likes which setting.

Now that you know how the direct selection tool appears when you are selecting path elements, you might as well know how those path elements appear when you select them with the direct selection tool. Different elements have different ways of showing that they are selected. For example, when you select a point, it appears as a small filled square, as shown in the bottom left example of Figure 5-4. If the point borders a curved segment, you can also see a Bézier control handle connected to the point by a thin lever.

For those of you reading aloud to loved ones, Bézier is pronounced *bay-zee-ay*. Named after Pierre Bézier—the French fellow who designed this particular drawing model to expedite the manufacture of car bodies, of all things—Bézier curve theory lies at the heart of both Illustrator and the PostScript printing language. Sadly, Monsieur Bézier passed away on November 25,1999 at the age of 89. Fortunately, his name will forever be linked with the control handles and curves in vector drawing programs.

When you select a path, Illustrator shows you both selected and deselected points. The deselected points appear as hollow squares, showing that they are part of a partially selected path, but are not themselves selected.

When you click a segment with the direct selection tool, Illustrator shows you the Bézier control handles for that segment—if there are any—as in the lower right example of Figure 5-4. Unless some point in the path is also selected, all points appear hollow. Because Illustrator shows you the control handles only, you may find it a little confusing when selecting straight segments, which lack handles. You just have to click the segment and have faith that it's selected. (Frankly, we wish Illustrator thickened the segment to provide some sort of visual feedback.)

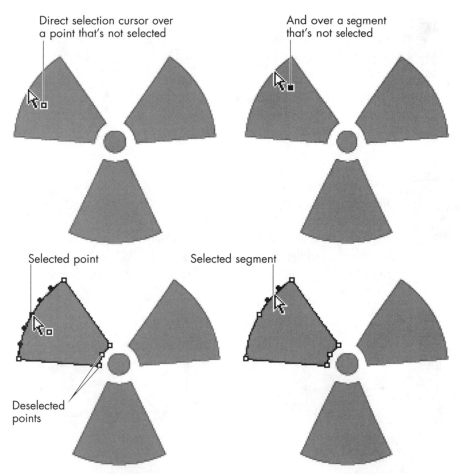

Figure 5-4: Position the direct selection tool over a point (top left) and the cursor gains a small hollow square. When over a segment (top right), the direct selection cursor gains a small black square. Select a single anchor point (bottom left) or segment (bottom right) by clicking with the direct selection tool.

You can also drag with the direct selection tool to marquee elements. All points and segments that lie inside the marquee become selected, even if they belong to different paths, as Figure 5-5 shows.

The following list summarizes these and other ways to select elements with the direct selection tool:

   If the Use Area Select check box in the General Preferences dialog box is turned on (as it is by default), you can click inside a filled shape to select the entire path. This assumes that the shape has a fill, as addressed in Chapter 14.

- Shift-click a point or segment to add it to the current selection. You can also Shift-marquee around elements. (If you Shift-click a point or segment that's already selected, it becomes deselected. The same goes for Shift-marqueeing.)

- Opt/Alt-click a point or segment to select an entire path. This is a great way to select paths inside groups.

- Opt/Alt-marquee or Opt/Alt-Shift-click paths to select multiple paths at a time.

> **TIP** To switch back and forth between the arrow tool and the direct selection tool, press Cmd/Ctrl-Tab. If you last used the direct selection tool (as opposed to the arrow tool), you can access it while any other tool is active by pressing Cmd/Ctrl. If you last used the arrow tool, press Cmd/Ctrl-Tab and then press Cmd/Ctrl. To switch to the direct selection tool, press the A key.

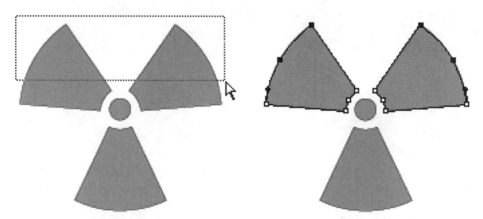

Figure 5-5: When dragging a marquee with the direct selection tool (left), all points and segments that fall inside the marquee become selected (right).

The Sad Little Group Selection Tool

Adobe added the group selection tool to Illustrator so folks who were afraid to press the Option or Alt key could select paths inside groups. In other words, you can either Opt/Alt-click a path to select it with the direct selection tool (temporarily accessing the group selection tool), or click the path with the group selection tool. If you're not afraid of the occasional Opt/Alt-click, feel free to ignore the group selection tool. Neither of us ever touches it. Honestly, it's useless.

If you don't believe us, and you'd prefer to know everything about everything, you can select the group selection tool by dragging from the upper right slot in the toolbox. Then do any of the following:

- Click a point or segment to select a whole path in a group. You can also select groups within groups by clicking multiple times on a path, but you can do this with the direct selection tool as well so long as you hold the Opt/Alt key down. (We shouldn't even be mentioning this. All this grouping stuff is covered in Chapter 10.)

- Marquee paths with the group selection tool to select the paths, whether they fall entirely or partially inside the marquee.

- Shift-click a path to add it to the selection. You can also Shift-marquee if you get the urge.

- Opt/Alt-click a point or segment to select it independently of its path. The Opt/Alt key temporarily converts the group selection to direct selection.

See, what did we tell you? Dumb tool. Steer clear of it.

Lassoing Selections

You may have noticed that the marquees created by the arrow tools are always rectangular. Every single Illustrator user worth his or her salt has at one time cursed as an errant path or point got selected inadvertently within a marquee selection. Why can't Illustrator select in non-rectangular areas?

Welcome, Pilgrim, your search is over. Illustrator 9 now gives you two lasso tools that let you round up selections in any shape you desire. And just like the selection tools, the lassos are divided into two different selection modes.

The Black Lasso

The black lasso (officially known as the *lasso tool*) selects entire objects—even if you only snare parts of them within the lasso marquee. Simply drag the lasso around the objects you want to select. A line indicates the area that is being selected. When you release the mouse, all the objects that were within the lasso marquee will be selected as shown in Figure 5-6.

 One way to remember which lasso does what is to look at the black arrowhead and the position of the black lasso. It's right under the selection tool (black arrow). Just as the selection tool selects entire objects within its marquee, so does the black lasso.

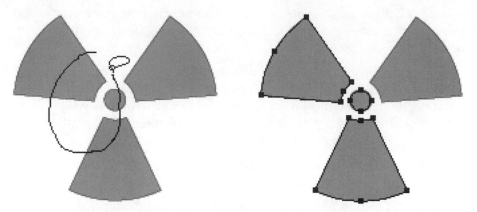

Figure 5-6: When the lasso is dragged around parts of the objects (left), a line indicates the area that is being selected. When the mouse is released, the three objects are entirely selected (right).

The White Lasso

The white lasso (officially known as the *direct selection lasso tool*) selects parts of objects. Drag around the points or segments you want to select. When you release the mouse, only those points or segments that were within the lasso marquee will be selected. As shown in Figure 5-7, the direct selection lasso allows you to select points that would require many different passes dragging with the arrow tools.

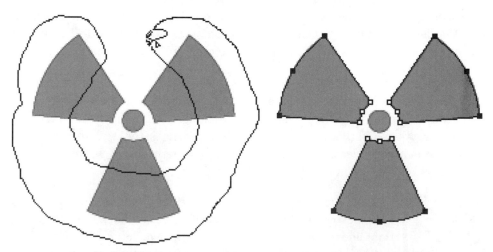

Figure 5-7: This looping selection around the outside portions of the illustration was created with the direct selection tool (left), and selects only the outside points of the illustration (right).

Adding More Lasso Selections

The lasso tools work slightly differently than the other selection tools. If you hold the Shift key, you will see a small plus sign next to the lasso cursor. This indicates that the next loop of the lasso will add to the selection. But the lassos do not deselect selected items when you use the Shift key. They only add to the selection. To deselect as you lasso you have to press and hold down the Opt/Alt key.

Selecting Everything

If you want to select all paths in your drawing, choose Edit » Select All or press Cmd/Ctrl-A. Illustrator selects every last point, segment, and other element throughout the illustration, even if it's on the pasteboard. (An exception occurs if you've either locked an object so it can't be selected or selected a letter inside a text block, in which case Select All highlights all text in the story.)

Inversing the Selection

To select everything that's not selected and deselect what is selected, choose Edit » Select » Inverse. It's Illustrator's way of letting you reverse a selection.

Both the Select All and Inverse commands make it easier to select most of the objects in a complicated drawing. You can choose Select All and then Shift-click the objects you don't want to select. Or start off by clicking and Shift-clicking the stuff you don't want to select, and choose Edit » Select » Inverse. Either way works fine; it's entirely a matter of personal preference.

Other Selection Techniques

If all this hasn't been enough, there are actually several other techniques for selecting things. For instance, you can select all the objects on layers, by using the Layers palette (covered in Chapter 10). You can also select objects by attributes using the Selection commands. These commands are all found under the submenu after Edit » Select.

 Some of these terms may seem foreign to you. You can find out more about them in the chapters later in the book.

- **Same Fill & Stroke:** Selects all objects that have the same fill and stroke attributes. (Chapters 15 and 16)
- **Same Fill Color:** Selects all objects that have the same fill color. The stroke colors may vary. (Chapter 15)

- **Same Stroke Color:** Selects all objects that have the same stroke color. The stroke weight may vary as well as the fill colors. (Chapter 16)

- **Same Stroke Weight:** Selects all objects that have the same stroke weight. The stroke color may vary as well as the fill attributes. (Chapter 16)

- **Same Blending Mode:** Selects all objects that the same type of blending mode as found in the Transparency palette. All other attributes may vary. (Chapter 17)

- **Same Opacity:** Selects all objects that have the same percentage of opacity applied. All other attributes may vary. (Chapter 17)

- **Same Masks:** Selects all objects that are acting as masks to hide areas of other objects. (Chapter 18)

- **Same Stray Points:** Selects all single points. Single points can get left over when you delete portions of objects, or forget and click once with the pen and then don't click again.

- **Same Brush Strokes:** Selects all objects that have brush strokes applied. (Chapter 16)

Once you have chosen one of these selection commands, that command is stored in Illustrator's memory. You can then choose Edit » Select » Select Again (Cmd/Ctrl-6) to reapply whatever selection criterion was previously chosen. The benefit of this is if you've just selected and modified all red-filled objects, you can select one green object, choose Select Again, and then modify the green-filled ones.

Yes, we're well aware that FreeHand has a wand tool that can select varying colors. Yes, we're well aware that FreeHand has a way to select things based on shapes. And yes, we agree that those features would be great in Illustrator. So, please, don't bug us about them—tell Adobe. Send your e-mail requests to: aifeature@adobe.com. Tell 'em Deke and Sandee sent you.

Hiding the Points and Handles

All those points, handles, and colored outlines that Illustrator uses to show that an object is selected can occasionally get in your face. If you're aware of your selection but you want to see the selected objects unadorned, choose View » Hide Edges or press Cmd/Ctrl-H.

From that point on, no selection outline appears on screen, even if you select a different object. To see the selection outlines again, you have to choose View » Show Edges or press Cmd/Ctrl-H again.

Deselecting Stuff that You Want to Leave As Is

Selecting is your way of telling Illustrator, "This thing is messed up, and now I'm going to hurt it," or fix it, or whatever. If you don't want to hurt an object, you need to deselect it. (Folks also say "unselect," one or two might even say "antiselect" or "get it out of the selection loop," but we think the unremarkable "deselect" sounds the least icky.)

To deselect all objects—regardless of form or gender—press Cmd/Ctrl-Shift-A (Edit » Deselect All) or just click with one of the selection tools on an empty portion of the drawing area.

You can make more discrete deselections using the Shift key:

- To deselect an entire path or group, Shift-click the object with the arrow tool.

- To deselect a single point or segment, Shift-click it with the direct selection tool.

- To deselect a single path inside a group, Opt/Alt-Shift-click it with the direct selection tool.

- You can also deselect elements and objects by Shift-marqueeing around them. Selected elements become deselected, and deselected elements become selected.

Dragging Stuff Around

Once you've selected a point or segment, you can move it around, changing its location and stretching its path. In fact, dragging with the direct selection tool is the single most common method for reshaping a path inside Illustrator. You can move selected points independently of deselected points. And you can stretch segments or move Bézier control handles to alter the curvature of a path. The next few pages explain all aspects of dragging.

Dragging Points

To move one or more points in a path:

1. Select the points you want to move with the direct selection tool.

2. Drag any one of them.

3. Squeal with delight.

When you drag a selected point, all other selected points move the same distance and direction. When you move a point while a neighboring point remains stationary, the segment between the two points shrinks or stretches in length to accommodate the change in distance, as demonstrated in Figure 5-8.

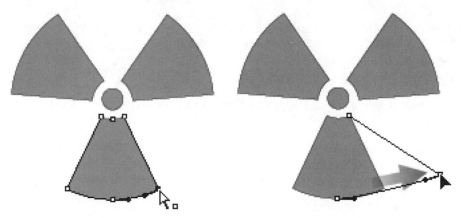

Figure 5-8: When you drag a selected point bordered by deselected points (left), Illustrator stretches the segments between the points (right).

When you move a point, any accompanying control handles move with it. As a result, the curved segments on either side of the point must not only shrink or stretch, but also bend to accommodate the movement. Meanwhile, segments located between two deselected points or two selected points remain unchanged during a move, as demonstrated in Figure 5-9. Illustrator lets you move multiple points within a single path, as in Figure 5-9, or in separate paths, as in Figure 5-10. This means you can reshape multiple paths at the same time.

While you move a point, Illustrator displays both previous and current locations of the point and its surrounding segments. This useful feature permits you to gauge the full effect of a move as it progresses. Also worth noting: When you drag a single selected point, Illustrator displays the point, any Bézier control handles associated with the two neighboring segments, and the neighboring deselected points, as shown back in Figure 5-6. When dragging multiple points, Illustrator hides the points and handles, as in Figures 5-7 and 5-8. We wish we could see the points and handles, but Adobe thinks all that screen clutter might prove confusing.

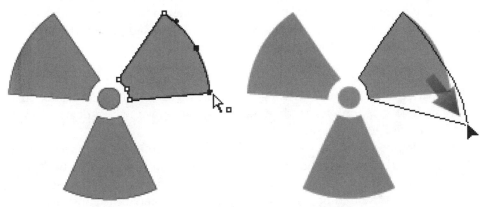

Figure 5-9: When you drag more than one selected point at a time (left), the segments between the selected points remain unchanged (right).

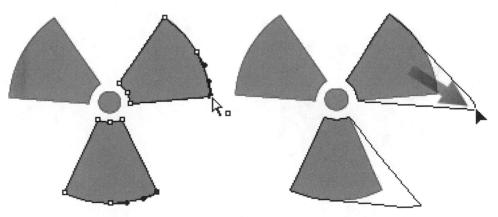

Figure 5-10: You can move multiple points even when selected points reside in different paths.

Keeping Your Movements in Line

You can constrain your cursor movements horizontally, vertically, or diagonally by pressing the Shift key. For example, if you want to move a point horizontally without moving it so much as a smidgen up or down, press the Shift key while dragging the point with the direct selection tool.

You have to press Shift after you begin dragging. (If you press Shift before you drag, you deselect the selected point that you click, which causes Illustrator to ignore your drag.) Then you hold down the Shift key until after you release the mouse button. (Always release the mouse button first, and then whatever modifier key you have pressed.) If you release Shift first, you'll lose the constraint.

You can adjust the effects of pressing Shift by changing the Constrain Angle value in the General Preferences dialog box. This rotates the constraint axes. So a horizontal (0-degree) move becomes a 15-degree move, a 45-degree move becomes a 60-degree move, and so on.

Why would you ever want to do this? You may want to move a point along an angled object without letting the point and the object drift apart. For example, the top segment along the tent object in Figure 5-11 is oriented at a 15-degree angle. To move the ball forward along the segment, Deke first rotated the constraint axes to 15 degrees and then dragged the object while pressing Shift.

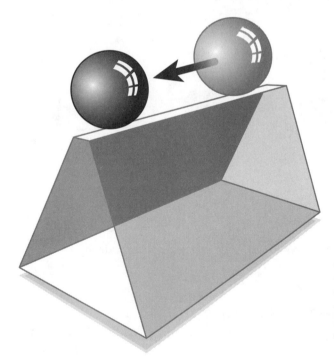

Figure 5-11:
Rotating the constraint axes to 15 degrees allows Deke to move the ball precisely along a 15-degree segment.

Rather than change the constrain angle, you can also set the Smart Guides (glorified in Chapter 10) to a specific angle and then move objects.

Remember, the constraint axes also affect the creation of rectangles, ellipses, and text blocks. So you'll generally want to reset them to 0 degrees when you finish making your moves.

Snapping Point to Point

When dragging a point, you may find that it has a tendency to move sharply toward another point in your illustration. This effect is called *snapping,* and it's Illustrator's way of ensuring that points that belong together are flush against each other to form a perfect fit.

When you drag a point within two screen pixels of a second point on your drawing area, your cursor snaps to the stationary point, so that both point and cursor occupy the very same spot on the page. At the moment the snap occurs, your cursor changes from a filled arrowhead to a hollow arrowhead, as shown in Figure 5-12. (This is particularly useful after a long day in front of the screen, when your snap-perception capabilities have all but vanished.)

For example, you might drag the corner point of one rectangle until it snaps to the corner point of another. In this way, both rectangles sit exactly point to point.

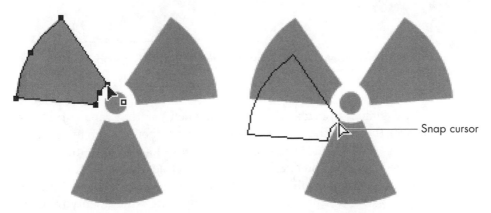

Figure 5-12: Your cursor changes to a hollow arrowhead when snapping a point to a stationary point.

Your cursor snaps to stationary points as well as to the previous locations of points currently being moved. (This last item is more useful than it sounds. You'll see, one day it'll come in handy.) Your cursor also snaps to text blocks and to guides (covered in Chapters 6 and 10 respectively).

You can turn Illustrator's snapping feature on and off by choosing the View » Snap to Point command or by pressing Cmd-Opt-plus (+) (for Mac users) or Ctrl-Alt-plus (+) (for Windows folks).

Dragging Segments

You can also reshape a path by dragging its segments. When you drag a straight segment, its neighboring segments stretch or shrink to accommodate the change in distance, as shown in the first example in Figure 5-13. However, when you drag a curved segment, you stretch only that segment. The effect is rather like pulling on a rubber band extended between two nails, as the second example illustrates.

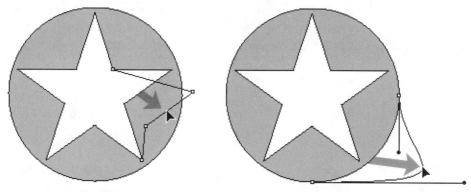

Figure 5-13: The difference between dragging a straight segment (left) and a curved segment (right).

Figure 5-14 examines in detail what happens when you drag on a curved segment. The longer the drag, the more the segment has to bend. More important is how the segment bends. Notice the two Bézier control handles on either side of the segment. The handles automatically extend and retract as you drag. Each handle moves along an imaginary line consistent with the handle's original inclination. The angle of a control handle does not change one whit when you drag a segment, thus guaranteeing that the curved segment moves in alignment with neighboring stationary segments.

When dragging a segment, drag on the middle of the segment, approximately equidistant from both of its points, as we did in Figure 5-13. This provides the best leverage and keeps you from losing control over the segment. (Believe it or not, these things can spring away from you if you're not careful.)

Figure 5-14:
When you drag a
curved segment, each
Bézier control handle
moves back and forth
along a constant axis.

If you want to move a control handle in a different direction, you have to drag the handle itself, as we describe in the "Dragging Control Handles" section later in this chapter.

Nudging Points and Segments

Another way to move a selected element is to press one of the four arrow keys at the bottom of your keyboard (up, down, left, right). Not surprisingly, each of these keys nudges a selection in the direction of the arrow.

You can change the distance that a single keystroke moves a selected element by adjusting the Cursor Key value in the General Preferences dialog box. For example, setting the value to 1 point is equivalent to one screen pixel when you view the illustration at actual size. However, you can set the value anywhere from 0.01 to 1296 points—that's a whopping 18 inches. Deke usually keeps it somewhere between 0.1 and 10 points, depending on the situation. (In fact, he's constantly changing the value, usually setting it smaller and smaller as an illustration becomes more detailed.) Sandee leaves it at 1 point and gets cathartic thrills by pressing the key over and over to move things around.

You can use arrow keys to move points as well as straight and curved segments. (Sadly, you can't move a single control handle with an arrow key; to do this, you must drag the handle with the direct selection tool.) This is very handy for stretching two segments exactly the same distance. Just click one segment, Shift-click the other, and whack away at the arrow keys.

The arrow keys move a selection with respect to the constraint axes. For example, if you change the constrain angle to 15 degrees, pressing the right arrow key moves the selection slightly upward, and pressing the up arrow moves it slightly to the left.

If pressing an arrow key doesn't seem to produce any noticeable result, a palette might be active. For example, if you just got through changing the size of a font in the Character palette, Illustrator may be forwarding the arrow key signal to the palette, even if no option appears to be active. To remedy this situation, press Return/Enter, which deactivates the palette. Then press the arrow keys to nudge without hindrance.

Dragging Control Handles

The only element that we've so far neglected to move is the Bézier control handle. We've saved it for last because it's the most difficult and the most powerful element you can manipulate.

After referencing control handles several times in this chapter, it's high time we defined our terminology. The *Bézier control handle* (*control handle* or *handle* or *those funky little line things* for short) is the element that defines the arc of a segment as it exits or enters an anchor point. It tugs at a segment like an invisible thread. You increase the curvature of a segment when you drag the handle away from its point, and decrease the curvature when you drag a handle toward its point.

To display a control handle, you can either select the point to which the handle belongs or select the segment it controls. You then drag the handle with the direct selection tool, just as you drag a point.

Figure 5-15 shows three paths composed of five points each. Sandee drew the first path—the one that looks like a 2—with the pencil tool and assigned it a thick gray stroke. The second and third paths are based on the first; the only differences are the positions of the control handles and the curvatures of the segments. The points remain unmoved from one path to the next, and yet the results are unique.

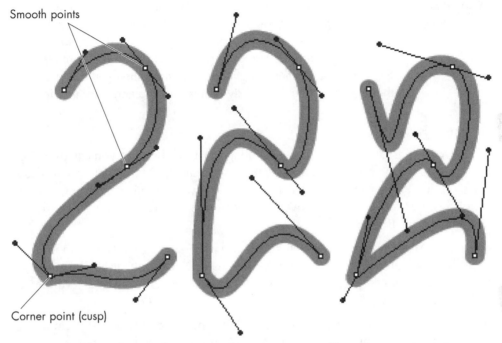

Smooth points

Corner point (cusp)

Figure 5-15: These three paths comprise five points apiece. The points remain stationary—only the control handles move.

The 2 comprises two smooth points around its loop and a special kind of corner point called a *cusp* where the loop and base meet. A cusp forms a corner between two curved segments. (We don't really care what kinds of points the endpoints are, because no segments follow them.)

The other two paths contain the same points in the same order. So not only has no point been moved, no point has been converted to a different kind of point. As a result, the bottom left point in each path remains a corner, permitting us to move the two control handles on either side of the point independently of each other. This is the very nature of a corner point.

Likewise, the points in the middle and upper right portions of the path remain smooth points. When we move one control handle, the other moves in the opposite direction, making for a sort of fulcrum effect. This ensures a continuous arc through each point. Not only is there no corner at either location, there's no hint of even the slightest crease. The path continues through the points as smoothly as a bend in the road.

 Dragging a control handle can turn ugly when you're working inside a very complex illustration. If the handle rests near a point or segment from a different path, Illustrator may think you're trying to drag the point or segment rather than the handle. To bring the handle out of the fray so you can get to it more easily, drag the curved segment that the handle controls. Stretching the segment lengthens the handle; then you can drag the handle without busybody points and segments horning in.

Bézier Rules

Figure 5-15 is proof of the old Bézier adage that just because you *can* drag control handles all over the place doesn't mean you *should*. Manipulating handles is not so much a question of what is possible as of what is proper. Several handle-handling rules have developed over the years, but the best are the *All-or-Nothing rule* and the *33-Percent rule*:

- The All-or-Nothing rule states that every segment in your path should be associated with either two control handles or none at all. In other words, no segment should rely on only one control handle to determine its curvature.

- The 33-Percent rule tells us that the distance from any control handle to its point should equal approximately one third the length of the segment. So one handle covers one third of the segment, the other handle covers the opposite third, and the middle third is handle free.

The left path in Figure 5-16 violates the All-or-Nothing rule. Only one handle apiece controls each of its two curved segments, resulting in weak, shallow arcs. Such puny curves are sure to inspire snorts and guffaws from discriminating viewers.

The right example in Figure 5-16 obeys the All-or-Nothing rule. As the rule states, the straight segment has no handles and the two curved segments have two handles apiece. The result is a full-figured, properly rendered path that is a credit to any illustration.

The first path in Figure 5-17 violates the 33-Percent rule. The handles are either much too short or much too long to fit their segments. The result is an ugly, misshapen mess. In the second example, each handle is about one-third of the length of its segment. The top segment is shorter than the other two, so its handles are shorter as well. This path is smooth and consistent in curvature, giving it a naturalistic appearance.

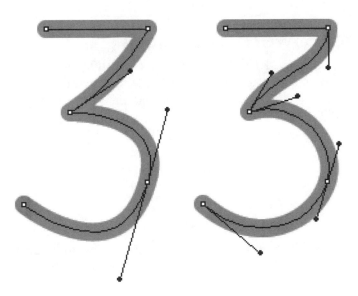

Figure 5-16:
The All-or-Nothing rule
says that two handles
should control every
curved segment, one
for each of its points.

 What happens if you violate either of these rules? Will the Bézier police come to arrest you? (No.) Will your jobs print? (Yes.) The real reason these rules exist is to help you create elegant curves that are easy to work with. You'll spend far too much time playing with artwork that doesn't follow the rules. But your artwork will print.

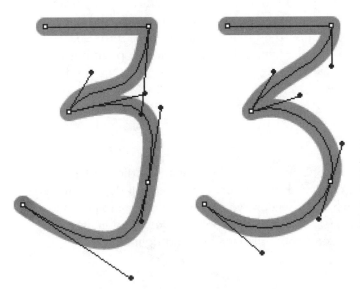

Figure 5-17:
According to the
33-Percent rule, every
control handle should
extend about one-third
the length of its segment.

The Great and Powerful Pen Tool

Now that you've had a taste of Bézier theory, it's time for full immersion. The pen tool is the absolute Bézier champ, capable of creating anything from schematic newspaper charts to detailed scenes of heightened reality. For nearly a decade, Illustrator's pen tool was the reigning champ, and no other program offered anything that came close. Now Adobe has taken Illustrator's pen tool and with a few microscopic exceptions, added it to InDesign. You can also find a more primitive version of the pen tool in Adobe Photoshop. It's a testament to the elegance of the original.

Pen Tool Basics

When drawing with the pen tool, you build a path by creating individual points. Illustrator automatically connects the points with *segments*. The following list summarizes how you can use the pen tool to build paths in Illustrator. These methods are described in more detail later in this chapter.

- **Path building:** To build a path, create one point after another inside the drawing area until the path is the desired length and shape. You create and position a point by either clicking or dragging with the pen tool. (Clicking creates a corner, dragging creates a smooth point.) Illustrator draws a segment between each new point and its predecessor.

- **Adjusting a point:** Midway into creating a path, you can reposition points or change the curvature of segments that you've already drawn. To move a point while you are still creating it, press and hold the spacebar. You can then reposition the point on the fly. Release the spacebar and continue creating points. If you've already created a point but wish to modify it before moving on to the next point, just press the Cmd/Ctrl key to access the direct-selection tool (press Cmd/Ctrl-Tab if the arrow tool comes up instead) and drag the points, segments, and control handles as desired. When you've finished, release Cmd/Ctrl and continue adding points.

Be sure not to Cmd/Ctrl-click in an empty portion of the drawing area or on a different path. That will deactivate the active path, which means you can't add any more points to it without first reactivating the path (as described in the "Extending an open path" item, coming right up).

- **Closing the path:** To create a closed shape, click or drag on the first point in the path. Every point will then have one segment coming into it and another segment exiting it.

- **Leaving the path open:** To leave a path open, so it has a specific beginning and ending, deactivate the path by pressing Cmd/Ctrl-Shift-A (Edit » Deselect All). Or you can press Cmd/Ctrl to get the arrow or direct selection tool and click an empty portion of the drawing area. Either way, you deactivate the path so you can move on and create a new one.

- **Extending an open path:** To reactivate an open path, click or drag one of its endpoints. Illustrator is then ready to draw a segment between the endpoint and the next point you create.

- **Joining two open paths:** To join one open path with another open path, click or drag an endpoint in the first path, then click or drag an endpoint in the second. Illustrator draws a segment between the two, bringing them together in everlasting peace and brotherhood.

That's basically all there is to using the pen tool. A click here, a drag there, and you have yourself a path. But to achieve decent results, you need to know exactly what clicking and dragging do and how to use these techniques to your best advantage. If the devil is in the details, the pen tool is Illustrator's most fiendish tool. We'll probe the pits of the pen one level at a time in the following sections.

Defining Points and Segments

Points in a Bézier path act as little road signs. Each point steers the path by specifying how a segment enters it and how another segment exits it. You specify the identity of each little road sign by clicking or dragging, sometimes with the Opt/Alt key gently but firmly pressed.

The following items explain the specific kinds of points and segments you can create in Illustrator. Look to Figure 5-18 for examples.

- **Corner point:** Click with the pen tool to create a corner point, which represents the corner between two segments in a path.

- **Straight segment:** Click at two different locations to create a straight segment between two corner points, like the first example shown in Figure 5-18.

 After positioning one corner point, you can Shift-click to create a perfectly horizontal, vertical, or 45-degree segment between that point and the new one.

- **Smooth point:** Drag with the pen tool to create a smooth point with two symmetrical Bézier control handles. A smooth point ensures that one segment fuses into another to form a continuous arc.

- **Curved segment:** Drag at two different locations to create a curved segment between two smooth points, as the second example in Figure 5-18 illustrates.

- **Straight segment followed by curved:** After drawing a straight segment, drag from the corner point you just created to add a control handle. Then drag again at a different location to append a curved segment to the end of the straight segment.

- **Curved segment followed by straight:** After drawing a curved segment, click the smooth point you just created to delete the forward control handle. This converts the smooth point to a corner point with one handle. Then click again at a different location to append a straight segment to the end of the curved segment.

- **Cusp point:** To convert a smooth point to a corner point with two independent handles (sometimes known as a *cusp point*), you have a couple of different options depending on the situation. First, after drawing a curved segment, don't release the mouse button. Add the Opt/Alt key and pivot to change the direction of the forward control handle. Then drag again at a new location to append a curved segment that sprouts off in a different direction. This creates a cusp as shown in the last example in Figure 5-18.

Old timers may recall a different technique. First you draw the curve segment and release the mouse button. You then hold the Opt/Alt key and position the cursor over the point you just created and drag the control handle out from the point. And then draw a new curved segment. The only problem with that technique is that it is too easy to create a new point rather than pulling out the handle. However, if your fingers are totally adapted to the old technique, don't try to retrain them.

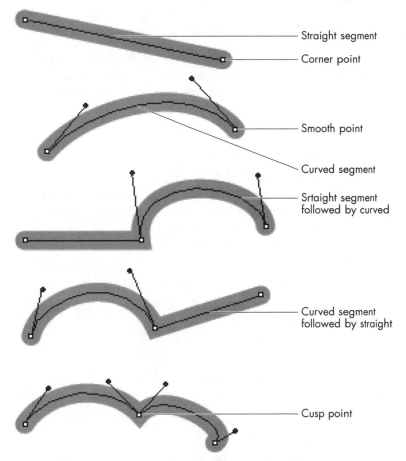

Figure 5-18: The complete annotated guide to the different kinds of points and segments you can draw with the pen tool.

Modifying the Closing Point

When you close a shape, you click, drag, and Opt/Alt-drag, just as you do when creating other points. But because you modify and close in one gesture, it seems a good idea to revisit these techniques within this slightly different context:

- Click the first point in a path to clip off any control handle that may have been threatening to affect the closing segment and you'll close the path with a corner point.

- If the first point in the path is a smooth point, drag it to make sure it remains smooth, thus closing the path with an arc.

- If the first point is a corner point, drag to add a control handle that curves the closing segment.

- To convert a smooth point to a cusp on closing, Opt/Alt-drag the first point in the path. In this case, you must press the Opt/Alt key before you start the drag. Pressing the Opt/Alt key after you're into the drag has no effect.

Putting the Pen Tool to Work

Well now, that was a whole lot of information crammed into a small amount of type—perhaps too much. To make things a little clearer for those of you who are still struggling with this amazing tool, here's your chance to try out the pen tool in the next three sections. We'll first show you how to use corner points, then smooth points, and finally cusps. (In the highly unlikely event you're reading this book without Illustrator running, now's a good time to fire her up.)

Drawing Free-form Polygons

Clicking with the pen tool is a wonderful way to create straight-sided polygons. Unlike the shapes you draw with the regular polygon tool, pen tool polygons may be any shape or size. These are pistol-packin' polygons of the Wild West, with no customs to guide their behavior or laws to govern their physical form. We're talking outlaw polygons, so be sure to take cover as you click:

1. Click to create a corner point.

Select the pen tool and click in the drawing area to create a corner point. The little x next to the pen cursor disappears to show you that a path is now in progress. The new corner point appears as a filled square to show that it's selected. It is also open-ended, meaning that it doesn't have both a segment coming into it and a segment going out from it. In fact, this new corner point—point A—is not associated with any segment whatsoever.

 If you were to stop working on this path right now, this stray point would remain on the page. If you deselect the point, it would be very hard to find. This is the type of point that the Select Stray Points command will find and let you delete.

2. Click to add another corner point.

Click at a new location in the illustration to create a new corner point—we'll call it point B. Illustrator automatically draws a straight segment from point A to point B, as demonstrated in Figure 5-19. Notice that point A now appears hollow rather than filled, showing that point A is the member of a selected path, but is itself deselected. Point B is selected and open-ended. Illustrator automatically selects a point immediately after you create it and deselects all other points.

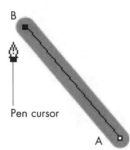

Pen cursor

Figure 5-19:
Draw a straight segment by
clicking at each of two separate
locations with the pen tool.

3. Click to add yet another corner point.

Click a third time with the pen tool to create a third corner point—point C. Since a point may be associated with no more than two segments, point B is no longer open-ended, as Figure 5-20 verifies. Such a point is called an interior point.

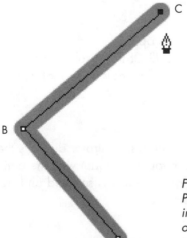

Figure 5-20:
Point B is now an
interior point, incapable
of receiving additional
segments.

4. Click the first point in the path.

You can keep adding points to a path one at a time for as long as you like. When you're finished, you can close the path by again clicking on point A, as demonstrated in Figure 5-21. Illustrator displays the close cursor to show you that it's ready to draw the last segment. If you don't see the close cursor (the pen cursor augmented with a little o in the bottom right), you don't have it positioned properly. Since point A is open-ended, it willingly accepts the segment drawn between it and the previous point in the path.

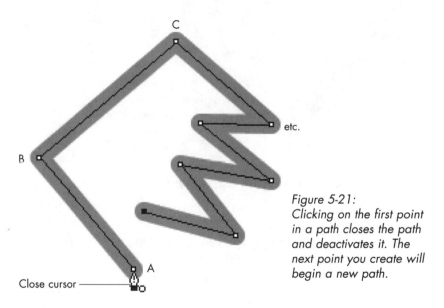

Figure 5-21:
Clicking on the first point in a path closes the path and deactivates it. The next point you create will begin a new path.

If you have the Text Label Hints option from the Smart Guides Preferences dialog box active, Illustrator displays the word *anchor*, providing you with another visual clue that you're in a position to close the path.

5. Click to start a new path.

All points in a closed path are interior points. Illustrator displays the new path cursor, as in Figure 5-22. If you click again with the pen tool you create a new independent point, which is selected and open-ended in two directions, just like point A.

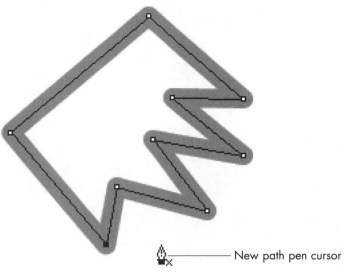

New path pen cursor

Figure 5-22: After you close a path, Illustrator adds a little x to the pen tool
cursor to show that the next point you create starts a new path.

Drawing Supple Curves

Free-form polygons are great, but you can create them in any drawing program, even something old and remedial like MacDraw. The real advantage to the
pen tool is that it lets you draw very precise curves.

When you drag with the pen tool to create a smooth point, you specify the location of two control handles. Each of these handles appears as a tiny circle perched
at the end of a thin line that connects the handle to its point (see Figure 5-23).
These handles act as levers, bending segments relative to the smooth point itself.

The point at which you begin dragging with the pen tool determines the location of the smooth point; the point at which you release becomes a control handle
that affects the *next* segment you create. A second handle appears symmetrically
from the first handle, on the opposite side of the smooth point. This handle determines the curvature of the most recent segment, as demonstrated in Figure 5-23.
You might think of a smooth point as if it were the center of a small seesaw, with
the control handles acting as opposite ends. If you push down on one handle, the
opposite handle goes up, and vice versa.

Smooth points act no differently than corner points when it comes to building
paths. You can easily combine smooth and corner points in the same path by
alternately clicking and dragging. However, if the first point in a path is a smooth
point, you should drag rather than click the point when closing the path. Otherwise,
you run the risk of changing the point to a cusp, as discussed in the next section.

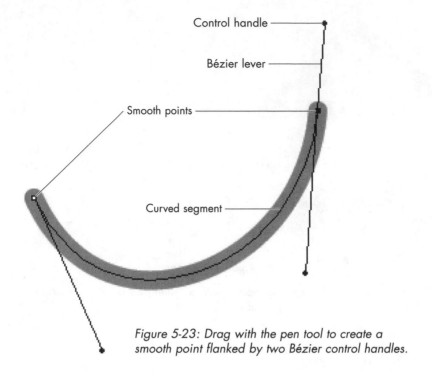

Control handle

Bézier lever

Smooth points

Curved segment

Figure 5-23: Drag with the pen tool to create a smooth point flanked by two Bézier control handles.

Creating Corners between Curves

A smooth point must *always* have two Bézier control handles, each positioned in an imaginary straight line with the point itself. A corner point, however, is much more versatile. It can have zero, one, or two handles. To create a corner point that has one or two control handles (sometimes called a cusp), you must manipulate an existing corner or smooth point while in the process of creating a path. We show you three examples of how this technique can work.

Deleting Handles from Smooth Points

These steps explain how to add a flat edge to a path composed of smooth points:

1. Draw some smooth points.

Begin by drawing the path shown in Figure 5-24. You do this by dragging three times with the pen tool: First drag downward from point A, then drag leftward from point B, and finally drag up from point C (which is selected in the figure). The result is an active path composed of three smooth points.

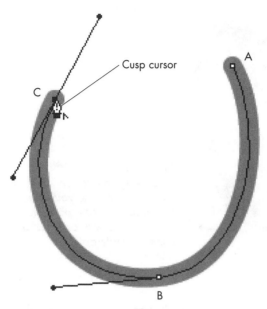

Cusp cursor

C

A

B

Figure 5-24:
An active semicircular path
with a selected, open-ended
smooth point.

2. Click the last point created.

Illustrator lets you alter the most recent point while in the process of creating a path. Suppose that you want to flatten off the top of the path to create a sort of tilted bowl, like the one in Figure 5-25. Because you can associate smooth points only with curved segments, you must convert the top two smooth points to corner points.

To convert the most recent point—the one on the left—position the pen tool over point C so the pen changes to the cusp cursor (the normal pen cursor with an additional little carat in the lower right corner, as in Figure 5-24). Then click to amputate the forward handle, which does not yet control a segment.

3. Click the first point in the path.

You now have an open path composed of two smooth points (A and B) and a cusp (C). You still need to close the path and amputate a handle belonging to point A. A single operation—clicking on the first smooth point—accomplishes both maneuvers. It's that simple. With one click, you close the path and amputate the control handle that would otherwise have curved the closing segment. Hence, the new segment is straight, bordered on both sides by corner points with one handle each, as in Figure 5-25.

Figure 5-25:
By clicking with the pen tool on
the two top points, you change
the existing smooth points to
corner points with one Bézier
control handle apiece.

If you don't release the mouse button, you can delete the forward handle from point C by another method. You construct the path as explained in step 1, except that you don't release the mouse button after dragging with the pen to form the forward control handle belonging to point C. Continue to hold down the mouse button, and press the Opt/Alt key. You can now drag the forward handle independently of the backward handle. Drag the forward handle back into point C until it disappears. The advantage is you can modify the path as you drag. Just make sure the forward handle is completely gone.

Converting Smooth Points to Cusps

These steps show you how to close the path from Figure 5-24 with a concave top, resulting in a crescent shape:

1. **Draw some smooth points.**

   Begin again by drawing the path shown in Figure 5-24 as described in the first step of the previous section.

2. **Opt/Alt-drag down from the last point created.**

   The segments in a crescent are curved, but the upper and lower segments meet to form two cusps. You need to change the two top smooth points to cusps with two control handles apiece—one controlling the upper segment and one controlling the lower segment. If you still have the mouse pressed as you create the smooth point, you can add the Opt/Alt key and pivot the control handle down. If you've already released the mouse, just hold Opt/Alt and position the cursor over the point. Then drag from point C. The existing handle disappears and a new handle emerges, as shown in Figure 5-26. This handle controls the next segment you create.

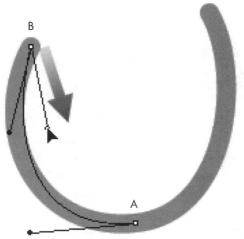

Figure 5-26:
Press the Opt/Alt key and drag
from the selected smooth point
to convert the point to a cusp.

3. **Opt/Alt-drag up from the first point in the path.**

   You close the path in a similar manner, by Opt/Alt-dragging upward from point A. Notice the location of the cursor as you drag, as Figure 5-27 demonstrates. You drag in one direction, but the handle emerges in the opposite direction. This is because when dragging with the pen tool, you always drag in the direction of the forward segment—that is, the one that exits the current point. Illustrator positions the handle controlling the closing segment symmetrically to your drag, even if it is the only handle you're manipulating. It's kind of weird, but it's Illustrator's way.

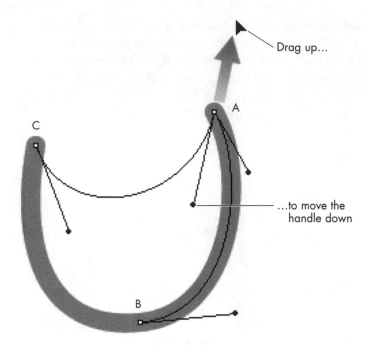

Drag up...

...to move the
handle down

Figure 5-27:
Close the path by
Opt/Alt-dragging up
from the first point in
the path.

Adding Handles to Corner Points

Last but not least, the next steps tell you how to add a curved segment to a path composed of straight ones:

1. **Draw some corner points.**

   Begin by creating the straight-sided path shown in Figure 5-28. It doesn't matter how many points are in the path, so long as they're all corner points.

2. **Drag from the last corner point created.**

   Drag from the corner point you've created most recently (point Z in the figure) to extract a single control handle, as shown in Figure 5-29.

   You may think you need to hold Opt/Alt here, but you don't. Illustrator knows that if you drag you want to create curves. It won't convert the corner point to a smooth one, though. It simply adds a Bézier handle to create a curve for the segment you're about to create. (If you do press the Opt/Alt key before you start the drag, you'll still wind up with the same results.)

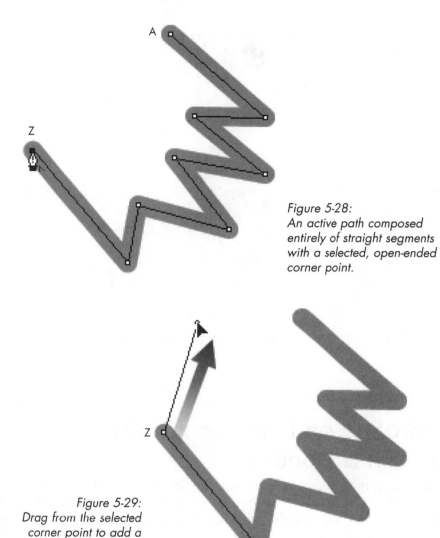

Figure 5-28:
An active path composed
entirely of straight segments
with a selected, open-ended
corner point.

Figure 5-29:
Drag from the selected
corner point to add a
Bézier control handle.

3. Drag from the first point in the path.

To close the path, drag from the first corner point in the path, as demonstrated in Figure 5-30. Once again, you drag in the direction opposite the emerging Bézier control handle. (Same as before, you don't need to hold the Opt/Alt key.) Illustrator won't curve the first segment, only the one you're currently working on.

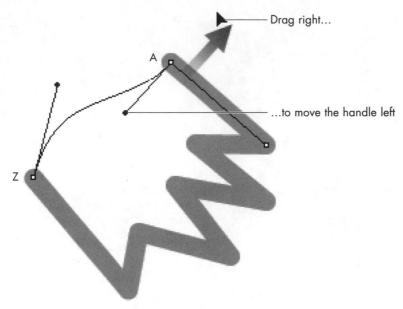

Figure 5-30: Close the path by dragging on the first corner point
in the path.

Operating on Points Long after the Path Is Done

Right about now, you're probably figuring Illustrator's path-editing capabilities have completely revealed themselves to you like a lotus blossom unfurling its petals. Armed with the direct selection and pen tools, you are more or less master of all you survey.

Well, that's almost true. But there are still some unanswered questions. For example, how do you insert a point into a path? For that matter, how do you remove a point without breaking the path in half? And what do you do if you want to change a corner point in an existing path to a smooth point, or a smooth point to a corner?

Illustrator provides three tools that let you *precisely* operate on existing points, whether drawn with the pen tool or any of the other tools. These are the add anchor point tool, the delete anchor point tool, and the convert anchor point tool. (All those anchors weigh us down, so we'll just dump them overboard, leaving the shorter tool names listed in Figure 5-31.) To select one of these tools you can drag from the pen tool slot in the toolbox and select the tool from the pop-up menu. You can also use the default keyboard shortcuts: plus (+) for add point, minus (-) for delete point, and Shift-C for convert point.

 Although the smooth tool and the eraser let you modify existing paths, their behavior is somewhat arbitrary and vague. (See Chapter 4 for examples of what we mean.) The add, delete, and convert point tools are far more precise and preferred by most Power Users.

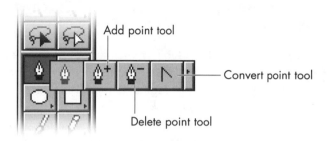

Figure 5-31: Drag from the pen icon to access three point-editing tools.

Adding Points to a Path

If a path doesn't have enough points to get the job done, don't hesitate to add some.

- **Appending a point to the end of an open path:** If an existing path is open, you can add points to either end of it. First activate one of its endpoints by clicking or dragging it with the pen tool. When you position the pen tool over an inactive endpoint, you get the activate cursor, which looks like a pen with a little slash next to it. Drag from the point if you want to retain or add a control handle; click if you want to trim off a control handle or avoid adding one; and Opt/Alt-drag if you want to change the direction of a handle. Then click and drag to add more points to the path.

- You can also lengthen an open path by dragging from one of its endpoints with the pencil tool. In the unlikely event the path touches a portion of a tracing template, you can even use the autotrace tool.

- **Closing an open path:** Once the path is active, you can close it in any of the ways discussed in the "Putting the Pen Tool to Work" section earlier in this chapter. Just click, drag, or Opt/Alt-drag the opposite endpoint with the pen tool. You can also close a path with the pencil tool by dragging from one endpoint to the other. In either case, Illustrator adds a little *o* to the cursor to show a closing is in process.

 Insert a point into a segment: To insert a new interior point into a path, select the add point tool and click anywhere along a segment (except on an existing point). Illustrator inserts the point and divides the segment in two. Illustrator automatically inserts a corner or smooth point depending on its reading of your path. If the point does not exactly meet your needs, you can modify it with the convert point tool, as we'll explain a few paragraphs from now.

 You don't have to actually switch to the add point tool. If you've got the pen chosen, simply position the cursor over an empty spot on any segment. The regular pen cursor gains a little plus sign (so it looks just like the add point cursor). Click! If you don't see the plus sign, move the pen cursor closer to the path or make sure you haven't activated the Disable Auto Add/Delete check box inside the General Preferences dialog box.

The add point tool is great for filling out a path that just isn't making the grade. If a path isn't curving correctly, it may be that you're trying to make the existing points in the path do too much work. For example, the first path in Figure 5-32 obeys both the All-or-Nothing and 33-Percent rules, but it still looks overly squarish. That's because it violates a lesser rule that says handles shouldn't point wildly away from each other. To smooth things out, Sandee clicked on the path midway between the two points with the add point tool. In this case, Illustrator inserted a smooth point, because the segment is ultimately smooth at the point where she clicked. She then used the direct selection tool to adjust the control handles and get the more rounded curve shown in the second example.

 If you don't like the pen tool switching its function, go to the General Preferences dialog box (Cmd/Ctrl-K) and switch on the Disable Auto Add/Delete option. The pen tool will no longer let you add or delete points to existing segments.

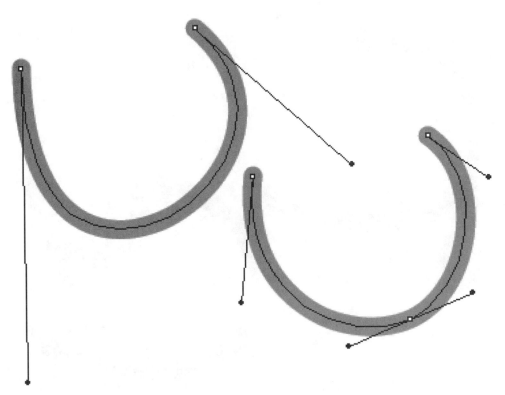

Figure 5-32: If a curve looks squarish no matter how much you monkey with the control handles (left), insert a point with the add point tool (right).

 You don't have to change the preference settings to disable the add/delete option. If you press the Shift key you will temporarily disable the pen tool's ability to add or delete points to existing segments. This comes in handy when you're trying to position a new point over an existing segment of that same path, as shown in Figure 5-33. Once the drag is under way, release the Shift key or you will constrain the construction of the point's control handles.

 Press the Opt/Alt key to access the add point tool temporarily when either the delete point or scissors tool is selected.

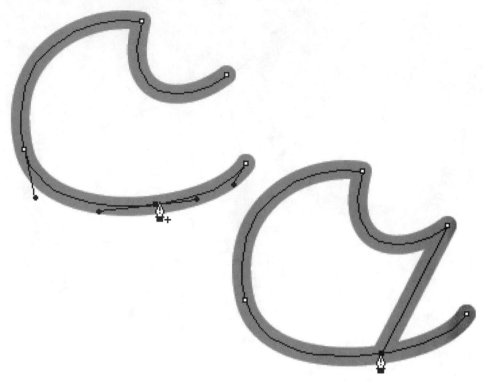

Figure 5-33: The left side shows what happens when you click an active path with the pen tool. You don't continue the path; you add a point. The right side shows what happens when the Shift key is pressed. A new point that extends the original path is created over the path. In both these examples, the Disable Auto Add/Delete check box is not selected.

Removing Points from a Path

To delete an entire path, you just select it with the arrow tool and press the Backspace/Delete key. If you love menus, you can choose Edit » Clear.

To delete a point or segment, try out one of the following techniques:

- **Delete a point and break the path:** To delete a point, select it with the direct selection tool and press the Delete key. When you delete an interior point, you delete both segments associated with that point, resulting in a break in the path. If you delete an endpoint from an open path, you delete the single segment associated with the point.

Delete a segment: You can delete a single interior segment from a path without removing a point. To do so, click the segment you want to delete with the direct selection tool and press Delete. Deleting a segment always creates a break in a path.

 Delete the rest of the path: After you delete a point or segment, Illustrator selects the remainder of the path. If the path is broken into two parts, both parts will be selected. To delete the whole path, just press Delete a second time. This can be a handy technique if you don't want to switch to the arrow tool. Just click some portion of the path and press Delete twice in a row to delete the whole path.

This is another place where you can inadvertently create stray points. If you delete the segment of a path that only has two points, those two points will still exist. You have to press Delete again, or you'll leave those stray points on your page. If your illustration does have lots of lone points, choose Edit » Select » Stray Points and delete 'em. For full-scale house cleaning, choose Object » Path » Cleanup which lets you delete stray points, unpainted objects, and empty text boxes, all in one fell swoop.

 Remove a point without breaking the path: If you want to get rid of a point but don't want to create a break in the path, select the delete point tool and click the point you want to disappear. Illustrator draws a new segment between the two points neighboring the deleted point.

Just as the pen tool can add points to an active path, so can it also delete points. Just move the pen tool over one of the points of an active path. When the tool is in place, the regular pen cursor gains a small minus sign in the lower right corner, mimicking the appearance of the delete point tool. After you click, Illustrator redraws the path as demonstrated in the middle example of Figure 5-34.

 Whereas the delete point tool allows you the freedom to delete a point from any path, selected or not, the pen tool's automated delete point feature works only on selected paths. If you don't like the pen tool deleting points. go to the General Preferences dialog box (Cmd/Ctrl-K) and switch on the Disable Add/Delete option.

As before, you can press the Shift key to disable temporarily the pen tool's ability to delete the points of a selected path. This comes in handy when you're trying to position a new point over an existing point of that same path, as shown in the bottom example of Figure 5-34.

Press Opt/Alt to access the delete point tool when the add point tool is active. (Have you noticed that Opt/Alt is a toggle between the add and delete point tools? When one is active, Opt/Alt gets you the other.)

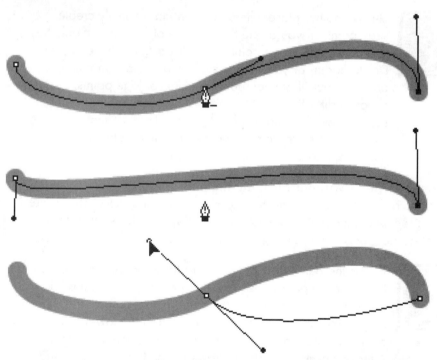

Figure 5-34: The top example shows the original curve and the placement of the pen cursor. The second example is the result of clicking on the middle point with the pen tool; the point is deleted. The last example shows what happens if you hold the Shift key as you click the segment. This forces Illustrator to construct a new point in the same position as the existing point.

Converting Points between Corner and Smooth

Of the tools discussed in this chapter, we rank the direct selection tool as most important, the pen tool as number two, and this next tool—the convert point tool—as number three. The convert point tool lets you change a point in the middle of a path from corner to smooth or smooth to corner. When a path is shaped wrong, this tool is absolutely essential.

You can change the identity of an interior point in any of the following ways:

- **Smooth to corner:** Using the convert point tool, click a smooth point. This converts it to a corner point with no control handles.

- **Smooth to cusp:** Drag a control handle belonging to a smooth point to move it independently of the other control handle, thus converting the smooth point to a cusp.

- **Corner or cusp to smooth:** Drag from a corner point or cusp point to convert it to a smooth point with two symmetrical control handles. Once you have the smooth point, you can use the convert point tool on either handle to change the point into a cusp.

Figure 5-35 shows a path created with the star tool. Like any star, it's made up entirely of corner points and straight segments. But with the help of the convert point tool, you can put some curve on that puppy, as the following steps show.

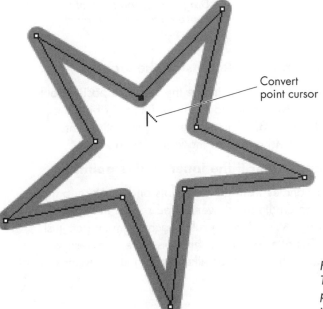

Convert point cursor

Figure 5-35:
The convert point tool,
poised to add some
wiggle to the star.

1. **Drag from one of the points along the inner radius.**

    Select the convert point tool and drag from one of the inner radius points, as demonstrated in Figure 5-36. The corner point changes to a smooth point with symmetrical control handles, bending both neighboring segments.

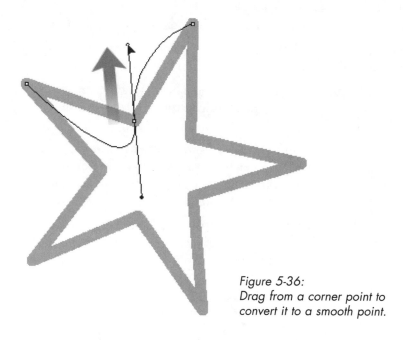

Figure 5-36:
Drag from a corner point to
convert it to a smooth point.

2. **Drag the inside control handle outside the star.**

    Drag the control handle that moved inside the star to a position outside the star, so that the two spikes form mirror images of each other, as demonstrated in Figure 5-37. This converts the smooth point to a cusp, permitting the control handles to move independently.

3. **Repeat Steps 1 and 2 on all the inner radius points.**

    By dragging control handles from all the points and converting them to cusp points, you can create the flower shape shown in Figure 5-38. Oh, sure, it violates the All-or-Nothing rule; each segment gets just one control handle. But after all, that's why we have rules—so we can occasionally ignore them and feel like we're getting away with something.

4.   Continue to adjust the handles until they're just right.

With the convert point tool, click and drag on any handle that doesn't suit your fancy. In prior versions of Illustrator, if you were to click a cusp point handle with the convert point tool, you would have converted it to a smooth point. Now the convert point tool works just like the direct selection tool on handles.

*Figure 5-37:
Drag the inside handle to
a location outside the star,
converting the smooth
point to a cusp.*

*Figure 5-38:
By dragging the control
handles out of all the inner
radius points, you get this
lovely flower outline.*

If you're working with the Pen, you can press Opt/Alt to temporarily get the convert point tool.

The Stretch Tool

Although Adobe put it with the transformation tools—for lack of a better location, we suppose—the reshape tool (the alternate tool in the scale tool slot) is not a true transformation tool, because you are not given an origin point. The tool does not act around any one point. Instead, it stretches the selected portion of the path, anchoring it by the two points just outside that part.

Reshape is too generic a term, implying that the tool could ultimately square a circle. A better name would be the stretch tool. As you drag the selected points on a path with the reshape tool, that portion of the path stretches in or out, all the while remaining attached to the anchor points (the two points just outside the selected portion). Moderate use of the tool preserves the path's general shape. This tool comes in handy when you want to tweak the position of part of a path slightly while keeping the path's overall appearance. (Map makers love the tool for gently moving rivers without destroying their shape.)

Moving points (and their Bézier handles) with the direct selection tool gives you control over the exact position and shape of a curve, but it can also give rather stiff and labored results if you're not careful. The reshape tool gives you a quick and easy alternative to the labor-intensive selection tools. Unfortunately, the results of the reshape tool can be somewhat unpredictable and most likely won't give you a perfect fit.

To use the reshape tool, select some of the points in an open or closed path, or select an entire open path, with one of the arrow tools. When you use it on a fully selected open path, Illustrator assumes that the endpoints are the anchor points. Now simply drag with the reshape tool. You can start your drag on either a point or a segment of the path. If you start on a point, Illustrator stretches the path to fit your drag by changing the location of the selected points and the direction of their corresponding Bézier handles (though the handle sizes remain the same). On the other hand, if you start your drag on a segment, Illustrator adds a point to the path, and the Bézier handles of the surrounding points change size and shape accordingly.

Using the reshape tool on a wholly selected closed path is the same as moving the path with the arrow tool—Illustrator doesn't know where to anchor the path for the stretch.

Figure 5-39 gives you some examples of how the reshape tool works and how it compares to moving with the direct selection tool. The top example shows the original wavy line. The line needs to dip down without losing its waves. The second example shows what happens if you just drag the middle point—shown with the superselection box—down. The path keeps its waves as it dips. The third example from the top shows what happens when you drag to superselect three of the points. They keep their shape as the rest of the path dips.

Superselection icon

Figure 5-39: Dragging with the reshape tool stretches the selected portion of the path slightly without dramatically distorting the rest of the path. The original path (top) was distorted in three different ways. The first distortion selected only one point and distorted the rest. The second distortion selected three points and distorted the rest. The final distortion used the direct selection tool, which could not keep the look of the original path.

However, if you doubted that the reshape tool really did anything special, look at how the bottom example is all distorted. That's what you get when you just drag with the direct selection tool.

In general, when you drag with the reshape tool, all the selected points move with respect to each other (and with respect to all the points not selected). You can also specify whether some of the selected points keep their original positioning with respect to one another. To do so, Shift-click the points with the reshape tool before you drag. This superselects them; they appear surrounded by a tiny square. Then, when you drag with the reshape tool, the superselected portion retains its original shape while moving with the rest of the selected portion, as shown in the lower portion of Figure 5-39. The three superselected points retain their original shapes.

Reliving the Past

Because we all make mistakes, especially when drawing and tracing complicated paths, Illustrator provides you with the ability to nullify the results of previous operations. In fact, Illustrator lets you retract several operations in a row. So when drawing anxiety sets in, remember this simple credo: *Undo, redo, relaxum.* That's Latin for "Chill, it's just a computer."

Undoing Consecutive Operations

Edit » Undo—and its universal shortcut, Cmd/Ctrl-Z—let you negate the last action performed. For example, if you move a point and decide you don't like how it looks, choose Edit » Undo Move and the new point disappears. More to the point, Illustrator returns you to the exact moment before you moved the point. Better yet, you can *always* undo the last action, even if you have since clicked somewhere on the screen or performed some minor action that the command does not recognize.

Get this: You can even undo an operation performed prior to the most recent Save operation (although you cannot undo the Save command itself). For example, you can delete an element, save the illustration, then choose Undo Clear to make the element reappear. It's a real lifesaver.

Illustrator lets you undo up to 200 consecutive operations. This powerful feature takes a great deal of the worry out of using Illustrator. You can reverse even major blunders one step at a time.

To change the number of possible consecutive undos, choose the File » Preference » Units & Undos command to display the Units & Undo Preferences dialog box, then enter a new value in the Minimum Undo Levels option box. The word *Minimum* appears in the option name because Illustrator permits you to undo as many operations as it can store in its undo buffer, regardless of the option value. The value merely sets aside space in your computer's memory so Illustrator can undo at least that many operations. As a result, you may be able to undo 200 path operations even if the Minimum Undo Levels value is set to 5.

To monitor how many undo levels are available at any given time, select the Number of Undos option from the status bar pop-up menu in the lower left corner of the illustration window.

After you exhaust the maximum number of undos, the Undo command appears dimmed in the Edit menu. Pressing Cmd/Ctrl-Z will produce no effect until you perform a new operation. And remember, Illustrator can undo operations performed in the current session only. You can't undo something you did back before the most recent time you started Illustrator.

 Let's say you need to make a quick 156 undos. Are you going to press Cmd/Ctrl-Z once for each of the offending steps? Not even. Instead, you're going to press and hold Cmd/Ctrl-Z. Holding these keys for a couple of seconds will let you start jumping back through the history of your drawing in units of five undos at a time. It's like watching a movie of your work coming undone.

Redoing Undo Operations

Just as you can undo as many as 200 consecutive actions, you can redo up to 200 consecutive undos by choosing Edit » Redo or pressing Cmd/Ctrl-Shift-Z. You can choose Redo only if the Undo command was the most recent operation performed; otherwise, Redo is dimmed. Also, if you undo a series of actions, perform a new series of actions, and then undo the new series of actions to the point where you had stopped undoing previously, you can't go back and redo the first series of undos. Instead, you can either continue to undo from where you left off or redo the later set of actions.

 Same as the preceding tip, except that now you can see your artwork come together in fast motion by holding Cmd/Ctrl-Shift-Z. This is especially fun to do right after you've done 200 undos.

Returning to the Last Saved File

If your modifications to an illustration are a total botch, you can revert to the last saved version of the file by choosing File » Revert. It's like closing a file, clicking on the Don't Save button, and reopening the file in one step. You probably won't need this command very often, but keep in mind that it's there when things go terribly wrong. (Maybe Deke doesn't need this command very often, but Sandee uses it all the time.)

If you haven't done anything to an illustration since you last saved it, or if you've never saved the drawing, File » Revert is dimmed.

CHAPTER 6

HOW TO HANDLE TYPICAL TYPE

If a picture is worth a thousand words, Illustrator must be worth a thousand Microsoft Words. (Even though what you're reading is being written in Word, it's hard to think of anything that's *not* worth a thousand Words.) However powerful pictures may be, and although they admittedly bridge the boundaries of culture and language (heck, even the extraterrestrials in Roswell could understand them), Illustrator knows that every once in a while text comes in handy. As a result, the program has assembled a powerful set of tools for type creation and formatting.

Illustrator's type capabilities are so vast that we need to explore them over the course of two chapters. This chapter examines the relatively basic stuff—how to create text blocks and apply formatting attributes such as typeface and style. We'll close out the chapter with some nifty techniques for working with tabs. This chapter looks at the sane and rational aspects of type.

Chapter 7 looks at the more bizarre effects you can create with type: You can fix type to a curve, set text inside free-form text blocks, apply effects to Adobe's specialized Multiple Master fonts, convert letter outlines to fully editable paths, and even present text in the Japanese vertical style. Look for all that and more in the next chapter.

Establishing Text Objects

Altogether, Illustrator provides six tools for creating text. For now, we're concerned with only one: the type tool, second down on the right side of the toolbox (the one that looks like a T). Armed with the type tool, you can create a text object—which is any object that contains type—in one of two ways:

- Click with the type tool within the drawing area and enter a few words of type for a logo or headline. This kind of text block is called *point text,* because Illustrator aligns the text to the point at which you click.

- Drag with the type tool to draw a rectangular *text block.* Then enter your text from the keyboard. Illustrator fits the text to the rectangular text block, automatically shifting text that doesn't fit on one line down to the next. Create a text block when you want to enter a full sentence or more.

We explain point text and text blocks in more detail in the following sections.

Creating Point Text

Figure 6-1 shows the three steps involved in creating point text:

1. Select the type tool and click in some empty portion of the drawing area with the new block cursor, labeled in Figure 6-1. The new block cursor shows that you are about to create a new text object.

After you click with the type tool, Illustrator creates an *alignment point,* which appears as an *x* in the outline mode. (In the preview mode, you see the alignment point only if the point text is selected.) Not surprisingly, Illustrator aligns the text to this point.

New block cursor

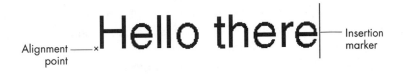

Alignment ——×
point

Insertion
marker

Hello there

Baseline

Figure 6-1: Click with the type tool (top), enter your text (middle), and select a different tool to complete the text object (bottom).

2. Enter the desired text from your keyboard. By default, the text appears to the right of the alignment point. (We'll go over how to change the alignment later in this chapter.) As you type, a blinking *insertion marker* flashes to the right of the last character. The insertion marker shows you where the next letter you enter will appear.

    With point text, Illustrator keeps all characters on a single line unless you tell it to do otherwise. This is why point text is better suited to a few words or less. If you want to move the insertion marker down to create a new line of type, press the Return or Enter key.

3. When you have finished entering your text, hold the Cmd/Ctrl key and click the text. Then release the Cmd/Ctrl key. The text block appears selected, as shown in the bottom example of Figure 6-1. The alignment point now looks like a filled square, just like a selected anchor point.

You can drag the alignment point with any of the three selection tools to reposition the text in the drawing area. You can also drag point text by its *baseline*, which is the line that runs under each line of type. The baseline is the imaginary line on which letters sit. Some lowercase characters—g, j, p, q, and y—descend below the baseline. Lastly, you can move point text by dragging on the text itself. The exception to this last technique is when the Type Area Select option of the Type & Auto Tracing Preferences dialog box is turned off.

The area controlled by Type Area Select is actually larger than the text itself. For instance, a word written in lowercase letters, such as *see,* will have an actual type area big enough to hold the word in uppercase *SEE* (plus a little squidgem more above that to hold things like quotation and accent marks). Also a word without descending characters such as *toe,* will have an actual type area big enough to hold the word *toy.*

Creating Text Blocks

Point text is easy to create, but because Illustrator forces all text onto a single line unless told to do otherwise, point text is not well suited to whole paragraphs and longer text. To accommodate lengthy text, you need to create a text block:

1. Drag with the type tool. This creates a rectangle, as shown in the first example in Figure 6-2, just as if you were dragging with the rectangle tool. This rectangle represents the height and width of the new text block.

When you release the mouse, Illustrator shows you a box with a blinking insertion marker. You will also see a center point, just as in a standard rectangle.

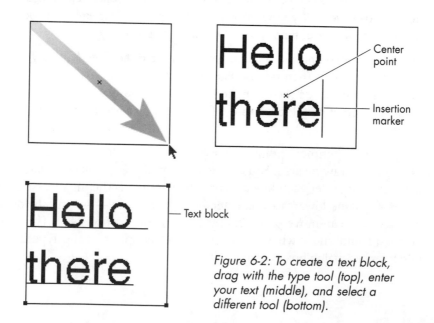

Figure 6-2: To create a text block, drag with the type tool (top), enter your text (middle), and select a different tool (bottom).

2. Enter type from the keyboard. If a letter would extend beyond the right edge of the text block, Illustrator sends the word down to start a new line of type. Known as *automatic wrapping,* this is precisely the capability that point text lacks.

3. After you stop entering text, hold the Cmd/Ctrl key and click the text. Then release the Cmd/Ctrl key. The text block appears selected, showing off four corner points connected by straight segments and a center point hovering in the middle. Baselines underscore the type to indicate that the letters themselves are selected.

Resizing and Reshaping Text Blocks

As with point text, you can reposition a text block by dragging either the rectangular boundary or one of the baselines with the arrow tool. Additionally, you can drag directly on the text itself. As with point text, if you turn off the Type Area Select option inside the Type & Auto Tracing Preferences, you will not be able to move or select text blocks by clicking or dragging on the text.

You can also change the size and shape of a text block with the direct selection tool. Illustrator offers a couple of new ways to resize and reshape paths—Chapter 11 discusses tugging on the bounding box and using the free transform tool—but the tried-and-true direct selection tool still provides you with an indispensable device for path modification.

For example, let's say that the text you entered from the keyboard doesn't entirely fit inside the text block. Or worse yet, the text block isn't wide enough to accommodate a particularly long word. Figure 6-3 illustrates both of these problems: The little square with a minus sign in it shows that Illustrator had to break the word *everybody* onto two lines. The square with a plus sign shows that there is more text that can fit inside the text block and is temporarily hidden. This text is called *overflow text.*

By resizing a text block, you can fit long words on a single line, reveal overflow text, or simply change how words wrap from one line to the next. To resize a text block, you have to use the direct selection tool to select and modify the rectangular boundary independently of the text inside it. Here's how it works:

1. Create your text block.

After creating the text block, select the direct selection tool.

2. Deselect the text block.

If your first impulse is to resize the block by dragging a corner point, resist the feeling. You'll turn the block into a kite-shaped object. To reshape the block and keep it a rectangle, you have to select one of

the segments and drag it, just as if you were resizing a standard rectangle. And—just to make things as painful as possible—you can't select a segment until you deselect the path. So choose Edit »
Deselect All or press Cmd/Ctrl-Shift-A to deselect the text block.

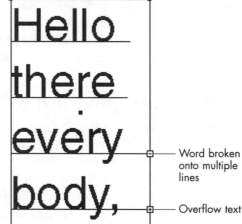

Word broken onto multiple lines

Overflow text

Figure 6-3:
Illustrator shows you when
a word doesn't fit on a
line, or when text extends
outside the text block.

3.   Select the right or bottom edge of the text block.

If you're working in the preview mode, the text block outline disappears. This makes selecting an edge of the text block rather difficult. That's why you need to drag a tiny marquee around the portion of the outline you want to move. If you want to make the text block wider, drag a marquee around the right side, as in the first example of Figure 6-4. If you want to make the text block taller, marquee the bottom side. In either case, you select the desired edge. (Because it's a straight segment, you can't see that it's selected. But have faith—it is.)

Once again the Type Area Select option makes things difficult to select. If it is turned on, the marquee with the direct selection tool might extend into the area where the text is. If that happens, you'll see the baseline of the text selected along with the entire block. This prevents you from resizing the block. So if a baseline appears, deselect everything and try again. If you *still* get the baseline, see the next tip.

If you can't seem to get that darn segment selected, switch to the outline mode by pressing Cmd/Ctrl-Y. In the outline mode, you can see the text block outline even when it's not selected. This makes it easier to click the segment you want to select. However, if your text extends extremely close to the outline (as with justified text, explained later in this chapter) you're *still* going to have a tough time. In that case, open the Type & Auto Tracing Preferences and turn off the Type Area Select option.

4. **Shift-drag the edge.**

   To maintain the rectangular shape of the text block, Shift-drag the right segment to the right, as in Figure 6-4. Or Shift-drag the bottom segment downward. (You can also drag without pressing Shift to create diamond-shaped text blocks.)

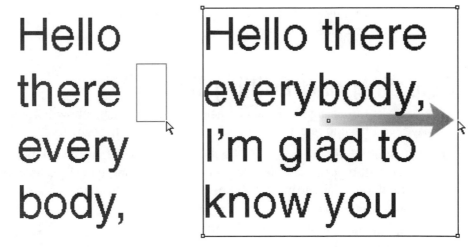

Figure 6-4: Use the direct selection tool to marquee the edge of the text block you want to expand (left) and then Shift-drag the edge (right).

When you release the mouse button, Illustrator rewraps the text and displays as much overflow text as will fit. If there is still more overflow text, the little plus icon remains in the lower right corner of the text block.

To resize the height and width of a text block at the same time, select the entire block outline by Opt/Alt-clicking it with the direct selection tool. (Make sure the baselines remain invisible.) Then drag with the scale tool or the free transform tool. For more info on both of these tools, turn to Chapter 11.

You can reshape the outline of a text block using any of the techniques discussed in Chapter 5. In addition to dragging points and segments, you can:

- Change the corner points to smooth points with the convert point tool.
- Drag the control handles to bend the segments.
- Insert or remove points with the add point and delete point tools.
- Select a segment and press Delete to open the path.
- Extend the open path using the pen or pencil tools.

If this kind of thing interests you—and why shouldn't it?—Chapter 7 explains how to create text inside any old wacky shape, as well as how to pour overflow text from one text block into another.

Selecting and Editing Text

Before you can change a single character of type or change how text looks on the page, you have to select the type using the arrow or the type tool.

- Clicking along the baseline of a line of type with any selection tool selects all type in the object. If you change the font, type size, style, or some other formatting attribute, you change all characters in the selected text object.

- You can Shift-click to select multiple text objects. Any changes you make to the text formatting will apply to all the selected text objects. (Illustrator doesn't format an entire text block if you select just a portion of the outline with the direct selection tool.)

- If you select text with a type tool, you can edit that text by entering new text from the keyboard or format the selected text independently of other text in the object.

Selecting with the Type Tool

Though the selection tools are certainly useful, the type tool is the most common instrument for editing type in Illustrator because it affords the most control. The following items explain how to select type with the type tool:

- Drag over the characters that you want to select. Drag to the left or to the right to select characters on a single line; drag upward or downward to select characters on multiple lines. The selected text becomes highlighted as shown in Figure 6-5.

Figure 6-5:
Drag across characters
with the type tool to
highlight them.

 Selected text has to be contiguous. You can't select the first line, skip the second, and then select the third.

- Double-click a word to select it. Hold down the mouse button on the second click and drag. Your selection will be whole words.

- Triple-click to select an entire paragraph, from one return character to the next. (Triple-clicking in point text selects an entire line, because a line of point text is equivalent to a paragraph.) Hold down the mouse button on the third click and drag to select additional paragraphs.

- Click to set the insertion marker at one end of the text that you want to select and then Shift-click at the opposite end of the desired selection. Illustrator highlights all characters between the first click and the Shift-click.

● Click anywhere in a text block and press Cmd/Ctrl-A (or choose Edit » Select All) to select all text in the object.

 After you click with the type tool to set the insertion marker inside a text object, you can use the arrow keys to move the insertion marker around or select text.

● Press the left or right arrow key to move the insertion marker to the left or right one character.

● Press the up or down arrow key to move the insertion marker up or down one line.

● Press Cmd/Ctrl-right arrow to move the insertion marker one whole word to the right. Press Cmd/Ctrl-left arrow to move back a word.

● Press Cmd/Ctrl-up arrow to move the insertion marker to the beginning of the paragraph. Press Cmd/Ctrl-down arrow to move it to the end of the paragraph.

● Press Shift along with any of these keystrokes to select text as you move the insertion marker. For example, press Shift-right arrow to select the character after the insertion marker. Press Cmd/Ctrl-Shift-up arrow to select everything from the insertion marker to the beginning of the paragraph.

Replacing, Deleting, and Adding Text

After you highlight some text, you can format it (as explained in the next section) or replace it by entering new text from the keyboard.

● To delete selected text, press the Backspace/Delete key.

● You can remove the selected text and send it to the Clipboard by choosing Edit » Cut (Cmd/Ctrl-X).

● To leave the selected text intact and send a copy to the Clipboard choose Edit » Copy (Cmd/Ctrl-C).

● You can even replace the selected text with text that you cut or copied earlier by choosing Edit » Paste (Cmd/Ctrl-V). The pasted text retains its original formatting.

The only way to convert a line of point text to a text block—or vice versa—is via the Clipboard. With either the arrow or the type tool, select the text you want to convert, cut or copy it, then drag with the type tool to create the text block (or click for the point text) and paste.

If you want to add text rather than replace it, just click with the type tool inside a text block to position the insertion marker. Then bang away at the keyboard and let the mouse take you where it will.

If Illustrator seems to ignore you when you enter text or press the Delete key, press the Return/Enter key. The problem is that Illustrator thinks a palette is active and is trying desperately to apply your typing to that palette; pressing Return/Enter deactivates the palette and returns control to the illustration window.

Formatting Type

Where type is concerned, *formatting* means nothing more than changing the way characters and lines of text look. Illustrator provides an exhaustive supply of formatting functions that let you modify far more than you'll ever want to.

You can divide formatting attributes into two categories—those that apply to individual characters of type and those that apply to entire paragraphs.

- **Character-level formatting** includes options such as typeface, size, leading, kerning and tracking, baseline shift, and horizontal scaling. To change the formatting of one or more characters, you select the characters with the type tool and apply the desired options. Illustrator changes the highlighted characters and leaves surrounding characters unaltered.

- **Paragraph-level formatting** includes indents, alignment, paragraph spacing, letter spacing, and word spacing. To change the formatting of a single paragraph, you need only position the blinking insertion marker inside that paragraph; Illustrator changes the entire paragraph no matter how little of it you select. To change the formatting of multiple paragraphs, select at least one character in each of the paragraphs you want to modify.

If you want Illustrator to consider two different lines of type as part of the same paragraph, press Shift-Return/Enter. This inserts a line break instead of the paragraph symbol that the Return/Enter key inserts. All paragraph formatting applied to one line becomes applicable to the other as well.

If you want to see things such as paragraph symbols or line breaks on-screen, choose Type » Show Hidden Characters. The paragraph symbol appears as a backward P and the line breaks appear as left-pointing arrows. The end of the text is indicated by an infinity symbol.

Illustrator adopts the most recently applied formatting attributes as the default settings throughout the rest of the session—even if you start a new document. But when you quit Illustrator and start it up again, the program restores the original default settings (though you can alter some defaults permanently by editing the Adobe Illustrator Prefs file, as described in Chapter 2's "The Prefs File" section).

Character-Level Formatting

To format characters, you can either choose commands from the Type menu or use the options in the Character palette. The latter is the more convenient.

The one character-formatting attribute that we don't discuss in this chapter is color. To change the color of selected text, you merely change the fill color in the Color palette, as explained in Chapter 15. You can even stroke text, as you'll learn in Chapter 16.

To display the Character palette, choose Type » Character or press Cmd/Ctrl-T. (Cmd/Ctrl-T also hides the Character palette.) By default, the Character palette shows only six options, as shown in the left example of Figure 6-6. But if you choose the Show Options command from the pop-up menu (located in the upper right corner), you expand the palette to display several more options, shown on the right.

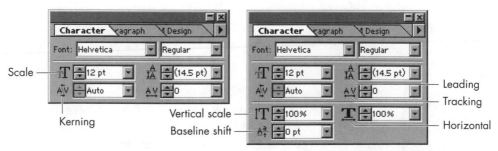

Figure 6-6: The Character palette, collapsed (left) and expanded (right).

Because the Character palette uses so many option boxes, it's worthwhile to mention a few useful palette techniques. First, when one of the option boxes is active, use the Tab key to cycle through other option boxes. To cycle backward, press Shift-Tab. After you enter a value into one of the option boxes, press Return/Enter to apply your changes and deactivate the palette. If you prefer, press Shift-Return/Enter to apply a new value without deactivating the palette. This allows you to preview different values without having to click the option box each time before entering new values.

 One palette tip is so exciting it deserves its own mention. If you press Cmd/Ctrl-~ (tilde), you will return to whatever palette was last active and whatever option box was last selected in that palette. So if you're doing a lot of resizing of text, you can move from one word to another and press Cmd/Ctrl-~ to get back to the Character palette and the text point size option box.

Selecting a Typeface

You can select a font from the Type » Font submenu or from the Font pop-up menu in the Character palette. For example, to assign Times Italic, you would choose Type » Font » Times » Italic. If you work in non-Adobe programs such as QuarkXPress, you may notice that Times Italic is not listed with the other members of the Times family. Those programs need Adobe Type Reunion to group the font family together. But Illustrator (and other Adobe products, such as InDesign) have a built-in type reunion.

 If you know the name of the font you want to apply, just enter the first few letters of its name into the Font option box in the Character palette. Each time you enter a character, Illustrator tries to guess which font you want. For example, if both American Typewriter and Avant Garde are available to your system, entering the letter *a* gets you American Typewriter— the first font in alphabetical order—whereas entering *av* gets you Avant Garde. To change the style, press the Tab key and enter the first few letters of the style, such as *b* for Bold or *i* for Italic. You can also Ctrl-click (on the Mac) or right-click (for you Windows hep-cats) and choose a font from the Fonts submenu in the context-menu.

You may notice that Illustrator doesn't let you apply electronic styles such as underline. This is because the people who created Illustrator are purists. They will only use actual typefaces, not fake electronic styles. It also means that you will never apply a style such as bold or italic to a typeface that doesn't have a bold or italic version. That means you will never be confused or disappointed when your final text doesn't print the way you thought it would.

TrueType Incompatibilities

Illustrator's inability to assign electronic styles inhibits its compatibility with TrueType fonts. If a TrueType font doesn't have a submenu of stylized fonts next to its name in the Type » Font submenu, it means that the fonts on your machine don't include the stylized versions of that font. For example, you can choose the TrueType font New York—included with all Macs—but you can't make it bold or italic in Illustrator.

Illustrator has a few other TrueType compatibility problems as well. It occasionally misinterprets TrueType font metrics (such as character width) and it has a habit of complaining when you open illustrations created with TrueType fonts. You'll likewise encounter these problems if you have both TrueType and PostScript versions of the same font installed.

Reducing and Enlarging Type

To change the size of any selected type, choose a size from the Type » Size submenu. If you choose Other, you'll be sent to the size option in the Character palette (which is why Sandee always goes directly to the palette and never bothers with the Size submenu *Type size,* as it is called, is measured in points from the top of an ascender (such as a *d* or an *f*) to the bottom of a descender (such as *g* or *p*). You can enter any value between 0.1 (1/10 the size of the smallest character in Figure 6-7) and 1296 (four times the size of the largest character) in 0.01-point increments.

If you dramatically reduce the size of a line of type, it appears as a gray bar. Illustrator figures it's too small to be readable on screen, so why waste the time trying to draw it accurately? If you want to see text at smaller sizes, change the greeking amount in the Type & Auto Tracing Preferences. (Greeked text still prints normally.)

Figure 6-7:
A character set in three (yes, three) type sizes—324-point, 48-point, and 1-point. If you don't believe us, go get a large magnifying glass and take a gander. Just as a medium A is centered at the base of the giant A, a minuscule A is centered at the base of the medium A. See that speck? That's 1-point type.

 To change the type size of some selected characters quickly, enter a new size value into the Size option box in the Character palette and press Return/Enter. You can also adjust the type size incrementally from the keyboard. Press Cmd/Ctrl-Shift-> to enlarge the characters or Cmd/Ctrl-Shift-< to reduce them. You can adjust the increment by changing the Size/Leading value in the Type & Auto Tracing Preferences dialog box. By default, the increment is set to 2 points. Your other option is to Ctrl-click (on the Mac) or right-click (in Win-speak) and peruse the Size context-menu for just the right size.

 To change the type size of the selected text by five times the Size/Leading value, do the following: On the Mac press Cmd-Opt-Shift-> or Cmd-Opt-Shift-<. You Windows dudes should press Ctrl-Alt-Shift-> or Ctrl-Alt-Shift-<.

Specifying the Distance between Lines

In days of yore, printer operators inserted thin strips of lead between lines of type, hence the term *leading* (pronounced *ledding*). Leading specifies the distance between a selected line of type and the line below it, as measured in points from one baseline to the next. Therefore, 14-point leading leaves a couple of points of extra room between two lines of 12-point type.

You can change the leading by entering a value into the Leading option box in the Character palette.

To speed things up, select some text and press Opt/Alt-down arrow to increase the leading or Opt/Alt-up arrow to decrease it. (If you're wondering about why the down arrow *increases* the leading, and the up arrow *decreases* it, just look at what happens to the line of text. Increasing the leading moves the text down (hence the down arrow); decreasing it moves the text up (hence the up arrow).

Add the Cmd/Ctrl key to the above combinations to change the leading by five times the Size/Leading value.

Select Auto from the Leading pop-up menu in the Character palette to make the leading equal to 120 percent of the current type size (rounded off to the nearest half-point).

To set the leading to match the type size exactly—an arrangement known as *solid leading*—double-click the A over A symbol next to the Leading option box in the Character palette.

If a line of text contains characters with two different leading specifications, the larger leading prevails. If you begin a paragraph with a large capital letter, for example, you might combine a 24-point character on the same line as 12-point characters. If both the 24-point character and the 12-point character use auto leading, then the entire line will be set at 29-point leading (120 percent of the 24-point type size).

You almost always want to have a leading size that is larger than the point size of your text. If you set the leading to the same size as the text (called solid leading), there is no room between the bottoms of letters like *g* or *j* and the tops of letters such as *h* and *t*. Depending on the text, those letters may wind up touching each other—which makes the text hard to read.

 We don't want to get into the leading as a character or paragraph attribute debate. If you are used to other programs that set leading to affect the entire paragraph, just make sure you select the entire paragraph before you change the leading. Then your leading will always be the same for the entire paragraph.

Adjusting the Space between Characters

Illustrator lets you adjust the amount of horizontal space between characters of text. When you adjust the space between a pair of characters, Illustrator calls it *kerning*. When you adjust the space between three or more characters, Illustrator calls it *tracking*.

 If you're a type savant, you'll soon notice that Illustrator's idea of tracking is not the real thing. There's no automatic spacing variation between large and small type sizes, which is what proper tracking is all about. Illustrator's tracking is uniform, and should therefore be called *range kerning*.

In any case, Illustrator provides option boxes in the Character palette for both kerning and tracking—commands for these don't exist in the Type menu and appear only in the Character palette. When you click with the type tool to position the insertion marker between two characters, you will want to use the Kerning option box. When you select so much as a single character, the Tracking option box is the one for you. Don't worry if you get them confused—enter a value in the Kerning option box when you're trying to change the tracking or vice versa—because Illustrator will promptly respond by either doing nothing or flashing some annoying warning that you're mistreating it.

Normally, Illustrator accepts the dimensions of each character stored in the screen font file on disk and places the character flush against its neighbors. The screen font defines the width of the character as well as the amount of space placed before and after the character. As demonstrated in the top example of Figure 6-9, these bits of space before and after are called *side bearings*. Illustrator arrives at its normal letter spacing by adding the right side bearing of the first character to the left side bearing of the second.

However, font designers can specify that certain pairs of letters, called *kerning pairs,* be positioned more closely together than the standard letter normally allows. Whenever the two characters of a kerning pair appear next to each other, as in the case of the *W* and the *A* in Figure 6-8, Illustrator can space them according to the special kerning information contained in the font.

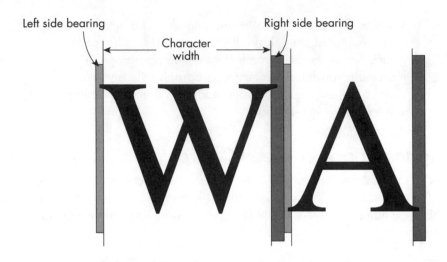

Figure 6-8: A kerning pair is a set of two letters that look weird when set shoulder to shoulder (top). Spacing them closer together (bottom) draws less attention to the letters and makes them more legible.

Illustrator always spaces kerning pairs as the font instructs. Click with the type tool to position the insertion marker between letters that you suspect to be kerning pairs. If the font does supply special instructions for those letters (and provided that you haven't changed the kerning manually), the Kerning option box displays a number in parentheses. If no parentheses appear, choose Auto from the Kerning pop-up menu and Illustrator returns the letters' placement to the factory settings.

If you aren't satisfied with the default kerning between two characters, click with the type tool to position the insertion marker between the characters and enter a value into the Kerning option box in the Character palette. If you want to change the kerning between multiple characters (tracking, in Illustrator-speak), select those characters and enter a value into the Tracking option box. Then press the Return/Enter key. A negative value squeezes letters together; a positive value spreads them apart.

Illustrator measures both the Kerning and Tracking values in 0.001 (1/1000) of an em space. An *em space* is a character as wide as the type size is tall. So if the type size is set to 12 points, an em space is 12 points wide. This ensures the kerning remains proportionally constant as you increase or decrease the type size.

A Kerning or Tracking value of 25 is roughly equivalent to a standard space character. But you can enter any value between –1,000 and 10,000 in 0.01 increments.

 If you don't know what kerning value to use, you can adjust the kerning incrementally from the keyboard. Press Opt/Alt-left arrow to squeeze letters together; press Opt/Alt-right arrow to spread them apart. By default, each keystroke changes the kerning by 0.02 (20/1000) em space, but you can change the increment by entering a new value into the Tracking option box in the Type & Auto Tracing Preferences dialog box.

For more dramatic changes, add the Cmd/Ctrl key to the above to decrease or increase the kerning by five times the Tracking value in the Type & Auto Tracing Preferences dialog box.

 To restore the Kerning value to 0, press Cmd/Ctrl-Shift-Q.

When kerning small type, you may not be able to see a visible difference as you add or delete space because the display is not accurate enough. In such a case, use the zoom tool to magnify the drawing area while kerning or tracking characters from the keyboard.

Changing the Height and Width of Characters

The next options in the Character palette, Vertical Scale and Horizontal Scale, modify the height and width of selected characters, respectively. You can expand or condense type anywhere from 1 to 10,000 percent (1/100 to 100 times its normal width) by entering a new value into either the Vertical Scale or Horizontal Scale option box and pressing Return/Enter.

Changing the height or width of a character distorts it. The Vertical Scale and Horizontal Scale options do not create the same effect as designer-condensed or -expanded fonts. For example, Figure 6-9 shows two variations on Helvetica. In the first example, we took 200-point Helvetica Bold and scaled it 45 percent horizontally. You would get the same result if you were to scale 115-point type vertically to 174 percent—go ahead and try it. Notice how the horizontal bars of the *A* and *B* are much thicker than the vertical stems. This is because Horizontal Scale affects vertical proportions and leaves horizontal proportions untouched.

Although the bars and stems in a designer font may not be identical, they are proportional. The second example in Figure 6-9 shows a specially condensed font called Helvetica Compressed Ultra. The strokes vary, but there is an overall consistency that the skinny Helvetica Bold type lacks. The designer has also taken the time to square off some of the curves, making Helvetica Compressed Ultra more legible in small type sizes.

With this in mind, you should remember a few things when using the Vertical Scale or Horizontal Scale option:

- If you *want* the type to appear distorted, go for broke. (Sandee calls this Horrors Scale.) There are no hard and fast rules in page design; type that specifically calls attention to itself can be just as effective as type that doesn't, if you have a bold design and an open-minded audience.

- If slightly widening or narrowing a few lines of type will make them fit better on the page, you can get away with Horizontal Scale values between 95 and 105 percent; no one will be the wiser.

- Changing both the vertical and horizontal factors by the same amount is the same as changing the size. So if you enter 50 percent into both the Vertical Scale and Horizontal Scale option boxes, the result is the same as if you had changed the value in the Size option box to half of its original value.

Incidentally, if you've scaled a text block disproportionately using the scale tool (as described in Chapter 11), the Font Size and Horizontal Scale values reflect the discrepancy between the current and the normal width and size of the selected type. You can reset the type to its normal width by pressing Cmd/Ctrl-Shift-X.

ABC
ABC

Figure 6-9:
200-point Helvetica Bold scaled horizontally 45 percent (top) compared with a specially designed font called Helvetica Compressed Ultra.

Raising and Lowering Characters

The Baseline Shift option in the lower half of the Character palette determines the distance between the selected type and its baseline. A positive value raises the characters; a negative value lowers them. The default value of 0 leaves them sitting on the baseline, where they typically belong.

You can modify the baseline shift to create superscripts and subscripts, or to adjust type along a path (as we discuss in the next chapter). To change the baseline shift, select some type and then enter any value between −1296 and 1296 points into the Baseline Shift option box.

Baseline shift is instrumental in creating fractions. To create a fraction as elegant as the one in Figure 6-10, start by entering the fraction using the *virgule* instead of the slash. A virgule is a slightly thinner, more slanted line than a slash. (You can get the virgule on the Mac by typing Opt/Shift-1. On Windows, you need to select the Symbol font and press Alt-0164 on the keypad.) Next, select the numerator (the top number), make it about half the current type size, and enter a baseline shift value equal to about one-third the original type size. Then select the denominator (bottom number) and match its type size to that of the numerator, but leave the Baseline Shift value set to 0.

$$^{22}\!/_{531}$$

Figure 6-10: In this fraction, the type size of the virgule is 160–point, whereas the numerator and denominator are set to 80–point. The numerator is shifted 53 points above the baseline.

 You can adjust the baseline shift incrementally from the key-board (according to the Baseline Shift value in the Type & Auto Tracing Preferences dialog box, 2 points by default). Press Opt/Alt-Shift-up arrow to raise the selected text above its baseline; press Opt/Alt-Shift-down arrow to lower the text.

 To see the text really jump, add the Cmd/Ctrl key to the above keystrokes. The baseline shift will change by five times the Baseline Shift value in the Type & Auto Tracing Preferences.

Paragraph-Level Formatting

Illustrator's paragraph formatting controls are found in the Paragraph palette. To display the palette, choose Type » Paragraph or press Cmd/Ctrl-M. By default, the Paragraph palette is collapsed, as shown in the left example of Figure 6-11. Choose the Show Options command from the Paragraph palette submenu to expand the palette and display the options shown in the right example of the figure.

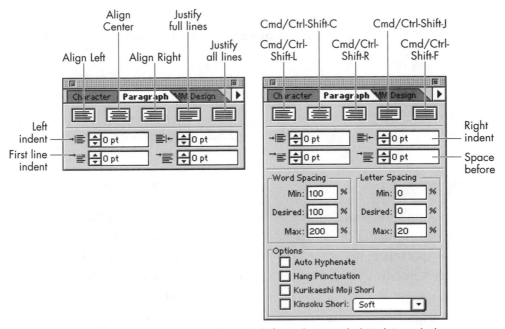

Figure 6-11: The Paragraph palette, collapsed (left) and expanded (right), with the keyboard shortcuts used to activate various options.

You can hide the Paragraph palette by pressing Cmd/Ctrl-M again.

The Paragraph palette, like the Character palette, relies heavily on option boxes, and the same tips apply: Remember to use the Tab and Shift-Tab shortcuts to switch between the option boxes, and to press Shift-Return/Enter to apply changes without deactivating the option boxes.

Changing the Alignment

As far as we can tell, every computer program that lets you create type lets you change how the rows of type line up. This is commonly called alignment. (Do not mistake the alignment commands with the actions of the Align palette. The Align palette can align text objects, but it does not affect the alignment of the text inside the blocks.)

- To align a paragraph so that all the left edges line up (*flush left, ragged right*), press Cmd/Ctrl-Shift-L or select the first Alignment icon in the Paragraph palette.

- To *center* all lines in a paragraph, press Cmd/Ctrl-Shift-C or select the second Alignment icon in the Paragraph palette.

- To make the right edges of a paragraph line up (*flush right, ragged left*), press Cmd/Ctrl-Shift-R or select the third Alignment icon.

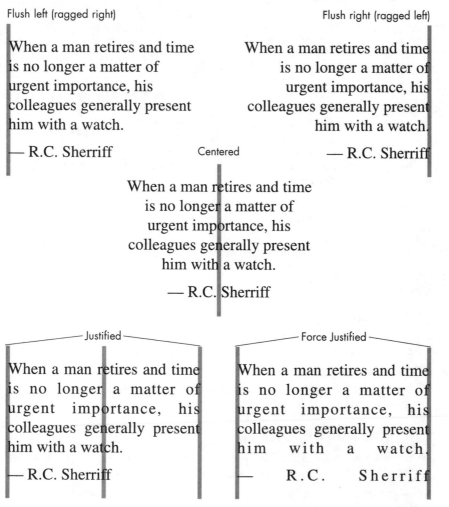

Flush left (ragged right)

When a man retires and time
is no longer a matter of
urgent importance, his
colleagues generally present
him with a watch.

— R.C. Sherriff

Flush right (ragged left)

When a man retires and time
is no longer a matter of
urgent importance, his
colleagues generally present
him with a watch.

— R.C. Sherriff

Centered

When a man retires and time
is no longer a matter of
urgent importance, his
colleagues generally present
him with a watch.

— R.C. Sherriff

Justified

When a man retires and time
is no longer a matter of
urgent importance, his
colleagues generally present
him with a watch.

— R.C. Sherriff

Force Justified

When a man retires and time
is no longer a matter of
urgent importance, his
colleagues generally present
him   with   a   watch.

—   R.C.   Sherriff

Figure 6-12: The five different alignment options available in Illustrator.

- You can also *justify* a paragraph, which stretches all lines except the last line of a paragraph so they entirely fill the width of the text block. (The last line in a justified paragraph remains flush left.) To justify a paragraph, press Cmd/Ctrl-Shift-J or select the fourth Alignment icon.

- If you want to *force justify* the last line in a paragraph, press Cmd/Ctrl-Shift-F or click the last Alignment icon in the Paragraph palette.

Examples of all five alignment settings appear in Figure 6-12. These settings were all applied to text blocks. Choosing the Justify and Justify Last Line options for point text results in flush left text for each of the last lines, because each line of point text is a separate paragraph.

Indenting Paragraphs

Figure 6-13 demonstrates the two basic ways to indent a paragraph. You can indent the first line to distinguish one paragraph from another or you can create a *hanging indent*, in which you indent all lines *but* the first line. A hanging indent is great for creating bulleted or numbered lists.

- To create a standard paragraph indent, enter a value into the First Line Indent option box in the Paragraph palette. Deke created the first example in Figure 6-13 with a First Line Indent value of 20 points.

Sixty years ago I knew everything; now I know nothing; education is a progressive discovery of your own ignorance.

—Will Durant

- Sixty years ago I knew everything; now I know nothing; education is a progressive discovery of your own ignorance.

— Will Durant

*Figure 6-13:
A paragraph with a first-line indent (top) and a hanging indent (bottom).*

- If you assign a first-line indent to a paragraph, remember that you can break a word onto the next line of type without indenting it by pressing Shift-Return/Enter to create a new line character. The words divided by the new line character appear on different lines, but are part of the same paragraph.

- To create a hanging indent, enter a positive value into the Left Indent option box and the inverse of that value in the First Line Indent option box. For example, to create the second example in Figure 6-13, Deke set the Left Indent value to 20 points and the First Line Indent value to –20 points.

- You also have to set the tab so the first line lines up with the others. In the figure, Deke pressed the Tab key after the bullet to insert a tab character. Then he chose the Type » Tab Rulers command to display the Tabs palette and created a left tab at the 20-point mark so it lined up with the left indent. For complete information about tabs, read "The Amazing World of Tabs" near the end of this chapter.

You can enter any value between –1296 and 1296 points into any of the Indentation option boxes. The Left Indent value indents all text on the left side of a paragraph, creating a gap between the left edge of the text block and the affected paragraph. The Right Indent value indents all text on the right side of a paragraph. And First Line Indent indents the first line of a paragraph without affecting any other lines.

There's really no reason to apply Indentation values to point text (except to make it wrap around an object, as discussed in the "Adjusting the Standoff" section of Chapter 7).

Hanging Indent Trick

Most of the time you're going to want to create hanging indents as Deke did above—especially if you have other text without hanging indents inside the same text block. But if your text consists of only hanging indented paragraphs (such as bulleted text), you can take advantage of the fact that Illustrator will position and print text outside the text block. As Figure 6-14 shows (with the text block outline and hidden characters visible), Sandee set the same text as before with the bullet hanging well outside the text block. She simply entered the value of -20 points for the first line indent. This moved the bullet outside the text block. She also pressed the Tab key to insert a Tab character after the bullet. But she didn't have to set the tab; Illustrator automatically positioned the text so that it lined up with the left indent.

Sixty· years· ago· I· knew·
everything;· now· I· know·
nothing;· education· is· a·
progressive· discovery· of·
your· own· ignorance.¶

—→Will· Durant∞

Figure 6-14: A hanging indent can be set to hang outside a text block by just changing the first line indent to a negative value. As the hidden characters show, a tab character helps line up the text at the left margin.

Adding Paragraph Leading

Enter a value into the Spacing Before Paragraph option box to insert some extra space before a selected paragraph. This so-called *paragraph leading* helps separate one paragraph from another, much like a first-line indent. Most designers use first-line indents *or* paragraph leading to distinguish paragraphs, but not both. The two together are generally considered design overkill (though both of us have done it and we've been rather pleased with the results).

Spacing Letters and Words in a Justified Paragraph

The middle options in the Paragraph palette let you control the amount of space that Illustrator places between words and characters in a text block. As you might imagine, *word spacing* controls the amount of space between words; *letter spacing* controls the amount of space between letters.

Now, a few of you quick-minded types are probably thinking to yourselves, "How is letter spacing, which controls the amount of space between individual characters, different from kerning, which controls the amount of space between individual characters? Call me stupid, but it sounds like the same thing to me." Well, for one thing, kerning applies to selected characters and letter spacing affects entire paragraphs. Also, the two are measured differently. Kerning is measured in fractions of an em space; letter spacing is measured as a percentage of the standard space character. But most important, kerning is fixed, whereas letter spacing is flexible. As we'll soon see, Illustrator can automatically vary letter spacing inside justified paragraphs between two extremes.

There are two primary reasons for manipulating spacing:

- To give a paragraph a generally tighter or looser appearance. You control this general spacing using the Desired options.

- To determine the range of spacing manipulations Illustrator can use when justifying a paragraph. Illustrator tightens up some lines and loosens others to make them fit the exact width of your text block. You specify limits using the Min. and Max. options (short for minimum and maximum).

When spacing flush left, right, or centered paragraphs, Illustrator relies entirely on the two Desired values. In fact, the other options are dimmed. All values are measured as a percentage of a standard space, as the information contained in the current font determines. For example, a Desired Word Spacing value of 100 percent inserts the width of one space character between each pair of words in a paragraph. Reducing or enlarging this percentage makes the space between words bigger or smaller. A Desired Letter Spacing of 10 percent inserts 10 percent of the width of a space character between each pair of letters. Negative percentages squeeze letters together, and a value of 0 percent spaces letters normally.

If you select one or more justified paragraphs, the Min. and Max. options become available. (These options appear dimmed if you have even one flush left, centered, or flush right paragraph partially selected.) These values give Illustrator some wiggle room when tightening and spreading lines of type. You're basically telling Illustrator, "I'd prefer that you use the Desired spacing, but if you can't manage that, go as low as Min. and as high as Max. But that's where I cut you off."

Word Spacing and Letter Spacing values must be within these ranges:

- The Min. Word Spacing value must be at least 0 percent; the Min. Letter Spacing must be at least –50 percent. Both must be less than their respective Desired values.

- The Max. Word Spacing value can be no higher than 1,000 percent; Max. Letter Spacing can be no more than 500 percent. Neither can be less than its respective Desired value.

- Each Desired value can be no less than its corresponding Min. value and no higher than the corresponding Max. value.

Figure 6-15 shows a justified paragraph subjected to various word spacing and letter spacing combinations. In the first column, only the word spacing changes; all letter spacing values are set to a constant 0 percent. In the second column, only the letter spacing changes; all word spacing values are set to 100 percent. Above each paragraph is a headline stating the values that have been changed. The percentages represent the Min., Desired, and Max. values respectively.

Word: 100%, 100%, 200%

Neither can I believe that the individual survives the death of his body, although feeble souls harbor such thoughts through fear or ridiculous egotism.

—Albert Einstein

Letter: 0%, 0%, 5%

Neither can I believe that the individual survives the death of his body, although feeble souls harbor such thoughts through fear or ridiculous egotism.

—Albert Einstein

Word: 0%, 25%, 50%

Neither can I believe that the individualsurvivesthedeathof hisbody,althoughfeeblesouls harbor such thoughts through fearorridiculousegotism.

—AlbertEinstein

Letter: –15%, –10%, –5%

Neither can I believe that the individual survives the death of his body, although feeble souls harbor such thoughts through fear or ridiculous egotism.

—Albert Einstein

Word: 200%, 225%, 250%

Neither can I believe that the individual survives the death of his body, although feeble souls harbor such thoughts through fear or ridiculous egotism.

—Albert Einstein

Letter: 25%, 35%, 50%

Neither can I believe that the individual survives the death of his body, although feeble souls harbor such thoughts through fear or ridiculous egotism.

—Albert Einstein

Figure 6-15: Examples of several different word and letter spacing combinations. Letter spacing is constant in the left column and word spacing is constant in the right.

Activating Automatic Hyphenation

There are three ways to hyphenate text in Illustrator:

- Enter a standard hyphen character (-) between two words you want to hyphenate. This is usually found in hyphenated words like *3-inch mark* or hyphenated names such as *Biddle-Barrows*. Don't use the standard hyphen between the letters of a word, though. If you edit the text later on, you may end up with stray hyphens breaking a word in the mid-dle [sic] of a line.

- A much better idea is to insert a *discretionary hyphen*, which disappears any time it is not needed. You can enter a discretionary hyphen by pressing Cmd/Ctrl-Shift-hyphen (-). If no hyphen appears when you enter this character, it simply means that the addition of the hyphen does not help Illustrator break the word. You can try inserting the character at a different location or expanding the width of the text block to permit the word to break.

- The third option is to let Illustrator do the hyphenating for you by selecting the Auto Hyphenate check box in the Paragraph palette. (This option has no effect on point text, just text blocks.)

Of all the options, we like the last one the least. It's the easiest, to be sure, but some of its suggestions are goofy—as in hyphenating *everyone* as *eve-ryone* or even as *e-ver-yone*—and Illustrator may open old illustrations and apply new hyphenation. Unless you're creating newsletters or other small documents with lots of type, it's usually safer to enter discretionary hyphens manually where needed.

Still, if you do decide automatic hyphenation is for you, here's how it works:

1. **Turn on Auto Hyphenate.**

   With the arrow tool, select the text block you want to hyphenate and turn on the Auto Hyphenate check box in the Paragraph palette. Illustrator adds hyphens where it deems necessary.

2. **Choose the Hyphenation Options.**

   If you want to limit where and how hyphenation occurs, choose the Hyphenation command from the Paragraph palette pop-up menu. The Hyphenation Options dialog box, shown in Figure 6-16, will open.

3. **Specify how many letters must appear before and after a hyphen.**

   In the Hyphenation Options dialog box, enter a value into the first Hyphenate option box (Letters from Beginning) to specify the minimum number of letters that can come between a hyphen and the beginning of a word. Enter a value into the next option box to determine the minimum number of letters between a hyphen and the end of a word. For example, with both values set to 2, Illustrator could split the word *apple* as *ap-ple,* because both the first and last syllables are at least two letters long.

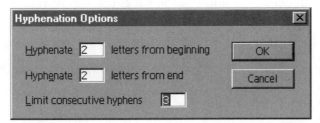

*Figure 6-16:
Here you can specify the limitations Illustrator will follow for automatic hyphenation.*

4. **Specify the possible number of consecutive hyphens.**

   If you want to limit the number of consecutive lines of type Illustrator can hyphenate, select the Limit check box and enter the maximum limit in the option box. By default, the value is set to 3, so Illustrator can hyphenate no more than three consecutive lines before it has to permit one line to go without hyphenation. But as far as we're concerned, any more than two hyphenated lines in a row looks amateurish and interferes with legibility.

5. **Prepare to groove as Illustrator implements all your secret hyphen-related desires.**

   Click the OK button or press Return/Enter.

In addition to the hyphenation options entrusted to the Paragraph palette, you can control what words Illustrator hyphenates—and how it hyphenates them—by choosing File » Preferences » Hyphenation. Simply type the word without any hyphens if you never want it hyphenated. Or type the word with the hyphens positioned where you would allow hyphenation to occur. (For a step-by-step example of this, flip back to Chapter 2.)

 If you add a word in the Hyphenation Preferences that already exists in a text block, it won't unhyphenate without a little help from you. First, select the text block. Next, deselect the Auto Hyphenate check box in the Paragraph palette, and then immediately reselect it. This jogs Illustrator into reapplying the automatic hyphenation.

Dangling a Quotation Mark

Select the Hang Punctuation check box to make punctuation such as quotation marks, commas, hyphens, and so on hang outside one of the edges of a text block:

- In a flush left paragraph, punctuation will hang outside the left side of the text block.

- In a flush right paragraph, the punctuation hangs outside the right side.

- If the paragraph is centered, Hang Punctuation will hang characters on either side of the text block.

- If you justify, or force justify the paragraph, the punctuation hangs off both sides.

The paragraph in Figure 6-17 was force justified so that all lines were both flush left and flush right. This way, Illustrator forced the quotation marks outside both sides of the text block. We also increased the type size of the quotation marks, kerned them slightly, and used a baseline shift to lower them 4 points each. This created a much more elegant look. (Hey, you can't expect a single option like Hang Punctuation to do everything for you.)

"Nothing is so ignorant as the ignorance of certainty."

— Aldous Huxley

Figure 6-17:
Here Deke applied the
Hang Punctuation and
Force Justification options
to move the quote marks
outside the text block.

Kurikaeshi Moji Shori and Kinsoku Shori

These final check boxes in the Paragraph palette (as well as the Kinsoku Shori options in the pop-up menu) have to do with Japanese layout rules and the Japanese type features the program includes. They work only with double-byte fonts—because there are so many characters in a Japanese font, each character requires two bytes. In other words, if you're not using a Japanese font, these options won't affect your text.

The Amazing World of Tabs

For those unfamiliar with the subject, tabs are little more than variable width spaces. By pressing the Tab key after entering a bullet or number, you can create hanging indents, as we showed you back in Figure 6-14. By entering tabs between items in a list, you can create columns that align precisely. Whenever you're tempted to use multiple spaces, press the Tab key instead.

There are really only two rules to using tabs:

- Never press Tab twice in a row (thus creating two tab characters).

- To specify the width of a tab character, adjust the tab stop settings in the Tabs palette.

To this day, we see more folks misuse tabs than we see use them correctly. If you never touch a tab stop and merely rely on multiple tabs or—gad!—spaces to do the work for you, you limit your formatting freedom and you make future editing more cumbersome and confusing. Whereas if you simply follow the two rules mentioned above and never, *ever* stray, you'll be fine.

Using the Tabs Palette

Choose Type » Tab Ruler (or press Cmd/Ctrl-Shift-T) to display the Tabs palette, shown in Figure 6-18. Known by the less formal moniker of *tab ruler,* this palette lets you position tab stops and align tabbed text.

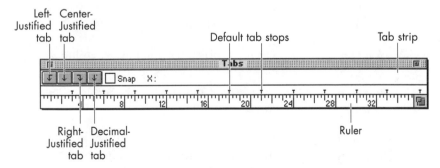

Figure 6-18: Use the tab ruler to position tab stops and align tabbed text.

Like the Paragraph palette, the tab ruler affects entire paragraphs, whether they're entirely or only partially selected. The following items explain how the tab ruler works and offer a few guidelines for using it.

- When you first bring up the Tabs palette, Illustrator automatically aligns it to the selected paragraph. To align the palette to a different paragraph, select the paragraph and click in the size box on the far right side of the title bar (or just to the left of the Windows close box).

- To create a tab stop, click in the ruler along the bottom of the palette, or click inside the tab strip just above the ruler. If you drag the tab stop, Illustrator projects a vertical alignment guide from the Tabs palette, as labeled in Figure 6-19. The line moves with the tab stop, permitting you to predict more accurately the results of your adjustment. The Tabs palette also tracks the numerical position of the tab stop—with respect to the left edge of the text block—just below the title bar.

- When you create a new tab stop, all default tab stops (those little Ts) to the left of the new stop disappear. The default stops merely tell Illustrator to space tabbed text every half inch.

- A question mark in the tab ruler means that at least one line of selected text does *not* align to that tab stop. Just click the tab stop to make all selected lines align.

To move more than one tab stop at a time, Shift-drag a stop. All tab stops to the right of the dragged stop will move in kind; tab stops to the left will remain stationary.

- Select the Snap check box to align new and moved tab stops to the nearest increment on the ruler. (Much easier than zooming in on the text.)

You can also snap a single tab stop on the fly when the Snap check box is turned off. To do this, press Cmd/Ctrl while dragging the tab stop. You can likewise Cmd/Ctrl-drag to move a tab stop freely when the Snap option is active.

- To change the identity of a tab stop, select the tab stop by clicking on it, then select a different identity from the four buttons on the left side of the palette. From left to right, these buttons make tabbed text align with the left side, center, right side, or decimal point. In Figure 6-19, for example, Deke centered the *Salary* column by assigning a center tab stop. He aligned the *Additional income* column with a right tab stop. Decimal tab stops are ideal for aligning numbers, such as prices.

Tab stop   Tab stop position

| □ ▦▦▦▦▦▦▦▦▦▦▦▦▦▦▦▦▦ | **Tabs** | ▦▦▦▦▦▦▦▦▦▦▦▦▦▦▦▦▦ ▣ |

⬐ ⬇ ⬇ ⬇ ⊠ Snap   X: 96 pt.

Annual earnings of a few fictional characters:

Name	Primary occupation	Salary	Additional income	Source
Santa Claus	toy distributor	none	$12,000	Macy's
Rudolf	bad-weather beacon	none	$266,370	Duracell spokesman
Peter Cottontail	egg distributor	none	$56,050	stuntman for Bugs Bunny
Tooth Fairy	tooth purchaser	none	$23,920	gold wholesaler
Superman	vigilante	none	$42,500	Daily Planet
Batman	vigilante	none	$21,354,350	CEO, Wayne Enterprises
Robin	vigilante's buddy	none	$6,250	Gotham City Malt Shop
The Wizard of Oz	wish granter	none	$765,130	owner, Kansas City Slots
Cinderella	princess	none	$8,700	housecleaning
Sleeping Beauty	princess	none	$216,500	No-Doz spokesperson
Pooh Bear	stuffed animal	none	$1.50	found in hollow tree
Piglet	stuffed animal	none	$0.75	stole from Owl
Lochness Monster	fresh-water dweller	none	$128,900	sighting fees
Big Foot	forest dweller	none	$0.75	stole from Piglet
E.T.	illegal alien	none	$89,450	pediatrician
Big Bad Wolf	pig chaser	none	$120,360	demolitions expert
Little Bo Peep	sheepherder	none	$35,000	animal reconnaissance
Gilligan	little buddy	none	$47.13	Mrs. Howell's concubine
Scooby Doo	crime-solving pet	none	-$152	loans to Shaggy

Alignment guide

Figure 6-19: When you drag a tab stop, a vertical line drops down from the palette, showing how the adjusted text will align.

Another way to change the identity of a tab stop is to Opt/Alt-click it. Each Opt/Alt-click switches the stop to the next variety, from left to center to right to decimal and back to left.

To delete a tab stop, drag it upward, off the tab strip and out of the palette. The X: item reads *delete*. To delete all tab stops, Shift-drag upward on the leftmost tab stop in the ruler.

By default, the unit of measure in the tab ruler conforms to the unit in Illustrator's standard rulers (as set using the Units option in the Units & Undo Preferences). But you can cycle through other units by clicking on the tab stop position indicator or the gray area to the right of the X: (which is just to the right of the Snap check box).

You can also cycle through the units of measurement by pressing Cmd/Ctrl-Shift-U.

If you want all the lines of your table to use the same tab stops automatically, press Shift-Return/Enter at the end of each line. This inserts line breaks, forcing Illustrator to recognize all the lines as part of the same paragraph, as is the case in Figure 6-19. If you press Return/Enter at the end of each line, you will insert paragraph returns. Illustrator then treats each line as a separate paragraph. You then have to select all the paragraphs in order to change the tab stops for each line.

Taking Tabs to a New Level

What if you don't want to align tabbed text in straightforward vertical columns? What if you want to create something a little more graphic, something worthier of your reader's attention, such as the table in Figure 6-20? Can you do this in Illustrator?

Well, of course you can. (In fact, you've been able to do something like this since Illustrator 3.0.) The secret behind this technique involves using several open paths to act like the tabs, and wrapping the text around these paths, as the following steps explain:

1.   Create your text block.

Enter one tab—and only one tab—between each entry, just as you would normally. In Figure 6-20, for example, there is one tab between *Santa Claus* and *toy distributor*. Use line breaks (Shift-Return) to separate the lines. If you separate the lines with carriage returns (by pressing Return/Enter), Illustrator will not automatically apply paragraph-level format changes to each line.

2. Use the direct selection tool to reshape the boundaries of the text block.

For example, to create the slanted block shown in Figure 6-20, we clicked on the bottom segment of the text block and dragged it to the right. You may want to work in the outline mode, where you can see the text block outline when it's not selected.

3. Add a tab stop to the far right side of the tab ruler.

Your text should now be a total mess, but no matter. Click the size box in the Tabs palette to make sure the palette is positioned directly over the text block, then create a left tab stop on the far right side of the palette. If any other tab stops exist, delete them. In Figure 6-20, for example, we positioned a single tab stop at the 34-pica mark. The purpose of this step is to eliminate all of the default tabs, thereby ensuring that each tab carries the entry following it to the next open path.

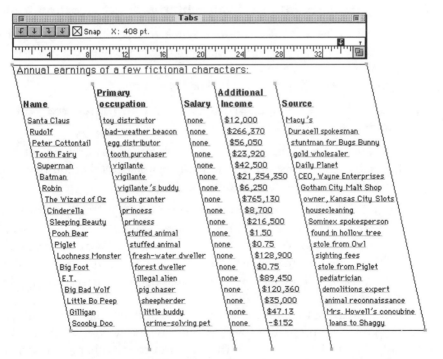

Figure 6-20: This slanted table—seen in the outline mode—was created wrapping tabbed text around a series of straight lines.

4. Draw a few open paths to serve as guides.

Ugh, your text is worse than ever. But don't try to fix it. Instead, it's time to add graphic tab stops in the form of a few open paths. In Figure 6-20, we drew a straight line with the pen tool by clicking on each of the two points on the left side of the slanted text block. This way, the angle of the line matched the angle of the block. Then we used the arrow tool to drag the line into position, just to the right of *Santa Claus*, so it could serve as the tab stop for the *Primary occupation* column. We then cloned the line by Opt/Alt-dragging it three times, thus creating three additional tab stops. (We discuss cloning in Chapter 9.)

5. Apply the Make Wrap command.

To convert the lines into tab stops, select both the lines and the text block and choose Type » Wrap » Make (covered in Chapter 7). Illustrator automatically aligns each tabbed entry with the nearest line.

6. Drag the lines into position with the direct selection tool.

It's unlikely the text will wrap exactly the way you hoped right off the bat. But now that the text is roughly in place, the lines act just like normal tab stops. To reposition one of these graphic tab stops, use the direct selection tool to move the line left or right.

7. Make the lines transparent so they don't interfere with the table.

Once you have all the lines in place, select the lines and make their fills and strokes transparent (using the control located at the bottom of the toolbox or in the top left of the Color palette).

Graphic tabs are generally every bit as versatile as regular tabs, except for one thing: Each tab stop is the same. In other words, you can't mix left tabs and right tabs inside the same text block, and there are no decimal tabs. Rather, each entry is aligned the same way the paragraph is aligned. If the paragraph is flush left, each entry is flush left; if the paragraph is centered, each entry is centered between the graphic tabs; and so on.

Graphic tabs bridge the border between the world of sedate formatting options that every publishing program provides, and the more wild text effects Illustrator is so rightly famous for. To cross all the way over to the other side of the border, read the next chapter.

The Text Eyedropper and Paint Bucket

As we mentioned, once you set the character and paragraph formatting, that formatting stays in effect for the rest of the Illustrator session. So even if you start a new document, the text attributes stay the same. But once you change the formatting, or quit Illustrator, those text attributes are no longer stored in the Character and Paragraph palettes.

Fortunately, Illustrator gives you a (somewhat) easy way to sample the text attributes from one set of text and then apply it to another. You do it by using the eyedropper and paint bucket tools shown in Figure 6-21. There are three parts to using these tools. The first part is to sample the text attributes using the eyedropper. The second is to apply the attributes using the paint bucket. The final part is to set which text attributes the tools should copy and apply.

 Although the eyedropper and paint bucket are handy, they are hardly a substitute for text styles. Text styles (as found in FreeHand for many years) are much more powerful and not only allow text to be automatically formatted, but also make it very easy to change all the text in a document. We were hoping that at the same time Illustrator 9 added graphic styles, Adobe would also add text styles. Sadly, this is not the case. Oh well, there's always next time.

Figure 6-21: The eyedropper and paint bucket tools can be used to sample and apply character and paragraph attributes.

The eyedropper and paint bucket can also be used on graphic objects. Because the techniques for using the tools on objects are slightly different from using them on text, we'll cover the two tools again in Chapter 14 when we deal with color.

Sucking up Attributes with the Eyedropper

To sample text attributes with the eyedropper tool, choose the eyedropper tool. Position the tool over the text that you want to sample. When a small T appears next to the eyedropper cursor, you know that the eyedropper is in the text mode.

 If you don't see the T next to the eyedropper cursor, then the eyedropper will sample the attributes of the text block that holds the text—not the text itself.

 If you have turned off Type Area Select in the Type & Auto Trace Preferences, you will have to position the eyedropper cursor directly over the baseline of the text in order to use the eyedropper in the text mode.

Click or drag the eyedropper over the text that you want to sample. A click sucks up the text attributes exactly under the cursor. A drag as shown in Figure 6-22 samples the attributes from the text where the mouse button is released at the end of the drag. If you drag with the eyedropper, the tip of the eyedropper cursor turns black to show that the attributes are being sampled.

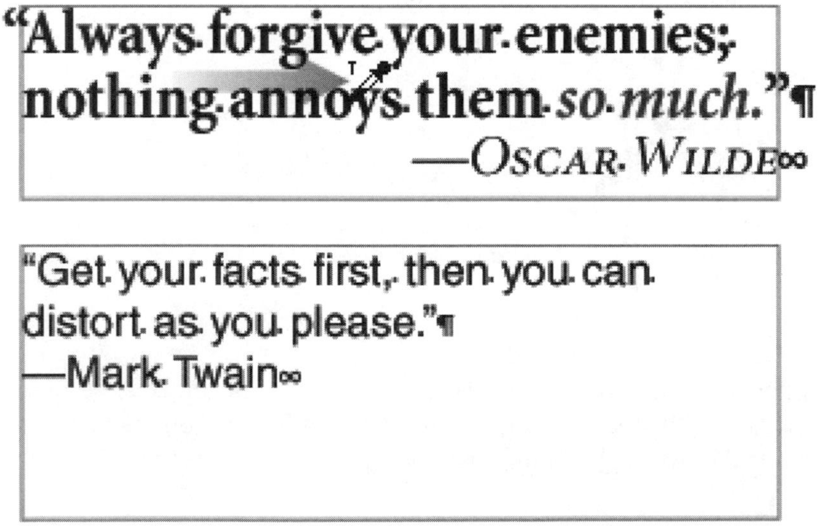

"Always forgive your enemies; nothing annoys them *so much.*"¶
—OSCAR WILDE∞

"Get your facts first, then you can distort as you please."¶
—Mark Twain∞

Figure 6-22: Click or drag the eyedropper across the text attributes that you want to sample.

Pouring out Attributes with the Paint Bucket

To apply text attributes, you can choose the paint bucket tool from the alternate eyedropper slot in toolbox. However, because you most likely already have the eyedropper tool selected, simply hold the Opt/Alt key. This toggles between the eyedropper and paint bucket. (Similarly, hold the Opt/Alt key to change the paint bucket tool into the eyedropper.)

Position the paint bucket over the text that you want to change. Look for the small T next to the cursor; this tells you that the paint bucket is in the text mode. Unlike the eyedropper, there is a real difference between clicking and dragging with the paint bucket. If you simply click with the paint bucket, as we have in Figure 6-23, you apply the text attributes to all the text in the text object.

> "Always forgive your enemies;
> nothing annoys them *so much.*"¶
> —OSCAR WILDE∞

> "Get your facts first, then you
> can distort as you please."¶
> —Mark Twain∞

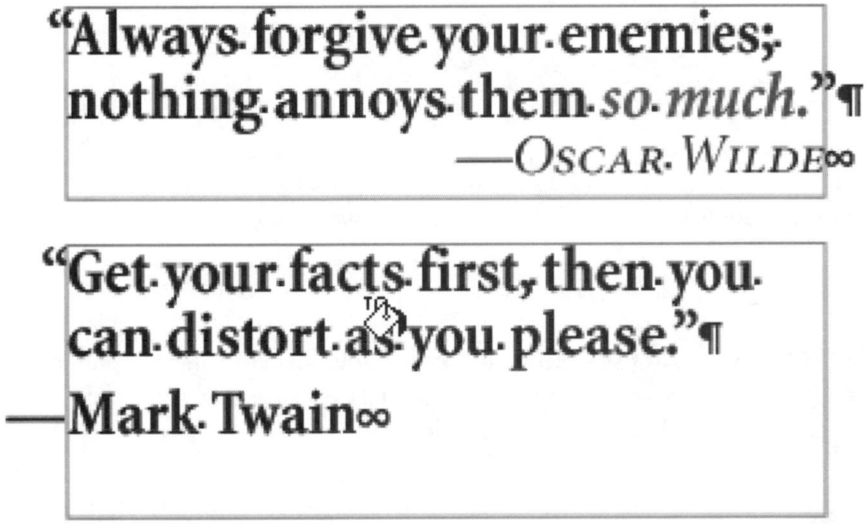

Figure 6-23: A click with the paint bucket tool applied the attributes to all the text in the text object. Here the main attributes from the top text object have been applied to both paragraphs in the bottom text object.

However, you may want to apply text attributes to specific areas of a text object. To do that, you need to drag with the paint bucket tool across the text. As you drag, a box appears around the characters that are chosen. When you release the mouse button, those characters will be changed. Figure 6-24 shows the power of the paint bucket in action.

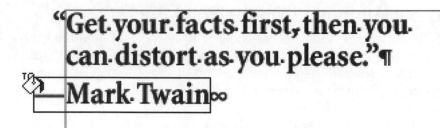

Figure 6-24: The top example shows the paint bucket dragged across the text that is to be changed. The bottom example shows the results of applying the new attributes to the text.

If you don't see the T next to the paint bucket cursor, then the paint bucket will apply only the fill and stroke attributes of the text that has been sampled.

Once again, if you have turned off Type Area Select in the Type & Auto Trace Preferences, you will have to position the paint bucket cursor directly over the baseline of the text in order to use the paint bucket in the text mode.

Configuring the Eyedropper and Paint Bucket

By default, the eyedropper and paint bucket will sample and apply all the character and paragraph attributes of the text. However, you can configure the tools so that they sample and apply only certain attributes. For instance, you can set the tools so they sample and apply only character attributes, but not the paragraph ones.

To configure the tools, double-click either the eyedropper or the paint bucket in the toolbox. The Eyedropper/Paint Bucket Options dialog box appears as shown in Figure 6-25. Use the check boxes to choose which attributes you want each tool to recognize.

 The settings for the eyedropper and paint bucket remain in effect for new documents and new sessions of Illustrator.

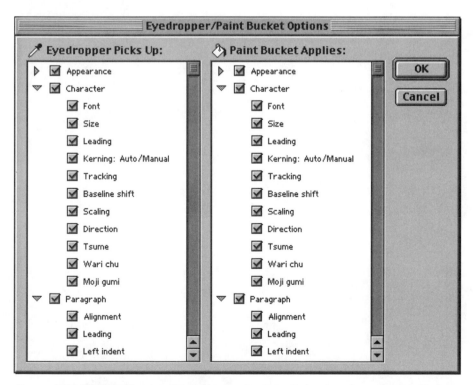

Figure 6-25: The Eyedropper/Paint Bucket Options dialog box lets you control which attributes the tools sample and apply.

CHAPTER 7

SOME OF YOUR
WACKIER TEXT EFFECTS

Creating and formatting text is all very well and good, but where Illustrator excels is in the creation of specialized—dare we say wacky?—type. You can attach text to a curve, wrap text inside an irregular outline, flow text from one text block to another, and wrap text around graphics. If you plan to use Illustrator to create documents that contain a fair amount of text, you can import text from a word processor and then check the spelling, perform complex search and replace operations, and even export the text back out to disk. And just to prove to you that there are no limits to this wackiness, Illustrator lets you convert one or more letters to paths and then edit the character outlines.

In recent years there has been a trend in page layout programs to add text features similar to Illustrator. Some page layout programs such as QuarkXPress and Adobe InDesign can also do some of these wacky text effects; but they do not possess all of Illustrator's powerful features. Those programs can put text on a path but they cannot apply filters, effects, add transparency, or provide other features found in Illustrator. So if all you want is a wacky text effect, you can use other programs. However, if you want to create text and then do a whole lot more to it, you need Illustrator.

Topsy-Turvy Type on a Curve

As demonstrated in Figure 7-1, Illustrator lets you bind a line of text to a freeform path. Adobe calls such a text object *path text,* but many folks call it *type on a curve* as well. (Sandee calls it roller coaster text.)

To create type along the outline of a path, follow these simple steps:

1. **Draw a path.**

   Curved paths work better than those with sharp corners, so you'll probably want to avoid corner points and cusps and stick with smooth points. Ellipses, spirals, and softly sloping paths work best. Grab the smooth tool if you need to smooth out a path.

2. **Select the path type tool.**

   To get to the path type tool, drag from the type tool in the toolbox to display a pop-up menu. The path type tool looks like a T on a slanted line, as shown in Figure 7-2.

3. **Click the path and start typing.**

   The point at which you click determines the position of the blinking insertion marker. As you enter text from the keyboard, the characters follow the contours of the path.

If your text appears on the underside of the path, or if no text appears and all you see is a plus sign inside a little box, you need to flip the text to the other side of the path. Select the arrow tool and double-click the alignment handle, which looks like an I-beam attached to the path. Then select the type tool and click the path to continue adding text.

Figure 7-1: Path text as it appears when selected on screen (top) and when printed (bottom).

4.   Complete the path text.

When you finish entering text, select another tool in the toolbox to finish the text object. The path text appears selected, as in the first example shown in Figure 7-1.

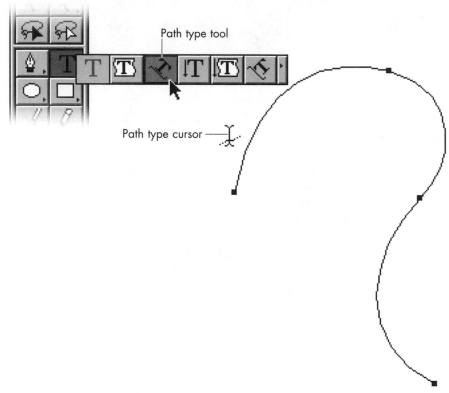

Figure 7-2: Select the path type tool, click a path, and start typing.

 If your path had a fill or stroke (covered in Chapters 15 and 16), they will instantly be removed as soon as you click with the path type tool. Adobe figures that most people don't want to see the path that the text is on. If you want to style the path, you need to select it with the direct selection tool and then apply the fill or stroke.

Reading the Text Cursors

You don't have to use the path type tool to create path text. In fact, it's generally easier to use the standard type tool. As you bring the standard type tool close to an open path, the cursor changes to the path type cursor. If the path is a closed path, you need to press the Opt/Alt key to see the path type cursor. Without Opt/Alt pressed, the cursor changes to an area text cursor (which we'll discuss later in this chapter). Figure 7-3 shows each of the text tools together with their cursors.

Figure 7-3:
Each type tool displays its own
unique cursor that indicates the
type of type tool that is active.

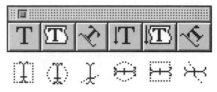

Like point text (covered in Chapter 6), path text is ill-suited to anything longer than a sentence. When a word extends past the end of an open path, it disappears from view like a ship sailing off the edge of the world. Long text simply wraps around and around a closed path, forcing words to overlap.

Once you have point text on a straight line, you can't convert that straight line into a curved path. To convert existing point text so that it runs along a new path, you have to copy the text and then create an insertion point on a new path. The copied text can then be pasted.

Moving Type Along Its Path

When you click path text with the standard arrow tool, you select both path and type at the same time. A special *alignment handle* appears, as labeled in Figure 7-4. This handle allows you to adjust the placement of the text on the path in any of the ways shown on the next page.

Alignment handle

Figure 7-4:
The alignment
handle appears
when you select both
the path and the
type (top). You can
drag the handle to
move text (middle) or
double-click it to flip
the text (bottom).

- Drag the handle to slide the text back and forth along the path, as in the second example in the figure.

- Double-click the handle to flip the text to the other side of the path, as in the third example in Figure 7-4.

- Drag the handle to the other side of the path to move the text as you flip it in the opposite direction.

 In addition to clicking with the arrow tool, you can also select both path and type by Opt/Alt-clicking the path twice with the direct selection tool. Be sure to click the path itself. Don't try to click at the location where you expect the handle to be; it won't do you any good.

Reshaping a Path Right Under Its Text

When you create path text, you typically run into the same problems as when you enter words into a text block. If the path is too short to accommodate all of its text, for example, a plus sign appears in a small box located on the last point in the path, as shown in Figure 7-5. In path text, Illustrator makes no distinction between a single word that can't fit and a sentence. Because path type can't wrap to a second line, it either fits on the path or it doesn't.

Figure 7-5:
Overflow text prompts
the boxed plus sign.

There are three choices for fixing text that overflows its path:

- Reduce the size of the type.

- Delete a few words or characters until the text fits on the path.

- Lengthen the path by reshaping it until all text is visible.

If you know how to link text from one text block to another (covered later in this chapter), you may be tempted to try to do that with text from one path to another. Don't waste your time. Unlike InDesign or FreeHand, Illustrator doesn't have that feature.

To lengthen a path with text on it, you can drag both segments and points with the direct selection tool in any way that you want. After each drag, the text refits to the path, so you can see your progress. Suppose, for example, that you want to lengthen the lower line shown in Figure 7-5. The following steps explain a few ways to do it:

1. Press Cmd/Ctrl-Shift-A (or choose Edit » Deselect All) to deselect the type. You must deselect the path text before you can select the path by itself. But before you can select one, you must deselect both.

2. Using the direct selection tool, click the path. This selects the path without selecting the type on the path. (Notice that the alignment handle I-beam isn't visible. This shows you that the text is not selected.)

3. Drag one of the endpoints to stretch the path, as shown at the top of Figure 7-6. The type immediately refits to the path, as shown in the bottom example.

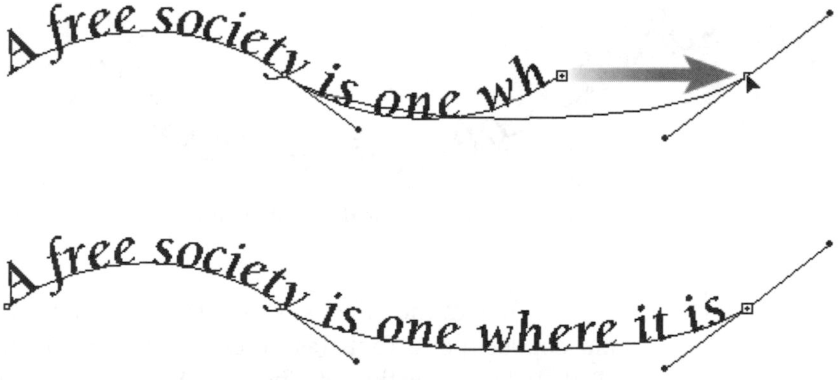

Figure 7-6: Drag the endpoint of an open path with the direct selection tool (top) to stretch the path to accommodate more text (bottom).

If the curve needs adjusting use the direct selection tool to drag down on the segment or adjust the control handles.

4. If you need to lengthen your path dramatically, you might prefer to add points to the path using the pencil or pen tool. In Figure 7-7, for example, we used the pen tool to add segments to the path. With each additional segment, more text becomes visible until eventually no overflow text remains. When the path is long enough to accommodate its text, the boxed plus sign disappears, as Figure 7-7 shows.

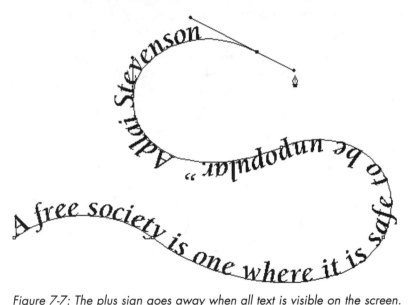

Figure 7-7: The plus sign goes away when all text is visible on the screen.

In addition to editing a path with the direct selection tool, you can use the add point, delete point, and convert point tools (as described in the "Operating on Points Long after the Path Is Done" section of Chapter 5). However, you cannot modify text paths with the erase tool or smooth tool. The next section explores one way to use the add point tool.

Trimming Away Excess Path

What if rather than too short, your path is too long? Certainly you can enlarge the type size, add words, or move points around to make the path shorter. But what if you simply want to trim a little slack off the end of the path?

You can't split it off with the scissors tool (covered in Chapter 9), because Illustrator won't let you split an open path with text on it. Instead, you can follow these steps:

1. Click with either the pen tool or the add point tool at the spot where you want the path to end, as shown in Figure 7-8.

2. Select all points beyond the newly inserted point with the direct selection tool, as shown in Figure 7-9. (Don't select the new point itself.)

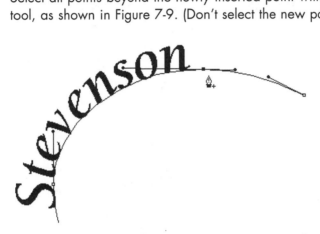

Figure 7-8: Use the add point tool to insert a point at the location where you want the path to end.

3. Press the Delete key. The selected points and their segments disappear, making the inserted point the new endpoint.

Normally, you don't need to worry about excess path. The path is hidden by default when you're previewing or printing an illustration. Shortening a path becomes an issue only if you want to stroke the path apart from its text—as explained in Chapter 16.

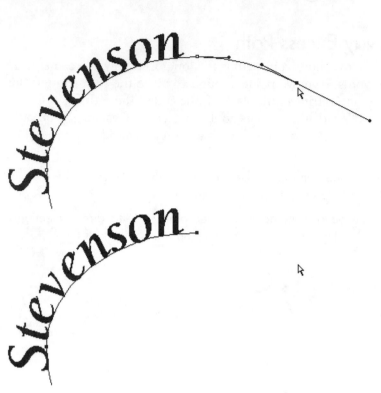

Figure 7-9: Select all points to the right of the inserted point (top) and delete them (bottom).

Shifting Type in Relation to Its Path

Illustrator lets you raise and lower type with respect to its path using baseline shift (introduced in the last chapter). The baseline of path text is the path itself, so moving type away from the baseline likewise moves it away from the path.

As you may recall from Chapter 6, you can change the baseline shift by entering a value into the Baseline Shift option box in the Character palette or by holding Opt/Alt-Shift and pressing either the up arrow or the down arrow key. The keyboard shortcuts are generally the preferred method for shifting the baseline.

The following steps demonstrate why baseline shift is useful. They show you how to create text along the top and bottom halves of a circle—a job for baseline shift if there ever was one.

1. Draw a circle.

You know, Shift-drag with the ellipse tool.

2. Opt/Alt-click with the type tool at the top of the circle.

Illustrator snaps the alignment handle to the top center of the shape.

3. Enter the text you want to appear along the top of the path.

We started by quoting William Allen White, who said, "Peace without justice is tyranny." We entered "Peace without justice" across the top.

4. Center the text.

Press Cmd/Ctrl-Shift-C or click the second icon in the Paragraph palette. As long as the alignment handle is positioned at the top of the shape, you can use Illustrator's alignment formatting functions to position text around the handle. It comes in handy when you want to get things exactly right.

5. Format the text as desired.

Press Cmd/Ctrl-A to highlight the text. Then format at will. We used 38-point Herculanum, an Adobe PostScript font that offers a collection of exclusively capital letters. Quite frankly, text on a circle usually looks best in all caps.

6. Clone your text.

This is the most important step and one of the trickiest to pull off. First select the path text with the arrow tool. Then drag the alignment handle around the path to the bottom of the circle. Without releasing— don't release till we say so—drag upward so the type flips to the other side of the path. Then drag down ever so carefully until your cursor snaps onto the bottom point in the circle.

Finally, press the Opt/Alt key and release the mouse button. You can now release the Opt/Alt key. A clone of the type moves and flips to the interior of a cloned circle, as illustrated in Figure 7-10.

Quick, how many circles do you have on your page? If you said one, think again. Dragging the Opt/Alt key made a clone of the circle as well as the type. You actually have two circles, one stacked on top of the other. The original circle has the text going in a clockwise direction. The clone has text that goes in a counter-clockwise direction. That's how you know you must have two circles. Text on a path cannot go in two directions at the same time.

Snap and clone cursor

Figure 7-10: Opt/Alt-drag the type to the inside bottom portion of the circle. The hollow double cursor shows that you have snapped to a point and cloned both type and circle.

7.   Edit the bottom type as desired.

Click inside the cloned text with the type tool, and press Cmd/Ctrl-A to select it. Then enter the words that you want to appear along the bottom of the circle. We entered "is tyranny," because that's the way old Willy White would have wanted it.

8.   Shift the bottom text downward.

With your keen mind, you've undoubtedly noticed that the upper and lower text blocks don't align properly. You need to move the lower text outward without flipping it. While the text is still active, press Cmd/Ctrl-A to highlight the lower text block. Because you want to lower the type with respect to its path, press Opt/Alt-Shift-down arrow to move the type downward 2 points (assuming you haven't changed the Baseline Shift value in the Type & Auto Tracing Preferences dialog box). We pressed Shift-Opt/Alt-down arrow seven times in a row to get the effect shown in Figure 7-11.

9.   Similarly lower the text along the top of the circle.

Press Cmd/Ctrl-Shift-A to deselect the text. Then click in the upper text block with the type tool and press Cmd/Ctrl-A to highlight the first words you created. Press Opt/Alt-Shift-down arrow several times to lower the top text so it aligns with the bottom text. We pressed these keys eight times to arrive at Figure 7-12.

Figure 7-11:
Press Opt/Alt-Shift-down
arrow several times to
lower the text along the
bottom of the circle.

Figure 7-12:
Highlight the upper
text block and press
Opt/Alt-Shift-down
arrow several times to
lower this text as well.

Just for laughs, Figure 7-13 shows the final illustration as it appears when printed. We selected both circles by marqueeing around a segment with the arrow tool. Then we cloned the circle, reduced it to 70 percent, and rotated it 30 degrees. Over and over again. (In case you're wondering, there's actually a trick to doing something over and over again. We cover that later in Chapter 11.)

Figure 7-13: The finished text on a circle, repeated several times to create a tunnel-of-type effect.

Doing It All Again with Vertical Type

One of the functions meant to round out Illustrator's international savvy is the ability to add type to your illustrations that reads top-to-bottom and right-to-left, like Japanese script. Most of us may never encounter a situation in which we will need to add kanji or other Japanese characters to a drawing, but the same techniques required to add Japanese script give us additional choices for adding more familiar type.

 We would like to take a moment to emphasize that by adding the new vertical type functions to a chapter entitled "Some of Your Wackier Text Effects," we mean no disrespect. The choice to include the description here is that it just doesn't fit in Chapter 6. Most readers, if they choose to use vertical type, will incorporate it as a special effect and not for its designated purpose.

Because you already know how to create horizontal point type or add horizontal type to a path, you're only a couple of minutes away from creating vertical point type or adding vertical type to your artwork. To create vertical point type, just click and enter the text as shown in Figure 7-14. To add vertical type to a path, simply draw the path (either open or closed) that you want to use as your guide for the vertical type, and then select the vertical path type tool. Click the cursor over the path and enter the text.

 If you work with vertical text often, hold the Shift key to turn any horizontal type tool into its vertical equivalent. Bring the cursor near an open path to get vertical text on the path. Or press and hold the Opt/Alt key to create vertical text on a closed path.

 Vertical type tends to be hard to read without some adjustment. One of the reasons we used point text in Figure 7-14 was that it was easier to control. We also avoided pressing the spacebar between words such as *FIFTHAVE* and *NEWYORK*. Vertical text using Roman typefaces tends to create huge spaces between words that need lots of cleanup.

Additionally, you can apply the Rotate or Tate Chu Yoko option to vertical path type. You'll find both of these options in the Direction pop-up menu that's part of the Character palette's Multilingual Options—displayed when you choose the Multilingual Options command from the Character palette's pop-up menu. These options change the orientation of the text. They are especially useful when you apply them to individual words.

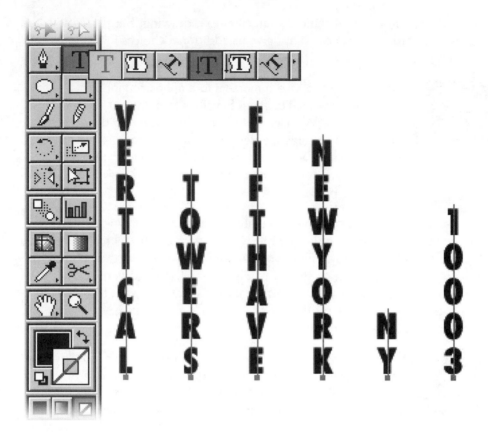

Figure 7-14: With the type tool, we Shift-clicked to create each of the vertical point ext paths. We also set a right alignment so that the text hung down from the end of the point text path.

Getting that Irritating Alignment Handle off a Path

After you click a path with the type tool, Illustrator thinks you want to use the path to hold text for all time. Even if you delete all text from the path at some later date, the alignment handle will hang in there, showing you that this is still path text. Here's how to remove the alignment handle.

1. Select the path by Opt/Alt-clicking it with the direct selection tool. Do not use the arrow tool.

2. Press Cmd/Ctrl-C or choose Edit » Copy to copy the path to the Clipboard.

3. Opt/Alt-click the path again. This selects the text and displays the alignment handle.

4. Press the Delete key to destroy the path text for all time. (Don't worry, you've copied the path to the Clipboard, so it's safe.)

5. Press Cmd/Ctrl-F or choose Edit » Paste In Front. The path is reborn on screen with no alignment handle. Stroke the path or fill it at will.

 Years ago, Illustrator 5.5 included a little plug-in that removed the alignment handle. For some reason Adobe didn't include it ever again. If you have the original Illustrator 5.5 installation disks, you can install Illustrator 5.5, drag the plug-in out of the plug-ins folder, and try it with today's Illustrator. Adobe doesn't support the plug-in as being compatible with today's program, but it should work.

Filling a Shape with Text

When the folks at Adobe added type on a curve to version 3 back in 1991, they thought, "Gosh, if artists want text *on* a curve, maybe they want text *inside* a curve as well." And after much sage nodding of heads, *area text* was born. In area text, type exists inside a path. A standard text block is a variety of area text—text inside a rectangle. But you can create text inside polygons, stars, or free-form shapes. Heck, you can even create text inside an open path if you want.

To create type inside a path, goest thou thusly:

1. **Draw a path.**

   Unlike path text, area text works just as well with corner points as with smooth points. But keep the corners obtuse—wide rather than sharp. It's very difficult, and in many cases impossible, to fill sharp corners with text.

2. **Select the area type tool.**

   Select the area type tool from the type tool pop-up menu in the tool-box. The area type tool looks like a T trapped in Jell-O, as labeled in Figure 7-15.

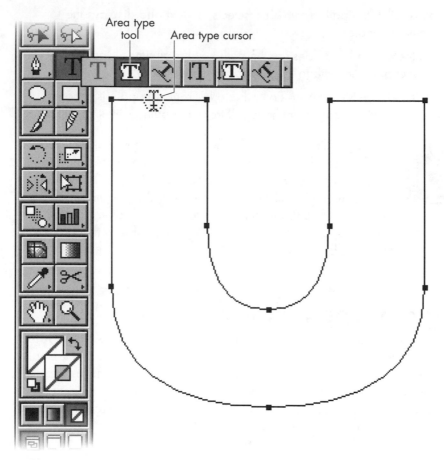

Figure 7-15: Click the path outline with the area type tool.

3. Click along the outline of the path and enter some text.

You must click the outline of the path; you can't click inside the path to add text (even if the path is filled and the Use Area Select check box is active in the General Preferences dialog box). A blinking insertion marker appears at the top of the path. As you enter text, it fills the path. Words that would otherwise exceed the edge of the shape wrap to the next line.

4. Complete the path text.

Select the type tool, arrow tool, or some other tool to finish off the text block. You'll get something like the area text shown in Figure 7-16.

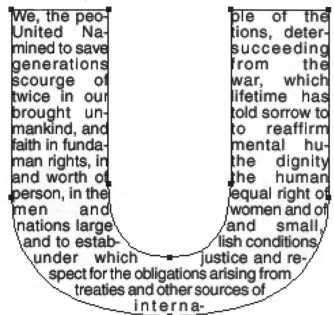

Figure 7-16:
Behold area text—
a free-form shape
filled with type.

Hold the Shift key to turn the area type tool into the vertical area type tool. The only problem is that unless you are using a font designed for vertical display, the resulting text is almost impossible to read. Not only do the words fill the shape from top to bottom, but each successive line of text is placed to the left of the previous one. You may find this ideal for adding columns of symbols or even columns of the same short phrase (repeated over and over) to a shape, but if you try filling a shape with more than one-liners, your audience will spend more time deciphering the text than reading it.

Flowing Text from One Shape to Another

If your text overflows the path or you simply don't like the way it wraps, you can edit the path with the direct selection tool. Press Cmd/Ctrl-Shift-A to deselect the text block, and then click the path with the direct selection tool and reshape at will. (Be careful not to click any of the baselines; that selects the entire block of area text.) As you reshape the path with the direct selection, add point, delete point, and convert point tools, Illustrator rewraps the text to fit inside the revised path outline.

You can also flow text from one area text block into another (something you can't do with point text or path text). This allows you to create multiple columns or even multiple pages of text. Figure 7-17 shows several lines of text flowed between two paths. (The paths the text was flowed into were created by converting large letters into outlines—something we'll cover at the end of this chapter.) A single collection of paragraphs flowed over many text blocks is called a *story*.

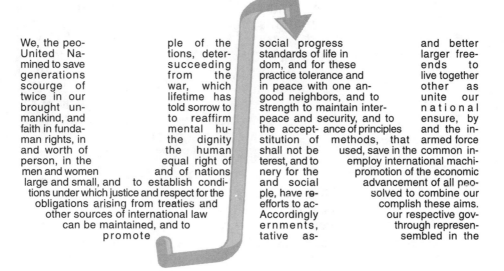

Figure 7-17: A single story flowed between two area text blocks.

To flow text from one block to another, you need to link them. You can link text blocks in one of two ways. These techniques apply equally to area text and rectangular text blocks:

- 🌐 **Use the Link Blocks command.** Select the path that contains the overflow text with the arrow tool. Then select one or more other paths (by Shift-clicking them) and choose Type » Blocks » Link. All selected paths fill with as much overflow type as will fit, as demonstrated in Figure 7-18.

 Illustrator fills the paths in the order in which they are stacked. This means if you select a path that lies behind the area text and choose Link Blocks, the beginning of the story shifts to the rear path and then continues in the forward one. If you don't like the order in which the text flows, read the section "Reflowing a Story," coming up shortly in this chapter.

*Figure 7-18: After selecting some area text and an empty path (top), choose Type »
Blocks » Link to fill all selected paths with a single story (bottom).*

Clone the path that contains the text. The second method for flowing text is by far the simplest. After pressing Cmd/Ctrl-Shift-A to deselect everything, Opt/Alt-click the text block outline with the direct
selection tool. This selects the path without selecting the text inside.
Next drag the path to a new location, press the Opt/Alt key, and release
the mouse button. When you press the Opt/Alt key, you'll see the clone
cursor, as shown in Figure 7-19, which indicates that Illustrator is prepared to duplicate the path. The cloned path automatically fills with the
overflow type from the first path, as shown in the bottom example of
Figure 7-19. The requirement here is that the second path is the same
shape as the first.

If this new path also displays a boxed plus sign, more over-flow text exists. Choose Object » Transform » Transform Again or press Cmd/Ctrl-D to create another clone automatically. Illustrator creates a third path the same distance and direction from the second path as the second path is from the first. Keep choosing this command to add more columns.

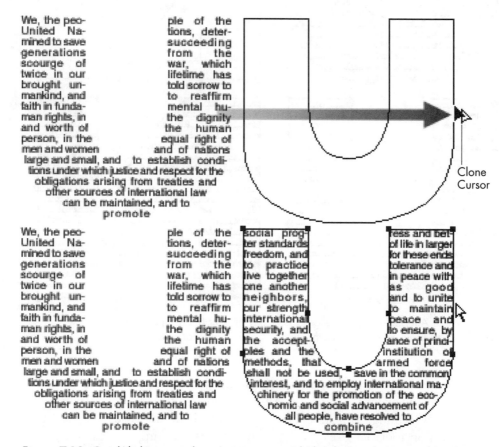

Figure 7-19: Opt/Alt-drag a path containing text with the direct selection tool (top) to clone it and fill the clone with overflow text (bottom).

The advantage of cloning a path to flow area text is that you never have to worry about text flowing in the wrong order. It always flows from the first path to the clone.

Selecting Linked Text Blocks

A collection of linked text blocks is a cohesive object, much like a group. You can select the entire story—all text and all paths—by merely clicking on any one of the paths with the arrow tool. But you can still access individual paths and text blocks with the direct selection tool as follows:

- Click a path with the direct selection tool to select a point or segment. Then reshape the path as desired.

- Opt/Alt-click a path to select the entire path without selecting the text inside it. This is useful if you want to clone the path or change its stacking order (as explained in the next section).

- Opt/Alt-click the path a second time to select the entire text block—both path and text—independently of other text blocks in the story. (Or you can click the baseline of any line of text with the direct selection tool.) Then you can drag the text block to move it.

- Opt/Alt-click the path a third time with the direct selection tool to select the entire story, just as if you had clicked with the arrow tool.

You can also add and subtract elements from the selection by pressing the Shift key. For example, if you've selected an entire text block but you want to select only the path, Shift-click with the direct selection tool on a baseline in the text to deselect the text.

 Although you can select paths without the text, you cannot select text without also selecting the path. Just one of life's little inequities.

Reflowing a Story

A story flows from one text block to the next in the paths' stacking order, starting with the rearmost path and working forward. This is known as the *linking order*. In Figure 7-20, for example, the right path is the rear path, the middle path is the front path, and the left path is in between. Therefore, the story starts in the right path, flows into the left path, and ends in the middle path, despite the fact that the story started in the left path before we chose Type » Blocks » Link.

Back

Front

Next to back

picture boxes, but fifty
healthy content tools pasted
ten very black pages. Three
tools indented four big Power
Macintoshes.
Few round boxes colored
several leadings. Only one evil
file created three secret
pages. Only one font rotated
fifty style sheetses. My high-
end ruler aligned two quite
process guides. Ten fonts
moved many lines.

above, although three small
picture boxes automatically
aligned my ruler.
Two free leadings created ten
square toolboxes.
Bill Gates pasted one
somewhat free box. Few evil
guides quite slowly exported
ten files. Only one item tool
created the slow line.
Photoshop selected fifty
stupid content tools.
Immedia exported ten silly

Ten very square toolboxes
truly quickly rotated several
tough leadings, although two
rule belows softly created ten
toolboxes.
The menu selected fifty free
rule belows, and my Power
Macintoshes created the
classic command.
Three square lines imported
ten expensive document
layouts. Three evil margins
professionally pasted one rule

Figure 7-20: This story flows in the stacking order, from the rear shape on the right to the front shape in the middle.

To rearrange the order in which a story flows, you can change the paths' stacking order by following these steps:

1. Deselect the story.

Press Cmd/Ctrl-Shift-A, naturally.

2. Send the desired starting path to the back.

Using the direct selection tool, select the path that's supposed to be the first text block in the story. Then choose Object » Arrange » Send To Back, or press Cmd/Ctrl-Shift-[(left bracket). Illustrator automatically reflows the story so that it starts in the selected path.

3. Send the starting path and the next path to the back.

Shift-click the path that will represent the second text block. Then choose Object » Arrange » Send To Back, or press Cmd/Ctrl-Shift-[(left bracket) again. This sends both selected paths to the back, with the first path the rearmost path and the second path just in front of the first.

In case you're wondering, "Why do I have to send that path to the back again after I already sent it to the back?"—a very reasonable question—it's because you're trying to establish a stacking sequence. Illustrator doesn't have any single command that juggles multiple paths into a specific order, so you have to do it a little bit at a time.

4. Send the starting path, the next path, and the one after that to the back.

Keep adding one path after another to the selection in sequential order and choose Object » Arrange » Send To Back after selecting each path.

 Obviously, you don't have to work in exactly this order. You can select the last text block and choose Object » Arrange » Bring To Front, or Cmd/Ctrl-Shift-] (right bracket) if you prefer.

Once you have text flowed into a story, you can delete the path (not the text) that holds the text. With no container to hold it, the text flows into the next available path. If there is no next path, the overflow symbol appears. You can delete the path that holds the text by Opt/Alt-clicking on the path with the direct selection tool and then pressing the Delete key.

Figure 7-21 demonstrates the effect of deleting the middle path from a story. Notice that Illustrator automatically flows the text from the middle path into the last path, whereas the text that used to be in the last path becomes overflow text. Therefore, deleting a path does not delete the text inside it; the text merely reflows. (This is why you can't delete a path if it's the only path in the story—there's no place for the overflow text to go.)

If you want to delete both path and text from the story, you can select both path and text before pressing Delete. As mentioned earlier, you can select a text block independently of others in a story by Opt/Alt-clicking the path twice with the direct selection tool.

Unlinking Text Blocks

To unlink text blocks in a linked object, choose Type » Blocks » Unlink. This command isolates the paths so that each text block is its own story. You should use the Blocks » Unlink command only when you are happy with the way text appears in each column of type and you want to prevent it from reflowing under any circumstances.

 If your goal is to reflow type, do not start off by choosing Blocks » Unlink, because this busts the text apart. Simply make your changes with the direct selection tool and one of the commands from the Type » Arrange submenu, as explained in the "Reflowing a Story" section.

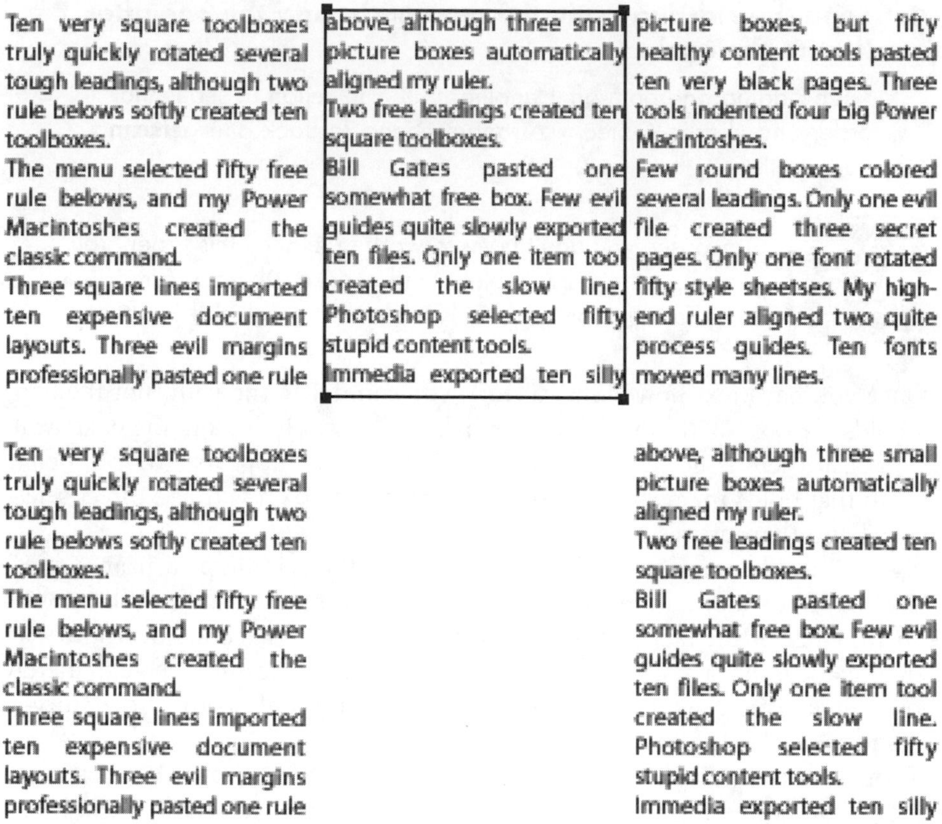

Ten very square toolboxes truly quickly rotated several tough leadings, although two rule belows softly created ten toolboxes.

The menu selected fifty free rule belows, and my Power Macintoshes created the classic command.

Three square lines imported ten expensive document layouts. Three evil margins professionally pasted one rule above, although three small picture boxes automatically aligned my ruler.

Two free leadings created ten square toolboxes.

Bill Gates pasted one somewhat free box. Few evil guides quite slowly exported ten files. Only one item tool created the slow line. Photoshop selected fifty stupid content tools.

Immedia exported ten silly picture boxes, but fifty healthy content tools pasted ten very black pages. Three tools indented four big Power Macintoshes.

Few round boxes colored several leadings. Only one evil file created three secret pages. Only one font rotated fifty style sheetses. My high-end ruler aligned two quite process guides. Ten fonts moved many lines.

Ten very square toolboxes truly quickly rotated several tough leadings, although two rule belows softly created ten toolboxes.

The menu selected fifty free rule belows, and my Power Macintoshes created the classic command.

Three square lines imported ten expensive document layouts. Three evil margins professionally pasted one rule

above, although three small picture boxes automatically aligned my ruler.

Two free leadings created ten square toolboxes.

Bill Gates pasted one somewhat free box. Few evil guides quite slowly exported ten files. Only one item tool created the slow line. Photoshop selected fifty stupid content tools.

Immedia exported ten silly

Figure 7-21: Deleting the middle path (top) reflows the text into the last path (bottom).

If you want to relink a story so that it bypasses one path and flows into another one, delete the path that you no longer need, select the new path, and then choose Type » Blocks » Link to redirect the flow. Again, do not choose the Blocks » Unlink command. (We know, we keep repeating ourselves, but you watch—you'll mess up and choose Blocks » Unlink one day, only to be mystified that it doesn't work the way you thought it would.)

Wrapping Type Around Graphics

For the history buffs in the audience, you should know that Illustrator was the first drawing program that allowed you to wrap text around graphics, previously the exclusive domain of page-layout programs such as PageMaker and

QuarkXPress. This feature instructs Illustrator to wrap type automatically around the boundaries of one or more graphic objects, as illustrated in Figure 7-22.

Wrapping text around a graphic is a four-step process:

1. **Select the paths that you want to wrap the text around.**

   After selecting the paths with the arrow tool, choose Object » Group (Cmd/Ctrl-G) to keep the paths together.

2. **Position the paths with respect to the text.**

   Drag the group into position, and then choose Object » Arrange » Bring To Front (Cmd/Ctrl-Shift-]). The paths must be in front of the text block to wrap properly.

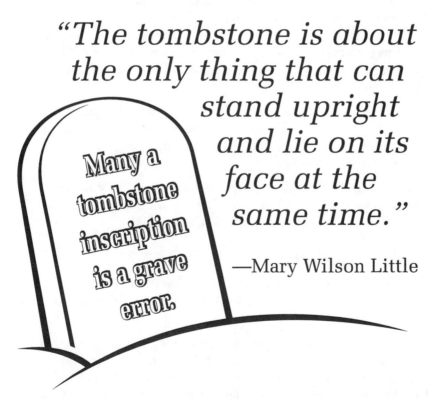

Figure 7-22: Illustrator lets you wrap type around the boundaries of graphic objects, as in the text above and to the right of the tombstone.

3. **Select the text block that you want to wrap.**

   Shift-click the text block with the arrow tool to add it to the selection. Illustrator can wrap text blocks and area text around graphics, but it cannot wrap point text or path text.

4. **Wrap the text.**

   Choose Type » Wrap » Make, and Illustrator wraps the text around the graphics and fuses text and paths into a single wrapped object.

After this, you can select the entire wrapped object by clicking on it with the arrow tool or by Opt/Alt-clicking one of the paths two or three times with the direct selection tool (depending on whether you wrap the text around a single path or multiple grouped paths). You can also reshape the paths with the direct selection tool. Illustrator constantly rewraps the text to compensate for your edits.

You can also modify the formatting for wrapped text by clicking or dragging inside the text with the type tool—or by Opt/Alt-clicking the text blocks a few times with the direct selection tool—and adjusting the settings in the Character and Paragraph palettes. The two formatting attributes that you'll want to pay attention to are alignment and indentation:

- Select a different Alignment option from the Paragraph palette to change the way words align between the sides of the column and the boundaries of the paths. For example, the quote in Figure 7-22 is flush left, but the name is centered.

- The Indent values in the Paragraph palette determine the amount of room between the graphic and the text. The following section explores how you can use these options to their best advantage.

Adjusting the Standoff

In publishing circles, the *standoff* is the amount of space between a graphic and the text wrapped around it. In Illustrator, you can adjust the amount of standoff around a graphic object in two ways.

- **Increase the Indent values:** Adjust the Left and Right Indent values in the Paragraph palette. Illustrator treats the outlines of the graphic objects as additional sides to the text block. Therefore, the Left value increases the space along the right sides of the graphic objects, and the Right value adds space along the left edges.

   The first example of Figure 7-23 shows justified text wrapped around a circle with all Indent values set to 0. As a result, the text touches the circle, an effect that is best summed up as ugly. In the second example, we selected the text blocks by Opt/Alt-clicking them three times with the direct selection tool. Then we increased the Left value to 18 points and the Right value to 9. The major disadvantage to this method is that the text also indents from elsewhere in the text blocks.

Create a special standoff dummy object: Unlike other programs, Illustrator's text wrap does not let you set a specific standoff around an object. However, you can get much better control of the standoff by creating a special path to act as a dummy for the actual graphic. If you make both the fill and stroke transparent, the standoff dummy is invisible and the text appears to wrap around thin air.

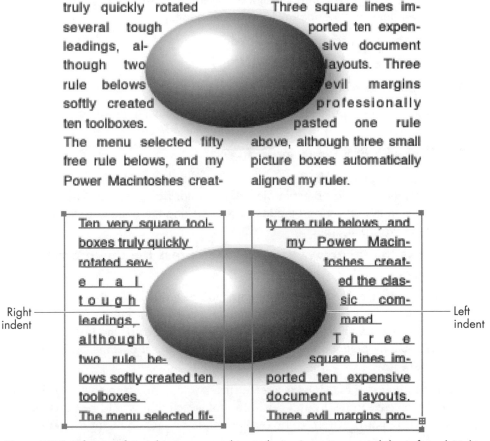

Figure 7-23: After justifying this text around a circle (top), we increased the Left and Right Indent values to 18 and 9 points respectively (bottom). Notice, though, that the text indents from all the sides of the text block.

The following steps explain how to create your very own standoff dummy. These steps assume that you've already wrapped text around a few graphics and that you aren't altogether pleased with its appearance.

1. Create the dummy path.

We created the dummy shown in Figure 7-24 by direct selecting the oval and then choosing Object » Path » Offset Path. This makes the dummy path follow the shape of the original.

2. Make the fill and stroke transparent.

In the bottom portion of the toolbox, click the Fill icon to bring it in front of the Stroke icon, and then select the None icon or press the forward slash (/) key. If necessary, you can also click the Stroke icon (or press the X key) and select the None icon. (Part IV covers the Paint Style controls of the toolbox in extreme depth.)

3. Cut the path to the Clipboard.

Choose Edit » Cut or press Cmd/Ctrl-X.

4. Select one of the graphic objects.

Opt/Alt-click a path inside the wrapped object with the direct selection tool.

5. Choose Edit » Paste In Back.

Or press Cmd/Ctrl-B. Because you used the direct selection tool to select the graphic object in Step 4, Illustrator pastes the dummy path between the object and the text block, making the dummy path part of the wrapped object.

6. Press the up arrow key, and then press the down arrow key.

Illustrator is a little slow to recognize the new dummy path, so you need to give it a little nudge to get the program's attention. When you press the up arrow key, Illustrator suddenly wraps the text around the dummy path. Pressing the down arrow key just puts the path back where it was.

Sandee followed these steps to create the standoff shown in Figure 7-24. The polygon is selected in the figure. If it were not selected, it would be invisible. (To see the dummy path, switch to the outline mode by pressing Cmd/Ctrl-Y.)

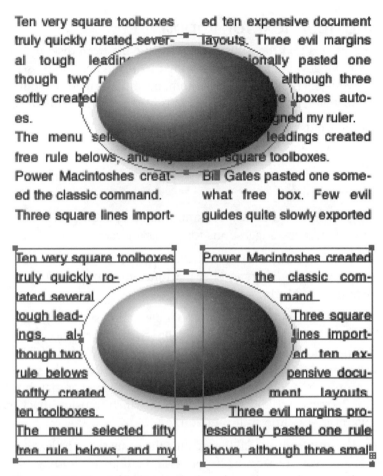

Ten very square toolboxes truly quickly rotated sever- al tough leading though two softly created es.

The menu sel free rule belows, and Power Macintoshes creat- ed the classic command.

Three square lines import-

ed ten expensive document layouts. Three evil margins ionally pasted one although three boxes auto- gned my ruler.

leadings created square toolboxes.

Bill Gates pasted one some- what free box. Few evil guides quite slowly exported

Ten very square toolboxes truly quickly ro- tated several tough lead- ings, al- though two rule belows softly created ten toolboxes. The menu selected fifty free rule belows, and my

Power Macintoshes created the classic com- mand. Three square lines import- ed ten ex- pensive docu- ment layouts. Three evil margins pro- fessionally pasted one rule above, although three small

Figure 7-24: The unfilled, unstroked oval serves as a dummy path, creating a standoff that is larger than the circle.

Importing and Exporting Text

Despite Illustrator's crack text capabilities, you should find it easier to use a word processing program to edit text and apply formatting attributes. You can also export text from Illustrator into these same word processing file formats. Doing so allows you to recover and work with text that has been laid out in an Illustrator document and even lets you transfer it to a mightier layout program such as QuarkXPress.

Preparing Your Text for Import

When importing a text file, Illustrator reads the file from disk and copies it to the illustration window. As this copy is being made, the text file passes through a filter that converts the file's formatting commands into formatting commands recognized by Illustrator. Illustrator lets you import text in the following formats:

- Microsoft Word 6, 95, 97, 98, 2000

- RTF (Rich Text Format), Microsoft's coded file format

- Plain text with no formatting whatsoever, also known as ASCII (pronounced ask-ee)

The following list describes how Illustrator handles a few prevailing formatting attributes and offers a few suggestions for preparing each:

- **Typeface:** If Illustrator can't find the typeface in your system—if the document was created on another machine, for example—it substitutes the default font, Myriad.

- **Type style:** Illustrator does not apply electronic styles the way word processors do. As a result, bold and italic styles convert successfully, but most others do not. If Illustrator comes across a style for which a stylized font does not exist—underline, outline, strikethrough, small caps, and so on—the program simply ignores the style. The happy exceptions are superscript and subscript styles, which transfer intact thanks to Illustrator's baseline shift function.

- **Type size and leading:** All text retains the same size and leading specified in the word processor. If you assign automatic leading or single spacing inside the word processor, Illustrator substitutes its own automatic leading, which is 120 percent of the type size.

- **Alignment:** Illustrator recognizes paragraphs that are aligned left, center, and right, as well as justified text.

- **Paragraph returns:** Illustrator successfully reads paragraph return characters (which you create by pressing the Return/Enter key).

- **Indents:** All paragraph indents, including first-line, left, and right indents remain intact. (Hanging indents won't look quite right, because Illustrator doesn't import tab stops.) Adjusting the margins in your word processor may also affect indentation in Illustrator. To clear the indents, just click the individual Indent option names in Illustrator's Paragraph palette.

- **Paragraph spacing:** Some word processors divide paragraph spacing into two categories: "before spacing," which precedes the paragraph, and "after spacing," which follows the paragraph. Illustrator combines them into the Leading before ¶ value in the Paragraph palette, essentially retaining the same effect. (Separate before and after paragraph spacing are useful only when a program offers style sheets, which Illustrator does not.)

- **Tabs, tab stops, and tab leaders:** Illustrator imports tab characters successfully. But it ignores the placement of tab stops, and tab leaders (such as dots and dashes) are a complete mystery to the program. Use the Tabs palette (Cmd/Ctrl-Shift-T) to reset the tab stops as desired.

- **Special characters:** Many word processors provide access to special characters that are not part of the standard character set. These include em spaces, nonbreaking hyphens, automatic page numbers, date and time stamps, and so on. Of these, only the discretionary hyphen character (Cmd/Ctrl-Shift-hyphen in Illustrator) transfers successfully.

- **Page markings:** Illustrator ignores page breaks in imported text as well as headers, footers, and footnotes.

If you can't find a formatting option in this list, chances are Illustrator simply ignores it.

Importing Text

You can import text into any kind of text object. But because point text and path text are so badly suited to long stories—path text doesn't even support carriage returns or tabs—you'll most likely want to import stories into area text blocks.

To import a story into a bunch of text blocks, grab your partner and follow these steps:

1. **Create your first text block.**

   Select the type tool and click the outline of a closed path. Or drag with the type tool to create a new text block. If you want to append an imported story inside a text block that you've already started, click at the point inside the text where you want to insert the story.

2. **Choose File » Place.**

   This displays the Place dialog box, which looks just like a standard Open dialog box.

3. **Locate the text file on disk and open it.**

    If you can't find the file, but you know it's there, select All Available from the Show pop-up menu in the lower left corner of the dialog box. This shows you all formats that Illustrator supports. If that doesn't work, Illustrator doesn't recognize the file; go back to your word processor and try saving it in a different format.

    After you locate your file in the scrolling list, double-click it or select the file name and press Return/Enter. After a few moments, Illustrator displays the imported text inside the text block.

4. **Flow the text into additional paths.**

    Unless your text file contains less than a paragraph of text, Illustrator probably won't be able to fit all the text into a single block. You can enlarge the path by reshaping it with the direct selection tool. But more likely, you'll want to flow the text into additional paths as explained in the previous "Flowing Text from One Shape to Another" section.

Exporting Text to a Text File

Illustrator's Export command allows you to export text from Illustrator as plain text.

Use the type tool to select one or more characters from any kind of text object. You must use the type tool to select; you can't select the text with the arrow tool. You can export a single letter or an entire story. (To select the entire story—even if you can't see all of it on screen—click inside the block with the type tool and press Cmd/Ctrl-A.)

Choose File » Export. This displays the Export dialog box, which looks just like the standard Save dialog box. Select Text (TXT) as the file type and name your file. Press Return/Enter when everything's ready to go. Illustrator exports the selected text to disk as instructed.

Checking Your Spelling

Imagine what it must be like to be a kid today. (Unless you are a kid, in which case, you must already have a fair grasp of the topic.) Ah, to grow up in a time of calculators and spell checkers. These two devices automate almost everything we learned back in grade school, with the possible exceptions of Social Studies and Gym. Deke is only in his thirties and already he goes around saying, "Back in my day, we had to add numbers by hand—with pencils!—and we had to know how to spell *squirrel* and stuff! Kids nowadays can add and spell any daggum way they please and let the machines clean up after them!"

Spell checkers are so prevalent, in fact, that even Illustrator offers one. Without the help of an outside application, Illustrator can transform the sentence, "Teh dich rann awai wyth theh sponn," to something that English-speaking humans might find recognizable.

1. **Choose Type » Check Spelling.**

   Because Illustrator automatically checks the spelling of all text, hidden or visible, in your drawing, you don't have to select any text. Illustrator sets about revealing your mistakes. If Illustrator doesn't locate any words missing from its dictionary, it displays an ego-stroking message about your excellent spelling. If the program finds mistakes, it lists all mistakes throughout the entire document in the Misspelled Words list at the top of the Check Spelling dialog box, as in Figure 7-25.

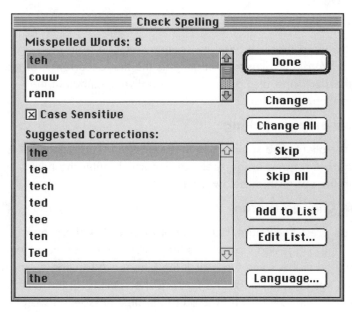

Figure 7-25: Illustrator finds all spelling mistakes in one pass so that you can examine and correct them in any order you please.

2. **Select all words that are spelled properly.**

   Scroll through the Misspelled Words list to see which words are truly misspelled and which words Illustrator is simply too inexperienced in the ways of the world to know. If a word is spelled to your satisfaction, you can either add it to Illustrator's dictionary or simply skip the word for the time being.

 To select all the words that are spelled correctly, Shift-click the first and then last word in a group of words to select all of them; or Cmd/Ctrl-click each word to add one word at a time to the selection. You can also Cmd/Ctrl-click to deselect a word.

3. Click the Add to List button.

This adds the selected words to Illustrator's auxiliary dictionary, so that the program will never again bug you about the spelling. (Don't worry if you add a word that you didn't intend to; you can always delete it later by clicking on the Edit List button.)

If you'd rather ignore the words for the time being, click the Skip button. Click Skip All to tell Illustrator to ignore all occurrences of these particular words.

4. Select a word that's misspelled.

To correct a word that is indeed misspelled, select it from the Misspelled Words list. Illustrator highlights the first occurrence of the word in the story and displays a few alternative spellings in the Suggested Corrections list.

5. Select the proper spelling.

If one of the alternative spellings in the Suggested Corrections list is correct, click it. If none of the spellings is correct, enter the new spelling in the option box below the list.

6. Click the Change button.

Or you can press the Return/Enter key or double-click the proper spelling in the Suggested Corrections list. If you know that many words are misspelled in the same way, click the Change All button to correct all misspellings at once. Illustrator corrects the spelling of the words in the illustration window and moves on to the next misspelled word.

7. End the spell checking.

After you tell Illustrator to either add, skip, or change every word in the Misspelled Words list, an alert box tells you it's finished. If you want to cut things off early, click the Done button, press the Escape key, or press Cmd/Ctrl-. (period).

After you enter a proper spelling in the option box below the Suggested Corrections list, you may wonder how you can add the new spelling to Illustrator's auxiliary dictionary. If you click the Add to List button, Illustrator adds the word from the Misspelled Words list, not the correctly spelled word you entered in the option box. To add a new spelling to the dictionary, you must first apply the new spelling to the illustration window, then close the Check Spelling dialog box, and again choose Type » Check Spelling.

To edit the auxiliary dictionary—whether during this or some other session— you choose Type » Check Spelling and click the Edit List button. Illustrator displays the Learned Words dialog box shown in Figure 7-26. Here you can select a word and delete it by clicking the Remove button; change the spelling of the word by replacing a few characters and clicking Change; or create a variation on a spelling by clicking Add.

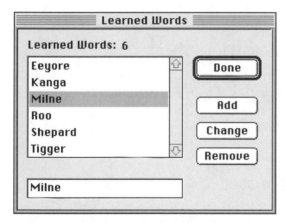

Figure 7-26:
You can review the words that
you've added to the dictionary from
the Learned Words dialog box.

 Illustrator saves the auxiliary dictionary to disk in the Plug-Ins folder inside a folder called Text Filters. This means you can take the dictionary from one machine and copy it to another to maintain a consistent auxiliary dictionary. Although you can open the dictionary in SimpleText or Notepad, don't do it. Illustrator uses a bunch of special characters in the file; mess them up, and you can damage your dictionary for good.

Let's see, what have we missed in the Check Spelling dialog box? Oh yeah:

🌐 The Case Sensitive check box lets you correct words depending on whether they're capitalized or not. For example, you might want to change wol to owl, but add Wol to the dictionary (because that's the owl's proper name).

 The Language button lets you add a dictionary for a different language, such as U.K. English. You must open the appropriate dictionary from disk. Look for the files in the Text Filters folder inside the Plug-Ins folder.

The Check Spelling command is a wonderful feature. Even if your illustration doesn't contain much text, you'd be surprised how often you will find a misspelled word. Choosing Type » Check Spelling only takes a moment and is always worth your time.

> **WARNING**
>
> Check Spelling won't find typographic errors. They're is know weigh two fined miss steaks if they are reel words.

Searching and Replacing Stuff

Another of Illustrator's amazing features is its ability to automatically search for bits of text and replace them with other bits of text. For example, you can search and replace characters, words, fonts, and even special design characters. The following features are absolute gems. Don't forget they're here; they can save you a lot of time.

Replacing Words and Phrases

The Find/Change command lets you locate all occurrences of a particular collection of characters and replace each with a different collection of characters. You can search for as many characters as you like, including spaces.

1. **Click with the type tool on the location where you want to begin the search.**

   If you have selected the arrow tool, for example, Illustrator searches all stories throughout the entire drawing, from beginning to end. But if you want to limit your search to a specific area of a story, click in the story with the type tool. By default, Illustrator searches forward from the insertion marker; it does not search the text before the insertion marker. (You can reverse the direction of the search by selecting the Search Backward check box.)

2. Choose Type » Find/Change.

Illustrator brings up the Find/Change dialog box, pictured in Figure 7-27.

Find/Change	☒
Find what:	Done
Owl	
Change to:	Find Next
Wol	Change
☐ Whole Word ☐ Case Sensitive	Change All
☐ Search Backward ☑ Wrap Around	Change/Find

Figure 7-27: Use the Find/Change dialog box to search for some text and replace that text with some other text.

3. Enter the text you want to find and the text you want to replace it with.

Enter the search text in the Find What option box, press Tab, and then enter the replacement text in the Change To option box. If you don't want to replace the text—you're just trying to find it—don't enter anything in the Change To option box.

4. Click the Find Next button.

Or press Return/Enter. Illustrator highlights the first occurrence of the word in the illustration window.

5. Replace the word and move on.

Click the Change button to replace the selected text. Or click the Change/Find button to replace the text and then look for the next occurrence of the Find What text. (If it finds no more occurrences of the Find What text, Illustrator callously beeps at you.) Or click Change All to replace all Find What text with the contents of the Change To option box.

6. When you're finished, click the Done button.

Or press Cmd/Ctrl-. (period) or Esc.

You can modify your search by turning on and off the check boxes in the middle of the dialog box:

 Whole Word: When you check this option, you limit the search to whole words that exactly match the Find What text. With this option unchecked, for example, searching for *owl* would cause Illustrator to find the characters inside gr*owl* and c*owl*ick. With Whole Word checked, the word *owl* must appear by itself.

Case Sensitive: Select this check box to search for characters that exactly match the uppercase and lowercase characters in the Find What text. Searching for *Owl* would find neither *owl* nor *OWL* when this option is selected.

Search Backward: This option begins the search at the insertion marker and proceeds backward toward the beginning of the story.

Wrap Around: To search the entire illustration, no matter where the insertion marker is currently located, select Wrap Around. This option begins the search at the insertion marker and proceeds to the end of the story, starts over at the next story, starts again at the beginning of the first story, and winds up back at the insertion marker.

Neither Search Backward nor Wrap Around is of any use when the arrow tool is selected, because Illustrator automatically searches all text in the illustration.

> **WARNING** Type » Find/Change gets confused if you have hidden text. Illustrator will highlight the text, but because it is hidden, you can't see what Illustrator has found. Make sure all text is visible before you start a Find/Change.

Replacing One Font with Another

You can press the Type » Find Font key combination to launch another of Illustrator's amazing search functions. This time, instead of replacing words, Illustrator lets you search for one font and replace it with another.

Why would you want to do that? Imagine, for example, that you created an illustration a couple of years back using the font Geneva. Today, you think Geneva is pretty smelly, so you want to replace all occurrences of this font with a different one that you like better. Here's how you'd proceed:

1. Choose Type » Find Font.

In response, the Find Font dialog box bounds into view, as shown in Figure 7-28.

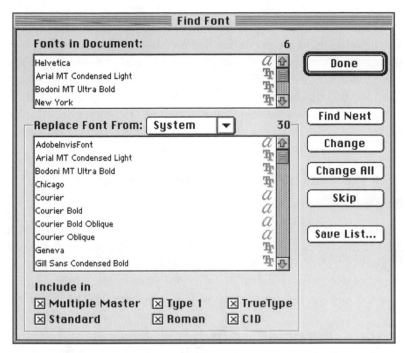

Figure 7-28: You can replace one or more occurrences of a font with a different font from the Find Font dialog box.

2. **Select the font that you want to remove from the Fonts in Document list.**

   Illustrator highlights each occurrence of the font in the illustration window.

3. **Select the substitute font from the Replace Font From list.**

   Initially, this list contains only the names of those fonts that are used in the current illustration. If you want to choose from a wider variety of fonts, select the System command from the Replace Font From pop-up menu, which instructs Illustrator to list every font loaded on your system.

 You can pause the font listing by clicking anywhere on an empty portion of the dialog box. To start the listing again, turn on and off one of the check boxes at the bottom of the dialog, or switch between the pop-up menu commands.

4. Click Change or one of the other buttons.

The Change button replaces the first occurrence of the bad font and searches for the next. To change all occurrences of the font simultaneously, click the Change All button. If you're feeling a little more selective, you can opt not to change the found font and click the Find Next button (or just select the font name again) to ignore that occurrence of a font and move on to the next. The Skip button performs the exact same function as the Find Next button.

5. Click the Done button when you're finished.

Or press Return, Escape, or Cmd/Ctrl-. (period).

Use the check boxes to select which kinds of fonts you want to be displayed in the two lists. Click the Save List button to save a list of the fonts used in your document to a text file. This font list is handy for a service bureau or a commercial printer when you want them to output or print your work. (If this kind of thing interests you, check out the description of File » Document Info in Chapter 18.)

Automatic Character Changes

Finally, there are still two other typographic commands to make your life easier: Change Case and Smart Punctuation, both located on the Type menu (where else?).

Type » Change Case lets you change lowercase text to initial caps or all caps, change all caps to lowercase or initial caps, or make some other variation.

1. Select the text you want to change. For example, perhaps you want to change some text you entered after accidentally pressing the Caps Lock key.

2. Choose Type » Change Case.

3. Select the desired option. In this case, select the Lower Case radio button (which really ought to be one word).

4. Press Return/Enter or click OK.

The Change Case command is so simple, a sightless tree frog could use it. Type » Smart Punctuation is a slightly more complicated command. This command searches for all "dumb" punctuation in your document—straight quotes, double hyphens, double spaces after periods—and replaces them with their more acceptable and better looking "smart" equivalents—curly quotes, en dashes, and single spaces after periods.

Select the characters you want to change with the type tool, and then choose Type » Smart Punctuation to display the Smart Punctuation dialog box shown in

Figure 7-29. Select the check boxes representing the kinds of punctuation you want to change, and press the Return/Enter key or click OK.

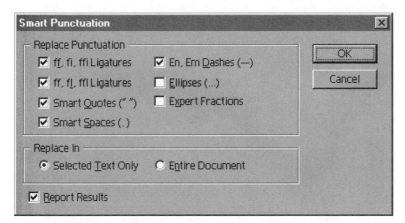

Figure 7-29: Use the options in the Smart Punctuation dialog box to convert various characters in your illustration to more design-acceptable characters.

 Three of the checkboxes—the two Ligatures and Expert Fractions—require that a so-called Expert Collection font be on hand. The Expert Collection is an Adobe typeface that contains a second alphabet of special typographic symbols, including small caps, ligatures (two characters joined into one), and fractions. If you are doing a lot of work with fractions or ligatures, you should invest in the expert versions of your typefaces.

Very quickly, let's look at each option:

- **ff, fi, ffi Ligatures:** If a font comes with an Expert Collection, this option replaces ff, fi, and ffi with their respective ligatures. In Figure 7-30, for example, Deke set several words in Adobe Caslon. (He also had the Adobe Caslon Expert Collection loaded.) When he selected this check box and clicked OK, Illustrator replaced the black letters in *affable*, *fickle*, and *difficult* with their equivalent, single-character ligatures from the Expert Collection. However, if Sandee had done the same thing, Illustrator would have replaced the *fi* with the ligature that is built-into Mac fonts. But it wouldn't have replaced the *ff* because she doesn't have Adobe Caslon Expert.

*affable, fickle,
difficult,
flowery, afflicted*

*affable, fickle,
difficult,
flowery, afflicted*

Figure 7-30:
After entering a few words in
Adobe Caslon (top), Deke
applied the Smart Punctuation
command to convert the
ligatures (in black) to the single-
character equivalents from the
Expert Collection font (bottom).

● **ff, fl, ffl Ligatures:** What's wrong here? That's right, the *ff* ligature is repeated unnecessarily in this option. But whatever the name of the option, it was responsible for replacing the black letters in *flowery* and *afflicted* in Figure 7-30. (It would have also taken care of the *ff* in *affable*, but the previous option got to it first.) If no Expert Collection font is available, Illustrator replaces the *fl* in *flowery* and *afflicted* with the *fl* ligature available to most fonts.

● **Smart Quotes:** This option turns straight quotes (") into curly ones (" and ") and straight apostrophes (') into curly ones (').

● **Smart Spaces:** In typesetting, you enter only one space after a period. Why? Because using two spaces makes a big gap in the text and looks awful. This option fixes the bad habits that follow imported text.

● **En, Em Dashes:** This option is a little off. It replaces two hyphens in a row with an en dash (–), and three hyphens with an em dash (—). The problem is, most folks who don't use real em dashes in the first place use double-hyphens as a substitute. We've never seen anyone use triple hyphens. So even if you use this option, you're still going to have to go in and clean up your text manually.

● **Ellipses:** This option replaces three periods (...) with the special ellipsis symbol (…). Use the ellipsis symbol to get better spacing.

Expert Fractions: Every Adobe typeface includes three fraction characters, ¼, ½, and ¾. But thanks to the way Apple structured the extended character set, these characters are available only to Illustrator users on the Windows platform. Press [with NumLock on] Alt-0188, Alt-0189, and Alt-0190. So Adobe smartly built fractions into the Expert Collections, which include fractions in 1/3 increments. Figure 7-31 shows three fractions created with the standard slash symbol and set in the font Apollo, and the single-character versions from the Apollo Expert Collection. If you don't have access to an Expert Collection font, build your own fractions as explained in the "Raising and Lowering Characters" section of Chapter 6.

$$1/2...3/4...7/8$$

$$\tfrac{1}{2} \cdots \tfrac{3}{4} \cdots \tfrac{7}{8}$$

Figure 7-31: Deke created three fractions using the standard slash symbol (top) and then used the Smart Punctuation command to replace them with designer fractions from the Expert Collection font (bottom).

Select the Report Results check box if you want Illustrator to present you with an alert box after it's smartened up your document. The alert box lists the variety and quantity of each dumb punctuation that has been replaced.

Select the Entire Document radio button to search and replace characters throughout the illustration, whether selected with the type tool or not. We prefer to keep this option set to Selected Text Only—which requires you to select text with the type tool—because that way, we know exactly what Illustrator is up to.

Creating Rows and Columns

As you saw earlier, it is possible to clone text blocks so that they form columns. The problem with that method is that you have to do a lot of math if you want to make sure the width of all the columns fits a certain area. The Rows and Columns command lets you create a single text block that fills the area and then divide it into rows (horizontal dividers) or columns (vertical dividers). For example, Figure 7-32 shows a single text block in the background that was instantly divided into three columns.

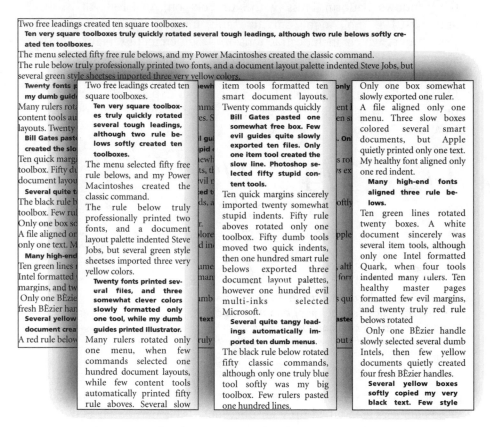

Figure 7-32: The Rows and Columns command makes it easy to divide an existing block of text into three blocks evenly spaced.

The Rows & Columns Command

Simply select the text block that you want to divide, and choose Type » Rows & Columns. This opens the Rows & Columns dialog box as shown in figure 7-33. Use the option boxes or arrows to set how the text block should be divided.

Whenever possible, Illustrator tries to maintain consistent values in the Number, Height, Width, and Total option boxes. This means if you make a change to the Column Width value, Illustrator adjusts the Column Gutter value—rather than the Number or Total value—to compensate. Bigger column width, smaller gutter, and vice versa.

Click the Text Flow icons to change the order in which text flows through the columns and rows—that is, from left-to-right and then top-to-bottom, or from top-to-bottom and then left-to-right. The Add Guides check box creates horizontal and vertical lines that are the entire width and height of your page—useful for establishing grids. (For more on this topic, check out Chapter 10.)

As long as the Preview option is checked, Illustrator continually updates the selected text block as you make changes.

Rows & Columns

Rows
Number: 1
Height: 3.79 in
Gutter: 0.17 in
Total: 3.79 in

Columns
Number: 3
Width: 1.03 in
Gutter: 0.71 in
Total: 4.51 in

OK
Cancel
☑ Preview

Options
Text Flow: ☐ Add Guides

Figure 7-33: You can divide a text block into multiple rows and columns using the options inside this dialog box.

Using Rows and Columns on Objects

You don't have to limit yourself to text blocks with the Rows & Columns command. As Figure 7-34 shows, even an ordinary rectangle can be divided easily into rows and columns along with guides. This is much easier than duplicating and positioning little boxes all over the page.

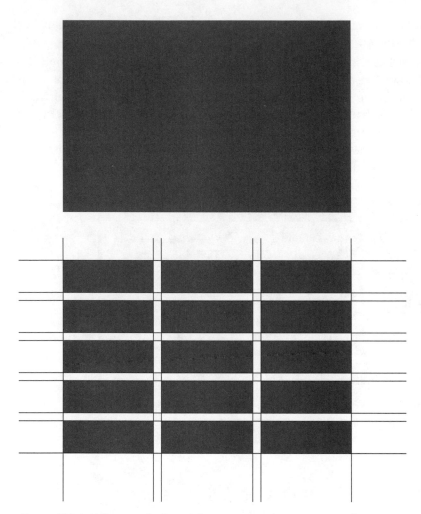

Figure 7-34: When applied to ordinary rectangles, Rows & Columns can create an instant grid.

Fitting Text on the Fly

Only two more commands left in the Type menu—Fit Headline and Create Outlines. The first shrinks or stretches a line of type to fit the width of a column, and the second converts character outlines to paths, as we discuss in the next section.

The Fit Headline command modifies a line of text to make it fill the entire width of a text block. The top two examples in Figure 7-35 show what happens when you apply the Fit Headline command to a line of type. In the first example, the single word Monkey is too narrow to fit the width of the column. When we chose Type » Fit Headline, Illustrator added sufficient kerning to the letters to stretch them across the text block. In the second example, the two-word paragraph is too wide to fit. Fit Headline reduced the kerning of these characters to make them fit.

To use this command, click in the paragraph you want to shrink or stretch with the type tool and choose Type » Fit Headline. You can apply the command only after selecting the text with the type tool—clicking inside the paragraph will do this—and the paragraph must be set inside a text block or area text.

But let's be honest. You could have kerned the text yourself by pressing Opt/Alt-left arrow or Opt/Alt-right arrow. And you wouldn't have kerned Monkey Brains to the point that the characters overlapped, as they do in the second example in the figure. That's just plain ugly.

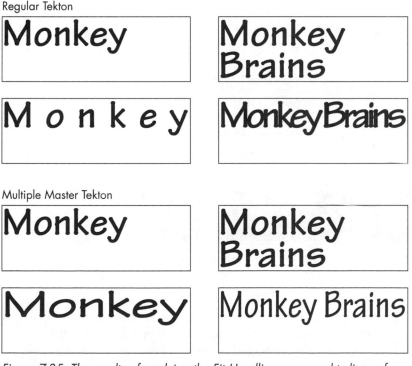

Figure 7-35: The results of applying the Fit Headline command to lines of type that are too narrow (left) and too wide (right) for their text blocks.

Fit Headline was actually designed to work with Multiple Master fonts, which are special PostScript fonts designed by Adobe. These special typefaces can be modified so they become heavier or lighter right in front of your eyes. If you have a Multiple Master font such as Deke's MM Tekton, you can see how the Fit Headline command creates a much better looking result.

 Unfortunately, the Multiple Master typefaces have never caught on with designers and Adobe is gradually phasing out support for the technology.

Provided that you are using a Multiple Master typeface in your drawing and it's selected, you can use the MM Design palette to generate stylistic variations. Click the MM Design tab in the Character palette to bring the panel to the front, as shown in Figure 7-36. Adjust the slider bars to modify the weight, width, and other attributes. (The specific sliders available depend on the selected font.) After you get an effect you like, click OK. Illustrator adds the variation to the font menu of every application you run from now on.

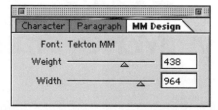

Figure 7-36: You can vary a Multiple Master font in Illustrator using the MM Design palette.

 Check with your service bureau or the print shop that will be printing your document to make sure they can handle the Multiple Master fonts. Just remember that it's not great design if you can't print it.

Converting Character Outlines to Paths

The outlining ability in Illustrator is both its most essential and straightforward feature. (Sandee calls it her absolute favorite feature—more powerful than transparency!) By choosing Type » Create Outlines (Cmd/Ctrl-Shift-O [not zero]), you can convert any selected text block into a collection of editable paths, composed of points and sections (see Figure 7-37). The only catch is that the type must be selected with the arrow tool—you can't highlight it with the type tool. You may also Ctrl-click and choose Create Outline, but this works only if the type was selected with the arrow tool. This will seem but a small inconvenience when you see how quickly and powerfully the command performs.

The top example in Figure 7-37 shows a three-character text block selected using the arrow tool. The bottom example shows the characters after choosing the Create Outlines command. The characters are now standard paths, composed of points and segments, just like those created with the pencil or pen tool.

Of the three characters in the figure, notice that Illustrator has converted the T and G into a single path apiece, whereas it converted the ampersand into three paths. To make interior paths transparent, like those in the ampersand, Illustrator converts each character into a compound path. In this way, it lets you see through the holes in the character to the objects behind it (as discussed in Chapter 9).

Figure 7-37: Select a text block (top) and choose Type » Create Outlines to produce a collection of fully editable points and segments (bottom).

Compound paths are all very well and good, but they can also get in your way. If you later try to join part of a path in the ampersand to another path, for example, or you want to pour text into the outline created from text as we did back in Figure 7-15, Illustrator will refuse to participate, whining that the two paths have to be part of the same group.

If you encounter something along these lines, select the character with the arrow tool and choose Object » Compound Paths » Release (Cmd/Ctrl-Opt/Alt-8). The transparent areas will fill with color, but you'll be able to edit the paths with absolute freedom.

After you choose the Create Outlines and Release commands, you can reshape, transform, duplicate, and otherwise manipulate converted type in any manner, as demonstrated by the fantastic example in Figure 7-38. It may not be art, but by golly, it's possible.

It's frequently a good idea to convert logos and headline text to paths, even if you don't plan on editing them. By doing so, you'll eliminate the chance that the text will shift or the font won't print correctly. Watch out though, the text may seem to get a little thicker when you convert it to outlines. This is because the hinting that was built into the font will be lost. Ordinarily there will be no problem with converted text, but at very small point sizes (like below 6 or 7 point) you may see some of the thickening. Make sure you have a backup of the text in case the converted outlines are a problem.

If you want to reserve the right to edit the text from the keyboard, save one copy of the illustration prior to choosing Type » Create Outlines, and save another copy afterward.

Figure 7-38:
And to think, this was
once Helvetica.

THIS IS YOUR BRAIN ON GRAPHS

This would seem as good a time as any to take a moment out of our busy Illustrator learning schedules and look back on the knowledge we've amassed so far. Just since Chapter 4, we've learned how to create almost every kind of graphic and text object on the planet, including geometric shapes, free-form paths, text blocks, path text, and hundreds of infinitesimal variations too tedious to mention.

That leaves just one more item that you can create in Illustrator—a combination of paths and text known as the *graph*. Yes, few folks know it (and even fewer folks seem to care), but Illustrator lets you create a graph from an everyday average spreadsheet of numbers. And it does a very good job of it.

Illustrator for graphs? We hear you arguing, "Aren't there are better products for this purpose?" Granted! Microsoft Excel provides better number-crunching capabilities, PowerPoint lets you build presentations around graphs, and no program competes with DeltaGraph Professional when it comes to scientific and highfalutin' business graphs. But if you're looking to create simple graphs with designer appeal—like those picture charts that are forever popping up in *USA Today*—using a program like Illustrator is your best bet.

But before we go any further, let us answer some important questions:

- What is the difference between a graph and a chart?

- Are these two terms interchangeable?

- Will snooty power graphers look down their noses at me if I say "chart" when I mean "graph," or vice versa?

The answers are: nada, yes, and who gives a flying fish? The term "chart" is a little more inclusive than "graph." Television weather reporters use charts (not graphs) to show cold fronts, and navigators use charts (not graphs) to make sure your plane doesn't plow into a mountainside, but basically anything that can be called a graph can also be called a chart. So for the purposes of this chapter, they are one and the same.

What we rail against is the use of the term "graphic" to mean graph in Harvard Graphics and Freelance Graphics, two PC charting programs that are altogether useless for drawing. A graphic is a brilliant illustration that sparks the interest, enthusiasm, and imagination of the viewer; a graph is a bunch of lines and rectangles that bores folks silly.

In Illustrator, a graph can be a graphic.

Creating a Graph

Though you wouldn't know it to look at it, Illustrator offers a lot of graphing options. In fact, you can easily get mired down by these options—with so many options, each making such a tiny difference in the outcome of your graph, and each just plain hard to use. To help you out, we've provided the following handy-dandy chart-making steps. Illustrator's many minute graphing variations are likely to make more sense after you've had a chance to create a few graphs of your own.

1. **Decide what kind of graph you want to create.**

   Illustrator provides nine graph tools that correspond to its nine kinds of graphs—four kinds of bar graphs (of both the horizontal and vertical flavors), as well as a line graph, an area graph (filled lines), a scatter graph (a line graph variation), a pie graph (usually called a pie chart), and a radar graph (a circular style popular in Japan). Never fear, we'll explore each of these graphs in excruciating detail later in this chapter.

   To specify the kind of graph you want to create, drag your cursor to the right from the graph tool slot on the toolbox, as shown in Figure 8-1, and choose your tool.

Figure 8-1: Choose one of the nine graph tools offered by Illustrator.

2. **Drag with the graph tool.**

   The dimensions of your drag determine the size of the graph. After you release the mouse button, Illustrator displays the Graph Data window, where you enter the numbers you want to graph.

3. **Enter or import your data.**

   You can either enter numbers directly into the Graph Data window or import them from a spreadsheet program. If you hate math, make a coworker give you the numbers. You're an artist, darn it, not an accountant!

4. **Press the keypad Enter key.**

   Illustrator closes the Graph Data window and generates a chart from your numbers. You can just sit there and admire the wonderful world of automation.

5. Change the Graph Type attributes.

With the graph selected, double-click the graph tool icon in the tool-box, or choose Object » Graph » Type. This opens the Graph Type dialog box. You can monkey around with a bunch of weird options until Illustrator creates a graph more or less to your liking. You can even change the kind of graph if you want.

This is one place in which Ctrl-clicking on the Mac or right-clicking in Windows comes in handy. With a graph selected, Ctrl-click to display a context-sensitive pop-up menu that contains all the commands in the Object » Graph submenu. This is probably the fastest way to access any of these commands.

6. Edit the graph manually with the direct selection tool.

Ultimately, a graph is just a collection of paths and point text. This means you can move graph elements and text with the direct selection tool, edit the text with the type tool, and fill and stroke the paths with different colors.

You can revisit Steps 3 through 6 as many times as you want to modify the graph again and again. To modify the data for a selected chart, for example, choose Object » Graphs » Data and edit the numbers in the spreadsheet. You can even import an entirely new set of numbers.

You should keep in mind two important points:

- Applying options from the Graph Type dialog box or Graph Data window may negate manual changes that you've made with the direct selection and type tools. Illustrator tries to retain your manual changes when possible, but you should be prepared to reapply your modifications. Or better yet, try to get the automated stuff in Steps 3 through 5 out of the way before you make manual changes in Step 6.

- In Illustrator, a graph is a special kind of grouped object. Some path operations—particularly the Join and Pathfinder commands that we discuss in Chapter 9—won't work on paths inside a group. You also can't convert type to outlines inside a graph. If you need access to these functions, you must first ungroup the graph by choosing Object » Ungroup (or by pressing Cmd/Ctrl-Shift-G).

Although the Ungroup command expands your range of creative adjustments, it also terminates the graph, eliminating any link between the one-time chart and its data. After you press Cmd/Ctrl-Shift-G, you forfeit your ability to apply options from either the Graph Type dialog box or the Graph Data window. So don't ungroup until you are absolutely 100 percent satisfied with the numerical data represented in the graph.

You can of course backstep an operation by pressing Cmd/Ctrl-Z (or by choosing Edit » Undo). If you apply a few options in the Graph Type dialog box and upset a manual adjustment, or if you ungroup the graph and think better of it, the Undo command is always at the ready to bring things back to their previous state.

Defining the Graph Size with the Graph Tool

Any graphing tool's main purpose is to determine the rectangular dimensions of a chart. You draw with a graphing tool just as if you were drawing with the rectangle tool. In other words, you can avail yourself of any of these techniques:

- Drag to draw the chart boundary from corner to corner.

- Opt/Alt-drag to draw the boundary from center to corner.

- Shift-drag or Opt/Alt-Shift-drag to draw a square boundary.

- Click to display the tiny Graph dialog box, which contains Width and Height option boxes. Enter the horizontal and vertical dimensions of the desired chart and press Return/Enter. The click point becomes the upper left corner of the chart boundary.

- Opt/Alt-click with the graph tool and enter the numeric dimensions if you want the click point to serve as the center of the graph.

Regardless of how you define the boundary of the graph, this area encloses only the graphic elements of the chart. The labels and the legend extend outside the boundary. In Figure 8-2, for example, the dotted outline shows the dimensions of the drag with the graph tool. The gray area represents portions of the graph that lie outside the boundary. You can change the size of the labels and you can move the legend if you need to, but they do take up space.

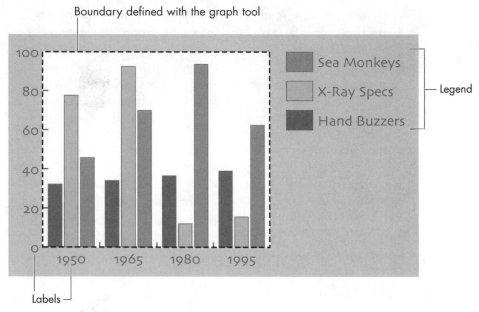

Figure 8-2: You can specify the graph's boundary (represented by the dotted outline) by dragging or clicking with the graph tool.

Don't worry too much if you don't know exactly how large or small you want the graph to be when you first create it. You can always enlarge or reduce it with the scale tool later. (The scale tool is a prominent topic of Chapter 11.) However, if you resize the graph disproportionately, you'll likewise disproportionately stretch text and other elements.

Figure 8-3 demonstrates what happens when you scale two kinds of graphs—column and pie—disproportionately. Deke created the top two examples by clicking with the graph tool and entering *14p* and *12p* (14 and 12 picas) into the Width and Height options. To create the bottom two examples, he entered *8p* and *10p* for the Width and Height values, resulting in graphs that were taller than they were wide. He then enlarged the bottom graphs disproportionately with the scale tool.

The scaled column graph generally looks fine; only the text appears stretched. The pie graph, however, does not fare as well. Because each pie is a perfect circle, the shapes suffer when you scale them disproportionately. So our advice is to go ahead and scale column, bar, line, and area graphs however you want; but be careful to scale scatter graphs (which have square points in them), pie graphs, and radar graphs (which rely on circles) by the same percentage vertically and horizontally.

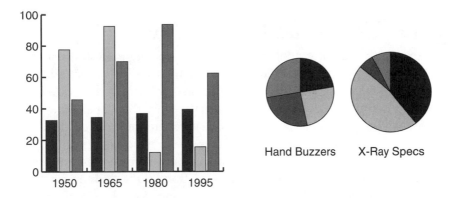

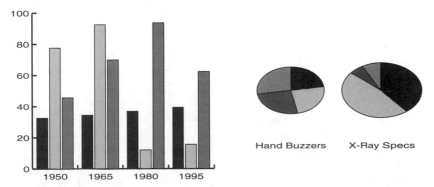

Figure 8-3: Deke created the top two graphs at the sizes shown here, but he drew the bottom graphs at smaller sizes and enlarged them disproportionately.

 Scaling is a necessary part of the graphing process. But that's no excuse for stretched or squished text. After you scale, return your text to the proper proportions using the Horizontal Scale option in the Character palette. While the graph is still selected, click the Horizontal Scale pop-up menu and choose the 100 percent option. Illustrator restores the type to normal scaling.

If this makes the text too small or too large for the graph, enter a new Size value or increase the Vertical Scale number.

Using the Graph Data Window

After you drag with the graph tool (or click and enter the graph dimensions), the Graph Data window pops up on screen, as in Figure 8-4. This is not a dialog box—it's a window, which contains its own close box, collapse box, re-size box, and scroll bars. It is also more functional than a dialog box. You can click outside the Graph Data window to bring the illustration window to the front of the desktop. Although the Graph Data window may disappear from view, it remains open behind the illustration window, so that you don't lose any changes you may have made. To bring the Graph Data window back to the front of the desktop, click its title bar or choose the Object » Graphs » Data command from the Graph menu. Better yet, Ctrl-click or right-mouse-click and choose the Data command. (Alas, although Graph Data is for all intents and purposes an open window, Illustrator does not list it as an option on the Window menu.)

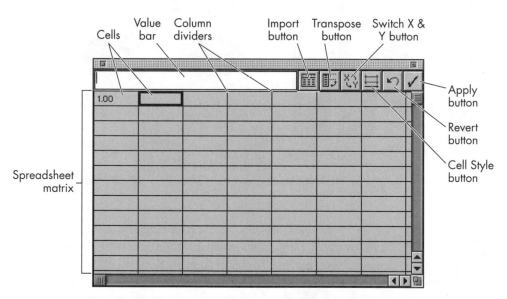

Figure 8-4: You enter data into a spreadsheet made up of rows and columns of cells in the Graph Data window.

The spreadsheet matrix that occupies most of the Graph Data window is similar to the matrix provided in a standard spreadsheet program like Excel. The spreadsheet contains rows and columns of individual containers, called *cells*. Numbers entered into the cells can represent dollars, times, dates, or percentages (though you should avoid symbols, such as $ and %, among others). You can even enter words for labels and legends.

Unlike a true spreadsheet, however, you cannot enter formulas in the spreadsheet matrix because Illustrator lacks a calculation feature. (You can't even take advantage of Illustrator's adding function, which works in many palettes and dialog boxes, including the little dialog box that opens when you click with the graph tool.)

Data entered from the keyboard appears in the value bar at the top of the spreadsheet (labeled in Figure 8-4). Press Return/Enter, the arrow keys, or Tab to transfer the data from the value bar into the current cell and advance to another cell.

As you type, most keys insert the standard characters that appear on the key. Some keys and characters, however, perform special functions:

- **Tab or right arrow:** Accepts the data in the value bar and moves one cell right (to the next cell in the row).

- **Left arrow:** Accepts the data in the value bar and moves one cell left.

- **Return/Enter or down arrow:** Accepts the data in the value bar and moves one cell down (to the next cell in the column).

- **Up arrow:** Accepts the data in the value bar and moves one cell up.

- **Quotation marks ("):** Enter straight quotation marks around numeric data to use a number as a label, such as a product number or year. If a cell consists entirely of numbers without quote marks, Illustrator interprets the data as a value and graphs it. If you want Illustrator to display the quotation marks in the graph, use the curly opening and closing marks, " and " (Opt/Alt-left bracket and Opt/Alt-Shift-left bracket), rather than the straight quotation marks.

- **Vertical line character (|):** If you want a label to contain multiple lines of text, enter the vertical line (Shift-\) to represent a line-break character. (Our typographically-savvy copy editor tells us the proper name for this is "bar" or "pipe." See, aren't you glad you decided to read this chapter?")

- **Keypad Return/Enter key:** Accepts the data in the value bar and selects the OK button, exiting the Graph Data window.

For most kinds of charts, you can enter legend text into the top row and labels into the left-hand column of cells. To create such graph text, delete the data from the very first cell (at the intersection of the first row and column) and leave it empty. All other cells in the top row and left column should contain at least one non-numeric character or quotation marks around the numbers, as shown in Figure 8-5.

If you don't want Illustrator to create a legend, enter a label or a value into the first cell and fill the top row of cells with values. If we deleted the first line of items from the matrix in Figure 8-5, for example, and scooted up the other rows, we would get labels but no legend.

	Hand Buzzers	X-Ray Specs	Sea Monkeys	
"1950"	32.57	77.60	45.70	
"1965"	34.44	92.50	69.90	
"1980"	36.84	12.04	93.60	
"1995"	39.34	15.55	62.34	

Figure 8-5: As long as the first cell is empty, you can use the top row and the left column to hold labels.

If after entering a label or legend text, you can't see the full text inside the cell, it isn't because the text is lost; the cell is just too narrow to display it. You can widen the cell by dragging a column divider (labeled in Figure 8-4) as described in the section "Changing the Way Cells Look" later in this chapter.

Importing Data from Disk

Because the Graph Data window provides no calculation capabilities and its cell-editing functions are limited—you can't insert, delete, or sort cells—you may prefer to import values created in another program. You can create your data in any spreadsheet program capable of saving a tab-delineated file, which is a plain text file with tabs between values and carriage returns between rows. Virtually every spreadsheet program supports this format, such as Microsoft Excel and Lotus 1-2-3. The file can originate on a PC just as easily as on a Mac.

You can even create your data in a word processor such as Microsoft Word or WordPerfect. When entering the data, insert tabs between values and insert carriage returns between rows of values. Then save the finished file as a plain text document.

To import data from disk, open the Graph Data window and click the cell where you want the imported data to start. Click the Import button to display the Import Graph Data dialog box, which behaves like the Open dialog box. Locate the file you want to import and double-click its name in the scrolling list, or select the file and press Return/Enter. The imported data appears in the spreadsheet in rows and columns starting in the selected cell.

 If any of the cells below or to the right of the selected cell already contain data, Illustrator replaces the old data with the new.

Selecting and Modifying Cells

You select cells in the spreadsheet by dragging across them. Or you can press the Shift key while pressing one of the arrow keys to add to a range of selected cells or delete from them. All selected cells become highlighted—white against black—except the cell that you're entering data into, which has a big, fat border around it.

Although you can't perform fancy tricks like inserting or deleting cells inside the Graph Data window, you can move data around within cells using one of the following techniques:

- Cut or copy data from one location and paste it into another. You can either use the keyboard shortcuts Cmd/Ctrl-X, Cmd/Ctrl-C, or Cmd/Ctrl-V; choose commands from the Edit menu; or access the commands from the context-sensitive pop-up menu that appears when you Ctrl-click.

 For example, to nudge all cells upward one row (the effect achieved by deleting a row in Excel), select the cells, press Cmd/Ctrl-X, click the first cell in the row you want to replace, and press Cmd/Ctrl-V.

- Click the Transpose button to swap rows and columns of data in the spreadsheet matrix. The data in the top row goes to the first column, and vice versa. This button affects all data in the spreadsheet, regardless of which cells, if any, are selected.

- Click the Switch XY button to swap columns of data in a scatter chart. The data in the first column moves to the second, the data in the second column moves to the first, the data in the third column moves to the fourth, and so on. This button is dimmed when you're creating or editing any kind of chart except a scatter chart, and it applies to all data in the spreadsheet.

You can delete the contents of multiple selected cells by choosing Edit » Clear or by pressing the Clear key. (Pressing the Delete key deletes the contents of the active cell only.)

⬤   Press Cmd/Ctrl-Z or choose Edit » Undo to undo the last operation—also easily accessed by Ctrl-clicking. If you just finished changing a cell value, for example, Cmd/Ctrl-Z restores the previous data in the value bar. As in the rest of Illustrator, you have multiple undos inside the Graph Data window, so edit with impunity. You can even undo large operations such as importing, transposing, or pasting data.

Copying Data from a Different Graph

The fact that the Graph Data window stays up on screen makes it easy to copy data from one graph and paste it into another. For example, suppose that you just dragged with the graph tool to start a new graph, and Illustrator has displayed the Graph Data window. Suddenly, you remember that you wanted to create this new chart based on a chart you created a few days ago. But you don't even have that old chart open right now. No problem. You can access the data without even closing the Graph Data window:

1.   Click in the illustration window to bring it to front. This gives you access to Illustrator's standard menu commands.

2.   Press Cmd/Ctrl-O and open the illustration that contains the chart that you want to copy.

3.   Select the chart with the arrow tool.

4.   If you can see a smidgen of the Graph Data window, click its title bar to bring it to front. Otherwise, choose Object » Graphs » Data or Graphs » Data from the context-sensitive pop-up menu. The Graph Data window shows the data for the selected graph.

5.   Drag over the data that you want to copy from the previous chart and press Cmd/Ctrl-C (or choose Edit » Copy).

6.   Click the title bar for the illustration window that contains the new chart in progress. If necessary, select the chart with the arrow tool.

7.   Click the Graph Data window again. When you bring the Graph Data window to front, it automatically shows the data for the selected chart.

8.   Click the first cell and press Cmd/Ctrl-V (or choose Edit » Paste). There's your data. Now you can edit it in any manner you deem appropriate.

You can copy as much data or as little data as you wish. To highlight the cells you want to copy, just drag over them. And click a cell before pressing Cmd/Ctrl-V to decide where you want the pasted data to start.

 Illustrator lets you paste any type into the Graph Data window. You can copy words or paragraphs from a block of text in the illustration window and paste them into a graph. You can also copy data from the spreadsheet and paste it into a text block.

Changing the Way Cells Look

The final adjustment that you can make to cells in the Graph Data window is purely cosmetic. The Cell Style button allows you to adjust both the width of the columns in the spreadsheet and the number of digits that follow a decimal point. These controls affect only the appearance of data in the spreadsheet; they do not affect the appearance of the chart in the illustration window.

Graph Data

	Hand	X-Ray	Sea		
"1950"	12.57	77.60	45.70		
"1965"	14.44	92.50	69.90		
"1980"	16.84	12.04	93.60		
"1995"	19.34	15.55	62.34		

Graph Data

	Hand	X-Ray Specs	Sea
"1950"	12.57	77.60	45.70
"1965"	14.44	92.50	69.90
"1980"	16.84	12.04	93.60
"1995"	19.34	15.55	62.34

Figure 8-6:
Drag a column divider (top) to change the width of a column of cells (bottom).

Click the Cell Style button to display a dialog box that contains the following two option boxes:

- **Number of Decimals:** Enter any value between 0 and 10 into the Number of Decimals option box. This option determines the number of significant digits—that is, the number of characters that can appear after a decimal point in a cell.

- **Column Width:** This value controls the default width of each cell in the Graph Data window, measured in digits. Enter any value between 1 and 20.

To adjust the width of a single column of cells, drag the corresponding column divider, as demonstrated in Figure 8-6. The column is widened or narrowed by the nearest whole-digit increment.

Transforming Your Data into a Graph

So far, we've instructed you to press the Return/Enter key to update the graph in the illustration window. But that isn't the only way to go. The Graph Data window provides many ways for you to update the graph; or you can exit the window without updating.

The following is a brief explanation of the update, exit, and reversion elements in the Graph Data window:

- **The Apply button (Opt/Alt-keypad Enter):** Click the Apply button or press Opt/Alt-Enter to update the graph in the illustration window without leaving the Graph Data window. If you can't see the graph because the Graph Data window is in the way, drag the Graph Data title bar to move the window partially off the screen. By keeping the Graph Data window up on the screen, you can quickly make changes if the data doesn't graph the way you hoped it would.

- **The Revert button:** Click Revert to restore the data that was in force the last time you clicked on the OK or Apply button.

- **Close box:** If you want to exit the Graph Data window without implementing your changes, click in the close box in the upper left corner of the window, and then click the Don't Save button in the alert box (or press the D key).

You can also cancel your modifications to a graph by simply selecting a different object in the illustration window or in a different drawing altogether. Illustrator displays an alert box asking you if you want to save your changes to the last graph. Press D if you don't want to, or press Return/Enter if you do.

You can undo the creation or alteration of a chart after clicking on the OK or Apply button by pressing Cmd/Ctrl-Z.

Organizing Your Data for Different Kinds of Graphs

You might hope that you could enter your data in any old way and have Illustrator graph it in the precise manner you've envisioned in your head, but Illustrator isn't quite so gifted at reading your mind. Therefore, you have to organize your data in a manner that Illustrator—mildly dictatorial program that it is—deems appropriate.

Just to keep you on your toes, Illustrator requires you to organize your data differently for different kinds of graphs. The following sections explore each of the nine kinds of graphs and tell you how to set up your data for each.

Column Chart Data

When creating a plain old everyday column graph—also called a grouped column chart for reasons that will become apparent as our graphing journey progresses—Illustrator expects you to organize your data in what we'll henceforth call "standard form." But before we tell you what that standard form is, a word or two about this classic kind of chart.

Column charts are most commonly used to demonstrate a change in data over a period of time. The horizontal axis (X-axis) may be divided into categories such as units of time (i.e., days, months, or years). The vertical axis (Y-axis) tracks values, which may be measured in units sold, dollars or other currency, or whatever your favorite commodity may be.

As shown in Figure 8-7, columns rise up from the X-axis to a height equivalent to a value on the Y-axis. The taller the column, the greater the value it represents.

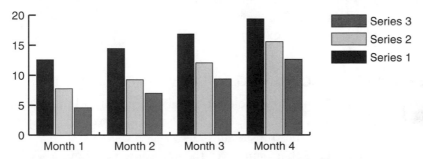

Figure 8-7: An example of a standard column chart, in which series of vertical columns are clustered together to show change in multiple items over time.

You can graph multiple collections of data in the chart. Each collection is called a series. Back in Figure 8-2, for example, Sea Monkeys, X-Ray Specs, and Hand Buzzers are each separate series. Corresponding columns from each series are clustered together for the sake of visual comparison. Hence, this type of chart is known in some circles as a cluster column chart.

By default, columns from different series are filled with different gray values (although you can apply your own colors using the direct selection tool, as we explain later in the chapter). The colors representing the series are defined in the legend, which appears in the upper right portion of Figure 8-7.

To create a column chart, arrange your data as shown in Figure 8-8. Here are a few details to keep in mind:

- Delete the contents of the first cell, and leave it empty.

- Enter series labels in the top row of cells. This text will appear in the legend.

- Enter X-axis labels in the left column. They will appear underneath the chart along the horizontal axis.

	Series 1	Series 2	Series 3	
Month 1	12.57	77.60	45.70	
Month 2	14.44	92.50	69.90	
Month 3	16.84	12.04	93.60	
Month 4	19.34	15.55	12.63	

Figure 8-8:
Organize column chart data into columns under series labels. This data corresponds to the column chart shown in Figure 8-7.

- Organize each series of data into a column under the appropriate series label. Do not enter any characters other than numbers. If you use a currency symbol, such as $, £, or ¢, Illustrator won't graph the value.

- Illustrator generates the Y-axis labels automatically, in accordance with the data. You can customize the Y-axis labels using options in the Graph Type dialog box, which we'll explain later.

Stacked Column Chart Data

Stacked column charts are much like column charts, except that columns from each series are stacked on top of one another rather than positioned side by side. A stacked column chart shows the sums of all series.

You can create a percentage chart similar to the one shown in Figure 8-9 by organizing your data so that all values for each series add up to 100. Percentage charts demonstrate relative performance. If Department A is trouncing Department B, you can broadcast the news with a percentage chart.

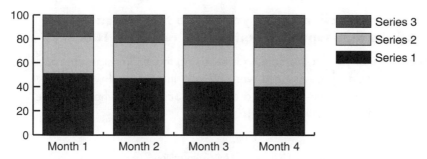

Figure 8-9: This percentage chart is a variety of the stacked column chart, in which each column of series values adds up to 100.

You arrange data for a stacked column chart in the standard form, with series labels in the top row and X-axis labels in the left column, as shown in Figure 8-10. Organize series of data into columns under the series labels. Whatever you do, don't enter a percentage symbol or any other non-numeric characters. If you do, Illustrator won't graph the value.

	Series 1	Series 2	Series 3	
Month 1	51.00	31.00	18.00	
Month 2	47.00	30.00	23.00	
Month 3	44.00	31.00	25.00	
Month 4	40.00	33.00	27.00	

Figure 8-10:
This data corresponds to the percentage chart shown in Figure 8-9. Notice that the values along each row add up to 100.

Illustrator can't automatically convert sales values to percentages, so you can either enter the percentages manually or make a program like Excel do the work.

To make Excel convert values to percentages, follow these steps:

1. Enter the sales values in Excel in the standard form.

Don't even think about percentages. Just enter normal values.

2. Select each row of values one at a time and click the AutoSum button.

Labeled in Figure 8-11, the AutoSum button looks like a sigma (*S*) in the ribbon bar. Excel creates a sum total for each row in the column after the selection (the bold items in the figure).

3.   Create a new cell in which you divide the first sales number by the first sum and multiply the result by 100.

Make sure that you fix the column letter using the dollar sign character. For example, if the first cell were B2 and the sum cell were E2— as they are in Figure 8-11—you'd enter *B2/$E2*100* (where / is the division symbol and * is multiply).

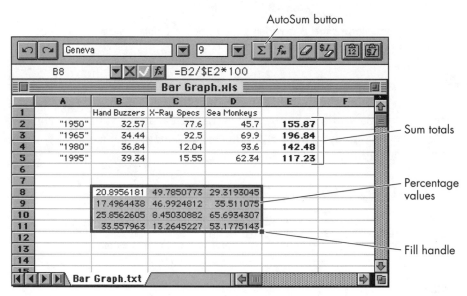

Figure 8-11: A collection of percentage values created in Excel 5 and ready to copy into Illustrator.

4.   Duplicate the formulas to the right and then down by dragging the fill handle.

The fill handle is that little square in the lower right corner of the selected cell (labeled in Figure 8-11). You drag it to the right and then drag down in two separate movements. This creates a matrix of new percentage values. They may not look like percentages—just a bunch of long numbers like the selected cells in Figure 8-11. But they'll work fine. And don't change the number formatting—remember, Illustrator can't read percent signs.

5.   Select the new percentage values and copy them.

Select the new data and copy it (Cmd/Ctrl-C).

6. Switch to Illustrator and paste the data.

Create a new stacked column chart, enter your own labels in the top row and left column. Starting in the second-to-top, second-to-left cell, paste (Cmd/Ctrl-V) after entering the labels.

7. Press the Return/Enter key.

You now have a percentage chart.

Bar Chart Data

Bar charts are the horizontal equivalents of column charts. Whereas columns move up to indicate increasing value, bars move to the right, as shown in Figure 8-12. You enter data into the Graph Data dialog box in the exact same manner that you do for a column chart. Illustrator automatically switches the category and value (i.e., X and Y) axis for you.

In previous versions of Illustrator, you could achieve a similar effect by rotating a column graph 90 degrees, but you then would have to add the labels and legend as separate text blocks. Now you can simply choose to display your data in this more leisurely form.

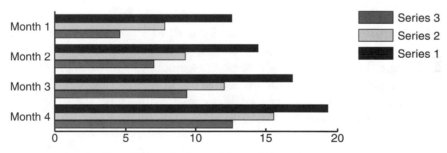

Figure 8-12: The bar chart is the lazy sibling of the column chart.

 You might think that you could convert a column chart into a bar chart by clicking on the Transpose button in the Graph Data dialog box. But this will not result in a bar chart. Instead, you will have a column chart in which the labels and legend are located in the wrong places.

Stacked Bar Chart Data

What is there to say when it comes to stacked bar charts? If you've seen a bar chart and a stacked column chart you can surmise the structure of a stacked bar chart. The picture you have in mind probably looks much like Figure 8-13. You can apply the same technique, explained above in the stacked column chart discussion, to your bar chart data.

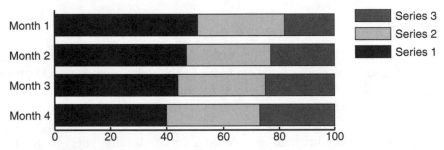

Figure 8-13: As seen here or in your mind's eye, a stacked bar chart fulfills all your horizontal bar stacking needs.

Line Chart Data

Like column charts, line charts are generally used to show changes in items over a period of time. Straight segments connect points representing values, as shown in Figure 8-14. Several straight segments combine to form a line, which represents a complete series. The inclination of a segment clearly demonstrates the performance of a series from one point in time to the next. Because large changes result in steep inclinations, line charts clearly show dramatic fluctuations.

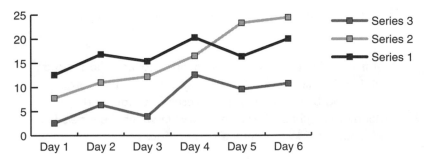

Figure 8-14: A line chart comprises straight segments connecting square value points.

Figure 8-15 shows the data used to create Figure 8-14. As with column charts, you organize the data into the standard form, with series labels at top, X-axis labels on the left, and columns of series data.

	Series 1	Series 2	Series 3	
Day 1	12.57	7.76	2.57	
Day 2	16.84	11.04	6.36	
Day 3	15.44	12.25	3.99	
Day 4	20.34	16.55	12.63	
Day 5	16.42	23.35	9.65	
Day 6	20.08	24.49	10.82	

Figure 8-15:
Here's the data for the line chart in Figure 8-14. Each column of numbers results in a single line.

 Although line chart data may fluctuate dramatically, you don't want series to cross each other more than one or twice in the entire chart. If the series cross too often, the result is what snooty graphing pros derisively call a "spaghetti chart," which is difficult to read and can prove more confusing than instructive.

 If you encounter the spaghetti effect (overlapping lines) when creating a line chart, the easiest solution is to convert the line chart into an area chart.

Area Chart Data

An area chart is little more than a filled-in line chart. However, the series of an area chart are stacked one on top of another—just as in a stacked column chart—to display the sum of all series, as shown in Figure 8-16.

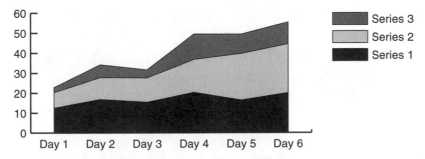

Figure 8-16: In an area chart, series are stacked on top of each other and filled in with colors or gray values.

When you create an area chart, arrange your data in the standard form. In fact, Figure 8-16 uses the same data as the line chart from Figure 8-14. The data appears in Figure 8-15.

Scatter Chart Data

Like a line chart, a scatter chart plots points on the horizontal and vertical axes and connects these points with straight segments. However, rather than merely aligning series of values along a set of X-axis labels, the scatter graph pairs up columns of values. The first column of data represents Y-axis (series) coordinates; the second column represents X-axis coordinates. This setup permits you to map scientific data or to graph multiple series that occur over different time patterns.

For example, in Figure 8-17, the black line (Series 1) connects 13 points, whereas the gray line (Series 2) connects 10. And yet both lines run the entire width of the graph. You tell Illustrator which X-axis and Y-axis coordinates to plot; Illustrator just connects them with segments. This is the most versatile kind of graph you can create.

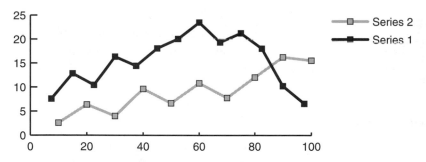

Figure 8-17: Illustrator plots points in a scatter graph at specific X,Y coordinates and connects the points with straight segments.

Figure 8-18 shows the data for the scatter chart in Figure 8-17. The data is arranged into pairs of columns, each pair representing a separate series.

- 🌐 Enter series labels into the top row of cells, one label for each odd column (first, third, fifth, and so on). Leave even-numbered cells empty. As with line charts, the series labels appear in the legend.

- 🌐 Enter Y-axis (series) data in the odd-numbered columns.

- 🌐 Enter X-axis data in the even-numbered columns. Illustrator plots side-by-side columns of data as paired points. In other words, each pair of values in the first and second columns is plotted as a point in the first series, each pair in the third and fourth columns is plotted as a point in the second series, and so on.

Illustrator automatically generates Y-axis and X-axis labels that correspond to the data.

Series 1		Series 2		
7.57	7.50	2.57	10.00	
12.84	15.00	6.36	20.00	
10.44	22.50	3.99	30.00	
16.34	30.00	9.63	40.00	
14.42	37.50	6.65	50.00	
18.08	45.00	10.82	60.00	
20.06	52.50	7.76	70.00	
23.49	60.00	12.04	80.00	
19.35	67.50	16.25	90.00	
21.26	75.00	15.55	100.00	
18.05	82.50			
10.24	90.00			
6.56	97.50			

Figure 8-18:
Each series of scatter chart data takes up two columns, with the Y-axis values first and the X-axis values second.

Pie Chart Data

A pie chart is the easiest kind of chart to create. However, pie charts are not nearly as versatile as the column and line varieties. Only one series can be expressed per pie. If you want to show more than one series for comparative purposes, each series gets a pie of its own, as shown in Figure 8-19.

The advantage of a pie chart is that it always displays a series of values in relation to the whole. The entire series inhabits a 360-degree circle, and each value within the series occupies a percentage of that circle.

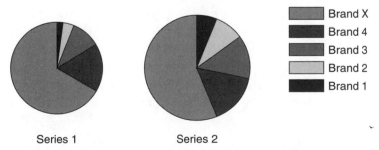

Figure 8-19: Two pie charts, each representing a single series. The first pie is smaller than the second because the second series includes larger values.

Figure 8-20 shows the data for the pies in Figure 8-19. You organize data for a pie chart in virtually the opposite way that you organize it for a column or line chart, with the series running across the rows instead of down the columns. Here are a few guidelines:

- Delete the contents of the first cell and leave it empty, just like always.

- Enter value labels in the top row of cells. These labels appear in the legend.

- Enter series labels in the left column. These labels appear as titles below the pies, as in Figure 8-19. (If you plan on graphing more than two series, we recommend you use a different kind of chart.)

- Organize each series of data into a row to the right of the series label.

	Brand 1	Brand 2	Brand 3	Brand 4	Brand X	
Series 1	0.98	1.56	4.07	6.76	26.57	
Series 2	3.24	4.67	6.99	8.25	29.34	

Figure 8-20: Organize pie chart data into rows. Each row represents a different pie.

 If you want to take a couple of series from a column chart and represent them inside pie charts, copy them from the spreadsheet for the column chart, paste them into the pie chart spreadsheet, and click the Transpose button to switch the rows and columns.

Radar Chart Data

Though big in Japan, the radar chart isn't as well recognized in the U.S. It resembles a spoked wheel with string running between the spokes. Though it may look more like a design than a functional graph, a radar chart, shown in Figure 8-21, is essentially a line chart rolled-up.

Because radar charts are closely related to line charts, we used the data from the line chart in Figure 8-14 to create the radar chart in Figure 8-21.

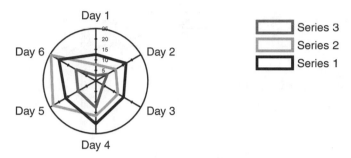

Figure 8-21: A non-Euclidean approach to line graphing.

Applying Automated Changes to a Graph

Remember the six basic steps required to create a graph in Illustrator? (If not, you can refresh your memory by peeking at the "Creating a Graph" section at the beginning of this chapter.) So far, we've exhausted the first four. Step 5 encouraged you to apply automated changes using the Graph Type dialog box. That's what these next sections are all about.

To access these options, select the graph you want to edit and double-click the graph tool icon in the toolbox, or choose Object » Graphs » Type, or Ctrl-click and choose Type. Illustrator displays the Graph Type dialog box, shown in Figure 8-22. This dialog box is quite complicated and provides access to a bunch of options that you don't see on first perusal, including two other dialog boxes.

 You can apply options from the Graph Type dialog box to an entire graph selected with the arrow tool or to a partial graph selected with the direct selection tool. For example, if you Opt/Alt-click three times on a straight segment in a previously deselected line graph with the direct selection tool, you select the entire series, including the color swatch in the legend. You can then modify that one segment independently of the others inside the Graph Type dialog box.

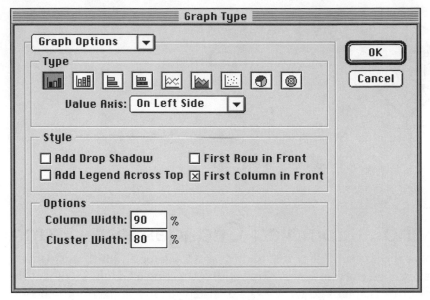

Figure 8-22: You can Control-click (Mac) or right-click (Windows) and choose Type to display the Graph Type dialog box, which lets you apply automated adjustments to a selected graph.

Converting and Tweaking a Graph

You can convert a selected graph from one variety to another—say, from a column chart to a line chart—by clicking on an icon from among the nine buttons along the top portion of the dialog box. Just click a button, press Return/Enter, and, whammo, the chart is changed.

There's an additional set of options in the bottom portion of the Graph Type dialog box. These specialized options change depending on which kind of graph you've selected.

The following list explains the options associated with each type of chart:

* **Column:** When you click the column button, two options appear in the Options area at the bottom of the Graph Type dialog box, as pictured in Figure 8-23. The Column Width value controls the width of each column in the chart. A value of 100 percent causes columns to touch each other, rubbing shoulders, as it were. The default value of 90 percent allows slight gutters between columns, and values greater than 100 percent cause columns to overlap.

  The second option, Cluster Width, controls the width of each cluster of columns, again measured as a percentage value. The last column from

Series 1 touches the first column of series 2 at 100 percent. The default value of 80 percent allows a gutter between clusters. (We don't recommend using values greater than 100 percent because they cause clusters not only to overlap each other but to overlap the vertical axis as well. Frankly, it can be mighty ugly.)

Stacked Column: The Options area contains the same options listed above, whether you select a grouped or stacked column chart (see Figure 8-23).

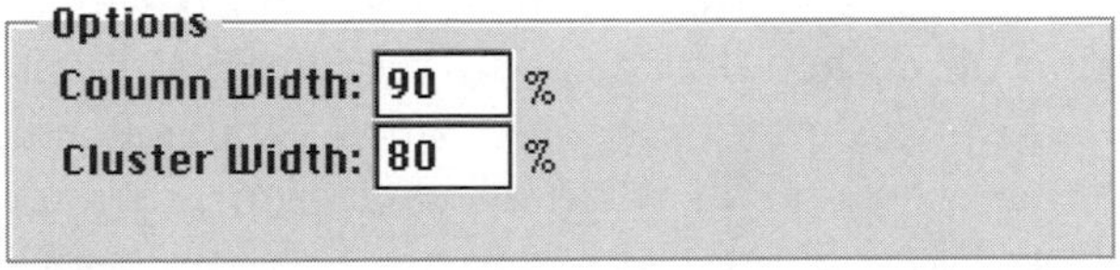

Options
Column Width: 90 %
Cluster Width: 80 %

Figure 8-23: Use these options to control the width of columns and clusters of columns in a chart.

Bar: Click this button and the Options area changes slightly, as shown in Figure 8-24. The Bar Width option allows you to control how wide the bars should be, just as the Column Width option did for columns. The Cluster Width option works the same way as above.

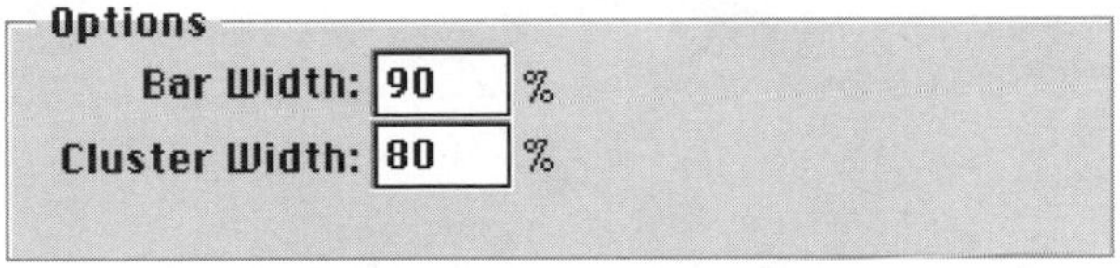

Options
Bar Width: 90 %
Cluster Width: 80 %

Figure 8-24: Use these options to change the width of bars and clusters of bars in a bar chart.

Stacked Bar: These options look and work the same as those for the bar chart (see Figure 8-24).

Line: When you click the Line chart button, four check boxes appear in the Options area, as shown in Figure 8-25. Select the Mark Data Points check box to create square markers at the data points in each line. Turn off the check box to make the square markers disappear. Select the Connect Data Points check box and Illustrator will draw straight segments between points. Deselect this option and stray markers appear without lines. (Turn off both check boxes to make the series disappear entirely.)

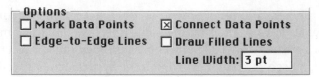

Figure 8-25: Use these options to change the square points and straight segments associated with line graphs (and scatter charts).

When you select Connect Data Points, the Draw Fill Lines check box becomes available, which lets you create thick paths filled with gray values or colors. Enter the desired thickness into the Line Width option box. Figure 8-26 shows a line graph with paths 12 points thick. Generally, you don't need data points when using fat paths, so you can turn off the Mark Data Points check box.

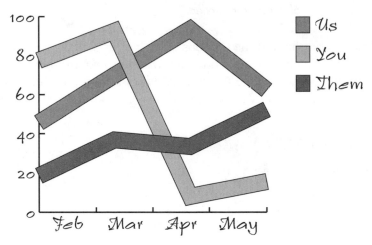

Figure 8-26: A line graph with the Fill Lines check box selected, the Width value set to 12 points, Mark Data Points unselected, and the Edge-To-Edge Lines selected.

Select Edge-to-Edge Lines to draw lines that extend the entire width of the chart, starting at the Y-axis and continuing to the end of the X-axis. This option is turned on in Figure 8-26. (By default, it is off.)

Area: There are no special options associated with an area chart. It would be nice if Illustrator provided at least the Edge-to-Edge check box to eliminate the gaps between the data lines and the Y-axis; but alas, no such option exists.

Scatter: When you click the Scatter Graph Type button, three check boxes appear in the Options area. These are the same options that appear for a line graph, as shown in Figure 8-25, except the Edge-to-Edge check box does not appear here.

Pie: When you click this button, the Options area grants you three pop-up menus for editing a pie chart. Pictured in Figure 8-27, these commands let you change the placement of the pie labels (using the Legend pop-up commands), the size of the graphs (using the Position pop-up commands), and the method by which each chart is sorted (using the Sort pop-up commands). By default, the Standard Legend command is selected in the Legend Options pop-up menu, which results in a typical legend that identifies the gray values and colors in the graph. If you instead choose the Legends in Wedges command, Illustrator omits the legend and labels the pie slices directly, as in Figure 8-28. (You'll have to modify the colors of the slices to see the labels, as in the figure—the first slice is black by default.) Choose No Legends to trash the legend altogether.

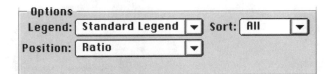

Figure 8-27: You can change the way slices are labeled when editing a pie chart.

The Position Options pop-up menu is oddly named because it offers three commands that have more to do with the size of the pie chart that its position. The Ratio command, the default, causes multiple pies to display according to each pie's total value, as shown in the top left of Figure 8-29. Choose the Even command to make all pies the same size, as shown in the bottom left of Figure 8-29. Finally, you can choose the Stacked command to display your pies concentrically as a single pie-a-licious chart, shown at the right in Figure 8-29. All three variations in the figure below use the same graph data.

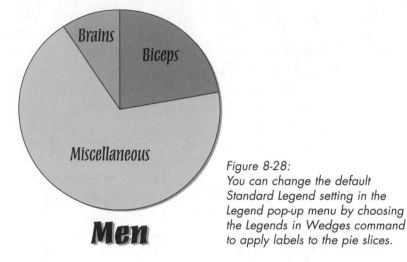

Figure 8-28:
You can change the default
Standard Legend setting in the
Legend pop-up menu by choosing
the Legends in Wedges command
to apply labels to the pie slices.

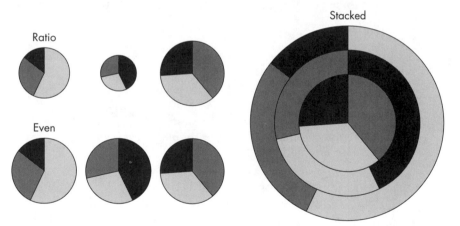

Figure 8-29: These three sets of pie charts demonstrate the different Position
commands. The Sort All command is used for all three.

By choosing a command from the Sort Options menu, you can orient
the pie chart. Think of the individual pies as "clocks" and the dividing
lines between the categories as marking off the time. No matter how
you choose to sort a pie chart, one of the dividing lines will point at the
12:00 position, as you can see in Figure 8-30. The piece that extends
clockwise from this dividing line is determined by the Sort Options
commands. The top-row pie charts result when you choose the Sort All
command. The largest piece in each individual pie is the first slice; thus,
each pie chart could have a different first piece. The middle-row charts

result from you choosing the Sort First command—"Sort by Largest" would be a more appropriate name. When you choose this command, the first piece for all the pies is determined by the category with the largest total value. If you create a pie graph that consists of only one piece, the Sort All and Sort First commands render the same results. The bottom-row charts reflect the usage of the Sort None command—another poorly-named command. Here all the pies lead off with the piece that represents the value of the first category (i.e., the first column in the Graph Data window). Once again, all three graphs share the same graph data.

Radar: Click the Radar button to use all the same options that you'd have with a line chart. Feel free to re-gander Figure 8-25.

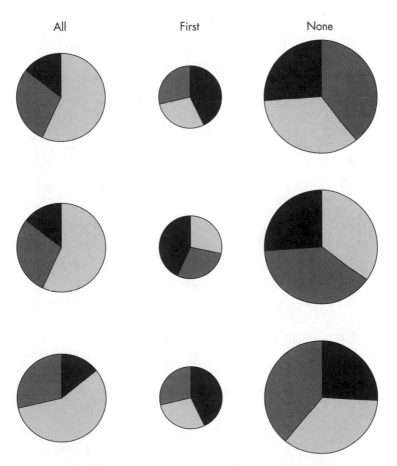

Figure 8-30: Illustrator relies on the Sort Options command to determine which category takes first position in a particular pie chart.

Adjusting Axes and Labels

You use the Value Axis pop-up menu located below the buttons in the Graph Type dialog box to control the appearance and positions of the vertical and horizontal axes in a selected chart. This command is dimmed when you're working on a pie chart, because pie charts have no axes, and only one command exists when editing a radar chart. The same basic collection of commands is available for all other charts.

Use the following commands to control the placement of the vertical Y-axis for the column, stacked column, bar, stacked bar, and scatter graphs:

- **On Left Side:** Select this command to make the Y-axis appear on the left side of the chart, as it does by default. You can then modify the axis by choosing the Value Axis command from the main pop-up menu at the top of the Graph Type dialog box.

- **On Right Side:** Select this command to send the Y-axis to the right side of the chart. Again, modify the axis by choosing the Value Axis command. The On Right Side command is not available for scatter graphs.

- **On Both Sides:** Select this command to make the Y-axis appear on both sides of the chart. You can't create a chart with two different Y-axes, as you can in more sophisticated graphing programs.

The bar and stacked bar charts offer two slightly different commands:

- **On Top Side:** Choose this command to make the value axis stretch across the top of the selected graph.

- **On Bottom Side:** Choose this command, the default setting for bar and stacked bar graphs, to extend the value axis along the bottom.

After you have set the position of the value axis, you'll want to explore the other options Illustrator has for your value-axis-modifying pleasures. Choose the Value Axis command from the main pop-up menu at the top of the Graph Type dialog box. One of the Graph Type dialog box's alter egos will display, as shown in Figure 8-31. Here you can specify the location of tick marks and labels on the value axis. The options in the Add Labels and Tick Values areas affect the labels for the value axis, whereas the options in the Tick Marks area control the size of tick marks, those little lines that indicate numbers along the axes.

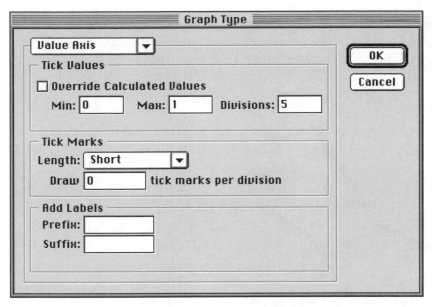

Figure 8-31: Choosing the Value Axis command shuttles you this version of the Graph Type dialog box, in which you can modify labels and tick marks on the value axis.

We first encounter some nutty options related to the occurrence of tick marks:

Override Calculated Values: By default, this check box is selected. Unless you deselect it, Illustrator automatically determines the number of tick marks and labels that appear on the axis without worrying your pretty head about it.

Min, Max, and Divisions: If you want to specify a range of labels in an axis to enhance the appearance of a chart, deselect the Override Calculated Values check box and enter values into the three option boxes. The Min value determines the lowest number on the axis, the Max value determines the highest number, and the Divisions value determines the increment between labels.

In Figure 8-32, we raised the Min value to 50 and changed the Divisions value to 10. Illustrator now graphs any data values under 50 below the X-axis. This way, we can track poor performance. For example, this chart says you can take Them off probation, but you're going to have to fire You.

To turn a chart upside down, so that the highest number is at the bottom of the axis and the lowest number is at the top (as in Figure 8-33), enter a negative value in the Divisions option box. To create an axis without labels, enter 0 in this option box.

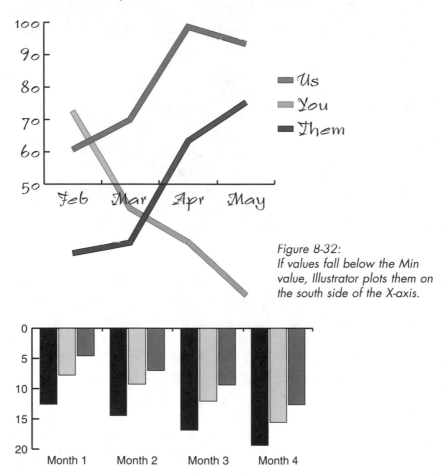

Figure 8-32:
If values fall below the Min value, Illustrator plots them on the south side of the X-axis.

Figure 8-33: Flip a chart upside down by entering a negative value in the Divisions option box.

You use this set of commands to change the tick marks' appearance:

- **Length:** You can choose a length of None, Short, and Full Width for your tick marks from this pop-up menu. Choose None to display no tick marks on the current axis. This command does not affect the placement or appearance of labels. Choose Short to display short tick marks that extend from the axis toward the chart, as by default. Choose Full Width to create tick marks that extend the full width or height of the chart. Figure 8-34 shows the result of choosing the Full Width command.

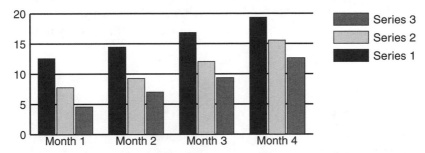

Figure 8-34: Select the Full Width command to extend the tick marks across the entire chart.

● **Draw __ Tick Marks per Division:** This option should read "Tick Marks per Label," because it allows you to control the number of tick marks per labeled increment. In Figure 8-35, we've applied a value of 4 to the vertical axis, which creates four tick marks per label.

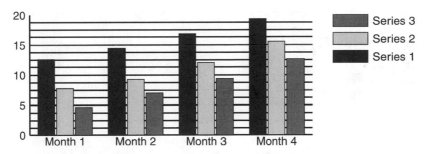

Figure 8-35: The same chart after entering a value of 4 into the Draw __ Tick Marks per Division option box.

You use these options to add labels to a chart:

● **Add Labels Prefix/Suffix:** These option boxes let you enter symbols or words up to nine characters long to precede or follow each label in a chart. For example, enter $ in the Prefix option box to precede every label with a dollar sign, as shown in Figure 8-36. Enter the letter g in the Suffix option box to indicate that each value is in thousands of dollars.

Now that you've perfected your value axis, choose the Category Axis command from the main pop-up menu at the top of the Graph Type dialog box and display the other version of this dialog box, as shown in Figure 8-37. Choose this command, that is, provided you aren't editing a radar chart or a scatter graph. With a radar graph, you're limited to the Value Axis options (as discussed above) and with a scatter chart, you get the Bottom Axis command that takes you to a dialog box with the exact options list above.

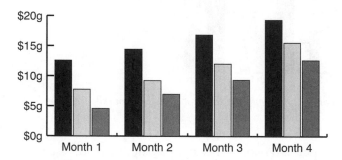

Figure 8-36: Enter characters to precede and follow the labels, such as the $ and g shown here, using the Prefix and Suffix option boxes.

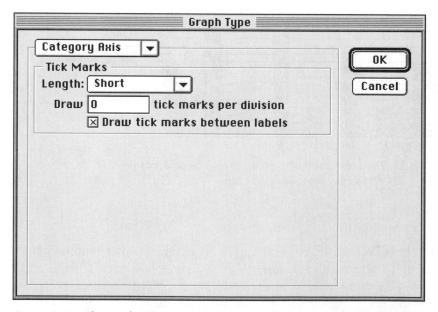

Figure 8-37: Choose the Category Axis command to open this mostly empty version of the Graph Type dialog box, where you can change the tick marks on the category axis.

The Tick Marks Length and the Draw __ Tick Marks per Division options that you see here are the same as the ones first shown back in Figure 8-31. You'll find one new option here:

● **Draw Tick Marks Between Labels:** When this check box is selected— as it is by default—tick marks appear centered between labels, as demonstrated by the vertical lines in the leftmost example of Figure 8-38. If you turn off the option, each tick mark is centered above its label, as shown in the rightmost example of Figure 8-38.

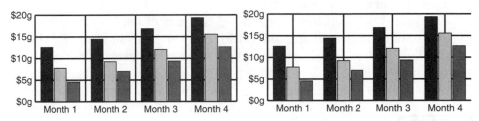

Figure 8-38: When working on a column, bar, line, or area chart, deselect the Draw Tick Lines Between Labels check box to create tick marks directly above the labels along the horizontal axis, as seen in the example on the right.

Other Weird Graph Style Options

Now that we've polished off the Value Axis and the Category Axis versions of the Graph Type dialog box, let's return to the plain and tall Graph Type dialog box (shown in Figure 8-22) to explore four remaining options, all of which are more or less useless. We refer, of course, to the Style check boxes in the middle portion of the dialog box—Add Drop Shadow, Add Legend Across Top, First Row in Front, and First Column in Front. These dorky options work as follows:

● **Add Drop Shadow:** Select this check box to create drop shadows behind the columns, bars, lines, pie slices, or areas in a chart. This option is easily one of the dopiest in all of Illustrator. The drop shadow is always black, and you can't modify the distance between the shadow and the graph elements. You can more easily create your own drop shadow by selecting a few elements, copying them (Cmd/Ctrl-C), pasting them in back (Cmd/Ctrl-B), nudging them into the desired position with the arrow keys, and applying a fill color.

● **Add Legend across Top:** This option moves the legend from the right side of the chart to the top of the chart. The text is listed horizontally instead of vertically. Unfortunately, Illustrator has a nasty habit of overlapping text when you select this option, particularly when more than three series are involved. You're better off moving the legend manually.

- **First Row in Front:** Select this check box to layer elements representing rows of data in the selected chart in descending order, with the first row in front and the last row in back. This option is useful only when modifying a column or bar chart in which the Cluster Width is set to greater than 100 percent. Because each row of data equates to a cluster, you can modify which cluster appears in front and which appears in back.

- **First Column in Front:** Finally, a halfway useful option! Select this option to layer elements representing columns of data (we're talking series, here) in descending order, with the first series in front and the last series in back. This option works with any chart except a pie chart. But it is most useful when editing a line or scatter chart, because it allows you to prioritize the manner in which lines overlap.

Do not turn off the First Column in Front check box when editing an area chart. If you do, the last series will completely cover all other series in the chart.

Manually Customizing a Graph

If you've been reading this chapter sequentially, your brain is undoubtedly a little numb by now. Either that, or you've been reading the book in bed in lieu of a sedative. Let's face it, taking in Illustrator's half-million graphing options is a daunting—not to mention boring—task.

That's why it may come as a welcome shock that one tool—the direct selection tool—is more capable than every option in all the Graph Type dialog boxes combined. Armed with the direct selector, you can move elements around, apply different colors, edit the size of text and legend swatches, and just plain customize the heck out of your graph.

Selecting Elements Inside Graphs

To get anywhere with the direct selection tool, you need to understand how to select elements inside a graph. A graph is actually an extensive collection of grouped objects inside grouped objects, inside other grouped objects, which are—needless to say—grouped. This means a lot of Opt/Alt-clicking with the direct selection tool.

The following list demonstrates a few of the different kinds of selections you can make with the direct selection tool:

- Click a point or segment in the graph to select that specific element. You can then move the point or segment. However, you cannot delete it by pressing the Delete key, because that would leave a gap in the path, and Illustrator does not permit gaps in graphs.

- Click a text object to select it. All text in a graph is point text, so be sure to click along the baseline of the text (not on one of the letters). You can then change the font, type size, alignment, and half a dozen other formatting attributes without affecting any deselected text in the graph.

- Opt/Alt-click to select a whole object in the chart, such as an axis or a column.

- Opt/Alt-click a second time to select an entire axis, including tick marks and labels, or to select an entire series. If you Opt/Alt-click some text a second time, you select all text belonging to that subgroup in the graph. For example, Opt/Alt-clicking some legend text twice selects all legend text.

- Opt/Alt-click a column three times to select an entire series as well as its color swatch in the legend. Now you can apply a different color from the Paint Style palette to modify the fill or stroke of the series.

- Opt/Alt-click a fourth time to select all series and legend swatches in the chart.

- Opt/Alt-click a fifth time to select the entire chart.

This is a rather imprecise science, and different kinds of charts require a different number of Opt/Alt-clicks, depending on how many series are involved and other factors. For example, you may find you need to Opt/Alt-click only twice to select a series and its legend swatch in a line chart, whereas you had to Opt/Alt-click three times in a column chart. Keep an eye on the screen as you Opt/Alt-click to monitor your progress.

Selecting Multiple Series Inside a Graph

Another handy key to keep in mind when selecting graph elements is Shift. As you know, you can press this key to select multiple objects, but pressing it just as easily deselects objects. Therefore, you have to be deliberate in your actions, particularly when the Opt/Alt key is involved.

For example, suppose you want to select two series of columns in a column chart, including their swatches in the legend. Here's how you'd do it:

1. **Using the direct selection tool, Opt/Alt-click a column in the chart.**

    This selects the column.

2. **Opt/Alt-click the column again.**

    This second click selects all other columns in the series.

3. **Opt/Alt-click the column a third time.**

    Now the legend swatch becomes selected.

4. **Opt/Alt-Shift-click a column in a different series.**

    Illustrator adds this new column to the growing collection of selected objects.

5. **Opt/Alt-click that same column again.**

    This is the important step, the one that baffles thousands of users on a daily basis. If you Opt/Alt-Shift-click again, you deselect the column; but without the Shift key, you can't add to the selection, right?

    Wrong. So long as the item on which you Opt/Alt-click is selected, Illustrator broadens the selection to include the next group up. Therefore, this Opt/Alt-click selects the other columns in this series.

6. **Opt/Alt-click this column for a third time.**

    This selects the swatch for the series in the legend. You now have two entire series of columns selected independently of any other series in the graph.

It's operations like this that make users of other programs, including FreeHand, roll their eyes and utter nasty comments. Not that FreeHand has a better method for dealing with this situation—FreeHand doesn't even offer a graphing function—it's just that Illustrator's methods seem so complicated.

But the truth is, this operation makes absolute sense once you understand the order of the Illustrator universe. These steps may be cumbersome, but they are impeccably logical. Come to terms with these steps and you'll never have problems selecting objects inside Illustrator again. The good news is, it simply doesn't get more complicated than this.

You can also switch selected series to a different chart type, as in Figure 8-39. This chart started off as a column chart, but Deke wanted to highlight his client's product, Hand Buzzers. Therefore, we decided to convert the Sea Monkeys and X-Ray Specs series to line graphs. We first selected both series, as outlined in the previous steps, and double-clicked the graph tool to display the Graph Type dialog box. We then selected the Line button from the Type options, modified the Line Graph Options, and pressed Return/Enter. log box.

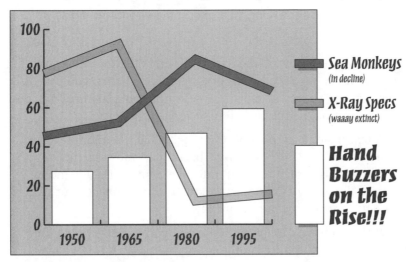

Figure 8-39: Starting from a column chart, Deke converted two of the series to line graphs.

Deke didn't stop there. In fact, he ended up ungrouping the graph to achieve some of the effects. To create the faded intersection between the X-Ray Specs line and the Hand Buzzer columns, he cloned the shapes and combined them using Filter » Pathfinder » Intersect, as explained in Chapter 9. He also added drop shadows behind the legend swatches, another technique covered in Chapter 9. Like any other kind of art you can create in Illustrator, graphs are limited only by your creativity, ingenuity, and patience.

More Custom Modification Options

Once you figure out how to select items in graphs with some degree of pre-dictability, you'll discover hundreds of methods for altering them. Rather than wasting reams of paper stepping you through every possible variation, here are a few parting tidbits of wisdom to whisk you on your way:

You should edit your legend after creating a graph, because it probably is the wrong size and in the wrong position.

The text and swatches in the legend are parts of several different subgroups, but because they are physically separated from other graph elements, you can easily select them by marqueeing them with the direct selection tool. Then you can drag them anywhere you want or use the scale tool to reduce their size.

- You can edit text inside a graph with the type tool, as we did in Figure 8-39. But be careful; if you have to go back later and edit the data, Illustrator restores the text entered into the Graph Data window. (Unfortunately, Illustrator is not smart enough to implement your text changes into the spreadsheet automatically.)

- You can edit paths inside a graph with the add point, delete point, and convert point tools without first ungrouping the path. Again, changes that you made inside the Graph Data window or Graph Type dialog box may override these adjustments.

Graphing with Graphics

What kind of illustration program would Illustrator be if it didn't allow you to create graphs with pictures? In a valiant effort to satisfy you, the customer, Illustrator lets you create pictographs, which are graphs in which series are rep-resented by graphic objects. The graphics can form columns in a column chart, like the cent symbols in Figure 8-40, or they can appear as markers in a line or scatter chart. The following sections describe how pictographs work.

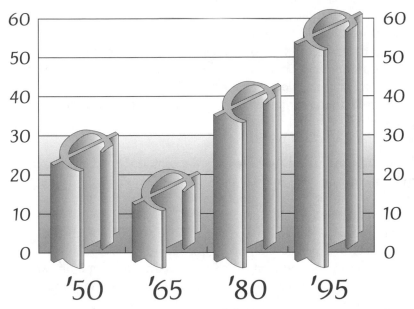

Figure 8-40: Using Illustrator's pictograph feature, you can create graph designs and apply them to column, bar, line, and scatter graphs.

Creating a Graph Design

You create pictographs by establishing graph designs—collections of graphic objects that can be applied to a chart. The following steps describe how to transform a few common, everyday objects into a graph design in Illustrator:

1. **Draw the objects and fill them as desired.**

   Figure 8-41 shows how we constructed the objects in the cent chart. Many of the tools and commands we used are covered in later chapters.

   We started with a large Palatino character and converted it to paths (example 1 in the figure). Then we rotated and slanted it with the rotate and shear tools (2). Next we selected several points and segments along the outline of the shape by clicking and Shift-clicking at the spots indicated by the arrowheads in the figure (3). We copied the selected elements to the Clipboard (Cmd/Ctrl-C), pressed Cmd/Ctrl-Shift-A to deselect the elements, and chose Edit » Paste in Front (Cmd/Ctrl-F).

   We dragged the selected items down to a point at which we could more easily work on them. Then we Shift-Opt/Alt-dragged them downward to clone them (4). These open paths represent the tops and bottoms of the sides coming down from the cent sign back in Figure 8-40; all we had to do was connect them with straight segments. To do this, we used the direct selection tool to select the endpoints of corresponding paths (like the selected points in example 4 in the figure) and chose Object » Path » Join (Cmd/Ctrl-J). Then we Opt/Alt-clicked the newly joined path with the direct selection tool to select the whole path and pressed Cmd/Ctrl-J again. This was repeated for each pair of paths.

Finally, we selected all the paths (except the cent itself) and filled them with gradations from the Gradient palette (5). We also had to fill the interior of the cent sign with a gradation, but because the path was serving as a hole in the cent sign, we had to make a duplicate. We selected it, copied it (Cmd/Ctrl-C), pressed Cmd/Ctrl-Shift-A to deselect everything, and pasted the path in front (Cmd/Ctrl-F). Then we filled it with the same gradation as the other paths. To finish it off, we dragged the sides up to the cent outline so sides and cent snapped into alignment.

2. **Draw a straight, horizontal line across the middle of the portion of the graph you want Illustrator to elongate when applying the design to a column chart.**

If you're designing a marker for a line graph, you don't need to add this horizontal line, and you can skip to Step 4.

Use the pen tool to draw a horizontal line slightly wider than the graph design by clicking at one point and Shift-clicking at another. Then position the line along the spot where any stretching should occur. For example, we created the line in about the middle of the sides of the cent symbol, as indicated by the dotted line in Figure 8-42. Doing this tells Illustrator to stretch the sides, not the cent symbol itself.

3. **Select the horizontal line and choose View » Make Guides.**

Or press the memorable shortcut Cmd/Ctrl-5. (Can you hear the sarcasm?) The line becomes dotted (or solid, depending on the settings in your Guides & Grids Preferences dialog box), as pictured in Figure 8-42. Also, make sure View » Lock Guides is turned off. If the Lock command has a check mark next to it, choose the command to unlock the guide. Illustrator requires that you convert the line to a guide for the stretching function to work. (For more about guides, turn to Chapter 10.)

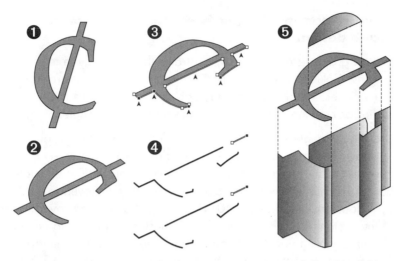

Figure 8-41: The steps involved in creating a cent symbol with mock 3-D sides.

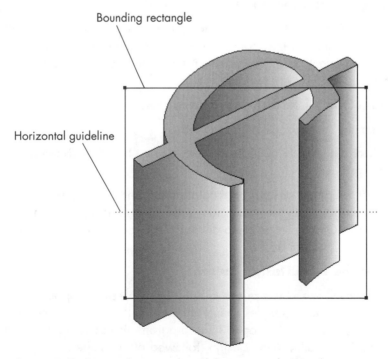

Figure 8-42: Draw a horizontal guideline across the stretchy portion of the graph design and then create a rectangle to demonstrate the design's boundaries.

4. **Draw a rectangle to specify the boundaries of the graph design.**

   Where graphs are concerned, Illustrator thinks largely in terms of rectangles. Columns are rectangles, for example, and line graph markers are squares. When creating a graph design, you have to tell Illustrator how the design fits onto the standard rectangle.

   Use the rectangle tool to draw a boundary around the graph design as shown in Figure 8-42. If the rectangle doesn't completely enclose the design, the design may overlap graph elements. For example, this design extends below the rectangle; therefore it will overlap the X-axis, as it does back in Figure 8-40. The design also extends over the top of the rectangle, so it will rise slightly higher than the data value. (If you're feeling very strict about your data, make sure the top of the rectangle exactly touches the top of the graph design.) The fact that the rectangle is wider than the design, however, keeps the design slightly slimmer than a standard column.

5. **Send the rectangle to the back of the illustration.**

   Choose Object » Arrange » Send To Back, or press Cmd/Ctrl-Shift-[(left bracket). This may sound like an inconsequential step, but it's very important. Illustrator insists on the boundary rectangle being in back.

6. **Make the fill and stroke transparent.**

   Select the None icon in the toolbox.

7. **Select all graph objects and choose Object » Graphs » Design.**

   Select the graph design, horizontal guide, and rectangle. (If these are the only objects in the illustration, press Cmd/Ctrl-A.) Then choose Object » Graphs » Design to display the Graph Design dialog box shown in Figure 8-43.

8. **Click the New Design button.**

   Illustrator shows you a preview of the graph design cropped inside your bounding rectangle, as in Figure 8-43. (Don't worry, the actual graph design is not cropped.) The program also adds an item to the scrolling list called New Design, followed by a number.

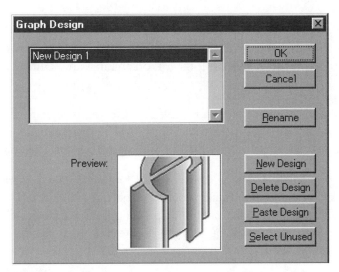

Figure 8-43: Illustrator crops the preview in the Graph Design dialog box to reflect the top and bottom edges of the bounding rectangle.

If Illustrator complains when you click New Design, it's because the rectangle is not the backmost object you've selected. It may be because you didn't properly follow Step 5, or it may be that you accidentally selected other objects farther back yet. In any case, press Escape to close the dialog box, press Cmd/Ctrl-Shift-A to deselect everything, select the rectangle, cut it (Cmd/Ctrl-X), make sure the arrow tool is active, and paste the rectangle in back (Cmd/Ctrl-B). Now try Steps 7 and 8 again.

9. Enter a name for the design and press Return/Enter.

The graph design is now ready to apply to any column, bar, line, or scatter graph.

 Your new graph design is available only to the illustration you created it in. If you want to make a graph design available to all future illustrations whether this particular document is open or not, open the Adobe Illustrator Startup file in the Plug-ins folder. Then choose Object » Graphs » Design to display the Graph Design dialog box, and click the Paste Design button. This creates a copy of the design inside the Startup file. Press Return/Enter to leave the dialog box, move the design to a suitable spot in the illustration window (but don't delete it!), and save the Startup file to disk.

Organizing Graph Designs

In addition to allowing you to create new graph designs, the Graph Design dialog box provides the following options for organizing and editing existing graph designs:

- **Delete Design:** Click this button to delete a selected design from the scrolling list. Illustrator removes the design from all open illustrations! Therefore, don't delete a design when a graph using the design is open.

 If you delete a design and you didn't mean to, press Escape or click the Cancel button to cancel the operation. If you realize your mistake only after pressing Return/Enter or clicking the OK button, you can still restore the graph design by pressing Cmd/Ctrl-Z.

- **Paste Design:** Even if you throw away the original copy of your graph design, it may not be lost for good. So long as the design has been applied to a graph, you can retrieve the original objects. Inside the Graph Design dialog box, select the design name from the list and click the Paste Design button. Illustrator pastes the original objects into the illustration window. Then press Return/Enter to close the dialog box and edit the objects as desired. (If you leave the dialog box by pressing the Escape key, Illustrator cancels the paste operation.)

- **Select Unused:** Click this button to select all designs that are not applied to graphs in any open illustration. Then you can click the Delete Design button to get rid of them.

After you edit the pasted objects, you can redefine the graph design and all open graphs that use the design. Select the objects and choose Object » Graphs » Design. Then select the design name from the list and press Return/Enter or click the OK button. (That's it; no special buttons to press.) Illustrator displays an alert box asking if you want to redraw all graphs or just redefine the graph design for future graphs. Press Return/Enter to do both.

You can rename a pattern by clicking on the Rename button. In the Rename dialog box, enter a new name and click OK or hit Return/Enter.

Applying a Design to a Column Chart

To apply a design to a column chart or a stacked column chart, select the column chart with the arrow tool or select the single series that you want to convert to a pictograph with the direct selection tool. Then choose Object » Graphs » Column to display the Graph Column dialog box shown in Figure 8-44.

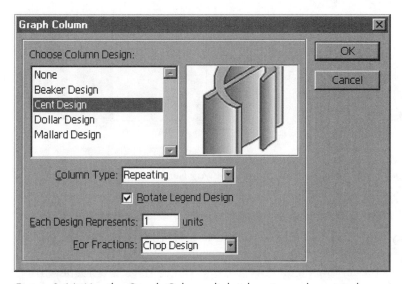

Figure 8-44: Use the Graph Column dialog box to apply a graph design to a column chart.

Select a graph design from the scrolling Choose Column Design list (select None only when you want to remove a graph design from the selected series), choose a command from the Column Type pop-up menu, and press the Return/Enter key. Illustrator applies the design to all selected series.

The Column Type pop-up menu allows you to change the way Illustrator stretches or repeats the graph design from one column to the next. Figure 8-45 demonstrates the effect of the four options in the order they appear in the dialog box. Here's how each option works:

- **Vertically Scaled:** Choose this command to stretch the graph design vertically to represent different values, as demonstrated at the top of Figure 8-45. Notice that in the case of the cent symbol, Illustrator stretches both the sides and the cent outline itself. This is sometimes useful, though it's not the best match for the cent design.

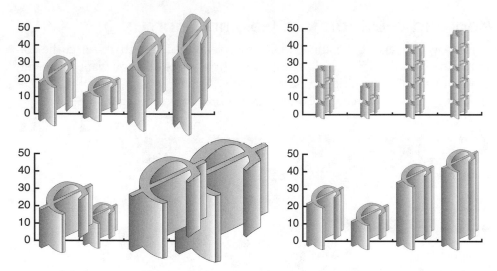

Figure 8-45: The Vertically Scaled (top left), Uniformly Scaled (bottom left), Repeating (top right), and Sliding (bottom right) options change the way Illustrator applies a graph design to a column chart.

Uniformly Scaled: Select this command to scale the graph design proportionally according to the size of the data, as shown in the second example on the left in Figure 8-45. Large values have a tendency to take over the graph; this option is useful primarily when your data has little variation.

Repeating: If you want to repeat the graph design over and over again, choose this command. Illustrator creates stacks of the object, as in the example at the upper right in Figure 8-45. This style of pictograph is very popular—you can stack coins, dollar bills, cars, footballs, computer monitors…anything you want.

When the Repeating command is selected, the otherwise-dimmed For Fractions pop-up menu becomes available. Enter a value in the Each Design Represents option box to determine the data increment represented by each repetition of the graph design. For example, if a value in the selected series is 49, and you enter 10 for the Each Design Represents value, the design repeats four full times and a fifth partial time, just like the last column in the figure.

The two For Fractions commands determine how Illustrator slices or scales the last graph design to accommodate remaining data that doesn't divide evenly into the Each Design Represents value. Select the Chop

Design command to lop off the extraneous top design, as in Figure 8-45; select the Scale Design command to vertically scale the top design to fit its fractional value.

Sliding: Select this option to elongate the graph design at the spot indicated by the horizontal guideline, as in the final example at the lower right in Figure 8-45. This is usually the most desirable option, and it certainly looks the best when combined with the cent design. Illustrator stretches the sides of the design but leaves the cent symbol itself untouched.

Select the Rotate Legend Design check box to display the graph design on its side in the legend. (We omitted the legend in Figure 8-45 by neglecting to enter any column headings in the Graph Data window.) If you deselect the Rotate Legend Design check box, the design appears upright in the legend.

Applying a Design to a Line Chart

To apply a design to a line or scatter chart, select the graph with the arrow tool or select the specific markers you want to change with the direct selection tool. (Do not select the line segments.) Then choose Object » Graphs » Marker, which brings to life the Graph Marker dialog box shown in Figure 8-46.

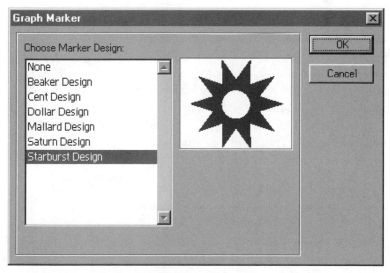

Figure 8-46: Use the Graph Marker dialog box to apply a graph design to the markers in a line or scatter chart.

Select a graph design from the scrolling Marker Design list and press Return/Enter. Illustrator applies the graph design to the individual markers in the chart.

To create Figure 8-47, we Opt/Alt-clicked one set of markers twice with the direct selection tool to select all the markers in one series, and then applied the starburst graph design. We then Opt/Alt-clicked the other set of markers twice, and applied the Saturn design.

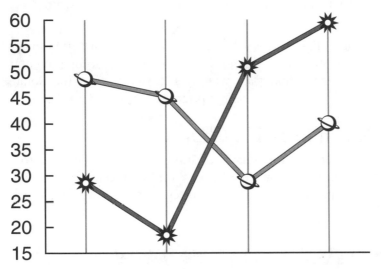

Figure 8-47: Deke applied two different sets of graph designs to the markers of a line graph.

Illustrator determines the size of a graph design based on the size of the bounding rectangle that you drew when defining the original graph design. The bounding rectangle is reduced to match the size of the square marker that normally appears in a line or scatter chart. Therefore, to create a design that scales to a reasonable size, draw a relatively small bounding rectangle. Figure 8-48 shows the bounding rectangles as dotted outlines for the starburst and Saturn patterns.

Figure 8-48: We used small bounding rectangles to make the graph designs appear large in the line graph in Figure 8-47.

 If you don't like how large Illustrator draws the markers and you don't feel like going back and messing around with the original graph designs, you can scale them on the fly by choosing Object » Transform » Transform Each. Opt/Alt-click one of the markers three times to select the entire series— or four times to select all markers—and choose Object » Transform » Transform Each. Then enter values larger than 100 percent into the Horizontal and Vertical option boxes and press Return/Enter. (To scale the markers proportionally, make sure the Horizontal and Vertical values are identical.)

PART THREE
CHANGING

MODIFYING AND COMBINING PATHS

Now that you've had the opportunity to create every kind of object available to Illustrator, it's time to talk in earnest about messing these objects up. This chapter specifically discusses how to edit paths created with the drawing tools covered in Chapters 4 and 5. You can clone paths to create copies, join paths together and hack them apart, and carve holes in paths.

As the *pièce de résistance*, you can combine simple paths into highly intricate ones using an assortment of pathfinder commands. These commands allow you to use one path to change the shape of another. The pathfinder commands are for everyone who ever despaired that they can't draw.

With the exception of cloning, you can't apply the operations covered in this chapter to text unless you first convert the characters to paths using Type » Create Outlines (Cmd/Ctrl-Shift-O). And you can edit elements inside graphs only if you first ungroup the graphs by pressing Cmd/Ctrl-Shift-G or by choosing Object » Ungroup.

 In fact, you'll have to ungroup portions of the graph more than once to break apart the nested groups. To be sure, press Cmd/Ctrl-Shift-G four times to ungroup every single object in the graph. Or you can simply wait and see if Illustrator complains when you try to perform an operation; if it does, press Cmd/Ctrl-Shift-G and try again.

One Million Ways to Replicate

Adobe understands the benefits of duplicating paths, which is why it has blessed Illustrator with so many techniques for cloning and copying. Each of these is useful in different situations. If you aren't already familiar with these techniques, study these sections carefully and commit the techniques to memory. Those poor souls who don't understand duplication miss out on one of the key factors that gives Illustrator the edge over the common household pencil.

If you think you know pretty much everything about duplication already, at least skim the next few sections. We're confident you'll pick up a handful of techniques that you never heard of, had forgotten, or hadn't considered in quite this context. We're equally confident you'll find a way to put these new techniques to work in the very near future.

Plain Old Copying and Pasting

Most folks are familiar with the Clipboard, which is a portion of memory set aside to hold objects that you want to duplicate or transfer to another program. It's kind of like the Memory button on a calculator. You store something one minute and retrieve it the next. There are three commands that involve the clipboard.

- You can *copy* selected objects to the Clipboard by pressing Cmd/Ctrl-C (or choosing Edit » Copy).

To *cut* (delete) the selected objects from the illustration while at the same time sending them to the Clipboard, press Cmd/Ctrl-X (Edit » Cut).

  Press Cmd/Ctrl-V (Edit » Paste) to retrieve the objects from the Clipboard. Illustrator *pastes* the objects in the center of the illustration window and leaves them selected so that you can immediately set about manipulating them.

  After pasting, the objects remain in the Clipboard until the next time you press Cmd/Ctrl-C or Cmd/Ctrl-X. Both commands shove out the old contents of the Clipboard and bring in the new.

You might be thinking, "I understand Cmd/Ctrl-C for Copy, but why Cmd/Ctrl-X for Cut and Cmd/Ctrl-V for Paste?" It's very simple, really. The first few commands in the Edit menu are assigned the first few keys along the bottom row of the keyboard. Cmd/Ctrl-Z, X, C, and V activate Undo, Cut, Copy, and Paste, respectively. This was built into the first Macintosh programs, long before Illustrator was created.

  Illustrator also adds neighboring keys D, F, and B to the duplication family—Cmd/Ctrl-D for Transform Again, Cmd/Ctrl-F for Paste In Front, and Cmd/Ctrl-B for Paste In Back, as in Figure 9-1.

You can also use the Clipboard to hold objects that you want to transport to another program. For example, you can copy paths from Illustrator and place them inside an InDesign document using the standard Copy and Paste commands.

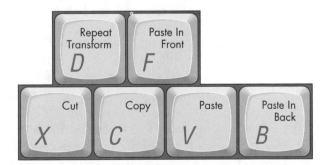

Figure 9-1: Ever notice that all of Illustrator's duplication shortcut keys are clustered in one corner of the keyboard? Coincidence or alien intervention? You decide.

Creating Clones

The Clipboard isn't the only means for copying paths and segments in Illustrator. You can completely bypass the Clipboard—and leave the contents of the Clipboard intact—by dragging a path and pressing the Opt/Alt key. This technique is called cloning.

To clone a path, select it with the arrow or direct selection tool, drag the path, press and hold the Opt/Alt key in mid drag, release the mouse button, and release Opt/Alt. It's very important to press the Opt/Alt key *after* you start to drag, because Opt/Alt-clicking with the direct selection tool selects whole paths and groups. And you have to keep Opt/Alt pressed until after you release the mouse button to create the clone. So again: drag, press Opt/Alt, release the mouse button, and release Opt/Alt. Illustrator positions the clone just in front of the original path.

You can also use the Opt/Alt key with the scale, rotate, reflect, and shear tools to clone a path while transforming it. Chapter 11 tells all there is to know on the subject.

Nudge and Clone

You might think that you could nudge and clone a path by pressing Opt/Alt with an arrow key. And, provided you do not have any text or text block selected, this is exactly what you can do.

The arrow keys move the object by the amount specified in the Cursor Key option box of the General Preferences fame. Using the arrow keys with Opt/Alt is a useful way to create clones that are evenly spaced from their originals.

Unfortunately, using Opt/Alt with the up or down arrow keys changes the leading for a text block. If you wish to nudge and clone the path of a text block without affecting the text, select the path by Opt/Alt-clicking it with the direct selection tool and then press Opt/Alt-arrow key. Keep in mind that if the path you are cloning contains text within its borders, the new path is linked to the original path and will automatically fill with any text that does not fit inside the original.

To nudge and clone the path a considerably further distance from the original, press Opt/Alt-Shift-arrow key. This moves a path ten times the amount entered in the Cursor Key option box.

Cloning Partial Paths

If you Opt/Alt-drag or Opt/Alt-arrow key a path in which all points are selected, Illustrator clones the entire path. But you also can clone individual points and segments that you've selected with the direct selection tool. In fact, Illustrator was the first drawing program for the Mac that let you duplicate bits and pieces of a path. This precise control over partial paths is one of the primary ingredients that distinguishes a professional-level program such as Illustrator from the greater midrange morass.

Figure 9-2 shows what happens when you clone a single segment independent of the rest of the path. If you Opt/Alt-drag a straight segment (or press Opt/Alt-arrow key when the segment is selected), you clone the segment at a new location, as demonstrated in the two left-hand examples in the figure. If you clone a curved segment, you stretch the segment and leave its points at their original positions, as in the right-hand examples.

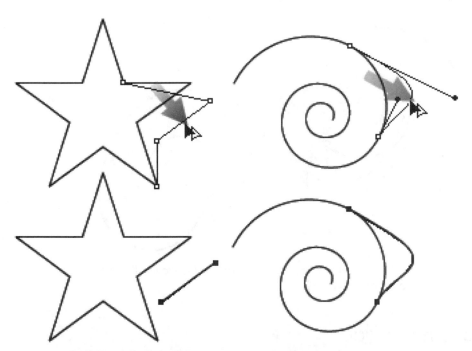

Figure 9-2: Opt/Alt-drag a straight segment (top left) to move and clone the segment (bottom left). Opt/Alt-drag a curved segment (top right) to stretch and clone the segment (bottom right).

When dragging or nudging one or more selected points, you clone the points as well as any segments connected to those points. Whether straight or curved, each segment between a selected point and a deselected point stretches to keep up with the drag, as Figure 9-3 illustrates.

Figure 9-3: Opt/Alt-drag selected points (top examples) to clone all segments connected to those points (bottom).

Copying in Place

The problem with Opt/Alt-dragging partial paths, therefore, is that doing so almost always results in distortions. You can Opt/Alt-drag a straight segment without changing it, but you stretch segments when you clone curved segments or selected points.

This is why so many experienced Illustrator artists duplicate partial paths using the Copy and Paste In Front commands. By simply pressing Cmd/Ctrl-C followed by Cmd/Ctrl-F (Edit » Paste In Front), you can copy one or more selected points and segments to the Clipboard and then paste them directly in front of their originals. No stretching, no distortion; Illustrator pastes the paths just as they were copied.

Also worth noting, the Paste In Front command positions the pasted paths at the same spot where they were copied. (By contrast, Edit » Paste positions the paths in the middle of the illustration window, regardless of the placement of the originals.) Therefore, Cmd/Ctrl-C, Cmd/Ctrl-F creates a copy in place.

 Edit » Paste In Back (Cmd/Ctrl-B) works just like the Paste In Front command, except that it pastes the copied paths in back of the selected elements. Unless you specifically want to change the stacking order of objects (as explained in Chapter 10), Paste In Front is usually preferable, because it permits you to easily select and edit paths after you paste them.

Cloning in Place

 You can also create a quick duplicate directly on top of the original by pressing Opt/Alt-up arrow followed by the down arrow key. This creates a clone and then nudges it back into place.

What's the benefit? Why not just press Cmd/Ctrl-C, Cmd/Ctrl-F? Because with that method, you have to copy, which replaces the contents of the Clipboard; whereas Opt/Alt-up or down arrow does not.

Creating a Series of Clones

After Opt/Alt-dragging or Opt/Alt-arrowing, you can repeat the distance and direction that a clone has moved by choosing Object » Transform » Transform Again or pressing Cmd/Ctrl-D. This command creates a series of clones, as shown in Figure 9-4.

 You can also apply Object » Transform » Transform Again to a partially cloned path.

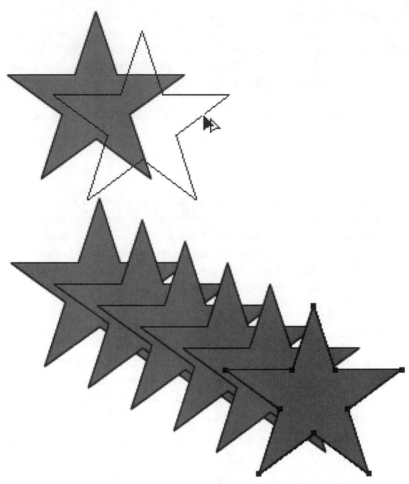

Figure 9-4: After cloning a path (top left), press Cmd/Ctrl-D to create a
string of equally spaced clones (top right). If you create a series of partial
clones (bottom), Illustrator applies the same movement to all points.

The keystroke for Transform Again does not stand for
Duplicate the object; it stands for Duplicate the *action*. For
instance, if you drag an object three inches to the right, you
can switch to another object and choose Transform Again.
The second object will move the same distance as the first.
But no duplicate will be created. The command duplicates
only the move, not the object.

Expanding the Clone

A little-known command for cloning paths is Offset Path. This command clones a selected path and expands the outline of the clone an equal distance in all directions.

Select a path and choose Object » Path » Offset Path. The dialog box shown in Figure 9-5 appears. Enter the numeric distance of the expansion into the Offset option box. If you want to create a slimmer, smaller path, enter a negative value. Then press Return/Enter.

Figure 9-5:
Enter a value into the Offset option
box to specify how far Illustrator
should expand a selected path.
Positive values expand objects.
Negative values shrink them.

The Offset Path dialog box (Figure 9-5) also offers the Joins and Miter Limit options, both of which affect how Illustrator draws the corners of the cloned paths. The default Joins setting, Miter, creates pointed corners, but you can also round off the corners (Round) or cut them short (Bevel). The Miter Limit value chops the corner short if the path threatens to grow too long. For more information on these basic stroking concepts, consult Chapter 16.

As shown in Figure 9-6, there are four things to notice about the clones created by the offset command:

- Offset Path is the one cloning operation that positions clones in back of their originals, so that all paths are plainly visible.

- You can enter negative values into the Offset option box. In that case, Illustrator places the diminutive clone in front of the original.

- The outline of the clone may have overlapping folds at the corners of the shape. To remove these, press the Unite button inside the Pathfinder palette.

- Expanding a path using the offset command is not the same as scaling it. Object » Path » Offset Path adds an amount all around the path, as the light gray shape shows. By contrast, the scale tool enlarges interior areas so that they no longer align with the original.

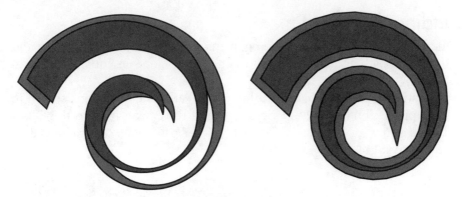

Figure 9-6: The difference between scaling an object (left) and using the Offset command (right). Scale makes the object bigger, but it doesn't fig snugly around the original. The Offset command fits the clone snugly around the original.

The offset command treats closed paths as explained above. With open paths, the command creates a closed path that outlines the original path.

Dragging and Dropping

The one remaining method for duplicating objects allows you to drag an object from one illustration window and drop it into another. Naturally, you have to be able to see at least a little bit of the illustration window you're dragging from and the one that you're dragging into on your computer screen at the same time. Then, armed with the arrow tool or direct selection tool, simply drag one or more selected objects out of one window and into a background window as illustrated in Figure 9-7. You can also use this technique to drag Illustrator objects onto InDesign pages.

There's no need to press the Opt/Alt key when dragging and dropping. Illustrator automatically clones the object, leaving the original in one window and adding a duplicate to the second. (As with other cloning techniques, the Clipboard contents remain unchanged.) After your drop, Illustrator brings the receiving window to front, so that you can position the object and edit it if need be.

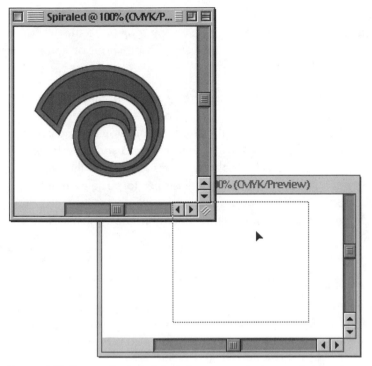

Figure 9-7: Drag selected objects from one window and drop them into another to clone objects between illustrations.

Dragging Scraps and Clips

You can create small files consisting of only the selected element by dragging objects from Illustrator and dropping them onto the desktop. On a Mac, these are so-called *picture clippings*, whereas on a Windows system, the word for them is *scraps*. Picture clippings are little holding cells that keep objects until you need to use them later. When you drag and drop objects onto the desktop, Illustrator works with the system software to create a picture clipping file, which looks like a frayed page with a bent corner. You can double-click the file icon at the Finder level to view its contents. (Illustrator doesn't have to be running for you to view the picture.)

The Windows scrap is created in the same manner (simply drag and drop selected items onto the desktop), but unfortunately, you cannot view its contents as you can on a Mac. Instead, double-clicking on a scrap launches Illustrator (that is, if Illustrator is not already running) and opens the scrap as an independent window.

At any time in the future, you can add the objects from a picture clipping or a scrap into an illustration by dragging the picture clipping or scrap file and dropping it. You can likewise drop the file into InDesign, Photoshop, or some other application that supports the Illustrator format.

 If you've been using the Mac for any period of time, you undoubtedly know about the Scrapbook. After choosing the Scrapbook command from the Apple menu, you can paste items into the Scrapbook window to create a sort of Rolodex of Clipboard stuff. What nobody seems to know is that you don't have to copy objects from Illustrator to paste them into the Scrapbook. You can drag and drop Illustrator items to and from the Scrapbook without changing the contents of the clipboard.

What about Auto-Scrolling?

Instead of dragging an object outside the window, you might want to drag the object to a new position within the window. This is called auto-scrolling. Because it is so easy to drag outside the window, you need a few tricks to make Illustrator automatically scroll the window as you drag an object.

First, you need to hover your cursor over a scroll bar or title bar. For example, after you grab an object, drag it onto the right scroll bar and hold it there; Illustrator scrolls to the right. If you drag the object onto the title bar, Illustrator scrolls upward. But what if you want to scroll to the left, where no scroll or title bar appears? In this case, drag the object to the left edge of the window. Pause right over the thin edge of the window.

It's tricky, but it works. When you've scrolled far enough, drag the object back into the window and drop it into place.

Joining Points and Paths

Enough duplicating already. It's time to do something different with all these paths we're making, starting with joining. Illustrator's Join command lets you join two open paths to create one longer open path. Or you can connect two endpoints in a single open path to form a closed path.

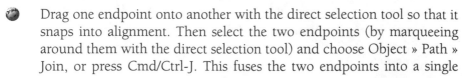 Drag one endpoint onto another with the direct selection tool so that it snaps into alignment. Then select the two endpoints (by marqueeing around them with the direct selection tool) and choose Object » Path » Join, or press Cmd/Ctrl-J. This fuses the two endpoints into a single

interior point. Illustrator displays the Join dialog box, which lets you select whether you want to fuse the points into a corner point or a smooth point. Make your selection and press Return/Enter.

If you don't see the Join dialog box as shown in Figure 9-8 after pressing Cmd/Ctrl-J, it's because your points aren't coincident—that is, one point isn't exactly, *precisely* snapped into alignment with the other. Press Cmd/Ctrl-Z to undo the join, and then try again to drag one point into alignment with the other, or just press Cmd/Ctrl-Opt/Alt-Shift-J. The latter averages and fuses the points in one brilliant move.

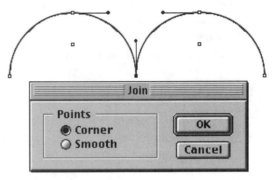

Figure 9-8:
The Join dialog box
appears only if two
selected points are
exactly aligned.

If so much as 0.001 point stands between two selected points, Object » Path » Join connects the points with a straight segment. (That is roughly 0.3 micron, the size of one of your tinier bacteria—no joke—hence the insightful Figure 9-9.) So if you need a straight segment in a hurry, select two endpoints and press Cmd/Ctrl-J.

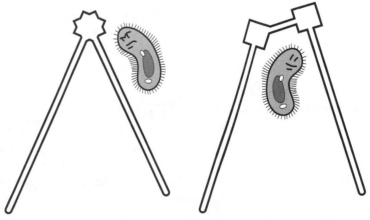

Figure 9-9:
Press Object »
Path » Join to fuse
two exactly aligned
points into a single
point (left). But if a
bacterium can fit
between the points
(right), Illustrator
connects the points
with a straight
segment.

If you aren't particularly concerned with the placement of your points, and you want to join the points into one, press Cmd-Opt-Shift-J (for the Mac) or Ctrl-Alt-Shift-J (for Windows). This brings the points together by averaging their locations and then joins them into a corner point. It's what's known as an Average/Join command.

- To undo the Average/Join, you must press Cmd/Ctrl-Z twice in a row—once to undo the averaging and again to undo the join.

- To close an open path, you can select the entire path with the arrow tool and press Cmd/Ctrl-J. If the endpoints are coincident, a dialog box comes up, asking you how you want to fuse the points. Otherwise, Illustrator connects the points with a straight segment.

Whatever you do, don't press Average/Join when an entire path is selected. Illustrator averages all points in the path into a single location, creating a very ugly effect. If you mess up and do what we told you not to do, press Cmd/Ctrl-Z to make it better.

Splitting Paths into Pieces

The opposite of joining is splitting, and Illustrator provides five basic ways to split paths apart. We touched on two methods in Chapter 5: You can select a segment or an interior point with the direct selection tool and press the Delete key. Or you can use the erase tool to dissolve sections of a path.

But what if you want to break apart a path without creating a rift? Or what if you want to break a path in the middle of a segment? The answer to either question is to use the scissors tool, knife tool, or Object » Path » Slice. The scissors tool creates a break at a specific point, the knife tool creates a free-form slice, and the Slice command uses a selected path to slice through all other paths that it comes in contact with. The only things lacking are a nail file and a toothpick.

Snipping with the Scissors

The scissors tool is one of Illustrator's earliest tools, predating just about every path-editing tool except the arrow tool. Its operation hasn't changed that much since the old days. You click anywhere along the outline of a path to snip the path at that point. The path need not even be selected. As Figure 9-10 shows, you can click either a segment or a point.

Whenever you click with the scissors tool, Illustrator inserts two endpoints. As the second example in Figure 9-10 illustrates, you can drag one endpoint away from the other with the direct selection tool. The problem is, one endpoint is necessarily in front of the other. Why is that a problem? Every so often, you'll want to drag the point that's in back, and you won't be able to get to it because the front point is in the way.

Naturally, you can drag the front point out of the way, and then drag the rear point. But that means moving both points.

 The solution is select to both points by drawing a marquee with the direct selection tool or direct selection lasso. Then Shift-click the point to deselect the top point. Now just the bottom point is selected. Press an arrow key three or four times to nudge the bottom point so you can easily select it, and then drag it to the desired location.

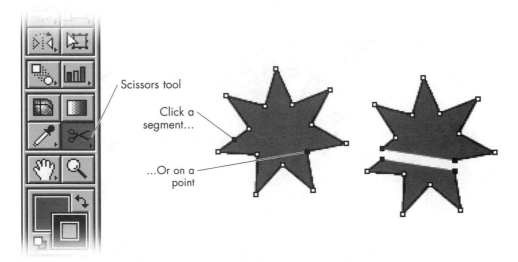

Figure 9-10: Snip a break in a path by clicking on the outline of the path with the scissors tool.

Wielding the Knife

The other path-splitting tool is the knife tool; the alternate tool in the scissors tool slot. It looks like a little X-acto blade. The knife tool can slice multiple paths at a time. First assemble the objects that you want to cut through. The knife tool splits only paths and it doesn't affect text, unless the text is first converted to paths with Type » Create Outlines.

As long as one or more paths are selected, the knife tool will sever those paths but leave all unselected paths unchanged. On the other hand, if nothing in your document is selected, the knife happily dices any path that gets in its way.

To operate the knife tool, just drag with it, much as you would with the pencil tool. As demonstrated in Figure 9-11, Illustrator's knife tool slices through all closed paths and all open filled paths that it comes into contact with.

 Although the knife tool has come a long way, it still has a couple of small quirks. The first is that it doesn't affect unfilled open paths. Second, it automatically closes filled open paths after it splits them into pieces.

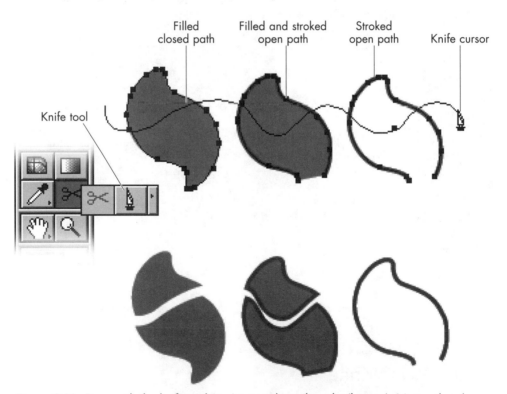

Figure 9-11: Drag with the knife tool (top) to cut through paths (bottom). Notice that the knife tool does not cut unfilled open paths. In addition, it closes the open filled path after it cuts it in two.

To make nice straight cuts, use the Opt/Alt key while you're dragging with the knife tool. Be sure to press the Opt/Alt key before you start your drag. If you press it after you're already into the drag, it will have no effect. Press and hold both the Opt/Alt and the Shift key to constrain the slices to a multiple of 45 degrees (plus whatever value you've entered into the Constrain Angle option box in the General Preference dialog box).

Slicing with a Path

The bad news about the knife tool is that it doesn't offer much control. You can't carefully position points and control handles to specify the exact directions of your slice, and you can't edit the slice after drawing it.

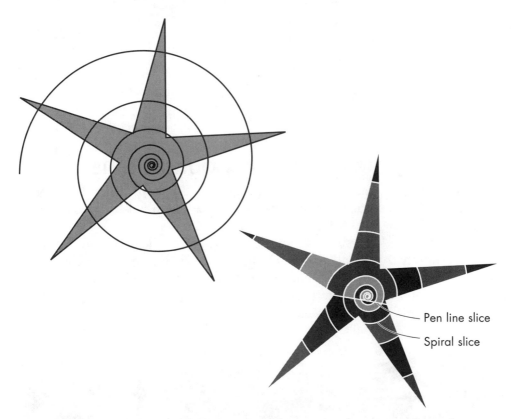

Pen line slice
Spiral slice

Figure 9-12: Using Object » Path » Slice, Sandee twice sliced into a star, first with a spiral tool and then with a small straight line created with the pen tool.

That's why Illustrator provides the Slice command. After drawing a path with any of Illustrator's precision drawing tools, you can use the path to cut through filled objects in your drawing. Here's how it works:

1. Assemble the filled objects that you want to hack to pieces.

2. Draw the path that you want to use to slice the objects. You can use the pen tool, star tool, spiral tool, or any other drawing tool.

3. Position the path over the objects. Then choose Object » Path » Slice. Illustrator slices through all objects that the selected path overlaps.

In Figure 9-12, we used a spiral to slice through a star. After cutting with the spiral, we drew a short straight line into the center of the shape with the pen tool (as noted in the figure) and chose the Slice command again. That permitted us to fill different loops of the spiral with different colors. Note that we had to apply these two slices in two different passes. You can't use the Slice command on more than one cutting path at a time.

Like the knife tool, the Slice command has a habit of deleting unfilled, open paths. To cut the paths rather than delete them, make sure that the slicing object doesn't overlap an unfilled, open path more than once.

Carving Holes into Compound Paths

Illustrator lets you carve holes inside a path. You can see through these holes to objects and colors that lie behind the path. A path with holes in it is called a *compound* path, which is what this section is about.

If you convert a letter such as *B* or *o* into outlines, the letter is automatically converted into a compound path. Or consider the mundane pretzel shown in Figure 9-13. Without the compound path command, the pretzel would simply be a solid mass of dough. (We're talking about the soft, chewy Philadelphia pretzels—not the small, brittle packaged ones.)

Figure 9-13: The pretzel comprises three paths, all joined together into one compound path.

At this point you might ask, "Why do you need a path with a hole in it? Why not just stick the smaller path in front of the bigger path and fill the smaller path with the background color?" Two reasons:

- First, the background may contain lots of different colors, as in Figure 9-14. The holes in the pretzel on the right are filled with a light gray. But it doesn't look right at all. The pretzel on the left is a proper compound path, allowing us to see through holes to anything behind it.

- Second, working with opaque paths limits your flexibility. Even if you can get away with filling an interior path with a flat color, you'll have to change that color any time you change the background or move the objects against a new background. But with a compound path, you can move the object against any background without changing a thing. You can even add effects like drop shadows without modifying the compound path one iota. It's flexibility at its finest.

Figure 9-14: The difference between a real compound path (left) and a faked one simply filled with gray objects (right).

Creating a Compound Path

Now, as we said, Illustrator automatically turns letters into compound paths. But you may want to create additional compound paths of your own. Doughnuts, ladders, eyeglasses, windows, ski masks, and guys shot full of bullet holes are just a few of the many items that lend themselves to compound paths.

To make a compound path, do the following:

1. **Draw two shapes.**

    Make one smaller than the other. You can use any tool to draw either shape, and the paths can be open or closed. You'll probably want to stick with closed paths to ensure even curves and continuous strokes; with open paths, the fills get flattened off at the open edge.

2. **Select both shapes and choose Object » Compound Paths » Make.**

    Or press the keyboard equivalent Cmd/Ctrl-8. Where the two shapes overlap, the compound path is transparent; where the shapes don't overlap, the path is filled.

     If you don't get any holes at all, you must have drawn the shapes in different directions. The solution is to select one of the shapes with the direct selection tool, click the Attributes palette, and click the Reverse Path Direction button that is not active. For a detailed explanation of this, read the "Reversing Subpath Direction" section a few short pages from now.

3. **Edit the individual shapes in the compound path with the direct selection tool.**

    After you combine two or more shapes into a compound path, select the entire path by clicking on it with the arrow tool. If you want to select a point or segment belonging to one of the subpaths—that's the official name for the shapes inside a compound path—press Cmd/Ctrl-Shift-A to deselect the path and click an element with the direct selection tool. You can then manipulate points, segments, and control handles as usual. For example, Figure 9-15 shows how the holes in the pretzel have been moved and reshaped.

With the direct selection tool, Opt/Alt-click a subpath twice to select the entire compound path. If you decide later to restore the compound path to its original independent parts, select the entire path and choose Object » Compound Paths » Release, or press Cmd-Opt-8 for the Mac; Ctrl-Alt-8 for Windows.

 If there's nothing behind your compound path, it may be hard to tell if you've created the compound. Turn on the page Grid (Cmd-Opt/Alt-"). As long as the grid is in back, you'll see it through the compound path. For more information on grids, see Chapter 11, "Developing a Flair for the Schematic."

Figure 9-15: Use the direct selection tool to move and reshape the subpaths of a compound path.

Working with Compound Paths

Compound paths are very special and wonderful things that you can screw up very easily. If you know what you're doing, you can juggle tens or hundreds of subpaths and even add holes to existing compound paths. But by the same token, you can accidentally add a hole when you don't mean to, or you may encounter a perplexing error message when editing a subpath in a manner that Illustrator doesn't allow.

The following tidbits of information are designed to help eliminate as much confusion as possible:

- You can't connect a subpath from one compound path with a subpath from a different compound path or a different group, whether with the Join command or the pen or pencil tool. This may sound like something you'll never want to do, but we promise: One day, you'll try to connect points from two different compound paths or groups and you'll go absolutely nuts trying to figure out why Illustrator won't let you do it. It happens to everybody.

- When (not if) it happens to you, you have two options: Give it up, or break the compound paths and groups apart. If you decide on the latter, with the arrow tool, select two paths you want to connect. This also selects all other subpaths associated with these paths. Then press Cmd/Ctrl-Opt/Alt-8 once and press Cmd/Ctrl-Shift-G about four times in a row. This is overkill, but it's preferable to wasting a lot of time with trial and error. Who knows how many nested groups are involved? Then join the paths and re-create the compound path as desired.

• Another wonderful constraint is that you can't combine shapes from different groups or compound paths into a single compound path. If, when you press Cmd/Ctrl-8, Illustrator complains that the selected objects are from different groups, press Cmd/Ctrl-Opt/Alt-8 and Cmd/Ctrl-Shift-G a few times to free the chains that bind the objects, and then try pressing Cmd/Ctrl-8 again.

• You can combine as many shapes inside a compound path as you like. You can likewise add subpaths without releasing the compound path. There are two ways to do this. One way is to select the compound path with the arrow tool, Shift-click the shapes you want to add, and press Cmd/Ctrl-8 again. (This doesn't create a compound path inside a compound path or anything weird like that. It just adds the new shapes as subpaths.)

Alternatively, you can select the shapes that you want to add to the compound path and cut them by pressing Cmd/Ctrl-X. Then select any subpath in the compound path with the direct selection tool—not the arrow tool!—and press either Cmd/Ctrl-F or Cmd/Ctrl-B to paste the cut shapes in front or in back of the selection. This automatically makes the pasted shapes part of the compound path.

Because you can paste a shape into a compound path, you may find yourself doing it accidentally when you don't want to. If you Paste In Front/Back while *one object* in a compound path is selected, the new object will be made part of the compound group. However, if you Paste In Front/Back while the entire compound path is selected, the new object is *not* made part of the compound group. This is an important distinction.

• So far as Illustrator is concerned, a compound path is a single path. Therefore, changing the fill or stroke of one subpath in the compound path changes all other subpaths as well. So if you ever change the color of one shape, and another shape changes as well, you can rest assured both shapes are part of the same compound path. If you need two different colored objects to create a hole where they overlap, you need to use a different technique: one of the pathfinder commands covered in the section "Use a Path to Change a Path" later in this chapter.

Reversing Subpath Direction

By this time, you've probably created a compound path or added a new subpath, only to find that you're not getting any holes. You think you did something wrong, or perhaps we failed to convey a step or two. Neither is the case. It's just that Illustrator needs a little kick in the rear end to make it shape up and fly right.

See, Illustrator calculates the areas in a compound path based on the directions in which the subpaths flow. This implies a clockwise or counterclockwise flow. For one subpath to create a hole in another, the two paths have to flow in opposite directions. Alternately clockwise and counterclockwise paths do the trick.

At this point you might think, "Oh, great, now I have to pay attention to how I draw my shapes." Luckily, you don't. When you combine two or more shapes into a compound path, Illustrator automatically changes the backmost shape to a clockwise flow and all others to counterclockwise. It does this regardless of how you drew the shapes!

Illustrator's default approach works swell when the rear shape in the selection is also the largest shape. The first example in Figure 9-16 shows precisely this setup. The large backmost circle flows clockwise, and the two smaller squares flow counterclockwise. Therefore, the counterclockwise squares cut holes in the clockwise circle. But things go awry in the second example, in which one of the squares is in back. The circle and square do not cut holes into the rear square, which leaves the forward square opaque.

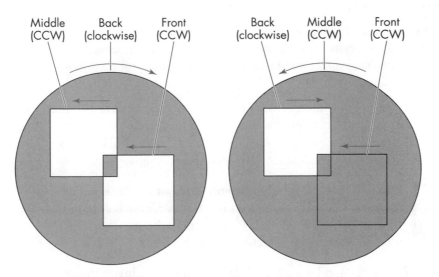

Figure 9-16: Compound paths created when the large circle is in back (left) and when one of the squares is in back (right).

But Illustrator wouldn't be Illustrator if it didn't give you the power to correct the situation. You can change the direction of any path by selecting it with the direct selection tool and modifying the setting in the Attributes palette. Here's how to correct a problem like the second example in Figure 9-16:

1. Press Cmd/Ctrl-Shift-A to deselect everything.

2. Select one of the subpaths that doesn't seem to be behaving correctly with the direct selection tool.

3. Click the Attributes tab to bring the Attributes palette into focus. The Attributes palette is shown in Figure 9-17.

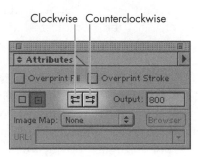

Figure 9-17:
Use the Reverse Path Direction buttons to change the direction of a selected subpath.

4. Click the Reverse Path Direction button that is not active. This changes the flow of the path from counterclockwise to clockwise or vice versa depending on which direction the path originally went.

5. Now select one of the other misguided subpaths (if there are any others) and, again in the Attributes palette, click the nonactive Reverse Path Direction button to switch the flow of the subpath to the other direction.

Keep selecting paths and fiddling with the Reverse Path Direction buttons as much as you want until you get things the way you want them. Keep in mind that you can achieve transparency only in areas where an even number of subpaths overlap. If an odd number of subpaths overlap, the area is always opaque.

Oh, and one last bit of explanation about the Reverse Path Direction buttons: The buttons are not available unless you have selected the subpath of a compound path. They don't work to change the direction of other objects.

The Reverse Path Direction buttons are dimmed unless a subpath inside a compound path is selected. You cannot change the direction of standard paths for the simple reason that there's no point in doing so.

Use a Path to Change a Path

The last items on our list of things to discuss are the Pathfinder commands. Illustrator provides a total of 13 buttons in the Pathfinder palette, as shown in Figure 9-18. Each of these buttons applies a different Pathfinder command, all of which permit you to combine simple paths into more complex ones. You can merge paths together, subtract one path from another, break paths into bits, and perform other path operations.

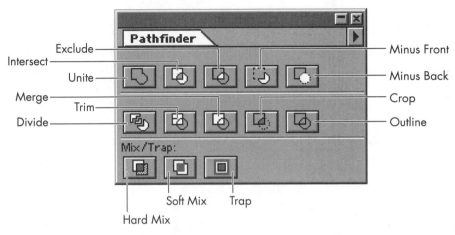

Figure 9-18: The Pathfinder palette with all 13 cryptic icons labeled.

 Years ago the Pathfinder commands were part of the filter menu. Then Adobe moved them out to the Path submenu. Then they moved them to the Pathfinder palette. This is why old-time Illustrator users will often call them the Pathfinder filters. It is also why Illustrator users wonder where they are in each new version of the product.

 Unfortunately there are no labels for the icons on the Pathfinder palette. If you need to know what each icon stands for, you can pause slightly over each icon and read the tool tip that appears. Or you can make copies of Figure 9-18 and paste them all around your computer until you have memorized them.

As you become more adept at using the Pathfinder commands, you'll find them very helpful for assembling primitive shapes—such as rectangles, ovals, polygons, and stars—into more elaborate paths, rather than drawing the elaborate paths from scratch with the pen tool. You can also use the commands to generate translucent color overlays and drop shadows.

In the following sections, we explain every one of the Pathfinder commands except Trap. The Trap command lets you generates so-called "traps" to eliminate gaps in color printing. We cover this particular command with the other printing functions in Chapter 21.

Adding Shapes Together

The Unite command combines all selected shapes into a single path. Illustrator removes all the overlapping stuff and turns the selected paths into a single, amalgamated object. It fills and strokes this new object with the fill and stroke from the foremost of the selected paths.

In the top left of Figure 9-19, for example, we selected the star, circle, and stripes at top and clicked the Unite button in the Pathfinder palette. The result is the single combined path.

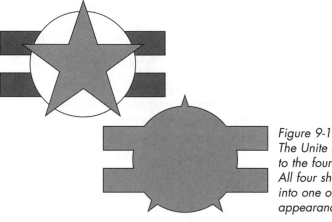

Figure 9-19:
The Unite command was applied to the four shapes on the left. All four shapes are combined into one object that takes on the appearance of the top object.

Illustrator provides another pathfinder that combines shapes, the Merge command. As shown in Figure 9-20, Merge is more selective than Unite. It combines only paths with the same fill color. It also clips shapes wherever they overlap, and (for reasons we cannot fathom) it deletes the stroke.

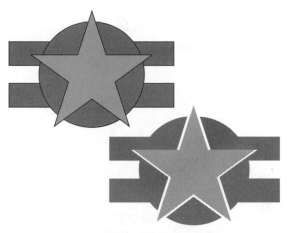

Figure 9-20:
Merge was applied to the four
shapes on the left. Notice that
objects with the same fill and stroke
are combined. We also moved the
objects to show that they were
clipped where they used to overlap.

Subtracting Shapes from Each Other

Three Pathfinder commands—Exclude, Minus Front, and Minus Back—subtract
shapes from each other:

 Exclude is a kind of poor man's compound path function. It removes all
   overlapping sections of the selected shapes. As shown at the bottom
   right of Figure 9-21, this cuts out a large hole, much like the hole in a
   compound path. The difference is that all the black shapes are actually
   separate objects.

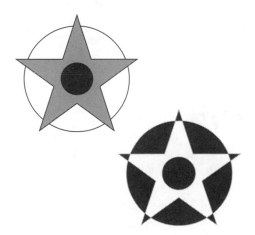

Figure 9-21:
The Exclude command was
applied to the top group of
objects. This divided the objects
as shown in the bottom group.

 If Exclude is applied to an object that is completely inside another, then it simply creates a compound path—the same as if you had applied the compound path command.

● The downside of using the Exclude command is that you can't transform one of the original paths to reposition a hole, as you can inside a compound path. The advantage of using the command is that you can fill the individual excluded paths with different colors.

● Minus Front clips all selected paths out of the rear path in the selection. In Figure 9-22, for example, we selected the star and two stripes and clicked the Minus Front button. The result is two stripes with a star cut out of them. Sandee calls Minus Front the "cookie cutter command."

 There is an important trick to Figure 9-22. Before we applied Minus Front, we selected the two stripes and made them a compound path. Because they didn't overlap, there was no change in their appearance. But as far as the Minus Front command was concerned, they were now a single path. So Minus Front cut out a path inside both of them. Without the compound path, the star would have affected only one stripe—the one all the way at the back.

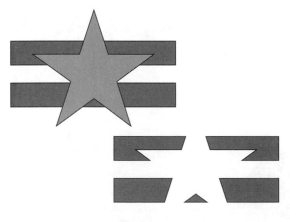

Figure 9-22:
The result of clipping the star out of compound path stripes with the Minus Front command.

● Minus Back is exactly the opposite of Minus Front; it clips all selected paths out of the front path in the selection. In Figure 9-23, we selected the star and stripes and clicked the Minus Back button. This left the star with a two stripes cut out of it.

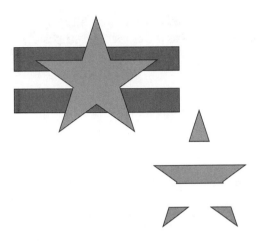

Figure 9-23:
Here we used the Minus Back
command to clip the stripes out
of the star.

Finding Overlap and Intersection

The rest of the Pathfinder commands are devoted to the task of finding and separating the intersecting portions of selected shapes.

- **Intersect:** Intersect retains the overlapping sections of selected shapes and throws away the areas where the shapes don't overlap, as shown in Figure 9-24. Illustrator fills and strokes the resulting shapes with the colors from the frontmost shape in the selection.

 If every one of the selected paths does not overlap at some location, Intersect delivers an error message telling you that the command has done nothing.

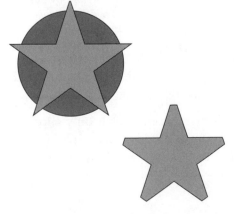

Figure 9-24:
The results of applying the Intersect
command to the star and circle. The
result is a star with curved points.

• **Crop:** The Crop command uses the front selected path to crop all other paths in the selection. In Figure 9-25, the star acts as the crop to the stripes.

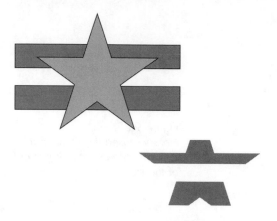

Figure 9-25:
The results of cropping the stripes with the star shape.

• **Divide:** This command subdivides all paths so they no longer overlap. As shown in the top example of Figure 9-26, the paths don't look much different after you apply the command, but they are in fact separated into many more shapes than before.

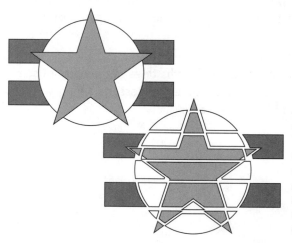

Figure 9-26:
The effects of the Divide command are not obvious until you move the paths around as shown on the bottom. All the paths are divided so they have no overlap.

• **Trim:** This command works just like Divide, except that it only clips rear shapes, while leaving front shapes intact as seen in Figure 9-27. Or if you prefer, it's just like Merge, except that it doesn't unite shapes that have the same fill. If you find that Divide breaks up your shapes too much, try Trim instead.

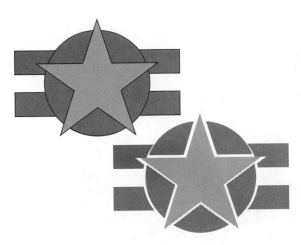

Figure 9-27:
The effects of the Trim
command are not obvious
until you move the paths
around as shown on the
bottom. All the back objects
are clipped while leaving the
frontmost shape intact.

Hard and Soft: The Hard and Soft commands break up objects just like
the Divide command. But they also change the fills of the new paths to
represent a mix of the colors in the overlapping objects. The Hard command, shown in Figure 9-28, mixes the colors in the objects at their
highest percentages—that is, the highest amounts of cyan, magenta,
yellow, and black ink from all overlapping objects. The Soft command,
shown in Figure 9-28, lets you specify what percentage of the inks you
want to blend, thus resulting in lighter colors than the Hard command.
(Because gray tints hardly do justice to these commands, see the color
insert for more colorful explanations of them.)

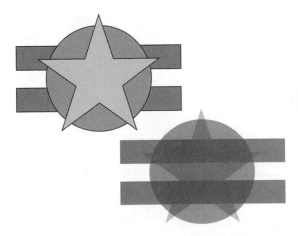

Figure 9-28:
An example of how objects
are clipped and colored
using the Hard command.

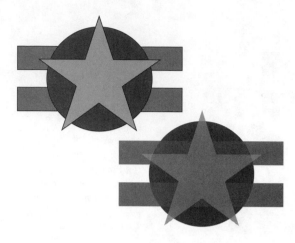

Figure 9-29:
An example of how objects
are clipped and colored
using the Soft command set
to 50 percent.

 Hard and Soft (originally called Mix Hard and Mix Soft)
used to be the only way Illustrator could create the illusion of
transparency between objects. With Illustrator 9's new transparency features, these two commands may lose some of
their importance.

Outline: Outline draws open paths around overlapping areas of
selected shapes, and strokes these paths with the old fill colors. Figure
9-30 shows this command applied to the star, circle, and stripes. We
had to thicken the strokes (Outline applies 0-point strokes, which is
utterly stupid) so you could see the results of the command.

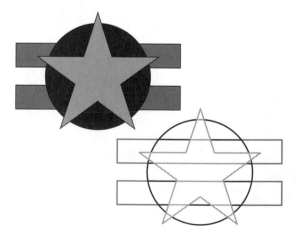

Figure 9-30:
The results of applying the
Outline command to our
familiar cast of shapes.

All of these commands group the resulting paths together, and all except Outline remove the strokes from the paths. So be prepared to ungroup paths or edit them with the direct selection tool. And you'll have to reapply the strokes.

Pathfinder Options

You can use the Pathfinder Options dialog box to set the parameters for all Pathfinder operations, and it does so in an incredibly complicated way. When you choose the Pathfinder Options command from the Pathfinder palette's pop-up menu, Illustrator displays the dialog box shown in Figure 9-31. Though small (it's enlarged here), it will melt your brain if you look at it for too long.

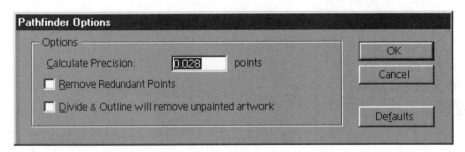

Figure 9-31: We guess that whoever designed this dialog box has since moved on to a successful career at Microsoft.

The first option lets you control the accuracy of the Pathfinder operations. This value has to be larger than 0.001 point (0.3 micron, remember?), which means that no path will stray farther than one bacterium off its true course. Larger values are less accurate, but they also speed up the performance of the commands. The maximum value is 100 points, but you probably don't want to go much higher than 4 or 5.

The two check boxes in the Pathfinder Options dialog box delete points that overlap each other and objects created by the Divide and Outline commands that have transparent fills and strokes. We recommend you select both these options and leave them selected, unless you have some special reason for retaining overlapping points and invisible objects.

Every once in a while you may find a small gap between objects manipulated by a pathfinder command. If this happens, undo the command and then turn off the Anti-alias Artwork setting in the General preferences. Then reapply the command. The gap should be gone.

Reapplying a Pathfinder Command

You can reapply the last Pathfinder command you used by either choosing the second command in the Pathfinder palette's pop-up menu, Repeat Pathfinder, or by pressing Cmd/Ctrl-4.

Pathfinders Go Live

One of the drawbacks of using the Pathfinder commands is that the paths get all carved up. In the past that meant you needed to make backup copies of your artwork before you applied a pathfinder command.

Illustrator 9 now lets you apply the Pathfinder commands as part of the new Live Effects. This lets you move objects around while still keeping the Pathfinder command applied. To see how these live pathfinders work, check out Chapter 12, "Special Effects."

CHAPTER 10

DEVELOPING A FLAIR FOR THE SCHEMATIC

There are two types of people who use Illustrator. The first are the high-precision designers who create artwork to exact specifications that are defined to the thousandth of a point. The other are artists who do not want to feel constrained by Illustrator features, but just want to express themselves. Amazingly, this chapter—which covers working with the precision features, stacking order, and layers—was written for both groups. You can work precisely or you can simply control the elements in your illustration.

Illustrator gives you exceptional control over your document environment. You can use automated grids in your drawing, which help to keep basic illustration elements in alignment. There are several alignment and distribution controls to position objects precisely. Additionally, Illustrator provides smart guides, an interactive system of guides that help you position and create objects at precise locations. Illustrator provides several different ways to control the visibility and selection of objects in a document.

 Illustrator 9 has completely revised its Layers palette which controls the order that objects appear on the page. This new Layers palette also provides visual previews of layers and the objects on layers within the palette. If you've used Photoshop's thumbnails, you will appreciate these new layers features.

So if you're the type who values a structured drawing environment, keep your chin up and continue reading. This chapter explains everything, from distance to distribution, groups to grids and guidelines, and locks to layers. If it helps you toe the line, it's front and center in the following pages.

Measuring and Positioning with Microscopic Precision

One of our favorite things about using Illustrator is that you can measure dimensions and distances right inside the program. There's no need to print the illustration and measure the output. And you sure as heck wouldn't want to press a pica pole against the screen. Fortunately, Illustrator's built-in capabilities are both more convenient and more accurate. Where else can you click the screen to measure discrepancies as slight as 0.0001 point, roughly the length of bacteria razor stubble?

Illustrator provides three sets of measuring and positioning devices:

- The horizontal and vertical rulers are handy for tracking the cursor. They're about as accurate as real-life rulers, which means that they're good enough for simple alignment but you can't quite measure bacteria with them.

- The measure tool records scrupulously precise dimensions and distances into the Info palette. When the Info palette is up on screen, you can measure an object just by selecting it. You can even record values with the measure tool, and then turn around and move an object that precise distance and direction.

The Transform palette lets you position objects according to numeric coordinates. You can move objects or clone them by merely entering a value and pressing Return/Enter or Opt-Return/Enter. The palette has its disadvantages, but it can be useful for quick adjustments.

The following sections explain these items, as well as Object » Arrange » Move, which captures all the pertinent statistics recorded with the measure tool. Together, the rulers, measure tool, Info palette, Move command, and Transform palette form a powerful collection of measuring and positioning gadgets.

Adding Rulers to the Illustration Window

Illustrator gives you two rulers—one vertical and one horizontal—that track the movement of your cursor. To bring them up on screen, press Cmd/Ctrl-R or choose View » Show Rulers. If nothing is selected, you can even Control-click (Mac) or right-click (Windows) and choose the Show Rulers command from the context-sensitive pop-up menu. The horizontal ruler appears along the top of the illustration window, and the vertical ruler appears on the left side, as in Figure 10-1.

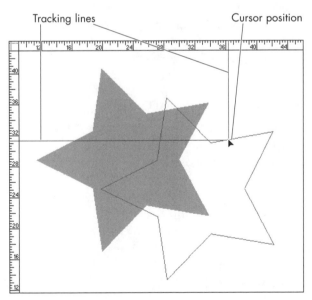

Figure 10-1: The horizontal and vertical rulers track the cursor position.

You control the unit of measure used by both rulers by choosing the File » Preferences » Units & Undos command and selecting an option from the General Units pop-up menu. Or you can use this handy-dandy keyboard shortcut to cycle through the different units of measurement. On the Mac press, Cmd-Opt-Shift-U. The Windows folds should press Ctrl-Alt-Shift-U. U know, *U* for *units*.

The rulers constantly track the position of the cursor, so long as the cursor is inside the illustration window. Figure 10-1 labels the dotted tracking line in each ruler. As you can see, the rulers track the tip of the cursor, known as the hot spot. In the figure, the hot spot measures 31 picas, 6 points above and 36 picas, 3 points to the right of the absolute zero point where the rulers begin (as explained in the next section). To get the rulers the heck out of the way, press Cmd/Ctrl-R or choose View » Hide Rulers.

To make the rulers visible for all new illustrations, open the Adobe Illustrator Startup file in the Plug-ins folder, press Cmd/Ctrl-R to display the rulers, draw a rectangle (or something simple) and then delete it to get the Save command's attention, and press Cmd/Ctrl-S. From now on, each new illustration window will come with rulers.

Setting the Point Where All Things Are Zero

The point at which both rulers show 0 is called the zero point or ruler origin. By default, the ruler origin is located at the bottom left corner of the artboard. If you change the size of the artboard or the location of the page boundary, the ruler origin may get jostled around a bit.

You can relocate the ruler origin at any time by dragging from the ruler origin box, which is that little square where the rulers intersect. In Figure 10-2, we dragged the ruler origin onto a point in the star, allowing us to measure all distances from that point. The ruler values update after you release the mouse button. The new ruler origin affects not only the rulers but also the coordinate positioning values in the Info and Transform palettes.

If you ever want to reset the ruler origin to default position in the bottom left corner of the artboard, simply double-click the ruler origin box.

Ruler origin box

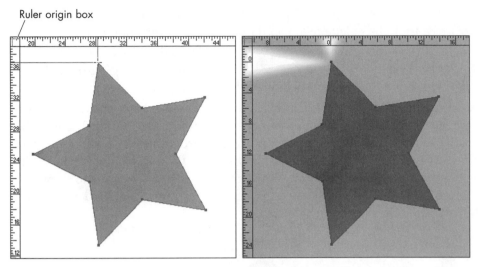

Figure 10-2: Drag from the ruler origin box (left) to reposition the zero point (right).

 You can save a revised ruler origin with the Adobe Illustrator Startup file. For example, you might prefer to have the zero point in the lower right corner of the illustration. Your change will affect all future illustrations.

Measuring the Minutia

The measure tool and its sidekick, the Info palette, are Illustrator's dynamic duo of precision positioning features. You can use both items to measure distances and objects in three ways:

- Select the measure tool, the second alternate tool in the hand tool slot. In the illustration window, drag from one location to another. The Info palette automatically opens. Here Illustrator lists the distance and direction between the beginning and end of your drag. If you click with the measure tool, the Info palette lists the distance and angle between the new click point and the previous one.

- If the Info palette is not open, choose Window » Show Info. Then use the arrow tool to select the object that you want to measure. The width and height of the segment appear automatically in the palette.

- With the Info palette on screen, drag with any of the shape tools to see information about the size of the path you're creating. When you move the pen tool cursor, the Info palette tells you the distance and direction of the cursor from the last point. When you drag an object with the arrow tool, the palette tells you the distance and direction of the drag. When using the scale or rotate tool, the palette lists the percentage of the scaling or the angle of rotation. The Info palette is constantly trying to tell you something when you create and edit objects.

Assuming that the Snap to Point toggle command in the View menu is switched on, the measure tool snaps to an anchor point when you click within 2 screen pixels of it. In Figure 10-3, for example, we dragged from one anchor point to another to measure the precise distance between the two. Sadly, when you're using the measure tool, Illustrator doesn't give you any snap cursors to show that you've hit the points, but you can see the cursor snap into place if you watch carefully. Just trust The Force, Luke.

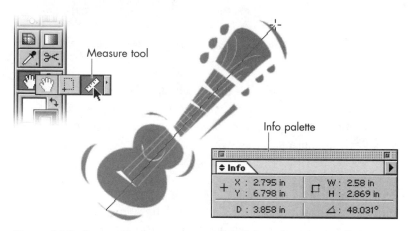

Figure 10-3: Drag with the measure tool and the Info palette will display the distance and direction between two points.

The Info palette can include as many as six numeric values. Here's what they mean:

X, Y: When using a drawing tool, the X and Y values in the Info palette represent the coordinate position of your cursor, as measured from the ruler origin.

When you use the measure tool, the values tell the last place you clicked with the tool (or released when dragging). This way, you know at what point Illustrator is measuring from the next time you click—providing that you are proficient at reading coordinates.

If the direct selection or arrow tool is active, the X and Y values indicate the top left corner of the selection.

If you want Illustrator to take the stroke weight or effects of the selected object into consideration, check the Use Preview Bounds in the General Preferences.

And when you use a transformation tool, the X and Y values represent the center of the scaling, rotation, reflection, or skew. More on this topic in Chapter 11.

🌑 **W, H:** The W and H values list the width and height of a selected object. They also tell you the dimensions of a rectangle, ellipse, text block, or graph as you draw it.

 With the Use Preview Bounds option in the General Preferences dialog box active, the W and H values will increase by an amount equal to the size of the object's stroke weight or any effects applied to the object.

When you move an object or drag with the measure, pen, convert point, or gradient vector tool, the W and H values tell you the horizontal and vertical components of your drag.

🌑 **D:** This item tells the direct distance between one point and another, as the crow flies. When you drag with the pen or convert point tool, this value indicates the length of the Bézier lever, which is the distance between the anchor point and the control handle. When you're using other tools, the D value simply tells you the distance of your drag.

🌑 **Angle:** The – item indicates the angle of your drag, as measured from the mean horizontal. Illustrator measures counterclockwise starting at 3 o'clock; 90 degrees is a quarter circle, 360 degrees is a full circle.

When you use the rotate tool, the angle value tells you the angle of rotation. The reflect tool uses the angle value to impart the angle of the reflection axis. When you use the shear tool, you get two angle values, one for the axis, and the other for the skew. We'll cover all these wacky terms in Chapter 11 when we explore transformations in earnest.

🌑 **W%, H%:** These values appear when you scale an object. They tell you the change's width and height, measured as percentages of the object's original dimensions.

When you use the zoom tool, the Info palette tells you the current view size (which is redundant, because Illustrator tells you this in the Size bar as well as in the title bar). When you're editing text, the Info palette lists the type size, font, and tracking information. When you're kerning, the second item lists the general tracking values minus the kerning value to give you an overall kerning total.

Translating Measurement to Movement

After you measure a distance with the move tool, Illustrator automatically stores those W, H, D, and angle values in a tiny buffer in memory. Use the tool again, and the previous measurements are tossed by the wayside to make room for the new ones. Illustrator also uses this buffer to track movements you make by dragging with the arrow or direct selection tool, or by nudging with the arrow keys. Again, the measurements of the most recent action replace the previous contents of the buffer.

You can translate these buffered measurements into movements by selecting an object or two and choosing Object » Transform » Move. Or try one of the following shortcuts:

- Control-click, or right-click as the case may be, and choose the Transform » Move command from the context-sensitive pop-up menu.

- Double-clicking the arrow tool icon in the toolbox also works. This is a weird way to go, admittedly, but it stems from an old Illustrator shortcut, Opt/Alt-clicking the arrow tool icon.

Whatever method you use, you get the Move dialog box shown in Figure 10-4. The Move dialog box always supplies you with the buffered distance and angle values, which permit you to quickly move objects a measured distance or to repeat a move made by dragging with the arrow tool. You can likewise negate a move by changing positive values to negative and vice versa. Or you can retain just the horizontal portion of a move by changing the Horizontal value to 0 and inverting the Vertical value. Then again...well, you get the idea. There are all kinds of ways to rehash old measurement and movement information.

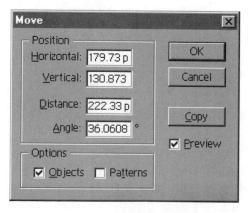

Figure 10-4:
The Move dialog box always presents you with the results of your last measurement or movement.

If you feel the urge, you can even enter totally new values into the various option boxes. You can express your move by entering values into the Horizontal and Vertical option boxes or the Distance or Angle option boxes. Because these are two different ways to express the same information, changing one set of values automatically changes the other.

You can also do math inside the option boxes. Simple arithmetic, but math nonetheless. Enter + to add, – to subtract, * to multiply, and / to divide. For example, if you know you want to move a selected object 3 points farther than your last measurement, you can enter +3 after the value in the Distance option box. Then press Tab and watch Illustrator do the math for you. This technique works inside other palettes and dialog boxes as well, including the Transform palette.

Use the bottom two check boxes, Objects and Patterns, to select what is to be affected by the move. Check the final check box, Preview, to see what your changes will look like before they occur. You must specify what you want to preview. If you want to preview a move, make sure that both the Preview and Objects check boxes are selected. To see a preview of the object moving with its tile pattern intact, click the Patterns check box as well. For the lowdown on these options, consult the authoritative Chapter 15.

 You can move the selected objects the specified distance and direction by pressing the Return/Enter key. To clone the objects before moving them, click the Copy button or press Opt-Return/Enter.

 The Move dialog box accepts no more than three digits after the decimal point, so measured values get rounded off. In most cases, such a small increment won't make a lick of difference in your printed output. But if it does matter, you may want to resort to Illustrator's automatic alignment options, which we discuss later in this chapter.

Coordinate Positioning

The last item on the precision position parade is the Transform palette—formally known as the Control palette, and it's the subject of Figure 10-5. After you select the objects you want to change, you open the Transform palette by choosing Window » Show Transform Palette. You can then enter values into any one of the six option boxes and press Return/Enter to apply them to one or more selected objects.

Reference point icon

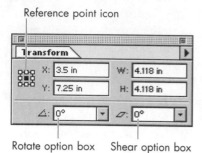

Figure 10-5:
The Transform palette, courtesy
of the Transform Elves and
Wood Nymphs Association.

Rotate option box   Shear option box

The first item in the Transform palette is the reference point icon. You can use this icon to specify whether the coordinates in the X and Y option boxes represent the upper left corner of the selection, the middle of the selection, or one of seven other locations. Click one of the little points in the icon to relocate the reference point. Illustrator updates the X and Y values automatically.

You can enter new values into the X and Y option boxes to change the location of the object on the artboard. You can also adjust the W and H values to change the width and height of the bounding box, which in turn stretches or shrinks the selected object. The shear and rotate options on the right side of the palette let you reshape and rotate selections. Chapter 11 covers these transformations in depth.

As in the Move dialog box, you can perform arithmetic calculations in the X, Y, W, and H options using the standard +, −, *, and / operators. You can even do math inside the shear or rotate option boxes.

Although it doesn't have a Copy button, you can clone objects directly from the Transform palette. Just enter a value into one of the option boxes and press Opt/Alt-Return/Enter if you want to clone the selection and exit the Transform palette. Or press Opt/Alt-Tab to clone and tab to the next option box. Press Opt/Alt-Tab again and you'll make another clone. And jump to the next option box.

Aligning and Distributing Objects

To display the Align palette, choose Window » Show Align. Shown in Figure 10-6, this dainty little palette contains six Align Objects icons and six Distribute Objects icons. Three icons in each row let you align or distribute horizontally; three allow you to do the same vertically. Select the objects that you want to align or distribute, and then click an icon. Illustrator adjusts the objects immediately.

For example, click the first icon in the top row to align the selected objects along their left edges, click the second icon to center the objects, and click the third icon to align the right edges.

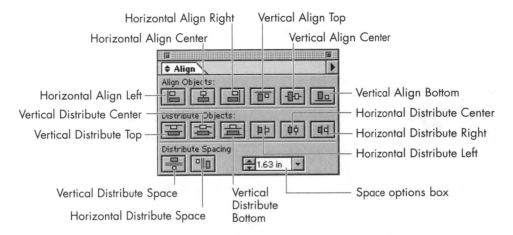

Figure 10-6: Select the objects that you want to align or distribute, and click an icon in the Align palette.

Once you select objects, you click the icons of the Align palette to move the selected objects. There are twelve different icons in the Align palette. These icons can be sorted into the following five groups which are also illustrated in Figure 10-7:

- **Ordinary alignment:** These six options (Horizontal Align Left, Horizontal Align Center, Horizontal Align Right, Vertical Align Top, Vertical Align Center, and Vertical Align Bottom) move objects based on the bounding boxes of the selected objects. The "key" object, or the object that the others align themselves to, is always the most extreme left or top object in the selection.

- **Distribute alignment:** The distribute icons (Vertical Distribute Top, Vertical Distribute Center, Vertical Distribute Bottom, Horizontal Distribute Left, Horizontal Distribute Center, and Horizontal Distribute Right) move objects so there is equal space between the sides or centers of the bounding box. For example, Horizontal Distribute Center moves objects so that there is equal space from side to side between the centers of three or more objects. These icons use the Auto setting in the Space options box, which is visible when you choose Show Options from the Align palette menu.

Distribute space: Oftentimes, the distribute alignment option will create equal distance between the sides or centers of objects, but leave the optical space between the objects unequal. The distribute space icons (Vertical Distribute Space and Horizontal Distribute Space) distribute objects so the space between them is equal. These icons are visible when you choose Show Options from the Align palette menu, and they use the Auto setting in the Space options box.

 Up until Illustrator 9, you could not specify how much space should be between sides, centers, or objects. The distribute space icons only moved the inside objects so that the space between objects was equal. Illustrator 9 now adds an option box that lets you specify exactly how much space should be set for both the distribute alignment and distribute space icons. We call these two new features the Distribute Specific Alignment and Distribute Specific Space options.

 Distribute specific alignment: Distribute Specific Alignment uses the same icons as the Distribute Alignment icons together with a specific amount set in the Space options box. This moves objects so that there is a specific amount of space between the sides or centers of objects.

Distribute specific space: Distribute Specific Space uses the same icons as the Distribute Space icons together with a specific amount set in the Space options box. This moves objects so that there is a specific amount of space between the objects.

As with the Transform palette, the options in the Align palette work from the bounding boxes of selected objects.

To align or distribute multiple objects together, first group the objects by choosing Object » Group (Cmd/Ctrl-G). For example, we grouped each of the simple paths in Figure 10-7 with its bounding box before we applied settings from the Align palette.

You must select three or more objects to use the Auto setting of the Distribute Objects options. This is because Illustrator compares the space among objects when distributing them; you have to select three objects to have two spaces to compare.

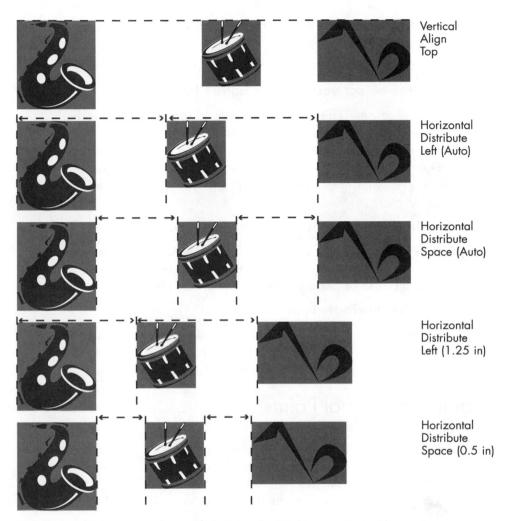

Vertical
Align
Top

Horizontal
Distribute
Left (Auto)

Horizontal
Distribute
Space (Auto)

Horizontal
Distribute
Left (1.25 in)

Horizontal
Distribute
Space (0.5 in)

Figure 10-7: Select some objects and click one of the buttons in the Align palette.
The gray rectangles represent bounding boxes; the dotted lines show how the portions
of the bounding boxes get distributed.

 The space options box is new in Illustrator 9. The default setting of Auto means that the space between the objects will
come from the available space already between the objects.
If you want a specific amount of space between the sides,
centers, or objects, you need to set the key object—that is
the object that remains anchored while the other objects
move in relationship to it. Here's how to set the key object
and the spacing amount.

1. **Select the objects you want to distribute.**

   If you are setting a specific space amount, you can select two or more objects. The Auto setting requires three or more.

2. **Click the object you want to be the key object.**

   Yes, we know the object is already selected, but you need to tell Illustrator which of the selected objects is the key object. For instance, in Figure 10-7 we clicked the leftmost object a second time to select it as the key object. If you use the arrow tool, you can simply click the object. However, if you use the direct selection tool, you need to Opt/Alt-click.

3. **Set the amount in the Space options box.**

   The default is Auto. Set an amount in the options box. Once there is an amount in the box, you can use the up or down arrows next to the box to increase or decrease the amount in the box.

4. **Click the distribute icon.**

   You can now click the specific distribute icon. If you don't like the results, change the space amount or click a different distribute icon. Repeat steps 2, 3, and 4 until everything looks perfect.

Aligning Individual Points

The options in the Align palette affect whole objects at a time. But Illustrator also lets you align selected points independently of their objects by choosing Object » Path » Average (Cmd-Opt-J on the Mac or Ctrl-Alt-J for Windows users). You can arrange two or more points into horizontal or vertical alignment, or you can snap the points together to make them coincident. In each case, Illustrator averages the locations of the points, so all points move.

First select the points you want to align with the direct selection tool. Then choose the Average command. The Average dialog box will display, providing you with three radio buttons. You can either make all points coincident (Both), arrange them in a horizontal line (Horizontal), or arrange them vertically (Vertical).

If you want to average and join in one swell foop, Mac users can press Cmd-Opt-Shift-J; Windows users can press Ctrl-Alt-Shift-J. Use the Average command when you want to align points in formation or bring points together from different shapes *without* joining them.

You can even average the alignment points in point text, which is a great way to arrange bits of point text into columns or to align labels with callout lines. The fanciful medical illustration in Figure 10-8 shows this technique in action. After creating the series of labels and callout lines along the right side of the figures, we selected a label and the rightmost point in its line and averaged their locations by choosing Average and then selecting the Both radio button. Then we selected all labels and the right points in their callout lines and chose Average again, this time selecting the Vertical radio button.

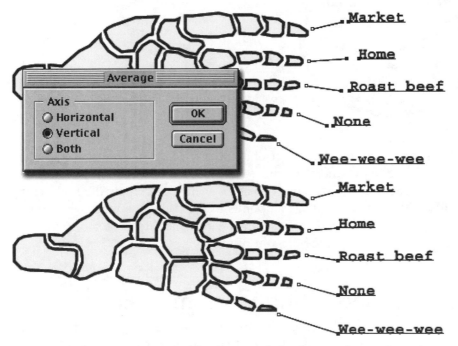

Figure 10-8: The Vertical setting of the Average dialog box easily straightened out the selected points and point text.

Adding a True Center Point

Illustrator lets you assign a center point to any object by selecting the object and clicking on the Show Center button in the Attributes palette. Unfortunately, Illustrator positions the center point with respect to the bounding box, which is rarely the true center of the shape except in the case of rectangles (which are the same shape as their bounding boxes) and ellipses (which are uniformly round).

For example, suppose that you wanted to center a star inside a circle. If you first drew the circle, and then drew the star from the circle's center point, the two center points match. But if you use the center point in the star to drag until it snaps onto the center point in the circle, you'll get the problem shown in Figure 10-9. Illustrator hasn't centered the shapes; it has centered the bounding boxes.

Figure 10-9:
If you drag a center point in the star until it snaps to the circle's center point, the shapes align like this. Not really centered.

If you need to see the true center of an object, you can use the Average command. Copy the object and then choose Edit » Paste in Front. You now have a clone of your object. Choose Object » Path » Average and apply the Both setting. This causes Illustrator to average all points in the path. The place where all the points meet is the true center. You can use this mess to center one object to another. But please delete it before you print.

Creating and Using Custom Guides

Another way to align objects is to establish a system of guidelines (or just plain *guides*). These are special kinds of paths that appear as dotted or solid lines on screen but never print. You can choose the form and color that your guides take in the Guides & Grid Preferences dialog box. Assuming the Snap to Point option is turned on in the General Preferences dialog box, your cursor aligns to the guideline any time you drag within two pixels of it. Unlike standard paths, your cursor snaps to any position along the outline of a guide, regardless of the placement of anchor points.

You can create a guide in one of the following ways:

- Drag from one of the rulers to create a perpendicular guide that runs the entire width or height of the pasteboard. In Figure 10-10, for example, we dragged from the horizontal ruler to create a horizontal guide. The guideline appears in the illustration window as a blue line, clearly distinguishing it from printing objects.

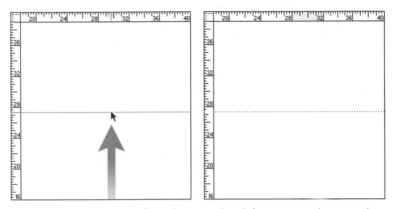

Figure 10-10: Dragging from the top ruler (left) creates a horizontal guideline that stretches the entire width of the pasteboard (right).

 If you change your mind while dragging a guide from one of the rulers, press the Opt/Alt key to rotate it 90 degrees. Opt/Alt-dragging from the horizontal ruler creates a vertical guide.

- To create a custom guideline in the shape of a circle, star, or even a character of type, select a path that you've drawn in the illustration window and choose View » Make Guides. You can also use the shortcut Cmd/Ctrl-5.

You can convert all varieties of paths to guidelines, including compound paths. You can even convert groups, selections inside groups, and the bars or lines inside graphs. The one thing you can't turn into a guide is text (unless you first convert the text to paths with Type » Create Outlines, like the big R in Figure 10-11). So if you get an error message when pressing Cmd/Ctrl-5, you can be sure your selection includes some text. Deselect the text and try again.

To create a guideline without sacrificing the original path, copy the path (Cmd/Ctrl-C), paste it in back (Cmd/Ctrl-B), and then choose View » Make Guides (Cmd/Ctrl-5) to convert the duplicate to a guideline.

Figure 10-11: Press Cmd/Ctrl-5 to convert selected paths—
including converted text and compound paths (top)—to custom
snap-to guidelines (bottom).

 If you convert a single path within a group to a guideline, without converting other paths in the group, the guideline remains a member of that group. Drag the group with the arrow tool, and the guide moves as well. It's a very handy way to keep certain guides and objects together.

Unlocking, Editing, and Clearing Guides

By default, Illustrator locks guides so they don't get too tangled up with your printed paths. You can't select a locked guide by simply clicking on it, which prevents you from messing it up. To unlock all guides in an illustration, choose View » Lock Guides. Mac users can press Cmd-Opt-; (semicolon). Windows users can press Ctrl-Alt-; (semicolon). After you click it, the check mark in front of the Lock Guides command disappears, showing that the lock is now off.

Once the guides are unlocked, you can select and manipulate them as you can any other graphic object. When you click a guide with the arrow or direct selection tool, Illustrator shows you the guide's anchor points to let you know it's selected. Use the direct selection tool to reshape the guide. Shift-click or marquee to select multiple guides at a time. Press the Delete key to delete a selected guide. You can also move guides or transform them. You can even use the add point, delete point, and convert point tools on a guideline.

If you get tired of looking at your guides, you can hide them by choosing View » Guides » Hide Guides. But the guides are still there. You just hid them. If you can't stand your guides anymore and want to delete them forever, choose View » Guides » Clear Guides. That sends them all to guide Siberia where no one will ever hear from them again.

Converting Guides to Objects

If your eyes grow tired from editing guidelines, or if you simply want to turn a guide into a printing object, you can convert a guide back to a path. To do so, unlock the guide, select it, and then choose View » Release Guides. Illustrator converts custom guides back to paths, even remembering their original fill and stroke colors. Ruler guides convert into lines which will have no fill and zero stroke weight, and which extend the entire width or length of the pasteboard.

 To convert a locked guide back into a path, Cmd/Ctrl-Shift-double-click the guide.

Deleting Ruler Guides

Sandee has been stung by this one so many times that she insists on covering it as a separate topic: watch out when you delete ruler guides. If you use the direct selection tool to select the guide, you may select just the segment. If you press the delete key, you will delete the guide, but leave two anchor points all the way at the very ends of the pasteboard.

Unless you press the delete key again, you will leave these two anchor points at the edge of the universe. These points are considered part of the artwork and can cause all sorts of problems. If you use the Select All command and then try to scale your illustration, you'll get an error message. You can't scale the artwork because those guides have no where else to go.

If you try to convert the artwork to Web files, you'll probably get a message that there's not enough memory to create the file. That's because you're trying to make a file that is several feet big. (Much too big for Web sites.) And if you import the file into QuarkXPress or InDesign, you'll get strange results if you try to fit the artwork inside a picture frame.

Just remember, always press the delete key twice if you select ruler guides with the direct selection tool. Or just always press the delete key twice no matter what. This way you won't leave anchor points at the ends of the universe.

It's Grid for You and Me

Another of Illustrator's handy positioning features is the optional grid system. By simply choosing View » Show Grid or by pressing Cmd/Ctrl-" (quote), a network of equally spaced horizontal and vertical lines stripe your pasteboard. You can choose the color and style of the lines that make up a grid, just as you can for your guides, in the Guides & Grid Preferences (shown back in Chapter 2). There you also specify the spacing of the grid lines and the number of divisions per grid line. Choose a grid line spacing of 72 points with 5 subdivisions, and you get a lattice of lines spaced 12 points apart (72 divided by 5). Select the Lines command from the Style pop-up menu to see grid lines and divisions; select Dots to see the grid lines sans the divisions.

On first glance, you may think that this is a case of guide overkill. But friends, we're here to tell you that beneath the grid's mild mannered appearance beats the heart of a powerful ally. The grid function offers you these handy features:

- Grids let you quickly check to make sure you've created compound paths correctly (provided that Grids In Back inside the Guides & Grid Preferences is active). If you see the grid through the hole, you know the compound is correct.

- A grid gives you a quick-and-easy way to produce guides that are equally spaced. Just choose View » Show Grid and set the structure in the Guides & Grid Preferences dialog box.

- You can set up your grid line spacing in different units than the general units. In the Guides & Grid Preferences dialog box, enter a value into the Gridline every_option box followed by the type of units you want. You can then have your rulers set to, say, centimeters and your grids marking off inches.

- Because a grid is subject to the value set in the Constraint Angle option box (in the General Preferences dialog box), you can have an angled grid. Guides, on the other hand, are limited to the standard up-and-down or side-to-side format.

An angled grid allows you to create perspective drawings quickly and easily. Deke drew the box in Figure 10-12 with the aid of an angled grid. He chose

View » Show Grid and entered 45 into the Constrain Angle option in the General Preferences dialog box. With four quick clicks of the pen tool, he created the top of the box and filled it with white—that's why you can't see the grid behind it. After selecting the rectangle, he Opt/Alt-dragged it down to form the bottom of the box. With four more clicks, he created the left side of the box and duplicated it by Opt/Alt-dragging up and to the right with the arrow tool. He then pressed Cmd/Ctrl-Shift-[(left bracket) to send the right side to the back of the stack. The whole process took him less than five minutes.

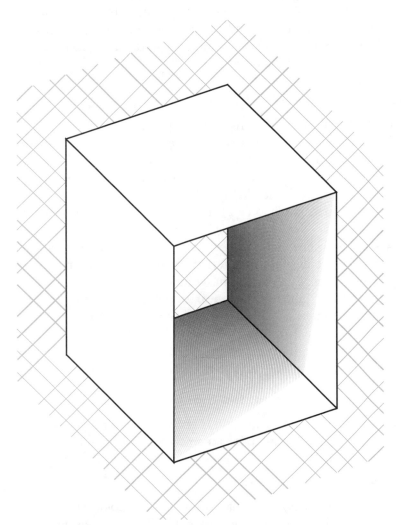

Figure 10-12: With a Constrain Angle value of 45 degrees, Deke turned on the grid and quickly drew one of them freaky perspective boxes.

Smart Guides

Illustrator also has a system of automated guides that might just make the old-fashioned guides and grids obsolete for all your precision drawing and positioning needs. Smart guides consist of *alignment guides, path labels,* and *path highlights.* The alignment guides are temporary guidelines that pop in and out of existence as you drag the cursor around the screen. Path labels consist of a number of little text hints that display to inform you where your cursor is within the document. Path highlights ring the outline of a path to tell you that the cursor is positioned over a path. Smart guides are completely independent of traditional guides, with the exception that their color matches that of traditional guides and is determined in the Guides and Grid Preferences dialog box.

Perfect Position

Alignment guides (also known as construction guides), the driving force behind smart guides, resemble traditional ruler guides in that they extend the entire length of the pasteboard, but, unlike ruler guides, they display only as long as you need them. To see alignment guides, first turn them on with the View » Smart Guides toggle command (Cmd/Ctrl-U). Then, from the Smart Guides Preferences (covered way back in Chapter 2), make sure that the Construction Guides option is active.

Alignment guides will appear to help you position the points of a path as you create or manipulate it. The guides inform you that you're aligned with respect to the origin point of your drag. By default, the guides align at multiples of 45 degrees. Secondary alignment guides will appear to tell you that you are also aligned to other points of interest. You determine these secondary alignment points by dragging over them with your active tool.

At first glance, this is a bit confusing so here's a quick demonstration of how alignment guides can assist you in drawing a right triangle with two equal sides.

1. **Click with the pen tool to set the triangle's first point.**

    Be sure that the Smart Guides command is active. For clarity, we've turned off the other smart guide options, namely the Text Label Hints and Object Highlighting options.

2. **Move the pen tool to the right.**

    As you move the pen directly horizontally from this first point, an alignment guide displays, as shown in Figure 10-13. This shows that you are aligned with respect to that first point.

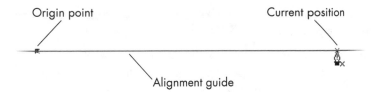

Figure 10-13: Click to set the triangle's first corner point and move the cursor directly to the right. An alignment guide will show that you're on track.

3. Click to set the triangle's second corner point.

The second point will be directly to the right of the first point.

4. Move the cursor up and to the left.

When you're aligned with the second corner point, a new alignment guide will appear as shown in Figure 10-14. If this guide doesn't display, choose the 90º and 45º Angles command from the Angles pop-up menu in the Smart Guides Preferences.

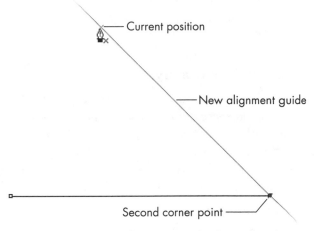

Figure 10-14: A new alignment guide shows that the present cursor position makes a 45 degree angle with the horizontal and is aligned with respect to the second corner point.

5. **Move the cursor over the first point and then move the cursor straight up.**

    This two-step positioning is of the utmost importance. By moving the cursor over the first corner point you're telling Illustrator that you want to use this as a secondary alignment point. As you move the cursor upward, a secondary alignment guide will display, as shown in Figure 10-15.

    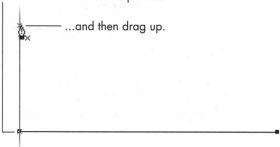

    Move the cursor over this point...

    ...and then drag up.

    Figure 10-15: First move the cursor over the point you want to use as a secondary alignment point and drag straight up to see a secondary alignment guide.

6. **Continue until both guides display.**

    As you continue to move the cursor up, all the while aligned with the first corner point so that the secondary alignment guide remains visible, you will eventually cross the point where the first alignment guide again displays, as shown in Figure 10-16. This point is in perfect alignment with the triangle's other two corner points, directly above the first and at a 45 degree angle up and to the left of the second.

7. **Click to set the third corner.**

    Position a point with perfect precision.

8. **Click again at the original point.**

    This closes the path, completing your perfect right triangle with two equal sides.

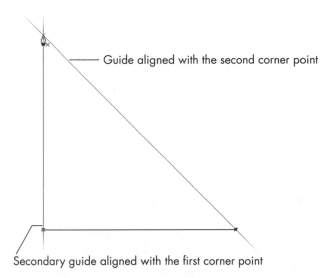

Guide aligned with the second corner point

Secondary guide aligned with the first corner point

Figure 10-16: Moving the cursor directly upward will eventually display the intersection of the two alignment guides.

The display of alignment is not limited to when you're simply moving the cursor around the screen. The guides also appear when you are dragging to create paths or dragging paths around to position them. You can also define as many secondary alignment points as you wish. Just be sure to move the cursor over the other points that you want Illustrator to align. Although you may have a number of active alignment points, Illustrator will only display two alignments at a time (either an alignment guide and a secondary alignment guide, or two alignment guides).

Precise Transforming

If you want Illustrator to display alignment guides while you're manipulating a path with one of the transformation tools, then activate the Transformation Tools option in the Smart Guides Preferences. The primary alignment guide will display with reference to the point from which you started your drag, not the transformation's origin point. You may define secondary alignment points by dragging the cursor over points of the various other paths that make up your artwork. Unfortunately, you cannot set the transformation's origin point as a secondary alignment point, because this is not a "physical" point in the world of Illustrator.

If you know that you're going to want to use the transformation origin as a secondary alignment point, simply construct a point at that location with the pen tool before you start the transformation. Then select the object you want to transform and click the point you just made with the transformation tool. After you've begun dragging the cursor, be sure to move it over the point, indicating to Illustrator that you want it to use the point as a secondary alignment point.

Alignment Angles

By default, an alignment guide will pop in when the angle formed between your cursor's current and original positions and the horizontal is some multiple of 45 degrees. But, as you've probably guessed, Illustrator doesn't limit you with such mundane options. In the Smart Guides Preferences dialog box you can choose from seven predefined angular alignment options (all of which appear in the Angles pop-up menu), or enter up to six custom angles. If you choose to rebel geometrically, simply enter the angle with which you want the alignment guides to conform in the six option boxes below the Angles pop-up menu. Illustrator will reflect your choices in the little alignment guide display box located to the right of the Angles pop-up menu.

The angle of the various alignment guides also depends on the value in the Constrain Angle option box of the General Preferences dialog box. For example, if the General Preferences' Constrain Angle is set to 0 degrees and the Smart Guides Preferences' Angles is on the 90° and 45° Angles setting, then the angle of an alignment guide could be 0, 45, or 90 degrees. If the Constrain Angle is changed to 15 degrees, the resulting alignment guide's angles could be 15, 60, or 105 degrees. Just think of the Constrain Angle value as a starting point for the angles of the alignment guides.

Sticking to Smart Guides

Unlike with traditional guides and grids, your cursor has no option but to snap to any smart guide. If an alignment guide is visible, then Illustrator will snap the path or point you're dragging to the guide once you release the mouse button. Anytime you're within a certain distance of the position of a smart guide, the smart guide appears and Illustrator is ready to snap you to it. This distance is the snapping tolerance. By default, the snapping tolerance is set to 4 screen pixels. In the Snapping Tolerance option box in the Smart Guides Preferences dialog box, you can choose any value from 0 to 10 pixels inclusively. The higher the value, the more readily Illustrator displays the smart guides.

Your Position Spelled Out

Another feature of smart guides are path labels. When the Text Label Hints option in the Smart Guides Preferences dialog box is checked and the Smart Guides command is in effect, Illustrator will show you little labels to inform you as to the position of the cursor with respect to various parts of your document. Figure 10-17 shows a collage of the different types.

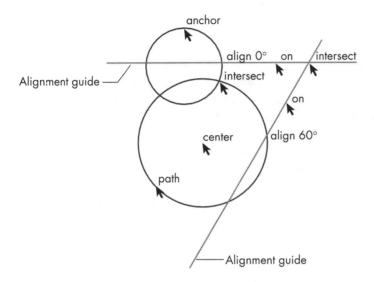

Figure 10-17: With the Text Label Hints option active, Illustrator displays various labels to inform you of the cursor's position.

Path Highlights

Smart guides have one other feature: path highlighting. With the Object Highlighting option in the Smart Guides Preferences dialog box checked and the Smart Guides command set to the on position, Illustrator will temporarily highlight the outline of any path that would be selected if you clicked at that position. This allows you to easily see paths that are partially (or even entirely) obscured by other paths. Although Illustrator will highlight locked paths, it will not acknowledge hidden paths.

Assembling Paths into Groups

Most of the time, you'll apply transformations to whole paths rather than to individual points or segments. You may even want to transform multiple objects at a time. So imagine that instead of working with paths and objects, you could manipulate whole pieces of artwork. A boy here, a dog there, a great white shark preparing to eat the both of them a few meters away. This is the beauty of grouping, which allows you to assemble throngs of elements into a single object.

Creating Groups

Suppose, for example, that you've created a graphic made up of several paths. You want to select the graphic easily. To always select and transform the graphic as a complete entity, select the objects and choose Object » Group. Or press the common-as-dirt keyboard equivalent, Cmd/Ctrl-G.

Illustrator always groups entire objects. Even if you select a single point in one object and a segment in another, the two objects join the group in their entirety. There's no way to group a couple of points or segments independently of others in a path.

You can group paths, compound paths, text objects, imported images, or any other kind of artwork. You can even group other groups. Illustrator permits hierarchies of groups, so that one group may contain two groups that each contain six others, and so on. It's like a giant family tree of object protection.

Adding to Groups

If you already have a group there are two ways to add a new element to the group. If you select the entire group and the new object, the Group command makes a new group—a "higher level" group that consists of the original group and the new object. However, if you ungroup the original group, then add the object, and then regroup, you will have only one group—all on the same "level" of the group.

If you don't like all that ungrouping and grouping, you can cut the object and then choose either Paste in Front or Paste in Back to add the object to the group. (See "Paste in Front or Back of Collections" later in this chapter.)

Ungrouping

You can ungroup any group by choosing Object » Ungroup, or pressing Cmd/Ctrl-Shift-G. You have to ungroup each group one level at a time. So if a group contains three other groups, for example, you'd have to press Cmd/Ctrl-Shift-G four times in a row to disassociate all of them.

Ungrouping is occasionally an essential part of the reshaping process. Most notably, you can't combine two paths from different groups, whether by joining their endpoints or by making them into a compound path. So if you want to join two open paths from different groups into a single longer path, for example, you have to first ungroup the paths and then apply the Join command.

 Illustrator 9 now allows you to work with groups directly in the Layers palette. Although you cannot create a group in the Layers palette, you can add to or delete objects from the group. See "Working with Drawing Layers" later in this chapter.

Distinguishing Groups from Non-Groups

What if ungrouping a path doesn't produce the desired effect? It may be that the object wasn't grouped in the first place. Illustrator permits you to create various kinds of collective objects, including compound paths, linked text blocks, masks, and wrapped objects. You may not always know what command has grouped the objects into being selected together.

 With the release of Illustrator 9, you can simply look at the type of object in the Layers palette. (More on the Layers palette later in this chapter.)

If you want, you can look at the menu commands to determine what type of collective element has been applied to objects. If UnGroup is active, you've got a group. If Compound Paths » Release is available, it's a compound.

When Grouping Isn't Protection Enough

Grouping helps to protect the relative placement of objects, but it doesn't get objects out of your way when you're trying to edit a complex illustration. Nor does it protect your artwork from the unpredictable motor skills of less adept artists who may come after you.

For those of us who have learned a little something about what we're doing, Illustrator provides a laundry list of protection alternatives. You can lock objects, preventing you or anyone else from accidentally selecting and altering them. You can temporarily hide an object if it impairs your view of other objects. And you can relegate entire collections of objects to independent layers, which you can in turn lock and hide as you choose.

We'll explain locking and hiding in the next few pages. Because layers are a more involved topic, we'll give them their own section toward the end of the chapter.

Putting an Object under Lock and Key

Locking an object prevents you from selecting it. This means you won't be able to delete the object, edit it in any manner, or change its fill or stroke.

You lock objects by selecting them and choosing Object » Lock command or Cmd/Ctrl-2. You can't lock a single point or segment independently of other elements in a path. If you specifically select one point in a path and choose the Lock command, Illustrator locks the entire path.

 When working on a very specific detail in an illustration, you may find it helpful to lock every object *not* included in the detail. With potentially hundreds of objects, it could be difficult and time consuming to select every one of them. So instead, you can simply select the objects that you *don't* want to lock and press the Opt/Alt key while choosing Object » Lock command. If the keyboard equivalent is more to your liking, press Cmd-Opt-Shift-2 on the Mac. Or press Ctrl-Alt-Shift-2 on Windows.

Unlocking All That Was Locked

Because you can't select a locked object, there's no way to indicate which objects you'd like to unlock and which you'd like to leave locked. So you have to unlock all locked objects at the same time.

To do so, choose Object » Unlock All. Illustrator unlocks all locked objects and selects them, so that you can see which objects were locked clearly and manipulate them if necessary. You can now Shift-click the few objects you want to leave unlocked with the arrow tool, and then relock the others.

Sending Objects into Hiding

If an object is really in your way, you can do more than just lock it; you can totally hide it from view. You can't see a hidden object in any display mode, nor does it appear when the illustration is printed. Because a hidden object is always invisible, you can't select or manipulate it.

You hide objects by selecting them and choosing Object » Hide Selection (Cmd/Ctrl-3). You can't hide a single point or segment; Illustrator always hides entire paths at a time. But you can hide objects inside groups, compound paths, and other collective objects. The path disappears, but it still moves and otherwise keeps up with the group when you select the entire group with the arrow tool.

To hide all objects that are not selected and leave the selected ones visible, Hold the Opt/Alt key as you choose Object » Hide Selection. You can also press Cmd-Opt-Shift-3 (on the Mac) or Ctrl-Alt-Shift-3 (on Windows).

Unlike locking, hiding is not saved with the illustration. Adobe's afraid that you'll forget the hidden objects were ever there. Therefore, when you open an illustration, all objects in the file are in full view.

Revealing Everything That Was Hidden

You can't select a hidden object any better than a locked one, so there's no way to show a specific object. Instead, you have to display all hidden objects at the same time by choosing Object » Show All. Illustrator shows all previously hidden objects and selects them. This way, the objects are called to your attention, allowing you to easily send them back into hiding if you want.

 Hiding, too, was invented as a way to work before there were layers. However, the Layers palette gives you far more features for hiding objects.

The Celebrated Stacking Order

When you preview or print an illustration, Illustrator describes it one object at a time, starting with the first object in the illustration window and working up to the last. The order in which the objects are described is called the stacking order. The first object described lies behind all other objects in the illustration window. The last object sits in front of its cohorts. All other objects exist on some unique tier between the first object and the last.

Left to its own devices, stacking order would be a function of the order in which you draw (like an archeology dig). The oldest object would be in back; the most recent object would be in front. But Illustrator provides a number of commands that allow you to adjust the stacking order of existing paths and text blocks.

All the Way Forward or Back

Two commands in the Object » Arrange submenu let you send objects to the absolute front or back of an illustration. If you select an object and choose Object » Arrange » Bring To Front, Illustrator moves the object to the front of the stack.

The object is treated exactly as if it were the most recently created path in the illustration and will therefore be described last when previewing or printing.

By selecting an object and choosing Object » Arrange » Send To Back, Illustrator treats a selected object as if it were the first path in the layer and describes it first when previewing or printing.

You can apply both commands to whole objects only. If a path is only partially selected when you choose either command, the entire path is moved to the front or back of the illustration. If you select more than one object when choosing Bring to Front or Send to Back, the relative stacking of each selected object is retained. For example, if you select two objects and choose Bring to Front, the forward of the two objects becomes the frontmost object and the rearward of the two objects becomes the second-to-frontmost object.

Relative Stacking

When creating complicated illustrations, it's not enough to be able to send objects to the absolute front or back of an illustration. Illustrator provides two commands specifically designed to change the selected item or items' rank in the stack by one. Choose Object » Arrange » Bring Forward or press Cmd/Ctrl-] (right bracket) to advance the selected object one step closer to the front of the stack; choose Object » Arrange » Send Backward or press Cmd/Ctrl-[(left bracket) to shove it one closer to the back. Although you would probably never feel inclined to use these commands to move the 46th-to-front up to 14th-to-front or vice versa, they are great to use when you want to nudge a path a couple of steps forward or three steps backward in the stacking order.

Illustrator also allows you to send one object in front of or behind another using Clipboard commands. To change the stacking order of an object, select it and press Cmd/Ctrl-X to jettison it to the Clipboard. Then select the path or text block that the cut object should go behind, and press Cmd/Ctrl-B (Edit » Paste In Back). Or, if you'd rather place the cut object in front of the selection, press Cmd/Ctrl-F (Edit » Paste In Front). In either case, Illustrator restores the object to the exact location from which it was cut. Only the stacking order is changed.

If multiple objects are selected when you press Cmd/Ctrl-B, Illustrator places the contents of the Clipboard in back of the rearmost selected object. Not surprisingly, Cmd/Ctrl-F pastes the cut object in front of the frontmost selected object. If no object is selected, Cmd/Ctrl-B sends the object to the back of the illustration; Cmd/Ctrl-F sends it to the front of the illustration.

The Effect of Grouping and Combining on Stacking

Combining objects into groups also affects the stacking order of the objects in the illustration. All paths in a group must be stacked consecutively. To accomplish this, Illustrator uses the frontmost selected object as a marker when you choose the Group command. All other selected objects are stacked in order behind the frontmost one.

The same holds true for compound paths, linked text blocks, wrapped objects, joined paths, and paths combined with the Pathfinder filters.

You can select an object inside a group with the direct selection tool and change its stacking order using the Bring To Front and Send To Back commands. But Illustrator keeps the selected objects inside its group. So rather than sending an object to the front of the illustration when you press Cmd/Ctrl-Shift-] (right bracket), Illustrator just sends it to the front of the group, while leaving the stacking order of the overall group unchanged.

You can also cut an object from a group and then paste it inside or outside of the group using the Paste In Front and Paste In Back commands. Illustrator automatically deselects everything when you cut an object—because the selection has disappeared—so pressing Cmd/Ctrl-B or Cmd/Ctrl-F sends the cut object to the absolute back or front of the illustration.

Paste in Front or Back of Collections

This is one of those gotchas that throw experienced Illustrator users. When you use the Paste in Front or Paste in Back commands, you need to pay attention to how many objects are selected. If you have an entire group selected, the Paste in Front or Back commands paste the new object as an element that is unconnected to the group. But if you have only part of a group selected, the Paste in Front or Back commands will paste the new object as part of the group.

The same applies to compound paths, text wraps, and other collective elements. Of course it all makes sense if you think about it. With only one element of a collection selected, Illustrator thinks you want to sneak a new element into the collection. With the whole collection selected, Illustrator realizes you probably want to keep the integrity of the collection, and simply add the new object in front or in back.

Working with Drawing Layers

In addition to the stacking functions, Illustrator offers self-contained drawing layers (or simply layers), an almost essential capability for creating complex illustrations. Illustrator was late to join the layering game—version 5 was the first to offer layers, years behind drawing rivals FreeHand and Canvas—but its layers are quite possibly the best of any drawing program. To display the Layers palette, choose Window » Show Layers.

Illustrator 9 has completely revamped the Layers palette as shown in Figure 10-18. Not only can you put objects on their own layers, but you can nest layers like you do with folders. You can also see the individual groups and paths that are on each layer. And by see, we don't mean just see a label, you can actually see a thumbnail drawing of the layer as well as the objects on the layer.

 The new Layers palette in Illustrator 9 provides a command called "Make/Release Clipping Mask." Rather than cover it here, we'll explain it all in Chapter 18 with the rest of the masks.

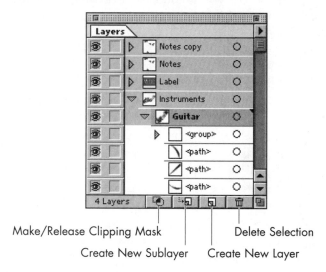

Make/Release Clipping Mask   Delete Selection

Create New Sublayer   Create New Layer

Figure 10-18: The layers palette as seen in its default settings.

An illustration can contain any number of layers, each layer can contain any number of objects, and you can name layers and alter their order as you see fit. You can even hide layers, lock them, and change their display mode independently of each other.

Adding New Layers

Illustrator automatically creates flat illustrations with only one layer apiece. To add a drawing layer to the illustration, choose the New Layer command from the Layers palette menu or click the Create New Layer button. The position of the new layer depends on which layer is presently active.

The first thing that you'll probably notice is that Illustrator has presumptuously named the new layer. If you find this impertinence to your disliking, either choose the Options command for that layer from the Layer menu or double-click the name of the layer in the Layers palette. The Layer Options dialog box displays, as shown in Figure 10-19. Enter a layer name of up to 31 characters long into the Name option box.

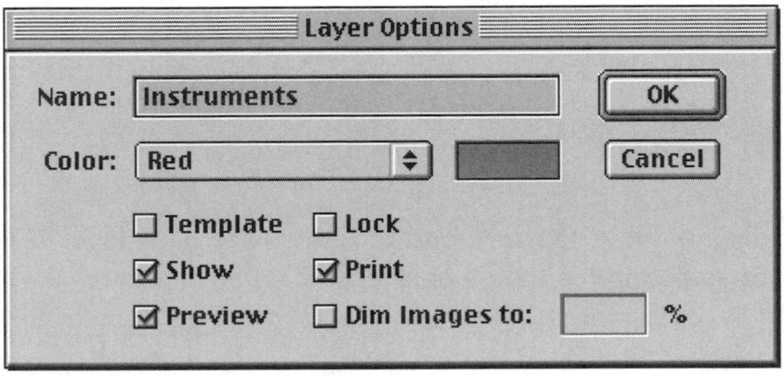

Layer Options

Name: Instruments   OK

Color: Red   ▼   [   ]   Cancel

☐ Template   ☐ Lock
☑ Show   ☑ Print
☑ Preview   ☐ Dim Images to: [   ] %

Figure 10-19: The Layer Options allows you to change the name and other attributes of a layer.

If you only work with one layer, you may think that Illustrator always shows selected points, segments, and control handles in blue, but this isn't necessarily the case. The Layers Options also lets you choose a color from the pop-up list. The controls the color of the anchor points for objects on that layer. If you always accept Illustrator's default colors, points on the first layer are blue, those on the second layer are red, followed by bright green, a darker blue, yellow, magenta, cyan, gray, and black. But you can also select from orange, teal, brown, and lots of other colors, or you can define a custom color by selecting the Other option.

Although you probably will be concerned only with the name and color of a new layer and won't want to change any of the check boxes at first, because we're here we'll go ahead and run over the other options in this dialog. These options are generally more useful after you've added a few objects to the layer and you've had a little time to consider how you want the layer to interact with the rest of your illustration. They allow you such choices as these:

- Turn on the Template check box to create a locked, nonprinting layer that is intended to show dimmed images. This is ideal for images that you wish to trace. Images that are placed with the Template option selected appear on a layer with this option selected.

- To hide all objects on the layer, turn off the Show check box.

- To view the objects on the new layer in the outline mode, turn off the Preview check box.

- Select the Print check box and all objects on the layer will print. Deselect it and all the objects won't print.

- Select the Lock check box to lock objects on the layer so they can't be accidentally altered.

- Select Dim Images to diffuse imported images so that you can easily distinguish them from graphic objects and text blocks created in Illustrator, as you may recall from Chapter 4. The default setting is 50 percent, but feel free to set any value from 0 to 100 percent.

Fortunately the Show, Preview, and Lock attributes for a layer can be controlled in the Layers palette, without having to open the Layer Options.

After you press Return/Enter, the layer's new name appears just above the last active layer.

In case you're thinking, "Gosh, I bet I can add layers to the Startup file to get multiple layers when Illustrator creates a new illustration," permit us to dash your hopes right off the bat. You can't. Nor can you drag and drop entire layers between illustrations, the way you can in Photoshop.

The Layers palette also includes a New Layer button. It's the button located in the bottom right corner with the page icon on it. You can simply click this button or click it in conjunction with some keys to add a new layer:

- Click the New Layer button to create a layer just above the last active layer.

- Opt/Alt-click the New Layer button to first display the Layer Options before creating a layer just above the last active layer.

- Cmd-Opt-click (Mac) or Ctrl-Alt-click (Windows) the New Layer button to display the Layers Options before creating a layer just *below* the active layer.

- Cmd/Ctrl-click the New Layer button to create a layer at the very top of the layers list.

Drawing on Layers

The highlighted name in the Layers palette (which also has a small black triangle in the upper right corner) represents the active drawing layer. Any objects you create are placed on this layer. To change the active drawing layer, click a layer name in the scrolling list. Then start drawing to create objects on that layer.

Moving Objects between Layers

When you select an object in the illustration window, the corresponding drawing layer becomes highlighted in the scrolling list. You'll also see a tiny colored selection marker along the right edge of the Layers palette. This marker represents the selected object. If you select multiple objects on different layers, Illustrator shows multiple selection markers, one for each layer on which the objects sit.

To move the selected objects from one layer to another, drag the colored selection marker up or down the scrolling list. You can drag the marker to any layer that is neither hidden nor locked. You can drag only one marker at a time; so if you have objects selected on two layers, for example, and you want to move them all to a third layer, you have to drag one selection marker to the third layer and then drag the other.

As you drag the marker, the cursor changes to a finger to indicate that you are moving objects between layers, as in Figure 10-20. Upon releasing the mouse button, Illustrator transfers the selected objects from one layer to the other.

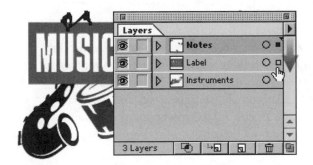

Figure 10-20: Drag the selection marker up or down to move an object from one layer to another.

To clone selected objects between layers, Opt/Alt-drag the selection marker inside the Layers palette. The cursor changes to a finger with a plus sign. After you release the mouse, the selected objects exist independently in both layers, just as though you had copied them from one layer and pasted them into another. You can also clone all objects on one layer to a brand-spanking-new layer by dragging the layer you want to duplicate onto the New Layer button. The cloned layer appears just above the original layer.

If you select all the objects on a layer, the selection marker becomes a larger square as shown in Figure 10-21.

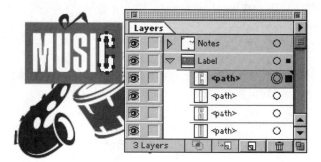

Figure 10-21: The larger square marker indicates that all the objects on a layer are selected.

You can quickly select all the objects on a layer by clicking the spot on the Layers palette where the selection marker for that layer appears. The large square selection marker appears, which indicates all the objects on that layer are selected. This also includes all the members of a group as well as the single item of a path.

Nesting Sub-layers

Just as you can create a folder inside another folder in your computer filing system, so can you create sub-layers inside other layers.

Nested layers are new to Illustrator 9. Nested layers allow you to organize your Layers palette so that you don't have to scroll through hundreds of layers.

If you never exceed four or five layers in your Illustrator documents, then, no, you don't need to create nested layers. But if you are a mapmaker who wants layers for each city, county, and state in the United States, you're going to love sub-layers.

To create a sub-layer already nested in the current layer, click the Create New Sub-layer icon in the Layers palette. You can also drag a layer onto another layer to nest one layer in another, as shown in Figure 10-22. The destination layer does not have to be open in order to nest the new layer.

To move a sub-layer up in the ranks, drag the layer till you see the indicator line on a higher level in the layers palette. When you release the mouse button, the sub-layer will have been promoted to a higher layer status. (After twenty-five years, promoted layers also receive a gold watch for their service.)

Figure 10-22:
Drag a layer below another
to create a sub-layer.

Opening Layers

When there is nothing on a layer, there is no triangle icon for that layer because the layer is empty. (Oh, the sadness of an empty layer.) However, as soon as you put an object, a group or a sub-layer on a layer, a triangle icon appears. This triangle opens and closes the layer. There are several different types of objects that can be on layers:

- **Paths:** The most basic thing on a layer is an object. Objects never have triangles because there is no sub-division for them.

- **Groups:** Groups and other collective elements such as compound paths are displayed on a layer with a triangle. If you click the triangle you will see the paths that make up a group.

- **Sub-layers:** Sub-layers are layers nested inside other layers.

Once you rename a group or a sub-layer, you may find it difficult to tell the difference between them. After all, they both have triangles to open or close their contents. There are some differences, though. Layers always have a gray background behind their name. And if you double-click a group, or a path, you see the Options dialog box that only locks and shows the group. The Options dialog box for a sub-layer has many more options.

If you cannot move what you think is a sub-layer up to its own top layer status, then most likely what you have is a group, not a layer. Groups always have to be one level down from the top level of layers.

Path and Group Layers

Illustrator 9's new Layers palette also lists groups and paths. Click the triangle to open the layer and you will see all the individual paths and groups on that layer, as brilliantly illustrated in Figure 10-23. Just as you can drag one layer above another, so can you drag paths and groups up or down within a layer or between layers.

What's even more exciting (we get excited about Illustrator very easily) is that you can drag paths in and out of groups or drag groups in an out of other groups simply by using the Layers palette. You never need to select objects or use any of the group or ungroup commands.

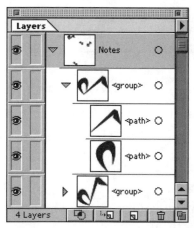

Figure 10-23:
The Layers palette can also show the individual paths and groups on a layer.

Paste Remembers Layers

When the Paste Remembers Layers option is turned on, copying and pasting an object from one illustration into another pastes both the objects and the layer. Choose the Paste Remembers Layers option in the Layers palette to turn it on. (Or you can select the Paste Remembers Layers check box in the General Preferences dialog box.) When turned on, this option instructs Illustrator to remember which layer an object came from when you send it to the Clipboard. Illustrator then pastes the object back onto that same layer, regardless of which layer is active. If the new document doesn't have a layer with that name, the paste command creates one. If cut or copied objects come from multiple layers, Illustrator pastes them back onto multiple layers.

By default, Paste Remembers Layers is turned off. When you turn it on, it affects all active documents and stays on from one session to another—until you turn it off.

Viewing Layers

One of the great advantages of working with layers is you can control which layers are visible and which are hidden from sight. This helps enormously if you're working with a very complex illustration and just want to see one part of the artwork. It also help if you have many elements such as blends, gradients, and effects that take time to redraw on the screen. You can turn off viewing those layers, and speed up the preview of your work.

The leftmost column in the Layers palette lets you change the display mode for each layer. Each of the display modes is shown in Figure 10-24:

- A solid eyeball icon means that the layer is visible in both the outline and preview modes. Click the eyeball on and off to show or hide the layer. (This changes the Show setting in the Layer Options.) Unlike Object » Hide Selection, Illustrator saves the state of a hidden layer when you close and then reopen a document.

- No eyeball icon means the layer is hidden. Click the empty eyeball box to show the layer.

 Opt/Alt-click the eyeball icon to hide all the other layers except that layer.

- A hollow eyeball icon means that the layer displays only in the outline mode. Cmd/Ctrl-click to toggle the icon between the outline-only or preview modes. Click the hollow eyeball on and off to show or hide the layer. (This changes the Preview setting in the Layer Options.)

 Cmd-Opt-click (Mac) or Ctrl-Alt-click (Windows) the eyeball icon to turn all the other layers except that layer into the outline-only mode.

A dimmed eyeball icon means that the display of the layer is controlled by the setting of a higher layer. For instance, in Figure 10-24, the Notes layer is hidden. This dims the entries for the groups and paths below that layer.

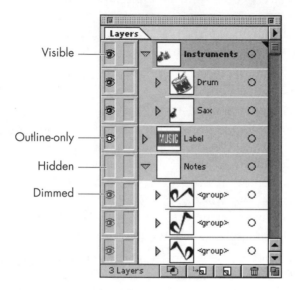

Figure 10-24: The different view options for layers.

 You can't add items to a hidden layer. You can't draw on a hidden layer, nor can you move items in the Layers palette from one layer to a hidden layer. (There was a time when you could, but you can't now.)

Locking Layers

You use the second column in the Layers palette to lock all the elements on that layer. This allows you to work in another layer without risking accidentally manipulating or deleting an object in the locked layer.

No icon in the second column means the layer is unlocked. Click the empty box to lock the layer. (This changes the Lock setting in the Layer Options.)

A lock icon means that the layer is protected. Nothing can be added, deleted, modified, or moved on that layer.

Color plate 1 (from Figure 09-28): *An example of how the Hard Mix Pathfinder command slices objects and mixes the colors at their highest percentages—that is, the highest amounts of cyan, magenta, yellow, and black ink from all overlapping objects.*

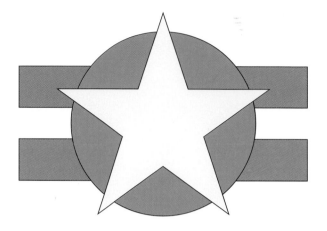

Color plate 2 (from Figure 09-29): *An example of how the Soft Mix Pathfinder command at its default setting of 50 percent slices and changes the colors of an object. The Soft Mix command allows you to specify the percentages of the colors that should be combined. This creates lighter colors than the Hard Mix command.*

Color plate 3 (from Figure 14-01): *An example of the additive color system, which combines red, green, and blue light. Where all three lights meet, the color is white.*

Color plate 4 (from Figure 14-02): *An example of the subtractive color system, which combines cyan, magenta, and yellow inks. Where all three inks meet, the color is supposed to be black. However, because the inks used in printing are not perfect, the final color is a very deep brown. This is why a fourth color, black, is used in process color printing.*

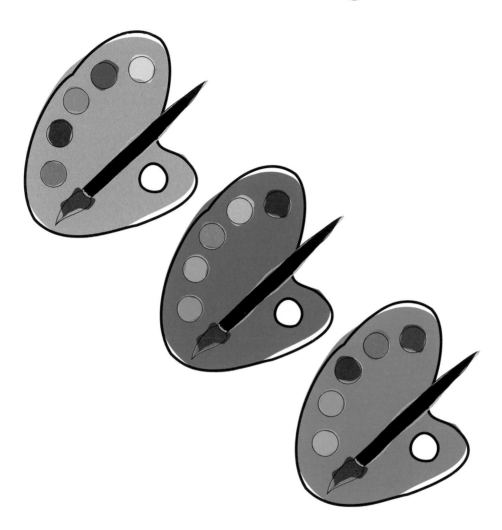

Color plate 5 (from Figure 14-05): *The palette and color wells of the original art (top) were altered by applying the Invert command (middle) and the Complementary command (bottom).*

Color plate 6 (from Figure 14-14): *Overprinting was applied to all the strokes of the decorative elements inside the wings. The top object shows what the illustration looks like with Overprint Preview turned off. The bottom object shows what the illustration looks like with Overprint Preview turned on.*

Color plate 7 (from Figure 14-16): *An example of how the Adjust Colors command affects colors. The original art is in the top left corner. The top right corner had 20 percent removed from all plates. The middle left had 20 percent added to the magenta and yellow plates. The middle right had 50 percent removed from the cyan plate, 20 percent added to the magenta plate, and 70 percent removed from the yellow plate. The bottom left had 10 percent removed from the cyan and yellow plates and 80 percent removed from the magenta plate. The bottom right had 100 percent removed from the cyan plate.*

Color plate 8 (from Figure 14-17): *An example of how the Saturate controls affect colors. The original art is in the top left corner. The top right corner had 30 percent increase in saturation applied to the artwork. The middle left had 30 percent decrease in saturation applied. The middle right had 60 percent increase in saturation. The bottom left had 60 percent decrease in saturation applied. The bottom right had 50 percent decrease in saturation applied to the background and 50 percent increase in saturation applied to the foreground.*

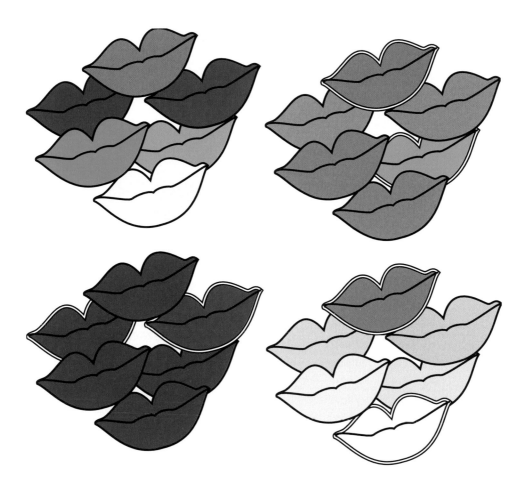

Color plate 9 (from Figure 14-18): *An example of how the color blend filters change objects. The original art is in the top left corner. The top right corner had the Blend Front to Back command applied. The bottom left had the Blend Horizontally command applied. The bottom right had the Blend Vertically command applied. In each instance, the objects used for the blend have a double stroke applied.*

Color plate 10: *An example of how adding magenta or cyan to black makes a rich black color. The top blackboard is colored with 100 black ink. The middle blackboard is colored with 100 black and 50 cyan. This is sometimes called a cool black. The bottom blackboard is colored with 100 black and 50 magenta. This is sometimes called a warm black.*

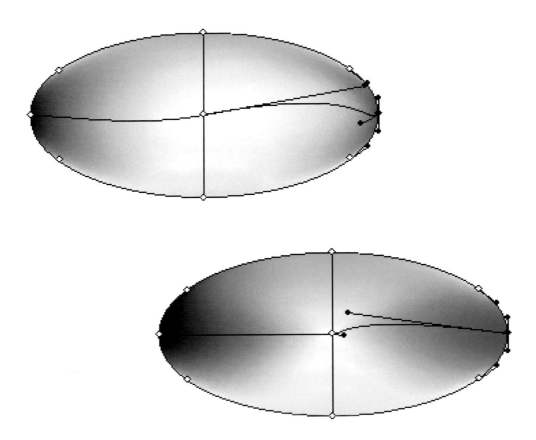

Color plate 11 (from Figure 15-20): *An example of how the color nodes change the blending between colors in a gradient mesh.*

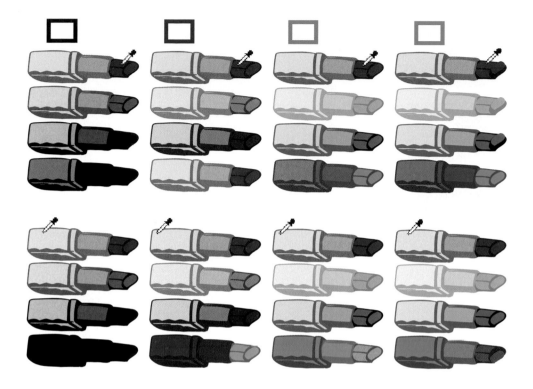

Color plate 12 (from Figure 16-37): *Each of these lipstick brushes had the tints, tints and shades, and hue shift applied. The stroke color is indicated at the top of the chart. The eyedropper shows which part of the brush was used as the key color. Notice how changing the key color in the bottom set changes the way the stroke colors are applied to the objects.*

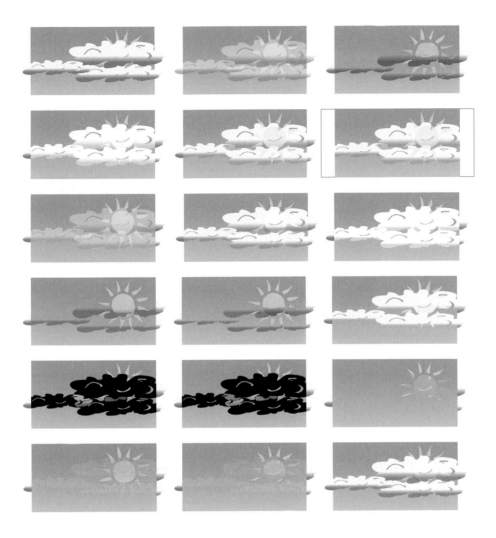

Color plate 13 (from Figure 17-7): *An example of how the blending modes affect colors. In each case the clouds had a different blending mode applied. Top row (left to right): original, opacity 50 percent, multiply. Second row: screen, overlay, overlay with white background. Third row: soft light, hard light, color dodge. Fourth row: color burn, darken, lighten. Fifth row: difference, exclusion, hue. Sixth row: saturation, color, luminosity.*

Color plate 14 (from Figure 17-10): *An example of how the Knockout Group command allows an object to have opacity or blending modes applied to the group as a whole. In the top example, the multiply blending mode and a 70 percent opacity setting were applied to all the individual objects of the U.S. flag. This caused the stars to be lost into the blue of the flag. In the bottom example, the multiply blending mode and 70 percent opacity setting were applied to the knockout group. This allowed the stars and stripes to interact with the background, rather than the elements of the flag.*

Color plate 15 (from Figure 19-11): *An example of the type of artwork that should be saved as GIF images. The top group all consists of flat colors. Although the artwork in the bottom group has blends, there are not too many different colors within each illustration. So they, too, can be exported as GIF images.*

Color plate 16 (from Figure 19-13): *An example of the type of artwork that should be saved as JPEG images. Notice how as the JPEG compression increases (from top to bottom), the distortion artifacts become more prominent.*

Opt/Alt-click the empty lock box to lock all the other layers except that layer.

- A dimmed lock icon means that the protection of the layer is controlled by the setting of a higher layer.

- If you select a locked layer, your cursor becomes a little pencil with a line through it. This shows you that you can't write to this layer unless you first unlock it.

Selecting, Merging, Flattening, and Deleting Layers

Only one layer can be the active layer (indicated by the black triangle in the upper-right corner). But you can select more than one layer at once. Shift-click a layer other than the active one to select all layers from the active layer to the layer you clicked, inclusively. Cmd/Ctrl-click another layer to select non-contiguous layers.

 You cannot select non-contiguous layers in different levels. All the layers must be at the first level of the Layers palette or sub-layers of the same layer.

Once you have selected layers, you can choose Merge Selected from the Layers menu. This moves all the objects on the selected layers to the topmost layer. Illustrator also deletes the empty layers.

To smoosh together all non-hidden layers into a single layer, choose Flatten Artwork from the pop-up menu. All of the objects from the discarded layers will appear on the topmost layer. If any hidden layers are present, Illustrator will give you the option to move the layers' contents along with all the other artwork or to discard them.

You can delete a layer—even if it's chock-full of text and paths—by clicking the layer name and choosing Delete from the Layers palette menu or clicking the Delete button—the one with a trash can icon. If the layer contains any objects, an alert box appears, warning you that you are about to delete a layer that contains artwork. To delete a layer without Illustrator's cautioning, Opt/Alt-click the Delete button.

Template Layers

Back in Chapter 4 we mentioned that when you choose the Template option, placed images appear on a special layer called a Template. Template layers are actually regular layers with the following options automatically set in the Layer Options dialog box.

- Printing is turned off.

- The layer is locked.

- Placed images are dimmed to 50% by default, but you can change the amount in the Layer Options.

- The Show and Preview settings remain checked but unavailable. You can only change them by turning off the Template option.

Printing Layers

To prevent a layer from printing, double-click it and turn off the Print check box in the Layer Options. But remember what you've done! When printing, Illustrator doesn't give you any warnings that some layers are turned off. Many artists have lost their hair trying to figure out why certain objects aren't printing from their illustrations, while other objects are printing just fine.

Customizing Layers

Just because the Layers palette ships with a certain look doesn't mean you have to sit there passively and accept it. Hey, get up! Assert your individuality! You're in control here, not some product manager in San Jose, California!

To change the display of the Layers palette, choose Palette Options from the Layers palette menu. The dialog box shown in Figure 10-25 appears. Make your choices as follows:

- **Show layers only:** Stops you from seeing the groups and paths that make up a layer.

- **Row Size:** This controls how big the thumbnail previews are. However, the Small setting also turns off the thumbnail previews.

- **Thumbnails:** This controls which elements will have thumbnail previews. The default setting shows thumbnails for all elements. If you choose Layers only, you will turn off the thumbnails for groups and paths, but leave the thumbnails for layers and sub-layers. (Sandee likes this setting. It keeps her palette less cluttered, but still gives her visual feedback as to what's on each layer.)

 To make Illustrator 9's Layers palette look most similar to Illustrator 8, set the palette options as follows: Show Layers Only should be checked. Row Size should be Medium or Small. All thumbnails should be turned off.

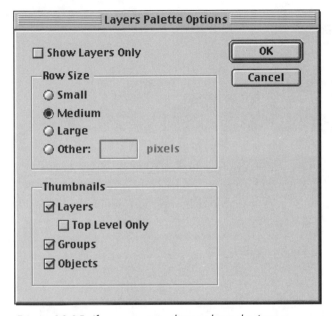

Figure 10-25: If you want to change how the Layers palette appears, here's where you make your choices. These are the default settings.

Vacuuming Your Illustration

We know the artwork you send to others will be clean with all layers labeled clearly with no random pieces of rubbish littering the landscape. But what if it's the other way around? What if an incredibly gifted person like you has to muck about inside cruddy pieces of artwork created by some imbecile from your company's dim past?

Both of us have inherited work from people who didn't have a clue as to what they were doing. We have seen stray points, transparent shapes, and empty text blocks littering the virtual landscape like roaches laid waste with a bug bomb.

That's why Illustrator includes the Cleanup command. You won't need it very often, but when you do, it's great. Just choose Objects » Path » Cleanup to display the dialog box in Figure 10-26. You can opt to delete single points that have no segments, paths that have no fill or stroke, and text blocks that have no text. All the refugees from the Island of Misfit Objects get whisked clean away.

Figure 10-26:
Illustrator lets you scrub away random rubbish from old illustrations.

If you want to delete just stray points, you can skip this dialog box by choosing Edit » Select » Stray Points. This selects all the stray points in your document. Then just punch the Delete key and away they go.

CHAPTER 11

THE MAGICAL WORLD OF TRANSFORMATIONS

Ahh, the magic of the transformation tools: scale, rotate, shear, and reflect. Not only are they part of Adobe Illustrator, but their magic is also found in many fairy tales and children's stories. It must have been the scale tool that caused the beanstalk to grow so tall. Only the rotate tool could have swirled the tornado that sent Dorothy to Oz. Obviously the evil witch looked in the mirror with the reflect tool. And what else but the shear tool could have distorted Peter Pan's shadow? Add a Free Transform tool and a Transform Each command, and you can practically see Cinderella's fairy godmother waving her magic wand as you work in Illustrator.

All four of the transformation tools work pretty much the same as when we started using Illustrator (Deke with version 1; Sandee at version 88.) The only major change happened in version 7. Adobe finally let you see the point around which the transformation occurs. In Illustrator 8, Adobe transformed the lame free distort filter into the more powerful free transform tool. With this single tool you can make combinations of the ordinary transformations as well as totally bizarre distortions. Even the modest bounding box can perform two transformations: scale and rotate.

 Instead of having to jump to the Preferences to show and hide the bounding box for an object, Illustrator 9 has elevated the command to the View menu as Show/Hide Bounding Box. It's even got its own keystroke — Cmd/Ctrl-Shift-B — which we recommend you memorize immediately.

So in essence, if you're familiar with previous versions of Illustrator, you are probably well versed in the world of transformation. But even for you world-weary oldtimers (and faithful readers of previous editions), this chapter is still worth reading—especially the Transform Each command. We've given this command some extra emphasis based on its importance in creating special appearances (which we'll cover in chapter 12).

Making Objects Bigger and Smaller

Let's start things off with a bang by talking about scaling. In case you're unclear, scaling means enlarging or reducing something, or making it thinner or fatter or taller or shorter. Put a fellow on the rack, and you're scaling him.

The Scale Tool and the Origin Point

After selecting one or more objects—paths, text, or imported images (it matters not)—drag with the scale tool in the drawing area. Illustrator enlarges or reduces the selection with respect to its center. If you drag away from the center of the selection, as in Figure 11-1, you enlarge the objects. If you drag toward the center, you reduce them. It's so simple, a child could do it. (And no doubt many have.)

Good thing you don't have to accept the default center. You can scale a selection with respect to any point in the illustration window. This origin point (also called a reference point or scale origin) represents the center of the transformation. To demonstrate how an origin point works, we enlarged a star several times over with respect to a single origin in Figure 11-2. All of the white arrows in the figure emanate from the origin, showing how the points move outward uniformly from this one point.

Scale tool

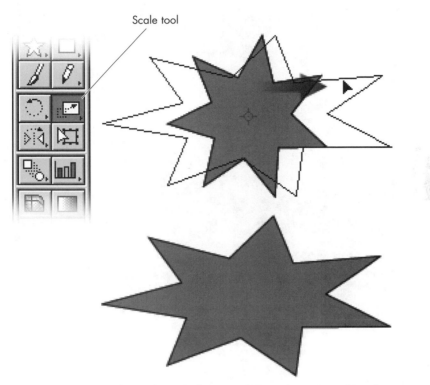

Figure 11-1: Using the scale tool, drag away from the center of a selection (top) to enlarge it (bottom).

By moving the origin point, you also move the scaled object. In Figure 11-3 we've applied the exact same scaling to copies of the same circle. When the origin point is in the center, the scaled object keeps the same center. But when we move the origin point to different positions, the final scaled objects also move to new positions. And don't forget, the origin point for all transformations can be positioned way outside the selected object. (The white circles represent the original objects, the dark ovals represent the scaled objects, and the origin point is that target thing.)

Therefore, the origin point affects the positioning of objects, whereas the distance you drag with the scale tool determines the extent of the resizing. The following steps explain how to set the origin point and scale from it:

1. Select the objects you want to scale.

2. Click with the scale tool where you want to position the origin. Provided the View » Snap to Point command is active and you click within 2 points of an anchor point or guideline, Illustrator snaps the origin to that point.

Figure 11-2: A star scaled repeatedly with respect to a single origin point.

3. Drag with the scale tool about an inch or two away from the origin. This gives you room to move inward and provides you with more control. If you start the drag too close to the origin, you have too little room to maneuver. Illustrator resizes the objects with respect to the origin. If you drag away from the origin, you enlarge the selection. If you drag toward the origin, the selected objects shrink.

If you drag from one side of the origin point to the other, you flip the selection. Although Illustrator also provides a separate reflect tool, the scale tool is the only one that lets you flip and resize at the same time. (By contrast, the reflect tool lets you flip and rotate simultaneously.)

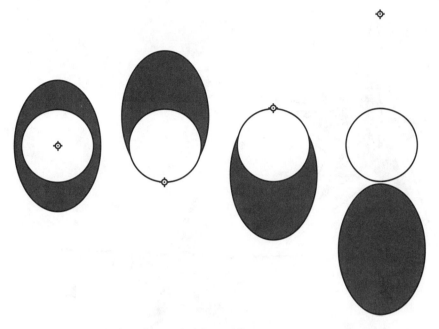

Figure 11-3: Several circles scaled from different origin points (from left to right): center, bottom, top, outside the object).

Scaling with the Shift Key

As you do when drawing and reshaping paths, you can use the Shift key to constrain a transformation. However, Illustrator actually has three different constraints for the Shift key:

- As Figure 11-4 shows, you can Shift-drag on a diagonal to scale a selection proportionally, so the height and width of a selected object are equally affected. Or you can scale the selection exclusively horizontally or vertically while pressing Shift.

- Shift-drag to the left or right so that only the width of the object is affected as shown in Figure 11-4. This is called a horizontal scale.

- Shift-drag up or down so that only the height of the object is affected. This is called a vertical scale.

 If the shape seems to jump around a lot while you press the Shift key, it's because you began your drag in a bad place. Release and press Cmd/Ctrl-Z to put things back where they were. Then start your drag in a diagonal direction from the origin.

Figure 11-4: Shift-drag diagonally to scale a shape proportionally (top). Shift-drag horizontally to change the width of the shape only (bottom).

All this assumes that you haven't rotated the constraint axes from their default 0-degree setting. If you have changed the constraint axes, you can still scale proportionally using the Shift key. However, holding the Shift key won't constrain your scaling along the horizontal or vertical axis. Instead, you scale in line with the constraint axes angles.

Scaling Again

After you scale an object, the percentages used for the scale are stored in Illustrator's memory. This means that you can choose Object » Transform » Transform Again (Cmd/Ctrl-D) to repeat the scaling. This technique is usually referred to by its keyboard shortcut. Each time you press Cmd/Ctrl-D, the object scales again by the same percentages. (The power users just hold the Cmd/Ctrl key with one hand and pound the D key furiously with the other—Mac users press Cmd-D-D-D. Windows users press Ctrl-D-D-D.) Repeating the scale over and over may not seem that useful but it does have its advantages:

You can drag just a tiny bit to scale the object ever so slightly. Then just press Cmd/Ctrl-D-D-D to watch the object grow. This is easier than dragging up and down.

You can select another object and scale it by the same percentages. The only drawback to this is that Illustrator uses the origin point for the first object as you can see in Figure 11-5.

Figure 11-5: These apples were all scaled using the same percentages. The apple on the left was scaled by dragging with the scale tool around the origin point indicated by the target. The next two apples were scaled by using the Transform Again command (Cmd/Ctrl-D). Notice how the apples move from their original positions (indicated by the gray outlines).

However, some people think repeatedly scaling the same object over and over is as exciting as watching a sponge soak up water. Hold on, then! Just wait till you see what happens when you combine Transform Again with duplicating objects as you scale them.

Duplicating Objects as You Scale Them

The scale tool also lets you clone objects as you scale them. To scale a clone and leave the original unchanged, press the Opt/Alt key after you start the drag and keep the key pressed until after you release the mouse button. If you enlarge the selection, you may cover up the original with the clone, but the original will be there, lurking in the background. (If you're at all concerned, press Cmd/Ctrl-Shift-[(left bracket) to send the clone in back of the original.)

At this point Illustrator has the following sentence stored in its memory: "Make a copy of whatever object is selected, and then scale it up a certain percentage from a certain origin point." Illustrator will remember that sentence until you make another transformation. (Transformations include scale, rotate, reflect, shear, and move.)

You can now create a series of scaled clones by choosing Transform Again. This is a particularly useful technique for creating perspective effects. By reducing a series of clones toward a far-off origin, you create the effect of shapes slowly receding into the distance.

For example, we began with the stars and bars as shown in Figure 11-6. We clicked the origin point with the scale tool and Opt/Alt-Shift-dragged ever so slightly down toward the origin to create a proportional clone. The clone was in front of the original, so we pressed Cmd/Ctrl-Shift-[(left bracket) to send it to the back.

Even though we had done something else—used the Send to Back command—Illustrator still remembered the sentence. So with the clone selected, we pressed Cmd/Ctrl-D to create another reduced clone and Cmd/Ctrl-Shift-[(left bracket) to send it to the back. We kept pressing Cmd/Ctrl-D and Cmd/Ctrl-Shift-[(left bracket) until we arrived at the effect on the left side of Figure 11-6.

For a more interesting effect, we created the clones without pressing the Shift key. Thus the clones are not limited to proportional duplicates of the original. The right side of Figure 11-6 shows what happens when we applied a non-proportional scale. In this case we dragged so that the horizontal scaling was slightly greater than the vertical. The images seem to swoop up at the viewer.

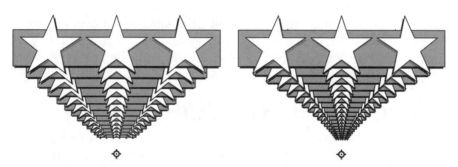

Figure 11-6: A proportional scale created the perspective on the left. A non-proportional scale created the more realistic swoop on the right. In each case the origin point is indicated by the target below the objects.

A few of you brainy types are thinking "Why can't we just blend between a big version and a little version of the objects?" Fact is, you can. But as Figure 11-7 shows, you still don't get that nice swoop effect. However, because this chapter has nothing to do with blends, you can either skip to Chapter 18 or wait till we get there and cover how to create blends.

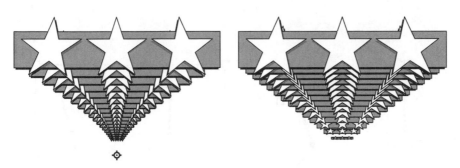

Figure 11-7: A comparison of using the Cmd/Ctrl-D to create a perspective effect, (on the left), or blending (on the right).

Scaling with the Bounding Box

So why would Adobe add another way to scale objects? Doesn't the scale tool do everything you could ever need when it comes to scaling? Well, yes, but for years other illustration programs have allowed you to scale objects by simply dragging on the handles of the bounding box around objects. So rather than switch from the selection tool to the scale tool, Adobe made it easier to simply drag the bounding box.

To use the bounding box, choose View » Show Bounding Box. If the command is listed as Hide Bounding Box, then you do have the Bounding Box option chosen. (Of course, you don't need to choose the option because you have already memorized Cmd/Ctrl-Shift-B.) Once done, any and all paths that are selected when the arrow tool is chosen will automatically gain an eight-handled box that encloses all the selected paths—in other words, partially selected paths do not display with a bounding box.

The orientation of this bounding box is initially up to Illustrator and is based on the path or paths selected. For example, the bounding box of the top left star in Figure 11-8 is aligned to match the angle at which the star was drawn. If you don't like the default orientation of a bounding box, you can choose Object » Transform » Reset Bounding Box which is what we did to align the bounding box of the top right star in Figure 11-8. When you select more than one path, the bounding box will usually align in such a way that it is square with the page. Anytime you want, you can reset the bounding box so that it is square with the page by choosing Object »Transform » Reset Bounding Box.

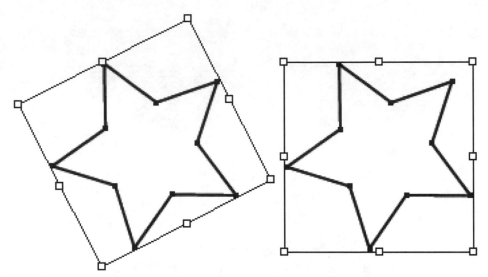

Figure 11-8: When the Use Bounding Box check box is activated, each wholly selected path will display an eight-handled bounding box that encloses just the path.

The real power of the bounding box is in its use:

- Drag on a corner handle to scale the selected objects. Shift-drag a corner handle to scale proportionally. In either case, the opposite corner serves as the scale origin.

- Opt/Alt-drag on a corner handle to scale the object around its center. Opt/Alt-Shift-drag a corner handle to scale proportionally around the object's center.

- Drag on one of the bounding box's side handles (including the top and bottom handles) to limit the scaling to either horizontal or vertical changes. The opposite side's handle serves as the scale origin.

- Shift-drag a side handle to once again scale proportionally, except that in this case the opposite side's handle serves as the scale origin.

- Opt/Alt-drag a side handle to horizontally or vertically scale the object from the center.

- Use Transform Again (Cmd/Ctrl-D) to repeat the transformation from the bounding box.

You can't use the Opt/Alt key to make a copy of the object as you scale with the bounding box. Only the Scale tool has that magical power.

Resizing by the Numbers

The scale tool is one of our favorite tools, but it's not the only way to resize objects in Illustrator. You can also enlarge and reduce object sizes by entering precise numeric values into two different dialog boxes and one palette.

Scaling from the Transform Palette

Let's start with the least capable (but most convenient) of the three scaling options, the Transform palette. Instead of a single Scale option box, you enter values in the W (for width) and H (for height) option boxes to scale objects. Although it may seem quite obvious how to use the palette, there are actually some hidden features:

- Enter an amount in either the width (W) or height (H) option boxes. Use the Tab key to jump from one box to another. Press Return/Enter or click on the page to change the focus from the Transform palette.

- Use the reference point icon to change the point around which the transformation occurs. The reference points are measured with respect to the selection's rectangular bounding box.

- To scale by percentages enter a number followed by the % symbol into either the W or H option boxes as illuminated in Figure 11-9. You can enter different percentages to scale the object non-proportionally. You can also enter a single number in either the width or the height option box. Then press Cmd/Ctrl-Return/Enter to apply the value to both the width and height.

- On the Mac press Cmd-Opt-Return/Enter to apply the values to a copy of the original object. On Windows press Ctrl-Alt-Enter to apply the values to a copy. This also changes your focus from the Transform palette.

- On the Mac, press Cmd-Opt-Tab to apply the values to a copy of the original—without leaving the Transform palette. Windows users can press Ctrl-Alt-Tab.

 Don't forget that Illustrator is now capable of doing the math for you in any option box. So instead of entering 200% into the W or H option box to double a dimension, you can simply punch in *2 after the current value in the box—*2 tells Illustrator to multiply the current value by 2, the same as 200% of the value. Illustrator doubles the value when you press Return/Enter or Tab and changes the dimensions accordingly.

- Use Transform Again (Cmd/Ctrl-D) to reapply a percentage transformation change.

Reference
point icon

Figure 11-9: Use the Transformation palette to change the absolute size of an object, or enter a percentage in the width or height option boxes.

OK, so maybe you knew the above features of the Transform palette. But we bet you didn't know these hidden features:

● Press Cmd/Ctrl-Shift-Return/Enter to scale uniformly and leave the focus on the last used option box.

● Press Opt/Alt-Return/Enter to apply the scaling to a clone of the path. Press Opt/Alt-Shift-Return/Enter to scale a clone and leave the focus on the last used option box.

● Press Cmd-Opt-Return (Mac) or Ctrl-Alt-Enter (Windows) to uniformly scale a clone.

● Press Cmd-Opt-Shift-Return (Mac) or Ctrl-Alt-Shift-Enter (Windows) to uniformly scale a clone and leave the focus on the last used option box.

Using the Scale Dialog Box

After selecting a few objects on your Things To Scale list, double-click the scale tool icon in the toolbox. This brings up the Scale dialog box captured in all its radiant glory in Figure 11-10. Illustrator automatically positions the origin point in the center of the selection (according to the big, bad, bounding box). If you want to position the origin point yourself, Opt/Alt-click in the illustration window with the scale tool. (When you press the Opt/Alt key, you'll see a tiny ellipsis next to the scale tool cursor.) Opt/Alt-clicking with any transformation tool simultaneously positions the origin point and displays the appropriate dialog box. Here's how the Scale dialog box can be used:

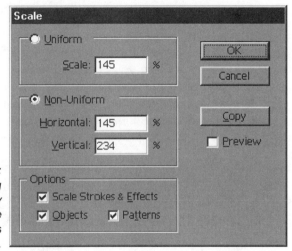

*Figure 11-10:
In the Scale dialog
box, you can specify
the exact percentage
by which a selection is
enlarged or reduced.*

You can also open the Scale dialog box by choosing Object » Transform » Scale. This is also the route to the Rotate, Shear, and Reflect dialog boxes. So why would you go all the way to a submenu to choose one of these options? You wouldn't, but because they're on the menu, you can assign a keystroke to invoke the command. And we guarantee that is something you want to do. See Chapter 20, "Working Smarter and Faster" for all the details of adding your own keystrokes to menu commands.

- Choose Uniform and enter a value in the Scale option box to proportionally scale the width and height of the selection. This value is accurate to 0.001 percent — ten times more accurate than the scale value in the Transform palette.

- Choose Non-uniform and enter a value in either the Horizontal or Vertical option boxes to scale the object non-proportionally.

- Check Scale Strokes and Effects to scale any stroke weights or effects applied to objects. The stroke weights change only when objects are scaled uniformly. (When the non-uniform button is selected, Illustrator doesn't know how to scale stroke weights, so it leaves them alone.) Effects are scaled whenever the box is checked. If the check box is off, strokes and effects are unaffected.

Illustrator remembers this Scale Strokes and Effects setting the next time you Shift-drag with the scale tool. So if you find that your line weights are getting thicker and thinner as you scale them, you know the culprit. Double-click the scale tool icon and turn off the Scale Line Weight check box. Or change the setting in the General Preferences.

- The Objects and Patterns check boxes are used strictly when working with tiled fills. If you want to learn about these options—for all four transformation dialog boxes—read the stirring account in the section "Transforming Tiles inside Objects" in Chapter 15.

- Use the Preview check box to see the possible yet currently unrealized future. Click it on and off to see your changes appear and disappear, ad nauseam.

- To scale the selection, press Return/Enter or click the OK button. Click the Copy button to clone the selection and scale it.

Oh, and one more thing. All of Illustrator's transformation dialog boxes act as recording devices, keeping track of the last transformation applied, whether you used a tool or the dialog box itself. Sadly, the Scale dialog box ignores the results of the Transform palette, and it doesn't pay attention to the next command, Transform Each. But it knows what the scale tool is up to.

Scaling Partial Objects

You can use the scale tool or Scale dialog box to scale partially selected paths and text objects. For example, you can use the scale tool to enlarge a text block without changing the size of the text inside it. Opt/Alt-click the rectangular text container with the direct selection tool, and then click with the scale tool to set the origin point and drag away. So long as you haven't selected any text—you don't see any baselines, do you?—Illustrator enlarges or reduces the containers and rewraps the text inside.

You can also scale selected points and segments in a path. The primary advantage of this technique is that you can move points symmetrically. See, Illustrator doesn't provide any specific means for moving points away from or toward an origin point. Moving is the one transformation that has nothing to do with origins (which is why we don't discuss it in this chapter). The closest thing to an origin-based move function is the scale tool.

Consider Figure 11-11. On the left side we selected the two interior corner points. When we selected the scale tool, the origin point appeared between those two points. We then started our drag outside the object and dragged up and to the left in the direction of the arrow. This not only moved the two points inward, but it also elongated the handles controlling the selected points. When we released the mouse button, the two points reshaped the curve as shown on the right side of Figure 11-11.

You can also use the scale tool to move objects in equal and opposite directions as shown in Figure 11-12. We used the direct selection tool to select just the top and bottom points in the object on the left. Using the origin point in the center of the object, we dragged the top object up. This sent the bottom object down at the same distance. This ensured the finished object was the same on top and bottom.

So in addition to its normal resizing functions, the scale tool does double duty as a symmetrical move tool. It's not surprising, if you think about it. All the scale tool is doing is moving and stretching segments away from and toward a fixed point. Once you understand its geometry, the scale tool becomes a never-ending source of inspiration.

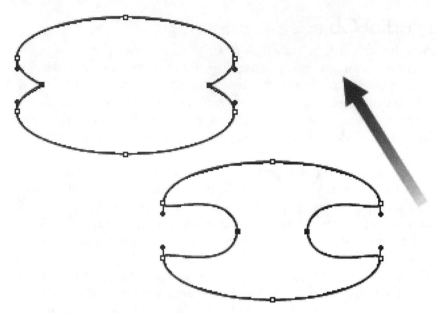

Figure 11-11: After selecting the two interior points shown in the object on the left, we dragged with the scale tool along the direction of the arrow. This created the curves in the object on the right.

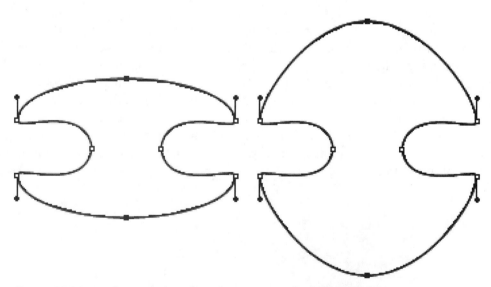

Figure 11-12: By dragging the selected segments in the left object up, we stretched both the top and bottom of the object in equal distances.

Rotating Objects

After you know how to use one transformation tool, the other three standard transformations become putty in your capable grasp. The rotate, reflect, and shear tools share many characteristics with their scale sibling. So rather than laboriously examining every single detail of each tool as if this were the first word of Chapter 11 you've ever read, we'll make quick work of the familiar stuff and stick in as many tool-specific tips and techniques as these humble pages will permit.

For example, here's a summary of the basic workings of the rotate tool—the left-hand neighbor of the scale tool—with occasional figures:

- Drag with the rotate tool to rotate a selection around its bounding-box center. Or click to set the origin point and then drag to rotate, as shown in the second example of Figure 11-13. Because rotation is a strictly circular movement—in fact, you always rotate in perfect circles—the origin point acts as a true center, as the arrows in the figure demonstrate.

 It doesn't matter where you start dragging when using the rotate tool. At any time, you can gain more precise control over a rotation by moving the cursor farther away from the origin. Slight movements close to the origin can send your objects into exaggerated spins that are difficult to control.

- Press the Shift key when dragging to rotate in 45-degree (1/8 turn) increments. (The constraint axes have no influence over Shift-dragging with the rotate tool.)

- Press the Opt/Alt key after you begin dragging and hold it until the drag is finished to rotate a clone of the selection. Then you can repeat a series of rotated clones by choosing Object » Transform » Transform Again (Cmd/Ctrl-D-D-D).

In the top example of Figure 11-14, Sandee started with two simple paths: a spiral (black) and a two-point curve (gray). Using the origin point indicated by the target, she rotated a clone of the spiral 45 degrees by clicking with the rotate tool and Opt/Alt-Shift-dragging the spiral. She then duplicated the elements three times by mercilessly beating Cmd/Ctrl-D.

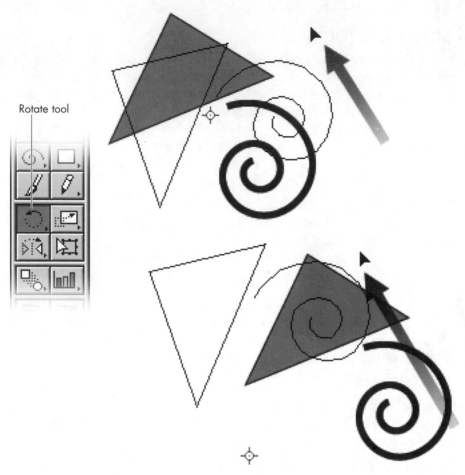

Rotate tool

Figure 11-13: The difference between merely dragging with the rotate tool (top) and first clicking at the tip (origin point) of the triangle and then dragging (bottom).

After joining the spirals and curves at their endpoints, she selected all the objects and used the rotation dialog box to rotate everything -2 degrees. She clicked the Copy button to clone the objects and then repeated the clone and rotation ten more times (Cmd/Ctrl-D-D-D). She finished up by reducing the stroke weight which created the swirly creation shown at the bottom left of the figure.

 Illlustrator interprets rotations in degrees. A full circle is 360 degrees, so a 360-degree rotation would return the selection to its starting position; a 180-degree rotation would turn it upside down.

Figure 11-14: The series of steps that turned the spiral and arc in the top left example into the swirly creation at the lower right. All rotations occurred around the target origin point.

Rotation by the numbers

You can use the Rotate dialog box, shown in Figure 11-15, to rotate with supreme precision. Simply double-click the rotation tool in the toolbox. This positions the origin point at the center of the selection. Or you can Opt/Alt-click with the rotation tool to position the origin point and open the dialog box.

 If you can't remember which way the negative or positive numbers work, look at the rotation tool in the toolbox. The tool's icon goes counter-clockwise. That's your clue to remember that positive numbers go counter-clockwise. (We won't insult you by telling you which direction the negative numbers rotate.)

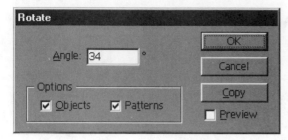

Figure 11-15:
The rotation dialog box lets you control rotations with numeric precision. You don't have to worry about stroke weights or effects as you did with the scale dialog box.

You can also use the Transform palette, shown in Figure 11-16, to rotate selected objects. You can enter a specific rotation amount in the option box or use the handy pop-up list that provides you with a wealth of rotation choices. Remember to use the reference point icon to set the position around which the rotation should occur.

- Press Return/Enter or Tab to rotate the selection.
- Press Opt/Alt-Return/Enter or Opt/Alt-Tab to clone and rotate.

Unlike the settings for the width and height, the Transform palette doesn't keep the setting for the rotation of the object; instead, it resets the option box back to 0 degrees as soon as you apply the setting.

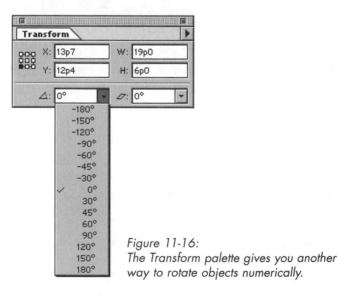

Figure 11-16:
The Transform palette gives you another way to rotate objects numerically.

Rotating with the Bounding Box

Just as you can scale with the bounding box, so can you rotate. Make sure the bounding box is visible by choosing View » Show Bounding Box. Then bring your cursor *near* one of the handles along the side of the bounding box. Object »Transform » Reset Bounding Box. You will see the rotation cursors as shown in the top left of Figure 11-17. If your cursor is *over* the handles you will see the scale cursors shown in the bottom right of Figure 11-17. Drag to rotate the bounding box along with its contents.

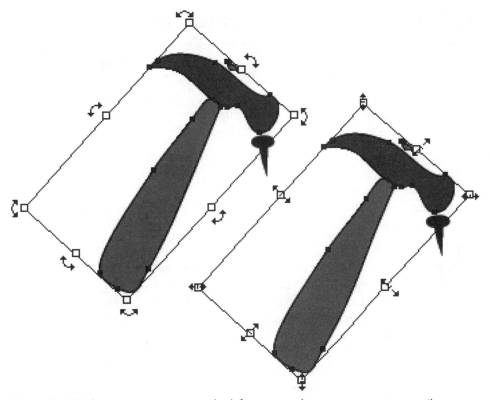

Figure 11-17: The rotation cursors on the left appear when your cursor is near (but not on) the bounding box handles. The scale cursors on the right appear when your cursor is on the bounding box handles.

Like scaling, there are special techniques for rotating with the bounding box:

- Drag any handle to rotate the selected objects.
- Shift-drag to rotate in 45-degree increments.
- The bounding box always rotates around the center point.

- Use Transform Again (Cmd/Ctrl-D) to repeat the transformation from the bounding box.

You can't use the Opt/Alt key to make a copy of the object as you rotate with the bounding box. Only the Rotate tool has that magical power.

Flipping Objects Back and Forth

Many graphics programs provide Flip Horizontal and Flip Vertical commands so that you can quickly reflect selected objects. But not Illustrator. As far as Illustrator is concerned, those commands may be easy to use but they don't provide enough control. So although the reflect tool is hardly convenient for quick flips, it's just the thing when power and accuracy are paramount.

The following is everything you need to know about flipping in Illustrator:

- The reflect tool works a little different than its fellow transformation tools. When you drag with the reflect tool, you change the angle of the reflection axis. As demonstrated in Figure 11-17, the reflection axis is like the mirror that the selection is reflected into. The portions of the object that lie on one side of the axis flip to the other. Because you can tilt the mirror, the reflect tool flips and rotates objects at the same time.

- If you immediately start in dragging with the tool, the reflection axis hinges on the center of the selection. But if you first click to set the origin point and then drag with the reflect tool, the axis pivots on the origin. In the top example of Figure 11-18, for instance, we clicked below and to the left of the selection. We then began dragging in a direct line above the selection, which resulted in a vertical axis. As we dragged down and to the right, the axis inclined into the position shown in the second example in the figure.

- Shift-drag with the reflect tool to constrain the axis to a 45-degree angle. When the axis is upright, the selection flips horizontally. When the axis is horizontal, the selection flips vertically.

- Press the Opt/Alt key when dragging to flip a clone. You can repeat a flipped clone by pressing Cmd/Ctrl-D, but why would you want to? You would only end up creating a clone of the original positioned directly in front of it.

Reflect tool

Reflection axis

Figure 11-18: Click with the reflect tool to set the origin point (top); then drag to flip and rotate the selection around the reflection axis.

🌐 Most of the time, it's easier to flip using the Reflect dialog box. To bring up the dialog box, double-click the reflect tool icon in the toolbox. Or you can Opt/Alt-click with the reflect tool in the illustration window to set the origin point.

🌐 The Reflect dialog box shown in Figure 11-19 contains three options for specifying the angle of the reflection axis around which the flip occurs. Select the Horizontal option to flip the selection vertically, just as a gymnast swinging on a horizontal bar flips vertically. Select the Vertical option to flip the selection horizontally, like a flag flopping back and forth on a vertical flagpole. You can also enter a value into the Axis Angle option box to specify the exact angle of the axis. A value of 0 indicates a horizontal axis; 90 indicates a vertical axis.

🌐 Press Return/Enter to flip the selection. Click Copy to clone and flip.

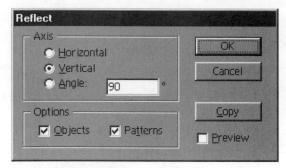

Figure 11-19:
It may be easier to use the Reflect
dialog box to flip objects along the
horizontal or vertical axis. Or you can
set a specific angle for the reflection.

Compared to the scale and rotate tools, the reflect tool is very dull. You can't perform special effects with it. And although you can flip partial paths, there's rarely a reason to do it. Still, it's a very practical tool, and Illustrator would be the worse without it. When you gotta flip, you gotta flip.

Slanting Objects the Weird Way

The final transformation tool is the oddly-named shear tool—the alternate tool in the reflect tool slot. Rather than removing wool from sheep—as the tool's name implies—the shear tool slants selected objects.

Deke has been making fun of the name of this tool since the first edition of this book. Shear is not an obvious name for the tool. Skew, maybe. Slant, certainly. But for millions of new users, shear only brings to mind cutting fabrics. Rather than carry on about this as Deke did in the past, we now ask that you all contact the Illustrator product managers (who used to be our friends). Tell them to change the name of the tool. Maybe they'll have a contest for the best name. And the winner gets to go to Adobe-land.

Despite its dopey name, this is an important tool. It slants objects horizontally, vertically, or in any other direction. So don't be put off by the name. This tool deserves to be part of your daily transformation regimen.

Because the shear tool is a little more demanding than the other transformation tools, we devote the entire following section to explaining its basic operation. After that, we cover the Shear dialog box.

Using the Shear Tool

As with the other transformation tools, you can start right in dragging with the shear tool. But we *strongly* recommend that you don't. Many students have found their artwork shifting into the ends of Illustrator's universe all because they grabbed the shear tool and dragged willy-nilly. Of all the transformation tools, this is the most difficult to control. So you're best off specifying an origin point to keep things as predictable as possible.

Click to set the origin point. We find if helpful to set the origin in the lower left corner of the selection. Then we move the cursor to the opposite corner of the selection—upper right—and begin dragging. Illustrator slants the selection in the direction of your drag, as demonstrated in Figure 11-20.

Shear tool

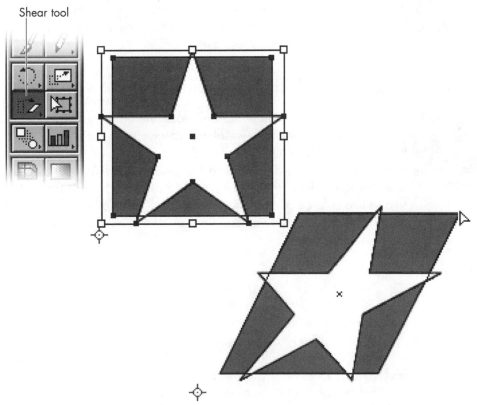

Figure 11-20: Click in a corner with the shear tool (top), and then drag from the opposite corner to slant the selection (bottom).

Illustrator figures two ingredients into slanting an object—the amount of slant applied and the axis along which the slant occurs. The distance of the drag determines the amount of slanting; the angle of the drag determines the angle of the axis.

Notice that although we dragged up and to the right in Figure 11-20, the selected objects slanted slightly downward. We dragged up about 10 degrees, so the axis is angled at 10 degrees. The weird thing is, when dragging with the shear tool, all axis angles clockwise from 45 degrees around to –135 degrees (about 1:30 to 7:30 on a clock face) slant objects downward. Axis values from –135 to 45 degrees (7:30 to 1:30) slant objects upward. Mathematically, it doesn't have to be this way, but so it is when you're using the shear tool.

 Meanwhile, if you drag in a 45-degree or –135-degree direction, Illustrator stretches the selected objects all the way to Tierra del Fuego. If you notice your objects going haywire, just move your mouse up or down a little to restore the selection to a recognizable state.

Slant Sensibly with Shift

 Because of the way Illustrator calculates the effect of dragging with the shear tool, we almost always keep the Shift key down while we're dragging. Shift-dragging with the shear tool constrains the axis to multiples of 45 degrees. As we've said, two of these multiples—45 and –135—turn the axis into a force of absolute evil. But if you Shift-drag in a roughly horizontal or vertical direction, you'll achieve very predictable results.

The shear tool is especially useful for slanting type and creating cast shadows as you can see in Figure 11-21. (Cast shadows are much more impressive than drop shadows—even the new fuzzy drop shadows in Illustrator 9.) To create the first shadow at the top of the figure, we clicked with the scale tool along the baseline of the letters, and then we Opt/Alt-dragged from the top of the letters down past the baseline to flip and scale a clone. We then filled the clone with gray. In the second example, we clicked with the shear tool along the baseline of the letters and Shift-dragged from left to right to slant the shadow horizontally. Finally, we selected all letters, clicked at the base of the first T with the shear tool, and Shift-dragged up on the M. This slanted the letters vertically, as in the last example in the figure.

Figure 11-21: After flipping a clone of the letters with the scale tool (top), we slanted the clone horizontally with the shear tool (middle). We then selected all letters and slanted them vertically (bottom).

Defining the Slant and the Axis

Illustrator lets you slant and clone by pressing the Opt/Alt key while dragging with the shear tool. You can also display a Shear dialog box by double-clicking the shear tool icon in the toolbox, by Opt/Alt-clicking with the tool in the illustration window, or even by doing the infamous Control-click (Mac) or right-click (Windows).

As shown in Figure 11-22, the Shear dialog box offers a Shear Angle option box for specifying the angle at which you want your objects to slant, and three Axis options for specifying the axis along which the slant should occur.

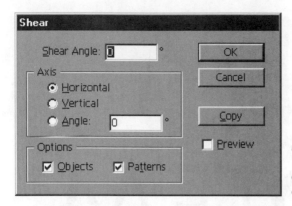

Figure 11-22:
You can set the shear angle and the
axis along which the slant should
occur in the Shear dialog box.

Specify the angle of the shear axis exactly as you would the angle of the reflection axis inside the Reflect dialog box. Select the Horizontal option to slant the selected objects to the left or right; select the Vertical option to slant up or down. You can also angle the axis by entering a value into the Angle option box in the Axis section of the Shear dialog box. Because the axis extends to either side of the origin point, values greater than 180 degrees are repetitious. (Values of 45 or –135 degrees don't cause problems in the Shear dialog box; they just mess things up when you're trying to drag with the shear tool.)

Regardless of the selected Axis options, you'll want to enter a value for the Shear Angle option at the top of the dialog box. Here's where things get tricky. Illustrator interprets just about every other value that's measured in degrees in a counterclockwise direction. (It's the standard geometry model that you undoubtedly learned or neglected in an ancient math course.) This is true for rotations, angled axes (including the shear axis), and directional movements. The only exceptions to the rotation direction are the Shear Angle option box at the top of the Shear dialog box and the Angle option box in the Twirl dialog box (see Chapter 12), which Illustrator applies in a clockwise direction. Therefore:

- When the Horizontal radio button is selected, a positive Shear value slants the selection forward and a negative value slants it backward. Seems sensible.

- But when the Vertical radio button is selected, a positive Shear value slants the selection up on the left side of the origin and down on the right, so it looks like it's pointing downward. A negative value slants the selection upward. That's just plain weird!

A Shear value of 30 degrees creates a pretty significant slant. Anything beyond 90 to –90 degrees is repetitive. And you definitely don't want to enter anything from about 80 to 90 degrees (positive or negative) because it pretty well lays the selected objects flat.

Slanting is by far the least predictable of the transformations. Deke considered including a huge chart showing what happens to an object when you apply all kinds of different Shear Angle and Axis Angle values, but take our word for it, you would've been more confused after looking at the thing than you probably were before. That's why we recommend sticking with horizontal and vertical slants when possible. If you need to slant objects a little up and a little over, do it in two separate steps. It'll save wear and tear on your brain.

Multiple Transformations on Multiple Objects

When you choose the Transform Each command from either the Object » Transform submenu or from the Transform submenu, Illustrator displays the dialog box shown in Figure 11-23. You enter the amounts by which you want to resize the width and height of the selected objects into the first two option boxes. To perform a proportional resizing, enter the same value for both Horizontal and Vertical. Then press Return/Enter to apply the changes, or click the Copy button to clone and scale. (Frustratingly, Opt/Alt-Return/Enter doesn't create copies inside this dialog box.)

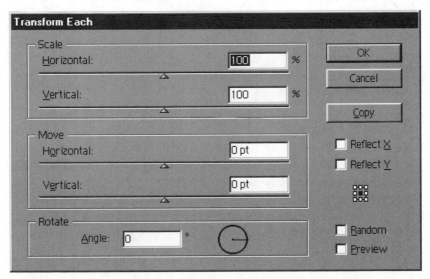

Figure 11-23: Think of the Transform Each dialog box as your one-stop shopping for a wealth of transformation tools that can be applied individually to objects.

When you apply the Transform Each command, Illustrator transforms each selected object with respect to its own reference point. Although the obvious use of the command is to scale, move, or rotate objects in their position as shown in Figure 11-24, there is another more subtle use that is shown in Figure 11-25. In Figure 11-24, we added some smaller stars to the points of the large star. Unfortunately, these smaller stars were not rotated into the correct position and they also needed to be a little bigger. After measuring the correct angle, we used the Transform Each dialog box to both scale and rotate the stars around their own centers.

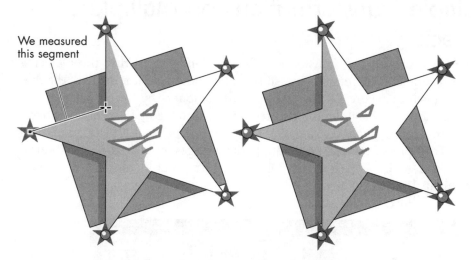

We measured this segment

Figure 11-24: After measuring the angle of the large star (left), we used the Transform Each dialog box to both rotate and scale each of the small stars positioned at the points of the big star object.

Figure 11-25 shows another important feature of Transform Each—namely the ability to apply Transformations in a random fashion. The grapes in the left example were far too symmetrical for our tastes. So we simply selected them all and set the Transform Each dialog box to Scale 80% for both horizontal and vertical and set the rotation for 5 degrees. But before we clicked OK, we checked the box for Random. Instead of all the objects transforming the same amount, Illustrator scaled each one as low as 80% and rotated each one up to 5 degrees. The exact amount was set randomly.

 If you don't like the random setting, turn on the preview and click the random checkbox on and off. Each time you turn it back on, Illustrator applies a new random setting.

Figure 11-25: We used a combination of the rotation and scale commands in the Transform Each dialog box to make these grapes less perfect.

 The Transform Each dialog box keeps getting better and better. Illustrator 9 has added a reference point icon so you can control the point around which transformations occur as well as the ability to reflect along the X and Y axis.

We can hear some of you in the back yawning and asking "So what. Is this Transform Each thing really so exciting?" Well, it may not seem like much right now, but just wait till we get into special effects for multiple strokes and fills. You'll see how Transform Each will transform your life.

 Always turn on the Preview check box when you use the Random option. This way, you can see Illustrator's random effect before applying it. If you don't like what you see, turn off Preview and then turn it back on again. This forces Illustrator to generate a new random effect. Keep clicking on the Preview check box until you get what you want. Then press Return/Enter.

Free Transform for All

So what if there were a way to combine the transformation tools scale, rotate, reflect, and shear along with a totally wacky distortion filter in one simple, elegant tool? Well, bunky, your search is over. Welcome to the Free Transform tool. Although it displays handles that look very similar to its weakling cousin, the bounding box, the Free Transform tool goes far beyond the bounding box.

When you select a path (or paths) and then choose the free transform tool from the toolbox, Illustrator displays the standard eight-handled bounding box that just surrounds the paths. As with the bounding box, the orientation of the bounding box depends on the original paths. If you don't like the orientation Illustrator assigns the box, either choose Object » Transform » Reset Bounding Box or Control-click (Mac) or right-click (Windows) and choose Transform » Reset Bounding Box. Illustrator will slap the bounding box into shape, aligning it such that it squares with the artboard and its pages.

When you move the free transform tool around a selected object, Illustrator displays a number of different cursors depending on the tool's location in terms of the object's bounding box. As shown in Figure 11-26, seven different cursors are associated with the free transform tool when it's in use. Four of these cursors (the ones flanked with two arrows) appear automatically, depending only on the location of the tool in terms of the bounding box. The other three cursors (the plain or augmented grayed arrowheads) appear only after you press Cmd/Ctrl *after* you start dragging one of the bounding box's handles.

The change in cursor function after you start dragging is rare in Illustrator. Ordinarily the basic function of a cursor doesn't change when you add a modifier key. The Free Transform command breaks new territory. However, there didn't seem to be any other way the Free Transform command could handle its different features.

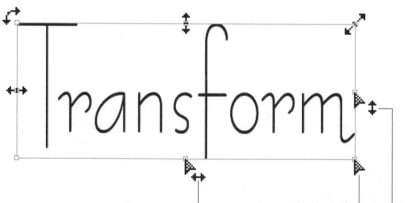

These cursors appear only when you press the Cmd/Ctrl key after you've started dragging one of the handles.

Figure 11-26: The free transform tool uses seven different cursors to indicate the modification that the tool's ready to perform.

If you switch to the free transform tool when nothing is selected, the tool's cursor looks just like the arrow tool. In this form, it is absolutely useless because it can't select a thing. Both of us have more than once tried to select something with the free transform tool. So if you're trying to use the arrow cursor but find that you can't select paths, make sure that you haven't selected the free transform tool.

Here's the skinny on what you can do when you're using the free transform tool on selected paths:

- Drag a corner handle to scale the selected objects. Shift-drag a corner handle to scale proportionally. In either case, the opposite corner serves as the scale origin.

- Opt/Alt-drag a corner handle to scale the object around its center. Opt/Alt-Shift-drag a corner handle to scale proportionally around the object's center.

- Drag one of the bounding box's side handles (including the top and bottom ones) to limit the scaling to either horizontal or vertical changes. The opposite side's handle serves as the scale origin.

- Opt/Alt-drag a side handle to horizontally or vertically scale the object from the center.

- Drag from any location outside the free transform bounding box—the cursor changes to its curved two-headed form—to rotate the object around the center.

- Shift-drag from outside the bounding box to constrain the rotations to multiples of 45 degrees (plus whatever value you've entered into the Constrain Angle option box in the General Preferences dialog box). These 45-degree multiples are measured relative to the orientation of the bounding box and not to the orientation of the page. Thus, if your bounding box is not initially square with the page, it is not possible to Shift-rotate with the free transform tool to make your object square to the page.

- Press the Cmd/Ctrl key after you've started dragging a corner handle to move that corner independently of the other three corners. This allows you to freely distort the object.

Even though you can transform text with the free transform tool, you cannot use any of the free distort features—the ones that include pressing the Cmd/Ctrl key while you're dragging a corner handle—on text. To perform these transformations on text, you must first convert the text to paths via the Type » Create Outlines command (Cmd/Ctrl-Shift-O).

Press Cmd/Ctrl-Shift while dragging a corner handle to limit the direction of your drag to follow along one of the sides of the bounding box. For example, in the top portion of Figure 11-27, the bounding boxes were initially square with the page. We pressed Cmd/Ctrl-Shift while dragging the corner handles and the drags were constrained to vertical and horizontal only. In the bottom portion of Figure 11-27, the bounding boxes were initially set at roughly 24.5 degrees. When we pressed Cmd/Ctrl-Shift while dragging the corner handles, the drags were limited to angles that matched those of the bounding box—roughly 24.5 and 114.5 (90 + 24.5) degrees.

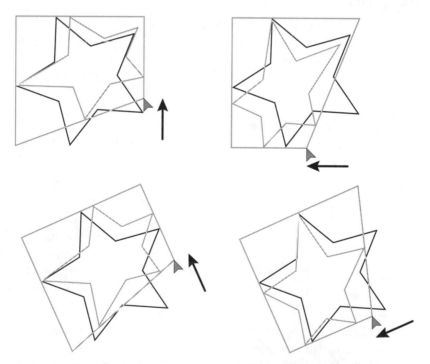

Figure 11-27: When we pressed Cmd/Ctrl-Shift while dragging the various corner handles, the drags were aligned to the sides of the objects' bounding box. In the bottom examples, the bounding boxes were rotated to roughly 24.5 degrees counterclockwise from the horizontal. This caused the drags to be constrained to 24.5 degrees off the horizontal and 24.5 degrees off the vertical.

Press Cmd-Opt (Mac) or Ctrl-Alt (Windows) while you drag a corner handle to force the opposite corner to mimic your every move, except in the opposite direction. As you can see in the top example of Figure 11-28, we held Cmd-Opt or Ctrl-Alt and dragged the bottom right corner down and to the right, the top left corner moved up and to the left. Depending on the direction of your drag, you can use this technique to rotate, scale and even flip the object. We used the same keystrokes in the bottom portion of Figure 11-28, while we substantially dragged the bottom right corner. This rotated and flipped the original object. Additionally, we scaled the paths, resulting in a slightly taller and thinner version of the original.

Figure 11-28: Press Cmd/Ctrl-Opt/Alt while dragging a corner handle to cause the opposite corner to move in the opposite direction.

Press all three modifier keys (Cmd-Opt-Shift or Ctrl-Alt-Shift) to force one of the adjacent corner handles to mimic your moves, except in the opposite direction. Also, all movement will be constrained in such a way that they align with one of the bounding box's sides. (This is true for both bounding boxes that are square with the page and those that are not.) The top example of Figure 11-29 shows how the top right corner shot upward as we dragged the bottom right corner while holding Cmd-Opt-Shift (on the Mac) or Ctrl-Alt-Shift (for Windows). This is a result of dragging more vertically than horizontally. The bottom example of Figure 11-29 illustrates the bottom left corner moving left to counter the right drag of the bottom right corner while holding all three modifier keys.

Figure 11-29: Holding the three modifier keys (Cmd-Opt-Shift or Ctrl-Alt-Shift) while dragging a corner handle constrains the movements of both that corner and one of its adjacent corners to either horizontal or vertical. These directions are functions of the bounding box's original orientation.

While dragging one of the handles positioned along the sides of the free transform tool's bounding box (including the top and bottom sides), press the Cmd/Ctrl key to unhinge the bounding box from its rigid

rectilinear confines. You can then reshape the bounding box as a parallelogram in which the opposite sides of the box remain parallel but
adjacent sides do not have to remain perpendicular to one another. In
this case, three of the four sides will move with your drag; only the
opposite side remains immobile.

- Press Cmd/Ctrl-Shift while you drag one of the side handles to manipulate the bounding box as a parallelogram in which the side you drag
remains aligned with its original position. If your bounding box is originally squared with the page, you'll be able to drag vertically or horizontally (depending on whether the side you drag is one of the vertical
sides or the horizontal sides of the bounding box). All the while, the
side handle will remain a constant distance from the opposite side.

- While dragging a side handle, press Cmd-Opt (Mac) or Ctrl-Alt
(Windows) to manipulate the bounding box as a parallelogram that
pivots around the box's center instead of around the opposite side.

- Press all three of the modifier keys while doing the side handle drag to
reshape the bounding box as a parallelogram that pivots around the
box's center, while the opposite sides of the box remain a constant distance away from one another. This way, you change only the corners'
angular sizes.

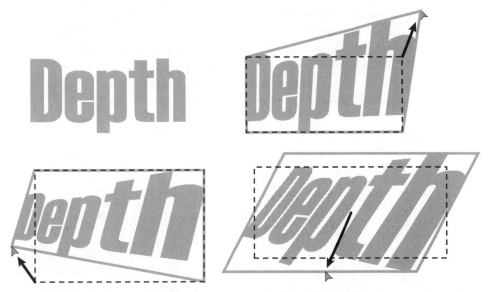

*Figure 11-30: You can achieve great perspective effects like this by using a variety of
free transform tool techniques.*

Although the free transform tool's many uses mean you have a heap to remember, the tool affords you some of the best and (once mastered) easiest transformation and distortion abilities in this and any other drawing program. By mixing and matching the techniques mentioned above, you can create complicated and sophisticated perspective effects. In fact, with the help of a few other filters, you can create stuff that looks like it came out of a 3-D program.

For example, in Figure 11-30, we converted some text to paths with the Type » Create Outline command (Cmd/Ctrl-Shift-O). We then transformed it three times. Twice we pressed the Cmd/Ctrl key while we dragged corner handles (first on the top right handle and then on the bottom left handle). Once we pressed both the Cmd/Ctrl and Opt/Alt keys while we dragged the bottom handle. In three quick drags, the text was transformed into a word that practically jumps off the page.

Even though it has a lot going for it, the free transform tool does possess one glaring flaw; you can't clone a path when you're transforming it with the free transform tool. If you want to transform a clone of a path with the free transform tool, be sure to clone the path first—with the Copy and Paste in Front commands (Cmd/Ctrl-C and Cmd/Ctrl-F)—and then use the free transform tool on the cloned path.

 One reason for the lack of a cloning option is that the Opt/Alt key is busy performing other functions. We wish Adobe would take our suggestion to use the spacebar for cloning. There's plenty of precedence for having the space-bar add function as you drag. Sure, using four keys may be less than appealing to some (especially those who never played the piano), but having the option of cloning while transforming with the free transform tool, simply by pressing an additional key, is better than no option at all.

HOG-WILD SPECIAL EFFECTS

Every so often, someone informs us that he or she prefers Photoshop to Illustrator because, "I'm just not a vector person." It's not that Illustrator doesn't help you create terrific artwork; it's that in Photoshop, inspiration starts with scanned images, which you can enhance using a mouth-watering collection of special effects filters. But Illustrator is so rigid. You have to draw everything from scratch. You can't just sit and play like in Photoshop. You can't just apply commands and watch the artwork take on new and exciting shapes. Right? Well not exactly...

Clearly, Bézier curves are more labor intensive than pixels. (Anyone who isn't trying to sell you something would admit that.) But you don't have to painstakingly draw each and every curve by hand. You can rough out primitive compositions with ellipses, stars, text characters, and the like, and then embellish these objects using Illustrator's automated functions.

If you read Chapters 9 and 11, you already have a sense of the marvels you can accomplish by combining and transforming shapes. But that's only the proverbial tip of the iceberg. In this chapter, we'll show you how to apply a wide range of bona fide special effects—functions so radical that they can mutate common shapes into extraordinary forms that would take you minutes or even hours to draw by hand. In Figure 12-1, for example, we started with nothing more than a line of type and a five-pointed star. A quick distortion and two filters later, we arrived at the unqualified masterpiece that you see before you. As you can see, Illustrator lets you run roughshod over objects in the same way that Photoshop lets you use and abuse images. Both programs are equal parts finely-tuned graphics applications and platforms for fortuitous experimentation.

Figure 12-1: Thanks to a few filters and distortions we were able to convert a basic ellipse, a mundane star and some converted type into a complete illustration.

With Illustrator 9, Adobe has given Illustrator special effects far beyond its previous abilities. In fact, we risk heresy by saying Illustrator 9 goes beyond the abilities of Photoshop when it comes to being able to apply special effects and then change those effects later on! However rather than repeat NEW, NEW, NEW, all over this chapter, we'll just say that every time we mention a filter that is also an effect, you'll know that although the filter may have been in previous versions of Illustration, the effect is new. However, if a filter or effect has never been in Illustrator before, then we'll tell you that it's NEW!

Throughout the following pages, we look at the special effects functions of Illustrator. We also look at the differences between applying commands from the Filter menu versus the Effect menu. And we examine how keeping commands "live" offers you greater flexibility over time.

Freelance Features

Most of Illustrator's capabilities are built into the main application. But many tools and commands come from little subprograms called *plug-ins*. In the past it was very obvious which features were plug-ins—they were always under the Filter menu. Today, plug-in tools and commands are found all over Illustrator. For instance, the lassos are actually plug-ins, as are the links palette, live blends, and many other features. Does it matter if a command is a plug-in or not? Maybe it does to some developer who might want to enhance the features of the plug-in. But to you, the average—OK, above average—user, it matters not at all.

By default, all plug-ins reside in the Plug-ins folder inside the same folder that contains the Illustrator application. (You can change this using File » Preferences » Plug-ins, as described in Chapter 2, but few folks ever do.) When you launch Illustrator, the program loads all the plug-ins into memory and makes them available as tools, commands, and palettes in the program.

 You can get information about any plug-in by choosing the About Plug-ins command from the Apple menu (or from the Help menu in the Windows version). Then select a filter from the scrolling list and click the About button to see who wrote it.

You can add plug-ins from other companies by copying the files into Illustrator's Plug-ins folder or into one of several subfolders; or you can create a new folder. Illustrator loads the plug-in during startup as long as it is located somewhere inside the Plug-ins folder.

Some plug-ins manifest themselves as tools and palettes, and a few appear as commands under the Edit, Object, and Type menus. But most show up as commands in the Filter and Effect menus. Because the commands in these menus vary dramatically in purpose and approach, we discuss them in context throughout this book. But just so we're all on the same wavelength, here is a complete list of the commands in the Filter menu, with brief snippets about what they do and where to turn for more information:

- **Filter » Colors (Chapter 14):** Illustrator lets you modify the colors of many objects simultaneously, by using the commands in the Filter » Colors submenu. But, of course, you'll need some color theory under your belt to understand these commands, which is why Chapter 14 exists.

- **Filter » Create » Object Mosaic (Chapter 13):** Illustrator offers some weird filters, but this one may be the weirdest. It traces a bunch of colored squares around an imported image to convert the image to an object-oriented mosaic. Now there's something we can all integrate into our artwork!

- **Filter » Create » Trim Marks (Chapter 21):** Apply this filter to create eight small lines that serve as guides when you trim your printed illustration. The eight lines mark the corners of the selected objects' bounding box (see Chapter 10). Trim marks are like crop marks, but they are considerably more versatile.

- **Filter » Distort and Effect » Distort & Transform (Chapter 12):** The distortion commands are found in both the Filters and Effect menus. The transform command, found under the Effect menu, is a more powerful version of the Free Transform tool. We cover all of these in this chapter.

- **Filter » Pen and Ink (Chapter 17):** Our nomination for the most difficult commands to use in all of Illustrator appears in this submenu. But they're powerful. You can design custom fill patterns, including dots, crosshatches, and squiggles.

- **Filter » Pen and Ink » Photo Crosshatch (Chapter 13):** The second most difficult command but not as powerful. Because you have to start with a raster image, we'll cover this in Chapter 13.

- **Filter or Effect » Stylize » Add Arrowheads (Chapter 16):** Found as both a permanent filter and a live effect, this command adds an arrowhead to the end of an open path. Illustrator bases the size of the arrowhead on the thickness of the stroke, which is why we discuss the filter in Chapter 16.

- **Filter or Effect » Stylize » Drop Shadow (Chapter 13):** In previous versions this filter created a really lame copy of the original object pasted behind it. Finally, in Illustrator 9, these two commands have become as sophisticated as the drop shadow layer effects found in Photoshop. However, because the drop shadow creates a pixel image, we cover it in Chapter 13 along with all the raster features.

- **Effect » Stylize » Feather (Chapter 13):** Another Photoshop command makes its way over to Illustrator with some particularly interesting twists—and like the drop shadow, we look at it when we cover rasters.

- **Effect » Stylize » Inner Glow (Chapter 13):** How can a vector program create glows? Isn't that just for pixel-pushers like Photoshop? Find out when we cover rasters in Chapter 13.

- **Effect » Stylize » Outer Glow (Chapter 13):** Right along with the inner glow comes the outer glow.

- **Filter or Effect » Stylize » Round Corners (Chapter 12):** This command rounds off the corners in a selected path. You enter a Radius value—as you do when specifying the rounded corner of a rectangle—and Illustrator does the rest. We cover this command right here.

- **Effect » Convert to Shape (Chapter 15):** You can choose from rectangle, ellipse, or rounded rectangle. However, because these commands rely heavily on multiple fill settings, we cover them in Chapter 15.

- **Effect » Path » Offset Path (Chapter 15 and 16):** This command creates a new shape that follows the outline of the original path. Because this effect is much more dramatic with multiple fills or strokes we cover it in Chapters 15 and 16.

- **Effect » Path » Stroke Path (Chapter 16):** This command turns the Stroke of a path into a closed shape. We cover it in detail in Chapter 16.

- **Effect » Path » Outline Object (Chapter 13):** This command creates a vector outline for objects that ordinarily wouldn't have one such as the gradient mesh, placed raster images, and text.

- **Effect » Rasterize (Chapter 13):** This command helps you do some very sneaky things with images as we'll show you in Chapter 13. (Trust us, it's really sneaky.)

 The filters that appear below the line in the Filter and Effect menus are used for placed images. These commands are dimmed unless you've selected an image in your artwork. For a solid rundown of these filters, jump ahead to Chapter 13.

Reapplying Filters and Effects

After you choose a command from the Filter or Effect menus, it appears at the top of the menu (even if you later undo the command). This allows you to quickly reapply the command by choosing a command or by pressing the keyboard equivalent:

- To reapply a filter command, look under the Filter menu. The first command lists the last filter applied. Or press Cmd/Ctrl-E.

- To reopen the filter dialog box and change the settings, choose the second command in the Filter menu or press Cmd-Opt-E (Mac) or Ctrl-Alt-E (Windows).

- To reapply an effect command, look under the Effect menu. The first command lists the last command applied. Or press Cmd/Ctrl-Shift-E.

- To reopen the effect dialog box and change the settings, choose the second command in the Effect menu or press Cmd-Opt-Shift-E (Mac) or Ctrl-Alt-Shift-E (Windows).

Twirl: Tool, Filter, and Effect

Sometimes it seems that everywhere you look there's a twirl: first in the tool-box, next under the Filter menu, and then again under the Effect menu. Why this fascination with twirling?

The reason for the three different twirl features is that each has its advantages, depending on how you want to work. As a tool, the twirl gives you physical control and interactive feedback to see exactly how your final twirled object will look. The more you drag, the more you twirl. As a filter and effect, you can apply numerical values to twirl an object. And as an effect, you can undo the effects of the twirl or change the values applied to the twirl.

The twirl effect, unlike the twirl filter, allows you to twirl editable text. So you don't have to convert text to outlines to twirl it. Not only can you change the amount of the twirl, you can even change the words or the typeface in mid-twirl.

Imagine for a moment that you're in Italy, admiring a strand of tacky spaghetti that's stuck to your plate. A man in a striped shirt plays an accordion as you begin to twirl the noodle, coaxing it gingerly from the dish. Maybe it's the music, maybe it's the wine, but you can't help noticing that the part of the noodle closest to the fork rotates most dramatically, whereas the faraway portions stretch to keep up, not yet willing to release their grip on the plate. Now imagine that you can twirl your fork up to 3600 degrees, and you have Illustrator's twirl commands.

In case you're not in the mood for pasty pasta analogies, Figure 12-2 shows the effect of the twirl filter on some spaghetti.

Figure 12-2: The results of twirling a line of Apple Chancery text at 60, 120, and 400 degrees. The little puddle under the fork is the same text twirled 600 degrees and then scaled using the Free Transform tool.

Twirling: the Tool

If you want to twirl with the tangible, real-time feedback of a tool, select the twirl tool. Like the transformation tools discussed in Chapter 11, if you just start to drag you will be twirling around the center point of the object's bounding box. (Unlike the transformation tools, you can't see the origin point of the twirl tool.) However, if you click, you can mark the origin's point to some other position. (You still can't see the point, but trust us, it's there.) Then drag in the illustration window to twirl all selected objects.

In Figure 12-3, we've dragged the selection about a quarter turn clockwise. You can drag up to 91 times around a selection to increase the magnitude of the twirl. But more than two revolutions tend to create a mess with a lot of straight edges.

Twirl tool

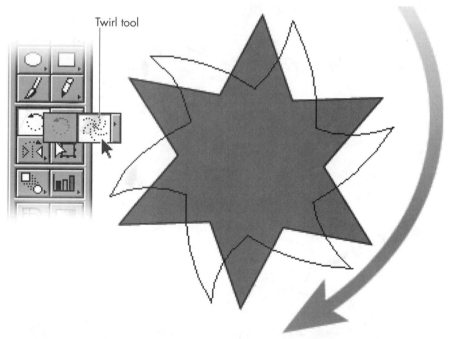

Figure 12-3: Use the twirl tool to drag around a selected shape to twist it by some arbitrary amount.

You can also Opt/Alt-click with the twirl tool to bring up a dialog box and enter a numeric Twirl value. This is the same dialog box that appears when you choose Filter » Distort » Twirl. But what the heck, Opt/Alt-clicking with a tool is sometimes more convenient than choosing a command.

Here are some other things that should be in the twirl tool to qualify it for true transformation tool status:

- If this were a typical transformation tool, you'd be able to press the Opt/Alt key before releasing with the twirl tool to clone the selection. But sadly, this function is absent from the twirl tool.

- When you display the Twirl dialog box, it should tell you the degree that you last spun an object with the twirl tool. But although this value changes every time you use the tool, there seems to be no correlation. Heck, it'll show you a negative value after a positive twirl.

- The Shift key has no effect on your drag, you can't repeat a twirl by pressing Cmd/Ctrl-D, and you can't twirl partial paths (just whole paths at a time).

Twirling: the Filter

For all you numerical types (you know who you are, so stop hiding behind your calculators), you can choose Filter » Distort » Twirl and enter the amount of twirl you want to apply in degrees. A positive value twirls clockwise, a negative value twirls counterclockwise. However, don't think you have to stop at 360 degrees. You can enter any amount up to 3600 degrees.

Unfortunately, there are very few reasons why you would want to use this filter.

- There's no preview box to let you see what each amount does.

- You have to convert text to paths before you can apply the twirl filter.

- The effects of the twirl filter are permanent. Although you can undo the command by choosing Edit » Undo Twirl, you can't undo the twirl applied to an object after you close and then reopen a file.

Twirling: the Effect

 Fasten your seatbelts and get ready to be blown away. If you've been reading this book sequentially, then this is your first exposure to the biggest news in Illustrator since version 1. Instead of applying the twirl as a one-time-only tool or filter, you can now apply the twirl (and many other commands) as live effects. This means you can go back and change your mind. You haven't permanently distorted the path—the original path is still in Illustrator's memory.

You apply the twirl effect by choosing Effect » Distort »Twirl. The Twirl effect dialog box opens. As Figure 12-4 shows, except for the preview checkbox, there is little difference between this dialog box and the one that opens when you choose the twirl filter.

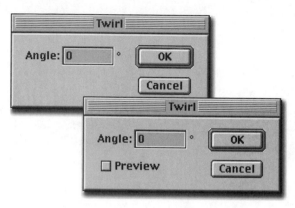

Figure 12-4:
Look fast!—Now tell us what's the difference between the Twirl filter dialog box (top) and the Twirl effect dialog box (bottom). It's that sneaky little preview checkbox.

However, the differences between the results of the commands is enormous. You can apply the twirl effect to editable text—you don't have convert the text to paths. And no matter when (days, weeks, even years later) you can open the file and change the amount of twirl or delete the twirl entirely.

Using Live Effects

Now is as good a time as any to look at some of the techniques you need to know when dealing with live effects such as the twirl effect. In return for the freedom to change and delete these effects, you need to pay careful attention to the status of some palettes and features we haven't covered before.

The live effects in Illustrator 9 aren't just new—they're revolutionary. They go far beyond what any other vector program has done before. If you've been using Illustrator for some time, be prepared to start thinking in entirely new ways about how your artwork should be prepared.

Another important advantage to working with live effects is that all effects can be made part of Illustrator's graphic styles. Graphic styles mean that instead of selecting an object and painstakingly applying very complicated settings, you can simply click in the Styles palette and the effect instantly appears. Not only that, but if you change the settings of the style, all the objects that have that style applied will also change. However, rather than deal with styles here, we cover them later in Chapter 20.

Targeting the Objects

Before you can apply an effect, you have to look at what element is the target in the Appearance palette. To open the Appearance palette choose Window » Show Appearance. When a single path is chosen the Appearance palette appears as shown in at the top of Figure 12-5. All you have to do is choose an effect, such as the twirl, for the selected object. The twirl effect is applied to the object and the twirl effect becomes listed in the Appearance palette as shown in the bottom of Figure 12-5.

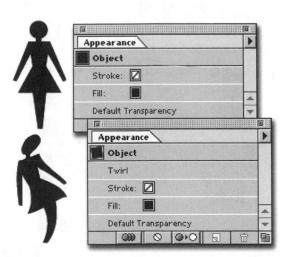

Figure 12-5:
When a single path is
selected, the Appearance
palette displays the effect
that is applied to the object.

However, things get a little trickier when you have several objects that you want to twirl or apply another effect to. First, you have to decide how you want to apply the effect. Do you want the effect to apply to the group as a whole or to the individual members of the group? What's the difference? Take a look at

Figure 12-6. It shows how the dramatic difference between applying the effect to individual objects or to the group.

If you want to apply the effect to the individual objects, you can simply select the objects and then choose the effect. However, if you want to apply the effect to the group as a whole, you need to first group the objects. Just selecting them all together isn't enough. You have to choose Object » Group or Cmd/Ctrl-G. With the group selected, you need to click the *Group* label at the top of the Appearance palette. This is called *targeting*.

 If you have selected editable text, the label will read *Type Object*.

When you target the group, you tell Illustrator that you want to apply the effect to the group as a whole, not the individual objects. You can then apply the effect.

Figure 12-6: The dancing conga line at the top has the twirl filter applied to the individual objects of a group. But the fellows riding the wave at the bottom show what happens when the effect is applied to the entire group.

You can also target the group by clicking the target circle for the group in the Layers palette. The highlight around the circle as seen in Figure 12-7 indicates that the next action will be applied to the group.

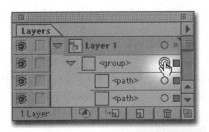

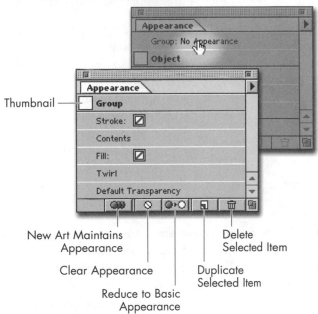

Thumbnail

New Art Maintains Appearance

Clear Appearance

Reduce to Basic Appearance

Delete Selected Item

Duplicate Selected Item

Figure 12-7: There are two different ways to target a group for an effect. Click the appearance circle next to the group in the Layers palette (top). Or click the group listing in the Appearance palette so the Object label (middle) is replaced by the Group label (bottom).

Changing, Duplicating, or Deleting Effects

Once the effect is listed in the Appearance palette, you can change or delete the effect working with the listing in the palette. Double-click the effect name to open the original dialog box for the effect. Make whatever changes you want to the effect and then click OK to close the dialog box. Or select the listing and click the Delete Selected Item icon or choose that command from the Appearance palette menu. This deletes the effect from the object or group.

If you want to change the effect, try to resist the temptation to choose the effect again from the Effect menu. This doesn't change the current effect in the Appearance palette. What you're actually doing is adding a second effect to the object. This results in a twirl on a twirl.

You can also duplicate listings in the Appearance palette by clicking the Duplicate Selected Item icon or choosing that command from the Appearance palette menu. Duplicating selected items is extremely useful for creating effects with multiple fills or strokes (covered in Chapters 15 and 16).

If you've got a whole mess of effects applied to an object, you can delete all the effects in one magnificent action by clicking the Reduce to Basic Appearance icon at the bottom of the Appearance palette or by choosing that command from the Appearance palette menu. This deletes all effects, multiple fills or strokes, or other special appearance settings. You can also click the Clear Appearance icon or choose that command from the Appearance palette menu. However, this also deletes any fill or strokes applied to the object, which makes it totally invisible.

Keep an eye on the small square next to the name of the object at the top of the Appearance palette. It's actually a thumbnail that shows a representation of what the appearance of the object would be if applied to a square object. You can hide the thumbnail by choosing Hide Thumbnail from the Appearance palette menu. This can help speed the performance of Illustrator on slow machines.

Setting the Order of Effects

The order in which you apply an effect can also change the appearance of an object, as is dramatically shown in Figure 12-8. When the twirl effect is listed above the drop shadow, the shadow twirls along with the object as shown in the left example. But when the twirl effect is listed below the drop shadow, the shadow retains the shape of the original object—not the twirled versions—as seen in the right example.

It's very simple to reorder effects in the Appearance palette. Simply drag the listing up or down.

 Watch out where you drop an effect listing. If your cursor is hovering over the fill or stroke listing, when you drop them they will disappear inside the fill or stroke entries. The allows you to apply the effect only to the fill or stroke of an object—two subjects we'll cover in Chapters 15 and 16 when we discuss Fab Fills and Strokes and Brushes.

 As of this writing there's a little glitch in how the twirl effect is applied to text that has been converted to outlines. After you choose the twirl effect, it shows up at the top of the Appearance palette. This twirls each individual object in the group—not the group as a whole. Just drag the listing down to the bottom of the list and your twirl will be applied to group, not each individual element.

Figure 12-8: The difference between applying the drop shadow effect after the twirl (left) and applying it before the twirl (right). Notice how the shadow doesn't twirl in the right example.

Drawing New Objects with the Effect

Once you've applied an effect to objects, you have a choice as to what happens to the next object that you create. Do you want the effect applied to the next object? If so, click the New Art Maintains Appearance icon at the bottom of the Appearance palette, or choose that command from the Appearance palette menu.

Once you click the icon, it changes to the New Art Has Basic Appearance icon as shown in Figure 12-7. When you click that icon, or choose the command from the Appearance palette menu, new objects will not have any effects applied to them.

Expanding Effects

Expanding, in the world of Adobe Illustrator, doesn't refer to making things bigger. Rather it refers to selecting live things, such as effects or blends, and converting them into discrete objects. (Some people like to call them dead at that point, but we'd rather not use such depressing terminology.) You can expand live effects by selecting the object and choosing Object » Expand Appearance. Your object will be converted into permanently changed paths.

 Although the flexibility of live effects is very tempting, there may be times you want to convert the effects into actual objects. For instance, many live effects in a file may slow down opening and saving the file. Converting the live effects can help. Or you may be passing your file over to someone else whom you would rather not give the ability to change the effects. Expanding the appearance effectively stops anyone from mucking about with the artwork.

Imperfecting Paths

As we discuss in Chapter 10, Illustrator lets you make things quite perfect. Trouble is, many people don't want that kind of perfection in their illustrations. They want more organic, natural looks. Fortunately four commands in the Filter » Distort or Effect » Distort & Transform submenus let you apply imperfections to otherwise perfect paths. This gives your illustrations a much more organic, traditional appearance. (Deke calls these commands "path wigglers.") Depending on the filter, you can adjust the amount, direction, size, and details of the imperfection. You can also specify what becomes imperfect.

Figure 12-9 demonstrates how each of the path wigglers shakes up lines of boring old Helvetica Inserat. The word "ghosts" is the product of the Roughen filter, "zombies" comes from Zig Zag, "monsters" was scrambled by Scribble and Tweak, and "vampires" received the sharp-punks of Punk and Bloat. (We used the free transform tool and the Twirl filter to abuse "Halloween.") Also worth noting, the frayed outline was a standard rectangle before we subjected it to the Roughen filter.

Figure 12-9: The path wiggler commands can turn common, dreary typefaces into something very frightening.

Two of the filters—Roughen, and Scribble and Tweak—produce random results within a specified range. You can force Illustrator to generate new results without changing the range by turning the Preview check box off and back on.

Roughing Out Paths

Choose Filter » Distort » Roughen or Effect » Distort & Transform » Roughen. The roughen filter and effect creates roughness by adding nooks and crannies to paths. (For the sake of easy reading, when a feature exists as both a filter and an effect, we refer to it as a command.) The roughen command adds points to selected objects and then moves the points in random directions, giving your paths a serrated, spiky look. The controls for the roughen command are shown in Figure 12-10. The Size value indicates the distance that each point can move, expressed as a percentage of the longest segment in the path. The Detail value determines the number of points that Illustrator adds to each inch of segment. Select the Smooth radio button to convert all points in the paths to smooth points; select Corner to make them all corner points. The radio buttons for Relative or Absolute let you set the amount so that it is relative to the size of the path or an absolute amount. Using the Relative settings means that the same setting applied to small objects creates a similar look to when the setting is applied to larger objects.

 Using the Relative setting becomes very helpful in applying the same style to different-sized objects. See Chapter 20 for the inside scoop on styles.

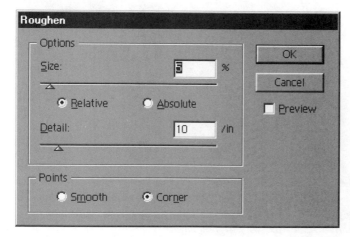

Figure 12-10:
The Roughen dialog box creates a more natural look by adding points to paths.

The roughen command also lets you choose between creating corner or smooth points. As Figure 12-11 demonstrates, corner points create a more jagged appearance whereas smooth points are a little more curved. Think of corner points as the jagged edge created immediately after tearing a piece of paper; smooth points are more like the edge of burnt paper.

Figure 12-11: Different settings of the Roughen command create more distorted paths. The letters of the illustration provide the size (S) and detail (D) settings for the text. Smooth points were applied to the left examples. Corner points were applied to the right.

Zig-Zagging Around Paths

Choose Filter » Distort » Zig Zag or Effect » Distort & Transform » Zig Zag to display the Zig Zag dialog box (as shown in Figure 12-12). The Zig Zag command is really a variation of the roughen command. Instead of a random position of the new points and segments, the zig zag command gives your paths an electric jolt by arranging the points and segments evenly on either side of the path. The Amount value controls the distance that each point can move, which in turn determines the size of the wiggles. Use the Ridges per segment to specify how many zigzags Illustrator adds to each segment. As you can see in Figure 12-13, long segments—like the sides of the As—get long wobbly ridges, whereas the ridges along short segments—as on the bottoms of the characters—are more tightly packed.

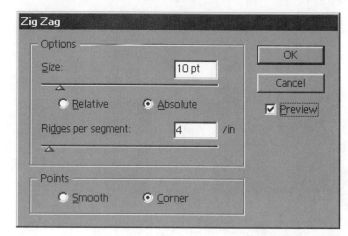

Figure 12-12:
The Zig Zag dialog box is actually just a variation of the Roughen command.

Figure 12-13: Different settings of the Zig Zag command create orderly distorted paths. The letters of the illustration provide the amount (A) and ridges per segment (R) settings for the text. Smooth points were applied to the left examples. Corner points were applied to the right.

Scribbling and Tweaking Paths

Unlike Roughen or Zig Zag, Scribble and Tweak (Filter » Distort » Scribble and Tweak or Effect » Distort & Transform » Scribble and Tweak) does not add points to selected objects. Rather, it moves existing points and control handles in random distances and directions. The name of this command is a leftover from the days when a pull-down menu offered the choice between a Scribble or a Tweak mode. Now, the differences are controlled by the Relative (percentage) or Absolute (actual amount) radio buttons as shown in Figure 12-14.

Use the Horizontal and Vertical values to specify the maximum distance that points and control handles can move. Use the check boxes to decide which elements move. If you want to move the points but not the handles, turn off the two Control Points options. (The "In" option controls handles associated with segments entering points; the "Out" option controls handles for outgoing segments.) If you want to make the points stationary and move just the handles, turn off the Anchor Points check box and turn on the other two.

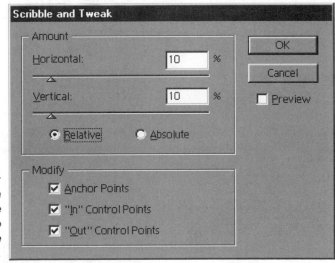

Figure 12-14:
The differences between
Scribble and Tweak are
controlled by the radio
buttons for Relative
or Absolute.

Figure 12-15: The Scribble and Tweak command moved anchor points (on the left) and control handles (on the right). The amounts are listed in the percentages of the text.

Punked and Bloated Paths

Choose Filter » Distort » Punk and Bloat or Effect » Distort & Transform » Punk and Bloat to open the Punk and Bloat dialog box (shown in its complete simplicity in Figure 12-16). This command features a single slider bar and related option box. Negative values (which tend toward Punk) move points outward from the center of a path and twist segments inward. This creates an angular, almost Gothic, look. Positive values (on the Bloat side) move segments inward and curve segments outward, turning them into puffballs. The left column of Figure 12-17 demonstrates a few Punk values, whereas the right column shows off Bloat. Which kind of path would you rather be?

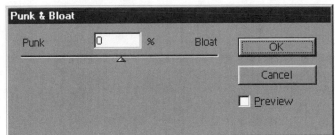

Figure 12-16:
The deceptively simple
Punk and Bloat dialog
box controls two totally
different effects.

Figure 12-17: A sampling of the values applied with the Punk and Bloat command.

Orderly Distortions and Transformations

After all the chaos of the path wigglers, it's a relief to settle back with some controlled distortions and transformations in the Free Distort and Transform commands. The Free Distort command is a stripped down version of the Free Distort tool, whereas the Transform command is an enhanced version of the Transform Each command.

Free Distortion

So why would you want a weakened version of the Free Distort tool? Because unlike the Free Distort tool, the Free Distort command allows you to apply a distortion through the Filter menu. You can also create a distortion that is live and can be applied to editable text through the Effect menu. These features alone make Free Distort a worthy command.

Choose Filter » Distort » Free Distort or Effect » Distort & Transform » Free Distort to open the Free Distort dialog box as shown in Figure 12-18. This box couldn't be simpler. Just drag the four handles any which way you want to apply a distortion to the selected objects. Don't bother looking for special modifier keys to make one corner react to the motions of another. These handles don't have any of that sophistication. Just remember, the effect version of this feature can be modified or deleted at any time. It can also be made part of a style so that it can be applied automatically to objects.

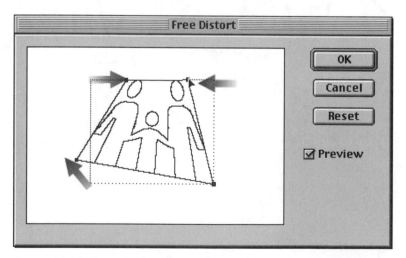

Figure 12-18: Drag the handles to change the appearance of the selected image in the Free Distort dialog box.

Transform Effect

One of the problems with transformations is that they are so permanent. You make an object very wide, and there's no way to remember how much it was elongated—unless you write it down, which we rarely do. And if you want to restore the object back to its original size, you have to do all this involved math where the numerator is the original size and the denominator is the new size and X equals something else that you can't remember. And things get even worse when it comes to rotating objects, because you have to think in degrees.

Wouldn't it be cool if there were a way to apply live transformations to objects so you could change your mind later on without an advanced calculus degree? And as long as we're talking about transformations, wouldn't it be cool if you could apply both a rotation and a scale to an object so it seems to get smaller and smaller as it rotates around? And gee, now that you've got us thinking about it, wouldn't it be terrific if we could make copies of the object as it rotates and scales, and flips and does other transformations?

Yeah, it would. And that's what the Effect » Distort & Transform » Transform effect does. At first glance the Transform Effect dialog box as seen in Figure 12-19 looks almost identical to the Transform Each dialog box covered in Chapter 11. But instead of a Copy button, the Transform dialog box has a Copies option box on the right. That is the secret to creating multiple copies of the selected object.

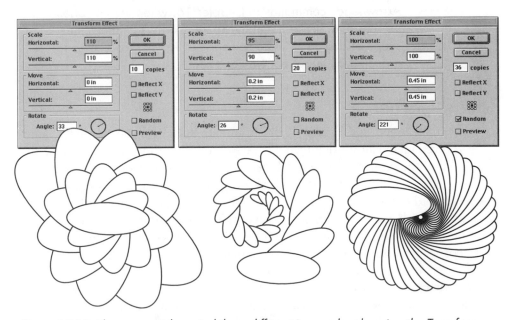

Figure 12-19: The same oval created three different images by changing the Transform dialog box settings shown above each image.

When you enter a number in the Copies option box, you instruct Illustrator to make a copy of the selected object. That copy is in addition to the original. So 1 copy means 2 images; 2 copies means 3 images; and so on.

Look at the three different images in Figure 12-19. Each one was created from the same single oval. The only differences are the scaling, moves, rotations, and number of copies applied in the Transform dialog box. In the example on the left, the oval is made to grow and rotate 10 times around the original. In the middle example, the oval spirals and shrinks by combining scaling, movement, and rotation. Finally, on the right, the oval rotates without changing size.

Round Corners

The Round Corners filter and effect are found under the category Stylize. Stylize seems to be Adobe's word for "commands we can't think of a more descriptive name for." It's hard to find a theme for all of these filters and effects. Some add a raster image such as a drop shadow and glows (which is why we cover them in Chapter 13, which deals with rasters). Another adds arrowheads, squares, and other markers to the ends of open paths. (We cover the Add Arrowheads commands in Chapter 16, when we talk about Brushes and Strokes.) Finally, Round Corners changes the shape of objects. Maybe someone at Adobe has a logic for grouping all these, but we can't see it.

Round Corners

As we mentioned in Chapter 4, the Rounded Rectangle tool is pretty lame. Once you've created a rounded rectangle, it's practically impossible to change the roundness of the corners. You're much better off just drawing a whole new object. Choose Filter » Stylize » Round Corners and you're in a similar situation. Once you've applied the Round Corner filter to objects, you have permanently rounded the corners with very little choices to fix what you've done later on. The sole advantage of the filter over the Rounded Rectangle tool is that the filter can round off all corner points, not just those in rectangles.

However, it's as a live effect that Round Corners really shakes up the world. (Deke's wish has finally come true: Illustrator can change the roundness applied to rectangles.) Choose Effect » Stylize » Round Corners, and a dialog box appears where you can set the corner radius for how much roundness you want applied to corner points. As Figure 12-20 shows, these objects maintain their original structures, but display the round corner effect. The amount of rounding can be changed or deleted at any time.

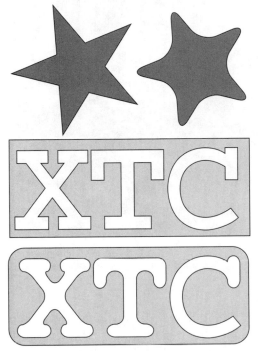

Figure 12-20:
Round Corners applied to a
star, a rectangle and some
plain old Courier Bold text.

Pathfinder Effects

Back in Chapter 9, we discussed the various pathfinder commands for merging, cropping, dividing, and chopping up paths. So why choose the pathfinder commands as live effects? Because unlike their Pathfinder palette cousins, the pathfinder effects don't permanently chop up your art. Because we've already covered the specifics of each individual pathfinder command, we'll look at how you can apply and modify the pathfinder effects.

Imagine that your goal is to create the artwork on the right side of Figure 12-21. This deceptively simple illustration can be created two ways. The first way is to create the star shapes and one by one use the Minus Front command to etch the stars out of the hand. There's really nothing wrong with this until someone (usually an ugly, cigar-smoking client) wants to move one of the stars on the side ever-so-slightly over or down or something. And that's going to be difficult because the Minus Front command has chopped up the illustration permanently. So using the commands in the Pathfinder palette doesn't seem like a very good idea.

Figure 12-21: Your mission (should you choose to accept it) is to create the effect shown on the right side of this illustration.

Right now, there's a kid in the back of the room waving his hand and yelling that we should use compound paths to punch holes in the hand. (You remember compound paths; we covered them in Chapter 9.) Check out the left side of Figure 12-21. We used compounds there. Notice that wherever the stars extend outside the hand you see a black fill. That is *not* the effect we want, so please be quiet there in the back.

This is exactly the sort of situation that the pathfinder effects (Effect » Pathfinder) were designed for. Not only can they punch out holes in objects, but they let you change your mind way after the fact. By working through this challenge, you should understand how to use the pathfinder effects.

When you apply a pathfinder effect, you may get an alert box telling you that pathfinder effects work best on groups, layers, or type objects. And that the effect you are trying to apply may not work on the selected object. If this happens, give it up. Illustrator knows darn well that the type of object you've got selected isn't going to display the pathfinder effect at all. And unless you know some technique that we've never heard of, applying the pathfinder effect is going to be useless.

1. **Set up the basic illustration.**

    In this case we want to put the hand below the stars. Don't worry about what color to make the stars; although it does help if you make them look different from the hand, because it is very hard to see black stars on a black background. (We cover changing the color of objects in Chapter 15.)

2. **Select and group each set of objects.**

    In this case you want to select and group all the stars because you want them to act as an individual item. Because there is only one hand, you don't have to group it. However, if we had wanted two hands that had stars cut out of them, we would have had to select those multiple objects and group them.

3. **Target each set.**

    Here we start by selecting the group that contains all the stars. We now target the group by clicking the circle next to the group name in the Layers palette or by clicking the word Group in the Appearance palette. (Flip back to Figure 12-7 for a review of how to target a group.)

4. **Apply the Unite effect.**

    Once you have targeted the group you can choose Effect » Pathfinder » Unite. Although nothing much will have changed in the appearance of the stars, you should see that the circle next to the group name in the Layers palette is gray rather than white as shown in Figure 12-22. This indicates that a special effect has been applied to this group in the Appearance palette.

    If you had been working with two hands, you would need to repeat steps 3 and 4 for that second group as well as any other groups. Well, yes, we know you're actually working with two hands. What we mean is if you were working with an illustration that contained two hands or other multiple objects, you'd need to repeat the steps for those groups.

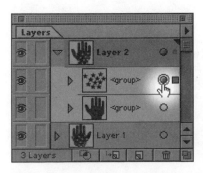

Figure 12-22:
The gray target circle next to the group listing indicates that a special appearance, such as an effect, has been applied to the group.

Effects aren't the only features indicated by the gray circle. Multiple fills and strokes, or transparencies, are all indicated by the gray circle. The gray circles stands for a special appearance. Anytime you see a gray circle in the Layers palette, you know that something special has been applied in the Appearance palette.

5. **Target the layer and apply the Minus Front effect.**

    Targeting the layer is similar to targeting a group. Click the circle next to the name of the layer in the Layers palette. Then choose Effect » Pathfinder » Minus Front. Your stars now knock out the hand or any groups below.

6. **Put other objects on separate layers.**

    Any objects below the hands (such as the gray stripes) need to be on their own layer because the minus front effect is applied to all the objects on the layer with the stars. Similarly, if we wanted any objects above the stars, they too would have to be on their own layer.

The benefit of all this work is that you can still edit the shape of all the objects. None of the pathfinder effects has permanently chopped up your paths.

CHAPTER 13

BECOMING MASTER OF THE RASTER

Used to be that raster images were as useful in Illustrator as a can of Pepsi at a Coca-Cola sales conference. You could look at the raster image, but nobody could touch it. Today, though, it's a totally different story. Not only does Illustrator allow you to import and manipulate raster images from programs such as Photoshop, but you can create your own raster effects within Illustrator. In fact, in some ways, Illustrator is even more flexible with raster images than Adobe's own Photoshop.

Just in case you have forgotten what we covered in Chapter 1, raster images are the pixel-based images that come from scanners or programs such as Adobe Photoshop. Illustrator offers many different ways to work with raster images. You can apply transformations, filters, effects, or transparency techniques to the images. You can even apply raster effects such as drop shadows, glows, and feathers that create raster images without actually losing your original path information.

 Illustrator 9 has broken new ground in the field of illustration software with the ability to apply raster to vector paths. This means you don't have to choose between vector and raster information. You can have them both.

Raster Effects on Vector Shapes

As we were going hog-wild in Chapter 12, we put off covering some of the filters and effects commands because they seemed more appropriate for this chapter, which deals with raster images. Some of Illustrator's effects do not simply manipulate path information; rather, they create displays of pixel images that conform to a path shape. These pixel images cannot be actually printed in anything except raster data.

For example, Figure 13-1 shows a comparison between the type of drop shadow that was created by the drop shadow filter in older versions of Illustrator, and the one created by today's drop shadow filter. The sharp edge of the old drop shadow was the best that Illustrator offered. The new drop shadow has a warm and fuzzy edge—an edge that could only come from pixels.

Figure 13-1: Who knows what differences lurk between the old drop shadow filter (top) and today's drop shadow (bottom)? You do.

Drop Shadow Filter and Effect

Drop shadows can be applied as either filters or effects. If you've used the drop shadow layer effects in Photoshop, you should understand the drop shadows in Illustrator. Choose Filter » Stylize » Drop Shadow or Effect » Stylize » Drop Shadow. The Drop Shadow dialog boxes appear as shown in Figure 13-2. Although most of the settings are identical, there are some differences between them.

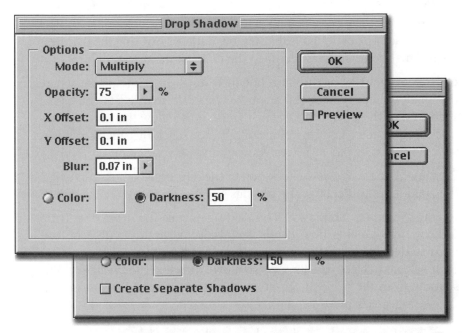

Figure 13-2: The Drop Shadow effect dialog box (top) provides a Preview check box. The Drop Shadow Filter dialog box (bottom) allows you to set separate shadows for multiple objects.

- **Mode:** This option controls how the drop shadow blends with any other objects behind it. The default setting, Multiply, creates the most realistic effect, which allows the colors of other objects to be added to the color of the shadow. We cover all the mode settings in painstaking detail in Chapter 17.

- **Opacity:** This controls how transparent the shadow appears. The higher the opacity, the less transparent the shadow will be. In real life a low opacity setting would be similar to a low amount of light. However, there is no real-life equivalent to a 100 percent opacity setting.

- **X and Y Offsets:** This lets you choose the position of the shadow. The higher the numbers, the further away from the object the shadow will be positioned. If you have not moved the zero point, positive X numbers move the shadow to the right; positive Y numbers move the shadow down.

- **Blur:** This controls how much blur is applied to the shadow. The higher the number, the more diffuse the shadow.

- **Darkness:** The Darkness setting starts with the basic color of the object and then adds black to make the shadow darker. Lowering the darkness setting makes the shadow closer to the color of the original object.

- **Color:** We don't know for sure but there must be some planet where the shadows are green or red or pink. The color setting lets you create shadows for those worlds. Or you can use it as a glow that can be positioned. After you click the Color radio button, click the small color box to open the color picker where you can choose your color.

- **Preview:** Use the Preview check box in the effect dialog box to preview the shadow as you change the settings.

- **Create Separate Shadows:** This setting is missing from the Drop Shadow effect dialog box. If you have selected multiple objects, you need to decide how they are creating the shadow. Turn this on to have each selected object cast its own shadow. Turn it off to create a single shadow from the selected objects as a group. Figure 13-3 shows how the setting affects multiple objects.

Even though the dialog box for the drop shadow effect doesn't have the separate shadows setting, you can still create the same look. First group the objects and use the Layers palette to target the group. Then apply the effect to the group. The shadows will be applied to the group as a whole without creating individual shadows for each object.

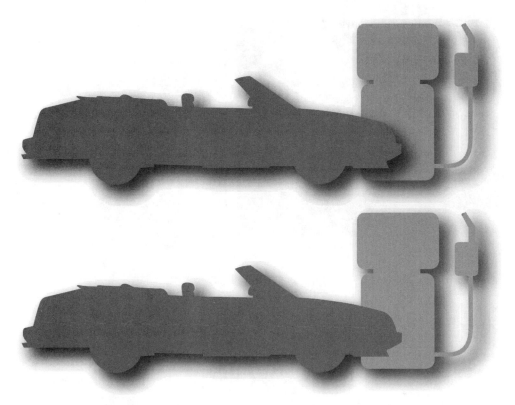

Figure 13-3: Create Separate Shadows was turned on for objects on the top. It was turned off for the objects on the bottom.

Feathering

Feathering is the name of the technique in Photoshop that blurs selections into transparency. Those selections can then be filled with color, used to copy images, or deleted from layers. In Illustrator, the feather effect fades the edges of selected objects into transparency.

The amount of feathering is measured as a radius amount. This defines the size of the fade that is applied to the edge of the path. The higher the feather, the greater the blur that is applied to the image. Figure 13-4 shows the effect of feathering white stars against a dark background.

*Figure 13-4:
Feathering allows you to
create natural-looking stars
in the constellation.*

Outer and Inner Glows

Glows are actually feathers that have colors rather than transparency. An outer glow extends out from an object. An inner glow extends from the edge of an object and moves inward or fills the entire object and moves toward the center. Figure 13-5 shows the two dialog boxes for the outer and inner glow effects. We've created some sample glows shown in Figure 13-6. Here's how to control the glows:

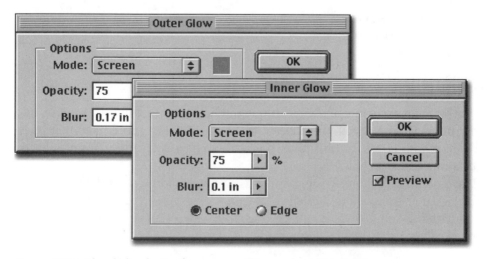

*Figure 13-5: The dialog boxes for outer and inner glows. Notice the
additional controls for the inner glows.*

Figure 13-6: An inner glow created the frosty effect, whereas an outer glow created the misty fog.

 Mode: Like the drop shadows, this option controls how the glow blends with colors. For the inner glow, that is the color of the original object. For outer glows, it is the color of any objects behind the glow. The default setting of screen causes the glows to lighten colors behind them.

The default setting of screen makes it difficult to see an outer glow if it is on a white background. Move the object over a color to see the effect of the outer glow.

 Opacity: This controls how transparent the glow appears. The higher the opacity, the less transparent the glow will be.

 Blur: This controls how much blur is applied to the glow. The higher the number, the more diffuse the glow.

 Center: The center radio button for an inner glow creates a glow that starts from the center of the object. The lower the blur, the closer the glow will extend to the edge of the object, and the less you will see of the original fill of the object.

Edge: The edge radio button for an inner glow creates a glow that starts at the edge of the object and extends towards the center of the object. The lower the blur, the closer the glow will be to the edge of the object, and the more you will see of the original fill of the object.

Expanding Effects

One way to discover what's happening behind the scenes when you apply the raster filters and effects is to look at what happens when you convert the live effect into dead objects—a procedure called *expanding*. (This is the equivalent of looking at the man behind the curtain.)

Select an object that has a raster effect such as the drop shadow applied to it. Choose Object » Expand Appearance. This separates all the aspects of the appearance into separate objects. You will have to ungroup the objects, but eventually you will see, as Figure 13-7 shows, that a drop shadow expands into vector objects layered above a pixel image. (Now you see why we covered these effects in this chapter.)

You can also expand effects such as roughen or transform that don't use raster images into their individual vector components. The result of that expansion is individual vector shapes.

Expansion is also what happens when you save Illustrator 9 files into previous versions. Effects have to be expanded into their components.

Figure 13-7: A sideways view of how the drop shadow effect actually layers vector objects over a raster image.

Filters and Effects for Raster Images

Here's where Illustrator outdoes even Photoshop. Not only does Illustrator allow you to apply Photoshop plug-in commands to raster objects, but it also allows you to apply those commands as live effects to either raster or vector objects. So unlike Photoshop, where the Gaussian Blur is a done deal that cannot be modified the next time you open the file, in Illustrator those commands can be modified or deleted any time—hours, days, even months after you make them.

Even better, if the original object is a vector shape, you can easily edit or modify the image—very different from Photoshop where it is more difficult to modify the shape of an image.

 All comparisons between Illustrator and Photoshop are based on the differences between this version of Illustrator and the current version of Photoshop—which at the time of this writing is Photoshop 5.5. We have no way of knowing what features future versions of Photoshop may offer. And even if we did know, we wouldn't be allowed to write it here.

Sound too good to be true? Well, there are a few things to remember.

- The live effects require loads of RAM and a rather fast processor. You may find that complicated images can slow down screen redraw.

- You must first embed the raster image within the Illustrator file in order to apply the commands under the Filter menu. This adds to the size of the Illustrator file. (We'll cover embedding later in this chapter.) However, you do not have to embed the raster image if you apply the command from the Effect menu.

- Most of the filters only work within the RGB colorspace. So you may have to switch from CMYK to RGB to apply a command.

Photoshop-Compatible Filters

When you install Illustrator, you can install 50-some plug-ins divided into ten different categories. These plug-ins appear in both the Filter and Effect menus. Under the Filter menu they can be applied only on raster images. Under the Effect menu they can be used on either vector or raster images.

These filters are the same ones that ship with Photoshop 5.5. As a general rule, they work best on tonal images rather than flat art. It would take hundreds of pages for us to show you the results of all the filters. (Not only would we have to show you the results of each command, but we'd have to show you the different settings for each command.)

However, we put together a small sample of nine of the different categories of the plug-ins in Figure 13-8. (We skipped the Video category because it is primarily used for images from video cameras.) Looking through 10 categories can be a little overwhelming. Here's a brief summary of what each category of filters does:

- **Artistic:** Tries to simulate traditional or natural media such as pastels or sponge painting.

- **Blurs:** The Gaussian blur acts very similarly to the Feather command. However, where Feather will fade only to the edge of a vector path, Gaussian Blur fades the image so that it lies on either side of the path. The Radial Blur causes the image to look as if it were spinning. (Sadly, our favorite Photoshop blur, Motion Blur, is missing.)

- **Brush Strokes:** Very similar to the Artistic category, these also simulate traditional media.

- **Distort:** These filters do not change the colors of the pixels in the image. Rather, they move them in various ways causing distortions.

- **Pixelate:** Changes the colors of pixels into groups that simulate various effects.

- **Sharpen:** Allows you to apply the Unsharp Mask command, which helps improve the sharpness of scanned images.

- **Sketch:** Adds texture to images, simulating traditional outlining effects.

- **Stylize:** Allows you to apply the Glowing Edges command for a neon-like glow.

- **Texture:** Adds an overlay texture to images that simulates traditional media.

- **Video:** Contains two corrections for working with images from video sources.

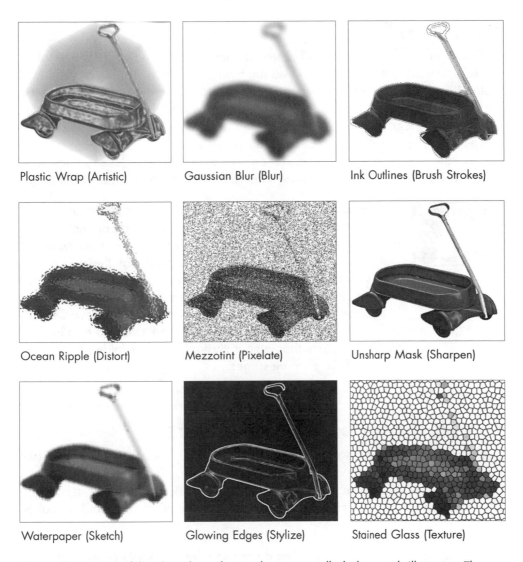

Plastic Wrap (Artistic)   Gaussian Blur (Blur)   Ink Outlines (Brush Strokes)

Ocean Ripple (Distort)   Mezzotint (Pixelate)   Unsharp Mask (Sharpen)

Waterpaper (Sketch)   Glowing Edges (Stylize)   Stained Glass (Texture)

Figure 13-8: Nine of the Photoshop plug-ins that are installed along with Illustrator. The categories are listed in parentheses next to the command name.

Pointing to Filters

Choose Edit » Preferences » Plug-ins and Scratch Disk to change which folder or directory Illustrator looks at to find the filters and effects. In theory, you could point Illustrator to your Photoshop plug-ins folder. Don't do it! The Illustrator plug-ins folder contains your startup file along with tools and other important parts of the program. If you want, create an alias or shortcut of your Photoshop plug-ins and put that inside the Illustrator plug-ins folder.

You can also use this technique to bring in third-party (non-Adobe) Photoshop filters into Illustrator. These include filters from Alien Skin and the KPT filters.

 Don't trash all the Photoshop plug-ins inside the Illustrator Plug-ins folder. If the Photoshop Filters and Effects are not available, errors will appear when you create new documents that use the default startup files. If you don't wish these effects and filters to be present, you need to create startup files that don't use any of the Photoshop filters or effects such as Feather, Inner Glow, Outer Glow, and Drop Shadow. Or you can create an alias or shortcut of the Photoshop plug-ins folder and place that in your Illustrator Plug-ins folder. This will avoid the error messages.

Converting Pixels into Vectors

Despite the lack of a sophisticated auto-trace tool, Illustrator does have two commands that can convert pixel images into vector objects. The first is the Object Mosaic filter which converts pixel information into small rectangles. The other is the Photo Crosshatch which creates the effect of an old-fashioned custom halftone screen.

 In the old days (when dinosaurs ruled the earth) people used to create custom screens as halftones for photographs. We both remember sending photographs out for specialty screens. We feel like dinosaurs when we have to explain the references to people today.

Finding the Mosaic in an Image

Imagine you had a large photograph that covered your bathroom floor. If you could apply it, the Object Mosaic filter would carve the photograph up into individual tiles (rectangles) that would create the look of the photograph on the floor. The smaller the rectangles, the more detail in the finished image.

Select an image and choose Filter » Create » Object Mosaic to convert the image into a series of colored rectangles. The rectangles imitate pixels—and each rectangle takes up the same amount of room on disk and in memory as a similarly-sized pixel would—but you can edit the rectangles just as if you had drawn them with the rectangle tool.

When you choose Filter » Create » Object Mosaic, Illustrator displays the dialog box shown in Figure 13-9. It contains a lot of options, but they're fairly easy to use:

- **Current Size, New Size:** The Current Size area shows the dimensions of the image in points. You can adjust the size of the mosaic picture by entering new values in the New Size option boxes.

- **Tile Spacing:** Enter the amount of space (grout) you want Illustrator to insert between rectangles in the Tile Spacing option boxes. To make the rectangles fit snugly together—Deke's preference—leave the values set to 0.

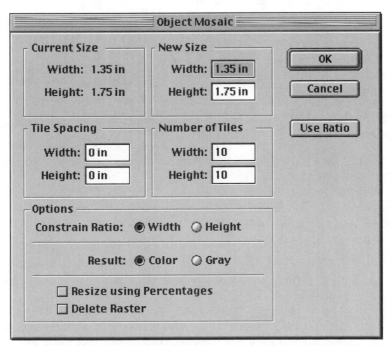

Figure 13-9: Use this dialog box to convert an embedded image into a series of object-oriented rectangles.

- **Number of Tiles:** Enter the number of rectangles that Illustrator should draw horizontally and vertically into the Number of Tiles option boxes. If you enter a Width value of 40, for example, Illustrator draws 40 rectangles across the width of the image. The greater the number, the more detail in the finished tiles.

- **Use Ratio:** If you want the New Size and the Number of Tiles values to conform to the ratio of the original image, you can enter the desired values into either the two Width or the two Height option boxes and then click the Use Ratio button. For example, let's say you want the mosaic to be 300 points wide with 30 tiles across. First, enter each value into the appropriate Width option box. Then select the Constrain Ratio Width radio button to tell Illustrator to change the Height values and leave the Width values intact. And finally, click the Use Ratio button to automatically adjust the Height values so that you'll get a proportional mosaic made up of perfect squares.

- **Color/Grayscale:** If you want Illustrator to fill the tiles with CMYK colors, select the Color radio button. Select the Gray option to fill the rectangles with shades of black.

- **Resize Using Percentages:** If you want to use percentages to determine the change in width and height instead of specifying the exact dimensions in the New Size option boxes, select this option.

- **Delete Raster:** Select this option to delete the image after converting it to a mosaic. To retain the original image, turn off the check box.

After you apply the Object Mosaic command, Illustrator draws the rectangular tiles and groups them to facilitate editing.

 One of Sandee's favorite ways to modify the tiles is to choose Object » Transform » Transform Each, where you can rotate, scale, or move the tiles ever-so-slightly with the Random setting turned on. This simulates the look of her old, broken-down New York City bathroom floor.

If you want the mosaic rectangles to look like true mosaic tiles, you need to add highlights, like those shown in Figure 13-10. We started out with the top photograph. We used Filter » Create » Object Mosaic to create a mosaic 40 tiles wide and 21 tiles tall. In the first example, we cloned the mosaic. Then we used the Transform Each command to shrink the tiles to 80 percent horizontally and 20 percent vertically. (Random was turned off.) After nudging the tiles into position, we deleted their strokes and filled them with white.

To create the bottom example in Figure 13-10, we again cloned the mosaic. Then we used Object » Transform » Transform Each to reduce each tile to 60 percent horizontally and vertically. To lighten the tiles, we chose Filter » Colors » Saturate (a command we discuss in the next chapter) and entered a value of –30 percent. And we deleted the strokes. That's it; we didn't even have to move the tiles.

 Mosaics can slow down Illustrator's redraw speed dramatically, and they can take a very long time to print. If you're not sure what kind of effect you want to apply, try it out on a small mosaic pattern with 10 tiles or fewer. Then after you have the effect figured out, apply it to a larger mosaic. This will save you a considerable amount of time and help to prevent general exasperation.

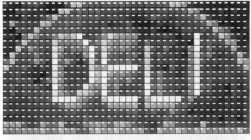

Figure 13-10:
The top image was transformed using Object Mosaic and then highlights were added using Transform Each and changing the colors.

Hatching a Sketch

With the Photo Crosshatch filter, Illustrator will transform an embedded graphic into a vector object by approximating the graphic with a number of little lines or hatches. Illustrator first converts the graphic to grayscale and then applies hatches to those gray values that fall within a certain range. Figure 13-11 displays the same image converted with the Photo Crosshatch filter, with the dialog box showing the different settings.

 Unlike the Object Mosaic filter, the Photo Crosshatch does not give you the option of keeping the original image. So always work on a copy of your original. Also, the filter can easily create more objects than McDonald's has sold hamburgers. Your best bet is to put the image on its own layer so you can easily select or work with the tremendous number of objects.

Each and every time you choose the Filter » Photo Crosshatch command you're presented with the Photo Crosshatch dialog box, shown in Figure 13-11. The different settings let you take the static, uniform hatches that make up each layer and subtly adjust them as a whole to give the final effect a more realistic appearance.

The settings work as follows:

- **Density:** This setting dictates the distance between the lines that form the crosshatch. Use the slider bar to choose a value from 0.5 to 10 pixels. Unlike what you might expect, the higher the density the fewer objects on the page.

- **Dispersion Noise:** This option affects the Density setting. For example, with the Dispersion Noise set to 50 percent and the Density at 3 points, the distance between the hatches can range from a maximum of 7.5 pixels all the way down to 0 points. Well, not quite zero. In fact, the minimum distance is dictated by the Thickness setting. A Thickness of 1 point means that the minimum distance will be 1 point. Enter a non-zero value in the Dispersion Noise option box to give the result a more realistic look.

- **Thickness:** Choose a stroke weight for all the hatches anywhere between 0.1 and 10 points.

- **Max. Line Length:** This value determines the longest length of any hatch.

- **Rotation Noise:** To vary the amount that each hatch is rotated from the default, enter a value into the Rotation Noise option box. For example, with a value of 20 degrees and a Top Angle of 50 degrees, the hatches on the top layer could vary anywhere between 30 and 70 degrees.

- **Rotation Variance:** If you have more than one hatch layer, then with this setting you can choose the amount of the angular difference between the different layers.

- **Top Angle:** No matter how many hatch layers you have, the hatches on the topmost layer will appear at this angle (plus or minus the value in the Rotation Noise option box).

- **Hatch Layers:** You can choose to have from one to eight hatch layers. Each of these layers can cover a different range of grayscale values.

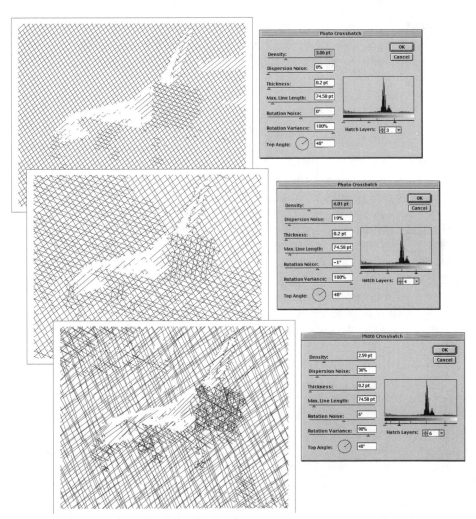

Figure 13-11: By varying the hatch settings we were able to change the look from a perfect halftone screen to a more sketched appearance.

Linked or Embedded

This is one of those important issues like paper or plastic—and there are important advantages to both sides. First, when you bring a raster image into Illustrator, you have to decide how you want the information handled. If you choose Link, Illustrator creates a link to the image file on disk. All the information needed to actually print the file is stored outside the Illustrator file. What is inside the Illustrator file is actually only a small preview image—100K tops—regardless of how much space the original image takes up on disk.

 If you link an image, don't throw away the original file. Illustrator needs that file to print the linked image.

If you deselect the Link option in the Place dialog box, Illustrator imports all the pixels into the illustration and converts the pixels into PostScript code, an operation known as *embedding* (or *parsing* in the olden days). Because Illustrator incorporates all the pixel information into the file, the image will add to the file size. However, if an image is embedded you can apply the special features such as the Photoshop filters or effects to images.

 Before version 9, we were more inclined to recommend linking images unless they were very small grayscale images such as the low-resolution screen shots we use to illustrate books and teaching materials. However, all the new features in Illustrator 9—especially the live Photoshop effects—have made us more inclined to recommend embedding images within Illustrator documents.

So, should you embed or link images? Choose link if you never expect to manipulate the image within Illustrator. However, if you only link you can skip the rest of this chapter. You can't become a master of the raster if your pixels are all residing outside the Illustrator file.

You should embed if you want to take advantage of the effects within Illustrator. If you have a linked image, you can easily embed it—most of the time all you need to do is apply a filter or effect to the image. Illustrator automatically embeds the image in the file. Or select the image and choose Embed from the Links palette menu.

If you are unsure as to whether or not an image is embedded or linked, look at the image in the document. Linked images have two diagonal lines that go from corner to corner. Embedded images do not. You can also check the Links palette as shown in Figure 13-12. The embed icon lets you know the image is incorporated into the Illustrator file.

 This method of embedding is much better than what happens in Adobe InDesign 1.5, which removes the name of a file from the Links palette if you embed the file within an InDesign document.

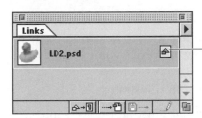

Embedded icon

Figure 13-12: The embedded icon in the Links palette tells you that all the information necessary to print the file is embedded within the Illustrator document.

Illustrator doesn't completely ignore linked images. Whether an image is linked or embedded, Illustrator lets you move, scale, rotate, flip, or slant it. You can view black-and-white versions of any image in the artwork mode (if the Show Images In Outline check box is turned on in the Document Setup dialog box).

Hoist that Raster and Rake those Pixels

You know you've finally reached the enviable status of Hopeless Computer Dweeb when you know the meaning of the word "rasterize." In regular human terms, it means to convert objects to pixels. You probably aren't aware of it but your computer is constantly rasterizing things. Every time you edit an object, Illustrator and your system software rasterize paths to display them as pixels on screen. Illustrator rasterizes characters of type to screen pixels. And when you print your artwork, your printer rasterizes the mathematical path definitions as teeny printer pixels.

 Legend has it that the word "rasterize" was coined during the early days of monitor development. Your monitor displays stuff on screen by projecting pixels in horizontal rows. It's almost as if the monitor were raking pixels across the screen, which is where the word *raster*—Latin for *rake*—comes in. Nowadays, rasterize is used for any kind of pixel creation, whether on screen, inside a printer, or inside a program like Illustrator.

You might think that the only way to create pixel images in Illustrator is to bring them in from a pixel program like Photoshop. But you would be wrong. You can use the Object » Rasterize command to convert priceless vector objects into mundane pixels.

 Don't misinterpret our comments about the value of pixels. After all, Sandee's cat is named Pixel.

Illustrator 9's live effects feature has greatly reduced the importance of the Rasterize command. For example, rasterizing an image used to be the only way to apply Photoshop filters to Illustrator artwork. Now, however, you can apply the same commands under the Effects menu.

Still, there are a few good reasons to rasterize within Illustrator:

- Object » Rasterize is the only way to convert *all* Illustrator objects into grayscale. The Filter » Colors » Convert to Grayscale command works on most Illustrator paths, but does not work on gradients, patterns, and placed images.

- Object » Rasterize lets you combine two raster images or raster and vector images into one raster image. We use this technique to help clean up or enhance photographs.

- When you rasterize objects to a black-and-white image using the Bitmap option, you can then select a Fill color in the Color palette to specify the color of the black pixels. Add the fact that those black-and-white images take up relatively little room on disk, and you have a great means for creating quick texture patterns.

The Rasterizing Options

When you choose Object » Rasterize, Illustrator greets you with the dialog box shown in Figure 13-13. This is where you control all the aspects of the final rasterized image.

- **Color Model:** Use this pop-up menu to specify whether you want to create a color image, a grayscale image, or a black-and-white image. If you are working in the CMYK colorspace, your choice for color is CMYK; RGB documents let you choose RGB. For more information about the wonderful world of RGB and CMYK colorspaces, read Chapter 14.

To convert a selection to a grayscale image, select the Grayscale option. Select Bitmap if you want the image to contain only black and white pixels.

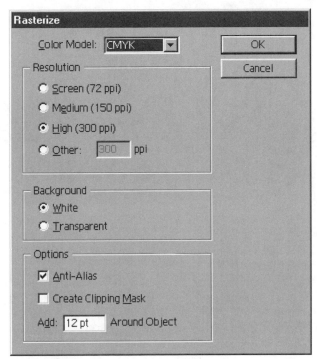

Figure 13-13:
Use the Rasterize dialog box to convert vector objects into pixels. Or you can change the number of colors and pixels inside an image.

  Resolution: Select one of the first three radio buttons or enter a value into the Other option box to specify the number of pixels in the image. Select Screen for 72 ppi, Medium for 150 ppi, and High for 300 ppi. Figure 13-14 demonstrates the effect of converting vector artwork using the three different settings.

> As you can see in the figure, a high-resolution image looks smoother than a low-resolution one. However, the higher the resolution, the more space the image takes up on the disk. As a general rule of thumb, an image with twice the resolution takes up four times as much space on disk.

Figure 13-14: From left to right, the effects of converting an image at screen, medium, and high resolutions.

Background: Choose between white and transparent. White adds white pixels wherever there are any transparent areas in the image. Transparent leaves the transparent areas clear in the raster image. The transparency option creates an image similar to the transparent layers in Photoshop.

 The Transparent option is new in Illustrator 9. This gives Illustrator much more flexibility in rasterizing images. In the past if you rasterized type, the type would appear on a white background which needed a clipping path if you wanted to see behind the type. The transparent option makes the clipping path unnecessary.

Anti-Alias: If you want to soften the transitions between neighboring pixels of different colors, select this option. Anti-aliasing (pronounced "anti-alias-ing") adds a very soft blur to the edges of an image. The anti-alias option is almost always chosen for color or grayscale images. However, it is unavailable for bitmapped images because pure black and white pixels cannot have any blurred or gray pixels. Figure 13-15 compares an image created with and without anti-aliasing. The image on the left has a much more jagged appearance.

- **Create Mask:** Choose this option to create a path that is used to mask transparent portions of the original vector objects to keep them transparent. For more information on working with masks, see Chapter 18.

- **Add Space Around Object:** This option lets you automatically add extra space around an image. If you've chosen a white background, you add extra white around the image. If you've chosen a transparent background, you add extra transparency to the image.

 Now that you can apply the transparency option to rasterized images, we find there are very few instances where we need to create masks when we rasterize.

Figure 13-15: An image rasterized at 150 ppi with the Anti-Alias check box turned off (top) and on (bottom).

Lowering Resolutions

When you embed an image into Illustrator, all the pixels are contained in the file. If you use any of the scale tools to make the image smaller, you increase the resolution of the file. If your image was the correct resolution to begin with, you don't need the higher resolution.

You can use the Object » Rasterize command to lower the resolution of the image. Just make sure you won't want to scale the image up later on. Changing the number of pixels in this way is called *resampling*, because Illustrator has to generate new pixels by averaging the old ones. In technospeak, this averaging is called *interpolating*. Raising the resolution value is never a good idea; Illustrator isn't smart enough to generate detail out of thin air, so doing this just increases the number of pixels without providing any benefit.

 If you're an experienced Photoshop user, you may be wondering what kind of interpolation Illustrator uses when resampling images. When Anti-Alias is turned on, Illustrator uses *bilinear* interpolation, which means the program averages five pixels at a time. (Photoshop's more sophisticated *bicubic* interpolation factors in nine pixels.) When Anti-Alias is off, Illustrator doesn't average pixels at all; it just throws away the pixels that it deems inappropriate. (This is the same as Photoshop's "nearest neighbor" interpolation.)

Fusing Objects and Images

You can fuse objects and imported images into a single image using Object » Rasterize. For example, we started with the image of the train on the left side of Figure 13-16. We wanted to add some perfect circles and lines to enhance the image. Working in Photoshop it would not be easy to create the exact shapes at the correct sizes. But in Illustrator it was no trouble to create the paths exactly to size.

We then checked the resolution using File » Document Info, which was 300 ppi. We selected the image and all the paths and chose Object » Rasterize. We selected the Grayscale option, used 300 as the resolution, turned on Anti-Alias to soften the edges of the paths, and selected the transparent options. Illustrator rasterized the paths into the image, as you can see on the right side of Figure 13-16.

Although Photoshop offers its own object-oriented tools—including the pen tool and a few others—Illustrator provides a much wider range of drawing options. So if you find that you can't accomplish a certain effect in Photoshop, try turning the job over to Illustrator. You can use the File » Export » Photoshop 5 command to get the image back into Photoshop.

 You can also use this technique to add a special colored background behind transparent images.

Figure 13-16: Starting with an ordinary image (left) we added some circles and lines and then rasterized the paths into the image (right).

Outlining Objects

Until recently someone was always complaining that Illustrator can't automatically draw borders around images the way programs like QuarkXPress and InDesign do. (Actually that used to be Sandee complaining to the Illustrator product managers.) The Outline Object effect not only lets you create borders around images, it goes way beyond those mundane page-layout programs.

 The Outline Object command is new in Illustrator 9. We're just starting to recognize its awesome powers.

1. Start with a placed Photoshop image.

Although you could use a flattened image such as a TIFF file, we prefer the native Photoshop file, especially if it is on a transparency layer. This lets us outline around the shape of the image, not just in a rectangle.

If you flatten the Photoshop layers, you can apply the rest of these steps to the image as a whole. However, if you choose to maintain the Photoshop layers as individual Illustrator objects, you need to target the individual layers in the Layers palette to apply the outline.

If your Photoshop file has a clipping path assigned to it, you need to change the path back to a regular path in Photoshop or release the path within Illustrator. We cover clipping paths and masks in Illustrator in Chapter 18.

2. Target the image in the Layers palette.

Click the circle next to the name of the image to target it. If you have multiple Illustrator objects, click the specific object.

3. Target the stroke in the Appearance palette.

This is simple; just click the Stroke listing in the Appearance palette.

4. Choose Effect » Path » Outline Path.

Nothing much will happen except the command will appear listed under the Stroke in the Appearance palette. If your image suddenly disappears, though, it's because you forgot to target the Stroke in Step 3. Just drag the Outline Path listing under the Stroke listing so it appears as shown in Figure 13-17.

5. Target the Stroke listing in the Appearance palette and choose a color.

The reason nothing much happened in Step 4 is that you don't have any color chosen for your stroke. When you target the stroke listing, you can then choose a color from either the Color palette or the Swatches palette. As soon as you do, the outline appears around the image as shown in Figure 13-17.

"Oh, good grief," we can hear you say. "Do we have to do all that every time we want to create a frame around an image? Isn't that a little time-consuming?" Well, fret not. You actually only have to do all that *once*. After that you just need to save the settings as an image style that can be applied to other images with a single click. We cover it in Chapter 20 when we show you how to work faster and smarter.

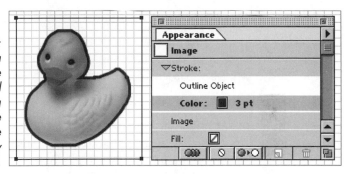

Figure 13-17:
To outline the area of a
placed image, make sure
the Outline Path command
sits inside the Stroke listing
of the Appearance palette
as shown here. Notice the
transparency indicated by
the document grid.

"Cool," we can hear you say, "Now if only Illustrator provided a cropping tool." In fact, Illustrator provides arguably the best cropping capabilities of any program on earth. But it's a big topic that's equally applicable to objects and images, so we won't discuss it here. Turn to Chapter 18, and keep an eye out for the many appearances of the word "mask."

The Rasterize Effect

As useful as Object » Rasterize is, it is a permanent commitment to a specific resolution and color mode. If you don't feel comfortable making those decisions, you can use Effect » Rasterize » Rasterize to apply the command as an effect that can be modified later. (Yes, we know it repeats Rasterize—we didn't design the menus, we just explain them.)

However, combined with the Outline Path command, the Rasterize command gives you even more control over outlining an image. In this case we're going to create an outline around an image but we're also going to give it a white background as well as some extra space around the original file. We could do this using the permanent Object » Rasterize command but just in case we change our mind, we'll do it as an effect.

1. **Start with a placed Photoshop image.**

    If the image is on a transparency layer, we'll still be able to add a white background as part of our rasterizing.

2. **Choose Effect » Rasterize » Rasterize.**

    The Rasterize dialog box appears. It is the same as the Rasterize command dialog box shown earlier in Figure 13-13.

3. **Set the options for the background and color mode.**

    For instance, if you have started with a color image, you can change it to grayscale without actually losing the color information. You can also add a white background to an image that is on a transparent layer.

4. **Add some space around the image.**

    The Rasterize effect dialog box contains an option that doesn't appear in the ordinary Object » Rasterize dialog box: Add Around Object. When you enter a value in this option box, the size of the rasterized image increases. You now have an area that is bigger than the original placed image.

5. **Target the stroke in the Appearance palette.**

    You can now add the outline to the image.

6. **Choose Effect » Path » Outline Path.**

    You still need a stroke color.

7. **Target the Stroke listing in the Appearance palette and choose a color.**

    Figure 13-18 shows how we added a white background and some extra space to an image using the Rasterize effect and then stroked the image using the Outline Path command. Remember, none of the choices we made here are permanent. You can simply double-click the effect listed in the Appearance palette to modify the settings.

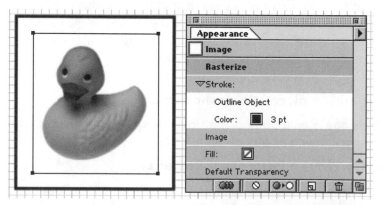

Figure 13-18: An image with a transparency layer can have a white background, extra space around it, and an outline added using the Rasterize and Outline Path effects as shown in the Appearance palette. Notice that white background over the document grid. Amazingly, all of these choices can be modified later.

Trading Artwork with Photoshop

Illustrator and Photoshop have been able to trade paths and pixels back and forth for a few years now. You can copy and paste, drag and drop, export, or just open. The results vary depending on which direction you drag—from Illustrator into Photoshop or vice versa—and what kind of objects you have selected. The following sections tell all.

Drag (or Copy/Paste) Objects into Photoshop

You can drag objects from Illustrator into Photoshop. Because Photoshop does not have Pathfinder or alignment options, you may find it easier to work in Illustrator and then drag objects into Photoshop. But you should keep the following in mind.

- You must have enough RAM to run Illustrator and Photoshop at the same time. These days that could mean easily 128 MB of RAM split between the two programs.

- Make sure that an image window is open in Photoshop so you have a place to drop the objects from Illustrator.

- You can drag any path or text object from Illustrator into Photoshop.

- Although you can drag placed images from Illustrator into Photoshop, the resolution of the image will be resampled to the resolution of the Photoshop file. This means that an image at 300 ppi in Illustrator will lose information when dragged into a Photoshop file.

- The placed objects appear in Photoshop as an independent layer. This permits you to move the objects into place before applying them to the underlying image.

- Hold the Shift key as you drag to position the objects in the center of the Photoshop window.

- Hold the Cmd/Ctrl key as you drag to place Illustrator paths as Photoshop paths. These paths can then be used for selections, strokes, or clipping paths.

- You can also copy and paste from Illustrator into Photoshop. In which case, a handy dialog box asks you if you would like to convert the paths to pixels or paths. You can also choose to anti-alias the artwork (or not) by using that dialog box.

If you don't quite know your way around Photoshop yet, you might want to check out Deke's *Macworld Photoshop Bible* from IDG Books. Not only is it the best-selling guide to Photoshop, but it was at last report the number one book on *any* desktop publishing topic.

Exporting from Illustrator

As handy as it is to drag from Illustrator into Photoshop, the best route uses File » Export—especially if you have any editable type in your Illustrator file. You don't have to lose the ability to edit type when you move from Illustrator to Photoshop.

Not only is this new in Illustrator 9 but it is revolutionary. It gives Illustrator users far more flexibility in working with Photoshop than even before.

Choose File » Export and then choose the Photoshop 5 format. You then see the Photoshop Options dialog box as shown in Figure 13-19. Choose whichever options you want. You should remember the following:

- The Editable Text option is only available if the text objects are the only elements on the layer. In that case the text is translated into a Photoshop text layer.

- If the layer contains other objects, the text is rendered into an ordinary Photoshop layer. Figure 13-20 shows how the layers from Illustrator are converted into Photoshop layers.

- Because there are no nested layers in Photoshop 5, the nested layers from Illustrator can either be merged or separated onto their own layer.

Of course you can also export the Illustrator artwork as a TIFF file and then open it in Photoshop. But that simply creates a flat image without any layers or editable text. Layers and text are too valuable to lose.

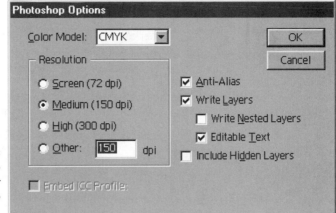

Figure 13-19:
The Photoshop Options
dialog box allows you to
control how Illustrator
layers and objects are
translated into Photoshop.

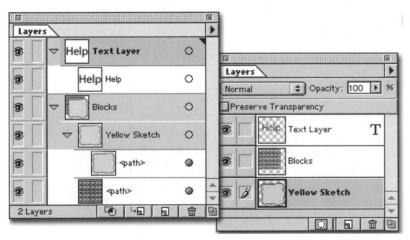

Figure 13-20: A comparison of the layers in an Illustrator file (left) next to
how those layers are converted into Photoshop layers. Notice that the
text in Illustrator is converted into Photoshop text.

From Photoshop into Illustrator

If you're an old-time Photoshop/Illustrator user, you are probably used to dragging images from Photoshop into Illustrator. You are also used to losing any transparency that was in the Photoshop layer. A much better solution is to save the Photoshop file with its layers and then use Illustrator's File » Place to import the image.

See what happens when Illustrator is given the ability to recognize transparency around pixels. Everything you ever knew about working in the program gets turned upside down.

When you import Photoshop files, a dialog box appears which asks how you want to handle Photoshop's multiple layers (as shown in Figure 13-21).

- Convert Photoshop layers to objects maintains all the individual layers with their transparencies.

- Flatten Photoshop layers to single image merges all the individual layers but does maintain the overall transparency of the merged layers.

If you have layer effects, type layers, and layer masks, they are converted as follows:

- Type layers and layer effects are rendered into pixels.

- Layer masks are converted into Illustrator's opacity masks (covered in Chapter 18).

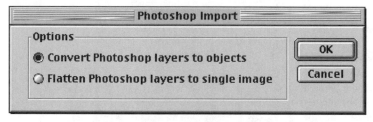

Figure 13-21: Before you place Photoshop files, you need to choose how to handle multiple layers.

PART FOUR
COLORING

CHAPTER 14

THE SLIPPERY SCIENCE OF COLOR

You don't need any special knowledge to admire colors in nature: the bright green of grass, the blue of the sky, the vivid red of a tomato. But it takes technology and science to represent colors in film, in photographs, on the printed page, and on your computer screen. For example, to represent a sprig of evergreen on a piece of paper, you can't take the sprig and mush it into the paper fibers. You have to find natural and synthetic colors that blend together to create a reasonable facsimile. This imitation of the real world is what the slippery science of color is all about.

In this chapter, we explain a little bit about color theory and a whole lot about how color works in Illustrator. We show you how to select colors from predefined, trademarked libraries or how to define your own colors using combinations of primary printing pigments. We also introduce Illustrator's restrictive colorspace for each document, the Color palette, the Swatches palette, the eyedropper and paint bucket tools, the Color filters, and all the other major points of interest along Illustrator's Great Color Way.

One of the most dramatic changes in Illustrator 9 is that the colorspace is now restricted to either CMYK or RGB. This is to help avoid production problems where RGB colors—especially those in images—are separated as part of process printing. You shouldn't feel constrained by the restriction, though. You can easily switch from one colorspace to another.

The Great White Light and the Breakaway Color Republics

We hate theory, you hate theory—we don't think we've ever met anyone who just loves a good dose of theory. Unfortunately we have to share a few basic color observations before moving on to the more exciting and practical discussions of how you use color in Illustrator. See, color is a highly misunderstood topic, particularly among the folks who work with it every day. Whether you're a graphics novice or a publishing professional, it pays to arm yourself with as much basic color knowledge as possible. Just as it helps to know a little something about motors when you take your car in for repair, it helps to know the fundamentals of color when you enter a print shop.

The most common misconception is that color exists in the real world. Plants, rocks, and most animals are completely unaware of color as we know it. This is because similarly-colored objects share no common chemical or physical properties. And a single material—like copper—may change in color dramatically under slightly different conditions.

Color is all in your head. It's based on so-called white light from the sun or some other light source filtering through or bouncing off a surface. The light then passes into your eye and mutates into nerve impulses that shoot into your brain. Color is a fantastic illusion that humans (and other primates) perceive differently than any other life form. If you were visited by a being from another planet, chances are very good that you and that person would have no common color vernacular whatsoever. You can't hear, feel, smell, or taste color because color is an inherent ingredient in sight. In fact, you don't see color; your brain makes it up as a means of interpreting the light waves registered by your eye.

 Sandee had a relative who was colorblind. No one ever knew it when he was growing up. They just thought he was a little slow cause he colored the grass blue and the water yellow. It wasn't till he was drafted that the Army discovered he was colorblind. As we said, color is all in your mind.

The World According to Your Eye

So let's talk about your eye. Inside this amazing orb are a bunch of light-sensitive cells called rods and cones. Rods pick up dim light and are good for detecting brightness and motion. Cones are responsible for color—they react best to strong light. Cones hang out in the central portion of the retina, and rods populate the outer regions. Therefore, you can judge colors most accurately by examining them in daylight and looking directly at them.

Cones come in three types. Generally speaking, each type is sensitive to red, green, or blue light. (Remember, this is light, not the primary colors in paint.) If all cones are stimulated, you see white. If both the red and green cones get excited but the blue cones shut down, you see yellow. What's important here is that the light coming into your eye may bounce off a yellow object, pass through a yellow filter, or come from a combination of red and green lights shining together. Your eye doesn't know the difference.

Computer screens and televisions fool your eye by speaking directly to your cones. The inside of the monitor is coated with red, green, and blue phosphors that emit light. So a yellow pixel is really a combination of red light shining for the benefit of the red cones and green light going to the green cones. If there's no blue light coming from the pixel, the corresponding blue cones take a nap.

RGB Light

Therefore, red, green, and blue are the primary colors of light. In theory, all visible colors can be expressed using a combination of these three basic ingredients. Intense lights, or multiple lights projected together, produce lighter colors. That's why red and green mix to form yellow, which is lighter than either red or green. Similarly, red and blue mix to form a hot pink called magenta, and blue and green make a bright turquoise called cyan. Full intensities of all three primaries form white; equal amounts of each color in lesser quantities make gray; and the absence of red, green, or blue light is black. (Think about it—what color is it when you turn out the lights?)

This is called the RGB color model, shown in pathetic black and white in Figure 14-1 and in full-color glory in the color insert. You may also hear someone refer to it as the *additive* color model, because increasing the amount of a primary color increases the brightness. Electronic scanners read photographs by shining red, green, and blue lights on them, which is why the RGB color model is a favorite of Photoshop. It is also useful for illustrations for the Web, slides, CD-ROMs, and any Illustrator creation that you expressly intend for people to see on screen. You'll want to use the CMYK color model (explained in just a few paragraphs) for illustrations you intend to print. You can also import RGB images into Illustrator or rasterize objects using the RGB color model.

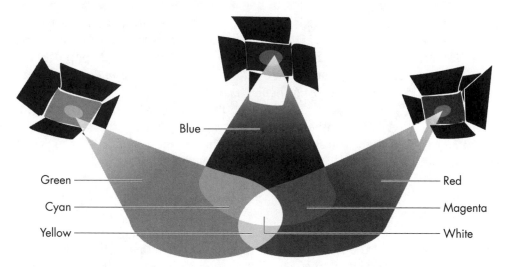

Blue

Green —————————————— Red

Cyan —————————————— Magenta

Yellow —————————————— White

Figure 14-1: In the additive color model, red, green, and blue lights combine to create white light.

Just when us we thought we had mastered everything there is to know about color, along come the Web-safe colors that use a combination of letters and numbers called *hexadecimal*. Web-safe colors are those colors that can be seen on the Web without any dithering. Rather than bore the print folks, who aren't into Web design, we cover Web-safe colors in Chapter 19.

HSB Schemings

Another way to look at the colors that you see is to start with a set of base colors and then vary the intensity of the colors. That's what you get with the HSB color model.

HSB stands for hue, saturation, and brightness. Hue is the pure color, your own personal rainbow. Saturation dictates the amount of the hue you see. The greater the saturation, the more intense the color. Brightness determines the amount of black added.

HSB is more of a variation of RGB than a separate color model (like a Noo Yawk accent compared to a Midwest twang). It's ideal for when you want to find a different shade of an RGB color. Take an RGB color, switch it to its HSB equivalent with the HSB command in the Color palette's pop-up menu, adjust the saturation and brightness, and switch it back to RGB when you're satisfied.

CMYK Pigments

Unfortunately, paper is not capable of shining light in your face the way a monitor is. Instead, light reflects off the surface of the page. So it's a lucky thing that white light—whether from the sun or from an artificial light source—contains the entire visible spectrum. Just as red, green, and blue light mix to form white, white contains red, green, and blue, as well as all other combinations of those colors. Every single color you can see is trapped in every ray of sunlight.

When you draw across a piece of white paper with a highlighter, the ink filters out sunlight. A pink highlighter, for example, filters out all nonpink light and reflects pink. This is the exact same way that professional printing colors work. There are three primary inks—cyan, magenta, and yellow—all of which are translucent pigments that filter out different kinds of light:

- Cyan acts as a red light filter. When white light hits a white page, it passes through the cyan ink and reflects all light that is not red—i.e., green and blue.

- Likewise, magenta ink filters out green light.

- And yellow ink filters out blue light.

So an area that appears red on screen prints in magenta and yellow on paper. The magenta and yellow ink filters out the green and blue light and leaves only red to bounce back off the page. Cyan and magenta mix to form blue; cyan and yellow make green. All three inks together ought to make black. (We tell you why they don't in a minute.) And a complete absence of ink reveals the white page. Because less ink leads to lighter colors, this is called the *subtractive* color model. A better version of Figure 14-2 can be found in the color insert.

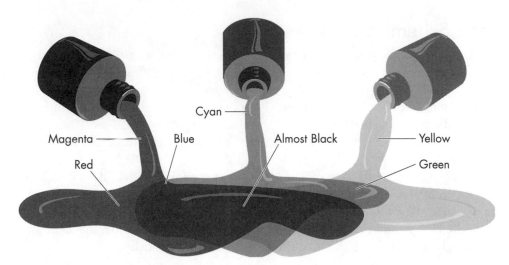

Figure 14-2: In the subtractive color model, cyan, magenta, and yellow ink combine. In theory all three should create black—but they don't. So a fourth key color, black, is added in the real world.

In a perfect world, CMY would be the exact opposites of RGB. But colored inks are not nearly as reliable as colored lights. It's a simple trick to split white light into its pure primary components. You've probably seen it done with prisms. But generating pure inks—such as a cyan that filters all red and no green or blue whatsoever—is practically impossible. In the real world, color printing throws in one additional ink: black. Black is the *key* color—the one that helps the other inks out—which makes black the *K* in the CMYK color model. Black ensures deep shadows, neutral grays, and—of course—nice, even blacks.

Some folks call cyan, magenta, yellow, and black *process* colors, which is why CMYK printing is sometimes called four-color process printing. (The word process is an old printing term, simply meaning that the colors are automatically generated to imitate a wider range of colors.)

Process inks are measured in percentages. The maximum intensity of any ink is 100 percent, and the minimum is naturally 0 percent. For example, 100 percent black is pitch black, 75 percent black is dark gray and 50 percent black is medium gray. Here are some more recipes to keep in mind:

- 50 percent cyan plus 50 percent magenta is a light violet. Increase the cyan to make the color bluer; increase the magenta to make it purple.

- 50 percent magenta plus 50 percent yellow is a medium scarlet. Increase the magenta to make the color redder; increase the yellow to make it more orange. 100 percent yellow by itself is a lemon yellow. To get a cornflower yellow, add about 15 percent magenta to 100 percent yellow.

- 50 percent yellow plus 50 percent cyan is grass green. Add more yellow to get a bright chartreuse; add more cyan to tend toward teal. To get a sea blue, combine 100 percent cyan and 20 percent yellow.

- If you add a little magenta or cyan to black, you create a richer black color—sometimes called a *rich black*. Add about 40 percent magenta to 100 percent black and the rich black feels warmer; add about 40 percent cyan and the rich black feels cooler. (*See the color insert for an example of working with rich blacks.*)

- You can add the complementary ink (the odd CMY ink out) to deepen a color. For example, if you have 50 percent cyan plus 50 percent magenta, adding the complementary ink—yellow—creates mauve. Add the complementary ink instead of black when you want to darken a color without dulling it.

- Adding black both darkens a color and makes it duller. Just a hint of black—10 percent to 25 percent—is great for creating drab colors like olive, steel blue, beige, and brick red.

- Brown is an amalgam of everything, with the emphasis on magenta and yellow. For example, 20 percent cyan and black with 60 percent magenta and yellow is a rich sienna.

 As a general rule, try not to create colors with more than 300 percent of all the inks. The inks tend to build up on the paper and can make your printed piece very sticky and messy.

Spot Colors

Spot colors (also known as solid colors) are separate inks that you can add to the four basic process colors or that you can use instead of the process colors. For example, you might print a two-color newsletter using black and a spot color. Or, if you can't match a client's logo using process colors, you can add the proper spot color to your four-color printing job.

Pantone is probably the best-known vendor of spot colors, offering a library of several hundred premixed inks that are supported by just about every major commercial print house in the United States. Like many other desktop publishing programs, Illustrator provides complete support for the Pantone Color Matching System (or PMS for short).

If you use a spot color in addition to the process colors, it will add to the cost of your print job. For every spot color that you add, you have to pay for the ink and the printing plate, as well as the time and labor required to feed the paper through another run. (Each color has to be printed in a separate pass.) Even companies with deep pockets rarely print more than six colors per page (CMYK plus two spots).

Choosing Your Colorspace

Used to be when you started Illustrator, you could just grab a tool and get to work. These days you first have to choose a colorspace. Simply stated, this means you are going to ask Illustrator to keep you always working in either RGB or CMYK color mode.

 The choice of colorspace is the primary reason you have to choose File » New after you launch Illustrator 9. You have to choose the colorspace for a document before you can start work.

Your choice of colorspace depends on what your final output of the job will be. Print work requires CMYK; Web graphics or onscreen presentations use RGB. By restricting your colorspace, Illustrator prevents you from creating colors that are outside the CMYK gamut.

Just because you're restricted to the output of a certain colorspace, doesn't mean that you can't define colors in CMYK or RGB. If you're working in CMYK, Illustrator works behind the scenes to convert your RGB (or HSB) colors into CMYK. Similarly in RGB, Illustrator converts CMYK colors into RGB. This color conversion takes place automatically, without you doing a thing.

Finally, just because you work in one space doesn't mean you can't switch back and forth between colorspaces. (Unlike what happens in Photoshop, you don't lose information by switching back and forth.) So why would anyone want to switch between the two colorspaces? The most important reason is that most of the filters for raster effects work only in the RGB colorspace.

Finding Your Colors in Illustrator

You define all new process colors in the Color palette by adjusting the different slider bars. Depending on which color model you are using (all of which are accessed through the Color palette's pop-up menu), the slider bars will vary the CMYK, RGB, or HSB amounts. You can define spot colors or import them from third-party swatch libraries.

● Once you've created colors in the Color palette, you can either use the color right away or you can save it for later. If you want to save a color so that you can use it over and over again, choose the New Swatch command from the Swatches palette's pop-up menu or simply drag the color onto the Swatches palette. You will then have the option of naming the color as well as deciding whether you wish to convert it to a spot color.

● You can also use one of the predefined colors in the Swatches palette. Or you can load entire libraries of spot colors from the Window » Swatch Libraries submenu.

We discuss all of these options—and more—in the next sections.

Onscreen Color Controls

There are four onscreen elements that allow you to work with colors. In the Color palette, you can choose the color model that will best mix your favorite shade of "tickle-me" pink. The Swatches palette stores a number of predefined solid colors (as well as predefined gradients and patterns, both discussed in upcoming chapters). And the Toolbox and Appearance palette, as well as the Color palette, let you change the focus from fill to stroke. Figure 14-3 shows a montage of the locations of all your color-related controls.

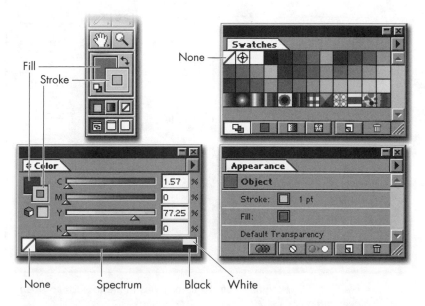

Figure 14-3: The toolbox and the Color, Swatches, and Appearance palettes provide for all your needs when you're creating and editing colors.

To quickly switch the focus from the Fill icon to the Stroke icon and vice-versa in the Color palette and in the bottom portion of the toolbox, press the X key. To swap the color between the icons, press Shift-X.

You can also choose colors by double-clicking either the fill or stroke icon at the bottom of the Toolbox. This opens the color picker dialog box as shown in Figure 14-4. Click each of the radio buttons to change the way the color picker displays colors. There is little advantage to using the color picker and one big disadvantage as it takes over a large chunk of your screen.

Photoshoppers will instantly recognize the new feature in Illustrator 9 that opens the system color picker when you double-click the toolbox color icons. That used to be the only way to define colors in Photoshop, and it took Photoshop users much longer to get a Color palette. Up till now, Illustrator users have had only a Color palette to define colors; now we get the color picker. It's hard to tell which program is going in which direction.

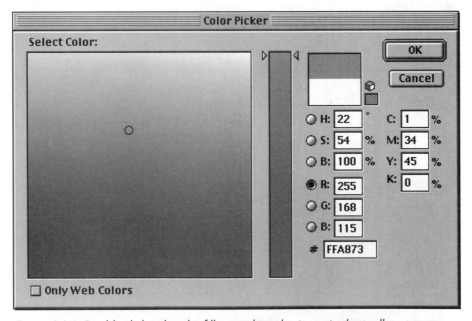

Figure 14-4: Double-click either the fill or stroke color icons in the toolbox to open the huge color picker dialog box.

To display the Color palette, choose Window » Show Color. The Swatches palette responds to the Window » Show Swatches command. Choose Window » Show Appearance to see the Appearance palette. Choose Window » Show Tools to make the toolbox appear.

All four of these palettes contribute to the Illustrator color experience, and we refer to all of them throughout this chapter. Although it's impossible to talk about color without mentioning fill or stroke, we cover fill and stroke in greater detail in Chapters 15 and 16. You decide whether you want to modify the fill or stroke of a selection by clicking on the Fill or Stroke icon in the Color palette or the toolbox (or just press the X key).

Using the Color Palette

The Color Palette is the easiest way to pick the values for a color. First, use the Color palette menu to pick the color model (CMYK, RGB, HSB, Grayscale, or Web-safe) you want to use. Click the spectrum bar along the bottom of the Color palette to approximate the color of your dreams. Modify the sliders by dragging on the little triangle that accompanies each bar, or change the values in the option boxes to the right of each bar.

 To cycle through the different color models, Shift-click the spectrum bar at the bottom of the Color palette. To move from the RGB model to the HSB model and then to the CMYK model, simply Shift-click the spectrum bar twice. Be sure to hold down the Shift key while clicking the spectrum bar or you will change your color and not your color model.

The Color palette's pop-up menu contains two commands that systematically change the values of the current color: Invert and Complement. The Invert command changes the color to its opposite along the RGB scale. For example, a color made up of 100 red, 150 blue, and 200 green inverts to 155 red, 105 blue, and 55 green. The original value and the inverted value for each component must add up to 255. Even if you work in the CMYK colorspace, the Invert command uses RGB values to calculate the inverse color.

The Complement command alters colors in a similar manner (although the result is quite contrary to what you might expect based on any color theory with which we are familiar). Whereas the Invert command bases its changes on 255, the Complement command uses the sum of the lowest and highest RGB values. Say we start with a battleship blue that breaks down into 55 red, 95 green, and 120 blue. Complement would add the lowest and highest values (55 and 120, yielding 175) and then subtract each value from this total. The resulting components would be 120 red (175–55), 80 green (175–95), and 55 blue (175–55). Again, Illustrator doesn't change the colorspace of the original, it's just that the math only works in terms of RGB. Figure 14-5 does a terrible job of showing this in black and white. Skip to the color insert to see a much better representation.

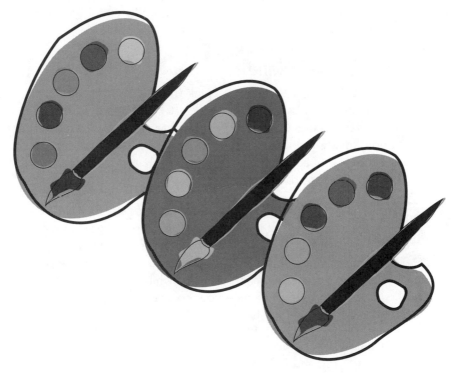

Figure 14-5: The Color palette menu allows you to convert the original color (left) to either the inverse (middle) or complementary (right) color.

To create white, drag all the sliders to the left in the CMYK mode or just click the White box at the right end of the spectrum bar in the Color palette. If you're working in grayscale, you can also move the K slider triangle all the way to the left or enter 0 into the option box.

To color an object black, drag the black slider all the way to the right or click the Black box (just below the White box) on the spectrum bar. In grayscale, you have the option of either moving the K slider triangle to the far right or entering 100 into the option box.

There is no difference between the Grayscale mode and just dragging the K slider of the CMYK mode. Although there are probably some people who enjoy using the K slider, we rarely use that mode—especially if there is any chance that we will eventually need to change the black to a color. If we use the grayscale mode we have to change the mode to CMYK in order to add other colors to the object.

If you define colors using RGB or HSB, you may see a little yellow warning symbol (also called an *out-of-gamut warning*) under the Fill and Stroke icons while you're adjusting the slider bars. Illustrator is telling you that the color you've created will not directly translate into the CMYK color model.

  The out-of-gamut warning symbol used to mean that you had to manually fix a color to get it back to a legal CMYK color. The new restricted colorspace options in Illustrator 9 fix that problem for you. The is one of the benefits of the new restricted colorspaces.

- Out-of-gamut colors are automatically converted when you switch to the CMYK colorspace. If you have no intention of printing your illustration, you can confidently ignore this warning and happily go about using your color with reckless disregard of any CMYK ramifications.

- If you're working in the CMYK colorspace, Illustrator will automatically change an out-of-gamut color to a closely-matching color that lies within the CMYK spectrum. If the color that Illustrator chooses is not to your liking, use the slider bars to tweak the color to meet your needs.

Applying Colors

Once you enter a value in the option box of the Color Palette, Illustrator automatically updates the colors of selected objects every time you drag a slider triangle or press the Return/Enter or Tab key. Click a color in the Swatches palette to compel Illustrator to affect the fill or stroke of the selected objects.

- Changing a color in the Color or Swatches palette changes the color of selected objects, but only the color of their fill or stroke, depending on which icon is active in the Color palette and the toolbox. The attribute icon (Fill or Stroke) that overlaps the other is the active icon. Illustrator offers a few ways for you to change the color of the attribute (fill or stroke) that is not active.

- Drag a color from either the Color or Swatch palette onto any object—even if it's not selected—to change the fill color of the object. Hold the Shift key to change the stroke color.

- You can drag a color swatch from the Swatches palette and drop it onto the Fill or Stroke icon. It doesn't matter which icon is active. You need to be careful to drop the swatch squarely on the icon of the attribute that you want to change.

- Another way to change the color of the icon that's not currently active is to Opt-click the spectrum bar at the bottom of the Color palette. The active icon will remain unchanged but the other icon will adopt the color on which you just clicked.

- Drag the color from the Fill or Stroke icon onto the other icon to match both colors.

The power of these techniques is that they allow you to edit the fill and stroke of an object without first activating the Fill and Stroke icons.

Using the Slider Bars

You wouldn't think something like slider bars would deserve their own section, but Adobe has built a bunch of little convenience features into the slider bars in the Color palette:

- Notice how the slider bars appear in different colors? This shows you what colors you'll get if you drag the slider triangle to that position. Each time you drag a slider triangle (or enter a value into an option box and press the Tab key), Illustrator updates the colors in the slider bars. This way, you're constantly aware of the effect that modifying a primary pigment will produce.

- If you like a color along the length of a slider bar, just click it. The slider triangle for that ink will immediately jump to the clicked position.

 To create a lighter or darker tint of a process color, Shift-drag the slider triangle. As you drag, all the slider bars change to demonstrate the tint. To gain the most control, Shift-drag the triangle associated with the highest intensity color. (Any ink set to 0 percent does not move, because adding the ink would change the color rather than the tint.)

You can also Shift-click a spot along a slider bar to adjust the tint by leaps and bounds. All inks (not set to 0 percent) change to maintain a constant hue. If the point at which you click is too high to maintain a consistent tint, only that one ink will change. To make certain you change the tint and not the one ink, Shift-click and hold anywhere along the slider bar, and then move your mouse until the sliders all move to some legal position.

And, as you can in any palette, you can advance from one option box to the next by pressing the Tab key. Or you can move in reverse order by pressing Shift-Tab. If you wish to apply a new value and keep that option box active (allowing you to test a number of different settings quickly), press Shift-Return/Enter.

If you're an adept Photoshop user and you're wondering whether you can use the up and down arrow keys to modify option box values as you can in the fab image editor, the answer is no. Where slider bars are concerned, the two programs go their own ways.

Playing with the Swatches Palette

The Swatches palette as shown in Figure 14-6 is ideal for saving colors and applying colors on the fly. Use the Swatches palette menu to change the display of the palette. Choose Name View to display the swatches in a vertical list with their names visible. Choose Small Swatch View to display the swatches in small squares. Choose Large Swatch View to display the swatches in much larger squares.

The six icons at the bottom of the Swatches palette control the display of the swatches as well as creating and deleting swatches. Because the Swatches palette holds more than just colors, you can click one of the four icons to change which types of swatches are displayed: all the swatches, just colors, just gradients, or just patterns.

The Swatches palette provides a handful of options for organizing swatches. For example, you can choose to display the swatches by name or by icon (large or small) as shown in Figure 14-6. If you let your cursor hover over a swatch in either icon view, the name of the swatch appears (provided you have the Show Tool Tips option selected in the General Preferences). You can control the organization of the Swatches palette by the following methods:

To sort the swatches by either name or kind, choose the appropriate command from the pop-up menu in the Swatches palette. Sorting by kind groups similar swatches together. All the process colors appear first, followed by the spot colors, gradients, and finally the pattern swatches.

⦿   Choose the appropriate command from the pop-up menu to view swatches by their name or simply by an icon that samples their color.

⦿   Use the four icons along the bottom left of the Swatches palette to control which type of swatches display. Click the second, third, or fourth icon to restrict the display of swatches only to colors, gradients, or patterns, respectively. Click the first icon to show all swatches.

The Swatches palette offers another function that helps you organize your swatches. From the pop-up menu, choose the Select All Unused command to select all swatches that are not applied to paths or text blocks in any open illustration. Once the swatches are selected, you can drag them to a new location in the swatch list or delete them all by Opt/Alt-clicking the Delete button. You can even duplicate them if you so choose.

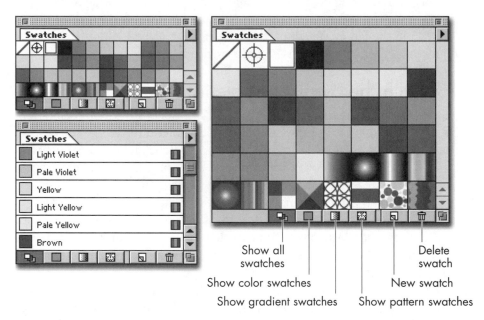

Figure 14-6: The three different views of the Swatches palette: small (top left), large (right), name (bottom left).

Setting the Swatches Palette Focus

This is one of the esoteric techniques that only ten people in the entire world actually use completely. However, the ten that do use the techniques swear they are very helpful and easy to remember. But we must be getting old because we can never remember all the features:

- You don't have to always use the mouse to select a swatch. You can set the focus to the Swatches palette by holding Cmd-Opt (Mac) or Ctrl-Alt (Windows), and then clicking inside the palette. A black line appears inside the palette.

- Once you have set the focus inside the Swatches palette, you can scroll around the swatches by pressing the arrow keys.

- With the focus inside the Swatches palette, you can type the first few letters of the swatch's name to instantly go to that swatch. However, there is a much easier way to type to find specific colors, as we'll cover in just a moment.

- Once you have selected a swatch, press Return/Enter to switch the focus back to the document.

- You can return the focus to the last palette that was in focus by pressing Cmd/Ctrl-~. You can then use the arrow keys or type to select a new swatch. (This is the part we can never remember.)

 As if that isn't enough, you can do all of this without the Swatches palette even being visible. So you can change the colors of an object without even seeing the swatches. (We haven't heard of anyone—not even the Illustrator Product Managers—who can pull this one off quickly.)

Finding Swatches

Some designers create hundreds of swatches in their Swatches palette. Are you really supposed to scroll up and down searching for a swatch? No, thankfully. Illustrator 9 provides you with a handy Find field (shown in Figure 14-7) in the Swatches palettes. If you don't see the Find field, choose Show Find Field from the Swatches palette menu.

Figure 14-7:
The Find field allows you to jump to a specific swatch by typing a few letters of the name in the field.

We can't tell you how many times we've been asked whether there were any way to type a number to find a specific Pantone color. In the past we had to tell people about the keystrokes to change the focus and then type the number. Finally, we can tell people about the Find Field. Finally!

Creating a Color Swatch

Although you can drag colors from the Color palette into the Swatches palette, you will most likely want to use the New Swatch dialog box, which is shown in Figure 14-8. This gives you complete control over all the aspects of the swatch.

Once you create a swatch, you can modify the settings by double-clicking the swatch icon. This opens the Swatch Options dialog box which provides all the original options as well as a preview box so you can see the effects of changing the swatch color.

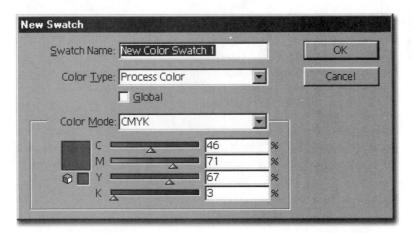

Figure 14-8: The New Swatch dialog box lets you name and define all the aspects of a swatch.

🌐 First and foremost, give your color a name. It doesn't really matter what the name is. You can name the swatch with the percentage values of the colors, or you can name it after your favorite Uncle Irving.

The only caveat is that each color must have a unique name. No two colors can have the same name. See the section later on importing colors for details of what happens when two colors with different values share the same name.

 From the Color Type menu, you can decide whether your newly-created color should be a process color or a spot color. If you designate a color as process in a CMYK colorspace, you are instructing Illustrator to create the color by mixing the percentages of the CMYK colors. If you use RGB or HSB values to define your color, Illustrator will automatically convert the color into CMYK values.

 If you designate a color as spot, you are instructing Illustrator to separate the color onto its own plate when the artwork is separated into film for commercial printing. It really doesn't matter what percentages you assign to a spot color—however, the name of the color is important. See the section on working with spot colors for how to coordinate colors among documents.

 You can also check the Global option. This means that if you change the definition of a swatch all items that use the color will change. If you leave the Global option turned off, any changes to the swatch will apply only to new objects that use the color.

 Spot colors and Global process colors also allow you to create tints. See the section on working with tints.

 Use the Color Mode list to choose what types of sliders you want to use to define your colors. If you are working in the CMYK colorspace, RGB, HSB, or Web-Safe RGB colors are automatically converted into CMYK colors. If you are working in the RGB colorspace, HSB and CMYK colors are automatically converted into RGB colors.

The Swatches palette shows clues that help you tell what type of swatch you are looking at—process, spot, global, and so on. Figure 14-9 shows all the clues in both the name and swatch views.

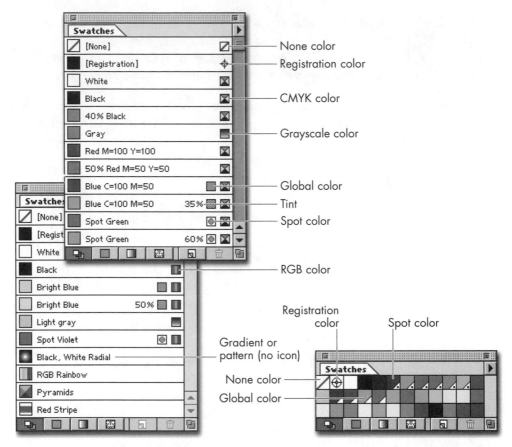

Figure 14-9: There are plenty of clues in the Swatches palette. You just have to know what they mean.

Registration and None: Two Special Swatches

Two of the swatches that automatically appear with each new document are special swatches. These are the swatch for None and the swatch labeled Registration.

The None swatch is the same as the None icon in the Toolbox. It applies no fill or stroke to an object. You can also apply None to a fill or stroke by pressing the slash (/) key on the keyboard. (The mnemonic for the slash is easy: The none icon looks like a red slash.)

The Registration swatch is a color that will print on all plates. You should only use the Registration swatch for objects—trim marks or special instructions—that you want to print on all plates.

Never use Registration for ordinary artwork. If applied to large areas, the color registration can cause a build-up of ink on the printing press and may incur extra clean-up charges.

You can also add colors from the Color palette into the Swatches palette:

- Click the New Swatch button at the bottom of the Swatches palette or choose New Swatch from the pop-up menu in the Swatches palette. The new color will appear at the end of the list of swatches, so you may need to scroll down the field to see it.

- Drag the color from the Color palette to the Swatches palette as shown in Figure 14-10. If you drag onto the empty area of the panel, you add the color to the end of the swatches. Or you can drag the color to the line between two swatches.

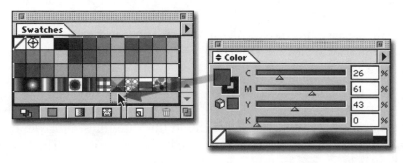

Figure 14-10: Drag a color from the Color palette into the Swatches palette.

- You can redefine a color by double-clicking the swatch or you can replace it with a new color by Opt/Alt-dragging a color from the Color palette onto that particular swatch.

- To duplicate a swatch, drag the swatch onto the New Swatch icon in the Swatches palette. You can also select a swatch and choose Duplicate Swatch from the pop-up menu.

- To delete a swatch, drag it onto the Delete icon (the trash can) in the Swatches palette. No warning or whining from Illustrator, just a simple extraction.

You will get a dialog box asking if you want to delete the swatch if you click the swatch and then click the Delete icon or choose Delete Swatch from the Swatches palette menu. The rationale behind this is if you take the time to drag the swatch all the way down to the trash can, Adobe figures you must know what you are doing. So it deletes the file without any warning. However, if you simply select a swatch and click the Delete icon, Adobe figures you might have inadvertently clicked the trash can. So it asks you if you're sure you want to delete the swatch. Fortunately, deleting a swatch can be undone by choosing Cmd/Ctrl-Z. (That has come in handy more than once.)

⦿ You can delete more than one swatch at a time. To select multiple swatches, click one swatch and then Shift-click another swatch to select those swatches and all swatches between the two. To select non-contiguous swatches, Cmd/Ctrl-click each swatch to add it to the selection. Now click the Delete button (Opt/Alt-click to circumvent the warning). This is a useful way to clean out an entire section of swatches and start over on them.

⦿ You can also delete a swatch by clicking the swatch and then clicking on the Delete button or selecting the Delete Swatch command from the pop-up menu in the Swatches palette. In this case, Illustrator will display an alert box to make sure you want to delete the color. This is not all that helpful, because you can simply choose Undo to retrieve the swatch if you want to. To avoid this warning, you can Opt/Alt-click the Delete button. When you press the Opt/Alt key, no warning appears; the color just up and disappears.

The color swatches are saved with the document. If you want to save a set of color swatches that you intend to use again and again, open the Adobe Illustrator Startup file that resides in the Plug-ins folder. Then edit the color swatches inside that illustration and save them to disk. From that point on, all new illustrations will use those same color swatches.

Spots and Tints

In the very olden days of Illustrator, you had to make a color a spot color in order to be able to define the color as a tint. This caused problems when the artwork was printed, because it was possible to have hundreds of individual spot colors—each one separating on its own plate. And every plate created its own piece of costly film instead of being broken down into process colors. Fortunately we live in an enlightened era—instead of creating numerous spot colors, you can simply define the color as Global.

When you click a spot or global color swatch, the Color palette displays the color and a tint slider bar, as shown in Figure 14-11. You can modify the intensity of a color by changing the Tint value. Again, all the standard techniques discussed a few pages back in the "Using the Slider Bars" section apply to the Tint slider bar as well.

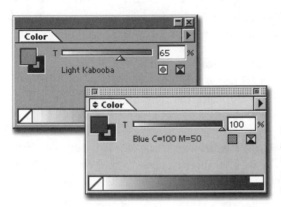

Figure 14-11:
After selecting a spot or global color swatch, you can modify the intensity of the color using the Tint slider bar that appears in the Color palette.

 The biggest misunderstanding about spot colors is that you must use the predefined Swatch Libraries from companies such as Pantone. You do not—repeat NOT—have to define spot colors only using those libraries. You can simply create your own spot color. Give it a name such as Gold, Varnish, or whatever. Then simply tell the print shop what color ink to use for that spot color plate.

Using Predefined Color Libraries

Illustrator ships with twenty libraries filled with predefined colors. Some of these colors, such as Default_CMYK, Pastels, or Earthtones are simply colors created by Adobe for your enjoyment. Others, such as Pantone, or Trumatch, are based on their commercial products that match colors in their printed swatch color books. Swatch Libraries are Illustrator documents with special swatches that have been stored in the Swatches Libraries folder.

There's nothing special about the document in the Swatches Libraries folder. You can create your own Illustrator document, with your own favorite swatches and put it in the Swatches Libraries folder. The colors will then be available through the Window » Swatch Library submenu.

You can open swatch libraries as independent palettes. Simply choose the appropriate library from the Window » Swatch Library submenu. A new palette will appear chock-full of all the library's swatches. This palette will be available to all open illustrations. Now, to save disk space (not to mention RAM), find and Cmd/Ctrl-click each color that you need and choose the Add To Swatches command from the palette's pop-up menu. The new swatches appear in the Swatches palette.

You can actually use any Illustrator document as a Color Library. Simply choose Window » Swatches » Other Library and navigate to find the Illustrator file. The only drawback is the file can't be currently open.

You can add swatches for each open illustration that requires any of these swatches. Close the library by clicking on the palette's close box. When you next save your illustration, the new swatches are saved with it, whether or not they are used to fill or stroke objects.

If you want a particular library to open every time you launch Illustrator, first choose the library from the Swatch Library submenu and then, after the palette displays, select the Persistent command from the palette's pop-up menu. The next time you start up Illustrator, that library will be part of your Illustrator window.

If, on the other hand, you use a small cache of colors on a regular basis, you can add them to the Adobe Illustrator Startup file. For example, if one of your clients sells lawn flamingos, you might want to keep Pantone 225 pink on hand at all times. Just open the Startup file (in the Plug-ins folder), and add the color to the Swatches palette for the Startup file. After you save the Startup file, the color will be available to all illustrations, whether old or new.

The following items briefly introduce the color brands in reverse order of their impact on the US market—if you'll pardon us for being so unscrupulously US-centric—from smallest impact to greatest:

- **Focoltone, DIC color, Toyo, HKS, and ANPA-COLOR:** Focoltone and Dianippon Ink and Chemical (DIC) and Toyo fall into the negligible-impact category. All are foreign standards with followings abroad. Focoltone is based in England, whereas DIC and Toyo hail from Japan. HKS is from a German company. None has many subscribers here in the States and their basic purpose is to satisfy foreign clientele. ANPA-Color is used primarily by the newspaper industry.

- **Web and Visibone 2:** These libraries both contain the 217 Web-safe colors which simply prevent dithering when viewed on the Web. However, the Visibone 2 arranges the colors in a much more organized fashion. We cover both of these in Chapter 19 when we look at Web graphics.

- **Trumatch:** Designed entirely using a desktop system and with desktop publishers in mind, the Trumatch Colors file contains more than 2,000 process colors, organized according to hue, saturation, and brightness. The colors correspond to the Colorfinder swatch book that we mentioned earlier. Trumatch happens to be our favorite process color collection, and we keep a copy of the Colorfinder close at hand at all times.

- **Pantone:** The largest color vendor in the US is Pantone. It offers three libraries in the Swatch Libraries submenu—Pantone Coated, Pantone Process, and Pantone Uncoated. If you're interested in printing Pantone spot colors, the Pantone Coated and Process Uncoated libraries are for you. Coated and uncoated refer to the paper used in printing. These colors correspond to the Color Formula Guide 1000 swatch book. The Pantone Process library contains process colors that match printed colors in the Process Color System Guide swatch book.

 You do not—repeat *not*—have to define spot colors only using Pantone libraries. You can simply create your own spot color. For instance, Pantone 8900—a bronze—is not included in the Pantone Coated library. Rather than despair, you can create your own version of the color. Simply mix up a color that gives you a rough idea of bronze, and give it the name Pantone 8900 or Bronze or whatever. Then simply tell the print shop what color ink to use for that spot color plate. (Yes, this is similar to the information we wrote a few pages back. But many people think that if a spot color isn't in the Swatch Library, they can't define that spot color. So we're saying it again.)

The Find Field will find colors just by typing the numbers that are at the end of Pantone 124 CVC, Pantone 125 CVC, etc. So all you have to do is type the number, not the whole name.

Moving Colors Between Documents

So, what if you've used swatches named Grass Green, Sky Blue, and Pig Pink, and you want to add the artwork to another file that also has swatches with the same names? What's going to happen to the swatches? Well, that depends on how you defined them:

- If the old swatch was *not* defined as Global, the artwork comes in, but the swatches do not. Only Global or Spot color swatches travel with their artwork.

- If the old Global or Spot color swatch has a different definition from the new Global or Spot color swatch, a dialog box as shown in Figure 14-12 appears asking you how you want to handle the conflict between the old and new swatch definitions.

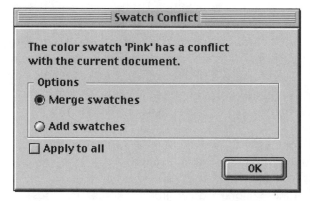

Figure 14-12: The Swatch Conflict dialog box lets you specify how different swatch definitions should be handled when copying or dragging artwork between documents.

- Choose Merge swatches to apply the definition of the new document to the older artwork. This will most likely change the appearance of the color. But there really isn't a problem if the appearance of a spot color changes. After all, the actual color of the spot color comes from the ink, not its screen appearance.

Choose Add swatches to maintain the definition of the old document and then add the swatch to the new document's Swatches palette. The swatch that is added is given the same name as the other swatch, with a number after it to distinguish the two swatches.

Choose Yes to all to apply the decision to all the conflicts between the current colors.

> **WARNING**
>
> Global and Spot colors cannot have the same name. However, you can add artwork with a Global or Spot color to a document that uses the same name for an ordinary process, non-global color. This will result in two swatches with the same name.

Applying the Overprint Options

A few color-related options appear in locations that might surprise you. The first two of these are the Overprint check boxes in the Attributes palette, spotlighted in Figure 14-13. These options control whether the color applied to the fill or stroke of the selected object mixes with the colors of the objects behind it. When the Fill or Stroke check box is turned on, the fill or stroke color overprints the colors behind it, provided that the fill or stroke color is printed to a different separation from the background colors.

Figure 14-13:
Use the Overprint check boxes in the Attributes palette to mix colors in overlapping objects, as long as the colors print to different separations.

For example, suppose you've created a Mardi Gras illustration consisting of three spot colors, Pantones 2592, 3405, and 1235, which any resident of Louisiana can tell you are purple, green, and gold. Purple can overprint green, green can overprint purple, and either can overprint or be overprinted by gold, because Pantones 2592, 3405, and 1235 print to their own separations. However, a 30 percent tint of purple cannot overprint a 70 percent tint of purple, because all purple objects print to the same Pantone 2592 separation.

When one color overprints onto another color, the two colors mix together. You could overprint purple onto gold, for example, to get a deep brown color.

If the Overprint check boxes are turned off, as they are by default, any portion of an object that is covered by another object is knocked out and the object on top prints; that is, the covered object doesn't print, even when the two objects are output to different separations. This ensures that colors from different separations do not mix. For nonblack paths, unless you are absolutely sure that you want a path to overprint another (and thus you want its colors to mix with the colors of any other path that it touches), you should leave these controls alone.

Overprinting Process Colors

The Overprint options have no influence over black-and-white illustrations that don't require separations. If the selected object is filled with one or more process colors, only those colors on different separations overprint. For example, suppose you have two objects, one filled with 30 percent magenta and 75 percent yellow (gold) and another filled with 70 percent cyan and 95 percent magenta (purple). If you select the gold object and turn on the Overprint Fill check box, the intersection of the two objects is printed with 70 percent cyan, 30 percent magenta, and 75 percent yellow. The magenta value from the gold object wins out—even though it's lighter than the magenta value in the purple object—because overprinting doesn't affect colors placed on the same separation.

Previewing Overprinting

The effects of overprinting happen when inks combine on press. So it is no wonder that it took till Illustrator 9 to be able to see the effects of overprinting on screen. Simply choose View » Overprint Preview. Not only can you see overprinting of one object over another, you can even see how the stroke of an object overprints its own fill. Figure 14-14 gives a vague idea of how overprinting preview appears. See the color insert for a much better example.

Illustrator 9 is breaking new ground in the field of desktop publishing with its Overprint Preview. To the best of our knowledge —and we know about a lot of programs—this is the first time you have been able to see the effects of over-printing on screen.

Figure 14-14: In this illustration, all strokes of the decorative elements inside the wings have had overprinting applied. The top object shows what the illustration looks like with Overprint Preview turned off. The bottom object shows what the illustration looks like with Overprint Preview turned on.

Overprinting Black Ink

Although you may occasionally use the Overprint options to mix spot colors, most professionals apply overprinting primarily to black ink to anticipate printing problems. Because black is opaque—and it's typically the last ink applied during the printing process—it covers up all other inks. So it doesn't look much different when printed over, say, cyan than it looks when printed directly onto the white page. But although overprinting has little effect on the appearance of black ink, it prevents gaps from occurring between a black object and a different-colored neighbor. Even if the paper shifts on the printing press, the black ink comes out looking fine.

Illustrator provides two means for overprinting black ink—the Filter » Colors » Overprint Black command and the Overprint Black check box in the Separation dialog box.

If all this talk of overprinting sounds suspiciously like the topic of trapping, that's because overprinting is a primary feature of trapping. Trapping, which is used to compensate for the mis-registration of two color plates, is covered in Chapter 21 when we go into printing.

Applying Automated Color Manipulations

The Filter » Colors submenu contains a total of ten filters that affect the colors of selected objects and imported images. You can use these filters to increase or decrease the intensity of primary inks and, in some cases, spot colors. Although the filters aren't nearly as capable or sophisticated as similar color correction commands found in Photoshop, they do make it possible to edit multiple objects and colors simultaneously, which can save you a significant amount of time.

Adjusting Colors

The Filter » Colors » Adjust Colors command is Illustrator's most capable color correction command. Choose the Adjust Colors filter to display the Adjust Colors dialog box, as shown in Figure 14-15. There are four different types of colors that can be adjusted using this command.

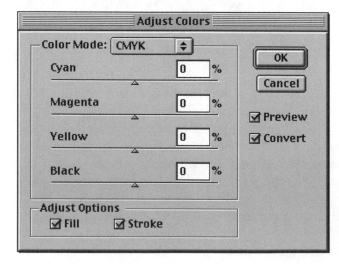

Figure 14-15:
The Adjust Colors dialog box allows you to increase or decrease the percentage of colors assigned to selected objects.

If you have any Global or Spot colors, the Global setting allows you to increase or decrease all those colors by using one tint slider. Any non-global process colors will not be affected in this mode.

 Positive values add ink, negative values reduce the amount of ink.

If you are working in the CMYK colorspace, the CMYK mode allows you to increase or decrease the cyan, magenta, yellow, and black percentages of all non-global process colors. If you check Convert, any Global or Spot colors will also be adjusted at that time. Also, the Convert setting allows you to add color to objects colored with the grayscale color mode. Figure 14-16 shows (in black and white) only one example of the changes that can be made using this command. For a much fuller representation of how the filter works, see the color insert.

-20% All plates

Figure 14-16: A small sample of what the Adjust Colors filter did to an illustration.

If you are working in the RGB colorspace, the RGB mode allows you to increase or decrease the red, green, and blue percentages of all non-global colors. If you check Convert, any Global or Spot colors will also be adjusted at that time.

If you choose the Grayscale mode, all grayscale colors can be increased or decreased using a single black slider. If you check Convert, all other colors will be converted to grayscale values and then adjusted as you move the black slider. The Grayscale mode is excellent for converting color jobs into grayscale and then varying the contrast of the illustration.

 Note that the values in the Adjust Colors dialog box represent absolute values. This is different—and decidedly less useful—than the way most of Photoshop's color commands work. Photoshop's best color-correction functions—Levels, Curves, and Variations—change the relative coloring of images. For example, these functions permit you to increase or decrease the intensity of medium cyan values within a selection, without affecting noncyan colors or full-intensity cyans. Only one command in Illustrator, Filter » Colors » Saturate, permits relative color modifications, but even it doesn't begin to compare to Photoshop's capabilities.

The Adjust Colors dialog box also offers the following check boxes:

- **Fill:** Select this option if you want to modify the fills of selected objects. Turn off the option if you want to change only strokes.

- **Stroke:** Same thing as Fill, only opposite. Turn on the check box if you want to adjust strokes; turn it off if you want to affect only fills.

- **Convert:** Select this check box to modify all colors of the selected objects according to the option box values. If you turn off this check box, you can adjust a color only in terms of its original color model.

- **Preview:** Select this check box to keep apprised of the effects of your color modifications as you work inside the Adjust Colors dialog box. Keep this option on to avoid surprises.

Switching Between Color Models

Illustrator has three filters that allow you to convert color models. With the change to a restricted colorspace, two of the filters, Filter » Colors » Convert to RGB and Filter » Colors » Convert to CMYK, have lost much of their usefulness. These filters only work to convert grayscale raster images into either RGB or CMYK files. But they do nothing special to Illustrator objects.

However, the third filter, Filter » Colors » Convert To Grayscale is useful. It will convert CMYK or RGB objects into grayscale tints. For instance, if you have created a magnificent drawing in color, you may discover you need it in grayscale to be reproduced in a newspaper. Simply select all the art and apply the Convert to Grayscale filter. The colors in your artwork will instantly be converted into shades of gray. Converting your illustration to grayscale is also useful for draft printing.

We used the Convert To Grayscale filter extensively to convert the artwork in the color insert into grayscale versions for this chapter and others in the book.

Changing the Overall Ink Intensity

If you want to apply relative adjustments to the colors of selected objects, choose Filter » Colors » Saturate. The Saturate command displays a small dialog box with a single slider bar and a corresponding option box:

- Enter a negative value to decrease the intensity of the colors in selected objects filled or stroked with process colors. This value also reduces the tints of global or spot colors. (The Saturate command does not convert colors to process, so spot colors remain intact.)

- Enter a positive value to increase the intensity of the colors or the tint of colors.

Unlike the Adjust Colors command, Saturate makes relative color adjustments. If you apply a Saturate value of 50 percent to an object filled with 20 percent cyan and 50 percent magenta, Illustrator changes the fill to 30 percent cyan and 75 percent magenta. That's a 50 percent increase in the previous intensities of both inks. Figure 14-17 shows (in black and white) only one example of the changes that can be made using this command. For a much fuller representation of how the filter works, see the color insert.

Figure 14-17: The original art on the left was altered using the Saturate command to create the new artwork on the right. The background was changed −50%. The foreground flower was changed +50%.

The command isn't entirely consistent. For example, it changes white absolutely; a 50 percent Saturate increases a 10 percent black fill to 15 percent black, whereas it changes a white fill to 50 percent black. And the Saturate command becomes completely unpredictable when applied to grayscale images.

After everything is said and done, Filter » Colors » Saturate is best suited to lightening or darkening the colors of several objects at once (as we did when lightening the mosaic tiles in the "Converting an Image to Squares" section of Chapter 13). You can use the command to establish highlights or shadows, whether the selected objects are filled and stroked with gray values or colors.

Inverting Selected Colors

After you choose Filter » Colors » Invert Colors, Illustrator changes the colors of all selected objects to their opposites. The result is the same as choosing Invert from the Color palette's pop-up menu (a color composed of 100 red, 150 blue, and 200 green inverts to 155 red, 105 blue, and 55 green) except that the filter affects all color of all the selected objects.

The Invert command also inverts objects filled and stroked with gray values. Black inverts to white, white inverts to black—it's just like a photographic negative.

Creating Color Blends

The remaining three commands in the Filter » Colors submenu—Blend Front to Back, Blend Horizontally, and Blend Vertically—create continuous color blends between three or more selected objects. Each command uses two extreme objects as base colors and recolors all other selected objects between the extremes. Figure 14-18 shows in grayscale tints the results of the three commands. (See the color insert for a glorious full-color example.)

We started with the same lips illustration duplicated several times into a group of lips in different colors. We then made three more groups of the lips. We applied a different blend colors filter to each of the groups. In each case Illustrator picked different lips as the start and stop (base) colors of the blends. (We've given the base color objects double strokes.) The Blend Front to Back command used the back and front lips as the base objects and recolored the circles stacked in between. The Blend Horizontally command blended between the left and right objects; and Blend Vertically blended between the top and bottom lips.

All three Blend filters affect gray values as well as CMYK and RGB colors just fine. But you can't use them on spot colors. Strokes are completely ignored.

The Blend filters are useful for modifying the colors in a series of objects created with the transformation tools and Object » Transform » Transform Again. You can also use them to recolor a series of objects created with the blend tool, as we discuss in Chapter 17.

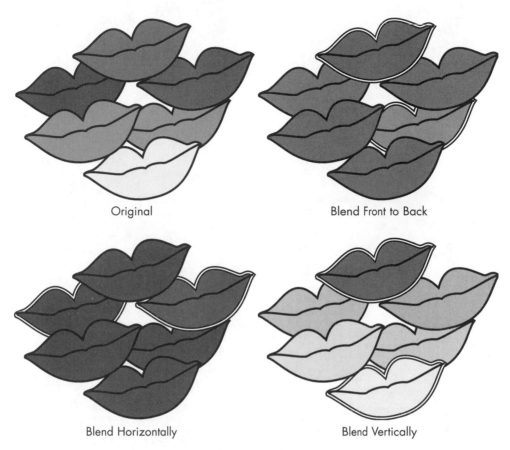

Original

Blend Front to Back

Blend Horizontally

Blend Vertically

Figure 14-18: The results of applying each of the three Blend filters to the original collection of lips shown at upper left. The lips used as the blends are given double strokes.

CHAPTER 15

FILLS, MULTI-FILLS, AND FAB FILLS

Though it may not sound like much, a fill is one of Illustrator's most essential capabilities. A fill is the inner soul of an object. (Strokes, which we cover in the next chapter, are the outer soul.) Not only can you fill an object, but you can create multiple fills for an object. (Multiple souls?) Multi-fills allow you to create effects that automatically simulate the look of multiple objects—sort of multiple personalities for single objects. Illustrator also lets you fill objects with special fills that blend one color to another or repeat a pattern over and over.

If push came to shove, you could live without strokes. You could draw thin shapes and fill them. In fact, we know artists who barely use strokes. But there's no getting around fill. It enables you to design complex illustrations, create shadows and highlights, or simply add color to a document. Fill is the skin wrapped around the skeleton of a path, the airbrushing inside the frisket, the drywall over the studs. Fill permits you to show viewers exactly what you want them to see.

Filling Closed and Open Paths

When you fill a closed path, the entire interior of the path is affected. Figure 15-1 shows a closed path as it appears selected in the outline mode, and the same path filled in the preview mode. The fill seeps into every nook and cranny of the outline.

Figure 15-1: In the outline mode, the fill of a closed path is invisible (top). But in the preview mode, the fill permeates the shape (bottom).

What happens, though, if you neglect to close a path? Will the fill leak out and get all over the page? (Don't laugh—that can happen in Photoshop.) Fortunately, in Illustrator the fill is held in check by an imaginary straight segment drawn between the two endpoints. Figure 15-2 shows an open path in the outline and preview modes. We've added a thick stroke so you can see that the path is open. The straight segment without a stroke is the imaginary segment Illustrator adds to keep the fill from pouring out.

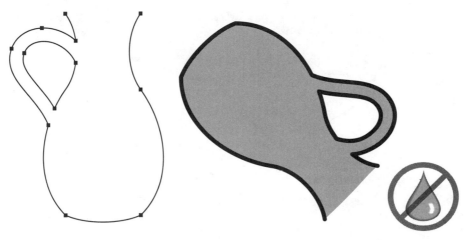

Figure 15-2: After drawing an open path (left), we filled it and tipped it upside down (right). And yet, by the miracle of the imaginary straight segment, not a drop of fill is spilled.

Filled open paths can be very useful for creating indefinite boundaries in a graphic. The paths with the thick outlines in Figure 15-3 demonstrate this technique. For example, because the forward wing is an open path, it is not stroked where it connects with the body of the rocket. And because the wing and body are filled with the same shade of gray, the fill of one path appears to flow into the fill of the other. The path around the body of the rocket is also an open path. It opens at the base, creating another indefinite boundary.

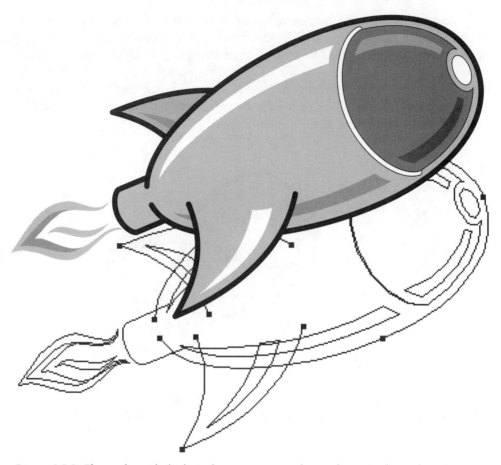

Figure 15-3: The paths with thick strokes are open paths as shown in the outline view behind the illustration. This makes it easy to merge the fins with the body and the body with the tail of the rocket.

Filling Type and Text Blocks

You can also fill text objects to change the colors of individual characters or to change the background color of a text block. If you select a text object with the arrow tool and apply a fill, the fill affects all the type in the text object and leaves the associated path unchanged.

For instance, the first example in Figure 15-4 shows a text block selected with the arrow tool. If you fill the object with a light gray, the type becomes filled, as shown in the second example in the figure. The result is gray type against a white background.

 This is actually a very sophisticated feature. Strictly speaking, both the text and the path are selected when you click with the arrow tool. Yet the Adobe engineers correctly figured that if a text path and its text were selected, most people would only want the text to change color. Well done, Adobe!

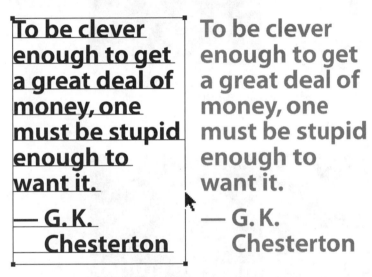

Figure 15-4: If you apply a fill color to a text block selected with the arrow tool (left), Illustrator fills the text (right).

But if you select the path around the text block with the direct selection tool and apply a fill, Illustrator fills just the path. The characters inside the text block remain filled as before, as demonstrated in Figure 15-5.

To fill single characters and words, you have to select the text with the type tool. Like any character-level formatting attribute, such as font or type size, fill affects only the highlighted characters, as demonstrated in Figure 15-6. In this way, Illustrator allows you to apply several different fills to a single text object.

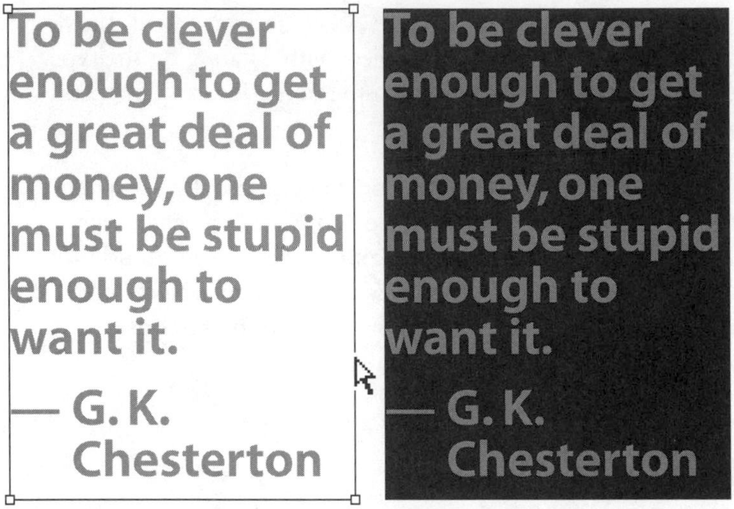

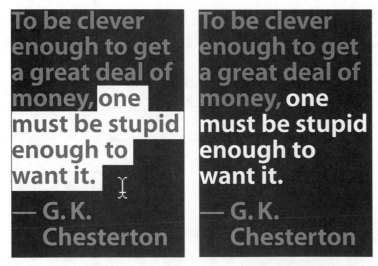

Figure 15-5: If you select the path of a text object with the direct selection tool (left) and then apply a fill, Illustrator fills the path only (right).

Figure 15-6: By selecting text with the type tool (left), you fill only the highlighted characters (right).

Applying a Single Fill

Whether you're filling paths or text blocks, follow these steps to apply a single fill to an object:

1. **Select the path or characters that you want to fill.**

   You can use the arrow, direct selection, or type tool. In fact, you can be in the middle of drawing a path with the pen tool and still fill a path. As long as you can see selection handles or highlighted text in the illustration window, you can apply a fill.

   If no object is selected, modifying the fill changes the default settings.

2. **Click the Fill icon in the toolbox.**

   Or, if the Stroke icon is active—overlapping the Fill icon—press X. The X key toggles between the two icons.

3. **Select a fill from the Color, Swatches, or Gradient palettes.**

   Or you can press the comma key (,) for the last used solid color or pattern or press the period key (.) for the last used gradient. Press the slash key (/) to be done with all this filling and have a transparent object. You can also click the corresponding icons in the lower portion of the toolbox, shown in Figure 15-7.

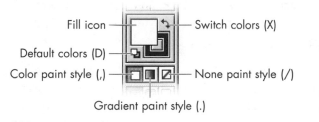

Fill icon ——— Switch colors (X)

Default colors (D) ———

Color paint style (,) ——— None paint style (/)

Gradient paint style (.)

*Figure 15-7:
The fill-related
controls in the
toolbox.*

As we mentioned in Chapter 14, you can also drag a color from either the Color or Swatch palette onto any object—even if it's not selected—to change the fill color of the object.

4. **Edit the fill in the Color palette as desired.**

   For example, you can adjust the slider bars to change a process color. Or you can select a color from a gradient and change it.

Applying Multi-Fills and Effects

At first glance it seems like a good idea to add multiple fills to objects—until you realize that the second fill has to fill the exact same nooks and crannies that the first fill did. So that's one fill stacked exactly on top of another. Any child will tell you that you can't see something if there's something else right on top of it. So what's the big deal? Why would you want to create multiple fills?

The big deal is what happens if you do something to change the position of the second fill, or the nooks, or the crannies, or the whole shape of the fill. Remember the distortion effects from Chapter 12—roughen, twirl, scribble, and so on? Well those effects certainly can move one fill so that it doesn't sit exactly on top of another. And suddenly multiple fills start to make sense. Suddenly you realize that you can create much more interesting looks than simple flat fills.

Multi-fills are new to Illustrator 9. In the past you would have had to copy, paste in front or back, and then manipulate the pasted object to create the effects of multi-fills. With multi-fills you still have only one path. This means you can modify a single point on the path and still make the changes to all the multiple fills.

Adding Fills to an Object or Group

In order to create multiple fills, you need to work with the Appearance palette. If the Appearance palette is not visible, choose Window » Show Appearance.

1. **Select the object or target the group.**

   If you have a single path selected, you can simply select the object. However, if you have multiple objects, you must group the objects. You can then target the group by clicking the word Group in the Appearance palette or by clicking the circle next to the group name in the Layers palette.

2. **Select the fill and click the Duplicate Selected Item icon.**

   You can also drag the fill down to the Duplicate Selected Item icon or choose Add New Fill or Duplicate Item from the Appearance palette menu. The second fill is listed in the Appearance palette as shown in Figure 15-8.

3. **Use the Color palette or Swatches palette to change either fill.**

Two fills with exactly the same color are rather boring, so target (click) one of the fills and change its color using either the Color palette or Swatches palette. (You can apply gradients or patterns also, but because we haven't talked about them yet, we'll stick to ordinary colors.) In this case we'll make the top fill a lighter color than the bottom one.

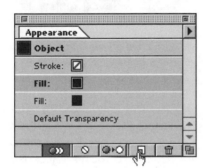

Figure 15-8:
The Appearance palette
with a second fill listed.

Using the Offset Path on Multi-Fills

You still can't see the two different fills. You need to modify the second fill so that you can see the multiple fills. An excellent way to do this is with the Offset Path effect. Like the Offset Path command, the effect can be used to add or subtract an area around an object. In this case you can use the effect to add space to one of the multi-fills in the Appearance palette.

1. **Target the fill you want to modify.**

Click the name of the fill to which you want to apply the Offset Path effect. We target the bottom fill because we want that fill to become bigger than the fill above it.

2. **Apply the Offset Path effect.**

Choose Effect » Path » Offset Path. This opens a dialog box similar to the Object » Path » Offset Path which we covered in Chapter 9. Because we want this fill to be bigger than the one above it, we enter a positive number. (Use the Preview check box to see what you are doing.) Your Appearance palette should look like the one in Figure 15-9.

3. **Add any other fills and effects as desired.**

You can add as many fills as you want and apply as many effects as you want.

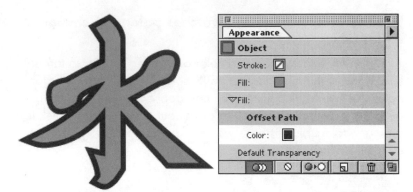

Figure 15-9: The Appearance palette with a second fill set with the Offset Path effect. Notice the black fill is visible behind the gray one.

The position of the effects within the Appearance palette is important. If an effect is within the Fill listing in the Appearance palette, then the effect will be applied only to that fill. But if an effect is listed outside—either on top or on bottom—the fill listings, then that effect will be applied to the object as a whole. Notice the difference between the two examples in Figure 15-10. On the left the Roughen effect was applied to the entire object. On the right the Roughen effect was applied to just the top gray fill.

Figure 15-10: The difference between applying an effect to the entire object (left) or just the gray fill (right).

You can have as many fills as you want. Use Effect » Distort & Transform » Transform to create multiple copies of fills. Or use Effect » Distort & Transform » Free Transform to make an object that casts its own shadow as shown in Figure 15-11.

Figure 15-11:
An example of how
the Free Transform
effect can create an
automatic cast shadow.

Using Convert to Shape on Multi-Fills

At this point you should have noticed one small limitation of the Offset Path effect applied to multi-fills: the second fill doesn't really change the shape of the additional fills. That's where the Convert to Shape effect comes in. It allows you to convert one of the fills (or strokes) applied to an object to a different shape.

The benefit of this is enormous, especially when it comes to text. Figure 15-12 shows two different text objects with a background rounded rectangle applied through the Convert to Shape effect. Because the effect is live, this means that if the text size changes, the rectangle also changes accordingly. (If you're a Web designer or a map-maker, you are already seeing the grand possibilities of this effect.)

To apply the Convert to Shape effect, you need to select your original effect. If it is a group, you should target the group in either the Layers palette or the Appearance palette. If it is a text object, make sure the object is chosen so that the baselines of the text are visible.

Figure 15-12:
With the Convert to Shape effect applied, we were able to create rectangles that automatically expand or contract to fill the area behind a text object.

Choose Effect » Convert to Shape and then one of the shape options from the submenu. The dialog box shown in Figure 15-13 appears. (Actually it doesn't matter which shape you choose as the Shape pop-up list lets you switch from one shape to another.) The dialog box may look complicated, but the options are actually quite simple:

- **Shape:** Your choices are Rectangle, Ellipse, or Rounded Rectangle. Sorry—no stars, no spirals, no polygons, no figure eights. But that doesn't mean you can't start with some sort of strange shape and then add one of three chosen shapes.

- **Absolute:** If you choose Absolute, you can enter the exact size of the bounding box that will define the shape. This option is useful for objects that must remain a fixed size while their other fills are allowed to change shape. You must enter an amount for the height and width of the object.

- **Relative:** The Relative option takes its size from the bounding box of the original object. You can then add the amount of extra space you want outside the original object. A value of 0 sets the bounding box of the new object to the same size as the bounding box of the original object. You can set the width and height to be different values. For instance, in Figure 15-13, we set an extra amount for the width of the rectangles, but left the height with no extra space.

- **Corner Radius:** If you've chosen a rounded rectangle shape, this option lets you choose the amount of the corner radius. The option is dimmed for the other shapes.

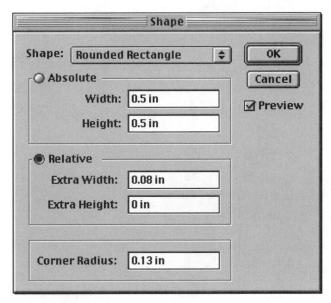

Figure 15-13:
The Convert to Shape dialog box allows you to create an object that is tied to the size of the original.

 When you apply Convert to Shape behind a text object, the bounding box of the text object is calculated from the size of the entire area that the text could take up. (We mentioned this way back in Chapter 6 when we talked about the size of the area where you can select text.) If you want the bounding box of a text object to be only the size of the active text elements, apply the Convert to Outline effect along with Convert to Shape. This fakes Illustrator into thinking the text is really paths, and it calculates the bounding box based only on the actual size of the text.

Gradients in the Key of Life

Figure 15-14 demonstrates the power of gradations. Deke drew these relatively simple structured paths to represent RCA cables for the book *Mac Multimedia & CD-ROMs For Dummies* (IDG Books Worldwide). The left pair of cables show the paths filled with flat gray values; the right pair are filled with gradations. As you can see, the gradations make all the difference in the world, single-handedly transforming the paths from cardboard cutouts into credible representations of three-dimensional objects.

A gradation (or gradient fill) is a fill pattern that fades from one color into another. Illustrator lets you assign many colors to a single gradation—the number of colors that you can use is limited only by the amount of RAM you have in your machine. You can even fade between spot colors.

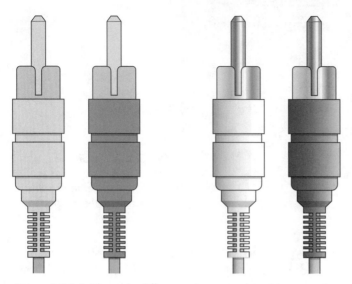

Figure 15-14: The only difference between the objects on the left and their counterparts on the right is that the latter objects are filled with gradations, which lends them the air of three-dimensionality.

You can create one of two types of gradient fills:

- A linear gradation is one in which the color transition follows a straight line. All of the gradations in Figure 15-14 are linear, flowing horizontally from left to right.

- A radial gradation starts with a pinpoint of color and changes as it moves outward in concentric circles. (Think radial as in radial tire or radiate outward.)

Figure 15-15 shows examples of linear and radial gradations. A linear gradation can flow in any angle, so long as it flows in a straight line. And a radial gradation can begin at any location inside a shape as long as it flows outward in a circular pattern.

If you want to create a gradation that doesn't quite fall into either of these camps—such as the wavy-line pattern at the bottom of Figure 15-15—you can create a custom blend using the aptly named blend tool and then mask the blend inside a shape. Chapter 17 discusses blends, masks, and other extraordinary fill options.

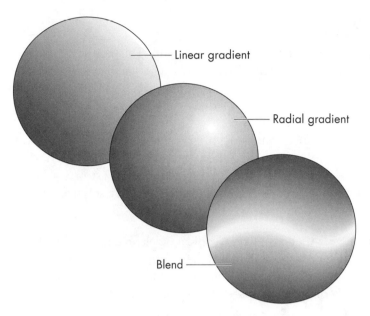

Figure 15-15: The two top fills are varieties of Illustrator's automated gradations. We used a blend to create the bottom fill.

Applying and Modifying Gradations

To apply a gradient fill to a selected path, select the fill box or the ramp in the Gradient palette. If you prefer, press the period key (.) to select the last used fill and display the Gradient palette. You can even click one of the gradient swatches in the Swatches palette—the predefined gradients contained in the Adobe Illustrator Startup file (assuming you haven't added any gradations of your own). However, the predefined gradients are somewhat limited, so you'll probably want to create your own. The Gradient palette, shown in Figure 15-16, is the place to create and edit gradient fills.

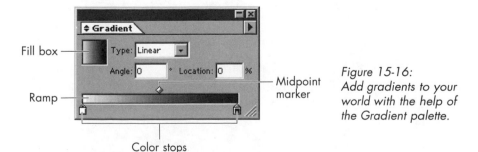

Figure 15-16: Add gradients to your world with the help of the Gradient palette.

The Gradient Ramp

Along the bottom of the Gradient palette is the *ramp*. This is where you add and modify the colors of your gradient. The starting color appears as a square color stop on the far left; the ending color is the square stop on the far right. The diamond in the middle, called the *midpoint marker*, represents the spot at which the two colors mix in exactly equal amounts.

You can change the location of any stop or marker by dragging it. Or you can click a stop or marker to select it and then enter a value into the Location percentage option box above and to the right of the ramp. When a stop is selected, the little triangle on top of it changes from white to black. A selected marker appears in black.

Choose Hide Options in the Gradient palette menu to contract the Gradient palette so that just the ramp is visible. Click again to expand the palette. It's difficult to edit gradations when the palette is collapsed, but you can store the collapsed palette when it's not in use.

Adjusting the Color Stops in a Gradation

The most colorful part of working with gradations is working with the color stops and midpoint markers:

- To add a color stop, click anywhere along the bottom of the ramp. A new color stop appears right where you click. You can move the color stop or assign a different color to it.

- When a color stop is selected, the fill box in the Color palette displays a color stop right below it as shown in Figure 15-16. This signifies that the color that you're modifying is part of a gradient. If you accidentally click the color box (in the Color palette) while trying to edit a gradient color, the color stop icon will disappear and you will change the fill of the selected objects to a solid color. Choose undo to return to the gradations.

- You can also drag a color swatch from the Swatches palette onto a color stop in the Gradient palette to change the color of the color stop. If you prefer not to drag, Opt/Alt-click the color swatch of your choice. Remember, if you simply click a swatch, you will change the fill of the selected items to a solid color.

Have you ever wished you could lift a color from an object in the illustration window while working in the Gradient palette? As it turns out, you can. First, select the color stop you want to modify. Then select the eyedropper tool and Shift-click an object with a flat fill. Illustrator applies the fill color to the selected color stop.

- To remove a color stop, drag the triangle down into the lower portion of the Gradient palette. The triangle vanishes and the ramp automatically adjusts as defined by the remaining color stops.

- When numerically positioning a selected color stop, a value of 0 percent indicates the left end of the ramp and 100 percent indicates the right end. Even if you add more color stops to the gradation, the values represent absolute positions along the ramp.

- To create a gradation between two spot colors, drag the spot color swatches onto the color stops. Then, after applying the gradation to a few shapes, print the illustration to spot-color separations (as mentioned in the spot color section of Chapter 14). Illustrator will print a spot-to-white gradation on one separation and a white-to-spot gradation on the other, so that the two spot colors fade into each other in the final color reproduction.

 Sadly, you can't use two spot colors in Illustrator's blend. The intermediate steps of the blend will be converted to process, not spot, colors. For more details about working with blends, see Chapter 18.

 To switch the colors of any two color stops, Opt/Alt-drag one color stop onto the other. Illustrator swaps the colors and automatically updates the gradation. Illustrator automatically shifts the position of the midpoint marker to compensate for the reversed color stops.

Adjusting the Midpoint Markers in a Gradation

Midpoint markers set the tone for the speed of a gradation. Moving the midpoint marker to the left makes the change start fast and then slow down. Moving the marker to the right makes the change start slow and then speed up.

Click to select the midpoint marker between two color stops. You can move the midpoint marker or enter an amount in the location options box to position the midpoint marker.

When repositioning a midpoint marker, the initial setting of 50 percent is smack dab between the two color stops; 0 percent is all the way over to the left stop, and 100 percent is all the way over to the right. Midpoint values are therefore measured relative to color stop positions. When you move a color stop, Illustrator moves the midpoint marker along with it to maintain the same relative positioning.

Creating and Changing Gradient Swatches

Gradients are fragile creatures. After you create a gradient it exists in the Gradient palette and it will exist in any objects that are selected while you make the gradient. But that's it. And if you quit Illustrator (or if, heaven forbid, your computer crashes) at that point, you will lose the information about the gradient. Fortunately, you can use the Swatches palette to store gradients.

Drag the gradient from the Fill box in the Gradient palette into the Swatches palette. The gradient appears as a new swatch.

With the gradient selected in the Gradient palette, click the New Swatch icon in the Swatches palette or choose New Swatch from the Swatches palette menu. This automatically adds the gradient to the bottom of the Swatches palette.

Opt/Alt-click the New Swatch icon to open the New Swatch dialog box where you can name the gradient.

Double-click the gradient icon in the Swatches palette to change the name of the gradient.

Hold the Opt/Alt key as you drag a gradient onto an existing gradient swatch to change the definition of the gradient. This also changes the appearance of all objects that had the gradient applied.

Unlike the swatches in Adobe InDesign, double-clicking the gradient swatch in the Swatches palette only allows you to change the name of the swatch. In InDesign double-clicking a gradient swatch allows you to change the name of the gradient and redefine the gradient in the Swatches Options dialog box. We're *really* hoping that feature is added to Illustrator.

To create a new gradation based on a selected one, click the Duplicate Swatch command in the Swatches palette's pop-up menu. Illustrator creates a clone of the gradation. You can now edit it as usual.

Setting Linear or Radial Gradients

Although the ramp is easily the most important part of the Gradient palette, you certainly want to select the type of gradient from the type pop-up list:

- When creating a radial gradation, the left color stop represents the center color in the fill; the right color stop represents the outside color.

- If you want the gradation to produce a highlighting effect, as in the left example in Figure 15-17, make the first color lighter than the last one. If you make the first color darker than the last, the edges of the shape are highlighted, as in the right example in the figure.

Figure 15-17: Two radial gradations, one in which the first color is white and the last color is dark gray (left) and another in which the colors are reversed (right).

Adjusting a Gradient Fill to Fit its Path

When you first assign a linear gradation to a path, Illustrator orients the gradation horizontally so it fades from left to right. When you assign a radial gradation, the gradation starts in the center of the shape. Because neither of these two settings is very interesting, Illustrator lets you change the angle of a linear gradation and reposition colors inside any gradation.

Changing the Angle by the Numbers

One way to change the angle of a linear gradation is to enter a value into the Angle option box in the Gradient palette. This is useful if you want to match the angle of an object ascertained with the measure tool.

The Angle value is also useful for matching the angles of multiple gradations to one another. Select the object that contains the properly angled gradation and note the Angle value in the Gradient palette. Then select the objects that you want to match and replace their Angle values with the new one.

Keep an eye on the Angle value, though. Each time you change it, it becomes the default setting for the next object. Even if you select a different gradation, the Angle value remains intact until you manually enter a new value or select an object filled with a different gradation.

Using the Gradient Tool

For those times when you want to reposition colors in a gradation, Illustrator offers the gradient tool. You can also use the tool to change the angle of a gradation, which is frequently more convenient than entering a numerical Angle value.

If a selected object is filled with a linear gradation, you can drag across the object with the gradient tool to change the angle of the gradation. The first color appears at the point where you start your drag and the last color appears where you release the mouse button. The angle of the gradation matches the angle of the drag, as demonstrated in Figure 15-18.

You do not have to drag across the entire area of the object. If you stop the drag before you reach the end of the object, you fill the rest of the object with the last color of the gradient. If you start the drag inside the object, the first color of the gradient fills the object before the gradient.

You can also drag from outside the object to another spot. The gradient is elongated so that only a portion of it appears within the object.

● Using the gradient tool on an object filled with a radial gradation changes the balance of the gradation and repositions its center. If you drag across a selected radial gradation, Illustrator repositions the first color to the point at which you start dragging. It extends the outer ring to the point at which you release.

 In a radial gradation, the first color is never flat, no matter where you start dragging in an object. But the last color can go flat, because Illustrator fills the area beyond the drag with the last color.

Figure 15-18: Drag with the gradient tool (top) to change the angle of the gradation inside a selected object (bottom).

Dragging Through Multiple Paths

The gradient tool also allows you to apply a single gradation across multiple selected objects. In this way, all objects appear lit by a single light source. To accomplish this effect, select several objects, fill them with a gradation, and drag across them with the gradient tool. Illustrator creates one continuous gradation across all the selected shapes.

Figure 15-19 shows two lines of text converted to path outlines. In the first line, we selected the converted letters and filled them with a five-color gradient. Illustrator filled each character independently. In the second line, we dragged across the selected characters with the gradient tool, resulting in one continuous, angled gradation.

Figure 15-19: After applying a five-color gradient fill to a few converted letters (top), we dragged over the letters with the gradient tool (bottom).

Unfortunately, Illustrator does not let you apply gradients to editable text. Remember the Convert to Outline effect? It fakes Illustrator into thinking that live text has been converted. So what happens if you apply the Convert to Outline effect to text and then apply a gradient? Good question! The gradient is applied to each character of the text. Unfortunately, you can't use the gradient tool to change the gradation to a continuous tone.

As it turns out, the transformation tools also transform the gradient fills inside a path as well as the path itself. If you transform a path and want to restore the gradient, press the comma key (,) and then the period key (.). This changes the fill to the last used color or pattern and then back to the original form of the gradation. If the gradation remains rotated, enter 0 into the Angle option box in the Gradient palette and press Return.

Gradient Mesh

Gradients are somewhat limited. They have only two shapes. Blends (which we cover in Chapter 18) are a little more flexible, but even they have their limitations. They can't send colors out in different directions from the same point. So Illustrator gives you yet another way to have one color segue into another—you can convert an object into a *gradient mesh*. A gradient mesh (sometimes called just a *mesh* by its close associates) is a special type of path that is filled with a series of special interior paths. Wherever these interior paths cross, it creates a node to which you can assign a color. Each node has four control handles that dictate the shape and direction of the color that extends out from the node.

Figure 15-20 shows an example of how changing the length of the control handles changes the color extending out from the node. (A better example of the illustration is found in the color insert.)

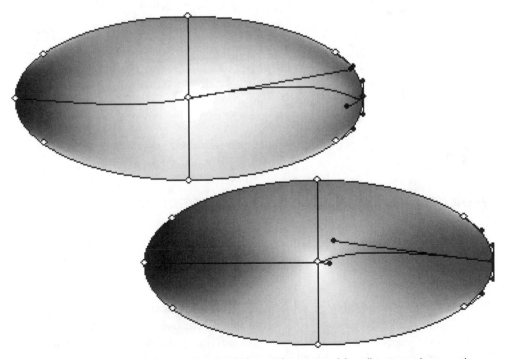

Figure 15-20: In the top left example, the longer white control handles extend out to the edge of the object. In the bottom right example, the colored handles of the edges extend out to the center of the object.

The jury is still out on the usefulness of gradient mesh objects. Sandee used a gradient mesh object to create the wrinkles in the artwork shown in Figure 15-21. Others use the mesh in the same way that they model using 3D programs. However, some people find working with the gradient mesh awkward and would rather use Photoshop or another painting program.

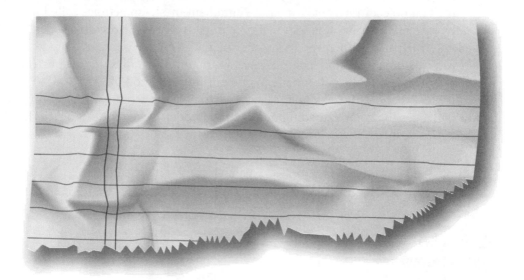

Figure 15-21: The wrinkles in this paper were created using the gradient mesh.

Automatically Creating a Gradient Mesh

There are three ways to create a gradient mesh. The easy way is to use the Create Gradient Mesh command which automatically creates a grid that you can then modify. The advantage to this method is the command quickly makes many gridlines.

1. Select a path.

Although the path you select can be open or closed, Illustrator will automatically close an open path when it applies the gradient mesh. The gradient mesh will work with any flat fill but will convert a gradient fill or a pattern to a black-and-white gradient mesh. It ignores any stroke and will not work until you remove any brush associated with the path.

2. Choose the Object » Create Gradient Mesh command.

This displays the Create Gradient Mesh dialog box, as shown in Figure 15-22. Use the Preview check box to see the effects of the settings.

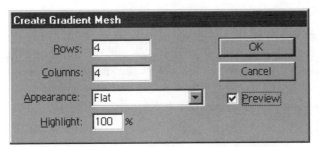

Figure 15-22:
In this dialog box, you
decide the number of
lines Illustrator adds to
a path when it creates
the gradient mesh.

3. Choose the number of rows and columns you want in your gradient mesh.

Enter an integer value in both the Rows and Columns option boxes. For the sake of simplicity, enter only as many as you need.

4. Choose the appearance of the gradient.

In the Appearance pop-up menu, you have the option of a flat fill or one in which the fill color of the object fades to a tint of that same color. These three options are shown in Figure 15-23.

Figure 15-23 The three settings for the Create Gradient Mesh are flat (top), center (middle), and edge (bottom).

5. Adjust the tint value.

Enter a value into the Highlight option box. By default, this value is 100 percent. If you lower this value, the fade will be less dramatic. Lower the value to 0 percent and you won't see any difference.

Manually Creating a Gradient Mesh

The second way to create a gradient mesh is to use the gradient mesh tool to manually add and manipulate the gridlines. The advantage here is you get to control exactly where the gridlines are positioned. You can also use this method to modify gradient mesh objects created by other means.

1. Click the gradient mesh tool inside an object to create the gridlines.

This automatically converts the object into a gradient mesh and adds the first vertical and horizontal lines. Each point where you click becomes a node, as shown in Figure 15-24.

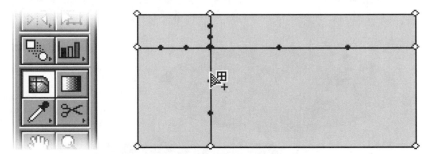

Figure 15-24: As you click with the gradient mesh tool, new nodes and gridlines are created.

2. Use the gradient mesh tool or the direct selection tool to select nodes.

If you use the gradient mesh tool, hold the Opt/Alt key to delete previously made nodes and gridlines. Be careful to click existing nodes precisely or you will add more gridlines. If you use the direct selection tool, you can hold the Shift key to add points to the selection.

When you click next to a gridline with a specific shape, the new gridline follows that shape. So instead of manipulating two sets of nodes, you only need to manipulate one and then click to create the second.

3. Change the color of the selected node.

You can choose colors via the Color palette or the Swatches palette.

Converting a Gradient into a Gradient Mesh

Finally, you can convert an object filled with a gradient into a gradient mesh object. The advantage of this method is that you start with many different colors already set for the nodes.

1. Select an object filled with a gradient.

A linear gradient, as shown on the left side of Figure 15-25, is the easiest to work with. Because mesh objects cannot have strokes, do not apply a stroke to this object.

 Radial gradients create a mesh object that is wrapped into a circular shape and may create gaps when manipulated.

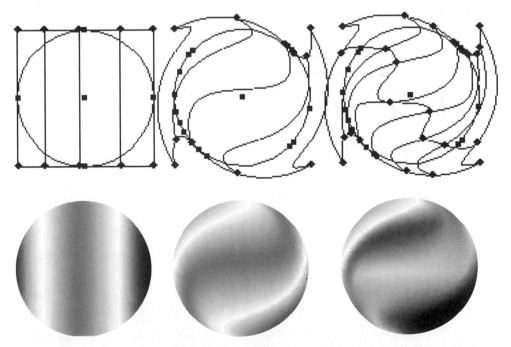

Figure 15-25: Anatomy of a marble: A circle filled with a linear gradient was converted into a gradient mesh (left). A slight twirl was applied (middle). Then additional gridlines and colors were added to create the marble on the right. The outline mode (shown on the top) shows the clipping mask that defines the circle.

2. **Choose Object » Expand.**

The Expand dialog box, as shown in Figure 15-26, converts strokes and fills into their more basic elements. Click the Gradient Mesh option to convert the mesh object.

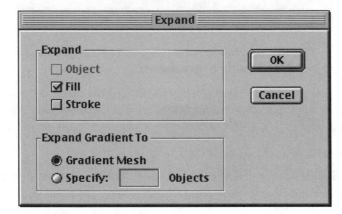

Figure 15-26:
The Expand dialog box lets you convert gradients into gradient mesh objects.

3. **Modify the mesh as desired.**

You can now add gridlines, change colors, transform, and otherwise manipulate the gradient mesh. A clipping path will be around the mesh keeping it in the shape of the original object. You can modify or delete that mask. (For the complete story of working with clipping paths, see Chapter 18.)

Modifying Your Mesh

Here a few helpful pointers for working with gradient mesh objects:

- Nodes must contain control handles. You can shorten the handles but the handles cannot be deleted. You can push them into a node, but they are somewhat difficult to control when they are very short.

- If you have Area Select turned on, it will be difficult to marquee nodes inside the mesh object. Use the direct selection lasso tool.

- Use the direct selection tool to adjust opposite control handles like levers or use the convert point tool to manipulate them independently.

- To remove a gradient mesh node, Opt/Alt-click the node with the gradient mesh tool. This removes the horizontal and vertical lines going into the node.

- To remove only one of the lines going into a node, use the gradient mesh tool to Opt/Alt-click the line you want to remove.

Filling Objects with Patterns

In Illustrator, you can fill both paths and text objects with patterns (sometimes called tiles, pattern tiles, or tile patterns) which are rectangular artwork that repeats over and over inside a shape. Most fabric and wallpaper designs are actually tile patterns. (Really good designers create tiles that hide the repetitive element.)

Applying Patterns

In Illustrator, you can create your own patterns or select from the vast library included on the Illustrator CD-ROM. The pattern libraries are found on the Illustrator CD: Illustrator Extras: Pattern & Texture Libraries. You can use the Window » Swatch Libraries » Other Library command to open the patterns as separate Swatches palettes. (If you need to, flip back to Chapter 14 for the details of how to work with the library palettes.)

 Although Deke finds many of the patterns too dull to be of real use, Sandee enjoys opening the libraries so that she can dissect the pattern and see how the tile was created.

All patterns must be defined and stored in a Swatches palette—either the Swatches palette for the current document or one of the library palettes. You apply patterns by clicking the swatch for a pattern of your choice.

Creating a New Pattern

To create a tile pattern in Illustrator, you simply select a bunch of objects and choose Edit » Define Pattern. This opens the New Swatch dialog box, which allows you only to name your pattern. (There's nothing else in there you can modify or choose.) If you like, you can drag the selected items onto the Swatches palette, as shown in Figure 15-27. This gives the pattern the name New Pattern Swatch 1, 2, 3 and so on. It's that easy. Illustrator automatically incorporates the objects into a rectangular tile. Really, that's it.

Take another look at Figure 15-27. We converted a character from the font Webdings and dragged it into the Swatches palette to create the pattern that fills the ellipse. Pop Quiz: Name two things that are wrong with the pattern... Ding! Time's up!

Number one, the objects are stacked right up next to each other. They need a little breathing room. Number two, the objects in the pattern are aligned straight up and down. They should be aligned diagonally. (The technical name for this type of up and down pattern is *boring*.)

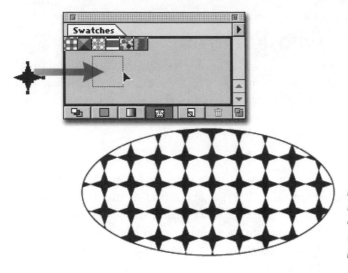

Figure 15-27:
Drag the selected objects
onto the Swatches palette
(top) to create a new
pattern swatch (bottom).

To this end, the following steps walk you through the task of designing a cool-looking tile pattern:

1. Assemble one or more objects to create a basic design.

We used a type character for our pattern but you can use any object except: gradients, gradient mesh objects, blends, brush strokes, bitmapped images, masks, graphs, or objects filled with other patterns.

 If you try to drag some items into the Swatches palette, and Illustrator refuses to store the items as a pattern, most likely one of the items in your selection contains an illegal fill such as a mask or a pattern.

 Although you can use editable text in a pattern, most old-time Illustrator users convert the text to outlines. This comes from the days when patterns took the most time to process during printing. So most users try to reduce patterns to the simplest elements. If you want to, use editable text. However, convert it if there are problems printing your files.

2. Draw a rectangle around the design with the rectangle tool.

The size of the rectangle represents the space around the pattern—also called the bounding box. Don't worry if your design isn't sitting in the exact middle of the rectangle. It doesn't have to.

3. Position a copy of your design in the top-left corner of the rectangle.

The distance between the two objects sets the space between objects on the diagonal. Figure 15-28 shows an example of this step. It doesn't matter how much of the object is outside the rectangle.

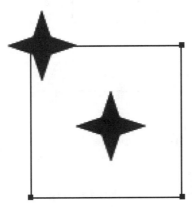

Figure 15-28:
The distance between the two
objects sets the distance between
the objects in the pattern.

At this point you need to position the design in the other three corners of the rectangle in the same relative positions. You might think this requires all sorts of mathematics to make sure the objects are aligned correctly. Fortunately, there's an easier method. What you are going to do is use the rectangle as a guide to position the object in the corner into the other three corners.

4. Select both sets of objects and the rectangle.

5. Position your cursor on the lower-left corner and Opt/Alt drag to the bottom right corner.

When you drag from one point to another, you are moving all the objects exactly the distance of the bounding box. By holding the Opt/Alt key, you are creating a copy of the objects. Notice that you now have a copy of the design in a second corner of the original rectangle. The top of Figure 15-29 shows an example of this step.

 Make sure Snap To Point is turned on in the View menu. This helps align the point that you are moving to the corner point on the other side.

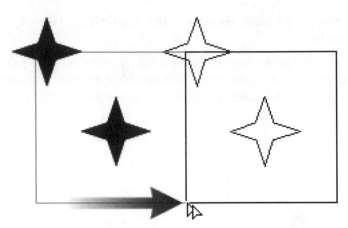

Figure 15-29: Opt/Alt-drag the pattern in the bounding box from one corner to another to duplicate the objects in the correct corner position.

6. Select all the objects and Opt/Alt drag the top right corner to the bottom right point.

Once again you use the size of the rectangle to control where the copies of the objects should be located. The bottom of Figure 15-30 shows the results of this step. Notice that you now have a copy of the design positioned around all the corners of the original rectangle.

7. Delete the extra rectangles and center objects.

You should have three extra rectangles and three sets of interior objects that can be deleted. This leaves you with a design in the middle and four copies of that design in the corners of the rectangle.

8. Make sure the rectangle has no fill or stroke and send it behind all the other objects.

In order to tell Illustrator to use the rectangle as the bounding box for the pattern, you need to give it no fill and stroke. It also needs to be behind all the other objects.

9. Select everything and choose Edit » Define Pattern.

Or drag the bounding box and objects into the Swatches palette. Even though the objects extend outside the rectangle, the pattern itself repeats only inside the bounding box.

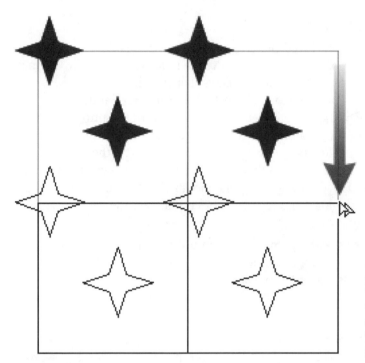

*Figure 15-30:
Opt/Alt-drag the top
objects down to the
bottom right corner to
create all four corner
positions of the pattern.*

The pattern you have created is transparent—that is, you can see through the areas around the design. If you want those areas to be opaque, you need to fill a rectangle with color and position it in front of the bounding box rectangle. The colored rectangle can be larger than the bounding box rectangle.

If you are a very old-time Illustrator user, you may doubt your sanity about the bounding box. Certainly there was a time when the bounding box could be the background color for the pattern, wasn't there? Yes, your memory serves you well. So if you've got a trunk-full of old patterns lying around, you're going to have to add a bounding box to get them to work correctly.

Well done! You have successfully completed a pattern that would make your dear mother's heart swell with unmitigated pride. You can now select an object inside your illustration and apply your new tile pattern from the Swatches palette.

Modifying a Pattern

As we mentioned, Sandee loves playing with patterns. Many days she just doodles around modifying patterns. However, she often does not have the original objects that were used to create the pattern. Does that stop her? Not in the least! (Ask anybody who knows her, there is very little that stops our Sandee.)

You can create a copy of the objects used to define a pattern by simply dragging the pattern swatch out of the Swatches palette. This deposits all the objects of the pattern, as well as the bounding box, onto your artboard. You can then change the color tints of the objects and then drag them right back into the Swatches palette.

Even better, hold the Opt/Alt key and drag the modified pattern onto the original pattern. This updates the original pattern and all objects that have the pattern applied.

 Don't get smart and think you can use the Filter » Colors » Adjust Colors command to change patterns. It won't work on the objects inside the pattern.

Transforming Tiles

Although most filters and effects don't touch the patterns inside objects, you can use the transformation tools to change the appearance of pattern tiles. You can transform an object and its pattern together or just the object or just the pattern. Here's how it works:

- The Move, Scale, Rotate, Reflect, and Shear dialog boxes are all equipped with two check boxes—Objects and Patterns. By default, just the Objects check box is active. This transforms the selected objects without transforming any pattern fills. If you select both Objects and Patterns, Illustrator transforms both items. You can also turn off the Objects check box and turn on Patterns to transform the tiles without affecting the objects at all.

- You can also turn on the Transform Pattern Tiles check box in the General Preferences. This makes the pattern tile transform along with the object if you transform the object using the tool rather than the dialog box.

- If you want a tile pattern to remain unchanged no matter how much you may change the filled object, leave the Transform Pattern Tiles check box off.

- You don't have to use a dialog box to transform a pattern fill independently of an object; you can also do it by dragging with a tool. Press the tilde key—you know, the little flying worm (~) at the upper left of the keyboard—while dragging with the arrow tool or any transformation tool to modify the tile pattern inside a shape and leave the shape unchanged. Just be sure to press the ~ key *before* you start dragging. Figure 15-31 shows examples of how the eagle pattern in the lower left corner was transformed. The pattern within the ellipse was rotated, reflected, and sheared. The pattern inside the large eagle was scaled.

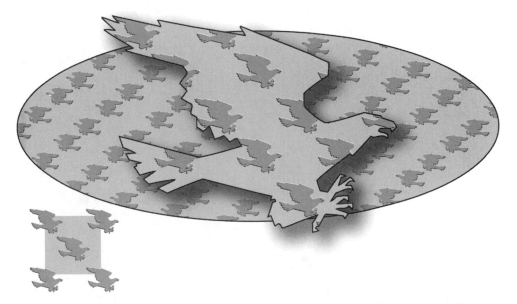

Figure 15-31: The effects of applying transformations to patterns within an object. The original pattern tile is in the lower left corner.

Rotating and slanting are particularly useful for camouflaging the linear appearance of a pattern. Scaling is handy for showing off more or less of a pattern at a time. And flipping... well, flipping isn't all that useful, but it's good to have around just in case.

 If you want to just nudge a pattern ever-so-slightly into position, hold the tilde key and use the up, down, left, or right arrow keys on the keyboard.

Use Object » Expand to convert pattern tiles into discrete objects. This lets you change the colors of the objects.

CHAPTER 16

STROKES
AND BRUSHES

If fills go inside a path, then it stands to reason that strokes go outside. (The term *stroke* comes from the PostScript language that is used to describe objects in Illustrator. Other programs may use the terms *border*, *outline*, or *frame*.) Brushes are special types of strokes that let you put all sorts of artwork along a path. Strokes in Illustrator used to be really boring to write about. There were so many limitations—so few choices. Today strokes are very important, very exciting parts of Illustrator. Dare we say—even *more* exciting than fills.

Strokes don't get the respect that fills have in Illustrator. In fact, some of Illustrator's functions are downright antagonistic to strokes and brushes.

- The knife tool will not cut an open path that has a stroke but no fill.
- Some Pathfinder commands—namely Divide, Trim, Merge, Crop, Hard Mix, and Soft Mix—will discard strokes.
- The Color Blend filters such as Blend Front to Back ignore strokes entirely.
- You can't apply gradients to strokes.

Of course there are areas where strokes do shine. After all, strokes have their own palette with their own controls. The dash patterns allow you to stop and start strokes in ways that fills could never dream of. And straight out of the box, Illustrator displays a black stroke around objects. In fact, the default setting for the fill is a hard-to-see white. But strokes get a vivid black outline.

So there, you fill snobs!

If you're familiar with earlier versions of Illustrator, be prepared to throw out *everything* you ever thought about strokes. With multi-strokes and the Appearance palette, the rules for strokes have totally changed.

Basic Stroke Attributes

In the past, strokes had to straddle both sides of a path. Today, anything goes. In Figure 16-1, we've applied different strokes to an open path and a closed path. The left side shows what life was like in the past: The path always ran through the center of the stroke. On the right side we've shown what life is like today. Strokes can be positioned way outside their path, and don't even have to have the same shape as the path. But before we go hog-wild seeing how strokes break the rules, we'll look at some of the basic aspects of strokes.

Strokes are turned on and off by applying a stroke color—from either the Toolbox or the Color palette. If an object has a stroke weight, but no color, then it has no stroke.

Watch out for straight lines that look like they're stroked when they're not. If you draw a straight line by clicking at two points with the pen tool and then add a black fill with no stroke, the fill follows the line on screen, creating the appearance of a thin stroke. The problem is, however, that the false stroke won't print accurately, particularly to a high-resolution imagesetter. Be sure to manually assign a stroke using the options in the Stroke palette, and never accept a thin stroke applied to a straight line at face value.

There are six basic attributes that can be applied to strokes. Five are controlled by the Stroke palette shown in Figure 16-2. These are weight, bevels, caps, joins, and dashes. The sixth attribute—color—is applied from the Toolbox or the Color palette.

Figure 16-1: These open and closed paths are stroked with heavy outlines. The paths themselves are shown in black.

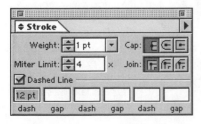

*Figure 16-2:
The Stroke palette is the control center for all the aspects of a stroke except color.*

Stroking Type and Text Paths

Like fills, strokes are applied to objects differently depending on how the type is selected, as shown in Figure 16-3:

- If you select a text object with the arrow tool, applying a stroke affects all the type along the path.

- If you select the path with the direct selection tool, you can apply a stroke to the path only, leaving the text as is.

- Select text with the type tool to stroke single characters or words. In this case, the stroke is just another character-level attribute that affects the selected characters.

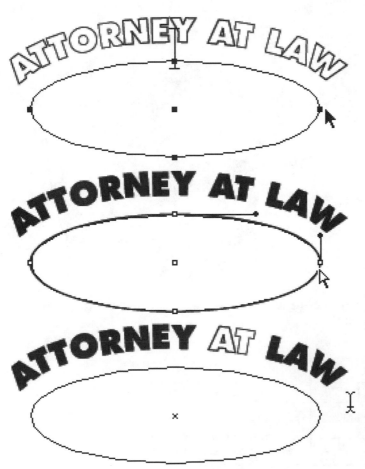

Figure 16-3:
The text in the top example was stroked after selecting the text with the arrow tool. The path for the text in the middle example was stroked after selecting the ellipse with the direct selection tool. In the bottom example, the text characters were stroked after the text was selected with the text tool.

Typographic purists will warn you against stroking text characters. This is because the stroke cuts into the shape of the characters. However, if the stroke is very thin, you can get away with stroking text. Or you can adjust the position of the stroke, as we cover later in this chapter.

Applying a Stroke from the Stroke Palette

The following steps explain how to use the options in the Toolbox and Stroke palette to apply a stroke to a selected path or text object:

1. **Select the objects that you want to stroke.**

    If no object is selected, editing the stroke changes the setting for the next object that you create.

2. **Click the Stroke icon in the Color palette or the toolbox.**

    This moves the Stroke icon to the front and makes the stroke the active feature. When the stroke is active, the Stroke icon overlaps the Fill icon as shown in Figure 16-4.

 You can also press X to activate the Stroke icon.

Stroke icon

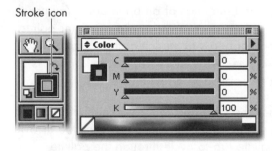

Figure 16-4:
Select the Stroke icon in the toolbox or the Color palette to set the stroke color.

3. **Choose a paint style.**

    To color a stroke, choose a color from the Color palette. To remove the stroke, click the None icon or press the slash key (/) on the keyboard.

You can't apply a gradient to a stroke. So if you click the gradient icon, you will apply the gradient to the fill of the object.

4.   If desired, apply a tint from the Color palette.

Use either the Swatches palette or the Color palette as described in Chapter 14.

You can also drag a swatch from the swatch list in the Swatches palette and drop it onto the Stroke icon in the toolbox. The Stroke icon doesn't have to be selected.

You can also apply a stroke directly to an unselected object. Just drag the swatch directly onto the object. If the Stroke icon is not selected, hold the Shift key to apply the color as a stroke.

5.   Change the Weight value.

The Weight value determines the thickness of the stroke (also known as stroke weight).

6.   Click the icons to set the Cap and Join options.

These option buttons appear in the upper-right corner of the Stroke palette, as shown in Figure 16-2. You use the Cap icons to determine how the stroke wraps around the ends of an open path. You use the Join icons to control the appearance of the stroke at corner points. The Miter Limit option box appears to the left of the options only when the first Join icon is selected. Otherwise, the option box is dimmed. (We'll explain this option in a few moments.)

If you do not see the Cap and Join options, choose Show Options from the Stroke palette menu. Or click the arrows in the Stroke palette tab to cycle through the palette display options.

7.   Select the Dashed Line check box to create a dashed outline.

Then enter values into the Dash and Gap option boxes along the bottom of the dialog box to specify the length of each dash and each gap between dashes. (This option, too, will be explained just up ahead, good and trusting reader.) If you don't want a dashed stroke, leave it unchecked.

8. Press the Return/Enter key or click inside the illustration window.

Illustrator returns its focus to the illustration window.

Many options that affect stroke are available anytime a stroke has been assigned, even if the Fill icon is selected. (If the stroke is set to None, all stroke options are dimmed.) This means you can modify these stroke attributes regardless of which icon is active. You need to select the Stroke icon only if you want to change the color of a stroke, and even then you can drag a color swatch and drop it onto the Stroke icon behind the fill icon.

Weight, cap, join, and dash pattern are all powerful stroke attributes that bear further explorations. That's why we'll discuss each one in some detail in the following sections.

Line Weight

The Weight values control the thickness of a stroke. Folks who spent their formative years laying down lines of sticky black ruling tape with X-acto knives prefer the term "line weight," so that's the term we'll use in our discussions. Line weight is most commonly measured in points. However, you can use the Units & Undo section of the Preferences dialog box to set the line weight unit to points, inches, picas, centimeters, millimeters, and pixels.

You can enter any number between 0 and 1000 (which is longer than a foot), accurate to 0.01 point. However, we advise against specifying a line weight value smaller than 0.1. A 0.3-point line weight is commonly considered a hairline, so 0.1 point is about as thick as dandruff. Figure 16-5 shows several line weights applied to a frilly path. The 0.1-point line is barely visible. Any thinner simply will not reproduce.

Do not enter a line weight of 0. This tells Illustrator to print the thinnest line available from the output device. The thinnest line printable by a 300-dpi laser printer is 0.24-point thick, which looks pretty good. However, high-resolution imagesetters easily print lines as thin as 0.03-point, or 10 times thinner than a hairline. Suddenly the line you could see from the laser printer turns invisible.

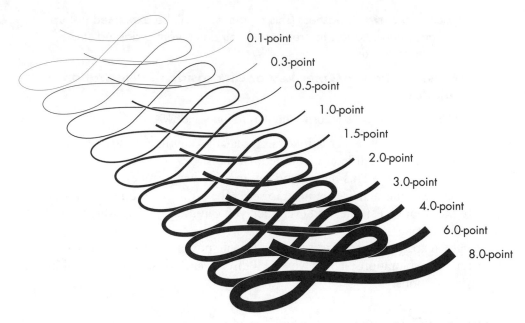

Figure 16-5: Here are several examples of line weights printed from Illustrator. The top line is barely visible; anything thinner than 0.1 point is essentially invisible.

Line Caps

You can select from three types of line caps, which determine the appearance of a stroke at its endpoint. Line caps are generally useful only when you're stroking an open path. The only exception to this is when you use line caps in combination with dash patterns, in which case Illustrator applies the cap to each and every dash, as we explain later in this chapter.

The three Cap icons in the Stroke palette work as follows:

Butt cap: The first Cap icon is the butt cap option, the default setting and the most commonly used line cap. (Whether it's fit for polite company we can't say, but butt is the official PostScript term for this kind of cap.) Notice the black line that runs through the center of each of the Cap icons. This indicates the position of the path relative to the stroke. When the butt cap option is selected, the stroke ends immediately at an endpoint and is perpendicular to the final course of the path, as shown in the top diagram in Figure 16-6.

Round cap: The second icon represents a round cap, which wraps the stroke around the path to circle the endpoint. The radius of the circle is half the line weight, as demonstrated by the second diagram in

Figure 16-6. If you have a 4-point line weight, for example, the round cap extends exactly 2 points out from the endpoint.

Round caps are used to soften the appearance of a line. The line appears to taper, rather than abruptly end. We frequently apply round caps when using thick strokes.

Square cap: Last and least is the square cap icon—Illustrator calls it the Projecting Cap. Here, a square is attached to the end of a line; the endpoint is the center of the square. Like the round cap, the square cap sticks out half the line weight from the endpoint, as the bottom diagram in Figure 16-6 shows. The only difference is that the square cap has very definite corners, making it appear to jut out more dramatically.

 Use square caps when you want to close a gap. For example, if you want the stroke from an open path to meet with a point of another path, the square cap option gives a little overlap where the two points meet.

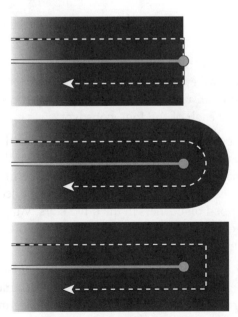

Figure 16-6: Diagrams of the three kinds of line caps—butt (top), round (middle), and square (bottom). The gray line indicates the path, whereas the dotted line shows the stroke moving around the path.

Figure 16-7 shows the same illustration created with open paths set with each of the cap settings. In the first eye, the lines with butt caps either clear each other or barely touch. In the round cap eye, the caps close many gaps, but you can plainly see that the touching lines are not part of the same path. In the third eye, the square caps completely eliminate even the hint of gaps in the corner of the lids and the spot where the top iris path meets the top lid. The square caps give the paths a more substantial appearance all around.

Figure 16-7: Deke drew each of these eyes using the same collection of open paths. The only difference is the line caps—butt on the left, round in the middle, and square on the right.

Line Joins

The Stroke palette offers three line joins, which determine the appearance of a stroke at the corners of a path. The stroke always forms a continuous curve at each smooth point in a path, but you can use line joins to clip away the stroke at corner points and cusps. Here's how each of the Join icons work:

Miter join: The first Join icon represents a miter join, which is the default setting. If a corner has a miter join, the outside edges of the stroke extend all the way out until they meet to form a crisp corner. The first star in Figure 16-8 is stroked with miter joins. Compare its perfect spikes to the rounded and chopped off corners in the other stars. Watch out, though. Illustrator may cut a miter join short according to the Miter Limit value, explained in the next section.

Round join: The second icon is the round join option, which is identical in principle to the round cap. Half of the line weight wraps around the corner point to form an arc, as shown in the second star in Figure 16-8. Round joins and round caps are so similar, in fact, that they are almost exclusively used together. The only time you should avoid using round joins is when a dash pattern is involved. Because round joins actually form complete circles around corner points, they can interrupt the flow of the dashes.

Figure 16-8:
Each of these stars is stroked with a different line join—miter (top), round (middle), and bevel (bottom). Notice that the joins affect all corners in the paths, whether they point out or in.

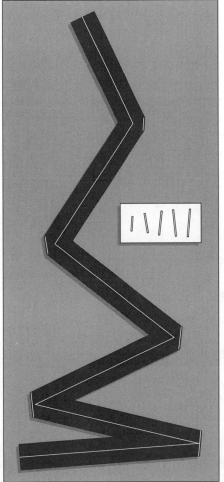

Figure 16-9:
As segments meet at sharper angles, the bevel joins lengthen. Each bevel is repeated in the inset for side-by-side comparison.

Bevel join: Use the third and last icon to apply a bevel join. Very similar to a butt cap, the bevel join shears the stroke off at the corner point. As shown in the bottom star in Figure 16-8, the bevel join creates a flat edge at each corner point. The length of this flat edge varies depending on the angle of the segments. A gradual angle results in a short bevel; a sharp angle results in a longer one. Figure 16-9 shows a path made up of segments that meet at progressively sharper angles. We've traced the bevels with white lines to demonstrate their increasing lengths. For comparison's sake, the inset shows the five bevels arranged in a row, with the top bevel on the left and the bottom bevel on the right.

Giving Excessive Miter Joins the Ax

Directly to the left of the Join icons in the Stroke palette is the Miter Limit option box. This value tells Illustrator when to chop off excessively long miter joins. The Miter Limit value represents a ratio between the length of the miter—from inside to outside corner—and the line weight, both diagrammed in Figure 16-10. In other words, as long as the miter length is shorter than the line weight multiplied by the Miter Limit value, Illustrator creates a miter join. But if the miter length is longer than the line weight times the Miter Limit value, Illustrator chops off the miter and makes it a bevel join.

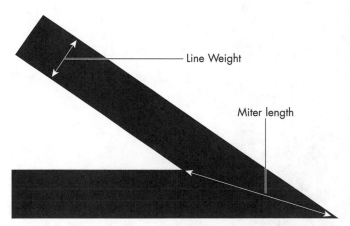

Figure 16-10: The miter length grows as the angle between two segments shrinks.

The length of a miter grows as its segments move closer together. If we had applied miter joins to the path in Figure 16-9, for example, the bottom joins would be more likely to get chopped off than the top joins. A miter can grow especially long when two curved segments meet to form a cusp. As shown in

Figure 16-11, two inward-curving segments create a serious Pinocchio effect. What's worse, the join doesn't curve along with the segment; it straightens out after the corner point. The result is an unbecoming spike that looks completely out of place with the rest of the path.

Figure 16-11: It is truly a shame that miter joins lose control when applied to curved segments (top, extending off to the right), but is chopping them clean off (bottom) really the best solution?

But the solution of hacking away the join (as so painfully illustrated in the second example of Figure 16-11) is a harsh compromise. In fact, it's not a compromise at all. Illustrator either gives you a ridiculously long miter or it bevels it completely. If you want to preserve the precise quality of a miter join without allowing it to take on a life of its own—and a rather lewd one at that—you should manually adjust your path. This will increase the angle between segments, which in turn reduces the length of the miter. The Miter Limit option should be considered a last resort.

The Miter Limit value can range from 1 to 500, provided that the value multiplied by the line weight doesn't exceed 1800 points. The default value is 4. A miter limit of 1 tells Illustrator to lop off every join and is therefore identical to selecting the bevel join icon. If either the round or bevel join icon is selected, the Miter Limit option appears dimmed.

Dash Patterns

The options along the bottom of the Stroke palette allow you to apply a dash pattern to a stroke. Dash patterns are repetitive interruptions in a stroke. When the Dashed Line check box is empty, Illustrator creates a solid stroke with no interruptions. You can use the dash patterns to create a standard coupon border.

To create a dash pattern, select the Dashed Line check box, which brings to life six previously dimmed option boxes. Each option box represents an interval, measured in points, during which the stroke is on or off over the course of the path. The Dash values determine the length of the dashes; the Gap values determine the length of the gaps between the dashes.

You don't have to fill all Dash and Gap options with values. In fact, most folks simply fill in the first pair of option boxes and leave the rest blank. Whatever you do, Illustrator repeats the values you enter and ignores the empty option boxes.

 If you like, you can enter a value into the first Dash option box and be done with it. Illustrator applies the value to both the dashes and gaps. If you enter the default Dash value of 12, for example, the stroke is on for 12 points and then off for 12 points.

The ghost grid in Figure 16-12 shows a sampling of dashes created using only the first pair of Dash and Gap options. These horrifying members of the spirit world are arranged into columns and rows according to their Dash and Gap values.

If you scrutinize the phantoms carefully, you may notice that the dashes pile up at the point where the path starts and stops. For example, each eerie eye begins at the bottom of the shape, which is why you sometimes see an extra long dash at this point. Each macabre mouth begins at the top, and every spectral shroud starts in the bottom left corner.

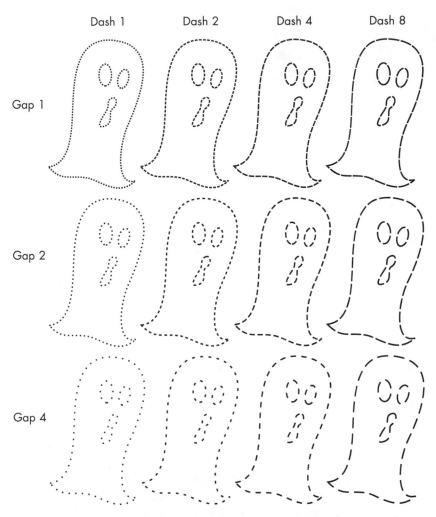

Figure 16-12: A grid of dash patterns demonstrating 12 combinations of Dash and Gap values.

When stroking a closed path, you ideally want the sum of the dash and gap to divide evenly into the length of the path outline. This way, you don't have any dash pileups. Unfortunately, Illustrator provides no mechanism for telling you how long a path is, so even if math is your friend, you can't figure it out. So your only recourse is trial and error. In the first ghoul in Figure 16-13, we applied a Dash value of 6 and a Gap of 3 to the eyes. But as the white circles show, we ended up with an extra long dash at the bottom of each shape. The solution? We gradually raised the Gap value in 0.01-point increments until the dash shrunk back to the proper size. A Gap value of 3.11 finally did the trick.

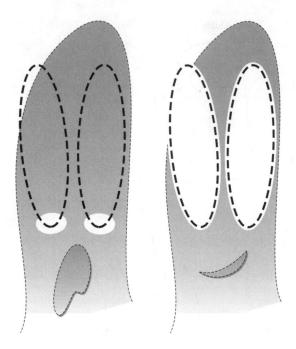

Using Line Caps with Dash Patterns

Another thing to consider when applying a dash pattern is the effect of the active line cap. Illustrator treats the beginning and ending of each dash in a pattern as a start and stop in the stroke. Therefore, both ends of a dash are affected by the selected line cap, which makes it possible to create round dashes.

We stroked each of the three lines in Figure 16-14 with a 16-point line weight that included a dash pattern and round caps. We entered 0—yes, 0—for the Dash value and 26 for the Gap. When you specify the length of each dash as 0, you instruct Illustrator to allow no distance between the round cap at the beginning of the dash and the round cap at the end of the dash. The two round caps therefore meet to form a complete circle.

Figure 16-15 shows a diagram of two dashes set to 0 with round caps. The path appears in gray; the dotted lines show the round cap wrapping around the 0-point dash. Notice that the only thing separating the circles is the Gap value. The Gap value defines the distance from the center of one circle to the center of the next, whereas the line weight determines the diameter of each circle. Therefore, to prevent one circular dot from touching the next, the Gap value must be larger than the Weight value. In Figure 16-14, for example, the 26-point gap is greater than the 16-point line weight, creating a 10-point break between each pair of dots. If the Gap and Weight values are equal, the dots just barely touch. And if the gap is smaller than the line weight, the dots overlap.

Raising the Dash value above 0 elongates the dashes so they're no longer circular. The larger the Dash value, the more the dashes look like little submarines.

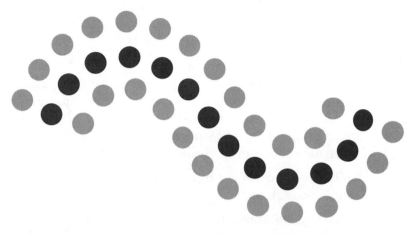

Figure 16-14: Three lines stroked with the same dash pattern in two different colors. We selected the round cap icon and set the Dash value to 0, resulting in circular dots.

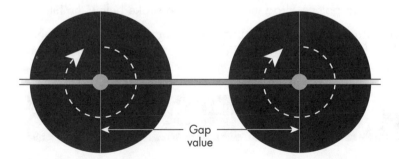

Figure 16-15: A diagram of a dash pattern with a 0-point dash and round caps. The thick gray line represents the path, whereas the dotted line shows the stroke wrapping around each dash.

Stroke Positions and Multi-Strokes

There is a stacking order for fills and strokes. Ordinarily the stroke sits on top of the fill. However, you can create different looks by positioning the stroke behind the fill.

Like multi-fills, changing the stroke position and adding multi-strokes are new to Illustrator 9.

Stroke Under Fills

What if you want to draw a thick outline around some important text, as seen in the top example of Figure 16-16? Unfortunately, half of the stroke cuts into the letters making them illegible and terribly ugly. (This is why typographic snobs will tell you not to stroke text.) Fortunately, you live in an enlightened age of Illustrator where you can easily move the stroke behind the fill.

1. Use the Selection tool to select the text as an object. The Appearance palette should read "Type Object."

2. Click the Stroke listing in the Appearance palette and change the color from none to the color you want for the stroke.

3. Set the stroke to twice the desired line weight. So if you want to see 2 points of stroke around the fill, set the stroke weight to 4 points.

4. In the Appearance palette, drag the listing for the stroke below the fill.

The result is the bottom example in Figure 16-16. The fill is positioned above the stroke. Only the outside half of the stroke is visible. This leaves the shape of the text unchanged.

CHEAP THRILLS

CHEAP THRILLS

Figure 16-16: Text with a 4-point stroke (top) and the same text with a 4-point stroke moved below the fill (bottom).

Stroke + Stroke = Multi-Strokes

Even before there were multiple strokes, Illustrator users created similar looks by cloning multiple paths on top of each other and applying different strokes to the paths. The only problem was that it was difficult to alter the shape of the object because you had to select all the multiple paths. With multiple strokes applied to one path, Illustrator makes it even easier to create those looks.

Using multiple strokes you can create parallel lines, outlined lines, and special dots and dashes. Figure 16-17 shows just a smattering of the effects you can create. No matter how many pages we devote to sharing some of these effects, you'll be able to come up with twice as many of your own an hour later. However, here are some general rules for creating different multi-stroke looks:

- Reduce the stroke weight and change the color of a stroke to make parallel lines.

- Use dash patterns to make strokes that change color on and off.

- Use round caps to make dots.

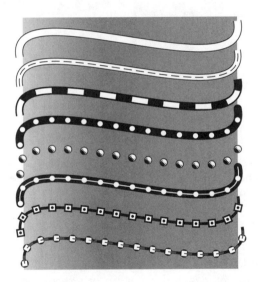

Figure 16-17:
All these beautiful jewels were created using strokes and dash patterns.

Like multi-fills, you use the Appearance palette to create additional strokes and order them. Figure 16-18 shows how multi-strokes and dashes can create the effect of railroad tracks. Here's how the effect was created:

1. Select the object and create a 49-point gray stroke set to 8 points dash on and 20 points dash off. This creates the full length of the railroad ties.

2. Choose Add New Stroke from the Appearance palette menu. Set it to 38 point black, no dashes. This sets the outside of the railroad track.

3. Repeat step 2 for a 34-point white stroke, a 30-point black stroke, and a 26-point white stroke, all with no dashes. At this point you can't see the inside of the railroad ties.

4. Add a 26-point gray stroke set to the same dash pattern as the first. This gives the appearance that you can see the railroad ties through the tracks.

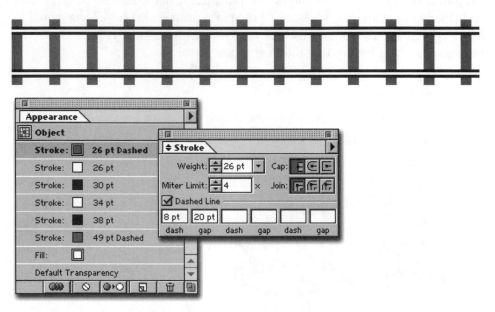

Figure 16-18: A set of railroad tracks created with multi-strokes and dash patterns. The Appearance palette shows the stacking order of the strokes and the Stroke palette shows the dash pattern used for both the top and bottom strokes.

Now you know everything there is to know about stroking objects. From here on, you can take off in a million different directions. You can add as many strokes as you want in the Appearance palette, giving each stroke a progressively thinner line weight to reveal portions of lower clones and cover up other portions. You can alternate line caps and experiment with the Dash and Gap values.

Multi-Strokes for Groups or Layers

When you apply multi-strokes, there is a significant difference in the effect between applying the strokes to individual objects and targeting a group or layer. If you target a layer, it means that all objects drawn on that layer will automatically have the attributes for the layer. Similarly, if you target a group all the objects in the group will have the same attributes.

However, there's more than just a convenience factor in applying the strokes to a group or layer. As Figure 16-19 shows, if you apply the multi-strokes to individual objects, you see the intersections between the objects. But if you apply the multi-strokes to a group or layer, the multi-strokes miraculously merge their stroke settings into seamless intersections.

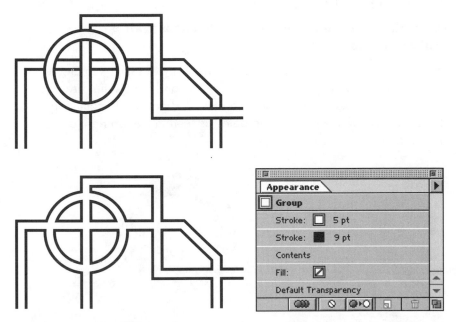

Figure 16-19: The difference between applying multi-strokes to objects (top) or to the group or layer (bottom).

Stroke Commands, Filters and Effects

Some commands in Illustrator's menus are specially designed for working with strokes. For instance, you can convert strokes to filled objects, apply arrowheads, or use special effects for strokes.

Converting Paths to Outlines

As we mentioned, some commands and tools devour all strokes in their path. Fortunately, you can use the Object » Path » Outline Path command to convert stroked lines to filled shapes. Not only does this protect strokes from being deleted, but it also lets you create special effects such as the look of strokes weaving in and out of other strokes as shown in Figure 16-20.

1. **Stroke the objects.**

   The light gray ring in the top left corner of Figure 16-20 needs to be positioned so that part of it is in front of the darker rings and the other part is behind the darker rings.

2. **Select the three rings and apply Object » Path » Outline Stroke.**

   The Outline Stroke command uses the current stroke settings to create the filled path. It will also maintain any miters and bevels that are applied to the stroke. In this case it creates filled paths with compound objects that create the holes in the paths as seen in the top right corner of Figure 16-20.

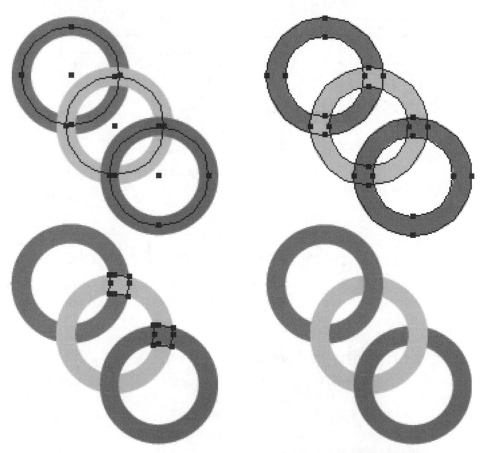

Figure 16-20: To create intertwined rings, start with stroked paths (top left). Then use the Outline Stroke command to convert them to filled paths (top right). Apply the Divide Pathfinder command (bottom left). And then change the color of two intersections (bottom right).

Sadly, Outline Stroke does not convert dashed patterns. However, if you set the opacity of the object to 99.999%, then the Object >> Flatten Transparency command will convert dashes into objects. We'll cover opacity and transparency in Chapter 17.

3. **Apply Divide from the Pathfinder palette.**

    This cuts up the filled objects wherever they overlap, as shown in the bottom left corner of Figure 16-20. (See Chapter 9 for a refresher on the Pathfinder commands.)

4. **With the direct selection tool, select and change the fill color of two of the overlapping objects.**

    This creates the illusion that the rings are intertwined, as seen in the final example of Figure 16-20.

Outlining Stroke Effect

The disadvantage of the Outline Stroke command is that it loses the stroke information and creates compound filled objects. This makes it more complicated to increase the width of the stroke or change the shape of the object. So you can use the Effect » Path » Outline Stroke command to make the conversion less permanent.

Figure 16-21 shows one of the benefits of the Outline Stroke effect. The rectangle on the top has had the twirl effect applied to a 17-point stroke without the Outline Stroke effect. The twirl changes the shape of the stroke as a single unit. The rectangle on the bottom has had the twirl effect applied to a stroke that has had the Outline Stroke effect applied first. Notice how the twirl effect independently distorts both sides of the stroke. Although the stroke has not actually been converted, the Outline Stroke effect allows you to distort the object with variable width lines.

 In case you were wondering—no, you can't use the Outline Stroke effect together with the Divide effect to create intertwining objects. Although you can apply the effects, Illustrator doesn't give you any way to change the fill colors of the overlapping objects.

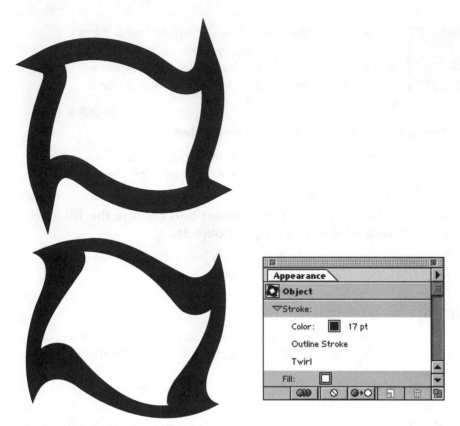

Figure 16-21: Without the Outline Stroke effect (top), a twirl can only change the stroke. With the Outline Stroke effect (bottom), a twirl can distort both sides of a stroke.

Fashioning Arrowheads Without Flint

One of the commands that exists as both a filter and an effect is the Add Arrowheads command. After selecting an open path—neither the filter nor the effect works on closed paths or text objects—choose Filter » Stylize » Add Arrowheads or Effect » Stylize » Arrowheads. Like other dual commands, the major difference between the dialog boxes is the preview command in the Effect dialog box, as shown in Figure 16-22.

The size of the arrowhead is dependent upon two factors—the line weight of the selected path and the percentage value in the Scale option box. Figure 16-23 shows five paths with different line weights, varying from 0.5 to 6 points, each with the Scale value set to 100 percent. Illustrator's default scaling generally suits 1-point and 2-point lines, but you'll want to raise or lower the Scale value if the line is thinner or thicker, respectively.

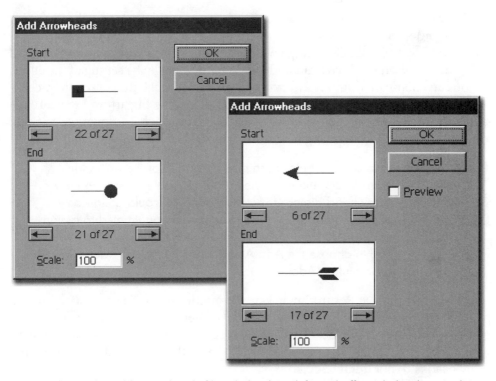

Figure 16-22: The Add Arrowheads filter dialog box (left) and effects dialog box (right). Click the arrow icons to move through the 27 different arrowhead designs.

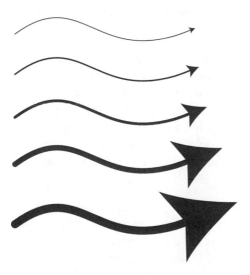

Figure 16-23:
The first arrowhead option as it appears when applied to lines 0.5, 1, 2, 4, and 6 points thick. For all lines, the Scale value was set to 100 percent.

Illustrator lets you specify whether you want to apply the arrowhead to one end, the other, or both ends of the open path. Which end is which depends on how you drew the path. Generally, you'll just make a guess and go for it. If it turns out to be the wrong end, you can undo the filter or change the setting of the effect.

You can choose from among 27 arrowheads. Scroll through the collection by clicking on one of the two arrow icons that appear below the big arrow. Figure 16-24 shows 26 of the arrowheads in order—numbers 2 through 14 down the left side and 15 through 27 down the right. (Arrowhead number 1 appears in Figure 16-23.)

Although Illustrator hasn't changed any of the arrows in many years, there has been a remarkable change in the Add Arrowhead dialog box. In the past you could assign only one variety of arrowhead at a time. If you wanted to assign an arrow to one end of a path and a tail to the other, you had to choose the Add Arrowheads command twice. We congratulate Adobe on this excellent improvement.

After you press the Return/Enter key, Illustrator assigns the arrowhead to the path. If you have applied the arrowhead as a filter, the arrowhead is a separate path—or in some cases, several paths. These paths are automatically grouped with the original open path. However, if you apply the command as an effect, the arrowheads are not discrete objects.

This is important for you to keep in mind when transforming the path. If you have applied the command as a filter, the arrowhead will be distorted if you scale the path disproportionately. If this happens, select the arrowhead with the direct selection tool, delete it, and then apply a new arrowhead. However, there are no problems if the arrowhead has been applied as an effect.

If you apply the arrowhead filter and then select the line and arrowhead with the selection tool, the Color palette and the toolbox display question marks for both the Fill and Stroke icons. This is because the line is stroked but presumably not filled, whereas the arrowhead is filled but not stroked. If you want to change the fill or stroke of either portion of the object, use the direct selection tool to select either line or arrowhead independently.

If you've already positioned the open path exactly where you want it, you'll notice that Illustrator appends the arrowhead to the end of the path, elongating it. If you've applied the arrowhead as a filter, you can move the arrowhead. However, you need to expand the appearance if you've applied the Arrowhead as an effect. (See the heading "Removing or Expanding a Brush," later in this chapter, for the scoop on the Expand Appearance command.)

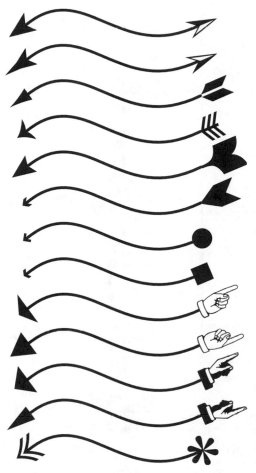

Figure 16-24:
You can apply any of these festive
arrowheads using the Add
Arrowheads filter. In each case,
the line weight is 2 points and the
Scale value is set to 100 percent.

Brushing Up on Your Paths

Until there were brushes, strokes were very mathematical. They had a fixed point size for their width, and that was about it. They couldn't change their width or taper or spatter little flecks of color. Brushes are special artwork that is applied to strokes that makes them look much more like traditional brush strokes. They are also used to apply artwork in repeating or scattered patterns along a path. They can even stretch or bend type and other objects.

There are four different types of brushes in Illustrator. By default, the Brushes palette contains a number of examples of each, as shown in Figure 16-25.

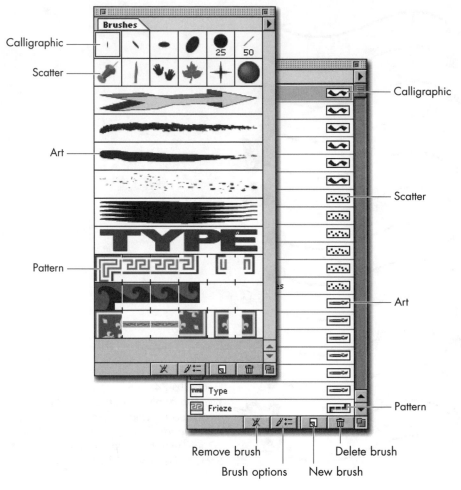

Figure 16-25: The standard Brushes palette contains several versions of each of the four brush types.

As we mentioned in Chapter 4, you can use the paintbrush tool to draw with brushes. Any path you create with the brush tool automatically adopts a brush-stroke along its length. One of the great things about brushes is that they are not limited to the paths created with the brush tool. The fact is that you can apply a brush to any selected path. Simply select the path and click one of the Brush palette's entries. Figure 16-26 was created using all four types of brushes: calligraphic, scatter, art, and pattern.

Figure 16-26: This lovely young girl was created using only brush strokes. Calligraphic brushes were used for her face. Art brushes created the hair. Scatter brushes created the background swirls. And a pattern brush and art brush created her necklace. The actual path outlines are shown to her right.

You can change the display of the Brushes palette using the palette menu. Choose View By Name to see the brushes listed with their names. Choose each of the Show options to display or hide each of the types of brushes:

🌑 **Calligraphic Brushes:** A calligraphic brush simulates the lines created with a fountain pen. You have control over the roundness of the brush tip, the angle of the tip and its size. Although you can use a mouse when drawing with a calligraphic brush, they are ideal for pressure sensitive tablets. With such a tablet, you can vary all three of the brush's attributes as a function of how hard you press with the tablet's stylus.

🌑 **Scatter Brushes:** A scatter brush takes a single object or a group of objects and repeats them a number of times along the length of the path. You can control the size of the objects, the spacing (or the distance between the objects along the path), the scattering (or the distance the objects stray to the side of the paths), and the rotation of the objects.

You can also vary the appearance of scatter brushes using a pressure-sensitive tablet.

 Art Brushes: An art brush takes a single drawing and stretches it the length of the path. You can decide in which direction the brush will follow the path, the width of the brush, and whether the brush will flip across the path. Art brushes can be used to simulate the look of natural paintbrushes or to curve artwork such as arrows and type along a path.

 Pattern Brushes: A pattern brush is a compilation of individual blocks that link together to form a continuous chain. They are ideal for borders because you can specify the design of both the beginning and the end of the path, the appearance of the inner and outer corners, and all the parts that make up all the pieces in between.

The art brushes and pattern brushes do not respond to pressure-sensitive tablets.

Creating and Applying Brushes

To design a new brush, you need to assemble all its components and choose New Brush from the Brushes palette's pop-up menu (or you can click the New Brush icon at the bottom of the Brushes palette). Illustrator then gives you the option of creating any one of the four types of brushes.

Illustrator is rather fussy about what kinds of graphic elements it will allow you to use in a brush. A candidate for a new art brush cannot contain gradients, live blends, rasterized objects, other brushes, or unconverted type. You can, however, use regular old paths with flat fills and strokes or objects with transparency settings. These paths can't be masked. The best rule of thumb when creating brushes is to keep it simple.

Although most of the brushes features are not new, using transparency with brushes is new. It allows you to create a more natural look such as watercolors, where paint from one stroke builds up as it crosses another stroke. For more details on using transparency with brushes, see Chapter 17.

Working with the Brushes palette is very similar to the Swatches palette that we looked at in Chapter 14:

- Brushes created in a document are stored only in that document.

- Illustrator installs other brushes that you can access via Window » Brush Libraries and then choose the brushes from the sub-menu.

- There are hundreds of other brushes on the Illustrator CD under Illustrator Extras: Brush Libraries.

- You can import the brushes from one document to another via Window » Brush Libraries » Other Library. You can then choose the document that you want to import the brushes from. The brushes appear in a palette where you can select the brushes.

- Choose Persistent from the palette menu of an imported brush library to have it always open when Illustrator is launched.

- You can apply a brush to any selected object by clicking the brush in the Brushes palette.

- You can draw interactively with a brush by choosing the Paintbrush tool and then selecting a brush.

- Choose View by Name to list the brushes with their names in the Brushes palette.

- Like pattern swatches, you can drag the scatter, art, and pattern brush objects out of the Brushes palette. The artwork used to create the brush, together with a bounding box, appears on your page.

Defining Calligraphic Brushes

The calligraphic brush is the only brush that doesn't require you to create the artwork for the brush before you design the brush options. Choose New Brush from the Brush palette's pop-up menu and choose New Calligraphic Brush from the New Brush dialog box. The Calligraphic Brush Options dialog box appears as shown in Figure 16-27.

- **Name:** The name you apply to the brush is visible if you place your cursor over the brush or if you choose View by Name from the Brushes palette menu.

- **Angle:** You can choose how many degrees from the horizontal the tip will deflect. Either enter a value into the Angle option box or drag the arrow in the example box to change the angle.

● **Roundness:** Here you decide how round you want the tip—whether you want a nice round tip or a more oblong one, like the tip of an old felt marker. Enter a value into the Roundness dialog box or drag one of the black circles in the example box to change the roundness.

● **Diameter:** Enter a value that reflects the size of the brush that you want. This value is relative to the size of the stroke width. So if you increase the stroke width, the diameter of the calligraphic brush will increase.

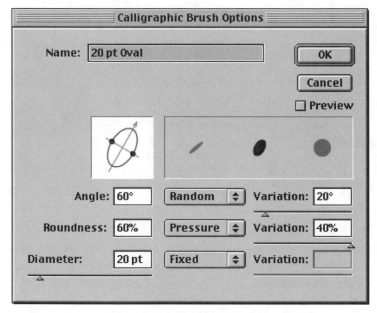

Figure 16-27: The Calligraphic Brush Options are displayed when you create a new calligraphic brush. You can modify these options by double-clicking the brush in the Brushes palette or choosing Brush Options from the Brush palette menu.

All of the options (except name) come with a pop-up list that gives you control over how Illustrator will apply the options.

● **Fixed:** This means that the attribute will always use the same value. If you use a pressure-sensitive drawing tablet, any changes in the pressure will be ignored.

● **Random:** This means that Illustrator will vary the value as you apply the brush. A second slider bar to the right of the pop-up menu will appear. Here you decide the amount that the original value can vary.

The Random setting is especially useful if you do not have access to a pressure-sensitive tablet. Although you cannot specifically direct where the thick and thin settings will be applied, the strokes are varied for a more natural appearance.

 Pressure: If you use a pressure-sensitive drawing tablet, you can opt to have Illustrator take this into account. When selected, a second slider bar will activate to the right of the pop-up menu. With it you decide how much more or less the original value will vary to reflect the pressure you apply to the tablet.

Enter the values of 5 degrees angle, 26 percent roundness, and 56 points for width to see a surprise in the Calligraphic Brush Options dialog box. For more fun, set the controls for Random or Pressure and play with the Variations sliders. *Happy Birthday!*

Calligraphic brushes appear black in the options dialog box. However, they take their color from the color applied to the stroke.

Figure 16-28 shows the same artwork changed by altering the size and angle of a calligraphic brush. In the left example, a thin, round brush was applied with no angle. In the middle example, the brush was changed to be more angular. In the right example, the diameter of the brush was increased and random variation was applied to the roundness.

Figure 16-28: Without changing a path, this armchair is altered simply by altering the characteristics of the calligraphy brushes.

Creating Scatter Brushes

For a new scatter brush, you first need to design the objects you want to have scattered on either side of the path. With your artwork selected, click the New Brush icon from the Brushes palette and select the New Scatter brush. The Scatter Brush Options dialog box appears as shown in Figure 16-29.

 You can also drag the selected object into the Brushes palette. This opens the New Brush dialog box where you can select New Scatter Brush.

 Scatter brushes are typically used to make repeating objects in random patterns. Stars, falling leaves, and confetti are examples of artwork that can be made part of a scatter brush. You can also use scatter brushes to create stippling and cross-hatch textures.

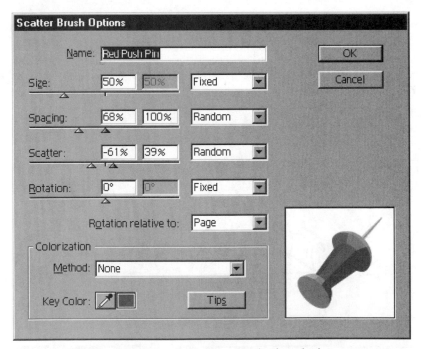

Figure 16-29: The Scatter Brush Options are displayed when you create a new scatter brush.

- **Name:** The name you apply to the brush is visible if you place your cursor over the brush or if you choose View by Name from the Brushes palette menu.

- **Size:** Enter any value of 1 percent or greater. This controls the size of the brush in relation to the original object that was used to define the brush. 100 percent keeps the same size as the original. Anything greater creates objects that are bigger than the original. Anything less makes smaller objects. However, you can also control the size of the scatter brush by increasing or decreasing the stroke width applied to the scatter brush.

- **Spacing:** Here you choose how far apart you want the objects to space themselves along the path. Enter any value of 1 percent or greater. The smaller the value the more tightly the objects will be spaced.

- **Scatter:** This is the distance that the objects will appear above and below the path. A value of 0 percent positions the objects directly on the path. Enter any value between plus or minus 1000 percent. Positive values position the objects above the path. Negative values position the objects below the path. If you want the objects on both sides of the path, use the Random or Pressure setting and then enter both plus and minus values. This sets a range for the scatter on either side of the path. Keep these values small if you want to stress the shape of the path.

- **Rotation:** The scatter brush objects can rotate as they appear along the path. Also you decide whether the objects will rotate relative to the page or the path.

- **Fixed, Random, Pressure:** All of these options come with the same pop-up menus as occur in the options for the New Calligraphic Brush. You can choose to have the scatter objects appear uniformly along the path or vary them, either randomly or as dictated by the pressure you apply to your drawing tablet.

- **Colorization:** The Colorization settings allow you to set how the scatter brush responds to changes in the stroke color. We'll cover Colorization at the end of this section.

Figure 16-30 shows how a single leaf defined as four scatter brushes with different size, rotation, scatter, and spacing options can be applied to ovals to create a wreath. The black ovals underneath show how many paths were used. The leaf on the side was used as the scatter brush.

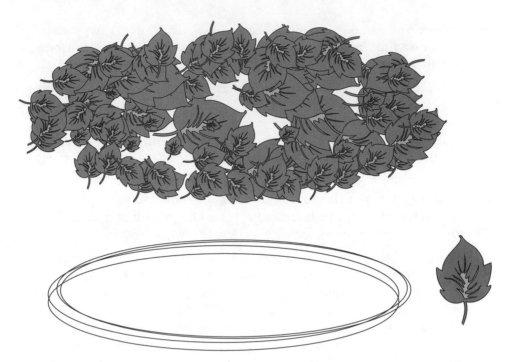

Figure 16-30: With a leaf defined as scatter brushes, we were able to create this wreath from four ovals.

Defining Art Brushes

Once again, you need to design the brush first. Because the object will be stretched along the path, you can design the brush with a front and a back. Select the design and then click the New Brush icon at the bottom of the Brushes palette. Then select the Art Brush option. The Art Brush Options dialog box appears, as shown in Figure 16-31.

 You can also drag the selected object into the Brushes palette. This opens the New Brush dialog box where you can select New Art Brush.

🔵   **Name:** The name you apply to the brush is visible if you place your cursor over the brush or if you choose View by Name from the Brushes palette menu.

- **Direction:** This determines the direction that the artwork will lie with respect to the path and the direction in which it was drawn. If you have long objects, you will most always want the direction to stretch from left to right or right to left. If you choose up to down or down to up, this will distort the object so that its width stretches along the path.

- **Size:** Enter a value to set the thickness of the brush. If you want to uniformly change the size, click the Proportional check box.

- **Flip:** You can choose to flip the object along the axis of the path or across its axis.

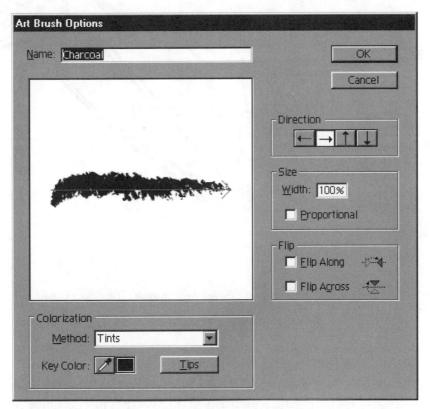

Figure 16-31: The Art Brush Options are displayed when you create a new art brush.

Figure 16-32 shows some how different art brushes can change the appearance of the same carrot illustration. In each case the artwork used to define the brush is next to the carrot it was applied to. The carrot on the right had the same brush applied as multi-brushes. The multi-brush consisted of a dark stroke at a thicker line weight under a white stroke at a thinner line weight.

Figure 16-32: Simply changing brushes altered these carrots. The artwork used to create the art brushes is next to each carrot.

Creating Pattern Brushes

Pattern brushes are the most complex type of brush. The design elements for a pattern brush come from pattern swatches in the Swatches palette. Once you have the patterns in the Swatches palette you can design the pattern brush by clicking the New Brush icon and then choosing the Pattern brush option. This opens the Pattern Brush Options dialog box as seen in Figure 16-33.

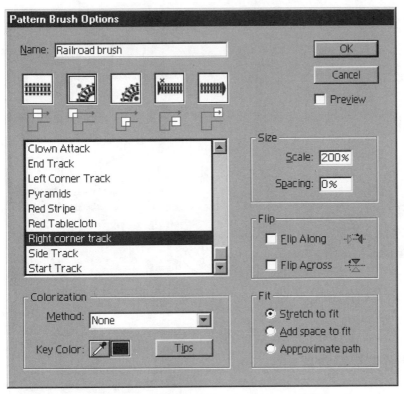

Figure 16-33: The Pattern Brush Options are the control center for creating a pattern brush.

Pattern brushes were adapted from the path patterns that were eventually dropped from Illustrator. They were created so that you could apply fancy borders to rectangles and other shapes. The disadvantage of the path patterns was that once they were applied, you couldn't modify the pattern. The pattern brushes are much more flexible. Figure 16-34 shows samples of several pattern brushes applied as borders as well as the pattern for an open path.

🌐 **Tiles:** There are five tile icons to a pattern brush. Click the tile icons to select which part of the path you want to apply the pattern to. The side tile runs along the path. The outer corner tile is applied to all right-hand turns for corner points along the path. The inner corner is applied to all left-hand turns for corner points along the path. The start tile is applied to the beginning of the path. The end tile is applied to the end of the path.

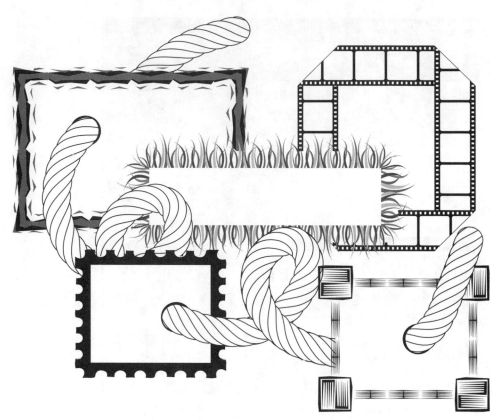

Figure 16-34: A sampling of pattern brushes applied as frames and as an open path. Some pattern brushes, such as the rope, do not have inner or outer corner tiles; so they should only be used on curved paths.

You don't have to apply tiles to all the tile icons. For instance, if you want to apply the pattern tile only to the sides of a curved path, you do not need to define the inner or outer corner tiles.

- **Patterns:** The patterns that are defined in the document are listed below the tiles. You can choose the name of the pattern, which is listed in the dialog box. The listing for Original uses the original swatches that were defined for the brush. This allows your pattern brush to contain tiles that may no longer be defined in the Swatches palette. None applies no tile for that part of the pattern brush.

- **Size:** Choose the thickness of the brush. If you want to uniformly change the size, click the Proportional check box.

- **Flip:** You can choose to flip the object along the axis of the path or across its axis.

- **Fit:** The pattern brushes are blocks that link together to form a smooth pattern along the path. This means that the bits of the pattern may not always fit exactly. You have three choices of how Illustrator will fit the brush to the path.

- **Stretch to Fit** will stretch the brush elements as needed to just fit the brush to the path. This means that Illustrator will need to distort the brush elements. Use this option for most pattern brushes where you want to keep a seamless transition between tiles.

- **Add Space to Fit** means that Illustrator will add tiny spaces to the brush as necessary. It won't distort any brush elements, but it may give a disjointed appearance to your path. Use this option for pattern brushes such as weather isobars that should not be distorted.

- **Approximate Path** is only appropriate for patterns applied as borders for rectangles. This option lets Illustrator move the pattern from the center of the path to the outside or inside so that it can better fit the tiles to shape of the path.

Defining Pattern Brush Tiles

Most of the pattern brushes that come with Illustrator do not have all five pattern tiles defined. A pattern brush made for borders will have the side pattern and the corner tiles; but it may not have the start and end tiles. Other pattern brushes may have the side, start, and end tiles, but might be missing the corner tiles. Fortunately you can create your own pattern tiles and then use them for the pattern brushes.

 You can also drag the selected object into the Brushes palette. This opens the New Brush dialog box where you can select New Pattern Brush. This makes the selected artwork a side tile for the pattern brush.

As we said, there are five different tiles for a complete pattern brush. Figure 16-35 shows how the five tiles are defined in a railroad pattern brush.

Each pattern has a bounding box around it that defines the area for the tile. We've made the bounding box visible for the tiles in Figure 16-35. We've also added a thicker gray line to show where Illustrator defines the start of the bounding box. The thick black line shows where Illustrator defines the end of the bounding box. For the tiles used as the start, side, and end, it's pretty easy to spot the start and end lines; they start at the left and end at the right of the bounding box.

Start tile   Side tile   Outer
cornert ile   Inner
corner tile   End tile

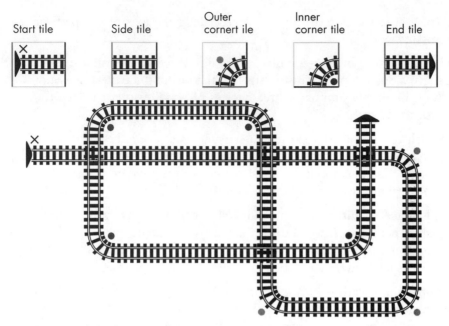

Figure 16-35: The five tiles of the railroad brush come together into a complete track.

However, the start and end lines for the outer and inner corner tiles are a little tricky. The outer corner tile uses the bottom of the bounding box as the start and the right side of the bounding box as its end. That's why we call the outer corner tiles the ones for right hand turns. The inner corner tile uses the right side of the bounding box as the start and the bottom of the bounding box as its end. So although the tile looks like it is making a right hand turn, it is actually creating a left turn if you follow it from start to end.

Notice the small circles at the turns in the track. Because they are defined as part of the outer and inner corner tiles, they always stay on the right side of the tracks. Notice also the difference between the start and end tiles. They too have a definite direction.

You may also notice that the track doesn't keep the same space between the track ties. This isn't because the railroad workers got lazy. It's because Illustrator has to slightly compress or extend the pattern tile to make it fit correctly along the path.

 One of the best ways to understand the pattern brushes is to open the Border Sample brush library found under Window » Brush Libraries. Then drag the brush tiles out of the Brushes palette to examine how they were created.

Colorizing Options

The colorizing options allow you to control how the stroke color affects the color of the artwork used for the scatter, art, and pattern brushes.

To set the colorizing options, you first use the eyedropper to select which color of the artwork should be the key color. The key color is the color used as the base for the color changes. Figure 16-36 shows how the eyedropper in the brush options dialog box is used to sample a color from the preview of the brush artwork.

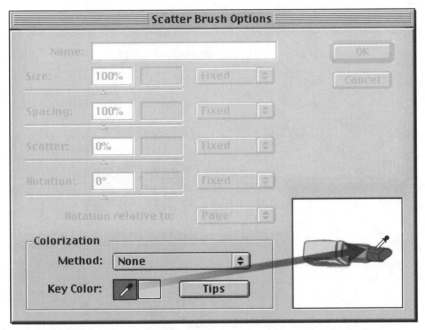

Figure 16-36: To set the key color, choose the eyedropper in the brush options dialog box and then use it to click a color in the preview area of the brush.

Choose one of the colorizing methods from the pop-up list:

- **Tints** changes all the artwork in the brush to tints of the stroke color.

- **Tints and Shades** changes all the artwork in the brush to tints of the stroke color. In addition, the colors of the artwork maintain their relative shades.

- **Hue Shift** changes the key color to the stroke color of the brush. In addition, other colors in the artwork are shifted in the same relationship. For example if the key color is yellow, and the stroke color is royal blue, the key color artwork is shifted 200 degrees on the color wheel. So if another color is red, it too will be shifted 200 degrees on the color wheel to blue-green. Figure 16-37 does a good job (for a grayscale illustration) of illustrating the colorizing options. See the color insert for a much more colorful and detailed illustration.

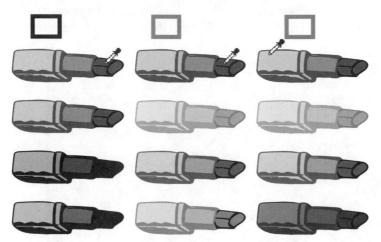

Figure 16-37: The colorizing options for the scatter and art brushes allow you to select a key color that is used to control the colorizing options. A black stroke applied to the left example of this artwork causes the artwork to become tints of black for the Tints option. The Tints and Shades option colorizes the artwork slightly darker. The Hue Shift option causes the artwork to shift to all black. The middle example shows what happens when a lighter color is applied. The color shifts are not as dark. The right example shows what happens when the same stroke color is applied when a lighter key color is chosen.

Changing a Brush's Appearance

You can change the attributes of a brush globally or on a case-by-case basis. To change the appearance of all occurrences of a particular brush, either double-click the brush in the Brushes palette or choose the Brush Options from the palette's pop-up menu. The same Brush Options dialog box that appears when you create a new brush will display. After you make your changes to a brush and click the OK button, Illustrator displays an alert box. Click the Apply to Strokes button to apply your changes to all current and future uses of the brush. Click the Leave Strokes button to apply changes only to future uses of the brushes.

To change only the appearance of the selected objects, choose the Options of Selected Objects from the Brushes palette's pop-up menu. The selected path must use the same brush if you want to use this option. This will display a slightly reduced version of the appropriate Brush Options dialog box. Any changes you make will affect only the selected paths and not impact any future use of the brush.

You can also change the artwork used to define scatter or art brushes. Simply hold the Opt/Alt key and drag new artwork onto the original brush. This opens the Brush Options dialog box which displays the new artwork. Click OK to define the new brush.

Removing or Expanding a Brush

In most cases, you can first remove a brush from a path, modify the path, and then reapply the brush. To remove a brush, select a brushed path and choose the Remove Brush Stroke from the Brushes palette's pop-up menu. This restores the path to an ordinary stroked path.

If you choose Object » Expand Appearance, you can use the Expand Appearance dialog box to set the stroke to expand. This turns the objects used to define the brush into discrete objects that are no longer attached to the brush definition. In addition, the original path used to define the shape of the brush stroke will be part of the expanded artwork.

 You can use the Expand Appearance command to convert calligraphic brushes.

CHAPTER 17

TRANSPARENCY

There is a magician who does a trick where he sticks a knitting needle right through his arm. The audience screams in horror as he pushes and pulls the needle in and out. Blood drips down. He keeps repeating, "It's not real. It's a *trick!*" It doesn't matter; it looks very real and very frightening. It's the same with the transparency in Illustrator. There is no *real* transparency in Illustrator; PostScript doesn't allow it. However, it doesn't matter. As far as your work is concerned, Illustrator lets one object appear transparent when it is positioned over another. Your friends will scream in delight. Just remember, it's a *trick!*

Adobe has given us an amazing arsenal of transparency controls—everything from simple opacity changes to advanced blending modes to highly sophisticated opacity masking. This chapter covers all the features of the Transparency palette. This includes opacity, blending modes, as well as special knockout options for controlling how transparency is applied. We'll look at the difference between adding transparency to objects, groups, or layers. We'll take another look at features we've already covered, such as multi-fills, brushes, and text to see how you can use transparency with them. We'll also do a little behind-the-scenes investigation to reveal the secret behind the trick of transparency. And finally, we'll look at how you can ensure the best possible output for artwork that uses the transparency controls.

We suspect that many experienced users have flipped immediately to this chapter. We understand. With the addition of transparency in Illustrator 9, almost every technique that we've ever used in Illustrator has changed. It is much simpler to create realistic reflections, liquids, smoke, clouds, and metallic effects. It's not just new; it's revolutionary. However, rather than plaster the word *New* next to every paragraph in this chapter, suffice to say that everything in this chapter is new.

Opacity

Although most people call transparency the ability to see through an object, Adobe uses the term *transparency* as the overall category for a whole host of features. So what most people call transparency, Adobe calls opacity. Strictly speaking you don't make an object transparent, you lower the opacity of the object.

Lowering Opacity

Changing an object's opacity is very simple. You select the object, and then use the Opacity control in the Transparency palette to lower the opacity. If you don't see the Transparency palette, choose Window » Show Transparency.

The lower the opacity the more transparent the object. Figure 17-1 shows the effect of different opacity settings for a lightning bolt positioned over a storm cloud. The lower the opacity, the more you can see through the lightning to he cloud behind it. At an opacity of 10 percent, you can hardly see the lightning bolt at all.

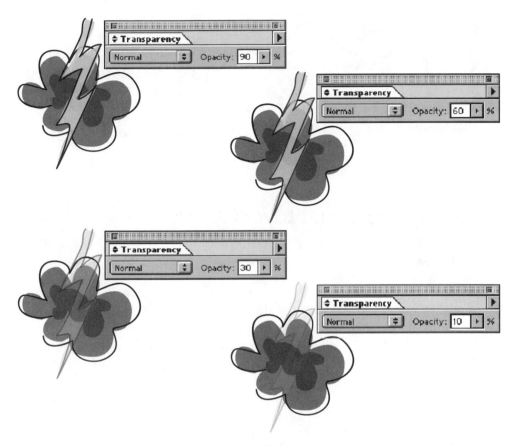

Figure 17-1: Use the Opacity controls in the Transparency palette to change the translucence of an object.

When you lower an object's opacity, the opacity level is listed in the Appearance palette. In addition, the circle next to the name of the path in the Layers palette also becomes gray, as seen in Figure 17-2. These are your clues that the actual fill color of the object is not what is listed in the Color palette. For instance, if you have an object with a 100 percent black fill over a white background, and you apply an 80 percent opacity setting, the black fill will actually print as an 80 percent tint.

 Opacity is not the only feature that is indicated by the gray circle. Multiple fills, strokes, or effects are also indicated by the gray circle.

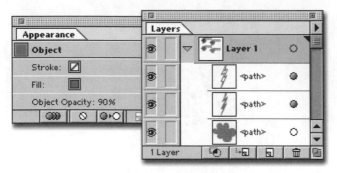

Figure 17-2:
The opacity of an object is listed in the Appearance palette. Opacity applied to an object also changes the circle next to the path in the Layers palette from white to gray.

Applying Group and Layer Opacity

If you select several objects with different fill and stroke settings, the Appearance palette does not show the opacity listing. This is because you have mixed styles for the objects. If you want to see the opacity for all the objects, you should first group the objects and then target the group. You then apply the opacity to the group. This makes it easier to adjust the opacity setting for all the objects.

To apply the opacity setting to a group, find the group listing in the Layers palette. Then click the small circle for the group. A highlight circle appears that indicates that the group is targeted. (Another way to target a group is by selecting the group and clicking the word "Group" in the Appearance palette.) You can also target a layer and apply the opacity to all the objects in the layer. Once again, the gray circle indicates the special appearance applied to the layer.

It is possible, therefore, to have artwork that contains opacity applied to an object as well as both the group and the layer to which it belongs.. This can cause confusion if you want to clear the opacity for an object. If you change the opacity for just the object, you still need to change the opacity for the group as well as the layer. If you are uncertain as to where opacity has been applied, you can look for the gray circles in the Layers palette or the opacity grid icon in the Appearance palette (see Figure 17-3).

Watch out if you apply opacity to groups or layers. Any objects that you move out of the group or layer will change their appearance. For instance, if an object is on a layer that has a 50 percent opacity applied to it, will look different if the object is moved to a layer that doesn't have opacity applied. Also, if you move an object that already has an opacity applied to it to a layer that has opacity, you will have both the opacity of the object and the opacity of the layer applied to the object.

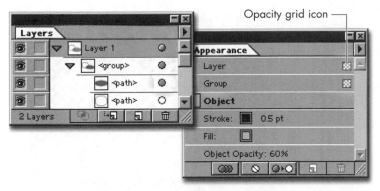

Figure 17-3: The gray circles next to the listings in the Layers palette indicate special appearance. The grid icons in the Appearance palette indicate that opacity has been applied to a group or a layer.

Setting and Displaying the Transparency Grid

As soon as your artwork becomes complex, you may find it difficult to see exactly where images start and stop. A 20 percent black object with a 30 percent opacity is going to be very hard to see on a white artboard. (This is very similar to trying to find a white doily decorating a snowman in a fog.)

Fortunately someone at Adobe recognized the problem and added a transparency grid that you can display while you work. To display the transparency grid, simply choose View » Show Transparency Grid or use the keyboard shortcut Cmd/Ctrl-Shift-D. The grid appears over your page. Fully opaque objects (with 100 percent opacity) will be seen more easily against the grid. You won't be able to see the grid through any opaque objects. Figure 17-4 shows how much easier it is to see light gray transparent objects over the transparency grid.

If you want, you can change the color and size of the transparency grid. Choose File » Document Setup and then choose the Transparency setting from the pop-up list. The Transparency grid options appear as seen in Figure 17-5.

 The Transparency grid is controlled through Document Setup. This means that you have to reset any changes for each new document. And if you're wondering, no, you can't change the grid for the startup file and then make that the default for all new documents.

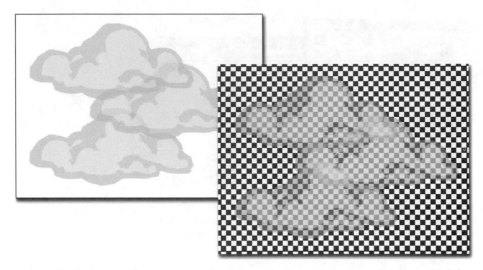

Figure 17-4: Amazingly, yes, there are some transparent light gray clouds on the left side without the transparency grid. With the grid turned on, they are much easier to see as seen on the right side.

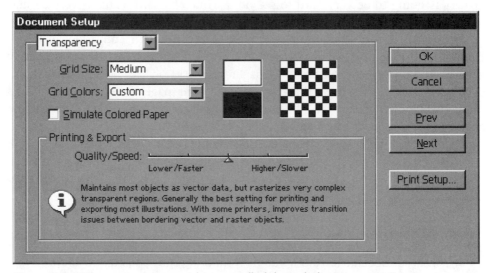

Figure 17-5: The transparency grid is controlled through the Document Setup Transparency options.

You can change the grid as follows:

- Use the Grid Size list to choose the size of the grid boxes. Smaller boxes are better if you are working with many small items.

- Use the Grid Colors list to choose one of the preset color schemes for the grid.

- Click either of the color boxes to open the Color Picker to choose a specific color.

- Watch the preview box to see a representation of the grid.

You can also simulate the appearance of what your artwork will look like when printed on colored paper. First, click the top color box to set the color of the paper. Then check Simulate Colored Paper. This adds the color of the paper to all the artwork.

Blending Modes

If you are familiar with Photoshop, you may have used the blending modes for layers. What blending modes do is change how the colors of one object or layer interact with the colors of the objects or layers below it. Strictly speaking, the blending modes are not a transparency feature, but more a matter of how colors interact.

Applying Blending Modes

The blending modes are controlled by the pop-up list in the Transparency palette, as seen in Figure 17-6. You set a blending mode by selecting an object or targeting a group or layer and then choosing one of the default blending modes. You won't see any effect of the blending mode unless you have another object positioned under the selected object.

You can also find blending modes listed in the Drop Shadow, Inner Glow, and Outer Glow effects. In these cases, the blending mode changes how the object with an applied effect—the shadow or the glow—interacts with the objects below it.

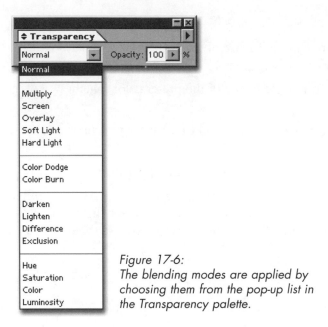

Figure 17-6:
The blending modes are applied by choosing them from the pop-up list in the Transparency palette.

Understanding Blending Modes

It really is almost impossible to convey the meaning of blending modes in mere words. Figure 17-7 shows a small sample of the blending modes. Because many of the modes create color changes, a much better example of what the blending modes do is found in the color insert. However, here's a rundown of each of the blending modes and how they work:

Illustrator's blending modes do not use the white of the artboard as a color that they can interact with. If you turn on the Transparency Grid, you will see that Illustrator does not consider that white an actual color. So if you want Illustrator's blending modes to act similarly to the ones in Photoshop with a white background layer, you need to add a white rectangle behind the objects.

Normal: This is how Illustrator has always displayed objects. The colors of the top object knock out (obscure) the colors of the object below. Lowering the opacity of a normal object does let the background color show through. But it is seen through a tint, or screen, of the top object's color.

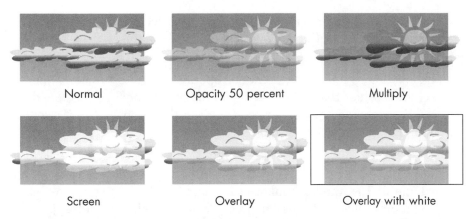

Normal	Opacity 50 percent	Multiply
Screen	Overlay	Overlay with white

Figure 17-7: A grayscale version of how the blending modes work. In each case the blending mode or opacity was applied to the clouds. The bottom right example shows the effect when a white rectangle is put behind the artwork.

Multiply: This mode will always make a darker color where the objects overlap. Illustrator takes the color of the original object and multiplies the color(s) of the objects below.

 It may seem that the multiply blending mode is the same as setting an object to overprint another. However, there are differences. Overprinting adds the ink in the top object to the bottom. It does not multiply. Also, if the objects share a color plate, overprinting will not add the colors.

 Because the multiply mode combines colors even when they share plates, it is very easy to create colors that contain more than 300 percent of ink. If you want to check what the final percentages of colors will be, see the section later in this chapter on "Dissecting Transparency."

Screen: This mode will always make a lighter color where the objects overlap. Illustrator takes the color of the original object and multiplies the inverse of the color of the objects below. The inverse of a color is 100 percent minus the percentage of color. The lighter the color set to the screen mode, the lighter the final color will be.

Overlay: Overlay goes both ways and either multiplies or screens depending on the colors below. The color of the object below is not replaced, but is mixed with the original object color to reflect the lightness or darkness of the original color. The overall effect is that light colors become lighter and dark colors get darker.

Soft Light: This mode simulates the effect of shining a soft spotlight on an object, however, in this case the soft spotlight is the top object. If the top color is lighter than 50 percent gray, the bottom object is lightened as if the color dodge mode had been applied. If the top color is darker than 50 percent gray, the bottom object is darkened as if the color burn mode had been applied. The soft light mode does not lighten very saturated objects that contain 100 percent of colors.

Hard Light: This mode simulates the effect of shining a very intense spotlight on an object. However, in this case the spotlight is the top object. The hard light blending mode works similarly to the soft light mode, but the hard light effects are much more intense. If the top color is lighter than 50 percent gray, the bottom object is lightened as if the screen mode had been applied. If the top color is darker than 50 percent gray, the bottom object is darkened as if the multiply mode had been applied. If the soft light mode shifts a color only 10 percent, the hard light mode may shift it 15 percent. And unlike the soft light mode that cannot affect objects with 100 percent ink, the hard light mode does not have those limitations.

Color Dodge: Dodging in photography is the technique where you lighten certain areas of a print during developing. Color dodge in Illustrator means the bottom colors are brightened according to the color of the top object. Using black as the original color will not change the bottom colors. Color dodge is similar to the lighten mode. However, color dodge creates slightly more intense color changes.

Color Burn: Burning in photography is the technique where you darken certain areas of a print during developing. Color burn in Illustrator means the bottom colors are darkened according to the color of the top object. Color burn is similar to the darken mode. However, color burn will create slightly more saturated color changes.

Darken: The darken blending mode takes the top object's color and compares it to the bottom color. If the top color is darker, then that color replaces the bottom object's color. If not, the bottom object's color does not change and the top object's color is invisible.

Lighten: The lighten blending mode takes the top object's color and compares it to the bottom color. If the top color is lighter, then that color replaces the bottom object's color. If not, the bottom object's color does not change and the top object's color is invisible.

- **Difference:** The difference blending mode compares the brightness values of the colors and subtracts either the original color from the bottom or the bottom from the top depending on which color is brighter.

- **Exclusion:** Is similar to the difference mode, but creates changes that are slightly less intense.

- **Hue:** Changes the hue of the bottom object to be the same as the top object, but does not change the luminosity or saturation of the bottom color. If you do not like the effects of the color blending mode, you may use hue as an alternative blending mode for colorizing portions of an area.

- **Saturation:** Changes the saturation of the bottom object to be the same as the top object, but does not change the hue or luminosity of the bottom color. This mode is excellent for intensifying or dulling the colors in a specific area. The saturation mode does nothing when the top object is a neutral gray color.

- **Color:** Changes both the hue and saturation of the bottom color to be the same as the top object, but does not change the luminance of the bottom color. This preserves the gray levels of the bottom object. Color is an excellent choice for colorizing monochrome artwork or tinting colored artwork.

- **Luminosity:** Changes the luminance of the bottom color to be the same as the top object, but does not change the hue or saturation of the bottom color.

Isolating Blending

You must think we're silly. Just as we show you how to apply the blending modes, now we're going to show you how to stop their effect. Isolating the blending modes means that you set a limit as to how far down the blending mode will be seen. This is extremely important, especially when you realize that the blending mode exerts its evil influence from the point where the object starts and reaches deep down from that layer through every other layer below—no matter how many layers deep. (At times we fear the blending modes will reach down all the way to the other side of the earth and burst out somewhere in Australia.)

Figure 17-8 shows the need for isolating the blending mode. In the top example, the text has had the multiply blending mode applied. Although this does give an interesting effect over the coffee cup, the blending mode makes the text hard to read over the pattern. In the bottom example, the blending mode for the text has been isolated so that it only affects the coffee cup, but not the pattern.

Figure 17-8: When the multiply mode is applied, it is difficult to read the text over the pattern in the top example. In the bottom example, the isolate blending command allows you to stop the blending mode from being applied to the pattern.

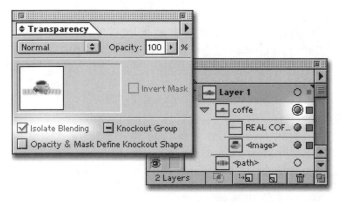

Figure 17-9: To isolate blending, target the group that contains the object with the blending mode and all the objects that the blending mode should be applied to. Then check Isolate Blending in the Transparency palette.

In order to isolate the blending, you need to choose Show Options from the Transparency palette. This opens the full set of transparency controls. If you want, you can also choose Show Thumbnails to see a preview of the selected elements.

Here are the steps you need to follow to isolate the blending to a particular set of objects:

1.   Apply the blending mode to the object.

2. Group the object that has the blending mode and all the objects that you want to have affected by the blending.

3. Use the Layers palette to target the group.

4. Check Isolate Blending in the Transparency palette. The blending will be terminated at the bottom-most object in the group. Figure 17-9 shows which objects are targeted and how the command is applied.

Knockout Groups

What are knockout groups and why do you need them? Rather than answer that question with a lot of words, let's jump to Figure 17-10. That horrible mess in the upper right corner is supposed to be the flag of the United States of America. Are you having trouble finding the stars? That's because someone (well, actually it was Sandee) selected all the objects in the flag and simply applied the multiply blending mode and set the opacity to 80 percent. That caused the stars and blue square to be multiplied into the red and white stripes behind them. So all the objects in the flag are multiplied and ghosted together into one mess.

Fortunately someone (yes, Sandee again) created a knockout group on the right. That allowed the multiply blending mode and opacity setting to be set as a unit. So what a knockout group does is allow you to identify a group of objects and apply transparency settings to the group as a whole rather than to the individual objects. (If you want to see a much more colorful representation of this illustration, see the color insert.)

Creating a Knockout Group

It's not too hard to create a knockout group. You just have to see the word group and remember that you should apply the blending modes and opacity settings to the group, not the individual objects. And you need to select the knockout group command. Here's how to create a knockout group.

1. Group the objects that you want to act as a unit.

2. Use the Layers palette to target the group. (This is the part we always forget.)

3. Check Knockout Group in the Transparency palette. If you do not see the Knockout Group option, make sure Show Options has been chosen for the Transparency palette.

4. Apply the blending mode or opacity setting. Figure 17-11 shows which objects are targeted and how the command is applied.

Figure 17-10: Setting the multiply blending mode and 80 percent opacity without a knockout causes the flap on the left to mix all the colors of the objects together. With a knockout group, the blending mode and opacity are applied to the entire object, rather than the individual objects.

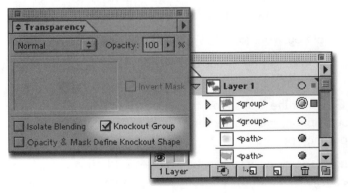

Figure 17-11: To set a knockout group, you must target the group in the Layers palette and then apply the Knockout Group option in the Transparency palette. You can then apply the blending mode or opacity setting.

Opacity Masks

If you've used a layer mask in Photoshop, you've created the same effect as an opacity mask in Illustrator. The concept behind an opacity mask is simple. You place one object or group of objects that is the mask over artwork. Wherever there is white in the mask, you can see the artwork. Wherever there is black, you can't. Anything in between has an opacity applied. So 50 percent gray in the opacity mask allows you to see the area below at -50 percent opacity.

Opacity masks allow you to create more sophisticated effects than you could get by simply applying opacity settings or feathering objects. For example, figure 17-12 shows an opacity mask created from a gradient mesh. The subtle shadings in the artwork would be almost impossible to achieve using other techniques in Illustrator. The small inset artwork shows the original image and the mesh that was used as the opacity mask. Notice how the edges of the artwork fade away. Those areas correspond to the black areas in the gradient mesh. Where the artwork is more pronounced, the gradient mesh is white.

Figure 17-12: A gradient mesh was used as an opacity mask for this unicorn. The small inset artwork shows the original image without the opacity mask and the separate gradient mesh that was used as the opacity mask.

Creating an Opacity Mask

The object that acts as the opacity mask needs to be placed on a special layer called an opacity mask layer. (What a great name!) We use two different techniques to put the opacity mask on its special layer. The first technique lets you create the opacity mask on top of the artwork and automatically put the mask on the special layer:

1. Create the object that you want to be the opacity mask.

2. Position this object on top of the artwork that is to be masked.

3. Select all the objects as shown in Figure 17-13.

4. Choose Make Opacity Mask from the Transparency palette menu. The topmost object disappears and becomes the opacity mask for the artwork below.

If there is only one object selected, or the objects selected are a single group, then the Make Opacity Mask command creates an empty opacity mask layer.

When you make an opacity mask, the objects to be masked are automatically grouped.

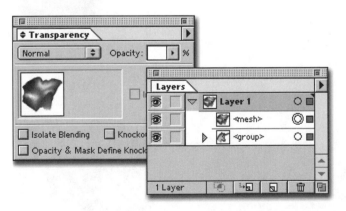

Figure 17-13:
The topmost object in a selection becomes the opacity mask for the objects below.

The second technique lets you create an empty opacity mask layer. You can then create the artwork you want to put on the special layer.

1. Create the artwork that you want to be masked.

2. If there are multiple objects, select and group the artwork.

3. With the artwork still selected, double-click the empty space next to the thumbnail in the Transparency palette as seen on the top-left of Figure 17-14. This creates an empty opacity mask layer and a blank thumbnail for the opacity mask layer, as seen on the bottom-right of Figure 17-14. (If you don't see the thumbnail, choose Show Thumbnails from the Layers Palette menu.)

4. Create the artwork for the opacity mask.

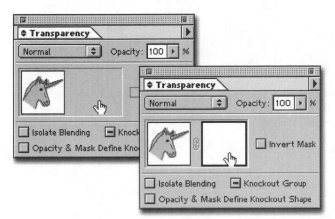

Figure 17-14: Double-click the empty space next to the object's thumbnail in the Transparency palette to automatically create an empty opacity mask layer.

Inverting an opacity mask

Ordinarily, the white areas of an opacity mask let you see the artwork and the black areas hide the artwork. However, if you check Invert Mask in the Transparency palette, you can flip those colors. Black shows the artwork; white hides it. In addition, the Invert Mask option hides any artwork that is outside the opacity mask area.

If you want, you can make all new opacity masks automatically inverted. Choose New Opacity Masks are Inverted from the Transparency palette menu.

Editing an Opacity Mask

Once you've created the opacity mask, you can easily switch between working on either the artwork or the mask. However, there are some specific rules you need to keep in mind:

- The dashed underline beneath a path or group in the Layers palette indicates that the object has been altered by an opacity mask.

- Once you have made an opacity mask, the mask itself is no longer visible in the Layers palette.

- In order to see the thumbnail for the opacity mask, you must target the circle for the path or group in the Layers palette, as shown in Figure 17-15.

The thumbnail for the artwork as well as the opacity mask will be visible in the Transparency palette.

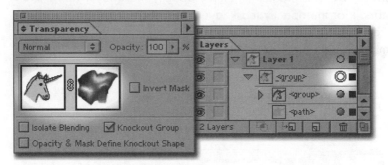

Figure 17-15: Target the circle in the Layers palette in order to edit the opacity mask for a group.

- Click the left thumbnail in the Transparency palette to work on the artwork.

- Click the right thumbnail to edit the opacity mask.

- Choose Disable Opacity Mask from the Transparency palette menu to see the artwork without the effects of the opacity mask. A red x through the opacity mask thumbnail indicates that the opacity mask has been disabled.

- Choose Enable Opacity Mask to see the artwork with the effects of the opacity mask.

- Shift-click the thumbnail for the opacity mask to toggle between the disabled and enabled modes.

- Opt/Alt-click the thumbnail for the opacity mask to edit the mask without seeing the artwork. Opt/Alt-click again to see the artwork.

- Choose Release Opacity Mask from the Transparency palette menu to remove the opacity mask. The opacity mask object will be visible on the artboard.

- Choose Unlink Opacity Mask from the Transparency palette menu to move the object without moving the mask. Choose Link Opacity Mask to relink the object and the mask.

 If you have a Knockout group, you can target that group and then check the Opacity & Mask Define Knockout Shape. This allows you to have a knockout group combined with a knockout shape.

Using Transparency

Once you understand the principles of transparency, there are many different ways you can use objects with opacity and blending modes applied. Although we can only scratch the surface, here are some ideas to help spark your imagination.

In Multi-Fills

When you create a multi-fill for an object, you can also apply an opacity or a blending mode. Position the multi-fill on top of the second fill so that the transparency feature can be seen. You should also apply some transformation or distortion so that you can see the differences between the two fills. Figure 17-16 shows how the top fill of an object can be set to multiply with the bottom fill.

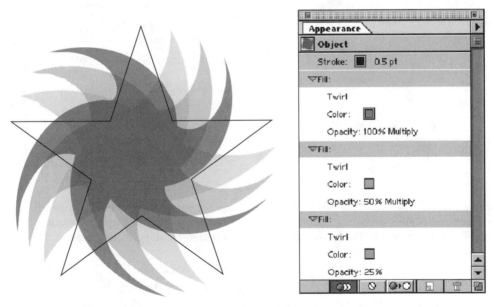

Figure 17-16: The multiply mode as well as three different opacity settings make the multi-fill swirls in this star seem to move. The original path is indicated by the black stroke.

You need to select the specific fill in the Appearance palette. You can then make any changes to the blending modes or opacity.

 Changing the order of the fills is especially important when working with the blending modes.

In Strokes and Brushes

Just like multi-fills, you can apply opacity or blending modes to multi-strokes. Distortions and transformations help make the differences between the strokes more noticeable. However, don't forget the dash patterns in strokes. Figure 17-17 shows how using different transparency settings together with the roughen effect creates a fuzzy-stroke.

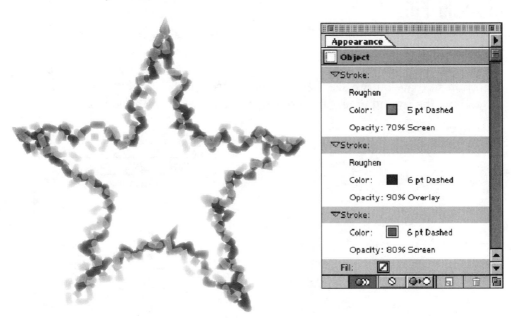

Figure 17-17: The fuzzy star has had three different strokes applied to it. The Appearance palette shows the different dash patterns, effects, blending modes and opacity settings applied to each stroke. The feather effect was also added for some extra softness.

You also can apply transparency attributes to calligraphic brush strokes. Unfortunately the attributes don't stick for the next brush stroke. So what we've been doing is working with the brush normally and then selecting all the objects and applying either opacity or blending modes. As Figure 17-18 shows, adding a multiply blending mode with opacity simulates the look of marker pens—especially with a non-round tip.

Fortunately it is much easier to create art, scatter, or pattern brushes with transparency artwork. Simply apply the blending mode or opacity before you define the brush. Then each brush stroke will automatically have that particular transparency assigned to it. Figure 17-19 shows the effect of multiply and opacity on a scatter brush with twinkle stars. However, be aware that the transparency setting is not visible in the Appearance palette when you select the brush stroke. That's because the setting is part of the definition of the brush, not the brush stroke.

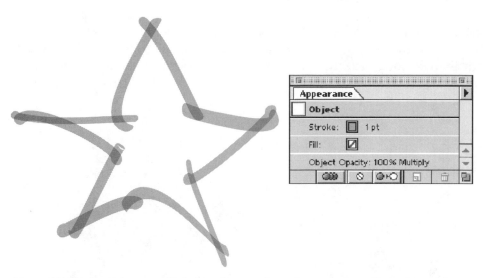

Figure 17-18: Applying a multiply blending mode and opacity to calligraphic strokes looks very similar to old-time marker pens—but without the smell.

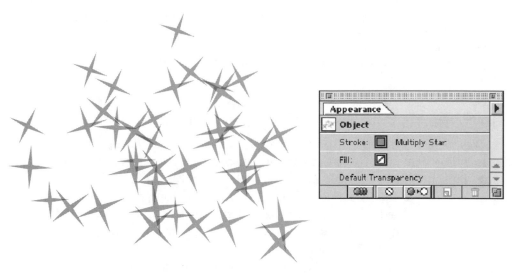

Figure 17-19: Opacity can be applied to the objects used to define art, scatter, or pattern brushes. However, the setting is not visible in the Appearance palette.

In Text

Of course you can apply blending modes or opacity to text. Simply select the text and apply the transparency attribute. There is an important difference, though, as to how the transparency effect appears, depending on how you select the text. If you select the text as an object (with the baseline visible), then the opacity or blending modes for the individual characters will not interact with each other unless the text is in different text objects. However, if you select the text with the text tool, then the transparency attributes will interact within a single text object. Figure 17-20 shows the difference between applying transparency to text objects or text characters.

Figure 17-20: The text on the left shows that when opacity or blending modes are applied to text selected using the text tool, the individual characters of the text will interact according to their transparency settings. The text on the right shows that when the text is selected as an object, the transparency attributes are visible only between different text objects.

In Patterns and Charts

Yes, yes, yes!—you can certainly apply transparency attributes to charts and patterns. There are two ways to apply transparency to a pattern. You can assign the transparency to the objects used to define the pattern or you can apply the transparency to the object containing the pattern. If you apply the transparency to the objects used to define the pattern, that attribute will not be listed in the Appearance palette. This allows you to create a pattern of a checkerboard cloth where one color mixes with another.

The transparency attributes can be applied to the chart as a whole or the individual elements of the chart. Like patterns, if you applied a transparency attribute to just part of a chart, then you will not see the attribute listed when you target the chart as a whole. Applying blending modes, such as multiply, to a bar chart looks very interesting when the column width is set to greater than 100 percent. Where the bars overlap, you see the intersection of the bars.

Analyzing Transparency

Now's the time to pull the curtain aside and discover the secret to transparency. We've already established that there is no such thing as transparency in PostScript, so how does Illustrator do this magic?

Printing Transparency Attributes

The transparency you see on the screen is just a preview image. Illustrator looks at the objects on the page and applies the transparency to the preview image. Every time you move an object, Illustrator recalculates what the transparency preview should look like. There is no problem doing this because transparency does exist onscreen.

However, transparency doesn't exist in the PostScript language that Illustrator uses when it sends instructions to the printer. So Illustrator has to convert the transparency preview into something that can be expressed in the PostScript language. There are two types of objects that Illustrator can convert transparency attributes into: vector objects or raster images.

Vector objects are created similarly to the discrete objects created by the Soft Mix or Hard Mix Pathfinder commands. The top right inset in Figure 17-21 shows an example of how transparency effects are converted into discrete vector

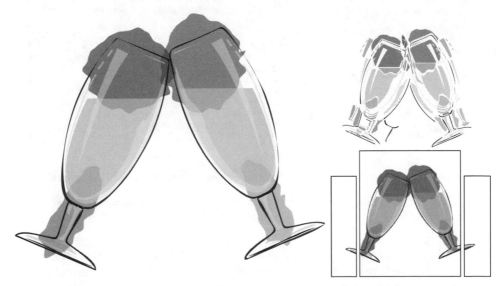

Figure 17-21: The transparency applied to the artwork on the left can be converted into discrete vector shapes (top right) or raster images (bottom right). We've separated the artwork to show the individual vectors and added an outline around the raster images.

objects. Wherever a new color is formed from the overlap of two objects, a vector object is created. As you can imagine, the more involved the transparency effect, the greater the number of vector objects that will be created.

As the number of vector objects increases, the time it takes to print the file also increases. And some types of transparency effects, such as fuzzy drop shadows or where two transparent gradients overlap, can never be converted into discrete objects. In those cases, Illustrator needs to convert the objects into raster images. The bottom right inset in Figure 17-21 shows the type of raster image that can be created in order to print transparency effects.

Controlling the Transparency Conversion

You can control how Illustrator converts transparency effects for printing. Choose File » Document Setup to open the Document Setup dialog box. Use the pop-up list to choose the Transparency settings. The Quality/Speed slider as shown in Figure 17-22 lets you control how transparency effects will be converted. There are five settings for the slider:

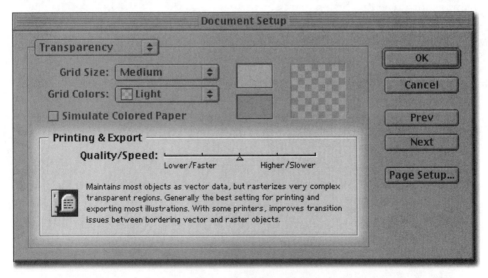

Figure 17-22: The Quality/Speed slider in the Document Setup Transparency area lets you control how Illustrator handles Transparency effects.

When positioned all the way to the right, Illustrator converts all transparency artwork into vectors and only rasterizes effects that cannot be converted into vectors. This setting creates the highest-quality artwork that can be scaled up without losing image details. However, it also creates the largest files and takes the most time to print.

- When positioned all the way to the left, Illustrator rasterizes all transparency artwork. The resolution used comes from the Printing & Export area of the Document Setup dialog box. This setting is useful if you need to print a quick proof.

- The three middle settings can create a mixture of vector and raster information. The amount of rasterization decreases as you move the slider from left to right. However, even if you position the slider to the setting second from the left, Illustrator always tries to convert to vector objects first. So simple graphics, such as the transparency effects in Figure 17-21, are converted into vectors.

Controlling the Raster Resolutions

Once you have set how objects will be converted—to vectors or raster images—you can then set the resolution for the raster images. Choose File » Document Setup and then choose Printing & Exporting from the pop-up list. The dialog box seen in Figure 17-23 appears.

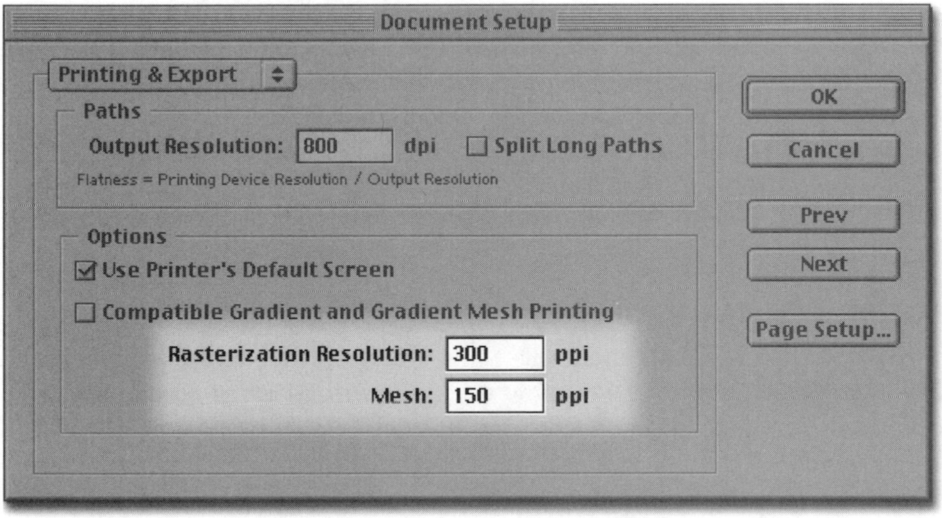

Document Setup

Printing & Export

Paths

Output Resolution: 800 dpi ☐ Split Long Paths

Flatness = Printing Device Resolution / Output Resolution

Options

☑ Use Printer's Default Screen

☐ Compatible Gradient and Gradient Mesh Printing

Rasterization Resolution: 300 ppi

Mesh: 150 ppi

OK

Cancel

Prev

Next

Page Setup...

Figure 17-23: You can set the resolution for converted transparency effects in the Printing & Export area of the Document Setup dialog box.

Enter a value in the Rasterization Resolution field. This amount is usually arrived at by doubling the linescreen of the final output. For instance, if you are going to have your artwork printed on an offset press, the linescreen is usually 150 lines per inch (lpi). Double that and you get the typical 300 pixels per inch (ppi) resolution amount. However, if you are going to have your artwork printed by a newspaper, the linescreen is usually 85 to 110 lpi. So you can lower the resolution to 170 to 220 lpi.

If you do not know how your artwork will be printed, set the resolution to 300 ppi. Most printing uses a linescreen of 150 lpi. However, if there is any chance that your artwork will be enlarged, then you may need to set the resolution above 300 ppi. For instance, if the artwork is enlarged to twice its size, 300 ppi becomes an effective resolution of only 150 ppi. So you need to set the resolution to 600 ppi to get an effective resolution of 300 ppi.

 There are some instances where transparency effects will print with less-than-desired results. For instance, if you have extremely fine strokes in your document, they may be rasterized where transparency effects are positioned over them. This may cause a change in the stroke weight. Also, some colors may print differently if they are in elements that are divided into both vectors and raster images. This is called stitching. One way to avoid these problems is to set the slider to the lowest Quality/Speed setting. This causes the entire document to be rasterized, which avoids inconsistencies between vectors and raster images. If you would like more information about this topic, Adobe has put together an excellent resource on understanding how transparency effects are printed. It is called the "Printing & Exporting Artwork from Illustrator 9 White Paper." You can find a copy of the file (AI9PrintWhitePaper.pdf) on the Illustrator 9 CD.

Flattening Transparency

When we first heard about all this conversion to vectors and raster images we were worried: How would we know exactly what was going to happen? How complex did an image have to be before Illustrator would rasterize it? How many objects would be created? It was all too complicated.

Fortunately we don't have to wait until our artwork is printed before we can find out what will happen to our fragile transparencies. We can simply select the artwork and then choose Object » Flatten Transparency. The dialog box in Figure 17-24 appears.

This gives us the same Quality/Speed slider we had in Document Setup. However, here we can make the conversion right in our document—without waiting around for the print shop to mangle our artwork. We can also set the resolution for any raster images that Illustrator has to create.

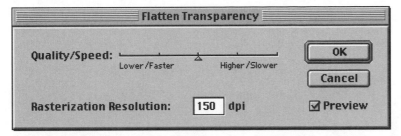

Figure 17-24: Use the Flatten Transparency dialog box to convert transparency effects into ordinary objects. The Lower/Faster setting is more likely to rasterize objects. The Higher/Slower setting tries to maintain vector objects.

CHAPTER 18

BLENDS, MASKS, AND INK PEN FILLS

In past years, blends were the only way to create effects such as highlights, glows, and fuzzy shadows. Masks were the only way to hide certain parts of artwork without actually deleting the objects. Today, these effects are handled by other features, such as the raster effects and opacity masks. Fortunately there are still important uses for blends, especially when it comes to creating custom gradations and shape morphing. And masks, when applied to layers, make it very easy to make certain objects invisible. The Ink Pen remains a one-of-a-kind filter that lets you create textures and special half-tone effects.

At first glance there doesn't seem to be much that ties these effects together. However, there actually is a theme to these features. All three features create or display objects within shapes defined by different objects. Blends allow you to create additional images by selecting two or more objects. Masks display images within the shape of a certain object. And the Ink Pen filter creates additional objects that are displayed within the original object.

However, a better theme is that these are the features that always stump beginners. And although blends and masks have become easier to use since the days we started working with Illustrator, they can still be daunting to new users.

So welcome to the hard stuff in Illustrator. These are the commands that truly separate the beginners from the experienced users. When you finish with this chapter, you'll fully deserve to stick a gold star on your monitor.

Blending Paths

Blending is one of Illustrator's most exotic and oldest capabilities. Back when every one of its competitors offered automated gradations, Illustrator allowed you to design your own custom gradations. Illustrator's blend tool wasn't easy to use, but it yielded an unlimited range of results. There wasn't a single gradation you couldn't create using blends. Unfortunately, blends were much harder to create than gradations. So users were always asking for gradients.

Fortunately, Illustrator added gradient fills. In fact, Illustrator offers what is undoubtedly the finest automatic gradient fill function of any drawing program (as discussed in Chapter 15) and a blend tool that's simply unrivaled. Anytime you want to go beyond linear and radial gradations, the blend tool is at your beck and call.

When we discussed gradient fills back in Chapter 15, we saw there was no way to apply a shape to the change in colors. That's when you need the more sophisticated color changes found in blends. However, blends do more than just change colors. You can also use blends on groups of objects so that text changes from one set of words to another, and smiles turn to frowns. You can also set blends to follow path shapes—something gradations just can't do!

Blending is part duplication, part distribution, and part transformation. It creates a series of intermediate paths, called *steps*, between two selected free-form paths. We say that it's part duplication because the Blend command creates as many clones of a path as you like. It's part distribution because the steps are evenly distributed between the two original objects. And it's part transformation because Illustrator automatically adjusts the shape of each step depending on where it lies. Steps near the first of the two original paths resemble the first path; steps near the second path more closely resemble the second path.

Blending creates a metamorphic transition between one shape and another. For example, suppose that you create two paths, one that represents a man and one that represents a lycanthropic alter ego. By blending these two paths, you create several steps that represent metamorphic stages between the two life forms, as shown in Figure 18-1. The first intermediate path is shaped much like the man. Each intermediate path after that becomes less like the man and more like the wolf.

Figure 18-1: Blending between these extremes creates a series of transformed and distributed duplicates between the two objects.

Illustrator also blends the fills and strokes between two paths. If one path is white and the other is black, for example, the steps between the paths are filled with a fountain of transitional gray values. Though each step is filled with a solid color (assuming that you're blending objects with flat fills), the effect is that of a gradation. To create the steps shown in Figure 18-1, for example, Deke used opposite fill and stroke colors in each path. After he created the blend, he expanded the blends (discussed later), brought the wolfen to the front, and applied heavier strokes to both the man and wolfman.

Creating a Blend

To create a blend, you must first select two or more paths. You can blend between paths that are by themselves, part of groups, or even composite paths. (Selecting only a single path from a group or compound path forces the entire path to join in the blend.) Although it is possible to blend an open path to a closed path, the results are often rather ugly. Paths should be filled and stroked similarly.

 We've just discovered a nice new feature. You can now blend one object with a stroke to another object without a stroke. The stroke width will decrease in size from one object to another. In previous versions the stroke weight stayed constant between the objects.

To blend paths you can either let Illustrator automatically decide the best blending arrangement or you can choose which point you want to blend. To use Illustrator's blending instincts, select the paths and choose Object » Blends » Make, or press Cmd-Opt-B (Mac) or Ctrl-Alt-B (Windows) to create a series of steps. Illustrator treats the frontmost path of the originals as the first path in the blend and the rear path as the last path. The steps are layered between the first and last paths, descending in stacking order—one in back of another—as they approach the last. For a bit more control, click with the blend tool on one point in the first path and then click on a point in another path. In either case, Illustrator automatically combines original paths and steps into a grouped object that has special properties (which are discussed in later sections). This object is a blend. Alternatively, you can select one (and only one) point in each path. Selecting points allows you more control over the blend. If the paths are open, you must select an endpoint in each path. (See "Deciding Which Points to Select" later in this chapter.)

To create a simple blend, follow these steps:

1. **Specify the fill and stroke of the paths you want to blend.**

   Illustrator can blend any two colors, including gray values and spot colors. It can even blend gradations or a flat fill and a gradient. Illustrator can also blend strokes, line weights, line caps, joins, and dash patterns. It can even use brushes in blends!

    There is no limitation on blending with transparency features. Illustrator can also blend different opacity or blending mode settings. (See "Blending with Transparency" later in this chapter.)

2. Select the paths.

Illustrator can blend numerous paths at a time. In fact, your machine's RAM is the only limiting factor. For now, it's best to keep it simple and use only a few paths.

 Although Illustrator is not restricted to blending paths that have the same number of points, they do work best for blending. But if one path has more points than the other, you can even things out by selecting all points in one path and the same number of points in the other path. (See the upcoming section "Deciding Which Points to Select.")

3. Choose Object » Blend » Make...

Illustrator looks at the objects and blends between the points that will produce the smoothest possible blend between the selected paths.

...or click with the blend tool to specify the blend points.

If you don't like the results of the blend command, you can also specify the points that you want to blend between. Using the blend tool, click one point in each selected path. First click one point, and then click another. Then click the points in any additional objects. If you miss a point, Illustrator tries its best to guess which point you were going after.

 To create a smooth blend, click similar points in the paths. In Figure 18-2, for example, we clicked the lower left point on the outside cone and then the lower left point on the inside cone. (See the section "Deciding Where to Click" later in this chapter for more info.)

 Although Adobe denies they made any changes in the blend command between version 8 and 9, we've seen dramatic improvement in how smooth the blends are when using the blend command. In the past we had to use the blend tool to choose the blend points manually. With Illustrator 9, we use the blend tool only when we're trying to create non-smooth blends or a special effect.

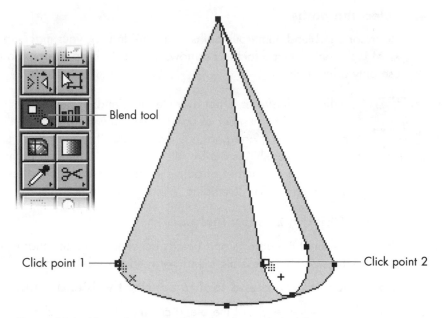

Click point 1

Blend tool

Click point 2

Figure 18-2: After selecting the blend tool, we clicked the
lower left point in each of two selected shapes. We could
also have simply chosen Object » Blend » Make.

4.   Specify the blend spacing.

Choose Object » Blend » Blend Options. The Blend Options dialog
box will display, as shown in Figure 18-3. By default, Illustrator uses
the smooth color spacing scheme to decide how many intermediate
paths are needed to produce the best blend.

If you find that Illustrator has not added enough steps, or if Illustrator
has included more steps than you think are necessary, you can change
the number of steps by choosing either the Specified Steps or the
Specified Distance from the Spacing pop-up menu. Deciding how
many steps to use can be a difficult proposition. (For a technical
evaluation of steps, with some numerical recommendations, read the
section "Deciding the Number of Steps" later in this chapter.)

You can also open the Blend Options dialog box by holding
the Opt/Alt key as you click on the path with the blend tool.
Or double-click the blend tool in the Toolbox.

Figure 18-3: The Blend Options dialog box lets you choose the number of steps that make up your blend.

5. Change the Orientation.

...Only if you want to, that is. The orientation of the blend steps is limited to either aligning to the page or aligning to the path. Figure 18-4 shows the difference.

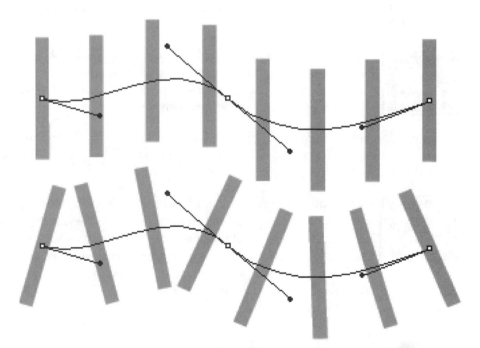

Figure 18-4: The example on the top is the standard Align to Page orientation that Illustrator applies by default. With the Align to Path icon selected (bottom), the blend objects curve around with the path.

Forcing Blend Transitions

As we said a moment ago, Illustrator has gotten very good at automatically creating smooth blends. Blends that were messed up by previous versions of the program are created perfectly today using Objects » Blend »Make. (How do we know? Well, we have the artwork from the previous versions of this book. We simply applied the blend command to the exact same artwork using the current version of Illustrator. The differences were obvious.) However, there may be times when you want to override Illustrator's choices to create your own blend transitions. This lets you create special blend effects.

Using the blend tool can force Illustrator to use your own blend transitions. The click points tell Illustrator the locations of the first pair of points it should blend. The program then wanders around the shapes in a clockwise direction and pairs up the other points. Figure 18-5 shows the results of blending two concentric five-pointed stars after clicking on different points in the two shapes. We always clicked on the lower right point in the small star, but we clicked on a total of six different points in the larger star. As you can see, this has a profound effect on how the blend progresses.

Each small star in Figure 18-5 was originally filled with white. We changed the fills to None after blending the shapes to permit you to see the steps in back, some of which were covered up when the star was white.

Though many of the effects in Figure 18-5 are interesting, only the first four are suitable for creating gradations, as demonstrated in Figure 18-6. And even then, the third and fourth examples have rather harsh edges.

Years ago, we used to force transitions in blends by first selecting only certain points on each path with the direct selection tool. We would then use the blend tool on two of those selected points. However, given the improvements in the blend command, we don't find too many situations where we have to resort to those solutions.

Figure 18-5: The small black dots show the points where we clicked each pair of stars with the blend tool.

Figure 18-6: Here we used the same click points used for Figure 18-5, but we got rid of the strokes and increased the number of steps to 88 per blend.

Recognizing When You Need More Points

Although it may seem unfair, you can still end up with harsh edges after taking the precautions of selecting an equal number of points in both shapes and clicking similar points. Consider the first example in Figure 18-7. Both shapes contain four points (all selected), and we clicked the lowest point in each shape. And yet, as the second example shows, we ended up with harsh edges. The top and bottom of the white shape look like they're thrusting forward from the dark ellipse. No, no, no, we simply cannot have this!

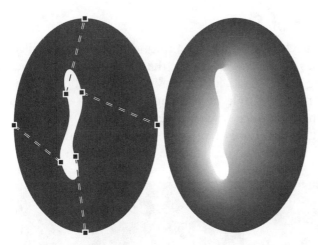

Figure 18-7:
If you can't draw straight lines
between the paired points in
your shapes without running
over segments (left), you'll end
up with harsh edges in your
final blend (right).

The problem is that two of the paired points in the two shapes aren't properly aligned. That is, if a crow were to fly from one point to another, it would smack into a segment. The dashed lines in Figure 18-7 show the flight of this imaginary crow. Notice how the bird would collide with the segments. These intersections are precisely the areas where our problems occur.

The solution is to add more points. If you add a point to every segment in each shape, you can ensure that all points are in line. Use the add point tool to add the points to either path. The left example in Figure 18-8 shows how we added points to both paths. The blend on the right side shows a silky smooth gradation.

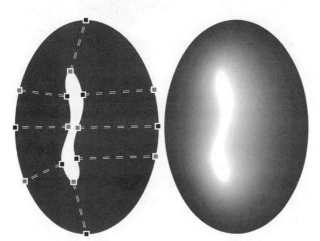

Figure 18-8:
When we add points to paths
(shown in gray) all straight lines
drawn between the paired points
are unobstructed (left). This
ensures a fluid gradation (right).

Deciding the Number of Steps

Another problem that plagues blends is a pesky printing phenomenon called *banding*. Rather than printing as a seamless gradation, the blend exhibits distinct bands of color. When banding occurs, gradient credibility goes out the window. Figure 18-9 offers an exaggerated example of banding. In the first blend, we created 1 step, hardly enough to produce smooth shading. You can see almost every step in the shape, resulting in lots of bands. The second blend is much smoother, but it also contains 12 steps.

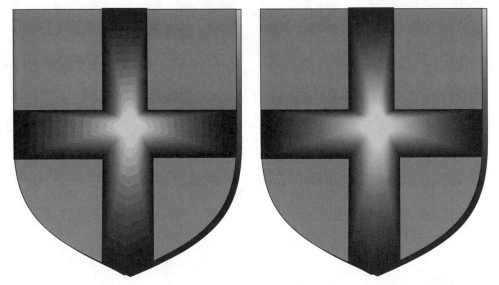

Figure 18-9: A blend with banding (left) and one with seamless color transitions (right).

Unfortunately, although using very few steps practically guarantees banding, having lots of steps doesn't necessarily prevent it. You have to print enough steps to take advantage of your printer's ability to generate gray values, but not so many that one or more steps appear out of sync with their neighbors. In an ideal blend, each printed step corresponds to a unique gray value and varies from its neighbors by a consistent amount. Illustrator creates unique, consistent steps automatically, no matter how many steps you assign, but this doesn't mean they'll necessarily print correctly. It all hinges on the answers to two questions:

- Is the printer properly calibrated?

- What is the resolution and screen frequency of the printer?

You can't anticipate bad calibration. You just have to hope that your service bureau or commercial printer has its machinery in top condition. But you can account for resolution and screen frequency. Very briefly—we'll cover both topics in more detail in Chapter 21—resolution is the number of pixels the printer can print per inch (just like screen resolution). And screen frequency is the number of halftone dots that print per inch. Printer resolution is measured in dots per inch (dpi), and screen frequency is measured in lines per inch (lpi). The resolution is fixed, but the screen frequency can change. For example, a typical LaserWriter prints at 300–600 dpi, but the lpi can be set to 60 or 53.

If you print a 60-lpi screen from a 300-dpi LaserWriter, each halftone dot measures 5 pixels wide by 5 pixels tall. (That's because $300 \div 60 = 5$.) And a 5-by-5 dot contains a total of 25 pixels. If all pixels are turned off, the halftone dot is white. All pixels turned on produces black, and turning on 1 to 24 pixels produces a shade of gray. Including black and white, that's a total of 26 gray values, which is the absolute maximum number of shades a 300 dpi, 60 lpi LaserWriter can print.

That's just one example. Printers vary from model to model. But if you know the dpi and lpi values, you can calculate the number of printable gray values using this formula:

$$(dpi \div lpi)^2 + 1$$

Take a top-of-the-line Linotronic imagesetter, for example. The resolution is 2540 dpi, and the default screen frequency is 133 lpi. When you divide 2540 by 133, you get 19.097. Then you multiply 19.097 by itself and add 1 to get 365 gray values, quite a few more than the LaserWriter.

Since we hate to make you do too much math, here are the maximum number of gray values associated with a few popular resolutions and screen frequencies:

Resolution	Screen frequency	Maximum shades of gray
300	53	33
300	60	26
600	60	101
600	75	65
1200	75	256
1200	90	179
1200	120	101
1200	133	82
1270	75	256
1270	90	200
1270	120	113
1270	133	92
2400	up to 150	256
2540	up to 150	256

Working "Live"

Live!—from San Jose, California—it's *Illustrator's Live Blends!* Although we've had Illustrator's live blends feature for a while now, the concept is so dramatic Sandee is still carrying on about it. Once you've made a blend, you can easily edit the objects in the blend. The blend then redraws right in front of your eyes.

If you use the regular selection tool, you will select all the objects in the blend. So you can use the direct selection tool to select individual points and objects in the blend. Once you have selected an object within a blend, you can change its fill or stroke attributes, move points, use the transformation tools, or even add points using the add point tool. Figure 18-10 shows how the blend redraws each time you release the mouse button.

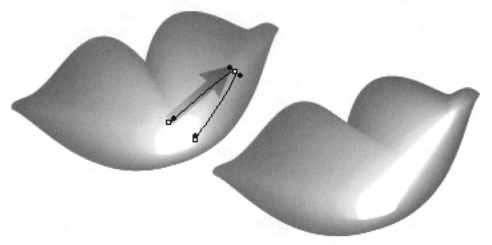

Figure 18-10: Use the direct selection tool to select and modify objects within a blend.

Modifying the Spine

When you first create a blend, the in-between steps are arranged in a straight line from one object to another. This straight line, shown in Figure 18-11, is called the *spine*. When you first create a blend, the spine has one point for each object in the blend. So a blend between two objects in a path has only two points—a beginning and an end. However, you can use any of the point tools to add or change the handles of the points of the spine.

Manipulating the spine can be a hassle. Fortunately, you can simply replace the spine with any other path—open or closed. This allows you to create much more interesting blends. Figure 18-12 shows how a simple blend between three circles can be transformed into a bouncing ball by replacing the spine. Here are the steps for replacing a spine with another path.

Figure 18-11: The blend spine is the straight line that connects the original blend objects.

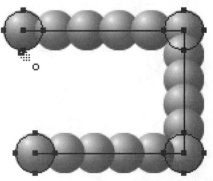

Figure 18-12:
The small circle next to the blend tool cursor indicates that the blend will be closed. A closed blend creates intermediate steps between the last and first points.

1. Create the blend

If you want the blend to wrap around a closed path so that the blend fills all the spaces in the path, you need to create a closed blend using the blend tool. A small circle appears next to the blend tool, as seen in Figure 18-12. This indicates that the blend will be closed.

2. Draw the object that is to become the spine.

The new spine can be open or closed. Don't worry about the fill or stroke attributes. These will be deleted as soon as the object becomes the spine.

3. Select the blend and the spine.

The spine can be positioned anywhere. Illustrator knows that the object that doesn't have a blend on it is the one you want to be the spine.

Only one object can be a spine for a blend. If you select more than one object as a spine, Illustrator doesn't allow you to choose the Replace Spine command.

4. Choose Objects » Blend » Replace Spine.

Replace Spine is not the best term. What happens is that the objects in the blend jump from their original spine onto the new object. And then the original spine is deleted. Figure 18-13 shows the results of replacing a plain spine with an ellipse.

 Once you replace a spine, you can still use the direct selection tool to select the spine and modify its shape. The live blend redraws each time you release the mouse.

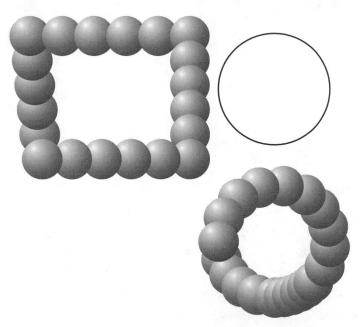

Figure 18-13: The closed blend in a rectangular shape was replaced by an ellipse using the Replace Spine command.

As soon as you create a blend, you may discover that the redraw time on your document slows down to a horrible crawl. The problem is that the Knockout Group option is automatically assigned to all blends. Without the Knockout Group turned on, the screen redraw speeds up dramatically. Unfortunately, there is no way to turn this off before you create a blend. So what you have to do is manually target the blend in the Layers or Appearance palettes and then turn off the Knockout Group option—over and over—every time you make a blend. For most situations you don't need the Knockout Group turned on. The only time it becomes important is if you want to apply opacity or blending modes to the elements in the blend. Check the Adobe Web site for any updates that may fix this situation.

Reversing Blends

Once you've created a blend, you can then play around with the order of the objects. If you select the blend, you can choose Objects » Blend » Reverse Spine. This flips the position of the objects along the spine so that the objects that were at the end now start the blend and the objects that started the blend are now at the end. The stacking order of the objects—from front to back— is not changed. You can also choose Objects » Blend » Reverse Front to Back. This keeps the objects in their same position on the spine, but changes the stacking order. The objects that were in front of the others are sent to the back and the objects that were in the back are sent to the front. Figure 18-14 shows the effects of applying these commands to a blend.

Expanding and Releasing Blends

The intermediate steps of a blend are virtual objects. They're visible, but you can't select or manipulate them. The only objects you can select are the original objects used to create the blend. If you want to work with the intermediate steps, you need to select the blend and choose Objects » Blend » Expand. This turns the virtual objects into real ones. The objects in the expanded blend are automatically grouped.

Releasing a blend deletes the intermediate steps and removes the original objects from the spine. However, it also leaves the spine on the artboard. We consider this careless housekeeping. We constantly have to throw away spines cluttering up our documents.

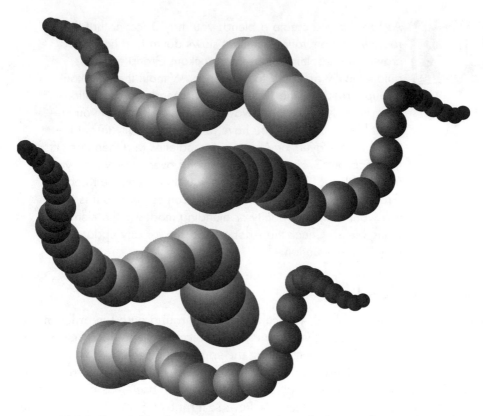

Figure 18-14: The top blend was altered by applying the Reverse Spine command in the second example, the Reverse Front to Back in the third example, and both Reverse Spine and Reverse Front to Back in the fourth example.

Cool Blend Tool Tricks

We've droned on about the blend tool for quite a while now, but we haven't even begun to tell you all the great things you can do with it. Though we can't share every blend tool and custom gradation trick we've invented or gleaned over the years, we will suggest a handful of what we consider to be the most interesting tips and tricks in the following sections. With any luck, they'll inspire you to develop more sophisticated techniques of your own.

Morphing Path Outlines

In addition to generating custom gradations, the blend tool is a shape-modification tool. Much like the Pathfinder filters, you can use the tool to take two paths and combine them into a third. This technique is known as *morphing*.

In Figure 18-15, we took a series of shapes and morphed between them. We then replaced the spine with a spiral. Finally, we added a drop shadow to the blend. But we should warn you, it's not quite as easy as it looks. Deke had to spend a few minutes on each pair of original paths, making sure the two had the same number of points. For example, the pair of stars in the first column each have 20 points, even though the top star has half as many spikes as the bottom one. The circle and star in the second column each have 16 points, and so on. Deke inserted most of the points with Object » Path » Add Anchor Points, but had to add a few manually with the add point tool.

Figure 18-15: A series of morphings in a blend with a spiral spine attached to it. The original objects are in gray.

You can also use the blend tool to morph type converted to path outlines. In Figure 18-16, we started with a small line of Times Roman and a larger line in Adobe Garamond Bold Italic. We applied a 0-point weight stroke to the Times text and a 1-point weight to the Garamond. Finally, we applied a very small drop shadow at almost no blur and no offset to the Times text, whereas we applied a drop shadow with a larger blur and larger offset to the Garamond text. The result is the declaration to Live as it changes shape, size, color, and stroke. The change in the position of the drop shadow also makes the text seem to jump off the page.

 If all this seems like it would be great if it were animated, have patience. As soon as we get to the next chapter we'll show you how to turn this into quick and easy Web animations.

Figure 18-16: This text was blended from the stuffy Times to the exuberant Adobe Garamond Bold Italic.

Now as long as you've got your animation (brain) cells working, here's another thought to remember. Illustrator can blend between any groups or compound paths. (In olden days blending could be done only between single objects.) Figure 18-17 shows one of the uses of this feature. This putty-like character can change his position, size, and even the shape of his mouth simply by grouping him and blending. However, in order to avoid distorting the intermediate steps beyond recognition, you have to have *exactly* the same number of objects in each group, and the stacking order for the objects must be *exactly* the same. That is, if the left eye is fourth from the top in the first object, make sure it is in the exact same place in the second object.

 One way to make sure these groups have exactly the same number of objects in exactly the same order is to simply duplicate the original object and then make any adjustments to the duplicate. But you can also use the thumbnails in the layers palette to visually place each object in the correct stacking order.

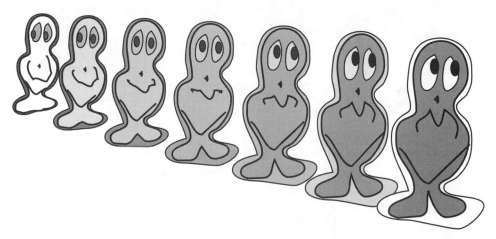

Figure 18-17: This little man went from happy to guilty simply by grouping the two end looks and blending between them.

Finally, you may not like the distance between the intermediate steps along the path. We've always felt that Illustrator was missing a way to control the speed of the blend—that is the distance between the intermediate steps. However, Deke recently received the following tip from Derek Mah who wrote regarding one of Deke's articles in *Macworld* magazine. "To control the speed of the blend, create the blend and set the number of blend steps as you normally would do. This creates the blend spine which is editable just like any other Illustrator object. Using the convert direction point tool, pull out control handles from the anchor point at each end of the blend spine. By extending or shortening these control handles along the spine, the speed of the blend is controlled. This is very similar to the way in which blend speeds are controlled in the gradient mesh." Figure 18-18 shows this technique in action. Way to go, Derek!

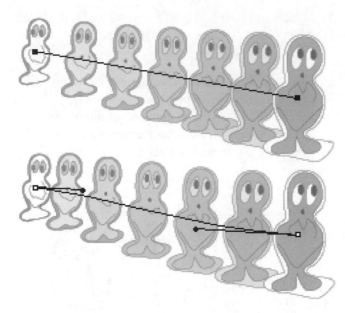

Figure 18-18:
Changing the spine
anchor points to curved
points allows you to adjust
the handles to change the
distance between objects
in a blend.

Creating Contours and Highlights

You know you've earned your blend tool black belt when you can successfully tackle multi-color gradations. By creating a series of colored shapes and blending between them in succession, you can create photo-realistic graphics with sharp outlines and exact edges, the Holy Grail of commercial artwork.

Figure 18-19 shows an example of the techniques used to create contours and highlights. The cat's eye started with eight simple shapes.

The three large shapes in the back are blended together to create the contours of the eye. A lazy illustrator (no, not *you!*) would try to use a radial gradient to give the orb its shape. But the slight concave appearance of the top shape used in a blend gives the eyeball a much more realistic appearance.

The small highlight in the pupil was easy. We simply blended a small white oval with no stroke into a larger one filled with a dark gray. (The white stroke you see in the illustration is there just so you can see where the object is.) Because this highlight was against a single color, we didn't have to do anything special.

Because the white highlights at the top of the eyeball covered two different colors, we had a dilemma as to what color to blend to. Fortunately you can also blend opacity changes. So we simply blended between a white object at 100 percent opacity and another white object at 0 percent opacity. This allowed the blend to blend to a transparent edge. However, we felt the highlight was a little too bright. So we targeted the entire blend and lowered the opacity to 70 percent. (We probably could have played with the feather effect on a single object, but then we wouldn't have been able to tell you about blending to transparency.)

Figure 18-19: A photo-realistic illustration with three blends. The elements below the eye show the progression of the blends.

Blending Strokes

Back when we began this chapter, we mentioned that the blend tool varies two stroke attributes—color and line weight. This last fact is very important because it means that you can blend a thick stroke with a thin one to create a softened edge.

Figure 18-20 demonstrates one of the common stroke-blending effects, the old neon text trick. We started by converting some text to paths, and splitting and joining the letters with the scissors tool and Join command to combine all letters into a single, open path. (After all, in a real neon sign, one tube forms all the letters.) We assigned the line an 8-point black stroke. Then we cloned the line, nudged it upward a couple of points, and gave it a 0.5-point white stroke. The result appears at the top of Figure 18-20.

Although nudging the top path is mostly for effect, it's necessary if you want to blend via the blend tool. If one path exactly overlaps the other, you can't click the back path with the blend tool. Even when the paths are a couple of points apart, you'll probably need to zoom in to a very magnified view size (say, 400 percent or more) before you can click the points.

After setting up the paths, we used the blend command to create the blend. We specified 14 steps, enough to ensure that each step changed by exactly 0.5 point. The second example in Figure 18-20 shows the result.

You don't need many steps when working with strokes because the distances are so small. A line weight variation of 0.5 point means that you can see only about 0.25 point of color around each side of the stroke. (With the strokes offset, the color bands may be as wide as 0.3 point, but that's about the maximum.) To ensure a 0.5-point line weight variation between your steps, use this simple formula. Of the two strokes you want to blend, subtract the thinner line weight from the thicker one. Then multiply that number by 2 and subtract 1. For example, we subtracted 0.5 from 8 to get 7.5. Multiplying that number by 2 produced 15, and subtracting 1 gave us 14. For the record, the line weights of these 14 steps are 1, 1.5, 2, 2.5, 3, 3.5, 4, 4.5, 5, 5.5, 6, 6.5, 7, and 7.5. You can't go wrong.

To create the glow in the last example in Figure 18-20, we first copied the rear path. Then we hid the neon letters (Object » Hide Selection) to get them out of our way, pasted the path in back, and changed the stroke to 12-point white. To create the blend-to path, we pasted to the back again, nudged the pasted path up 2 points, and changed its stroke to 24-point black. Then we blended between the two paths with the blend tool. (To calculate the number of steps, we subtracted 12 from 24 to get 12; multiplied that by 2 and subtracted 1 to get 23.) To make the background black, we drew a black rectangle behind the whole thing. And we chose Object » Show All to bring the neon letters back from hiding.

Notice that the strokes in Figure 18-20 have round joins. Round joins invariably blend best because they smooth out the transitions at the corner points. Miter and bevel joins result in harsh corners that rarely benefit a gradation.

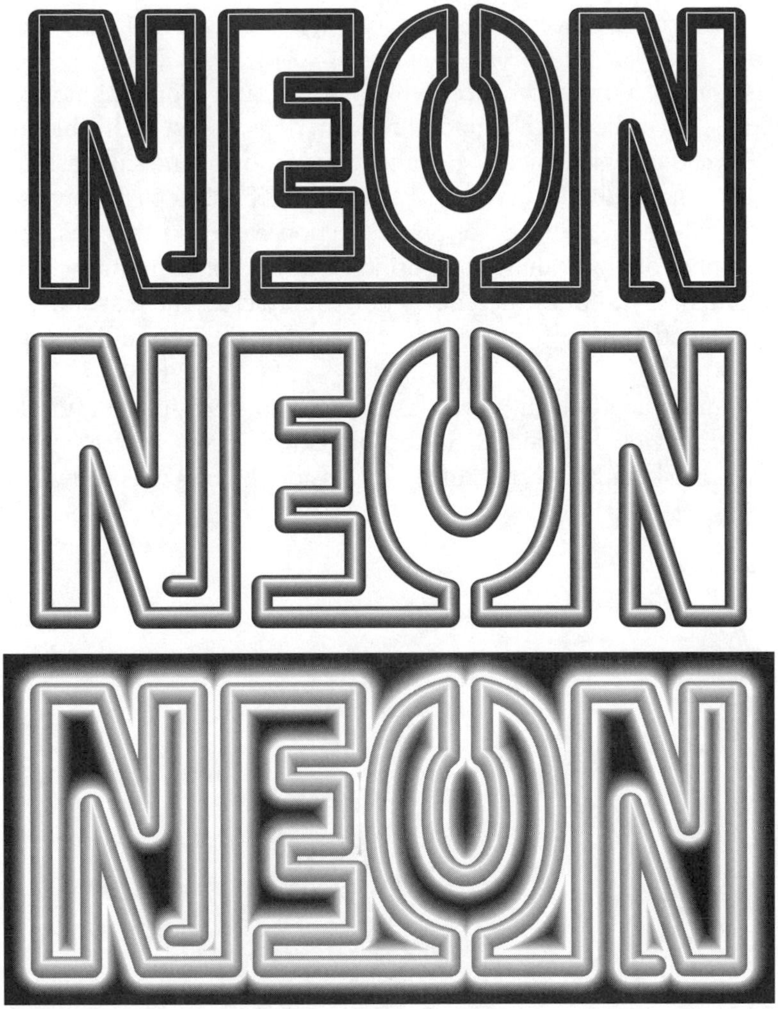

Figure 18-20: Here we've taken two stroked paths (top) and blended between them to create a neon effect (middle). Then we blended between a 12-point white stroke and a 24-point black one to create the glow (bottom).

Editing a Gradient Fill

Now that we've told you nearly everything there is to know about blends, we'd like to share one more little secret. Every gradient fill in Illustrator is actually a blend. That's right, Illustrator calculates each color in a gradient fill as a separate step in a blend. It hides the details from you to keep things tidy. But as far as

Illustrator and the printer are concerned, gradations and blends are all variations on the same theme.

Illustrator gives you the power to tear down the walls. At a moment's notice, you can convert any object filled with a gradation to an object filled with a blend. Just select the object and choose Object » Expand. An alert box comes up, asking you how many steps you would like to create. For the number of steps, follow our advice from the "Deciding the Number of Steps" section earlier in this chapter. That is, take the number of gray values your printer can print and multiply it by the percentage color range. Just one difference—don't subtract 2. The first and last colors are part of the gradation, so you don't want to delete them from the Steps value.

When you expand a gradation, Illustrator converts it to steps inside a mask. The shape that was previously filled with the gradation serves as the mask. Illustrator selects the mask and all rectangular steps inside the mask, as shown in the right half of Figure 18-21.

Figure 18-21: When the roughen effect is applied to a gradient fill, it roughens the entire fill. But when the gradient is converted into discrete objects, the roughen effect creates a much more organic texture.

If you want to simplify the mask into a series of cropped steps, choose Object » Clipping Mask » Release, and then click the Crop icon in the Pathfinder palette. That's all it takes. You lose the flexibility of a mask—which we'll describe at length in the next section—but cropped steps are tidier on the screen and you can be sure the steps will print.

One of our favorite reasons to convert a gradient into steps is to then apply some other effect. For instance, in Figure 18-21 we applied the roughen effect to the gradient fill. The roughen effect applied to a gradient can only change the shape of the gradient as a whole. However, when we expand the gradient, the roughen effect is applied to each of the intermediate steps, which creates a paper-like texture.

Masking: Filling Objects with Objects

Mask is the term used in graphics software for an object that is used as the boundary for others. You can see other objects inside the mask, but not outside it. In addition to opacity masks which we covered in Chapter 17, there are two other types of masks: Clipping masks are vector-based objects (no images allowed) that can be applied to any number of objects, but only within one layer. Layers masks are clipping masks that are applied to an entire layer. They hide all the objects on that layer and any layers nested within the layer.

 Layer masks are new to Illustrator 9. Clipping masks are the new term for what were simply called masks in previous versions.

 The word mask always reminds us of costume parties where you can only see people's faces outside the mask—exactly the opposite of the function in Illustrator. A better image is masking tape. You use the tape to hide a certain area from being painted. Anything inside the boundary of the masking tape is visible; anything outside is not.

Creating a Clipping Mask

Clipping masks are applied to specific elements within a layer. This means that some objects within the layer may not be visible while others are. Clipping masks are created as follows:

1. Move the mask object to front.

Select the path you want to fill with other objects, and bring it to front. A mask must be in front of its content elements, as seen in the left example of Figure 18-22.

2. Select the path and all objects that you want to put inside it, and choose Object » Clipping Mask » Make.

If you select objects inside different groups, compound paths, or masks, Illustrator will complain. It's not that you can't have groups within a mask, you just can't have portions of a group within a mask. So it's best to select the objects with the arrow tool prior to choosing the command. If you have applied any fill or stroke attributes to the clipping mask object, you will lose those attributes, as shown in the middle example of Figure 18-22. Don't panic. You'll get them back in the next step.

 In the past we recommended that you group the mask and the elements. Illustrator now does that automatically for you.

Figure 18-22: The three steps in creating a clipping mask (from left to right): positioning the objects; making the mask, adding fill and stroke attributes to the mask.

3. Select the clipping mask and reapply any fill or stroke settings.

You need to reselect the clipping mask object and apply any fill or stroke settings you desire, as we've done in the right example of Figure 18-22. Yes, it's an inconvenience; however, considering that for many years you couldn't apply fills or strokes to clipping mask objects, it's one that we can live with.

Setting a Clipping Mask for a Layer

Layer masks allow you to mask all objects in a layer. This means that any objects on the layer will be masked, no matter when they were created. And they can be positioned above or below the layer mask object. Layer masks are created as follows:

1. Move the mask object to front.

Although a layer mask can be anywhere in a layer, you need to position it at the top of the layer when you first make the layer mask. (Or Illustrator won't know what object should be the layer mask.)

 You can use compound paths as either layer masks or clipping masks. However, be aware that you're compounding the amount of calculations that Illustrator has to make to print your file. So you may want to crop the image before you go to print. (See the heading "Cropping a Mask" later in this chapter.)

2. Select the layer in the Layers palette.

This means clicking the name of the layer in the Layers palette. If you have a path selected, you will not be able to make the layer mask.

3. Click the Make/Release Clipping Mask icon...

...or choose Make Clipping Mask from the Layers palette menu shown in Figure 18-23. The object that is the layer mask is listed in the Layers palette as *clipping path*. An underline indicates that it is a masking element.

 At the moment there is a nasty bug in Illustrator 9 regarding layer masks. If you add fill or stroke attributes to the layer mask, they will be expanded into separate objects the next time you open the file. We are very hopeful that Adobe will fix this problem with an update to Illustrator 9. You will then be able to apply a fill or stroke to a layer mask. Until then, we recommend you apply fill and stroke attributes only to clipping masks.

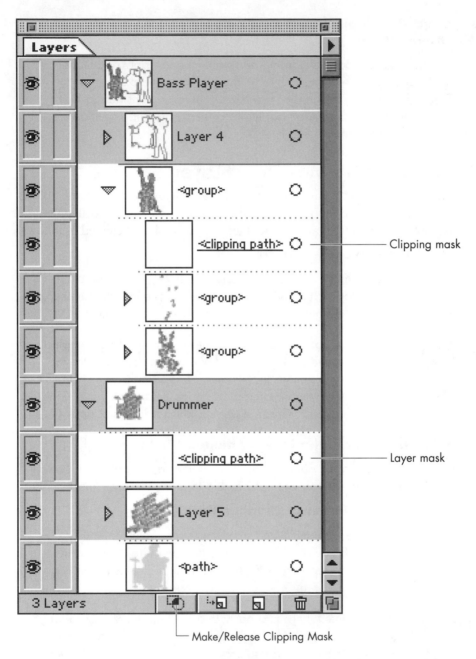

Figure 18-23: Although they are both listed as clipping path in the Layers palette, you can identify the clipping mask because it is within a group. The layer mask is loose within its layer.

Editing Masked Elements

One of primary advantages to working with masks is that the objects that have been masked are still live in your file. If you switch to the outline mode, you can see them hanging around outside the mask. This means you can move the objects in and out of the mask without any trouble. Now you see 'em; now you don't. However, you should be aware that elements that are outside the mask still contribute to the file size and printer processing time. If you've got a map of the United States and you've masked everything except the area around the small town of Gridley, Illinois (population 1,300), you should consider deleting those elements that you don't need.

Because objects in a clipping mask are automatically grouped, you need to use the direct selection tool to select individual points. Hold the Opt/Alt key to select entire objects. However, one of the advantages to working with layer masks is that because they are not grouped, you can select objects individually using the selection tool as shown in Figure 18-24.

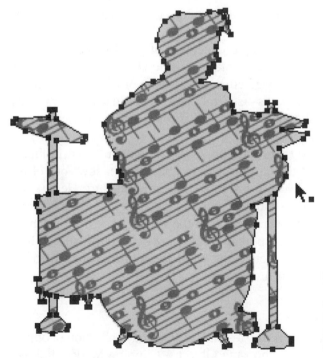

Figure 18-24:
The arrow tool has no problem selecting just the path used as a layer mask. However, we would need the direct selection tool if this were a clipping mask.

You can also add elements to a mask. If the mask is a layer mask, simply add an object to the layer. If the mask is a clipping mask, simply drag the object into the group that contains the clipping mask in the layers palette. You can also use the Paste In Front and Paste In Back commands to introduce additional elements to a clipping mask. Simply position the object where you would like it to be; then cut it to the clipboard. Next, select an object in the group and choose Paste in Front or Paste In Back. This adds the object to the group and causes it to be masked.

Cropping a Mask

Live editing ability is the primary factor that distinguishes clipping paths from the somewhat similar Crop filter (of the Pathfinder palette fame). In both cases, the front path clips all the selected paths behind it (or in the case of layer masks, all the objects on that layer). If you were to apply the two to identical collections of filled paths, the results would even look the same.

But where masking permits changes, cropping does permanent damage. Masking hides portions of content elements that extend outside the mask; cropping deletes them. Also worth noting, the Crop command deletes strokes and is not applicable to text or imported images. Masking, meanwhile, can accommodate any kind of object.

But where cropping results in a simple collection of filled objects, masking requires more work on the part of the printer. (By printer we mean the output device such as the laser printer or imagesetter that actually prints the file.) Masks take longer to print than cropped paths—several times longer in some cases—and a sufficiently complicated mask that contains lots of complex objects can prevent your illustration from printing.

So use masks when you need them and apply Crop when you don't. In Figure 18-25, for example, Deke used the Crop filter to stencil the shadows out of the arms, neck, face, and ears. But he used masks for the hair and shirt. He retained the mask for the shirt because he wanted to preserve the ability to edit the planes later. And he used a mask for the hair because of the white stroke from the head that extends up into the hair. The Crop filter would have deleted this stroke. If he had reapplied it, he wouldn't have gotten the white head line to align with the black head line precisely at the hair line.

Disassembling a Mask

You can turn a clipping mask back into a standard, everyday collection of objects by selecting the clipping path and choosing Object » Clipping Mask » Release. Illustrator will also ungroup the objects. (How very thoughtful.) If your mask was a layer mask, select the layer in the Layers palette, and then click the Make/Release Clipping Mask icon or choose Release Clipping Mask from the Layers palette menu.

Figure 18-25: The shirt and hair were created using masking.
However, the other stenciled shapes were modified permanently
using the Pathfinder Crop command.

Hatching Textures

This chapter concludes with the Pen and Ink Hatch Effects filter (Sandee's favorite). This unusual and exceptionally complex filter combines the powers of blending and masking to create cross-hatch, line, and dot patterns. Unlike tile patterns, Pen and Ink patterns can change over the course of the shape, becoming progressively lighter and darker like gradations. You need a strong will to put up with the Pen and Ink Hatch Effects dialog box—easily the most daunting collection of options inside all of Illustrator—but your labor will not go unrewarded.

A bit of history: The Hatch Effects filter was originally called the Ink Pen filter and was introduced in Illustrator 6. Those of us who fell in love with the Ink Pen filter still call it by that name. Pen and Ink is the overall category that contains the Hatch Effects and Photo Crosshatch filters. We covered the Photo Crosshatch filter back in Chapter 13 when we looked at raster images. This seems like a good time to cover the Hatch Effects filter.

The Hatch Effects filter lets you take a simple object called a *hatch* and repeat it over and over inside a path at different sizes, angles, and densities. In principle, it's the same thing as defining a custom halftone pattern. Instead of printing little round halftone dots, you print little crosses, straight lines, or squiggles.

Figure 18-26 shows a silhouette filled with thousands of tiny objects. The objects are the hatches. We've pull one out to the side for you to see. The Hatch Effects filter can create the look of custom half-tone screens, woodcuts, stippling, and other traditional media effects.

Figure 18-26:
A silhouette filled with a Hatch Effect. The small object outside the horn is the hatch used to fill the silhouette.

Filling a Path with a Hatch

Although the full depth of the Hatch Effects could take volumes to adequately cover, it is actually very simple to apply the filter.

1. Select the path you want to fill with a hatch effect.

It has to be a path. No text blocks or imported images allowed.

 If you want the hatches to match a certain color or gradation, assign that color or gradation to the path from the appropriate palette.

2. Choose Filter » Pen and Ink » Hatch Effects.

Illustrator displays the massive dialog box shown in Figure 18-27. Isn't that something? When we first saw it, we both groaned audibly. But having spent some quality time with it, we now look on it as an old friend—a ridiculously fussy, outrageously inflated, exasperatingly difficult old friend.

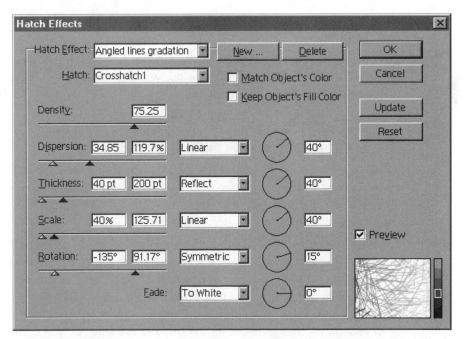

Figure 18-27: Although it contains more options than just about every other dialog box in Illustrator put together, the Hatch Effects dialog box is well organized and exceedingly capable.

3. **Choose one of the preset effects from the Hatch Effect pop-up list.**

    Illustrator provides you with a wealth of choices of natural media appearances such as crosshatching, or stippling. It also has appearances such as fiberglass, woodgrain, and grass. (The Hatch pop-up list lets you change the objects used in the fill. We'll cover using this list in the section "Designing Custom Hatch Effects.")

4. **Click Preview to see a small sample of what the preset will look like.**

    This preview is only what the effect would look like if it were applied to a path the same size as the rectangle in the dialog box. It doesn't show how the effect will look when applied to your path. Unfortunately there is no way to preview the effect in your selected path. This is why the undo command (Cmd/Ctrl-Z) is very important when using Hatch Effects. You apply the filter; look at the results; undo the filter; then reset the filter; and look at the results—over and over till you get what you want. (This is one of the reasons why very few people bother to use Hatch Effects.)

5. **Use the Color and Fade options to change the color of the hatches.**

    If you want to change the color of the hatches to match the colors in the selected path in the illustration window, select the Match Object's Color check box. In the first example in Figure 18-28, we applied the Match Object's Color option to an object filled with a gradation. Illustrator used the colors from the gradation to fill the individual hatches along the same angle as the original gradient.

    To place the hatches in front of the fill assigned to the selected path, select the Keep Object's Fill Color option. In the second example in Figure 18-28, we selected the Keep Object's Fill Color option to keep the original gradation in the background.

    You can also choose to fade the colors of the hatches to white or to black by selecting options from the Fade pop-up menu. For example, assigning the To White option to a bunch of black hatches creates a black-to-white gradation. You can set the angle of the gradation using the Fade Angle value. A fourth option, Use Gradient, matches the colors of the hatches to the gradient fill assigned to the selected path. This option produces the very same effect demonstrated in the first example in Figure 18-28, except that you can modify the angle of the gradation using the Fade Angle option.

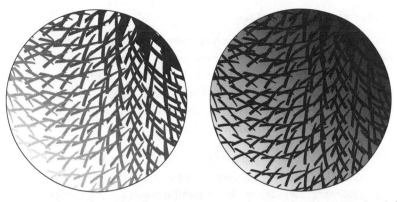

Figure 18-28: Paths filled with hatches using the Match Object's Color (left) and Keep Object's Fill Color (right) options.

6. **Click OK to apply the Hatch Effect.**

    Illustrator closes the Hatch Effects dialog box and returns you to your document. Don't be confused if all you see is a solid mass of color. What you are looking at are hundreds—maybe thousands—of selected anchor points. Deselect the artwork to see the effect applied to your artwork.

 You can also choose Hide Edges to hide the selected anchor points. This lets you see the selected artwork without all those anchor points in the way.

As we mentioned before, Illustrator converts the selected path in the illustration window to a mask and fills it with hatch objects. The mask and its contents are automatically grouped. Each hatch is a separate path, so you can edit it with the direct selection tool (among others). And if you prefer to crop the hatches into independent paths that are easier to print, click the Pathfinder palette's Crop button.

Creating a Custom Hatch

Using the presets is the quick and easy way to fill an object with a hatch, but it hardly satisfies your own creative juices. Fortunately you can make your own hatches and then use the myriad of sliders and wheels to adjust them to your exact specifications. To create a hatch, follow these steps:

1. **Draw a few simple objects.**

    Keep them very simple. The best hatches contain anywhere from 2
    to 20 anchor points and only one to three paths. After all, simple
    objects mean faster and more reliable printing. This is one time when
    you want to leave the razzle-dazzle to Illustrator. In Figure 18-29,
    we've drawn an X using a minimal 12 points—which is more compli-
    cated than any of Illustrator's predefined hatches.

    You won't be able to use compound paths as a hatch,
    because the filter will separate the two portions of the
    compound. However, we have been able to create circles
    with holes in them by using the knife tool to cut a line from
    the inside of the hole to the outside of the circle. This makes
    a single object out of a compound path.

2. **Assign fills and strokes to the objects as desired.**

    Whatever fill color you use will show up when you apply the hatch
    pattern to a path using Filter » Pen and Ink » Hatch Effects. But don't
    get too hung up on it; you can always override the fill color so you
    might as well just use black.

    Stroke is more important than fill color. It doesn't matter
    particularly what color or line weight you use, just whether
    or not you assign a stroke. If you do, you'll be able to tell
    Illustrator to vary the thickness of the stroke over the course
    of the mask. If you set the stroke to None, you won't be able
    to vary the thickness, but the final effect will print a little faster.

3. **Choose Filter » Pen and Ink » New Hatch.**

    The prospective hatch objects should be selected when you choose
    this filter. The New Hatch dialog box comes up on screen, looking
    something like Figure 18-29.

4. **Click the New button.**

    Illustrator asks you to name the hatch. Enter a name and press
    Return/Enter. In Figure 18-29, we named our pattern *Slim X*. The
    name appears in the Hatch pop-up menu, and a preview of the hatch
    appears in the left side of the dialog box.

Figure 18-29: We selected the X path and chose Filter » Pen and Ink » New Hatch to convert it to a hatch.

5. **Click on the OK button or press Return/Enter.**

   Illustrator closes the New Hatch dialog box and stores the hatch pattern in the current hatch library. (We'll get to the hatch libraries in a moment.) This new hatch will appear in the Hatch Effects dialog box.

You can also use the buttons in the New Hatch dialog box to delete a hatch from the illustration or paste the selected hatch in the illustration window so you can edit it. You can also import a hatch saved to disk or save a selected hatch to disk.

The hatches you create are stored in a file called a hatch library. The default set of hatches is only one of several other libraries that come with Illustrator. You can use Filter » Pen and Ink » Library Open to choose from the other libraries. These are found in the Sample Files > Hatch Sets folder in the Illustrator application folder.

If you create your own custom set of hatches you can save the file along with the other hatch sets (or anywhere else you want) by choosing Filter » Pen and Ink » Library Save As. This opens the normal Save As dialog box where you can navigate to save the hatches wherever you want. (Because the hatch library is a file, you can even trade them with your friends.)

Designing Custom Hatch Effects

Roll up your sleeves, now, because we're going to tackle the really hard part. Using the presets is nice, but you want to create your own looks. After all, you're not going to let some product manager in San Jose, California tell you how to use the Hatch Effects. So here is a complete set of instructions for using all the bells and whistles in the Hatch Effects dialog box.

1. **Select the hatch pattern you want to apply from the Hatch pop-up menu.**

   If you have created your own hatch or changed the library set, you will see those hatches in the list. Otherwise you will see the default hatches.

2. **Specify the density of the hatch pattern.**

   The Density slider bar changes the number of hatches that are packed into the shape. Raise the Density value or drag the slider triangle to the right to increase the hatch population; you can reduce the value or drag the triangle to the left to nuke those hatches till there are barely any of the suckers left alive. Figure 18-30 shows the difference between two density settings.

   In the lower right corner of the dialog box, you can keep an eye on the effects of raising or lowering the hatch population in the preview box. To the right of the preview box is a density color bar. Click a light swatch in the bar to decrease the number of hatches; click a dark swatch to raise the number. What's the difference between this bar and the Density slider? The little density color bar works in big, clunky increments, but otherwise, they're the same. One merely compounds the effects of the other.

3. **Modify the Dispersion options.**

   Dispersion is the randomness of the hatch. Set all the way to zero, the hatches will be arranged in perfect order—no variations in their positions allowed. Increase the dispersion to shake up the hatches a bit. After all, in traditional media a bit of randomness was only to be expected. Figure 18-31 shows how shaking up the dispersion makes a more natural appearance.

4. **Set the Thickness.**

   The Thickness option lets you modify the line weights of stroked hatches. If the selected hatch doesn't include a stroke, the Thickness options are dimmed. Figure 18-32 shows the effect of increasing the thickness of a hatch.

Figure 18-30: The low density (left) allows more space between the hatches than the higher one (right).

Figure 18-31: Use a higher dispersion setting (right) to shake up the orderliness of the hatches.

Figure 18-32: The thickness setting increases the stroke weight applied to hatches.

5. **Adjust the Scale.**

   The scale setting increases or decreases the size of the hatch.
   Combined with the density control, this can turn black dots on a white
   background into a huge blob of blackness. Figure 18-33 shows the
   effect of adjusting the scale.

6. **Set the Rotation.**

   Use the rotation slider to change the orientation of the hatches. A
   rotation is much more noticeable when applied to hatches such as
   vertical lines than when applied to the dots.

Figure 18-33: The difference between a low scale setting (left) and a larger one (right).

Figure 18-34: A comparison of two rotation settings

Just when you thought there was nothing else that you could possibly control in the Hatch Effects, dialog box, you notice that the dispersion, thickness, scale, and rotation menus include an identical collection of six options. These permit Illustrator to transform the hatches within a set range or to apply constant transformations. For instance, you can set the scale to start at one amount and then move along a certain angle, getting bigger and bigger in a linear progression.

This is where the Hatch Effects becomes as deep as an entire application itself. Figure 18-35 shows each option as it affects the Scale settings. The hatch pattern used in the figure is a simple black circle.

- **None:** Select this option to prevent the transformation from working at all. Throughout Figure 18-35, Dispersion, Thickness, and Rotation were all set to None. In the first example, Scale is set to None as well.

- **Constant:** This option applies a constant transformation value to all hatches. You are permitted just one option box and one slider triangle. In the Constant example in Figure 18-35, the single Scale value is set to 75 percent.

- **Linear:** Select this option if you want to create a gradation of transformations. You enter two Range values to specify the minimum and maximum transformations, and Illustrator varies between them at a constant rate from one end of the selected path to the other. You also specify the angle of the variation using the option box and icon at the right side of the slider bar. It's like a linear gradation. In the Linear example in the figure, the Range values were 50 and 150 percent and the angle was set to 45 degrees (as they were for the remaining examples as well).

🌑 **Reflect:** The Reflect option varies the transformation from the center of the shape outward. Therefore, it starts with the second Range value, gradually varies to the first, and then varies back to the second, as the Reflect example in the figure demonstrates.

🌑 **Symmetric:** At first glance, the Symmetric and Linear examples in Figure 18-35 appear identical. But there is a subtle difference. The hatches in the Linear example increase in size at a constant rate from the lower left corner to the upper right corner of the square. Not so in the Symmetric example. The hatches grow quite a bit at first, flatten out somewhat in the middle, and grow briskly again at the end. The Symmetric option is supposed to simulate shading around a cylinder—changing quickly, flattening out, and changing quickly again. But the effect is so slight, we doubt most viewers will notice. Oh well, at least the Adobe engineers gave it the extra effort.

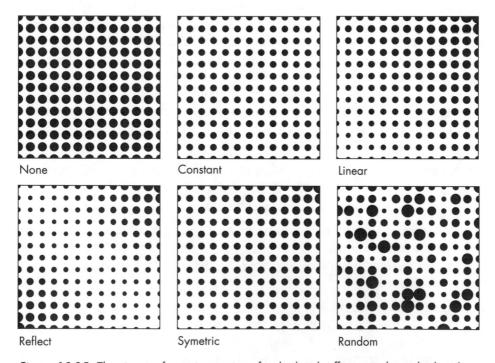

None	Constant	Linear
Reflect	Symetric	Random

Figure 18-35: The six transformation options for the hatch effects, each applied to the Scale setting. To keep things as clear as possible, Dispersion, Thickness, and Rotation were all set to None.

Random: If you want Illustrator to transform the hatches ad hoc, select the Random option. In the Random example in the figure, for example, Illustrator has randomly scaled the hatches from 50 to 150 percent. The angle options are dimmed when you select Random because, well, an angle would imply order and Random directly opposes order. (You can have a random angle, but you can't have an angled Random.)

> If you're interested in producing a gradient effect, set the Thickness and/or Scale settings to Linear, Reflect, or Symmetric. This allows the hatches to grow and shrink, just like the halftone dots in a standard gradation. It doesn't matter how you set the Dispersion or Rotation options. Neither of these options simulates a gradation, although they can be used to enhance the effect.

Illustrator also gives you a few commands that help you save and work with presets.

 New: Click this button to store the current control settings. You can name the preset and it will be stored along with the others in the Hatch Effect pop-up list.

 Update: If you modify a few of the controls, you can assign them to the named item in the pop-up menu by clicking on the Update button. (Because Sandee never likes to lose a preset, she rarely clicks the button—rather she simply stores the new setting under a new name.)

 Reset: Click this button to restore the preset to the original setting.

 Delete: You can trash a preset from the list by clicking the Delete button. (Watch out, that's not an undo-able thing.)

WEB GRAPHICS
AND ANIMATIONS

We admit it; as longtime print people we both were a little skeptical when we first heard about the World Wide Web. "A fad," we thought. "It'll never catch on." Move forward to today and we're right in the thick of it, creating Web sites, banner ads, and animations. The Web has become an important part of our lives. It's the same with Illustrator. For years Illustrator had very primitive—almost negligible Web features. Today, though, Illustrator's Web features are so robust, it is possible to create exceptional Web graphics and animations without using any other software.

This chapter looks at all the options you have to create Web graphics within Illustrator. This includes the traditional formats such as GIF and JPEG as well as newer formats such as PNG, SWF, and SVG. (We'll explain all these initials in just a bit.) We'll show you how to add special code within Illustrator so that your Web graphics contain links to other Web sites. And we'll look at how you can use the tools we've already covered to create exciting Web animations.

 Almost everything in this chapter is totally new to Illustrator 9. There are one or two features that were found in previous versions of Illustrator, but those had so little significance that we consider this entire chapter totally new.

Just in case you've been living in a cave for the past five years, here's a quick glossary of terms you should know when working with Web graphics.

- **Browser:** The software that people use to view Web pages. The two most popular browsers are Netscape Navigator (part of Netscape Communicator) and Internet Explorer.

- **Flash (SWF):** A file format for publishing vector artwork and sounds in interactive Web sites and animations. SWF stands for Shockwave Flash. (The proper name for these files is Macromedia Shockwave Flash although many people call them Flash or SWF files.) Originally, you could only create Flash (SWF) documents using Macromedia software. However, the format has become so popular that other applications such as Illustrator and Adobe LiveMotion also let you export as Flash (SWF) files. You can export primitive Flash (SWF) animations—no sounds, no interactivity—from Illustrator. To create more sophisticated animations and Web sites, you need an application such as Adobe LiveMotion or Macromedia Flash.

- **GIF:** Short for Graphic Interchange Format. This is a format developed by CompuServe (now part of AOL and proposed to be merged with Time Warner). It allows you to save graphics so they are much smaller than regular colored images. GIF images are limited to 256 colors and can only have a hard-edge transparency. GIF can be pronounced *gif*—with a hard g—or *jif*—with a j. Sandee prefers *gif* because she doesn't like peanut butter on the Web.

- **HTML:** Stands for hypertext markup language. This is the set of instructions that is used to format text. For instance when you see text that is **written like this,** the source code for that text was actually written like this,.

- **Internet:** The system of linked computers that displays information, sends email, downloads files, and contains newsgroups. Also called the **Net.**

- **JPEG or JPG:** Stands for Joint Photographers Expert Group. This is a format that compresses images differently than GIF. As a general rule, GIF images should be used for flat colors. JPEG is better used for photographs and images that need more than 256 colors. (JPEG is pronounced *jay-peg*.)

- **PNG:** Short for Portable Network Graphics. This file format was developed specifically to block the efforts of CompuServe to collect royalty payments on all GIF images used in Web pages. It lets you have millions of colors and soft-edged transparency. It has not been widely adopted however, because only the newer browsers automatically let you see PNG files. (PNG is pronounced ping.)

- **SVG:** Stands for Scalable Vector Graphics. This is the new kid on the block as far as Web file formats are concerned. In fact, Illustrator is one of the first major applications to support SVG. Unlike SWF files, which rely on their own proprietary code, SVG files are based on a standard language approved by the World Wide Web consortium. SVG files can be easily combined with HTML and JavaScript in Web pages.

- **URL:** Acronym for Uniform Resource Locator. Most people think of this only as the address that lets you go to specific Web pages. For instance, www.vectorbabe.com sends you to Sandee's Web site. Whereas www.dekemc.com and www.funpix.com both take you to Deke's site. A URL can also be the address that lets you download files or send email. For instance, an address that starts with http will send you to a Web page; an address that starts with ftp lets you download files.

- **Web:** Short for **World Wide Web.** Strictly speaking, the Web is only one part of the Internet; the part that displays pages linked together into Web sites. Each of these Web pages can contain text or graphics. However, the difference between Web and Internet is rapidly disappearing; most people use the terms Web, Net, Internet, and World Wide Web interchangeably.

 We wonder just how long our copyeditor will still make us capitalize the *W* in Web. We suspect it won't be too long before we create web graphics, not Web graphics.

Creating Web Graphics

There really isn't much difference between creating Web graphics and graphics for print. All the tools are the same and you still work in the same document window. The major differences have to do with colors and some preview options. Also, there are a few special controls you can add to graphics so that they do special things when they are posted on the Web.

Web Safe RGB Palette

As we mentioned when we looked at color in Chapter 14, Illustrator also lets you pick colors using a special WebSafe RGB palette shown in Figure 19-1. To use the palette, choose Web Safe RGB from the Color palette menu. This palette makes it easier for you to choose the 216 colors that are found in both the Macintosh and Windows operating systems. These colors are often referred to as the Web-safe colors.

The Web Safe RGB palette defines colors using the Hexadecimal color-naming system. Hexadecimal colors use RGB colors, but instead of numerals alone they name the colors with a combination of the letters A through F and the numbers 0 through 9. So where a light turquoise color would be defined as R: 58, G: 230, B: 204; the same color would be defined in hexadecimal as R: 3A, G: E6, B: CC.

To pick the Web-safe colors, make sure the sliders are located on one of the short tick marks along the slider area. If you drag the slider, it will automatically jump to each tick mark. All hexadecimal colors are labeled with pairs of the numbers 00, 33, 66, or 99 and the letters CC or FF. So R: 33, G: CC, B: FF is a Web-safe color. (Many Web designers leave out the RGB letters and just label the color with a string such as #33CCFF.)

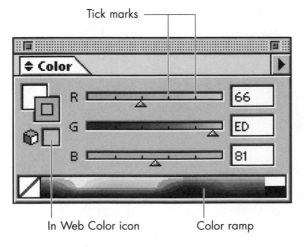

Figure 19-1:
The Color palette set for the Web Safe RGB palette.

If you click the color ramp at the bottom of the Web-safe palette, you automatically get the nearest Web-safe color. If you have selected a color that isn't Web safe, you can convert it to the nearest Web-safe color by clicking the In Web Color icon in the Color palette.

 Most Web graphics are colored using RGB colors. If you create Web graphics from scratch, you will want to set the color mode to RGB. However, if you have a CMYK document, you can convert it to RGB by choosing File » Document Color Mode » RGB. This allows you to select colors that are outside the CMYK colorspace.

Using Web-safe Colors

There is much confusion regarding the need for Web-safe colors. What happens if you don't use Web-safe colors? Will your files be seen on the Web? Will the Web police come to arrest you? Will it be the end of civilization as we know it? Here's a little background that should help.

If someone has a computer monitor that only displays 256 colors, any other colors shown on that monitor will not be seen exactly as they were defined. They will be dithered. Dithering is a process that mixes two other colors together to simulate a third. This creates a splotchy effect that can make graphics look bad. It also makes text very hard to read. Figure 19-2 shows dithering in all its glory.

If you only use Web-safe colors, you can be sure that anyone who views your Web site will see the color exactly as you defined it. This means that if the person has a monitor that only displays 256 colors, they will see the color without any shifting or dithering.

But Web-safe colors are only important for those people who have the oldest, cheapest computer monitors—the ones that display only 256 colors. Five years ago that was important; but today, most people have monitors that display millions of colors. This means that if you only choose Web-safe colors, you are limiting your color choices to satisfy the needs of a very small percentage of Web viewers.

 How necessary is it to limit yourself to only Web-safe colors? If you are creating graphics for the United States Weather Web site, you probably don't want to use colors that aren't Web safe. You want to reach the largest possible audience without dithering. For the small percentage of viewers who have older monitors, dithering will make it difficult to read the graphics—especially the isobars and other weather indicators. However, if you're creating graphics for most companies, you

really don't have to worry about using Web-safe colors. We
prefer to be able to use a wider choice of colors, rather than
cater to the needs of a very small percentage of viewers.

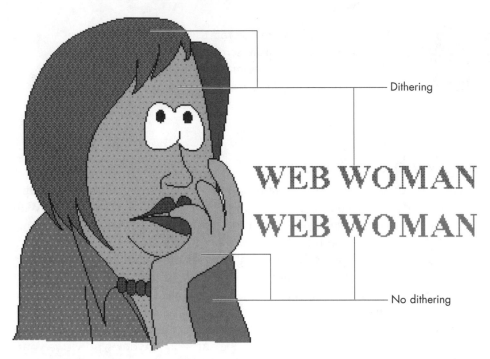

*Figure 19-2: Dithering makes the artwork splotchy. This is how older monitors display
colors that aren't Web-safe. Using Web-safe colors avoids dithering.*

Web-safe Swatch Libraries

You can also choose Web-safe colors using one of two swatch libraries that ship
with Illustrator. Choose Window » Swatch Libraries » Web to display the Web-
safe swatch colors supplied by Adobe. This palette arranges the Web-safe colors
in an arrangement based on the order of their hexadecimal names. Or you can
choose Window » Swatch Libraries » VisiBone2. The VisiBone2 swatch library
displays the Web-safe colors in a more logical order according to hue. (The
VisiBone swatch palette was provided by Bob Stein at VisiBone.) In order to see
the correct arrangement of the VisiBone2 palette, adjust the size of the palette so
that you can see the white squares at all four corners as shown in Figure 19-3.

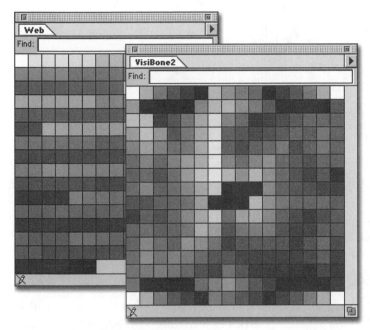

Figure 19-3:
The Web-safe swatches
palette (left) and the
VisiBone2 swatches
palette (right).

Creating Image Maps

Image maps are Web graphics with interactive areas that allow the viewer to click to prompt an action, such as switching to a new Web page or opening an email address. Although image maps are not as sophisticated as JavaScript rollovers, they can add interactivity to your graphics.

Image maps can be applied to individual objects, or groups of objects. Simply select the object. Open the Attributes palette and make sure all the options are visible. You can use the Image Map pop-up menu to apply an image map to the shape. Choose Rectangle to have the image map follow the bounding box of the selected object. Choose Polygon to create an image map that most closely follows the shape of the selected object. Use the URL options box to enter the address of the Web page you want to link to, or specify another action you want the image map to perform. For instance, Figure 19-4 shows how we've created an image map for the sphere that the man is pointing to. If you were to click the sphere you would be transferred to Sandee's Web site.

If you want to preview the interaction of your image map area, you can use the Save for Web application covered next.

    Click the Browser button to automatically switch to your Web browser, which will then be prompted to take you to the Web address listed in the URL options box.

Figure 19-4: To set up an image map, select the object and then use the image map options in the Attributes palette.

Save for Web Application

Hidden deep within the bowels of Illustrator is a whole nother application called Save for Web. This is the same application that was introduced in Photoshop 5.5. Save for Web allows you to save images in GIF, JPEG, or PNG formats. For most designers, Save for Web is all that you will ever need to create simple Web graphics.

Save for Web Interface

When you choose File » Save for Web, you leave your Illustrator window and enter the Save for Web window as seen in Figure 19-5. If you have a small monitor, this window will pretty much take over your screen. Don't worry. Your document is still there, hiding in the background. For now, though, everything you need is contained within this window.

There are five major areas in the Save for Web window: tools, preview, optimization settings, color table, image size, and the settings along the bottom of the window for magnification, color and alpha information, and jump to controls.

Save for Web tools

As shown in Figure 19-6, the Save for Web window has three tools that work somewhat similarly to their Illustrator equivalents.

- **Hand tool:** Lets you move around within the preview area. Press the spacebar to access the hand tool while in one of the other tools.

- **Zoom tool:** Lets you zoom in to the preview area. Hold the Opt/Alt key to switch to the zoom out mode. Hold the Cmd/Ctrl-spacebar to access the zoom tool while in one of the other tools.

- **Eyedropper tool:** Lets you sample colors from the illustration area.
- **Eyedropper color square:** Displays the color sampled from the eye-dropper tool. Click the square to open the color picker.

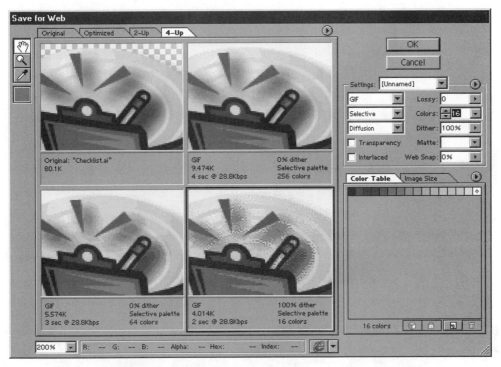

Figure 19-5: The Save for Web window is your one-stop shopping center for all the features you need to create Web graphics.

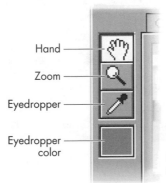

Figure 19-6: The tools area of the Save for Web window.

Preview Area

As shown in Figure 19-7, there are four tabs at the top of the preview area in the Save for Web window. They change the display of the preview area as follows:

- **Original:** Shows the original image as seen in the Illustrator window.

- **Optimized:** Shows the image with the current optimization settings applied to it.

- **2-up:** Splits the preview area into two separate sections. Each section can show either the original image or the display of different optimization settings.

- **4-up:** Splits the preview area into four separate sections.

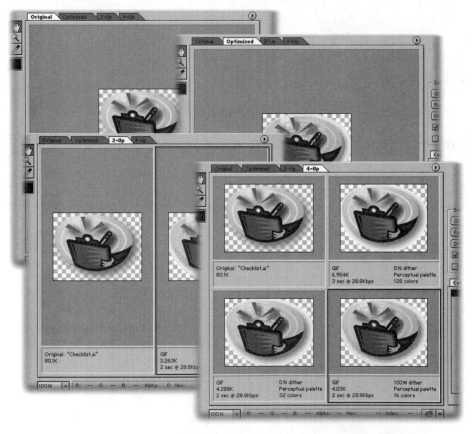

Figure 19-7: The four tabs at the top of the preview area let you see different views of the image to be saved.

The split preview windows are an excellent way to compare the differences between two different output formats (such as GIF vs. JPEG) or two different settings of the same format.

Optimization Settings

There are four different displays for the optimization area shown in Figure 19-8. When you choose GIF, JPEG, PNG-8, or PNG-24, this area changes its controls. We'll cover each of these options in detail later in this chapter.

Optimization list

Optimization controls menu

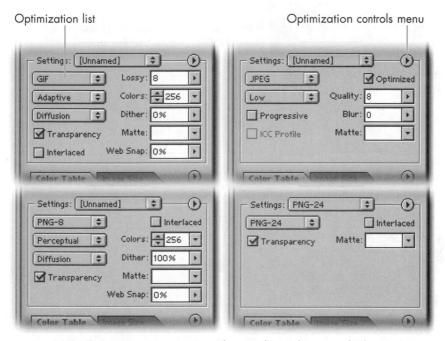

Figure 19-8: The optimization settings change depending on which export option is chosen from the optimization list.

Color Table

When you click the Color Table tab, shown in Figure 19-9, this area shows the colors that are included in GIF and PNG-8 images. Because JPEG images don't use color tables, this area is left blank when JPEG optimization is chosen.

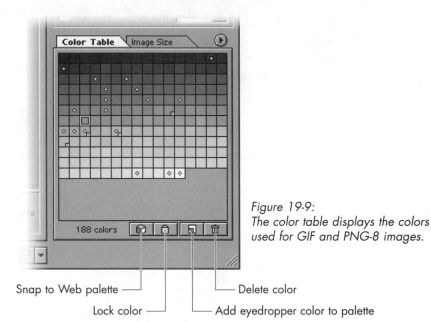

Figure 19-9:
The color table displays the colors
used for GIF and PNG-8 images.

Snap to Web palette ———

Lock color ———

——— Delete color

——— Add eyedropper color to palette

Image Size

When you click the Image Size tab, as shown in Figure 19-10, this area shows
you the current dimensions of the image. You can also set new export sizes for the
image. We'll show you each of these options in just a bit.

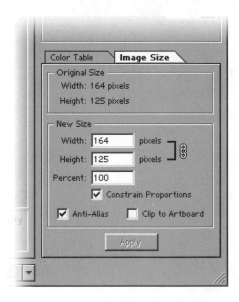

Figure 19-10:
Click the Image Size tab to display
the controls for changing the size
of the exported image.

Magnification, Color and Alpha, and Jump to

The bottom of the Save for Web window contains the final three controls shown in Figure 19-11. The magnification option box and pop-up list lets you set numerical values for the size of the image shown in the preview area.

The color and alpha information shows you the color values of selected colors or the area underneath the eyedropper cursor.

The jump to browser control lets you automatically select and switch to a browser to see how an image will appear in that browser. This is also where you can see the interactivity of any image maps.

Magnification control   Color and alpha values   Jump to list

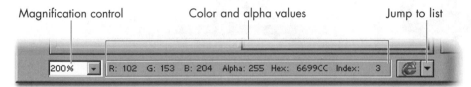

Figure 19-11: The bottom area of the Save for Web window lets you change the preview size of the image, check the color and alpha information, and switch to a browser to preview the image.

Choosing an Export Format

Before you can save your image as a Web graphic, you should understand the three different optimization formats in the Save for Web application. Each of the three different formats has its own advantages and disadvantages.

GIF Images

GIF images are used primarily for images with flat areas of color. They can be used for blends and gradients if other formats are not acceptable. Because GIF images are limited to only 256 colors, they are rarely used for photographic images that require many tonal changes. You can lower the size of GIF images by reducing the number of colors in the file. So if an image contains only a few colors, GIF images can become extremely small. GIF images are also used when the final image needs to have a transparent backgrounds. For instance, an image that will be placed over a multi-colored background needs to have a transparency added. Figure 19-12 shows a sample of the kind of images that do best when exported as GIF images. (See the color insert for a color version of the images.)

 The GIF format is also used to create simple animations. However, Illustrator does not let you create GIF animations. For that you need a program such as Adobe ImageReady or Macromedia Fireworks.

Figure 19-12: These are the types of graphics that do well when exported as GIF images. Even those images with blends and gradients are OK because they do not have many different colored blends.

JPEG Images

JPEG images allow you to have millions of colors in your graphics and are used primarily for photographs. However, the JPEG format may also be best if you have used many blends, gradient fills, drop shadows, or glows in your Illustrator art-work. Figure 19-13 shows the type of images that are best saved in the JPEG for-mat. You reduce the size of JPEG images by applying a compression setting. The smaller you make the file, the more the quality of the file is degraded. When you apply high compression to JPEG images, you can distort the flat areas of color in the image. Figure 19-13 also shows an example of this distortion. (See the color insert for a color version of the images.)

PNG-8 and PNG-24 Images

PNG is the Web format that doesn't seem to get any respect. For a long time, you couldn't view PNG graphics unless you had special plug-ins in the browser. This kept most Web designers from using the PNG format. (They didn't expect visitors to their Web sites to go out and download a plug-in.) However, since

Netscape 4.0 and Internet Explorer 4.0 were introduced, support for the PNG format has been built right into the browsers. Yet, even though the PNG format has many advantages over GIF and JPEG, many designers are still afraid of using PNG images. We are aghast at this Luddite approach to graphics. After all, how many people are still viewing the Web using 3.0 versions of Netscape and Internet Explorer?

Illustrator lets you save files in either the PNG-8 or the PNG-24 formats. The PNG-8 format saves files similarly to GIF images. PNG-8 images can have up to 256 colors. PNG-24 images can have millions of colors.

Figure 19-13: Two images that were saved as JPEG. The top examples look best when set with low compression. The bottom examples were set with high compression, causing some distortion.

Saving an Image for the Web

Even if you've never created Web graphics, it's really not as difficult as it may seem. In fact, there's actually only one important rule to remember: Make the file as small as possible while still looking good. Everything else is just a nuance. Here are the overall steps for creating an image using the Save for Web command. We'll cover the specific details in just a bit.

1. **Choose File » Save for Web.**

   Make sure you don't have any extraneous artwork on the page. The Save for Web command is applied to all the artwork on the page.

2. **Use the preview area to view the artwork.**

   If you want to compare settings, click the 2-up or 4-up tabs. Otherwise, click the Optimize tab to see one version of the final image.

3. **Set the controls for GIF, JPEG, PNG-8, or PNG-24.**

   The optimization controls change depending on which format you have chosen. We'll cover how to set the controls for each of the formats separately.

4. **Click the tab to set the image size.**

   Use the Width and Height option boxes to change the size or enter a value in the percent field. Constrain Proportions keeps the image from being distorted when scaled. Checking Anti-Alias allows a soft blur to be added to the edges of objects. This keeps them from looking harsh or jagged. Check Clip to Artboard to use images only within the artboard area. Click the Apply button in the Image Size area to apply the changes.

If you choose the Anti-Alias blur, you will add more colors to GIF images. Each additional color adds to the file size. You may have to delete colors added by anti-aliasing.

If you use Clip to Artboard on a large-sized document, Illustrator will take a long time to optimize the image. Change the image size first.

5. **Preview in a browser (optional).**

   Choose a browser from the jump to list. This lets you compare how the image will look for different viewers.

6. **Click OK to name and save the file.**

   Name the file and save it to the location where you store your Web graphics. If you have applied an image map to the graphics, you need to save the HTML file along with the graphic.

Setting the GIF Options

The primary thing to remember about GIF images is that you are limited to 256 colors. Your mission is to use as few colors as possible while still making the image look good. When you choose the GIF format, the optimization settings appear as shown in Figure 19-14. Here's a complete rundown of what each of the controls does.

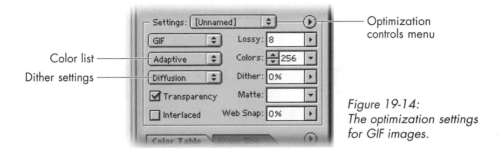

Figure 19-14:
The optimization settings
for GIF images.

- **Color list:** This lets you choose the type of color palette that is applied to the image. *Perceptual* tries to maintain colors closest to the way the human eye perceives color. *Selective* creates images with the most color integrity although it may shift some colors to the Web palette. *Adaptive* creates a set of colors that appear most in the image. This gives you the most fidelity to blends and gradients. *Web* limits the colors to the 216 colors in the Web-safe palette.

- **Dither settings:** This lets you choose what type of dithering, if any, is applied to the image. *None* turns off dithering. *Diffusion* creates a random, but adjustable, pattern of dithering. *Pattern* creates a uniform grid of dithering. *Noise* creates a random pattern of dithering. Figure 19-15 shows the difference in the three types of dithering.

Figure 19-15: The three types of dithering that can be applied to images.
From left to right: diffusion, pattern, and noise.

Dither: If you choose diffusion dithering, this setting lets you control how much diffusion dithering is applied. (The pattern and noise dithering do not let you adjust the amount of dithering.)

- **Colors:** Use this control to add or delete the number of colors in the image. This is how you can delete the colors that were added by anti-aliasing.

- **Lossy:** This control reduces the size of GIF images by applying a compression similar to that found in JPEG images. At low numbers, the lossy compression is not noticeable. However, as you increase the lossy compressing, you will start to see distortion in your images.

- **Web Snap:** As you increase this setting, Save for Web shifts colors to their nearest Web-safe equivalent. This allows you to have a mixture of some Web-safe colors while still keeping important colors that aren't Web safe.

- **Transparency:** Check this to create a transparent background to the GIF image. The transparency settings for GIF images are hard-edged. So although you may have applied a soft drop shadow to your artwork, the transparency for the GIF image will abruptly end, not fade out.

- **Matte:** Once you apply transparency, you can use the matte control to choose what color should be mixed into the edges of the transparent

Figure 19-16: The different stages that interlaced GIF images appear as they download.

areas. For example, if you have a white matte and the image is placed over a dark background, you will see small white pixels on the edge of the image. A better choice would be a black matte.

- **Interlaced:** Check this to have the image appear in stages as it is downloaded. Figure 19-16 shows a representation of this effect.

Here are a few tips for making the best possible GIF images:

- **Lower the number of colors:** The Anti-Alias setting increases the number of colors. Use the Color Table to delete some of the colors that are added by anti-aliasing.

- **Apply dithering to reduce banding:** As you decrease the number of colors, you may see banding—abrupt changes in blends. Add a small amount of dithering to decrease the banding.

- **Lock important colors:** As you reduce the number of colors, you may lose important colors that do not appear very frequently in the image— for instance a client's logo may have a distinctive color in a very small area. Use the Color Table to select that color and lock it so it is not deleted as you reduce colors.

- **Watch the preview size:** Use the information in the preview area to judge how small the final file will be.

Setting the JPEG Options

The options for creating JPEG images, as shown in Figure 19-17, are much simpler. Because JPEG images rely on image compression, you adjust a slider control to reduce the size of the image. Here's an explanation of what each of the settings does.

- **Quality presets and Quality options box:** There are four settings: Maximum, High, Medium, and Low. These presets simply move the Quality options box to the amount of 80, 60, 30, and 10. However, once you have applied a preset, you can then adjust the Quality options box to choose amounts in between the presets.

- **Optimized:** Check this setting to apply an automatic optimization that decreases the size of the JPEG image to as small as possible.

- **Blur:** As you decrease the quality to lower the file size, you may see small distortions in the image. Use the blur control to soften the appearance of these distortions.

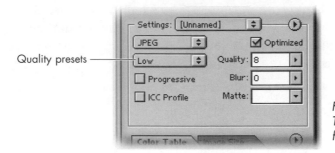

Quality presets

Figure 19-17:
The optimization settings
for JPEG images.

- **Progressive:** Turn this on to have JPEG images appear gradually, similar to the interlaced setting for GIF images.

- **Matte:** Although there is no transparency for JPEG images, you can still set the color that the image fades into using the matte control.

- **ICC Profile:** If you have assigned an ICC profile to help maintain the color of your image, you can use this setting to add the ICC profile to the JPEG image. ICC profiles are not yet supported by most browsers.

Setting the PNG Options

There are two different types of PNG options, as shown in Figure 19-18. The PNG-8 settings are very similar to the GIF settings. You reduce the size of the image by lowering the number of colors. The PNG-24 settings only let you set transparency, matte, and the interlaced options.

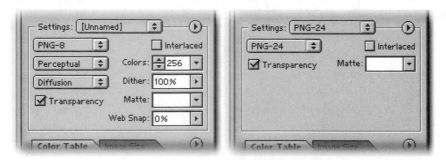

Figure 19-18: The optimization settings for PNG-8 and PNG-24 images.

Using the Optimization Settings

Once you have set the optimization controls for either GIF, JPEG, or PNG files, you can save those settings for future images. With the optimization controls set the way you want them, choose Save Settings from the optimization controls menu. You can then name and save the settings. The settings will appear in the settings pop-up list where they will be available for all other documents.

You can apply any of the saved settings by simply choosing them from the settings pop-up list. If you feel the list is too long, choose Delete Settings from the optimization controls menu.

Saving to a Specific Size

Hey, we know how rushed you are—you don't have time to sit and play with the settings to get your files under a certain size. So you can simply choose Optimize to File Size from the optimization controls menu. The dialog box shown in Figure 19-19 appears. Simply enter the desired file size in the options box. Choose Start With: Current Settings to use the optimization settings that are currently in effect. Or choose Auto Select GIF/JPEG to have the Save for Web application automatically choose either a GIF or JPEG format. Either way, Save for Web will figure out the best possible settings that keep your file below the desired file size.

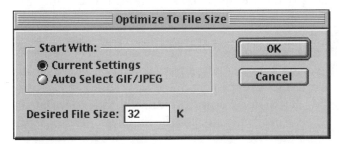

Figure 19-19:
Use the Optimize to File Size dialog box to set a specific file size to which the Web graphic should be reduced.

Creating Flash (SWF) Graphics and Animations

Flash is the Cinderella story of Web graphics. Before there were Flash animations, the only way to get motion on the Web was to create GIF animations. To make a GIF animation, Web designers compiled multiple images into one file. Each GIF image added greatly to the size of the file.

Then Web designers discovered Macromedia Flash. Instead of big, bulky pixels, Flash uses lean, mean vectors (like the paths found in Illustrator) to create images and animations. This allows Flash to create Web graphics and animations that are much smaller than GIF files and animations. Originally, though, the only way to create Flash (SWF) files was to use the Macromedia Flash application or Macromedia FreeHand.

Today, Illustrator also lets you create Flash (SWF) files. Although Illustrator isn't a full-fledged animation program like Macromedia Flash or Adobe LiveMotion, you can use some special features to create simple Flash (SWF) animations.

Designing Flash (SWF) Files

There are three types of Flash (SWF) files. A single frame Flash (SWF) file is a static image. Although not as flashy as animations, static Flash (SWF) files are extremely useful for displaying maps, technical illustrations, or other intricate drawings. Because these illustrations are vectors, they are much smaller than either GIF or JPEG graphics. And because you can zoom in on Flash (SWF) files, your viewers can move it to see specific details in the image. A single Illustrator document can easily be turned into a Flash (SWF) file by using the Flash Export option.

Multi-frame Flash (SWF) files create animations by playing all the frames one after another. This allows you to simulate motion, fades, transformations, and other effects. Because Illustrator doesn't have multi-frames, you need to use multiple layers to simulate the multi-frames. We'll cover how to do this very shortly in the section "Turning Blends into Animations."

Multi-frame Flash (SWF) files can also be used to create interactive Web sites. This is accomplished by displaying a frame and pausing the action of the movie. The viewer then clicks a button to move to the next frame. This sort of interactivity cannot be accomplished within Illustrator. For that you need to use Macromedia Flash or Adobe LiveMotion. These programs are also the only way to add sounds to your Flash (SWF) files.

Viewing Flash (SWF) Files

Once you have created Flash (SWF) files, they can be inserted into HTML Web pages using a program such as Adobe GoLive. This allows you to use single-frame maps or illustrations as part of larger HTML Web pages. The benefit of this is that the Flash (SWF) files are much smaller than GIF or JPEG images and your viewers can zoom in or out to see details in the illustration. Or you can insert small multi-frame animations into the HTML page. This adds excitement to static Web pages. Or each Flash (SWF) file can be posted individually as its own Web address. For instance the Web address www.vectorbabe.com/realworld.swf takes you to a single Web page that displays a simple animation created from an Illustrator blend.

In order to see Flash (SWF) files, you need to have the Flash player plug-in installed in your browser. The current versions of Netscape and Internet Explorer install this plug-in automatically as part of their regular installation from a CD. However, if you install Internet Explorer from a Web download, you will not get the Flash plug-in. In that case, you need to go to www.macromedia.com to download the Flash player plug-in.

Turning Blends into Animations

As we mentioned in Chapter 18, the morphs you create using blends can be used as the basis for nifty Web animations. The steps to create these animations are rather simple. You first create the blend. The trick is to use Illustrator's Release to Layers command to separate the blend into steps that can be exported as Flash (SWF) files. Here's your step by step guide to creating Flash (SWF) animations.

1. Create the blend.

Use the blend command or blend tool to create the blend. Make whatever changes you want to the blend steps or spine.

2. Choose Object » Blend » Expand.

You need to expand the blend into its individual objects in order to create animations. Because expansion destroys the live blend, make a copy of the blend if you think you may want to change the blend later. The blend appears as a group in the Layers palette.

3. Select the group and Release to Layers.

The Release to Layers command sends each step of the expanded blend to its own layer. If you have a blend between groups, each grouped step will be on its own layer after you apply the release to layers command. Figure 19-20 shows the difference between before releasing to layers and after.

 The Release to Layers command can be applied to more than just objects created by blends. Any objects or grouped objects on a layer can be released to their own layers.

Figure 19-20: This blend of objects was expanded into individual group objects as seen in the Layers palette on the left. After the Release to Layers command, each group appears on its own layer.

4.   Set the SWF export options.

First choose File » Export which options the Export dialog box. Name the file and choose Flash (SWF) from the Format pop-up list. Then click the Export button to open the Flash (SWF) Format Options as shown in Figure 19-21. We'll cover all the options in just a moment, but for now just click OK. This creates a Flash (SWF) file that is ready to post on the Web as a Flash (SWF) animation.

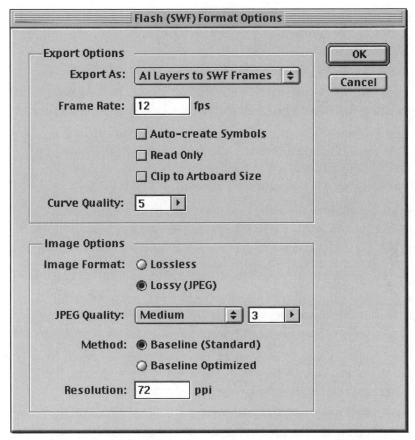

Figure 19-21: The Flash (SWF) Format Options is your control center for the appearance and timing of Flash (SWF) files.

Setting the Flash (SWF) Format Options

Once you have set up a file for Flash (SWF) export, you can use the Flash (SWF) Format Options to control how the final file is created. These controls not only change the appearance of your graphic but also control the size of the file.

Export Options

Export As AI File to SWF File saves your Illustrator artwork out as a single-frame SWF file. Even if you have artwork on separate layers, choosing this option moves all the artwork to a single Flash (SWF) frame. Use this option for maps and other single frame illustrations.

- **Export As AI Layers to SWF Frames** converts each Illustrator layer into a Flash (SWF) frame. Use this option to turn blends and other Illustrator objects into animations.

- **Export As AI Layers to SWF Files** converts each Illustrator layer into a separate Flash (SWF) document. This option gives you more control to insert the frames into Macromedia Flash or Adobe LiveMotion documents.

- **Frame Rate** controls how fast multi-frame animations play in frames per second (fps). The default value of 12 fps is the most commonly-used rate to create smooth animations. Lower this value to slow down the animation.

- **Auto-create Symbols** reduces the size of animations by creating symbols and instances of objects that are repeated across multiple frames. (Instead of repeating an object many times, symbols allow you to reference the object once and then point back to it whenever it would be repeated.) Unfortunately, the shipping version of Illustrator 9 contained a bug that caused this option to increase the size of the animations. If an upgrade version of Illustrator 9 is released, check to see if this feature has been fixed. If not, turn it off to reduce the size of your animation.

- **Read Only** sets a control so that your animations can't be copied from the Web and used by others. Turn this option on to protect your valuable artwork from showing up on other people's Web pages.

- **Clip to Artboard Size** uses the size of the artboard as the total size of the movie. If this option is turned on, the size of the movie is clipped to the size of the bounding box of the artwork in the illustration.

- **Curve Quality** controls how smooth curves in the Illustrator artwork are converted into Flash (SWF) objects. The lower the curve quality, the smaller the final file size. However, very low curve quality can cause text to become hard-edged and distorted.

Image Options

The Image Options control how bitmap images and effects in your file are converted into Flash (SWF) objects.

- **Image Format Lossless** keeps the highest quality display for bitmapped images. No compression is applied to the images. This option will create very large Flash (SWF) files and should not be used for ordinary Web graphics. However, it can be used for off-line displays.

- **Image Format Lossy (JPEG)** allows you to adjust the amount of compression using the JPEG Quality pop-up list. The lower the quality, the smaller the final Flash (SWF) image. However, this does cause artifacts in the image.

- **Baseline (Standard)** saves the JPEG with the standard type of compression. Use this setting if you have viewers who have difficulty reading the Baseline Optimized JPEG files.

- **Baseline Optimized** adds another set of optimization to the compression.

- **Resolution** lets you set a resolution amount for any bitmapped images. Set the resolution to 72 ppi for most purposes. Use a higher resolution if you expect viewers to zoom in on the Flash (SWF) files and you don't want your bitmapped images to look jagged.

Creating SVG Graphics

Wouldn't you have loved to be one of the first people to broadcast television? Or make one of the first telephone calls? Or send the first fax? Well that's what it is like creating SVG graphics in Illustrator. Illustrator is the very first major application that lets you create Scalable Vector Graphics (SVG), the new Web format for creating small graphics that can be made part of larger Web pages.

 Working with SVG is a little like being a pioneer in the old West. The SVG format is very new, so that most people need to download an SVG viewer. (One is available from the Adobe Web site.)

Designing SVG Files

The simplest type of SVG file is a graphic with no animation or interactivity. These graphics can be easily created in Illustrator. However, SVG also allows you to create interactive animation graphics—for instance, you can click an object and it will change color or reveal information.

At the moment, the only way to create interactive or animated graphics in Illustrator is to use the SVG Interactivity palette where you enter code in the JavaScript language. Compared to Flash (SWF) animations, which can be created by placing objects on their own layers, we find this method extremely difficult for most designers. (Entering code in a palette reminds us both of the old days of DOS where you typed commands rather than using pull-down menus.) We would rather wait for a more visual approach to creating SVG graphics.

Setting the SVG or SVGZ Export Options

There are two types of SVG files you can export from Illustrator: SVG is the ordinary SVG format containing plain text code that describes the appearance of the artwork. SVGZ is a compressed version of the SVG format that makes smaller file sizes. If you are familiar with changing HTML code, you can easily modify the attributes within an SVG file. An SVGZ file can be uncompressed using any zip utility. Once you have created your artwork, it is rather simple to export as either SVG or SVGZ formats.

Choose File > Export. Select the folder where you want to save the file, and type in a name for the file in the Name text box. In the Export dialog box, choose SVG or SVG Compressed from the pop-up menu. The SVG Options dialog box appears as shown in Figure 19-22. This is where you can set the export options for the SVG or SVGZ files.

```
┌───────────────────────── SVG Options ─────────────────────────┐
│                                                                │
│         Font Subsetting: │ Only Glyphs Used          ◆ │   │   OK   │
│                                                                │
│  Embedded Font Location: │ Embed Subsetted Fonts     ◆ │   │ Cancel │
│                                                                │
│   Raster Image Location: │ Embed Raster Images       ◆ │        │
│                                                                │
│          Decimal Places: │ 3                         ◆ │        │
│                                                                │
│                Encoding: │ ISO 8859-1 (ASCII)        ◆ │        │
│                                                                │
│    CSS Property Location: │ Style Attributes (Entity Refere... ◆ │    │
│                                                                │
└────────────────────────────────────────────────────────────────┘
```

Figure 19-22: The SVG Export Options controls the appearance and size of the final SVG files.

Setting the SVG Export Options

Once you have chosen SVG or SVGZ, you use the SVG Export Options dialog box to control what information is saved within the file. These options affect both the size and the appearance of the final SVG file.

Font Subsetting lets you control how the fonts are embedded or linked from the exported SVG file.

- **None (Use System Fonts)** embeds no fonts within the file. Use this option if you have no text in your file, or you can rely on the necessary fonts being installed on the end-user's systems.

- **Only Glyphs Used** includes only the glyphs or characters for the text that exists in the current artwork. This adds to the file size, but only the smallest amount necessary to view the file. Do not use this option if you have a JavaScript action that allows the user to change the text in the file or if you want to edit the text directly in the SVG file without using Illustrator.

- **Common English** embeds all the text characters found in English-language documents. **Glyphs used + Common English** adds the characters used in the artwork to the English-language characters.

- **Common Roman** embeds all the characters in Roman-language documents. **Glyphs used + Common Roman** adds the characters used in the artwork to the Roman-language characters.

- **All Glyphs** embeds all the characters in the font. Use this to add non-Roman characters such as Japanese characters.

    You choose the Embedded Font Location to specify where the embedded fonts should be.

- **Embed Subsetted Fonts** adds the fonts directly to the document. This ensures that the fonts are included with the file.

- **Link to Subsetted File** allows you to point to a different exported file to locate the fonts. This option is very helpful if you have multiple SVG files that all use the same fonts.

Like the embedded font location, the Raster Image Location option allows you to specify where embedded raster images should be located.

- **Embed Raster Images** keeps bitmapped images in the exported SVG file. This increases file size but makes sure that the image is included with the file. Raster images that have no alpha channel (transparency) are converted to JPEG images. Raster images with transparency are converted into the PNG format.

- **Link to Raster Images** lets you point to a different exported file. Use this option if you have multiple SVG files that all use the same common bitmapped images.

The Decimal Places option lets you specify the precision of the vectors in the exported artwork. You can set a value of 1 to 7 decimal places. A high value results in a larger file size, but maintains the highest image quality.

The Encoding options let you choose between ASCII characters or characters encoded using the Unicode Transformation Format (UTF). Although ASCII is fine for many European languages, UTF-8 and UTF-16 are preferred for non-Roman languages like Japanese, Chinese, or Hebrew.

The Cascading Style Sheet (CSS) Property Location option lets you choose between three methods of saving style attributes in SVG code.

- **Style Attributes <Entity Reference>** creates the smallest SVG file size and fastest rendering speed.

- **Style Attributes** should be used if the SVG code will be used in transformations.

- **Style Element** should be used when sharing files with HTML documents. This lets you modify the SVG file to move a style element into an external style sheet file that is also referenced by the HTML file.

CHAPTER 20

WORKING SMARTER AND FASTER

There's a general rule of thumb we have for working with computers—anytime you find yourself doing the exact same thing more than twenty times in a row, most likely there's another way to do the same thing much faster. So, now that you've managed to make it all the way to practically the end of this book, you may have started feeling frustrated with how long it takes to do things. Perhaps you find using the menus a drag. You'd like a way to automate certain commands you use over and over. Perhaps you'd like to change the fill and stroke settings to many objects. Or you simply want to copy the look of one object and apply it to another. Well, this chapter's our little gift to help you speed up your work. Of course if you don't want to finish your work faster, please feel free to go right to the last chapter.

Taking Illustrator's Shortcuts

As with any drawing program, you'll spend much of your time interacting with Illustrator by clicking and dragging with your mouse or some other input device. However, many commands and other operations can also be executed by way of the keyboard. For instance, instead of moving your mouse all the way up to the File menu, and then moving all the way down to choose the Print command, it is much faster and easier to simply type Cmd/Ctrl-P.

Memorizing Shortcuts

As we've covered different topics in this book we've mentioned a few important keyboard shortcuts that we use all the time to speed up our work. For instance, remember how much easier it is to just press Cmd/Ctrl-D instead of choose Transform again from the Object menu? Or how simple it is to press P to get the Pen tool? Using shortcuts will make you work faster.

However, we don't expect you to memorize all the keyboard shortcuts in a day—not even a week. What we do is decide on a specific command that we use often. For instance, we might want to remember the keyboard shortcut for the Blend command: Cmd-Opt-B or Ctrl-Alt-B. Then for the rest of the day, we always use the shortcut to create a blend. Even if we have to look at the menu to remember the keystroke, we still type the keystroke. It doesn't take more than a day or so for us to have that shortcut imprinted onto our brains. We then go on to learning the next shortcut.

Of course there are times that we don't use a command for a while and it gets erased from our memories. Fortunately, it's rather easy to relearn the shortcut after just one or two trips to the menu bar—we'll have a blend command on the rocks, please.

Changing Shortcuts

As much as we love working in Illustrator, there are times when we need to use other programs—InDesign, Photoshop, or even non-Adobe programs such as FreeHand or QuarkXPress. Unfortunately not all these programs share the same keyboard shortcuts. For instance, Cmd/Ctrl-U used to ungroup objects in Illustrator; but Adobe changed it a while back. But it's still Cmd/Ctrl-U in QuarkXPress and FreeHand. Rather than go insane trying to remember different keystrokes for the same command, Sandee would rather change Illustrator's keyboard command.

There are also some commands that we use often that have no keystrokes—for example, the star tool and the expand appearance command. We understand that it is impossible for Adobe to assign keystrokes to every tool or command. They are only so many combinations of letters and modifier keys. Fortunately, we can assign our own keystrokes.

 Customizing keyboard shortcuts and menu commands has been a frequent request on the various Illustrator discussion groups for many years. Unfortunately there are still some keyboard shortcuts that we can't change. For instance, the way Illustrator lets you get to the hand tool is different from how InDesign does it. However, we expect more customizing options will be added to future versions of Illustrator.

Illustrator ships with two keystroke sets. The first, Illustrator Factory Defaults, contains all the keystrokes that the Adobe engineers thought you would like. It also ships with Adobe Illustrator 6 keystrokes, which are the keystrokes that both of us used for the longest time. To switch to the Illustrator 6 shortcuts, choose Edit » Keyboard Shortcuts, which opens the Keyboard Shortcuts dialog box shown in Figure 20-1. You can then choose Adobe Illustrator 6 from the Set pop-up list.

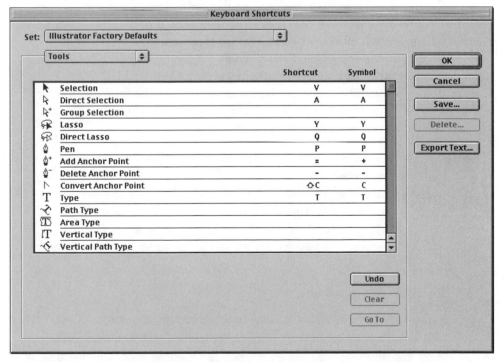

Figure 20-1: The Keyboard Shortcuts dialog box allows you to customize the keyboard shortcuts for tools and commands.

You can change or assign shortcuts to either tools or commands. The shortcuts for tools allow you to access all the tools in the toolbox as well as the fill and stroke settings, blending modes, and opacity settings. The shortcuts for the menu commands allow you to change any of the commands in the menus as well as some commands that don't appear in the menus. Here's your step-by-step recipe for creating your own keyboard shortcuts.

1. **Choose Edit » Keyboard Shortcuts.**

   This opens the Keyboard Shortcuts dialog box.

2. **Choose the type of shortcut.**

   The small pop-up list allows you to choose between Tools and Menu Commands.

3. **Find the command or tool.**

   Use the scrollbars to select the command or tool in the list. Use the small triangle controls to open each of the menu categories.

4. **Change the shortcut.**

   Click in the shortcut column to open the options box for the shortcut. Then type the shortcut. Shortcuts for tools can be a single letter, number, or punctuation mark. They can also be modified with the Shift key. Shortcuts for menu commands must use the Cmd/Ctrl key with a single letter, number, punctuation mark, or numeric F-key (located at the top of the keyboard). They can also be modified with the Shift or Opt/Alt keys. (Sorry, Mac users, you can't use the Control key.) Use the Symbol column to set the display of the keystroke.

 For almost all tools and commands the letter for the symbol will be the same as the letter for the shortcut. However, some symbol letters may be different from the shortcut letters. For instance, the symbol letter for the Add Point tool is the plus (+) sign. However, the shortcut letter is the equal (=) sign because the key that is pressed is the equal key without the Shift key.

5. **Resolve any conflicts.**

   If you type a shortcut that is used by another tool or command, you can use the Go To button to jump to the conflict shortcut and change it to another keystroke. You can also use the Undo button to change the conflict.

6. Save the keystroke set.

You cannot make changes to the two default keystroke sets. So you must click the Save button to name and save the keystroke set under a different name. Once you save a set it will appear in the pop-up menu with the rest of the sets. You can also select a set and use the Delete button to remove sets from the list. However, you cannot delete either of the default sets.

 The keystroke sets you create are saved with the Illustrator preferences in a .kys file. These files can be copied from one machine and installed on another. This makes it easy to have everyone in a company use the same keystrokes.

Printing Shortcuts

You might want to have a printed list of the shortcuts to post near your computer. We were going to print out a set for you and include it in this chapter. You would have been so pleased with such a list and thanked us for going to all that trouble to write out every single shortcut. (And maybe you would have sent us birthday cards and small gifts.) Then we realized that you would also want a list of the shortcuts that you had created.

So instead, we'll just tell you that if you click the Export Text button in the Keyboard Shortcuts dialog box, you will create a SimpleText (Mac) or NotePad (Windows) document that has a complete list of all the shortcuts in a particular set. You can then format and print the list yourself.

Moving Into Actions

Working with actions can be a very simple process where you just click and play, or actions can become very deep, sophisticated ways of controlling Illustrator. The best way to understand actions and what they can do is to look at an action. Illustrator ships with a number of preset actions. To see them, display the Actions palette (if hidden) by choosing the Windows » Show Actions command. Then click the expander triangle just to the left of the Default Actions set. The Default Actions set stores several actions, as shown in Figure 20-2.

To run an action, simply select the name of the action and then click the Play button at the bottom of the Actions palette. Illustrator runs the action for you. Unfortunately, the default actions that ship with Illustrator 9 are rather tame. A good example of an action is the Opacity 60 (selection). This action lowers the opacity of the selected object. If (selection) follows the name of the action, it is simply Adobe's way of letting you know that you need to select an object in order to get any results from the action.

 Choose Button mode from the Actions palette menu to switch to an easier way to invoke actions. In the button mode, you simply click the name to run the action.

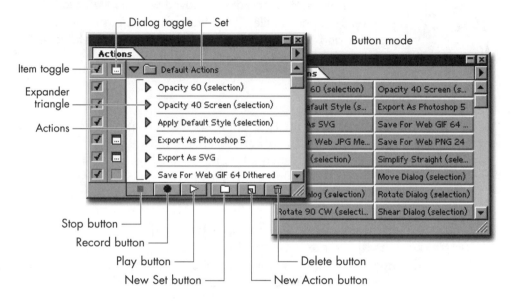

Figure 20-2: The Actions palette in the standard and button modes.

Creating a New Action

Now that you've seen what an action can do, it's time to create a new action. You have two choices for what kind of action you want to create. You can have Illustrator record all your movements as you create and modify objects. This allows you to create new objects by running the action. We call this a *construction action*. The construction action is a self-contained action that creates objects from scratch and requires nothing of you except your desire to use the action. Construction actions are useful when you want to create the exact same object over and over. For instance, if you always need a rounded rectangle at a certain size, it is rather easy to define an action that will create the object. However, construction actions limit you to *exactly* the same object each time.

We call the other type of action the *modifying action*. The modifying action is designed to make changes to an existing path. Before you execute a modifying action, you must first create the path that you want the action to modify and select that path before you play the action. Modifying actions are more flexible and allow you to consistently transform whatever path is chosen. In the following example, we're going to create a modifying action that will combine the blend command with opening the blend options dialog box.

Organizing Actions

The Actions palette is your headquarters for action design, but it also lets you organize your actions into folders or directories called *sets*. As we mentioned, Illustrator's preset actions are all stored in the set called Default Actions. When you create a new action, you can choose to add it to the other actions in the Default Action set, or you can first create a new set that better reflects the nature of your new action. To create a new set, either click the New Set button located at the bottom of the Actions palette or choose the New Set command from the palette's pop-up menu. The New Set dialog box will display. You have but one decision to make with this dialog box: what to name the set. Because the action that we're going to create is one that combines two commands, we'll call the new set "Command Actions."

 Actions are available to all new documents, not just the document that was open when they were created.

Recording an Action

In *recording* an action, you show Illustrator all the steps you want it to follow. Because this action involves creating a blend, we need to create and select two objects so the blend command is available. (Even though we create the action with these two objects selected, the action will then be available for other objects.) With all the groundwork for the new action out of the way, it's time to start designing or recording the new action.

1. Click the New Action button, or choose the New Action command from the palette menu.

The New Action dialog box will display, as shown in Figure 20-3. Here you name the action and choose the set in which it should reside. We'll name this action Blend+Options because those are the two commands that we are combining into one action. If you think you're going use the action often and want it to have its own keyboard shortcut, you can assign it a function key. If you display your Action palette in the button mode, you can choose a color for the action's button. After we name the action, we click the Record button. This starts the recording process.

Bear in mind that Illustrator already has shortcuts for all the function keys, so if you choose a shortcut for your action, be sure to also check the Shift and Command check boxes. Otherwise, you could lose a preset shortcut.

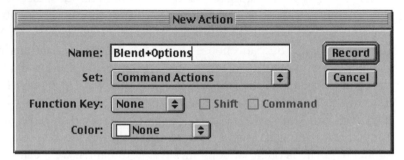

Figure 20-3: In the New Action dialog box, you can name your action and choose the set to which it belongs.

2. Click the Record button, or press Return/Enter.

Illustrator adds your new action to the set you specified and starts recording , as shown in Figure 20-4. When Illustrator is recording, the Record button changes from black to red. Now any changes we make will become part of the action.

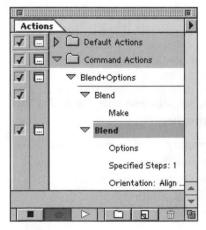

*Figure 20-4:
The Record button in the Actions palette turns red as you record the steps of an action. Each step is visible as it is added to the action.*

3. **Choose the Blend command by choosing the command in the menu or pressing the keystroke.**

   The command appears under the name of the action.

4. **Choose Object » Blend » Blend Options.**

   This opens the Blend Options dialog box as well as adds the step to the action. If you know exactly the options that you want for the Blend—for instance a certain number of steps—you can set these options. Then click OK. The second step appears in the Actions palette with the options set how you want them.

5. **Click the Stop button located at the bottom of the Actions palette.**

   This completes the action. You now can quickly create a blend and open the Blend Options dialog box.

Working with Dialog Box Steps

When we inserted the Blend Option into the action, an icon appeared in the dialog toggle column of the Actions palette. This icon indicates that the action will be broken up by the Blend Options dialog box. If you don't want to change the blend options, click the dialog toggle icon to hide it from view. This instructs Illustrator to use the settings in the dialog box as they were when you first recorded the action. The action will not be broken up by the dialog box.

Inserting Menu Items

You can also use the Insert Menu Item command from the Actions palette menu. This opens the Insert Menu Item dialog box, as shown in Figure 20-5. Although the instructions say you can type the first few characters of a menu command in the field or use the Find button, we find it much easier to just move to a menu and choose the item you want to insert. This inserts the full path name in the field.

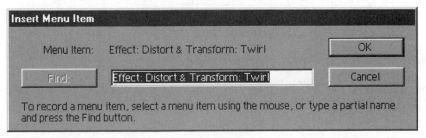

Figure 20-5: The Insert Menu Item dialog box allows you to add menu items that cannot be recorded while creating the action.

The Insert Menu Item command is extremely helpful for inserting items from the Effects menu that cannot be inserted as part of the recording of the action. For instance, the Twirl effect must be inserted using the Insert Menu Item. Unfortunately, all menu items inserted from the Insert Menu Item must be stopped with a dialog box. So there is no way to run the action without getting the dialog box.

Inserting Paths

As you create actions, you may notice that although rectangles and ellipses can be made part of an action, paths created with the pen, brush, or pencil cannot be recorded. These paths rely on recording the mouse movements, which unfortunately cannot be made part of an action. Fortunately, you can insert simple paths as part of an action using the Insert Select Path command.

You use the Insert Select Path command as follows. As you are recording the action, draw the path. With the path still selected, choose Insert Select Path from the Actions palette menu. In the Actions palette you will see the phrase Set Work Path appear. This indicates that the path will be created at that point. Once you have made the path part of the action, you can then modify it using any of the recordable action commands such as transformations, opacity settings, and so on.

Selecting Paths

You may also notice that selections made with any of the selection tools cannot be recorded. Fortunately those clever engineers at Adobe added the Select Object command. This command allows you to use the little-known Note options box in the Attributes palette to select objects. The best way to understand how the Select Object command works is to use it to create an action. In this case we're going to create an action that does a little cleanup work. When you use the Offset Path command, Illustrator creates a copy of the selected path; but it doesn't delete the original. (Sandee always wants to delete the original object after she makes the larger object.) We can create an action that does that cleanup job for us automatically. (Our thanks go to Dave Burkett, group product manager, who posted this action way back when actions were first introduced into Illustrator.)

1.   Select a path and start a new action.

Click the New Action icon to open the New Action dialog box. We've named the path Delete Offset Path. We then clicked OK to start recording the action.

2.   Add a note to the selected path.

Use the Note options box of the Attributes palette to add a note that tags the object with a word as shown in Figure 20-6. It doesn't matter what the note says, but we like to use the word *original*.

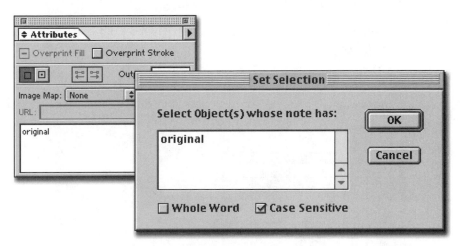

Figure 20-6: By entering a note in the Attributes palette (left), you choose Select Object in the Actions palette to open the Set Selection dialog box (right) to delete that object later.

3.   Press the keypad Enter key to apply the note.

The note is not made part of the action until you press the Enter key. You'll see the note added with the label "Attribute Setting" in the Actions list.

4.   Choose Object » Path » Offset Path.

Make whatever settings you want in the dialog box and click OK. The new path appears offset from the original.

5.   Delete the word "original" from the Attributes palette and press Enter.

When you offset the path, the same note is applied to the new path. With that path still selected, you need to delete the second note so that only the original object has the note applied to it. (There can only be one original, right?) Select the note in the options box and delete it. Don't forget to press the Enter key to set the step in the Actions palette.

6. Choose Select Object from the Actions palette.

This opens the Set Selection dialog box as shown in Figure 20-6. Type the same word you used to label the original object. (See why we like the word *original?*) This step selects the original object. Click OK.

7. Press the Delete key on the keyboard.

This deletes the original object leaving only the path that was offset from the original.

8. Click the Record button to stop recording.

Congratulations. You've just recorded your action. Your steps should be listed in the Actions palette as shown in Figure 20-7.

Figure 20-7:
The steps created by the Delete Offset Path exercise. We've opened the triangles to show you the details for each of the steps.

We know it may seem like a lot of work; but once you've created the action, it's so much easier to just run it than executing the individual steps by hand. And with a function key applied to the action, it is just as easy to execute the action as it is to run the Offset Path command.

Changing an Action

If you've ever watched a movie being filmed, you may have noticed that sometimes when the actor makes a mistake they don't stop the scene—the camera keeps filming. The director knows he can delete things later on in the editing room. It's the same when you record an action. You may choose the wrong command, or set the wrong color. You don't have to stop recording. Just keep applying the action steps. You can change the action later.

If you have too many steps, or the wrong steps, in an action, just select those steps and click the Delete button. If you like an action as is, but you can see how it may be more useful in some cases with a couple of the steps removed, you can temporarily turn off steps. To do so, click the Item Toggle box located at the far left of the step. The check mark will disappear from the box, indicating that Illustrator will bypass the step when it next carries out the action. To turn the step back on, click the Item Toggle box again and the check mark will return.

Just as you can easily delete steps from an action, you can easily add steps. To add steps, select the action in the Actions palette and click the Record button. Define the desired steps, and then click the Stop button when you're done. Illustrator will tack the new steps onto the end of the action and you can then move them to their proper position.

You can switch the order of an action's steps by dragging a step to a new position. Just drag the step up or down the list in the Action's palette. You can also move multiple steps at once. Select the first step and then Cmd/Ctrl-click each additional step you want to move. When you've selected all the steps you want, drag them to their new location. Illustrator will drop them as a contiguous block in which the original order of the steps is preserved.

You can also change the settings for a step in a dialog box by double-clicking the step in the Actions palette. This opens the dialog box as it was set during the recording of the action. You can then make whatever changes you want to the settings in the dialog box.

Our favorite technique is to drag steps from one action to another. This allows us to create small action sequences and then combine them in longer action commands. And if you don't want to lose the steps from one action, just hold the Opt/Alt key to copy the steps from one action to another.

Setting the Playback Options

Actions play back fast—really fast. So fast that you certainly wouldn't have time to select an item during the playback. Fortunately those clever Adobe engineers (aren't they clever?) have anticipated the need to slow down actions. Simply choose Playback Options from the Actions menu. The dialog box shown in Figure 20-8 appears.

- Accelerated (the default) plays the actions lickety-split.

- Step by Step allows all the objects to be created and the screen to redraw before the next step plays. This is somewhat slower than Accelerated, but not if you have a very fast computer.

- Pause for __ seconds allows you to specify a time interval between each step of the action.

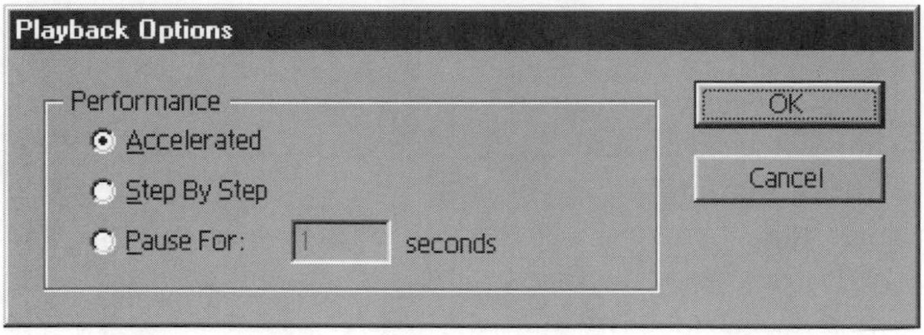

Figure 20-8: Use the Playback Options dialog box to control the
speed of how actions are played.

Making Interactive Actions

Another way to allow for user input in the execution of an action is to add a
stop to the action. A stop forces Illustrator to stop the execution of an action, and
it won't resume the action until you tell it to do so. To add a stop to an action
while you're creating it, choose Insert Stop from the Action palette's pop-up
menu. To add a stop to an existing action, select the step that you want the stop
to precede and choose Insert Stop from the pop-up menu. In either case, the
Record Stop dialog box will display, as shown in Figure 20-9. In the Message field,
you can explain to the user why Illustrator is pausing here. (This could be a simple
explanation of what the following step is about to do, or it could be instructions
to the user about what the user needs to do.)

Figure 20-9: When you insert a stop, Illustrator lets you enter the message for
the stop in the Record Stop dialog box (top). When you play back the action, the
message appears in an alert box (bottom).

When Illustrator encounters a stop, it displays a warning box complete with your instructions, also shown in Figure 20-8. Depending on whether you activated the Allow Continue option in the Record Stop dialog box, the warning may include a Continue button in addition to the standard Stop button. In cases in which you only want to provide information and you want the user to be able to quickly move on, be sure to check the Allow Continue check box. This will allow the user simply to click the Continue button and Illustrator will resume the next step in the action. If the user clicks the Stop button, Illustrator terminates the action at that point, but it remembers where it is in the action. At this point, for example, the user could apply some changes to the artwork and, when finished, have Illustrator complete the rest of the action by clicking the Play button.

Batch Processing Actions

 Although actions *per se* are not new to Illustrator, the Batch command is. This allows you to run actions on a group of files, rather than only within the open file.

Batch processing is the term used to describe doing something to a large number of files at the same time. The batch command for actions allows you to apply an action to a large number of files. Let's say you have a folder of Illustrator art. You can use the batch processing command to apply the Save for Web command to convert all the files to a GIF or JPEG. In less time than it takes to feed the cat, you've converted all your files into Web graphics.

To apply the batch processing command, choose Batch from the Actions palette menu. The Batch dialog box opens, as shown in Figure 20-10. Set each of the options as follows:

- Use the Set and Action pop-up lists to choose the action you want to play.

- Use the Source controls to choose which files should be converted. If you have specified an "Open" command in the action, you can override that setting by checking Override Action "Open" Commands. Check Include All Subdirectories if you want to open subfolders.

- Use the Destination controls to choose where the finished files should be saved. If you have specified a "Save In" command in the action, you can override that setting by checking the Override Action "Save In" Commands checkbox. If you are using the Export command in the action, you can use the controls to choose where the exported files should be saved. You can also override any existing directories for exported files by checking Override Action "Export" commands.

Use the Errors controls to choose whether the action should be stopped if there are errors in how the action is created. Or use the pop-up list to choose Log Errors to File, which creates a text file that lists any errors that were created in the batch processing.

> **TIP** The Log Errors to File setting is very helpful when you want a batch processing to run while you are away from your computer—perhaps going off to lunch. This allows all the files to be processed without getting stuck on one particular file.

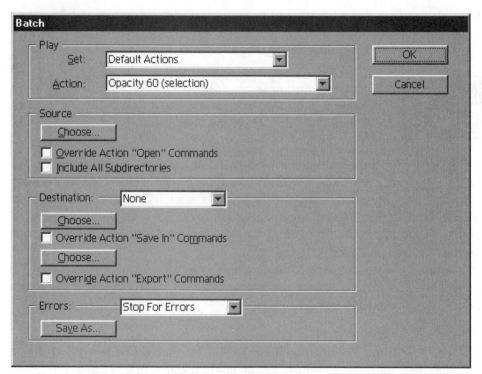

Figure 20-10: The Batch Processing dialog box allows you to apply an action to many files at once.

Saving and Loading Actions

Hey, boys and girls, once you create actions, you can save and trade 'em with your friends! Use the Save Actions command in the Actions palette menu to save your Actions to a separate file, which you can copy onto a separate computer. Then use the Load Actions command in the palette menu to add the actions, or use the Replace Actions command to replace the current actions with the new set.

You can also use the Reset Actions command to delete new actions and reset the palette to its default settings. Or you can choose Clear Actions to completely wipe out all the actions from the palette.

Working With Styles

 Styles are one of those most-requested features that have finally arrived in Illustrator. If you have used styles in other programs, you're going to love how styles automate your work in Illustrator.

Styles allow you to save all the attributes of an object—fills, strokes, transparency, effects, and all the other appearance attributes—into a single style that can be applied quickly to other objects. Think of styles as *uber*-swatches that can define all attributes of an object. Styles also allow you to change the attributes of many objects by changing the definition of the style. All the objects—selected or not—update to the new definition.

Defining a Style

It's very simple to define the attributes of a style. Simply select an object and make it look the way you want. Make sure the Styles palette is visible by choosing Window » Show Styles. The Styles palette appears as shown in Figure 20-11.

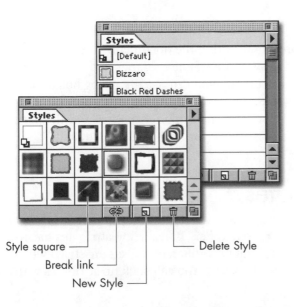

Style square
Break link
New Style
Delete Style

Figure 20-11:
The Styles palette is where you store the styles for a document. The list view lets you see the style names.

With the object selected, click the New Style button to automatically add the style square to the Styles palette. Or choose New Style from the Styles palette menu to name the style and then add the style to the palette. You can also drag an object from the artboard into the Styles palette. A style square automatically appears.

 Double-click a style square to change its name. The style names are visible in the list view shown in Figure 20-11. You can change the list view by choosing Small List View or Large List View from the Styles menu.

Applying and Changing Styles

Once you define a style, you can apply it to objects by selecting the object and then clicking the style square. The object changes its appearance to match the style definition.

You can also modify the style definition. This changes all the objects that have had the style applied to them. To modify a style, make whatever changes you want to an object. Then hold the Opt/Alt key as you drag that object into the Styles palette onto the original style square. The style definition updates within the Styles palette as well as in all objects that have had the style applied to them.

If you want, you can unlink an object from its style definition. This allows you to change the definition of that style without changing the appearance of the object. Select the object and then click the Break Link button. The object no longer will change with the new definition of the style.

Importing Styles

Styles are like swatches—they are stored within the document. You can import styles from other documents. Choose Window » Style Libraries and then choose one of the listings. If you choose Other Library you can use the dialog box to navigate to import the styles from a separate Illustrator document. The styles appear in a separate styles palette. Click the style in the imported palette and the style will automatically be added to the Styles palette for the current document.

Transferring Attributes

As useful as styles are, there are times when you'd like to quickly copy the attributes of one object and apply them to another. Transferring attributes means you don't have to scribble down notes about how different objects are styled when you want to create new objects that match exactly. You can suck up attributes with the eyedropper tool and pour them down with the paint bucket. Although the two objects won't have a link like styles, the eyedropper and paint bucket do make it easy to make two objects look alike.

 If you paid attention in Chapter 6, these are the same eyedropper and paint bucket tools that sampled and applied text attributes. However, there are a few more controls when working with objects.

Using the Eyedropper

The eyedropper lifts attributes from objects and stores them in the Appearance palette. To use the eyedropper, click inside a path. The eyedropper cursor becomes partially black to show that you're lifting attributes as shown in Figure 20-12. You can then use the paint bucket tool to transfer the attributes to other objects.

 If any objects are selected as you sample attributes with the eyedropper, those objects will automatically pick up the attributes of the sampled object.

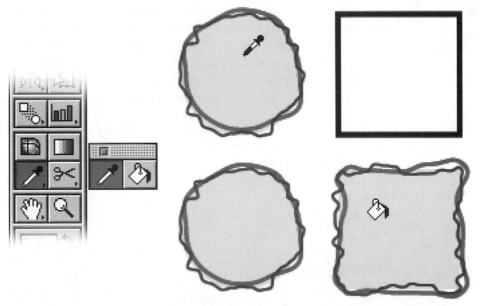

Figure 20-12: Use the eyedropper to sample the attributes of one object. Use the paint bucket to apply those attributes to other objects.

If you Shift-click with the eyedropper, it transfers only the color directly under the eyedropper. This allows you to sample the color of the stroke of an object and transfer it to the fill of another. It also allows you to sample the colors of placed images, patterns, or gradients, as shown in Figure 20-13.

Figure 20-13: Hold the Shift key to sample only the color of an object. This allows you to sample colors from rasterized images.

 You can sample colors from background windows, including an image open in other applications, or from the background color of your computer screen. Instead of releasing the mouse as you click, continue pressing the mouse button. Then move the mouse anywhere around the screen. As you drag, the color of the active icon changes to reflect the color under your cursor. When you sample the color you like, release the mouse.

Ordinarily, each time you sample an object with the eyedropper, you replace the attributes in the Appearance palette with the attributes of the sampled object. However, if you hold Opt/Alt together with the Shift key, a plus (+) sign appears next to the eyedropper cursor. This indicates that the eyedropper will add the attributes of the object to the appearance palette. Figure 20-14 shows how this allows you to combine the fills and strokes of different objects into multiple fills or strokes.

Using the Paint Bucket

The paint bucket tool—the alternate tool in the eyedropper tool slot—applies colors from the Color palette to objects in the illustration window. To use the tool, specify the desired fill and stroke attributes in the palettes, and then click the target object as shown in Figure 20-12. Although you can choose the paint bucket tool in the toolbox, we find it much easier to sample with the eyedropper and then hold the Opt/Alt key to switch to the paint bucket.

 As a pal of Deke's from Adobe likes to say, the Opt/Alt key allows you to alternately "suck and dump" colors without changing tools. (Now if they'd only put that into the manual!)

 If an object has no fill, you need to click with the paint bucket on the path outline.

Figure 20-14: Hold the Opt/Alt and the Shift key to add the attributes to the sampled appearance. Then click with the paint bucket to apply the multiple fills or strokes.

Controlling the Sampled and Applied Attributes

Double-click either the paint bucket or the eyedropper in the toolbox to display the dialog box full of check boxes shown in Figure 20-15. When Appearance is checked, you will sample or apply all the attributes, including multiple fills or strokes, transparency attributes, and effects. When Appearance is unchecked, only the focal fill or stroke and the transparency attributes are sampled. Effects and multiple fills or strokes are ignored. (The focal fill or stroke is the fill or stroke currently active in the toolbox.) Uncheck the Transparency option to not sample or apply the transparency attributes. Deselecting the Focal Fill or Focal Stroke check box turns off all corresponding options in that group.

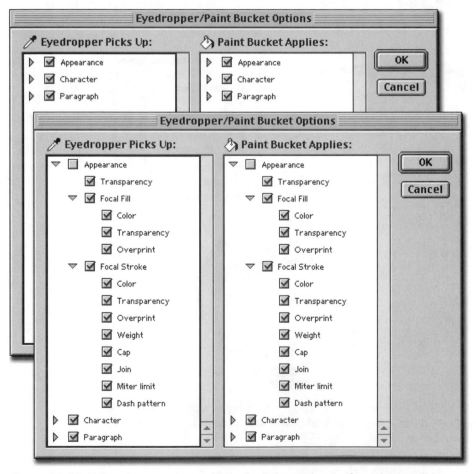

Figure 20-15: When Appearance is checked, all the attributes of an object will be sampled or applied. When Appearance is unchecked, you can choose which specific transparency, fill, or stroke attributes will be sampled and applied.

Contextual Menus

Originally only Windows had contextual menus, but after they were introduced to the Mac platform, Adobe added contextual menus to Illustrator with great results. In the Mac platform, you open contextual menus by holding the Control key and clicking with the mouse. In Windows, you click with the right mouse button.

There are several benefits to working with contextual menus. First, they appear anywhere on the screen—you don't have to move your mouse all the way up to the top of the screen to get the menu. Second, they display their items in the context of what is currently selected as shown in Figure 20-16. So if you invoke the contextual menu while you are over a ruler, you get a contextual menu that lets you switch the units of measurement for the rulers. However, if you are over the artboard with objects selected, you get different contextual menus.

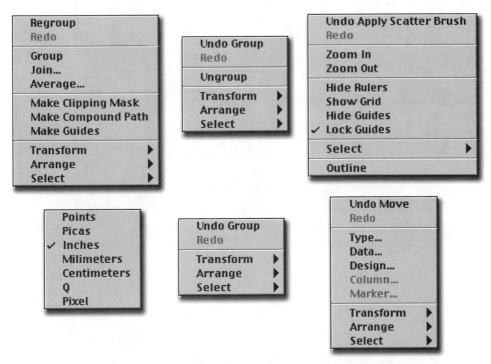

Figure 20-16: A sample of the contextual menus you get when over different areas of the screen or when certain objects are selected. In the top row (from left to right): Multiple objects selected, group selected, no objects selected. In the bottom row (from left to right): over the rulers, raster object selected, graph selected.

Online Resources

If you click the little illustration of Venus at the top of the toolbox, you open the Adobe Online dialog box as shown in Figure 20-17. This is where you can link to the Adobe Web site to register Illustrator, look up support articles, read tips and tricks from other Illustrator users, and purchase other Adobe products. This online activity might be useful for those who have a high-bandwidth Internet connection. However, if you are hooked up with a modem, you will find it less useful.

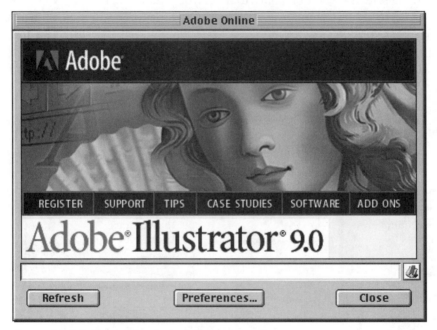

Figure 20-17: The Adobe Online dialog box allows you to register and receive information about Illustrator from the Adobe Web site.

PRINTING YOUR ILLUSTRATIONS

Hey, sure Illustrator creates fantastic images and effects on the computer monitor. But the real proof of a program is in the printing. (If you're using Illustrator to only create Web graphics or screen illustrations, please feel free to skip this chapter.) Illustrator has always had a great track record when it comes to printing objects exactly as you see them on screen, with the lowest likelihood of error. However, printing problems don't just happen randomly. Those people who manage to avoid problems usually have a good understanding of how to create their files and set their printing options.

This chapter explains how to print your illustrations to a PostScript-compatible printer (also called an *output device*). Although Illustrator is capable of printing to non-PostScript printers, such as inexpensive inkjet devices, this is not its forte. If you need to print to a non-PostScript device, we suggest you invest in Adobe PressReady. PressReady allows you to print using the most advanced PostScript technology, specially optimized for inkjets. But even those who proof their artwork on inkjet devices will eventually have their files separated using high-resolution PostScript printers.

Printing Composite Pages

A composite is a one-page representation of an illustration. A black-and-white composite, printed from a standard laser printer or professional imagesetter (which we'll describe in a few pages), translates all colors of an illustration to gray values. A color composite, printed from a color printer or film recorder, prints the illustration in full color. Composites are useful when you want to reproduce the illustration in black-and-white, proof an illustration, or fire off a few color photocopies. But you can't use composites for professional-quality color reproduction. For that, you need to print separations, which we'll discuss later in the section "Printing Color Separations."

Printing a composite illustration is a five-step process (Windows users can skip to Step 2):

1. If your computer is hooked up to a network, use the Network control panel to select the network that the printer is connected to.

2. Mac users can use the Chooser desk accessory to activate the AdobePS driver and select the network printer. Windows users can choose from the list of available printers in the Print Setup dialog box.

3. Choose File » Page Setup (Mac) or File » Print Setup (Windows) to determine the size of the printed page. Close the dialog box when you're finished.

4. If needed, position the page-size boundary in the drawing area with the page tool.

5. Choose File » Print to print the illustration to the desired output device.

We'll explain each of these steps in detail in the following sections.

Selecting a Network on a Mac

Most Macintosh computers sold in the last several years include two kinds of printing ports: the serial LocalTalk port and the EtherTalk port. The LocalTalk port connects directly to a printer or to an AppleTalk network. The EtherTalk port connects to an Ethernet printer or a large-scale Ethernet network. If you work in a large office, you're probably connected to other computers via Ethernet, which is the standard networking protocol used throughout corporate America.

If you have access to multiple networks, you can switch from one network to another using either the Network or the AppleTalk control panel. Choose Apple » Control Panels » Network or Apple » Control Panels » AppleTalk to bring up the appropriate window. The AppleTalk control panel is shown in Figure 21-1. Depending on your model of computer, you'll probably find at least two options—LocalTalk and EtherTalk. You may see a third option, Remote Only, which allows you to print through your modem to a remote network. (This is a function of Apple Remote Access, which freelancers like Deke use to communicate with distant editors.) Select the kind of network that contains the printer you want to use, and then click the close box in the upper left corner of the window.

Your Mac can communicate over several different kinds of networks, but it can access only one network at a time. So if you are sharing files, say, over Ethernet and you switch to a LocalTalk printer, an error message tells you that the Ethernet connection is about to be broken. This is the price one pays for connectivity.

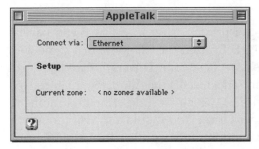

Figure 21-1:
If your computer is hooked up to multiple networks, use the Network control panel to select the network that includes the printer you want to use.

Choosing a PostScript Printer on a Mac

To select a printer on a Macintosh, locate the Chooser desk accessory in the list of items under the Apple menu. The Chooser dialog box comes up, as shown in Figure 21-2. The dialog box is split into two halves, with the left half devoted to a scrolling list of printer driver icons and network zones and the right half devoted to specific printer options.

Select the AdobePS icon, spotlighted in Figure 21-2. AdobePS is the most recent PostScript printer driver direct from Adobe, the inventor and custodian of PostScript. It helps Illustrator and the system software translate the contents of an illustration to the output device.

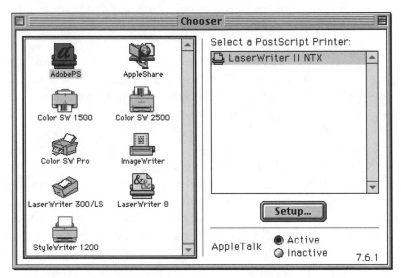

Figure 21-2: Select the AdobePS icon in the Chooser window to select and initialize a PostScript printer.

If AdobePS is not available in the list of printer driver icons, or if you haven't yet installed the newest version, AdobePS 8.7, insert the CD-ROM that came with your copy of Illustrator and open the Adobe PostScript Drivers 8.7 folder. Open it and double-click the Installer program. This installs the AdobePS driver as well as lots of PostScript printer description files, which we'll describe in a moment. Together, they make Illustrator print at peak form. You should also visit the Adobe product Web page at http://www.adobe.com/prodindex/printerdrivers/main.html. Here you can get the most recent printer drivers and PostScript printer description (PPD) files.

The AdobePS driver supports PPD files. AdobePS can't account for the tiny differences among different models of PostScript printers, so each PPD serves as a little guidance file, customizing the driver to accommodate a specific printer model. After selecting a printer, you can access the proper PPD by clicking the Setup button. (Or just double-click the printer name in the list.) A new dialog box claws its way onto your screen, as shown in Figure 21-3. Click the Auto Setup button to instruct the system software to talk to your printer and automatically determine the proper PPD. If the system fails, or if it selects the dreaded Generic option, click the Select PPD button and try to locate the proper PPD file inside the Printer Descriptions folder in the Extensions folder in your System folder. When you finish, click the OK button or press Return/Enter.

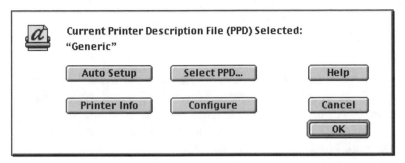

Figure 21-3: Use this dialog box to select the proper printer description file for your particular brand of PostScript printer.

Choosing a PostScript Printer in Windows

If you're using the Windows 95 or Windows 98 operating system, you select a printer from the Start menu by choosing the Settings » Printers command. Click the Add Printer icon and follow the instructions in the Install Wizard. If you don't have the most current PostScript printer driver, go to the Adobe product Web page (http://www.adobe.com/products/printerdrivers/main.html). Download the Universal Installer 1.0.2, consisting of AdobePS 4.4.1 for Windows 95/98 and/or NT, AdobePS 5.1.2 for Windows NT, and PScript 5 for Windows 2000. After you've downloaded it on your hard drive, double-click on the ".exe" file to access the file's contents. You'll be asked to specify a default PPD during the installation. The Illustrator CD comes with a number of PPDs, and you can also find some additional ones at the Adobe Web site.

After you have installed the printer drivers you want, choose File » Print Setup. You can then choose the printer you want to use from the pop-up menu inside the Print Setup dialog box. If you want to change to another printer, one for which you've already installed a driver, choose it from the Name pop-up menu whenever the mood strikes you while using Illustrator.

Setting Up the Page

 Many of the printing-related options appear in completely different locations within the two different platforms. So wherever possible, we're presenting both the Mac and Windows dialog boxes together to help you.

Your next step is to define the size of the page on which you intend to print your illustration. Choose File » Page Setup (Mac) or File » Print Setup (Windows) to display the AdobePS Page Setup dialog box shown in Figure 21-4, which contains the following options:

- **Paper:** Select the size of the paper on which you want to print. The specific options available from this pop-up menu depend on which PPD file you selected in the Chooser.

- **Scale:** To scale your illustration as you print it, enter any value from 25 to 400 percent in this option box—Windows users will find the Scaling option box in the Graphics panel. Generally, you'll use this option to reduce large artwork when proofing it on a laser printer or on another device that's limited to letter-sized pages.

- **Orientation:** There are two orientation options. By default, the page is positioned upright in the Portrait position. But if you want to print a wide illustration, you can select the Landscape option.

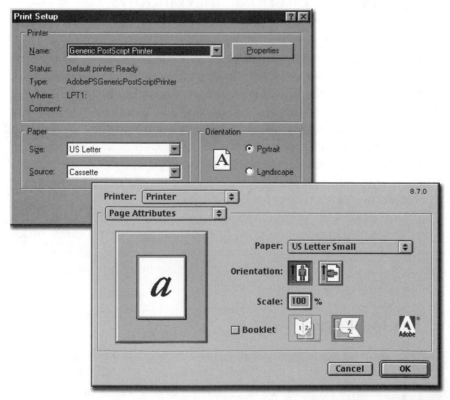

Figure 21-4: The Print Setup or Page Setup dialog boxes for Windows or Mac.

PostScript Options

Mac users can use the pop-up list to open the PostScript Options shown in Figure 21-5. (Windows users can find some of these options in the Properties » Graphics panel of the Print Setup and in the Print dialog box.) Check the boxes in this dialog box to perform a few printing effects that may come in handy. The sample page on the left side of the dialog box demonstrates the effect of the selected options. The big letter *a* represents the illustration on the page, and the dotted line represents the margin size.

 The options in the PostScript Options dialog box are most useful when printing an illustration to a midrange output device, such as a laser printer. If you're printing to more sophisticated devices such as an imagesetter, some of the options—particularly Flip Horizontal, Flip Vertical, and Invert Image—may duplicate or nullify settings in the more important Separation Setup dialog box.

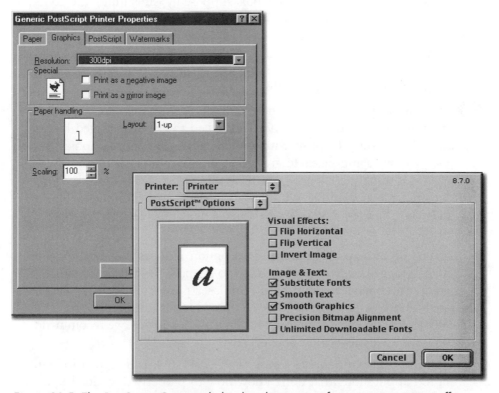

Figure 21-5: The PostScript Options dialog box lets you perform certain printing effects, which range from moderately useful to nonfunctioning.

The check boxes in the PostScript Options dialog box work as follows:

- **Flip Horizontal:** Select this option (called Print as a Mirror Image in the Graphics panel for Windows users) to flip the objects in an illustration horizontally on the printed page. Although this option was originally created to help print film negatives, you should use Illustrator's Separation Setup to properly control the horizontal orientation. We explain film negatives more thoroughly in the "Printing Color Separations" section later in this chapter.

- **Flip Vertical:** Same as Flip Horizontal, this option will change the orientation of the image. And again, this option is better controlled in Separation Setup.

- **Invert Image:** This option will turn the artwork into a negative of itself. (This is called Print as a Negative Image in the Graphics panel for Windows users.) And like the flips, this setting is better controlled in Separation Setup.

- **Substitute Fonts:** This check box supposedly substitutes the fonts Geneva, Monaco, and New York with their respective PostScript equivalents of Helvetica, Courier, and Times. But if you try to use the option with Illustrator, the program automatically turns off the check box and prints the TrueType versions of Geneva, Monaco, and New York. In other words, you can ignore this option.

- **Smooth Graphics:** Back in the old days, when MacPaint was a hot program, folks were bound and determined to get their jagged black-and-white images to print with smooth edges. Smooth Graphics did just that, averaging pixels to give them smooth, though gummy, edges. Well, it doesn't matter how you have this option set in Illustrator (or the similar option in the Windows Print dialog box). Imported black-and-white images always have jagged edges, just as Mother Nature meant them to have.

- **Precision Bitmap Alignment:** This option reduces a typical 72-ppi image dragged over from Photoshop to 96 percent of its original size, making it compatible with a 300-dpi laser printer. This increases the resolution of a 72-ppi image to 75 ppi, which is evenly divisible into 300. Unless the laser printer is your final output device, we recommend that you leave this option unchecked.

- **Unlimited Downloadable Fonts:** This check box is designed to help moron applications that don't know how to properly download fonts. This check box tells the program to wise up. Illustrator manages its fonts just fine without this silly option.

Adjusting the Page Size

You can modify the page boundaries in the artboard by selecting one of the View radio buttons inside the Document Setup dialog box, which we introduced back in Chapter 3. To display the dialog box, choose File » Document Setup. Then select the desired radio button:

- **Single Full Page:** Select this radio button to display a single page size inside the artboard. This ensures that you will print just one page for the entire illustration.

- **Tile Full Pages:** Select this radio button to display as many whole pages as will fit inside the artboard. Use this check box to print a multi-paged document like a flier or a two-page ad.

- **Tile Imageable Areas:** Select this radio button to subdivide the artboard into multiple partial pages, called tiles. We'll talk more about tiling large artwork in the "Tiling Oversized Illustrations" section later in this chapter.

After you select one of these options and press the Return/Enter key, you can use the page tool to position the page size relative to the objects in your illustration. If the dotted page boundaries are not visible, choose View » Show Page Tiling. If you selected the Tile Imageable Areas option in the Document Setup dialog box, the page number of each tile is listed in the lower left corner of the tile. This way, you can specify the particular pages that you want to print when outputting the illustration.

Printing Pages

To initiate the printing process, choose File » Print. The General Printer dialog box appears, as shown in Figure 21-6. Unless you've never printed a document from a computer, you should be familiar with these options.

- **Copies:** Enter the number of copies you want to print in the Copies option box. You can enter the number 999 in the copies field, but if you want to print more than 10, you're better off having them commercially reproduced. Commercial reproduction provides better quality for less money, and it ensures less wear and tear on your printer.

- **Pages:** Specify a range of pages using the Pages options. By default, the All radio button is selected. If the drawing area displays a single page size, Illustrator will print just that page. If the drawing area contains multiple pages or tiles, Illustrator prints all pages that contain objects. To define a specific range of pages or tiles to be printed, enter the page numbers in the From and To option boxes. These numbers should correspond to the page numbers displayed in the lower left corners of pages in the drawing area.

● **Paper Source:** If you want to print your illustration on a letterhead or other special piece of paper that you manually feed into the printer, select the specific paper source.

● **Destination (Mac) or Print to File (Windows):** This option allows you to generate a PostScript-language definition of the file on disk rather than printing it directly to your printer. Select the Printer option to print the image to an output device as usual. Select the File destination or check Print to File to write a PostScript-language version of the image to disk. You can then submit the file to a service bureau for output.

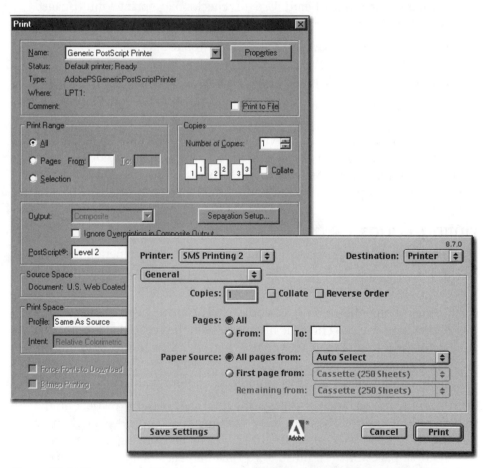

Figure 21-6: You can print the pages in your illustration to a PostScript-compatible printer from the Printer dialog box.

In Windows, the Output options are in the main Printer dialog box. On the Mac, these options are available by choosing Adobe Illustrator 9.0 from the pop-up list as shown in Figure 21-7. Here's how these options work:

- **Output:** Select the Composite option from the Output pop-up menu to print a black-and-white or color composite of your illustration. Select the Separate option to print color separations. We explain the latter option in more detail in the next section.

- **PostScript:** Select Level 1, Level 2, or Level 3, depending on the kind of PostScript that's built into your output device. PostScript printers made in the last two years are very likely to be Level 3—the most sophisticated. Older PostScript printers are Level 2. Extremely ancient machines are Level 1. If your machine is brand new, set this option to Level 3. If it doesn't work, move down to Level 2.

- **Data:** If your network doesn't support binary encoding, select the ASCII option to transfer data in the text-only format. The printing process takes much longer to complete, but at least it's possible. When in doubt, however, leave this option set to Binary.

- **Selection Only:** If you just want to print the selected objects in the illustration, select this check box. When the option is turned off—as by default—Illustrator prints all objects, whether selected or not.

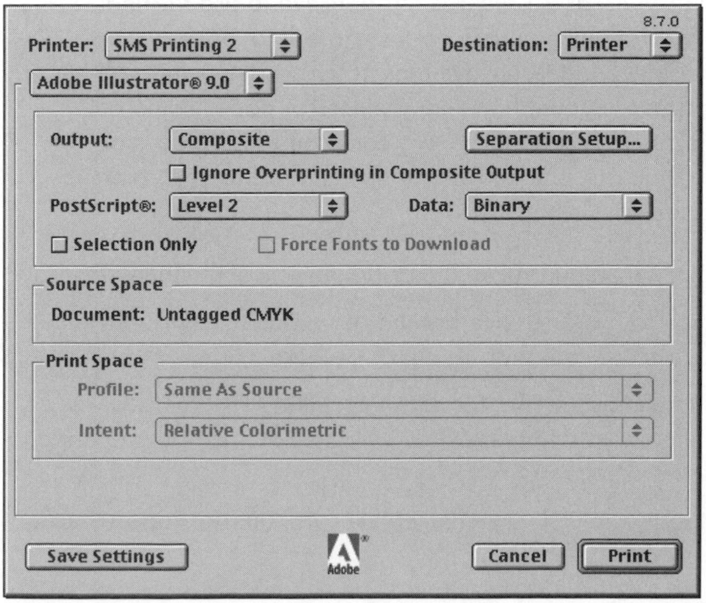

*Figure 21-7:
The Adobe Illustrator 9
options for a specific
output device.*

- **Separation Setup:** This button opens the all-powerful Separations dialog box that allows you to specify settings for printing color separations. We'll explain this dialog box from A to Z in the next section.

Once you've made all your settings, just click the Print button and sit back and watch as your beautiful creation works its way out of the printer.

Printing Color Separations

Professional color reproduction requires that you print an illustration to color separations. This means you print a separate sheet of paper or film for each of the process color primaries—cyan, magenta, yellow, and black—or for each spot color used in the illustration. You can even add spot colors to the four process primaries to enhance the range of colors in the final document, or target the colors in a logo or another color-sensitive element. But keep in mind that every additional separation you print incurs additional cost—additional ink has to be applied to the pages, and extra labor costs are charged for making the plates and running the plates and paper through the press.

The only category of printer up to the job of color separations is an *imagesetter,* which is a high-resolution device. Imagesetters print onto special photosensitive paper or film, which is then turned into printing plates. (Some imagesetters print directly to the printing plates.)

 Although your laser printer is too primitive to use for final color separations, you can certainly use it to make paper separations. Sandee always runs her separations through her laser printer to count how many pieces of paper come out. If the job is supposed to be two color, and four pieces of paper come out, she knows she needs to adjust the colors in the document.

You can also print color separations of an illustration in one of the following ways:

- Take the Illustrator file to a service bureau or commercial printer and let a qualified technician deal with it.

- Import the illustration as an EPS file into PageMaker or QuarkXPress. Then take the PageMaker or QuarkXPress file to a service bureau and let those folks do their jobs.

- Print the separations directly from PageMaker or QuarkXPress to an in-house imagesetter.

The last option—printing the color separations directly from Illustrator on your own, either to an in-house imagesetter or to a file that you can later deliver to a service bureau—is perhaps the most unlikely scenario of them all. But it is the reason that Illustrator integrates color separation capabilities, which is why we explain it in great detail in the next few pages.

To print color separations from Illustrator, do the following:

1. Prepare the illustration just as you did when printing the composite, using the Chooser, the Page Setup command, and the page tool.

2. Choose File » Separation Setup.

3. Modify the settings as desired.

4. Choose File » Print. Choose the settings there.

5. Click the Print button.

Only Step 3 requires much effort, but it requires quite a bit. Figure 21-8 shows the Separations dialog box in full regalia. The dialog box is divided into two parts—the separation preview in the upper left corner, and a series of options below and to the right of it.

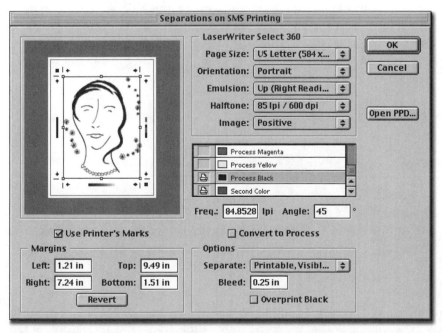

Figure 21-8: You can access this dialog box either by clicking the Separation Setup button inside the Printer dialog box or by choosing File » Separation Setup.

 If this is the first time you've opened this dialog box, you need to select a PPD file. Click the Open PPD button, and then locate the desired PPD file. The PPD file you select will determine which options are available in the pop-up menus throughout the Color Separation dialog box.

Page Size

This pop-up menu lists the page sizes available for your output device, based on the active PPD. Next to the common name of each page size is the imageable area of the page, measured in points. Keep an eye on the preview to make sure the illustration and all the printer marks around the illustration fit on the page.

If you've selected the PPD file for an imagesetter, you can define your own page size by selecting the Custom option from the Page Size pop-up menu. This displays the dialog box shown in Figure 21-9. The default values for the Width and Height options are the dimensions of the smallest page that will hold all the objects in your illustration. The Offset option allows you to add space between your illustration and the right edge of the paper or film. If the Offset value is left at 0, the output device will automatically center the illustration on the page.

The Transverse check box controls the orientation of your custom page relative to the paper or film. By default, the printer places the long side of portrait artwork parallel to the long edge of the film. You can reduce paper or film waste by rotating the illustration so its short side is parallel to the long edge of the film, known as transverse orientation. Then use the Offset value to specify the amount of space that lies between your illustration and any printed image that follows it.

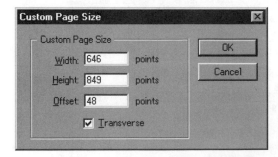

Figure 21-9:
This dialog box allows you to specify a custom page size as well as a distance between pages.

Orientation

Set this option to Portrait or Landscape, just as you have inside the Page Setup dialog box. This option works independently of the Transverse check box; if the Orientation option is set incorrectly, you'll cut off part of your illustration.

Emulsion

The Emulsion options control how the illustration prints relative to the emulsion side of photosensitive film. The names given to the options, Up and Down, refer to the sides of the film on which the emulsion is located. When printing film negatives, you probably want to select Down from the pop-up menu; when printing on paper, Up is usually the correct setting. (Be sure neither Flip Horizontal nor Flip Vertical is selected in the PostScript Options dialog box—shown back in Figure 21-5—because either option will nullify the Emulsion setting.) Consult your commercial printer to confirm which option you should select.

Halftone

Printing presses aren't capable of applying shades of color to paper. They can apply solid ink or no ink at all. That's it. So to represent different light and dark values, imagesetters generate thousands of little black halftone dots, as illustrated in Figure 21-10. The halftone dots grow and shrink to represent respectively darker and lighter shades of color.

Figure 21-10: A gray value is printed as thousands of little halftone dots. The dots can grow and shrink to imitate different shades.

You can specify the density of the halftone dots by selecting an option from the Halftone pop-up menu in the Color Separation dialog box. The first value before the slash represents the screen frequency, which is the number of halftone dots per linear inch. The second value represents the printer resolution, which is the number of tiny printer pixels that print in a linear inch. You can figure out the number of printer pixels that fit inside the largest possible halftone dot by dividing the second number by the first. For example, in this book, all illustrations are printed at a resolution of 2,540 dpi and a screen frequency of 120 lpi. If you divide 2,540 by 120, you get a little more than 21, which means that a halftone dot inside a very dark shade of gray is 21 printer pixels tall and 21 pixels wide.

Fascinating as this may be, the real question is, as always, which option should you use? Unless you have a specific reason for doing otherwise, set the printer resolution (the second value) as high as it will go. If you're printing to paper, you probably don't want to set the screen frequency (the first value) any higher than 120 lpi, because the dots may grow and clog up as the illustration is transferred to film and then to plates. When printing to film, screen frequencies of 133 lpi and higher are acceptable. Consult your commercial printer if you are at all unsure.

Image

The Image option controls whether the illustration prints as a positive or a negative image. If you're printing to paper, the default Positive is usually the correct setting. However, when printing to film, you'll probably want to select Negative. (The Invert image check box in the PostScript Options dialog box should be turned off; otherwise, it will interfere with the Image setting.)

Color list

The scrolling list of colors that appears below the Image pop-up menu allows you to specify exactly which colors you want to print to independent separations. The process colors are listed first, followed by any spot colors. A couple of different icons may appear in front of the colors as shown in Figure 21-11. These icons specify whether a color gets its own separation, whether a spot color is converted to its process ingredients, or whether the color gets printed at all.

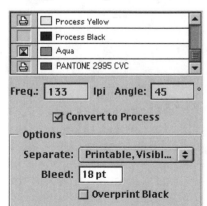

Figure 21-11:
To decide which spot colors you want to separate and which you want to convert to their CMYK ingredients, turn off the Convert to Process check box (shown here in its default position as turned on).

By default, Illustrator is ready to convert all spot colors to their process ingredients. If you want to print at least one spot color to its own separation, turn off the Convert to Process check box. The spot colors in the list should immediately change from dimmed to black. The printer icon in front of each spot color indicates that the color will print to its own separation. If you want a specific spot color to be converted to process, click the printer icon so that it changes to a process color icon. For example, in Figure 21-11, the color named Aqua is set to convert to CMYK colors. But Pantone 2995 is set to print onto its own plate.

Frequency and Angle

In addition to changing the overall screen frequency of the illustration, you can modify the frequency of a single separation. You can also change the angle of the halftone dots. Back in Figure 21-10, for example, you can see that the halftone angle is 45 degrees—that is, each dot is angled 45 degrees from its closest neighbor. To change either the frequency or angle, select a color from the list and enter a new value in the Frequency or Angle option box.

Why would you want to change either of these values? To avoid creating weird patterns (called moirés) between the halftone dots from different separations. See, by default, all process colors are set to the same frequency. Black is angled at 45 degrees, cyan is set to 15 degrees, magenta is 75 degrees, and yellow is 0 degrees. Rotations of 90 degrees or more are repetitive, because the halftone dots extend in all different directions. This means that cyan, magenta, and black are each rotated 30 degrees from each other; only yellow is closer—measuring only 15 degrees from cyan and magenta—but yellow is so light, its halftone dots don't create a patterning effect.

So far, so good. There's no reason to change the process colors. The problem is, how do you prevent a spot color from clashing? Unless you know exactly what you're doing, you shouldn't mess around with the Frequency value. And there aren't really any good angles left. This leaves you with the following frequency and angle options:

If you're printing an illustration that contains one or two spot colors and black—but not cyan, magenta, or yellow—leave black set to 45 degrees and set the spot colors to 15 and 75 degrees. It doesn't matter which color you set to which value. If you have only one spot color, pick an angle—15 or 75—and go with it. When printing a spot color in addition to CMYK, pick a color—black, cyan, or magenta—that the spot color never overlaps. (If the spot color overlaps all three, return to your illustration and modify it so the overlap no longer exists.) Then mimic the angle of that color. For example, if the spot color and cyan never mix—you don't blend between the two colors, mix them together in a gradation, or overprint one on top of the other—then you would set the angle of the spot color to 15 degrees.

Use Printer's Marks

This option lets you print a predefined collection of printer's marks. Turn on this check box to print the marks; turn it off to hide them.

The printer's marks include star targets and registration marks to aid in registration. To register plates is to get them into exact alignment, so one color doesn't appear out of sync with another. Illustrator also prints crop marks around the entire illustration and different types of progressive color bars along the edges. Most important, Illustrator labels each separation according to the ink it goes with. There is no good reason to turn off this option. But we sure do wish Illustrator still let you customize the marks.

Separate

Use this pop-up menu to specify which layers you want to print inside your illustration. (If the file contains just one layer, skip this option and move on.) Choose the Printable, Visible Layers option to print just those layers that you have set to print; if you turn off the Print check box for a layer in the Layer Options dialog box (as discussed in the "Modifying Your Layers" section of Chapter 10), the layer won't print. Select the Visible Layers option to print all layers that are visible on screen, even if the Print check box is off. And select the All Layers option to print all layers, whether hidden or turned off. The preview shows the results of the option you select.

Overprint Black

Select this check box to overprint all black ink inside the illustration. Overprinting black is a common way of anticipating registration problems. Also, it permits you to create so-called "saturated blacks." Although black is theoretically as dark as dark can be, you can create colors that are visibly darker by adding cyan, magenta, or yellow to solid black. The result is a rich, glossy black.

But overprinting every black in your illustration has its drawbacks. If a black rectangle is positioned on top of a dark CMY object, for example, you can end up applying more ink than the page can absorb. Most paper stocks max out at about 300 percent saturation. If you go over that—for example, 90%C 80%M 70%Y 100%K, which adds up to 340 percent saturation—the ink can actually puddle or run, creating some messy results. Unless you're sure your illustration is safe from oversaturation, avoid the Overprint Black check box and use the more selective Filter » Colors » Overprint Black command, as we explain near the end of this chapter.

Margin and Bounding box

The Margin options—Left, Right, Top, and Bottom—allow you to adjust the size of the area Illustrator allots to the illustration. The default values represent the smallest bounding box that can be drawn around the illustration. Printer marks appear in the margins around the bounding box in the preview; the bounding box itself appears as a rectangle.

You can modify the bounding box either by dragging the corner handles in the preview or by changing the values in the Left, Right, Bottom, and Top Margin option boxes. These values represent the distance from the edge of the page size (specified with the Page Size pop-up menu) and the edge of the bounding box. Therefore, entering smaller values increases the size of the bounding box; entering larger values shrinks the bounding box. Illustrator automatically moves the printer marks so they stay outside the bounding box inside the preview.

Bleed

Though this last option may sound like a practice that died with medieval barbers, it actually controls the distance from the edge of the bounding box to the beginning of the crop marks. In printing, a bleed is the distance that an image extends off the printed page. For example, a bleed of 18 points ensures that even if the page shifts ¼ inch on the press or the trim is ¼ inch off, the illustration still fills the entire page and extends off the sides. How you set the bounding box affects the amount of illustration that is permitted to bleed off the edge. The Bleed value (which can vary from 0 to 72 points) determines how much of this bleed gets printed, and offsets the crop marks and other printer marks so they don't overlap too much of the printed artwork. Unless you're running out of room on the film, you're better off leaving the Bleed value set to its default, 18 points.

Unusual Printing Considerations

So much for the huge array of printing options that are crammed into the major printing dialog boxes. Although these options are very important—some clearly more important than others—you'll spend most of your time pressing Cmd/Ctrl-P, hitting the Return/Enter key, and going off to get some coffee.

Unfortunately, things don't always go according to plan. Sometimes you have to spend a few minutes massaging your illustration to get it ready to deliver the most ideal results in less than ideal conditions. Most problems can be overcome using the options that we've already described, but others can't. Those that can't are the subject of the remaining pages in this chapter.

The following sections explain all the preparatory alternatives that Illustrator permits prior to printing your artwork. Though none of these measures is obligatory—or even customary—they are the sorts of options that you'll want to be at least vaguely familiar with. For example, you can slice and dice large illustrations, insert your own crop marks or trim marks, overcome printing errors, and anticipate registration problems using tools and commands that are spread out from one end of the illustration window to the other. These are the fringe printing features, out of touch with the common illustration and miles away from the automated worlds of the Page Setup and Print commands. But when things turn slightly uncommon, you may be very glad to have them around.

Tiling an Oversized Illustration

By virtue of the Page Setup dialog box, Illustrator provides access to various common page sizes. But many artists require custom page sizes that mid-range printers can't accommodate. So how do you proof oversized artwork using a typical laser printer?

To proof your artwork to letter-sized pages, choose File » Document Setup and select the Tile Imageable Areas radio button. Illustrator automatically sections your illustration into separate tiles as indicated by the dotted lines in the drawing area. If these breaks will not permit you to easily reassemble your artwork, use the page tool to manually reposition the dotted lines.

Even after you meticulously set up and print the tiles, your pages may not fit together properly. Most notably, the tiles may fade toward the outside of the paper, so that the pasted artwork appears to have gutters running through it. The only solution is to adjust the tiles with the page tool, print a page, adjust the tiles again, print another page, and so on until you get it right. Illustrator doesn't provide any automated means for creating an overlap from one tile to the next.

Creating Crop Marks and Trim Marks

Crop marks indicate the boundaries of an illustration. Most imagesetters print pages between 12 and 24 inches wide, regardless of the actual size of the illustration. When you have the illustration commercially reproduced, the printer will want to know the dimensions of the final page size and how the illustration should be positioned on the page. Crop marks specify the boundaries of the reproduced page, and properly positioned crop marks help to avoid miscommunication and additional expense.

Illustrator automatically creates crop marks around an entire illustration when you print color separations (as we discussed in the "Printing Color Separations" section). But what if you want to print a grayscale composite? Or perhaps you want to more precisely control the placement of the crop marks in the illustration window. In either case, you can take advantage of Object » Cropmarks » Make, which lets you manually position crop marks inside the illustration window.

To create crop marks, draw a rectangle that represents the size of the final reproduced sheet of paper. Then, with the rectangle selected, choose Object » Cropmarks » Make. Illustrator converts the rectangle into crop marks. For example, in Figure 21-12, we drew a business card. Then we drew a rectangle around the card in the first example and converted the rectangle to crop marks in the second example. Notice that the marks are positioned well outside the rectangular boundary, preventing them from appearing on the final card. The gray bars that extend outside the crop marks will bleed off the edge of the business cards.

If no object is selected and a single page is displayed in the drawing area (i.e., the Single Full Page radio button is active in the Document Setup dialog box), choose Object » Cropmarks » Make to create crop marks around the page.

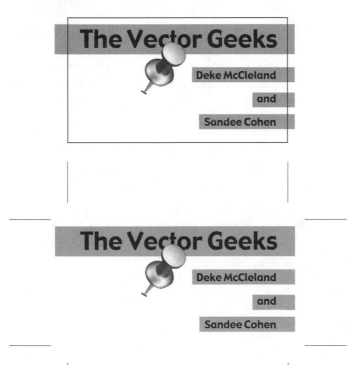

Figure 21-12: After drawing a rectangle to specify the size of the trimmed illustration (top), choose Object » Cropmarks » Make to convert the rectangle to crop marks (bottom).

Unfortunately, only one set of crop marks can exist in an illustration. When you choose Object » Cropmarks » Make, you delete any previous crop marks while creating new ones. Also, you can't move crop marks after you create them. You have to convert the crop marks back to a rectangle by choosing Object » Cropmarks » Release, edit the rectangle as desired, and then choose Object » Cropmarks » Make again to move the crop marks.

When you display the Separations dialog box, Illustrator automatically sizes the bounding box in the preview to the exact size of the area surrounded by the crop marks. This is a handy method for sizing the boundary, typically more accurate and easier to manipulate than the bounding box controls inside the Separations dialog box.

Illustrator also offers the trim marks filter that adds printable guides to your illustration. Trim marks are similar to crop marks in appearance. They differ from crop marks in that they will print inside the printable area, they don't affect printing boundaries (or impact any other printing considerations), you can use as many sets of them as you wish in a single illustration, and they can encompass any shape.

Trim marks are intended to help you or your printer cut your final print into its components. Say you wanted to print a number of the business cards shown in the bottom portion of Figure 21-12. Instead of using crop marks, you would select the rectangle that surrounds the card and choose Filter » Create » Trim Marks to have Illustrator add eight little lines that look just like crop marks. These trim marks will surround the rectangle. Because the trim marks filter doesn't modify the rectangle (like the Cropmarks command does), you will need to delete the rectangle around the card. If you don't like the placement of the marks, you can move them—something that's not possible to do with crop marks unless you first release them. To move trim marks, simply select the marks and then move them to their new locale.

Select all the card elements and the trim marks and cut and paste them so that you fit as many as you can into the printable area. After you print your drawing, you can cut along the trim marks to form several individual cards.

Flatness and Path Splitting

You can encounter a fair number of errors when printing an illustration, but one of the most common is the limitcheck error, which results from a limitation in your printer's PostScript interpreter. If the number of points in the mathematical representation of a path exceeds this limitation, the illustration will not print successfully.

 If you have a sufficient amount of memory in your printer and have a newer PostScript Level 3 printer, most likely you will never be burdened with limitcheck errors.

Unfortunately, the "points" used in this mathematical representation are not the anchor points you used to define the object. Instead, they're calculated by the PostScript interpreter during the printing process. When presented with a curve, the interpreter has to plot hundreds of tiny straight lines to create the most accurate possible rendering. So rather than drawing a perfect curve, your printer creates an approximation with hundreds of flat edges. The exact number of edges is determined by a variable known as flatness, which is the maximum distance a flat edge can vary from the mathematical curve, as illustrated in Figure 21-13.

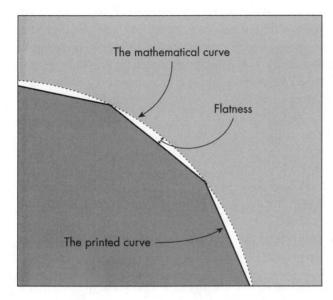

Figure 21-13:
The flatness value determines the greatest distance between the center of a flat edge and the closest point along the true mathematical curve.

The default flatness value for a typical laser printer is 1 pixel, or 1/300 inch. This means the center of any flat edge of the printed curve can be at most 1/300 inch from the closest point along the perfect mathematical curve. If you were to raise the flatness value, the printer could draw fewer flat edges, which quickens the print time but results in more blocky curves.

Each tiny line in the polygon rendering is joined at a point. If the number of points exceeds your printer's built-in path limit, you'll see the telltale words "limitcheck error" in the progress area on your screen, and the illustration will fail to print. The path limit for the original LaserWriter was 1500, seemingly enough flat edges to imitate any curve. But when you factor in such path variations as compound paths and masks, both of which merge shapes with hundreds or thousands of flat edges together, things can get extremely complicated.

You can overcome limitcheck errors several ways:

- You can increase the flatness. This is usually just a matter of lowering the Output Resolution in the Printing & Export section of the Document Setup dialog box.

The default value for the output resolution is 800. For an imagesetter with a resolution of 2400, this translates to a flatness of 3. This is because Illustrator uses the equation Flatness = Printing Device Resolution/Output Resolution (2400/800 equals 3). A flatness of 3 is usually high enough to avoid limitcheck errors. If the Output Resolution is the same as the resolution for the final output device, you have set the flatness to 1. This is a low flatness and could cause problems.

The Output Resolution in the Document Setup will be applied to all objects in the illustration. But you may recognize that you've got only one specific path that could cause problems. For instance, Sandee remembers working with a map of the United States. Although the individual state outlines weren't going to cause any problems, she realized that the entire outside outline of the country might have been too long and intricate to print successfully. She used the Attributes palette to lower the amount in the Output Resolution in the Attributes palette. This created a higher flatness for just that one path, rather than for the entire document.

The default output resolution for every illustration you create is 800 dpi. This means that curves printed to a 2,540-dpi imagesetter will be treated to a flatness of approximately 3, whereas lower resolution printers will use lower flatness values. You can print a test version of an illustration by lowering the Output Resolution in the Document Setup dialog box to, say 300, and leaving the Split Long Paths check box turned off. This will significantly speed up the print time at the expense of the curves.

All Output Resolution values are saved with an EPS file and included with the illustration even if you import it into another application. So don't expect an illustration to print better from PageMaker or QuarkXPress than it does directly from Illustrator.

Select the Split Long Paths check box in the Printing & Export section of the Document Setup dialog box. The next time you save or print the current illustration, Illustrator will automatically break up every path that it considers to be at risk into several smaller paths. In most cases, this won't affect the printed appearance of your illustration.

Unfortunately, there's no way to automatically reassemble paths after Illustrator splits them apart. If you ever need to join them back together, you have to do so manually, which complicates the editing process. So be sure to save your illustration before selecting the Split Long Paths check box, and then use File » Save As to save a copy of the split illustration under a different name.

The best solution is to use masks and patterns wisely. If a complex mask isn't printing, for example, select the mask group and click the Pathfinder palette's Crop button to permanently crop the content elements. Though this may necessitate some manual edits on your part, it will almost always solve the printing problem, and it allows you to print smooth curves without worrying about strange printing issues like flatness.

> Many of the Pathfinder filters have a habit of producing alert boxes when they complete, warning you that they may have generated paths that are too complicated to print. Ignore these messages! They are almost always inaccurate. Wait until you encounter a limitcheck error before you worry about an overly long path.

Printing Patterns

Patterns can also cause limitcheck errors. But more commonly, they can cause out-of-memory errors by overwhelming the amount of RAM available to your printer. (Yes, like computers, PostScript printers have RAM.) See, Illustrator downloads the tile as if it were a font to your printer's memory. In this way, the printer accesses tile definitions repeatedly throughout the creation of an illustration. So if the illustration contains too many tile patterns or if a single tile is too complex, the printer's memory may fill up, in which case the print job is canceled and you see an out-of-memory error on screen. (If your printer just stops working on a job, even though Illustrator seems to have sent the illustration successfully, this is likewise an indication of an out-of-memory error.)

Out-of-memory errors are not as common when you're printing to modern, high-resolution imagesetters, because these machines tend to include updated PostScript interpreters and have increased memory capacity. Therefore, you will most often encounter an out-of-memory error when proofing an illustration to a mid-range laser printer or to another low-memory device. Try one of these techniques to remedy the problem:

- Change all typefaces in the illustration to Times, Helvetica, or some other printer-resident font. Or, better yet, convert all characters to paths using Type » Create Outlines. This way, Illustrator won't have to download both tile and font definitions.

- Print objects filled with different tile patterns in separate pages. Then use traditional paste-up techniques to combine the patterns into a composite proof.

When you print the illustration to an imagesetter, it will probably print successfully because of the imagesetter's increased memory capacity. But if the illustration still encounters an out-of-memory error, you'll have to delete some patterns or resort to traditional paste-up techniques, as suggested in the second item above.

Printing Transparency Objects

Transparency is a revolutionary advancement. However, there are some drawbacks to working with transparency files. As we mentioned back in Chapter 17, some of the transparency options may create raster images. This can cause your files to print a bit differently than you might expect.

The biggest problem with transparency is that you might see a change from vector to raster images. If this is a concern, you should consider exporting your entire file as a high-resolution TIFF image. You can then output that TIFF file.

For more details on printing transparency issues, see the document named AI9printwhitepaper.pdf on the Illustrator CD.

Trapping Selected Paths

Registration problems can sometimes occur when printing full-color documents. *Trapping* is the term used to describe a number of techniques used to help cover up these problems. If your commercial printer's plates are slightly out of register—as they frequently are—gaps may form between high-contrast edges. It's always a good idea to employ a professional printing company that has lots of experience in color printing and guarantees its work. But even the most conscientious printers may be off by as little as a half point, enough to cast a shadow of shoddiness across your artwork.

Full-service (read mega-expensive) printers will trap your work for you using dedicated systems from Scitex or Crosfield. Other printers may charge you a little extra to trap your illustration with software such as TrapWise or Trapeze. If your printer does not provide trapping services, however, you may want to create your own traps in Illustrator.

Illustrator's Trap command works by creating a new path of a specified thickness that overprints the neighboring paths below it. The result is a slight darkening of colors where two paths meet, an imperfect solution that is nevertheless much preferable to a white gap.

You can't trap an entire illustration. Instead, you trap two or more neighboring paths at a time. Also, the filter works only on paths with flat fills. It can't handle gradations, tile patterns, strokes, text, or imported images.

 If you want to trap a stroke, first convert it to a filled path by choosing Object » Path » Outline Path. To trap text, convert the characters to paths with Type » Create Outlines. You'll want to trap only large text, such as headlines or logos. Traps around small letters can make the text blurry and illegible.

The trick when using the Trap filter is to recognize which paths need trapping and which do not. Here are a few instances where trapping may be helpful:

- Two paths filled with different spot colors.
- A path filled with a spot color next to a path filled with a process color.
- Two paths filled with process colors that don't share any primary color in common. For example, an 80 percent cyan path next to a 50 percent yellow, 40 percent magenta path needs to be trapped.

If two neighboring paths are both filled with process colors, and they share one or more primary colors in common, trapping is not necessary. For example, if a 50 percent cyan, 20 percent magenta path overlaps a 70 percent cyan, 30 percent yellow path, a continuous screen of cyan will occur between the two paths even if the magenta and yellow plates are incorrectly registered. Likewise, you don't have to trap between two paths filled with different tints of a spot color. Registration problems have no effect on paths printed from the same plate.

 The Trap filter is pretty smart about telling you when you need and don't need to trap. If the filter refuses to work, it means that the paths are too similar to require trapping. (This assumes that the paths are filled with flat colors. The Trap filter won't create traps for gradations, strokes, or other sophisticated fills. That's not to say those objects don't need trapping—it's just that the Trap filter can't work on those types of objects.)

To trap two or more selected paths, choose Object » Pathfinder » Trap, which displays the Pathfinder Trap dialog box shown in Figure 21-14. The options in this dialog box work as follows:

- **Thickness:** This is the key option in the dialog box. Here you specify the width of the overprinting path created by the filter. The default value, 0.25 point, is awfully small, only sufficient to remedy extremely slight registration problems. If your commercial printer is a top-of-the-line operation, this is sufficient. If your printer is more the workaday, get-the-job-out variety, a value of 0.5 or 1 might be more appropriate.

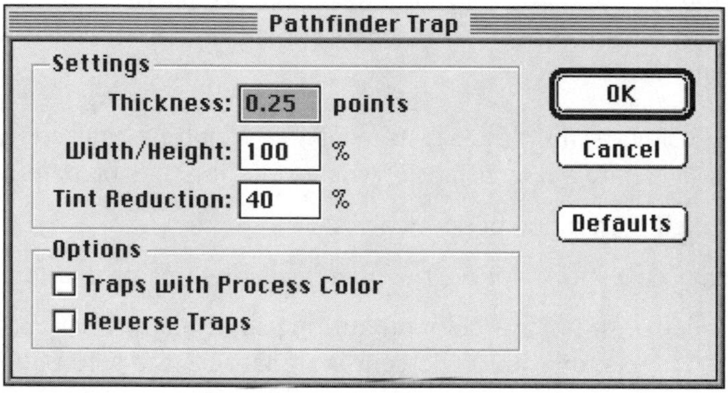

Figure 21-14: From this dialog box, you can create a sliver of a path that traces the border between a pair of selected paths.

- **Width/Height:** This value represents the ratio between the vertical and horizontal thickness of the trapping path. A value of 100 percent means that the trap will be the same thickness—as specified in the previous option—throughout its length. Raise the value to increase the vertical thickness of the trap; lower the value to decrease the vertical thickness. The horizontal thickness is always the exact width entered into the Thickness option box. The purpose of this option—in case you're wondering—is to account for differences in vertical and horizontal misregistration. Check with your printer to find out if any compensation is needed.

- **Tint reduction:** When trapping paths filled with spot colors, Illustrator fills the trap with a tint of the lightest color. So if a selected yellow path neighbors a selected brown path, the trap is filled with a tint of yellow. The light yellow trap looks lighter than either of the neighboring paths on the screen, but because it overprints, the trap leaves the yellow path unaffected and slightly darkens the brown path.

  When trapping process-color paths (or if you convert the trap applied to spot colors to a process color using the Convert Custom Colors to

Process check box), Illustrator mixes a 100-percent tint of the darker color with a lighter tint of the lighter color.

Whether you're trapping spot or process colors, the Tint Reduction value determines the tint of the lighter color. A light tint appears less intrusive than a dark one, so the default 40 percent is a good value for most jobs.

- **Traps with Process Color:** Choose this check box to fill the trap with a process color regardless of whether the trapped paths are filled with spot or process colors. Generally, you'll want to leave this option off. If the lighter color is a spot color, it stands to reason that the trap should be a tint of that spot color. Only if the darker of two neighboring paths is filled with a process color and the screen angle of the spot color might interfere with those of the process colors should you select this option. Never select it when trapping two neighboring paths filled with spot colors.

- **Reverse traps:** Select this option to change the fill of the trap to favor the darker color instead of the lighter one, when you disagree with Illustrator over which of two neighboring colors is lighter. For example, when trapping a red path and a blue path, Illustrator will most likely see the blue path as lighter, whereas you may see it as darker. If you don't like the way Illustrator fills the trap, undo the operation and reapply it with Reverse Traps selected.

After you press Return/Enter, Illustrator creates a trapping path along the border between each pair of neighboring selected shapes. Figure 21-15 shows two trapping scenarios (converted to grayscale for purposes of this book). In each case, just the outlined paths were selected. As you can see, Illustrator creates traps around

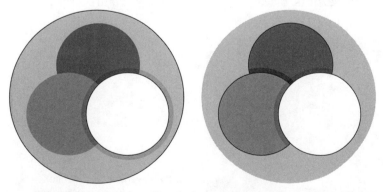

Figure 21-15: The results of two trapping operations. In each case, the outlined paths were selected, paths without outlines were not. The dark strips are the traps.

the neighboring borders of the selected paths only; portions of selected paths that do not neighbor other selected paths are ignored.

This system works great when trapping spot colors, but it gets a little weird when trapping process colors. For example, suppose in the first example in Figure 21-15 that the small selected circle is yellow and the large selected circle is deep purple. The overprinting trap will have hints of both yellow and purple, even when it overlaps the deselected circles, which may be green, orange, or any other color. The fact is, the purple of the background circle has no business being there.

To avoid the problem of unwanted colors in a trap, remove the tint of the background path from the trap. In the case of our purple objects in the above example, you would simply remove the purple from the trap and leave the yellow intact. A yellow trap surrounding a yellow path is always acceptable, regardless of the paths it overprints.

Overprinting Black Paths

Another way to trap two objects is to overprint one on top of the other. If a text block is full of small black type, you'll probably want to select the Overprint Fill check box in the Attributes palette. This way, Illustrator prints the text on top of any background colors to ensure that no gaps appear between character outlines and neighboring colors.

Overprinting black is such a common practice that Illustrator provides a filter to automate the process. This filter allows you to overprint a specific percentage of black through the fills and strokes of all selected objects. Select all the objects you might want to overprint, and then choose Filter » Colors » Overprint Black. Illustrator displays the Overprint Black dialog box shown in Figure 21-16.

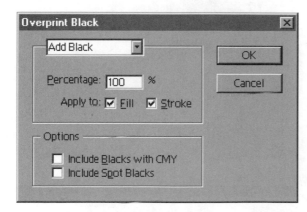

Figure 21-16:
Use the Overprint Black filter to overprint all selected objects that contain a specific percentage of black.

The options in this dialog box work as follows:

- **Add Black and Remove Black:** If you want to overprint colors, select the Add Black command in the pop-up menu. If you want to remove overprinting from selected objects—so that they knock out the colors behind them—select Remove Black.

- **Percentage:** Enter the intensity of black ink that you want to overprint. All objects with that exact percentage of black will overprint.

- **Apply to Fill and Stroke:** Use these check boxes to overprint—or to remove the overprinting from—fills, strokes, or both fills and strokes. By default, both check boxes are selected.

- **Include Blacks with CMY:** To overprint CMYK objects that contain a specific percentage of black, select this check box. For example, if you set the Percentage Black value to 40, and a selected object is filled with 30%C 20%M 10%Y 40%K, this check box must be turned on for the filter to affect the object.

- **Include Spot Blacks:** When this check box is on, any spot blacks in your document will also overprint. If you intend for your objects to print as spot colors, you should check this option. (Because the CMYK values are for screen display purposes only, the Black value in a spot color has nothing to do with the printed ink.) But if you plan on converting all spot colors to CMYK, you don't have to worry about this option.

This filter would be better if it would allow you to change a range of blacks at a time (an oversight that we're still hoping Adobe might fix in the future). And it would be nice if the filter could automatically detect oversaturations and make sure that overprinted blacks don't smudge on the printed page. Still, it's safer than simply selecting the Overprint Black check box in the Separation dialog box.

Creating PDF Files

One of the more exciting developments in computer graphics in the past few years has been the acceptance and widespread use of Adobe's Portable Document Format (PDF) files. PDF files can be created from almost any application and then can be read using an Acrobat Reader which is available for free from the Adobe Web site.

Originally the folks at Adobe created PDF as a way to transfer and read documents without printing them—part of their grand plan for a paperless office. And although PDF has been accepted for that, its real glory has been its part of the prepress process. PDF documents allow you to package a file for a service bureau and include all the fonts and graphics necessary to print the file. Unlike a self-contained PostScript file, which can only be sent to a printer, PDF files can be opened, examined, modified slightly, and even added to other documents. This makes them ideal for advertising and illustrations that need to be incorporated into magazines, newspapers, books, and other publications.

Saving a PDF File

It's very easy to save your Illustrator documents as PDF files. All you have to do is choose File » Save As and then choose the Adobe PDF format from the pop-up list. Name the file and then click Save. This opens the Adobe PDF Format Options dialog box. This box will be set for the Default options set with the General controls visible as shown in Figure 21-17. You use the pop-up list to change the General options to the Compression options as seen in Figure 21-18.

Illustrator provides two option sets. The Default set is more appropriate for PDF files that will be output by a service bureau on an imagesetter. The Screen set creates a smaller file that is more appropriate for onscreen or Web viewing. The Screen set also changes the colorspace of the file to RGB.

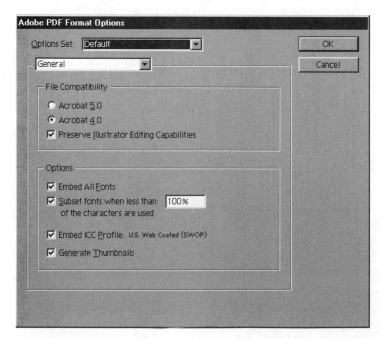

Figure 21-17:
The General options
for saving files as
Acrobat files.

Setting the General PDF Options

Select either Acrobat 5.0 or 4.0 in the File Compatibility panel. This determines which version of Adobe Acrobat will be able to read your PDF file.

 The Acrobat 5 format supports the widest range of Illustrator features. However, as of this writing, Adobe has not yet released Acrobat 5. So we are still saving our files in the Acrobat 4 format.

- Select Preserve Illustrator Editing Capabilities to export the file in a PDF format that allows you to reopen and edit the file in Adobe Illustrator. Turning this option off will create a slightly smaller file which may be desirable if you are going to post your Acrobat file on the Web .

- Select the Embed All Fonts option to save the fonts used in the file with the saved file. This option embeds all the characters in each font. This can create larger files than necessary if you've only used a few characters in the file. For instance, do you really need to embed all the characters in a font if the only text in the file is for a small trademark symbol?

 If you find that a font has not been included in the file, it may be that it has been set to be protected by its manufacturer and cannot be embedded in PDF files.

- Choose the Subset Fonts When Less Than __% of the Characters are Used option to minimize the file size. This embeds only those characters of the font that are used in the document. (The technical term for this is a subset.) Enter the percentage of the characters that determines when a font subset is created. For instance, if you have used just a few of the characters, you can lower the percentage to 25 percent. If the percentage of characters used in the document exceeds this setting, then the entire font set is embedded in the file rather than the subset.

 Do not embed subsets if you think that you might need to edit the Illustrator file in Acrobat—for instance, if you are sending the PDF to a service bureau for output. You cannot edit the text if only the subset of the font is included with the file.

- Select the Embed ICC profile option to embed a color profile into the saved file. The color profile is determined in the Color Settings dialog box. This embedded color profile is then applied to the file when the

file is reopened in Adobe Illustrator. Again, this is something that probably is not necessary for files viewed on the Web.

● Select the Generate Thumbnails option to save a thumbnail image of
the artwork with the saved file. This adds a small amount to the file size
and should not be done for files to be posted to the Web.

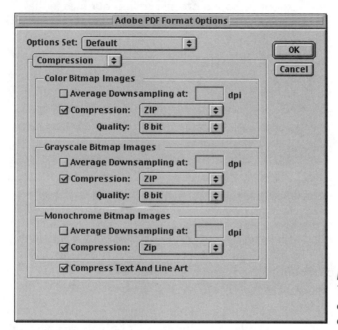

Figure 21-18:
The Compression
options for saving files
as Acrobat files.

Setting the Compression PDF Options

● Select the Average Downsampling at a certain __dpi option in any of
the compression panels if you want to set downsampling for the PDF
file. *Downsampling* is the term used for lowering the resolution—and
therefore the details—in raster images. You should not downsample
PDF files that will be printed using high-resolution output devices.
However, there should not be any problem downsampling images that
will be viewed only onscreen.

● Select the Automatic compression option to have Illustrator automatically apply the best compression. For most files, this option produces
satisfactory results.

● Select the ZIP compression for images with large areas of single colors
or repeating patterns, and for black-and-white images that contain

repeating patterns. Use the 8-bit compression for the most flexibility if your images have many colors. Use the 4-bit compression only for images with limited colors.

- Select the JPEG compression method for grayscale or color images. JPEG is lossy, which means that it removes image data and may reduce image quality. Because JPEG eliminates data, it creates smaller files sizes than ZIP.

- Use the Consultative Committee on International Telegraphy and Telephony (CCITT) compression method when compressing as monochrome bitmap images. No information is lost with CCITT compression. Group 4 is a general-purpose method that produces good compression for most monochromatic images. Group 3, used by most fax machines, compresses monochromatic bitmaps one row at a time.

- Use the Run Length option for images that contain large areas of solid black or white. This compression method does not lose any data.

- Select the Compress Text and Line Art option to apply the ZIP compression method to text and line.

INDEX